PENGUIN CLASSICS

# THE PENGUIN BOOK OF IRISH POETRY

PATRICK CROTTY is a critic and translator who works as Professor of Irish and Scottish Literature at the University of Aberdeen. He has published articles on many aspects of Irish, Scottish and Welsh writing and is a frequent contributor to the *Times Literary Supplement*. His *Modern Irish Poetry: An Anthology* appeared in 1995. He is currently editing the definitive *Complete Collected Poems of Hugh MacDiarmid*, the first volume of which will appear in 2013.

SEAMUS HEANEY was born in County Derry, Northern Ireland. *Death of a Naturalist*, his first book, appeared in 1966 and since then he has published poetry, criticism and translations which have established him as one of the most acclaimed writers of our time. In 1995 he was awarded the Nobel Prize for Literature.

# THE PENGUIN BOOK OF IRISH POETRY

*Edited by* PATRICK CROTTY
*with a Preface by* SEAMUS HEANEY

PENGUIN BOOKS

PENGUIN CLASSICS

Published by the Penguin Group
Penguin Books Ltd, 80 Strand, London WC2R 0RL, England
Penguin Group (USA), Inc., 375 Hudson Street, New York, New York 10014, USA
Penguin Group (Canada), 90 Eglinton Avenue East, Suite 700, Toronto, Ontario, Canada M4P 2Y3 (a division of Pearson Penguin Canada Inc.)
Penguin Ireland, 25 St Stephen's Green, Dublin 2, Ireland (a division of Penguin Books Ltd)
Penguin Group (Australia), 250 Camberwell Road, Camberwell, Victoria 3124, Australia (a division of Pearson Australia Group Pty Ltd)
Penguin Books India Pvt Ltd, 11 Community Centre, Panchsheel Park, New Delhi – 110 017, India
Penguin Group (NZ), 67 Apollo Drive, Rosedale, Auckland 0632, New Zealand (a division of Pearson New Zealand Ltd)
Penguin Books (South Africa) (Pty) Ltd, 24 Sturdee Avenue, Rosebank, Johannesburg 2196, South Africa

Penguin Books Ltd, Registered Offices: 80 Strand, London WC2R 0RL, England

www.penguin.com

This selection first published 2010
Published in this format in Penguin Classics 2012

013



Printed in Great Britain by Clays Ltd, Elcograf S.p.A.

A CIP catalogue record for this book is available from the British Library

ISBN: 978-0-141-19164-5

www.greenpenguin.co.uk

*In memory of Patrick Crotty (1910–80)*
*and Kathleen Burns (1913–94)*

*and for Brian, Ronan and Fergal*

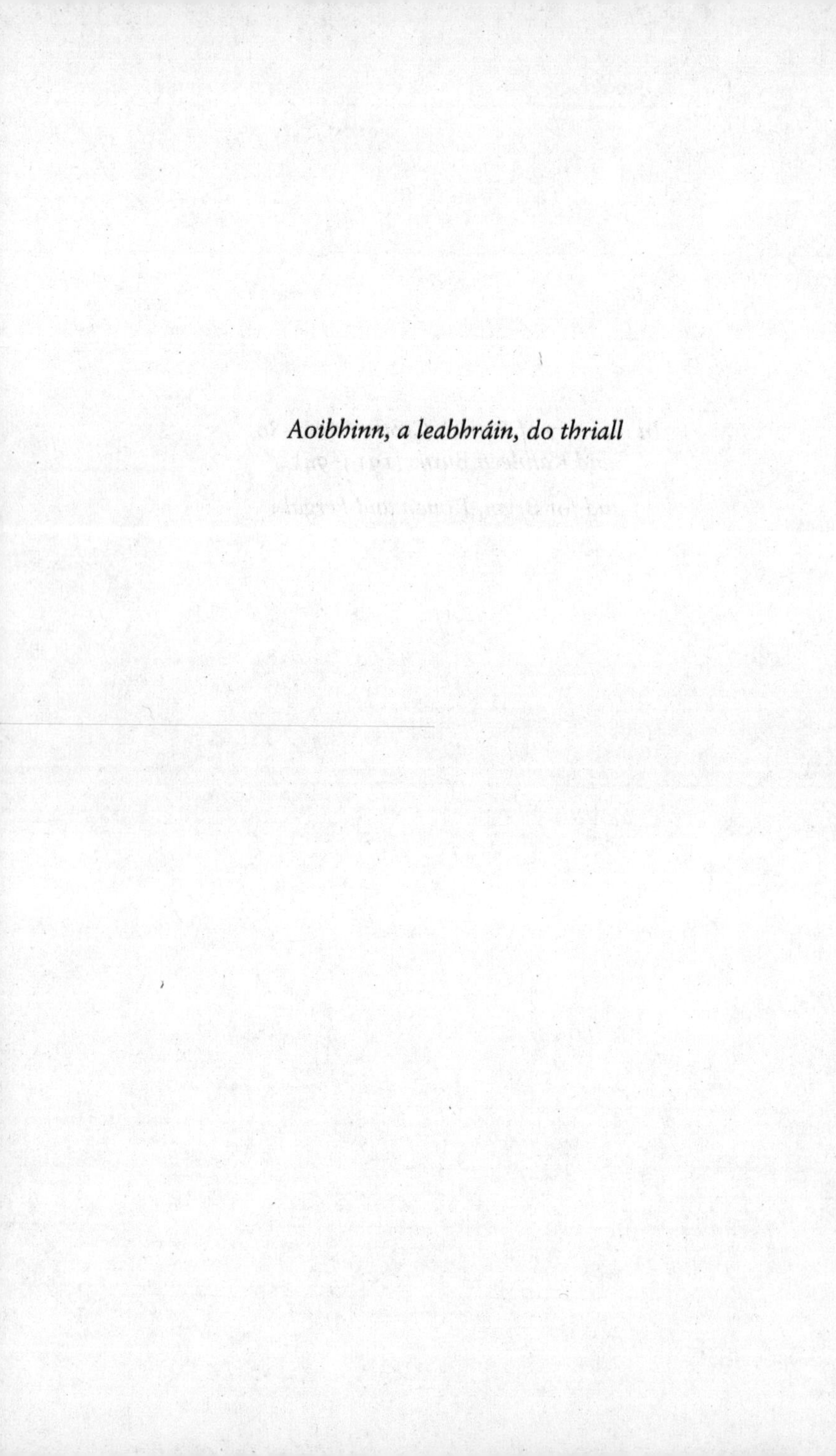

*Aoibhinn, a leabhráin, do thriall*

# Contents

## III CIVILIZATIONS: 1601–1800

## IX SONGS AND BALLADS SINCE 1801

# Preface

This is the most comprehensive and confident anthology of Irish poetry yet. The comprehensiveness is due to the inclusion of a much greater selection of work from the earlier periods, the confidence to sureness about the artistic quality and significance of that work and of writing done later, in Irish and English, in the decades since the death of William Butler Yeats. But the anthology also benefits from being compiled at the end of an era which has seen important new developments in the relationship between Ireland and Britain, between Northern Ireland and the Republic, and between the unionist and nationalist communities within Northern Ireland itself.

Patrick Crotty has a scholar's understanding and an insider's feel for the complications and rewards of the relationship between the British and the Irish islands, its causes and hurts and consequences. He is totally cognizant of the bitter histories lurking beneath the old familiar binaries – Planter and Gael, Protestant Ascendancy and Hidden Ireland – but a look at the contents list will show that he has an inclusive attitude. Translations of work from Latin, Old Norse and Norman French indicate that Crotty, like Leopold Bloom, takes it for granted that a person's birth in Ireland (or indeed a translator's feel for Irish poetry) is sufficient to make Ireland his or her nation.

Bloom's nation – 'the same people living in the same place' – starts off as those original Gaels whose myths and practices would subsist for centuries in a country that was destined to experience conversion by Christian missionaries, raids and eventual settlement by Viking adventurers, then conquest by Norman barons, annexation by the English crown and, finally, military and cultural defeat of the Gaelic order by that same English power. All of these great events are confronted and given expression in the poems included here, but the poems are not chosen only as commentary on that history. Their imaginative vigour, their technical pleasure in themselves as works, their artistic sufficiency and inner freedom are what earn them their literary place. And when we turn to the work of the nineteenth century and after, that resurgent energy of the writing *qua* writing becomes an aspect of a wider surge towards political and cultural independence.

Certainly the 'Irish' in Patrick Crotty's title does not induce in him the kind of anxiety detectable in the introduction to the earlier 1958 *Oxford Book of Irish Verse*. One of its editors spoke there of Irish poetry in English as 'a relatively novel art' and harked back to a phase of Irish history when 'the only English known by the majority was that minimum necessary to understand an order'. But if such old resentments have disappeared it is still worth remembering that the editor who wrote those words was Donagh MacDonagh, himself a poet and son of the poet-revolutionary Thomas MacDonagh who had been executed a mere forty-two years earlier because of his part in the 1916 Rising. Which is another way of saying that until relatively recently Irish poetry has often been implicated, and has sometimes very deliberately implicated itself, in 'the national question'.

When, for example, Yeats declared in 1937 that Gaelic was his national language, but not his mother tongue, he wasn't just making a fine linguistic distinction: he was clinching the argument that he owed his soul not only to the 'Irishry' – the quotation marks were his – but 'to Shakespeare, to Spenser and to Blake . . . and to the English language'. He was also detaching himself from the cultural nationalism of the new Irish Free State which his early work had done so much to foster, as well as from the early work of his friend Douglas Hyde, then president of the country, the man who had once written a manifesto on the necessity of 'de-anglicizing' Ireland. In similar and equally significant fashion, there was more than word choice involved when half a century later Paul Muldoon translated the title of Nuala Ní Dhomhnaill's poem 'Ceist na Teangan' not as 'The Language Question' but as 'The Language Issue', since 'issue' implies offspring from an ongoing intercourse between Irish and English rather than a barren stand-off.

In the history of Irish poetry, crisis and recuperation are recurrent features. Fifteen hundred years separate the 'Adze-head' who appears in the sixth-century poem which opens this anthology from the speaker of 'Pedigree', the last poem in the contemporary section, yet those poems are united in at least one respect: each is the utterance of a writer expressing a world in transition, the former poised between pagan/immemorial and Christian/other, the latter between local/domestic to pluralist/diasporic. In the intervening centuries much of the greatest work arises from similar, often far more extreme tensions and contestations: historical and cultural change due to defeat in war, the attendant cycles of dispossession and repossession, loss of language, of standing, of learning, of cohesion at local and national level, loss of physical and psychic security.

But equally important at every stage of this history is the sufficiency of poetry itself: the immense incantation of Dallán Forgaill's 'Amra Colm Cille', for example, proclaiming the heroic virtue of Colum Cille's epoch-defining life, the exhilaration and licence of Brian Merriman's *The Midnight Court* countervailing the oppression of penal laws, the jubilant defiance of Yeats's 'Lapis Lazuli' at a moment when things in Europe were falling violently apart. Moreover, when viewed in this context, the centuries-long tradition of bardic poetry can be understood as another case of imagination pressing back again the pressures of reality, a mighty constancy rather than a hidebound conservatism, and as such it is given proper representation here. Here, too, important emphasis is laid on the the song tradition, revealing how it has long functioned at individual and collective levels as a kind of spiritual survival kit. And the same could be said of the love poetry, ranging from the passion and strictness of early Irish voices – women's as well as men's – through the more euphonious styles of folk English and opulent vernacular Irish. Yet as is always the case, it is in the representation of the contemporary scene that the most testing decisions have to be made about who and what to include (or not) at the end of a millennium and a half of poetic achievement. Inevitably and understandably many readers, myself among them, will want to contest some of those decisions, but in making them, as elsewhere in the volume, the editor displays bold and independent judgement.

Patrick Crotty's anthology richly complements the achievements of the poet-editors Brendan Kennelly, John Montague and Thomas Kinsella in their respective volumes, *The Penguin Book of Irish Verse* (1970), *The Faber Book of Irish Verse* (1974) and *The New Oxford Book of Irish Verse* (1986), each of which contained translations from work in Irish as well as poetry written originally in English. His book is part of an increasingly successful effort to recuperate and reintegrate a literary history, an effort which gained significantly in strength and purpose in the course of the Irish Literary Revival. At the end of the nineteenth century, Yeats famously saw Ireland as soft wax, ready to take the imprint of his grand literary and cultural design; at the beginning of the twenty-first, this anthology reveals the depth and riches of the tradition which the arch-poet's intervention helped to retrieve and which his successors have so thoroughly and variously consolidated.

SEAMUS HEANEY

# Introduction

## An Ancient Practice

In 1995 Seamus Heaney became the fourth Irish recipient of the Nobel Prize for Literature. The international visibility of Irish writing in the modern period is a remarkable and continuing phenomenon, all the more so given that the Republic of Ireland and Northern Ireland share a smaller land mass than South Carolina, with a combined population only slightly larger. The global significance of writing from the island is nothing new, however: it is argued below that in world historical terms the achievement of the early medieval poets represented in section I of this book is at least equal in importance to the work of the sequence of famous writers that runs from Oscar Wilde through John Millington Synge, James Joyce and the Nobel Laureates William Butler Yeats, George Bernard Shaw, Samuel Beckett and Heaney to Edna O'Brien and Paul Muldoon.

Grand claims about the antiquity of Irish traditions recur in writings after the Act of Union of 1801, when it seemed the separate identity of the smaller of the two main 'British' Isles might be extinguished. Thus Horatio, the bewildered, love-struck Englishman who narrates *The Wild Irish Girl* (1806), the popular post-Union 'national tale' by Lady Morgan (1776?–1859), has his prejudices challenged by the heroine's protestations of the ancient lineage of the music she plays on her harp, a music said to be older than that of the Welsh, the English and more or less all other modern nations. The very ardour with which they are formulated can draw attention to the implausibility of some of the more vivid claims. In 1822 the radical aristocrat Roger O'Connor (1762–1834) published a fantastical narrative called *The Chronicles of*

*Eri, being the history of the Gael, Sciot Iber, or Irish people: translated from the original manuscripts in the Phoenician dialect of the Scythian language*, which reappeared in 1936 as *Six Thousand Years of Gaelic Grandeur – Unearthed.*

This penchant for high rhetoric marred works of genuine scholarship, too. In *The Aryan Origin of the Gaelic Race and Language* (1875), for example, the Irish language revivalist Canon Ulick J. Bourke (1829–87) cloaks the seriousness of his philological enterprise in pomp: 'The object and aim of the present work is to give a thorough critical account of the language of the Gael, to show its early origin; that it is Aryan, and comes to us down the great stream of migration that had begun to flow westward from the high country between the Tigris and the Indus, even before Abraham went forth out of his country . . .'

Yet for all of this, poetry in Ireland is a genuinely ancient cultural practice. Quite how ancient is difficult to determine. Ogham stones bearing witness to the existence of a form of writing and perhaps of Roman influence appear to predate the arrival of Christianity early in the fifth century. The first Irish poets are said to have undertaken composition in dark interiors, but there is no direct trace of their work, as poetry did not become a matter of record until some time after the scribal customs of Christian monks had spread throughout the island and the wider Gaelic world in the course of the fifth and sixth centuries.

The earliest surviving poetry is strongly Christian in character. The oldest Gaelic verses in the present volume are the selections from Dallán Forgaill's lament for the missionary monk Colum Cille, dateable (according to most scholars) to the fairly immediate aftermath of its subject's death on Iona in AD 593 (or 597). *The Penguin Book of Irish Poetry* opens with the lyric 'Adze-head', which affects to stylize an early fifth-century Irishman's proleptic contempt for bishops and their newfangled religion. (The prolepsis, however, may be fictive: in manuscript 'Adze-head' appears within the framework of the late seventh-century *Vita Sancti Patricii*, a hagiography by the monk Muirchú moccu Macthéni.) A more plausible representation of pagan perspectives is offered by the even later 'I Invoke the Seven Daughters', where the Christian elements are difficult to reconcile with the surrounding matter and are most readily understood as interpolations in an earlier, mythological poem.

The relationship between Christian and non-Christian outlooks in the literature of early Ireland is a vexed question, not least because the great bulk of the writing in the first half a millennium or so of literary production (the period represented in section I) was done by clerics. The *filid* – a powerful poetic caste trained in schools, and entrusted with legal and linguistic lore as well as other forms of traditional knowledge – were skilled in divination and appear to have been rivals to the clergy during the early years of Irish Christianity. An intervention on their behalf by Colum Cille at Druim Ceat near Derry in 575, in the context of a settlement brokered by the saint between the Ulster and Scottish territories of the Gaels, marked an accommodation between the old ways and the new that would be variously reflected in the literature of the following centuries. Though the schools waned in importance during the great period of Irish missionary Christianity, when they were absorbed into the educational function of the monasteries, they had resumed much of their former status by the twelfth century, and the later poems in section I were written by professional poets rather than clerics.

The renaissance of the pre-Christian social and cultural primacy of poetry in the 1210–1650 'bardic' period (sections II and III) is remarkable, and it is hardly fanciful to say that there are vestiges of that ancient primacy in the deference and public attention paid to poets and poetry in present-day Ireland. The residual pull of the pre-Christian world was being registered as late as the twelfth century, in the Fionn cycle through the witness of revenants like Oisín ('The Praise of Fionn', 'The Blackbird of Derrycairn') and Caoilte ('Caoilte Laments the Passing of the Fianna'), and in the protests of the dispossessed king Sweeney to the cleric Ronan in *Buile Shuibhne* (*The Frenzy of Sweeney*).

If an encounter between Christian and pre-Christian values was staged in much of the poetry of early Ireland, however, it was generally Christians who were doing the staging. Far from being a testament to the pre-Christian grandeur of the country (as Yeats and other figures of the late nineteenth-century Literary Revival liked to think) the Ulster prose-and-verse saga *Táin Bó Cuailnge* is pervasively Christian in vision. A clerical redaction (strictly speaking, two clerical redactions) of vernacular materials of unspecifiable antiquity, the *Táin* is informed throughout by the thinking of monks who did not merely put their gloss on events but inscribed their patristic values in the core narrative of the chaotic consequences of Queen Medb's challenge to the masculine order.

In 1936 the poet Austin Clarke referred to a persistent dichotomy between sex and religion in Irish writing as 'our native drama of conscience'. Clarke's comment attempted to cast his own difficulties with the sexual attitudes of the Catholic Church in the light of the conflict between body and spirit that is so marked a feature of early Irish poetry. Many social commentators have seen the puritanical character of twentieth-century Irish Catholicism as a hangover from the need to control reproduction in the aftermath of the Great Famine of the 1840s. For someone as steeped in Old and Middle Irish literature as Clarke was, however, continuities between the ascetic and celibate traditions of the early Gaelic church and the social ambience of the Irish Free State were too striking to ignore.

Asceticism is a central value of the poetry of section I – celebrated in 'The Hermit's Song', aspired to in 'Straying Thoughts', complained of in the agonized outcries of Sweeney. The magnificent tenth-century monologue 'Lament of Baoi, the Nun of Beare Island' internalizes the war against the body, while 'St Brigit's Housewarming' wittily employs alcoholic indulgence as a metaphor for self-denial. If the spirit/body opposition of the early period is recalled in the twentieth century in Patrick Kavanagh's *The Great Hunger* and the work of Paul Durcan, and, more self-consciously, in that of Nuala Ní Dhomhnaill and Clarke himself, the libertarian and occasionally anti-clerical posing of the dichotomy in the modern and contemporary period (sections VII and VIII) is radically at variance with the orthodoxy of the poetry of section I.

The beginnings of a more persuasive continuity – one that amounts to a characteristic theme of Irish poetry over nearly fifteen hundred years of verse-making – can be traced to 'Adze-head': this concerns neither the contestation between paganism and Christianity *per se* nor the narrower antagonism between Christian and pre-Christian apprehensions of corporeality that Clarke referred to, but rather the meeting of conflicting world views and of their underlying political power-bases. The clash of two value systems encapsulated in 'Adze-head' looks forward not only to the antithesis between Christianity and its antecedents in the Old Irish 'The Downfall of Heathendom' and Johannes Scottus Ériugena's 'Homer sang once of his Greeks and his Trojans' (a Latin repudiation of classical antiquity), but to later conflicts between the perspectives of Gael and Viking, Gael and Anglo-Norman, Catholic and Protestant, nationalist and unionist, and the Irish and English languages.

Section II opens with a Norman French account of the arrival of Strongbow (Richard de Clare) in Ireland in 1170 and includes Middle English animadversions on Irish mores from a hundred and fifty years later. These early centuries of the long drawn-out conquest of Ireland saw the flourishing of the bardic schools and the consolidation of native poetry in the work of some of the greatest practitioners of strict-metre syllabic verse. The complexities of the political and cultural milieu are illustrated here by the extract from Gofraidh Fionn Ó Dálaigh's 'Praise of Maurice Fitz Maurice, Earl of Desmond', which compares the exploits of a fourteenth-century Anglo-Norman lord to those of the god Lugh, thereby tactfully transposing from the literal and historical to the metaphorical and mythological planes the bardic duty to assert a patron's lengthy Irish pedigree. Though there are many trans-linguistic and trans-sectarian nuances in the poetry of the seventeenth and eighteenth centuries, this period saw the literature of Ireland split more decisively than ever before along ethnic and religious lines as a consequence of a series of historical cataclysms that brought the bardic tradition to an end, creating the conditions for the replacement of Irish by English as the everyday language of most of the population.

The failure of the late sixteenth-century rebellion of the northern chiefs; the Plantation of Ulster; the departure of many of the aristocratic Gaelic families to the courts of Counter-Reformation Europe; the defeat of the Confederacy that had held most of the country in the Catholic interest from 1641 to 1649; the ferocious military campaign led by Oliver Cromwell in 1649–50; the severity of the subsequent 'settlement'; the loss of the last remaining elements of the Catholic leadership caste after the end of the Williamite wars in 1691; the institutionalized denial of religious, economic and political rights to the majority Catholic population: all of these elements combine to lend an apocalyptic intensity to much of the Irish-language poetry of the period. Unsurprisingly, that poetry displays unprecedented bitterness in its delineation of relations between Gael and Gall ('foreigner'). Verse in English, meanwhile, almost exclusively the product of the new 'Protestant nation', grows in quantity and competence and is for the most part urbane and untroubled by the degradation that surrounded its making.

The contours of modern Ireland are already recognizable by the beginning of the nineteenth century. Though most of the population would continue to use Irish rather than English for decades after the Act of Union, English had already supplanted the older language as the medium of serious verse. If the contestation between Gael and Gall was more than ever a subject of poetry, the focus had become retrospective. There is a high degree of romanticization in the approach to the Irish past of Jeremiah Joseph Callanan, James Clarence Mangan, Samuel Ferguson and other poets represented in section V, and their work of imaginative retrieval frequently takes the form of translation (the earliest versions of Gaelic poems used in this book come from nineteenth-century writers).

The poetic engagement with the distant past ushered in by Ferguson intensifies in the Revival period (section VI), when it intersects with the gathering momentum of nationalist politics. Mediation of the Gaelic tradition is central to the poetry of Austin Clarke in the early years of independence (section VII), and the backward look is sustained in anglophone verse, in tones variously of realism, nostalgia and irony, up to the contemporary era (section VIII). One of the more remarkable developments in the poetry of our own day is the meeting between oral culture and modernity facilitated by the deployment of Gaelic folklore in the service of an egalitarian feminist politics in the resurgent Irish of the poems of Nuala Ní Dhomhnaill.

Another theme that emerges from a survey of the long history of poetry in Ireland is the land. 'Lament of Baoi, the Nun of Beare Island' is partly to be understood as the testimony of a naturalized sovereignty goddess. Hence the nun – returned to the temporal sphere and no longer protectress of the territory – mourns her separation from the timeless persistence of the land, figured in male terms:

To all the old I bear good will
Except wide-pastured Feven
Whose mane though as old as mine
Is sunbright still and golden.

Feven's Stone of the Kings has been battered
By winter's storms time out of mind
But like the Fort of Ronan's in Bregon
Its face is youthful, still unlined.

(Feven – or Femen – and Bregon are north Munster place names.)

The trope of the sovereignty goddess whose marriage to the king assures the land's well-being underlies the much later *aisling* ('vision') poetry of Aodhagán Ó Rathaille ('The Glamoured'), Art Mac Cumhaigh ('The Churchyard of Creggan') and Eoghan Rua Ó Súilleabháin ('A Magic Mist'). In these and related Jacobite poems and songs, the speaker encounters a beautiful maiden suffering the advances of a lout (or louts) identified with varying degrees of explicitness as representatives of the Protestant British succession; her overseas betrothed, the Stuart Pretender, is helpless to defend her. The figure of the young woman conflates territory and nation – land and Ireland.

Brian Merriman's comic masterpiece *Cúirt an Mheán-Oiche* (*The Midnight Court*) – the last major poem written in Irish before the tradition spluttered back to life in the twentieth century – opens with a parodic *aisling*. The poem's eponymous tribunal on the miseries of Merriman's native territory of East Clare is presided over by Aoibheall, an otherworld queen who can be seen as a late, very vivid embodiment of the sovereignty goddess. *The Midnight Court* is unusual in Gaelic tradition in seeming to respond to an English-language text, Oliver Goldsmith's *The Deserted Village*, the other long work represented entire in section III. 'Ill fares the land', the *leitmotif* of Goldsmith's idealizing portrait of vanishing rural simplicities, takes on additional resonance when heard in the context of Irish poetry's age-old concern with territory. The theme recurs in Allingham's *Laurence Bloomfield in Ireland*, a book-length verse narrative on post-Famine land agitation and the early stages of the challenge to landlordism that eventually resulted in the redistribution of the estates (most of them dating from the plantations of the colonial period) via the Wyndham Act of 1903.

In 1942 yet another agrarian long poem, Patrick Kavanagh's *The Great Hunger*, offered a glum rebuff to the idealization of rural Ireland in the drama of the Abbey Theatre and the political rhetoric of Éamon de Valera (1882–1975); significantly, it did so from the point of view of a poet sprung from the class of small ('peasant') proprietors who were the principal beneficiaries of the settlement of the land question. In the mid- and later twentieth century the ancient antagonism between Planter (an explicitly territorial term) and Gael cast a darker shadow over Ulster than Ireland's other three provinces (to say the least). Land is the central focus of two incisive Northern Irish treatments of continuing sectarian division, John Hewitt's historical allegory 'The Colony' and 'Broagh', Seamus Heaney's bravura lyric of linguistic excavation.

## Poetry and Women

A striking feature of verse in the Gaelic tradition – and one that helps identify a major tendency (if not a theme) in Irish poetry more broadly – is an openness to women's perspectives and experience. In the literature of early medieval Ireland this was countered by a strain of misogyny, evident for example in the *Táin* and the starkly patriarchal 'Instructions of King Cormac mac Airt'. Nevertheless, section I is alive with female voices – those of Eve, the mothers of the massacred Innocents, St Ite, St Brigit, Créide, Liadan, the battle goddess Morrígan, Gráinne and Baoi. Except for Eve and Morrígan, all the women are portrayed sympathetically and some of these poems were probably female in authorship. The scholar Máirín Ní Dhonnchadha has argued that Baoi's lament was composed by Digde, a tenth-century 'penitent spouse' (a woman who retreated to a convent on suffering widowhood or a succession of widowhoods). The seventh-century Liadan and her tragically rejected lover Cuirithir are strongly held by tradition to have been poets, and though the solitary surviving quatrain attributed to Liadan is not the tenth-century poem spoken by her persona in section I, the attribution suggests that in Ireland poetic composition by women is almost as old as poetry itself.

Gormlaith (*d.*947), who features centrally in section II, became a penitent spouse after the death of her third husband Niall Glúndub in 919. The extant verse that can confidently be ascribed to her is fragmentary, and the five monologues included here were written up to half a millennium after her death. (Tradition can operate somewhat like an eternal present in the Gaelic world – thus the suite of lyrics in section VII by another female poet, Máire Mhac an tSaoi – one of the leading figures in the contemporary revival of poetry in Irish – ventriloquizes its exploration of a mid-twentieth-century love affair through the character of the historical Máire Ní Ógáin, the proverbially foolish lover of the eighteenth-century poet Donnchadh Rua Mac Con Mara.)

It is notable that two of the Gormlaith monologues ('At Niall's Grave' and '3 × 30, 9 × 9') draw attention to the speaker's status as a poet. 'Icham of Irlaunde', one of the oldest English poems associated with the country, is (like so many poems in Irish) spoken by a woman. In the early 1600s Brighid Chill Dara, an aristocrat of mixed Irish and English lineage, could engage in self-assured poetic banter with the most renowned professional poet of her day in a manner suggestive of intimacy alike with the privileges and technical intricacies of bardic verse, and with the love of teasing paradox in Renaissance English poetry that was being brought to a new level of outrageousness in the contemporary work of John Donne (see her 'Response to Eochaidh Ó hEodhasa's Poem'). Long before the emergence of Restoration and 'Enlightenment' female poets like 'Philo-Philippa' and Dorothea Dubois, women were writing poetry of the highest sophistication in Ireland. Indeed, if we count Digde as the author of 'Lament of Baoi' and accept the suggestion of some scholars that there are traces of Gormlaith's originals in the later monologues spoken in her name, female-authored works can be said to appear in all nine sections of this anthology. Such sustained productivity by women is unusual in western Europe.

Women are prominent in popular as well as high literary art in Ireland. Anonymous folk songs first in Irish ('Donal Óg', 'My Grief on the Sea' and 'Shule Aroon'), then in English ('My Love is Like the Sun', 'I Know My Love' and 'The Butcher Boy'), are as hospitable to female perspectives as the Old and Middle Irish materials of section I, and identified women songwriters feature in sections IV and IX. In Gaelic culture, the public lamentation of the dead fell to women. Irish anthologies customarily include Éibhlín Dhubh Ní Chonaill's eighteenth-century keen 'Lament for Art O'Leary', a poem which, while of considerable power, is more generic and conventional than is often appreciated. In section V I have instead chosen a later example that shows the female poetic art of keening still vibrant in the middle of the nineteenth century.

It would be unfair to discuss women and poetry in Ireland without mentioning Charlotte Brooke (*c.*1740–93), whose dual-language *Reliques of Irish Poetry* appeared in 1789. Though her English renditions are too mannered for inclusion here (translations rarely have a lifespan of more than two centuries), her anthology not only provided the most remarkable Irish contribution to the vogue for literary antiquarianism associated with Allan Ramsay (1686–1758) in Scotland and Thomas Percy (1729–1811) in England, but also prefigured the nineteenth-century poetic rapprochement between Gaelic and Anglo-Ireland.

The characteristic cross-gendering of the early period is not maintained at the same frequency in later centuries, although male-authored poems featuring women's voices have continued to be written. The most celebrated and controversial of these is undoubtedly the semi-dramatic *The Midnight Court*, which has been condemned for indulging male fantasies, but also praised for recognizing female desire. If Jonathan Swift can be convicted of class as well as gender condescension in 'Mary the Cook-Maid's Letter to Dr Sheridan', later English-language poets have been as compassionate as the early Irish lyricists in their delineations of feminine subjectivity. Perhaps it is no coincidence that Ferguson's 'Deirdre's Lament for the Sons of Usnach', William Larminie's *Fand*, James Stephens's 'The Red-haired Man's Wife' and Padraic Colum's 'The Poor Girl's Meditation' are all works by poets deeply engaged with Gaelic tradition. Only Ferguson's and Larminie's poems are past-centred, 'Celtic' pieces; the other two protest against poverty and patriarchy in contemporary urban and rural settings respectively. Austin Clarke's 'Martha Blake at Fifty-one' deserves mention in this context as a fiercely engagé third-person portrait of the last days of a lower-middle-class Dublin spinster oppressed alike by her piety and its manipulation by the agents of a powerful institutionalized church.

Two harrowing poems in section VIII cross gender lines in the opposite direction to give intimate second-person portraits of male psychology *in extremis*. Medbh McGuckian's 'Monody for Aghas' dwells on the bodily suffering endured by Thomas Ashe, a hunger-striking republican leader killed by forcible feeding in 1917, while Rita Ann Higgins's 'Black Dog in My Docs Day' charts the suicidal depression of a young man in 1990s Galway.

## The Art of Poetry

The survival of learning in Europe in the aftermath of the collapse of the Roman Empire was in considerable measure due to Irish monks like Johannes Scottus Ériugena and Sedulius Scottus, whose perilous journeys across inhospitable continental terrain are memorialized in the latter's Latin lyric 'Safe Arrival', and to countless of their unnamed colleagues. Among them were the authors of the many Old Irish poems that have come down to us as marginal inscriptions on illuminated Latin manuscripts created in Irish monasteries in Britain, France, Germany and Switzerland. While the poetic attainment of the clerical scribes has its part in a much larger Irish contribution to early medieval culture, the imaginative and technical daring of the poems themselves makes that attainment perhaps the greatest and most historically significant of the country's many achievements in literature. The novelist Flann O'Brien (1911–66) wrote of the 'steel-pen exactness' of the monks' quill-inscribed lyrics, and Seamus Heaney has drawn attention to the extraordinary luminosity of their rendering of the natural environment, their 'sudden apprehension of the world as light'. Old Irish poets introduced a major innovation that verse from the Anglo-Saxon world would not catch up with for centuries: theirs were the first art poems anywhere to use end-rhyme, a procedure they appear to have adapted from Latin hymnody. The debt would be handsomely repaid in the distinctively Irish rhyme patterns of such Latin hymns as Cú Chuimne's eighth-century 'Let us sing daily', the oldest known hymn to the Virgin.

One of the most noteworthy features of the early poetry is its awareness of itself as writing, its sense not only of its own textuality but of the processes – simultaneously joyful and exacting – that went into its making. Poem after poem calls attention to the act of composition and to the material contexts alike of writing and reading. Thus, in section I we see an anonymous monk 'writing out of doors', and hear Colum Cille complain of the physical demands of the scribal life. Posthumous tributes by Dallán Forgaill and Beccán the Hermit praise the saint because he 'wove the word' and because he owned books. Secular and public life, too, held poetry in explicit esteem: King Cormac's 'instructions' list 'silence during recitals' as a key virtue. Even clerical poets who wrote in Latin rather than Irish are at their most animated when discussing the nature and scope of their art, 'Hibernicus Exul' striving to reconcile the idea of poetic immortality with the need to praise God, and Ériugena countering Graeco-Roman aesthetics with a Christian theory of poetry.

The most extended meditation in Irish tradition on the nature of the poetic impulse is to be found in *Buile Shuibhne* (*The Frenzy of Sweeney*), a twelfth-century account in prose and verse of the madness that overtook Sweeney at the Battle of Mag Rath (637) as a result of the curse of St Ronan, whose psalter he had thrown into a lake. Sweeney flies from perch to perch in Ireland and Scotland, living off berries and alternately cursing his condition and praising the landscape in a series of impassioned lyrics. The persistent linking of Sweeney's loss of his kingdom (territory again!) to the fluency of his art led the poet Robert Graves (1895–1985) to describe *Buile Shuibhne* in *The White Goddess* (1948) as 'the most ruthless and bitter description in all European literature of an obsessed poet's predicament'.

With the rise of bardic verse in the thirteenth century, poetry became even more conscious of its own artistry and cultural eminence. Muireadhach Albanach Ó Dálaigh's address to the Blessed Virgin is among the most fervent and ambitious of the many religious poems in this book. Yet it is not the work of a clergyman but of a professional poet so worldly that he killed a retainer who insulted him – and, as a consequence, was forced to make his career in the service of Scottish rather than Irish lords. Ó Dálaigh praises the Trinity and Mary as the ultimate aristocratic patrons, to whom he offers his services free of charge:

O Trinity, O gentle Mary,
every glory passes but yours.
Hear my poem, O Four Persons,
please offer no gold as reward.

His 'well-wrought verse', he insists, has a special sincerity: 'I say the truth, in poetry.'

More than a century later, Tadhg Óg Ó hUigínn's elegy for his brother and fellow poet Fearghal Rua asserts the dead man's importance by presenting poetry itself as the primary casualty of his death:

Poetry is daunted.
A stave of the barrel is smashed
And the wall of learning broken.

('A School of Poetry Closes')

The catalogue of consequences of the bard's impending demise in the anonymous verses on the last illness of Eochaidh Ó hEodhasa (*d.*1612) builds to the climactic identification of poetry as his soon-to-be-widowed spouse. The elevated status of poetry is illustrated again by Lochlainn Óg Ó Dálaigh, whose 'Praise for the Young O'Briens' pays its greatest compliment when it says that the boys are assured of lasting fame because they are friends of poets. In an extravagant defence of the bardic prerogative, Giolla Brighde Mac Con Midhe's thirteenth-century 'A Response to a Threat against Poetry' directs the magisterial eulogistic resources of the tradition to the praise of the art itself.

Later, throughout the period of Gaelic Ireland's terminal crisis and decline, complaints about cultural impoverishment focus on the degeneration represented by the native poetry's move away from strict syllabic metres. If Eochaidh Ó hEodhasa's 'The New Poetry' is gleefully sarcastic and snobbish on the subject, Dáibhí Ó Bruadair's 'To see the art of poetry lost . . .' rages in desperation at the increasing predominance of accentual song-measures, the slackness of which (in a characteristic racial insult) it associates with the coarse manners of the English. *The Midnight Court* – that least patrician of Gaelic poems – is by contrast relaxed about the status of poets and poetry. The coded identification of Merriman as protagonist and author near the conclusion suggests that the duties of the amateur versifier consist mainly of

> Playing his tunes, on sprees and batters
> With his intellectual and social betters.

The English-language poetry of Ireland is rarely as insistent on its own aesthetic status, but it is frequently self-reflexive. Eighteen of the twenty stanzas of the early fourteenth-century 'Hey!' close with a couplet complimenting the preceding lines on their formal ingenuity; these self-congratulations are presumably meant to be read as parodic jibes aimed by the Anglo-Normans at a distinctive literary habit of their Gaelic neighbours. In his elegy on the death of Garret FitzGerald (1559?–80), Richard Stanihurst self-consciously concedes the poverty of his powers compared to those of '*Homer* or *Virgil*' or '*Geffray Chauncer* in English'. The reflections of 'Philo-Philippa' and the Earl of Roscommon on the challenge of transmitting poetic effects from one language to another still seem cogent, especially when the present work relies so much upon poems translated from Irish and other languages.

In more recent times, too, there have been flurries of poetic self-consciousness: Goldsmith's touching valediction to his art near the end of *The Deserted Village*; Allingham's mordant couplet from *Blackberries* on the gap between aspiration and achievement in a poet's career; or Yeats's melancholy illustration of the undependably palliative capacities of poetry in his narrative of the fate of King Goll's borrowed tympan. ('The Madness of King Goll' can be seen as a sort of miniature *Buile Shuibhne*.) Some of the subtlest contemporary poems meditate on their own procedures: Michael Longley's deceptively simple 'Form' or Seamus Heaney's 'The Harvest Bow'; intricate verbal devices that define and embody the characteristic dialectic between presence and absence in lyric speech. Eiléan Ní Chuilleanáin's 'Gloss/Clós/Glas' and Nuala Ní Dhomhnaill's 'The Language Issue' explore the unstable foundations of poetry in a culture that remains to some degree bilingual. The latter poem is translated by Paul Muldoon, the contemporary anglophone world's most accomplished user of rhyme and arguably the greatest lyric innovator Ireland has produced in the millennium and a half since the tonsured scribes of the monasteries hit upon the idea of getting the syllables at the end of their lines to chime pleasingly.

## Organization of the Volume

Each of the nine sections in this anthology is prefaced by an epigraph taken from one of its constituent texts, and the seven poetry sections open with a poem that gives a historical signature to the material that follows. With the exception of the first section, the poems are arranged chronologically according to the poets' dates of birth. The prevalence of anonymous and undateable material in the Old and Middle Irish periods made a thematic approach more appropriate; the two song sections also depart from strict chronology, though to a lesser degree.

While each of the nine sections surveys a historical era and can be read as a free-standing mini-anthology, a degree of orchestration has been attempted across the volume as a whole. Thus, Alfred Lord Tennyson's version of 'The Voyage of Maeldune' – one of the Old Irish *immrama* (voyage tales) – is subjected to impish comment later on in the extract from 'Immram', a long poem by the ancient protagonist's contemporary namesake, Paul Muldoon. John Cunningham's 'The Ant and the Caterpillar' has been included both for its intrinsic interest and because it provided the model for Joyce's 'The Ondt and the Gracehoper'. Songs by Toirdhealbhach Ó Cearbhalláin, the 'Late Irish Orpheus' commemorated by Laurence Whyte in section III, can be found in section IV. Poems commune with other poems within sections also: Seamus Heaney's protest song 'Craig's Dragoons', for example, draws much of its angry force from its relationship with Thomas Davis's 'Clare's Dragoons'. If the reader discovers a wealth of such correspondences throughout the anthology, many of them will inevitably – given the richness of Irish tradition – be innocent of editorial intention.

The boundaries between sections are to some degree porous. A few of the anonymous love poems presented as a group in section II were composed after 1600, but the generic status of the *dánta grá* (as these lyrics of love and friendship are customarily called) meant that they demanded consideration together in a designated subsection. In section I the Gaelic text from which 'The Praise of Fionn' was translated appears to have been written as late as the 1500s, albeit on the basis of a much older Fenian lay.

The dividing line between 'poem' and 'song' is similarly permeable. Lyrics in Irish in the later seventeenth and eighteenth centuries were increasingly committed to the song metres that replaced the syllabic measures of the bards, and some of these poems might consequently have claims to inclusion in section IV rather than III. In the event, individual pieces were assigned to one section rather than another on the basis that poems are intended for recitation or private reading, while songs are primarily meant to be sung (or have entered the tradition in sung form).

The poems in *The Penguin Book of Irish Poetry* have been chosen mainly for their aesthetic interest, and the selections inevitably reflect early twenty-first century critical priorities. It is hoped, however, that the arrangement of the material facilitates the telling of a 'national tale' unfolding over many centuries. A few pieces – such as *The Song of Dermot and the Earl* and 'Raven's Rock', Joseph Campbell's rapt response to the 1916 Rising – have been included to help carry the historical narrative. Other poems – 'The Massacre of the Innocents', for example – appear because they represent a characteristic mode of their time.

On the whole this volume is restricted to work by poets born or brought up in Ireland, though again this has been a rule of thumb rather than a strict policy. Patrick, the Bishop of Dublin who was shipwrecked and drowned in the Irish Sea in 1084 (a fate which lends added poignancy to his 'Prologue' on marine travel) may have been English. If so, he was a compatriot of William Smith, a Catholic participant in the religious wars of the 1640s, whose eloquent commentary on the plight of strife-torn Ireland is reproduced in section III. The Norse material in section I originated outside the country, but is included for its vivid responses to Irish people and events.

## The Translations

Where it was possible to do so, the selections from Irish and Latin were made on the basis of the attractiveness of the poems in their first language, rather than the availability of English versions. Many new translations had to be written. (More than a third of the book's two hundred or so translations are printed here for the first time.) Efforts have been made to redress the significant under-representation in earlier anthologies of the bardic poetry that forms the core of Gaelic literary achievement in the late medieval and early modern periods. This volume is hugely indebted to Tiffany Atkinson, Kit Fryatt, Seamus Heaney, Kathleen Jamie, Bernard O'Donoghue, Maurice Riordan and David Wheatley for their splendid versions of bardic and other poems, and also to Peter Davidson and Michael Longley, who have brought unfamiliar Latin and eighteenth-century Irish material into distinguished English.

In my own contributions I tried to remain alert to the fact that although the originals were written in the past, they were not in the past when they were written. A translator's primary duty is to the poetic animation of the source text, so I sought to avoid the archaisms that can make cribs by some even of the twentieth century's most distinguished Celticists sound like amateur costume drama. (Some, not all: the translations here by Kuno Meyer, Robin Flower, James Carney and Patrick K. Ford demonstrate that philology and literary sensibility can coexist.) Ever since the controversies surrounding Ezra Pound's *Cathay* (1915) and *Homage to Sextus Propertius* (1919) there has been a sort of low-level war between scholarship and poetry in relation to the representation of other literatures in English, a disagreement rooted in conflicting understandings of fealty. The problem with the ideal of loyalty to lexical and grammatical nuance is that it rests upon a view of the original as a linguistic sample rather than a work of art. Almost without exception the poems in this book (those in English and Scots as well as the Old, Middle, Classical and Modern Irish, Latin, Middle English, Norse and French *ur*-texts of the translated pieces) are verbal engines designed to give pleasure. The purpose of translation is to carry something of the primary engine-thrum across the language barrier so as to make the non-anglophone poems 'go' in English.

Transposition of this sort must incur significant loss, even when most nearly successful. No one is likely ever to find a way of communicating (let alone replicating) in English bardic poetry's peculiar combination of stylized intricacy with dramatic immediacy, lacquered veneer with passionate utterance. Similarly, the fusion of assonantal sophistication and visceral rage in Aodhagán Ó Rathaille can only be gestured towards in a Teutonic language. To have despaired of transmitting the erotics of the Gaelic and other originals, though, and to have instead presented prose or otherwise unmetrical versions of them, would have been to betray their fundamental status as poems. In general the new translations are conservative – by Poundian standards at least. As literary renditions have done more or less in every age, they affect contemporary rather than historical idioms.

Not too contemporary, however: over-dependence on colloquialism and customary phrasing can detract from the otherness of the past. My version of Baoi's lament was attempted precisely because so many of the existing translations cancel the distance between our time and the tenth century, robbing the poem of its strangeness by downplaying its mythological dimension to emphasize the universality of the nun's predicament. It has not ultimately proved possible to be fully consistent in mediating ancient poetry. In a few cases, when a draft began to take on vitality by moving away from the original, I followed verbal impulse to a result founded upon rather than directly representative of the poem I had set out to honour. Thus 'St Ite's Song' and, to a lesser extent, 'Speak No Evil' are offered as 'versions after' rather than 'translations from' Old and Middle Irish. Elsewhere, the quest to convey the tonalities of 'Age' led away from the metrical structure of the Middle English text towards a shorter-lined, longer poem than the one in the so-called Kildare manuscript (British Library, Harley MS 913). These examples are not typical, it must be said, and the great majority of the translations stay as close to the source poems as the contingencies of verse-making allow.

**Section I** takes its title from the lyric that serves as its epigraph. The phrase draws attention to the early Irish monks' predilection for composing in broad daylight to distinguish themselves from the initially pagan professional poets who pursued their craft in darkened rooms. The characteristic sense of the sunlit beauty of the natural world and sensitivity to changes of weather and season in Old Irish lyric have been understood as fortuitous consequences of that preference. While the thematic arrangement and associated headings make the section more or less self-explanatory, a few comments may be helpful.

'The Song of the Sword of Cerball' is one of the earliest surviving poems in the bardic manner. It is likely that eulogistic verses were composed throughout the period of clerical hegemony, but that they found their way into manuscript much less readily than the religious poems of the monks, and did not move decisively from the oral to the written domain until well into the second millennium AD. (The situation is complicated by the fact that both the eventually literate *filid* and the non-literate poetic class known as *baird* became increasingly involved in monastic life in the centuries after Colum Cille's convention at Druim Ceat; a crucial consequence of this was the development of the monasteries as centres of Gaelic as well as theological learning.) Tennyson's 'The Voyage of Maeldune' is something of a curiosity, a versified reworking of a voyage tale that anticipates Yeats's 'The Wanderings of Oisin' by nearly a decade. The English poet adapts elements of the translation of *Immram Curaig Máele Dúin* in P. W. Joyce's *Old Celtic Romances* (1879), but in a manner flattering to his own Tory understanding of Irish 'character'. The poem is nevertheless a work of some vigour, and one that demonstrates the widening impact of Celtic antiquarianism in the lead-up to the Literary Revival.

The title and epigraph of **section II** come from the early fourteenth-century Anglo-Norman satire 'The Land of Cockayne', a poem intriguingly congruent with the Gaelic 'The Vision of Mac Conglinne' in the gastronomic if not the erotic features of its imagined earthly paradise. The section signature is provided by four extracts from *The Song of Dermot and the Earl*, a *chanson de geste* in crudely functional Old French couplets recounting the arrival of Strongbow and his Normans in Ireland. The *Song*'s narrative of that first act in Ireland's protracted drama of conquest and colonization is said to have been based on the reminiscences of Morice Regan, secretary and interpreter to the ousted king of Leinster, Dermot MacMurrough (1110–71), whose invitation to Henry II and his barons has made him a byword for treachery in Irish memory.

The confidence of the settler communities who followed in the wake of Strongbow is attested to by the only slightly more sophisticated (if decidedly more spirited) commemoration of the entrenchment of New Ross, written almost a century after the first Norman incursions and (like the *Song*) committed to the speech they brought with them. Though French would be retained as the language of officialdom throughout most of the period covered by section II, it increasingly gave way to Irish in the day-to-day lives of the Norman nobility. The distinctive dialect of Middle English employed by the poems transcribed beside 'The Entrenchment of New Ross' in the Kildare manuscript appears to have been used mainly by the lower orders in the Pale (the region around Dublin directly under the jurisdiction of the English crown) and in the fortified towns of the south-east of the country. This language, too, came under pressure from Irish, and most of the English speakers who stayed on in Ireland during the prolonged Gaelic resurgence of the fifteenth and sixteenth centuries followed the example of their overlords and adopted the linguistic and cultural habits of the more indigenous portion of the population.

The Middle English poems (composed *c.*1320) are unshadowed by this future, and conjure a fully articulated and secure society. Scholars are divided as to whether or not 'The Land of Cockayne' should be interpreted as lampooning the Gaelic monastic life which the invaders had received a papal sanction to reform. It is thought to have been written in the Franciscan (and therefore Norman) abbey at Kildare. The clergy and tradesmen comically evoked in the other major work in the Kildare manuscript, 'Hey!' (sometimes known as 'A Satire on the People of Dublin'), clearly belong to an Anglo-Norman world, even if the poem's procedures mock Gaelic literary practice.

The Kildare manuscript notwithstanding, the most ambitious and accomplished poetry produced in Ireland in the period under discussion was composed in Classical Irish. This poetic language became standardized some time after 1200 and was sustained over the next four and a half centuries by the stringent professional training undergone by its practitioners. The precise extent of the continuity between the bardic schools and the pre-Christian academies of the *filid* is obscure. It seems clear at least that the monastic reform attendant on the arrival of Cistercians, Franciscans and other European religious orders around the time of the Norman incursions broke the institutional link between Gaelic and Christian learning that had evolved over the centuries.

A new secular poetic class – drawn from the hereditary learned families – emerged out of these changed ecclesiastical conditions. Like their ancient forebears, the creators of bardic poetry composed indoors, in the dark. They were court poets and their primary duty was to praise their patron. Even so, there is a considerable variety of effect and a broad frame of reference in their work, allied to a sometimes tetchy awareness of the cultural and monetary value – as well as the difficult artificiality – of poetry. Elaborate rules with regard to the deployment in their syllabic quatrains of metre, rhyme, assonance, consonance and alliteration were formalized alongside regulations governing diction. As a consequence, poetic style in a Gaelic world that included north-western Scotland as well as Ireland remained more or less constant for nearly half a millennium, even though the Irish and Scottish Gaelic languages continued to develop and diversify, and to diverge from one another, both in everyday usage and prose literature.

The extraordinary conservatism of bardic practice becomes clear when considered alongside the transformations undergone by English poetry in the same period, the immense literary time-span running from 'Summer is Ycumen In' (*c.*1240) to the heyday of John Milton (1608–74) and Andrew Marvell (1621–78). If that comparison seems Anglocentric, it is no more so than the defence of traditional Irish mores in Laoiseach Mac an Bhaird's 'Brothers'. Perhaps nothing in the bardic material included here exemplifies the Gaelic reluctance to adapt to a changing world so vividly as Tadhg Dall Ó hUigínn's celebration of the continuing vitality of the ancient practices of hostage-taking and cattle-raiding in 'Enniskillen', a poem in praise of Cú Chonnacht Mág Uidhir, who was Lord of Fermanagh from 1566 to 1589.

Yet strict-metre verse is not necessarily insular in outlook. The love poems grouped together in section II are notable for their wit and grace, and for an economy of style that bespeaks a highly sophisticated, self-aware milieu. In some respects they belong to a European world, having elements in common both with late medieval courtly love poetry and a line of erotic playfulness in English verse that runs from Sidney and the Elizabethans through the Metaphysicals to the Cavalier poets. Worldly, cool and occasionally sly, the *dánta grá* are not averse to extreme sexual innuendo, as 'Piece Making' demonstrates.

The two most idiosyncratic poems in this section come from the appendix to Richard Stanihurst's translation of the first four books of Virgil's *Aeneid* (1582): his elegy for his student Garret FitzGerald and FitzGerald's own death-bed lyric of repentance both appear in their original eccentric orthography. Logician, aesthetician, philologist, historian, biographer, theologian, alchemist, pioneering pharmacist and diplomat, Stanihurst was even by the standards of the Renaissance an extraordinary polymath. He began life as a typically loyal member of an Old English family from the Pale, and his extravagantly written accounts of the Irish past in Holinshed's *Chronicles* (1577) are remarkable, *inter alia*, for their aspersions on Gaelic culture. Reformation politics created strange alliances, however, and the turn of the century found the poet representing Hugh O'Neill in the negotiations that led to the Spanish intervention at Kinsale. After the defeat of the Ulster chiefs, Stanihurst lived in the Spanish Netherlands, where he became a Jesuit. He had strong views on metrics as well as spelling, and his elegy on FitzGerald is as striking for its irregular syllable count as for its eschewal of rhyme, which he detested.

The Irish epigraph to **section III** sardonically comments on the 'turn for the better' involved in the supersession of strict-metre verse by the 'softer' art of the accentual poets, and on the yielding of the old Gaelic clan system to the English aristocratic order (whereby the O'Donnell become Earl of Tyrconnell, the O'Neill Earl of Tyrone, the O'Maguire Earl of Fermanagh, etc.). The signature poem is by the epigraph's author, Eochaidh Ó hEodhasa, bard to the O'Maguires of Fermanagh, whose chief's exploits in the long campaign that culminated in disaster at Kinsale in 1601 it celebrates. If the tonalities of James Clarence Mangan's rendering of 'Ode to the Maguire' are wild and vehement when compared to the austere classicism of the original, their apocalyptic fervour is appropriate to the catastrophe that overcame the Gaelic world in the new century. Poetry in Irish for a time retained and even increased its vigour, rather as the colours of the day reserve their finest display for sunset, and both the early seventeenth-century verse that marked the end of the bardic tradition and the accentual lyric poetry of the following hundred years or so are of consummate technical virtuosity. The dominant temper of both modes is querulous, indignant and – climactically in the work of Ó Rathaille – desolate.

As early as the twelfth-century chronicles of Ireland by Gerald of Wales, the colonizing classes attempted to justify their activities in terms of a mission to extend civilization to the barbarous Irish, while throughout the six hundred years that separated the arrival of the Normans from the death of the Ulster poet Peadar Ó Doirnín the Gaels in their turn felt little reason to doubt the antiquity and quality of their own civilization. After the Reformation the discourses of civilization and barbarism took on a murderous edge, as in the English poet Edmund Spenser's posthumously published *A View of the Present State of Ireland* (1633), where the dialectical presentation of the argument only partly mitigates a colonial enthusiasm for genocide.

Among the writers in section III, Dáibhí Ó Bruadair and Aodhagán Ó Rathaille believed that the English held a monopoly on barbarism in Ireland, while many in Jonathan Swift's circle (if not Swift himself) took it equally for granted that they (or their Anglo-Irish offshoot – the eighteenth century saw the emergence of a distinct Irish Protestant identity) held a monopoly on civilization. The Latin poems from the Confederation of Kilkenny, like the erudite Gaelic 'Dirge' of the poet-priest Pádraigín Haicéad and the scholarly prose achievement of Séathrún Céitinn (who is represented here by three pieces from his small but stylish and various corpus of poetry in Irish) remind us that, in some respects at least, Gaelic vs Anglo-Saxon antipathies are to be understood as local expressions of an overarching European conflict between Catholicism and Protestantism. (Donnchadh Rua Mac Con Mara's poised Latin epitaph for Tadgh Gaedhealach Ó Súilleabháin, composed in 1795, speaks for the long temporal reach of Counter-Reformation learning in Ireland – Mac Con Mara was educated in a hedge-school.)

Swift's little known and uncharacteristically ornate 'Verses Occasioned by the Sudden Drying Up of St Patrick's Well near Trinity College, Dublin' takes the form of a monologue by St Patrick. The poem provides an early example of what later would become a stock claim for the Patrician lineage of the Church of Ireland, but Swift develops his theme in a way unusual for an

Anglican clergyman, not only asserting the seniority of Irish to English civilization but arguing that the larger island was rescued from barbarism by missionary clerics from the smaller one. He also contrasts the benign Irish attitude to the country's British colony – Scotland – with the malign treatment of Ireland by Britain. Aodhagán Ó Rathaille, who died the year Swift wrote his poem, might have agreed; he would certainly have sympathized with the sense of Ireland's terminal decline that leads Patrick to relinquish his national patronage in the closing lines. However, Ó Rathaille would have found incomprehensible Swift's depiction of Catholicism as slavery, and his assumption that Gaelic high culture existed only in the distant past.

If some of the divisions of language, politics and culture in Ireland softened in the post-Reformation period it was only because a more fundamental difference – that between Catholicism and Protestantism – was growing ever more definitive. The extent to which long-standing affiliations could dissolve under the pressure of this dominant religious conflict is suggested by the disparity in circumstance and motivation separating the first two of the three Richard Nugents who are in turn referred to, heard and addressed in the opening part of section III. All belonged to the same extended family, a prominent Old English dynasty associated with Meath and Westmeath. The first – subject of Giolla Brighde Ó hEodhasa's tender bardic poem of consolation to the young man's bereaved mother – grew up Irish-speaking and fought alongside the Ulster chiefs before his early death; while the second – author of a witty English sonnet-epistle to the third – was content to present himself as a typical Renaissance fop, confessing to his namesake cousin that he left Ireland for the appropriately Petrarchan reason of the continued residence there of his 'sweete foe'.

The bards themselves had rather more pressing reasons for emigrating, as their patrons fled to the continent, where they struggled to maintain their aristocratic way of life at courts friendly to the recusant cause. In 1609 Giolla Brighde Ó hEodhasa, a kinsman of Eochaidh, renounced his poetic calling in favour of a religious one, taking the name Bonaventura on his ordination as a Franciscan priest at the College of St Anthony of Padua in Louvain. (In this new role he wrote important works on theology and Irish grammar to accompany an earlier treatise on bardic prosody.) Fearghal

Óg Mac an Bhaird tried to continue in his original profession, but died destitute in Louvain – his 'Letter of Complaint' is addressed to Father Flaithrí Ó Maolchonaire, the founder of St Anthony's College. Eoghan Rua, from the same poetic family (their surname means 'Son of the Bard'), fared somewhat better, travelling to Flanders with the O'Donnells of Tyrone during the Flight of the Earls in 1607 and later becoming an important member of the coterie of Hugh O'Neill in Rome, where he was granted a pension by Philip III of Spain. The child Aodh Ó Domhnaill whom Mac an Bhaird hailed in his brief poem of 1613 grew up not (as the poet later hoped) to lead a Catholic invasion of Ireland, but rather to pursue a career as a senior officer in one of the Irish brigades of the Spanish army.

Many of the miscellaneous lyrics in section III are shadowed not only by political antagonism but by violence. 'Love' is one of the shorter pieces in Faithfull Teate's *Ter Tria* (1658), a forceful if at times eccentric Irish contribution to the tradition of book-length arrangements of devotional poetry inaugurated by George Herbert's *The Temple* (1633) in England and extended by Henry Vaughan's *Silex Scintillans* (1650) in Wales. Teate, the father of Nahum Tate (who became England's poet laureate and whose work is represented here and in section IV), was a Church of Ireland clergyman who moved to England after three of his children died as a result of an attack on his property in County Cavan during the Catholic uprising of 1641. From the opposite side of Ulster's religious and linguistic divide, Peadar Ó Doirnín vividly conveys the horror of sectarian child-murder a century later in 'The Mother's Lament for Her Child'. The poem that closes section III is said to have been written by Robert Emmet in invisible ink in 1799, four years before he was hanged, drawn and quartered for leading a rebellion in pursuance of the aims of the United Irishmen he laments in 'Arbour Hill'.

Encounters between dominant and subaltern political formations were not always bitter in character, and one historical moment of great pathos is recorded here: Eoghan Rua Ó Súilleabháin is represented both by translations of his glitteringly musical poems and by the original of the rough-hewn ballad in English which he formally offered to Admiral George Rodney after the Battle of Les Saintes in the Caribbean in 1782, when this last of the great lyric poets in Irish was a common sailor in the British navy. Thomas Dermody's eccentric 'Odaic Epistle' in Scots to Robert Burns similarly crosses identity boundaries. Dermody was not a Presbyterian radical from Ulster, as his poem's language and sentiment might suggest, but a schoolmaster's son from Ennis in County Clare in Munster. He ran away to Dublin at the age of ten, published his first collection of poems four years later, won fame with his second at seventeen and spent most of the rest of his short life in alcoholic dissipation.

Two long works on agrarian themes dominate the closing pages of section III. *The Deserted Village* (1770) achieved wide popularity in Ireland. Though the poem explicitly mentions 'England's' rather than Ireland's 'griefs' (and contains a description of a decisively English rural tavern), many readers have been eager to agree with Goldsmith's sister Mrs Hodson, who identified Lissoy in County Westmeath, where the poet spent his childhood, as the model for the village of the title. Some of the details, certainly, seem to relate to the author's homeland. The 'wretched matron' who serves as 'sad historian of the pensive plain' has much in common with the *cailleach* figure of Gaelic poetry and mythology (the sovereignty goddess in her more melancholy aspect) and there are strong Irish resonances to the emigration scene of the closing verse paragraph. If the speaker's desire 'Here to return – and die at home at last' is read in terms of Goldsmith's biography, then 'home' becomes a reference to the Irish midlands. (Critics generally assume that the farewell to poetry which follows the emigration scene features Goldsmith writing *in propria persona*.) It might be objected that the characteristic Augustan universalizing tendency informing *The Deserted Village* robs arguments about the poem's setting of much of their relevance and renders redundant speculations about its possible citations of particular English and Irish instances of rural degeneration, clearance and 'improvement'. A counter-objection might say that Goldsmith uses the universalizing mode as a cloak that allows him to smuggle Irish concerns into an acceptably metropolitan and 'English' literary performance.

As noted above, *The Deserted Village* influenced the other long work in section III. *The Midnight Court*'s ambiguous relationship to Gaelic literary precedent has generated much comment, but one question has baffled critics. The huge expansion in population that would eventually set the scene for the Great Famine of the 1840s was already developing apace in Munster in the 1770s, not least in Brian Merriman's native county of Clare. Why then does *The Midnight Court*, composed in 1780, complain of rural depopulation? We know that the poet won prizes for his flax at the Royal Dublin Society in 1797 and that he made his living in his later years as a teacher of mathematics in Limerick: clearly he moved with competence between the two main linguistic cultures of the south of Ireland; it is inconceivable that such a bilingual intellectual was ignorant of the most popular English-language poem in Ireland at the time, so the simple answer to this question is probably 'because *The Deserted Village* does so'.

> Ill fares the land, to hastening ills a prey,
> Where wealth accumulates and men decay

wrote Goldsmith. Merriman's townland (rather than village) is deserted because wealth accumulates and *women* decay, their charms unappreciated and their reproductive faculties ignored by men interested only in economic advancement.

Stylistically, *The Midnight Court* marks a vernacular departure in Gaelic poetry that might have served as the foundation of an entirely new literature had not political and economic circumstances conspired to bring Irish near to extinction in the nineteenth century. The plenitude, slanginess and gargantuan inventiveness of Merriman's vocabulary constitute his most signal contribution to Gaelic poetic method, and it is extremely difficult to communicate in English this aspect of his achievement. Four separate translations have been drawn upon for the full text presented here, each highlighting a different facet of the immensely rich source. Ciaran Carson catches the exuberance and outrageousness of Merriman's mode of address, while Seamus Heaney honours the poem's thumping assonantal drive and rootedness in living speech. The matter-of-fact approach of *The Midnight Court* to love and marriage is most effectively conveyed by Thomas Kinsella's version. Frank O'Connor taps more traditionally English and canonical lexical resources to emphasize the Augustan qualities of a poem that to a degree (particularly in the *aisling* parody of the opening) shares a mock mode with Alexander Pope's *The Rape of the Lock* and such later British poems as 'Tam o' Shanter', and displays an unusual Gaelic partiality for rhyming couplets.

Manuscript references to vernacular songs occur throughout the bardic period, but as these works belonged to oral rather than literary culture they have perished, along with many popular poems and verses by women that also receive mention. If Columbanus wrote the Latin hymn to the Trinity preserved in the Antiphonary of Bangor during his time at that monastery, then this formally daring and theologically subtle work may be the oldest text not only in **section** IV but in this anthology. (The saint left Bangor *c.*589 for his mission to the continent; 'Rowing Song' seems to have been composed just over two decades later, as he made his way with his companions up the Rhine from Coblenz to Mainz on their journey towards the territory of the Alamannians.) The 'Hymn' was probably designed for use in the Easter liturgy – at any rate it is notable for the thoroughness with which it interstitches an imagery of darkness overpowered by light into its account of the chronology and meaning of the life of Christ.

The oldest vernacular piece in section IV is the only slightly later and still widely sung 'Be Thou My Vision', attributed to Dallán Forgaill, the reputedly study-blinded author of section I's lament for Colum Cille. The earliest secular song in the book, 'Donal Óg', is at least a thousand years younger, going back no further than the seventeenth century. Many of the Gaelic folksongs have a melancholy aspect, characteristically reinforced by the slow airs to which they are sung. 'From the Cold Sod that's o'er You' is unusual among them in its connection to international balladry (it can be seen as a variant of Child Ballad No. 78, 'The Unquiet Grave').

Otherwise, popular song in Irish developed in a somewhat insulated environment where theme is concerned. There is much comment, direct and indirect, on the calamitous politics of the period: the forest clearances that followed the triumph of William of Orange (1650–1702) are defiantly mourned in 'Shaun O'Dwyer of the Glen', while the Jacobite defeat of 1691 and its dispiriting aftermath are observed from ground level in 'Patrick Sarsfield, Lord Lucan'. Tomás Ó Flannghaile's seventeenth-century 'The County of Mayo' (exquisitely rendered in George Fox's 1834 translation) provides an early, unsurpassed treatment of the pains of emigration that would form a dominant motif in the experience of the Irish masses for three hundred years after Ó Flannghaile's time. The tender benediction 'Shule Aroon' – listed under the 'English' heading and given in a macaronic version that reveals a song in transition from the older language to the younger – is voiced by a girl on the brink of becoming camp follower of a recruit to the French military (Irishmen were allowed by the British authorities to join the armies of the European Catholic powers throughout most of the first half of the eighteenth century).

While the Gaelic love songs in general are characterized by a combination of emotional frankness with a stark dignity of utterance, they can also be playful: gently so in the exchange between Seán Ó Neachtain and Úna Ní Bhroin; more rambunctiously in Eoghan Rua Ó Súilleabháin's rakish dialogue 'The Volatile Kerryman'. (The celebrated composer Seán Ó Riada's translation puns on the adjective in the Irish title 'An Ciarraíoch Mallaithe' by rendering it homophonically as 'volatile' rather than literally as 'accursed' or, in this context, 'incorrigible'.) Cathal Buí Mac Giolla Ghunna's address to a bittern dead of thirst beside a frozen lake is playful in another way, blending pathos with slyness by deploying sympathy for the unfortunate bird in defence of the drinking that earned the poet both his complexion and his nickname ('*buí*' is Irish for 'yellow'). The two harp songs by Toirdhealbhach Ó Cearbhalláin, whose legendary skills as a composer and competence as an instrumentalist made him welcome in many of the 'big' houses of the Anglo-Irish, show Gaelic song in its more formal aspect.

The authored texts presented at the head of the English group are literary in character, perhaps to the point of politeness, although Nahum Tate's 'While Shepherds Watched' enjoys continuing currency as a Christmas carol. Most of the anonymous songs, like folksongs everywhere, give the point of view of the powerless. The oldest among them, 'The Boyne Water', is something of an exception in its raucous triumphalism. 'My Love is Like the Sun', doctored and de-Hibernicized by Burns (who removed the reference to the Curragh in County Kildare), has the distinction of being one of a tiny handful of traditional pieces disimproved by the great Scottish poet. ('My Love is Like the Sun' comes from a later point in the eighteenth century than 'Shule Aroon': the young woman's lover joins the British army.) The Jacobite 'The Blackbird' has obvious affinities with the *aisling*, while 'The Irish Phœnix' can be seen as a degraded, depoliticized exercise in the latter form, albeit one redeemed by the extravagant vigour of its language. The comic fatalism and lively Dublin street slang of 'The Night before Larry was Stretched' expresses the outlook of the urban poor – a class rarely represented in Irish poetry. (The expert versification of the piece may suggest genteel authorship, however.) 'Willy Reilly' – a tale of love triumphing over class and sectarian obstacles at their most extreme – draws on actual events and was widely popular in the northern counties of Ireland in the late eighteenth and early nineteenth centuries.

The songs associated with the 1798 rebellion reveal diverse aspects of that traumatic episode. 'The Shan Van Vocht' remains the best known and most politically influential of the many historical typifications of Ireland as a woman, while 'The Star of Liberty' expresses the internationalist revolutionary ideology that motivated the leadership of the United Irishmen and a still disputed proportion of their followers. No rebel song has greater pathos than 'The Croppy Boy', which circulated in broadsheet form in the immediate aftermath of the insurrection. 'General Wonder', a laconic and unforgiving narrative of the events surrounding the abortive French landing in Bantry Bay at the end of 1796 from the perspective of the eventual victors, stakes a formidable claim to being the most reactionary poem in this book.

James Orr – an Ulster Presbyterian United Irishman who took part in the Battle of Antrim (1798) and then fled to North America – returned to Ireland around the turn of the century and twice applied (without success) to join the yeomanry being raised to counter the threat of Napoleonic invasion. His substitution of British loyalism for Irish separatism was symptomatic of a widespread withdrawal into sectarian safe havens by people of all religions after the rebels' ideal of uniting 'Catholic, Protestant and Dissenter' under 'the common name of Irishman' broke down in the face of reports (exaggerated by the authorities, according to some commentators) of inter-communal outrage in the main theatre of fighting in Wexford and adjacent counties. Orr retained his radical views on social and economic issues, but relinquished them in relation to the 'connection with England', identified by the United Irish leader Wolfe Tone as 'the never-failing source of all our evils'.

*

'Donegore Hill', which provides the signature to **section V**, can be read as a muted expression of the new Unionist allegiance of the Ulster radicals. One of the few works in Ulster Scots to extend rather than imitate the literary traditions of Lowland Scotland, the poem is an important addition to the series of sardonic celebrations of public festivity that stretches from the fifteenth-century 'Peblis to the Play' through the slightly later 'Christis Kirk on the Grene' to Robert Fergusson's 'Leith Races' and (just before Orr's time) Burns's 'The Holy Fair'. On 7 June 1798 Orr joined thousands of his fellow rebels on Donegore Hill, a few miles east of Antrim, in preparation for the attack on the town. His poem (included in a volume of his verses published by subscription in 1804) conspicuously stops short of describing the ensuing battle, focusing instead on the cheerful chaos of the gathering and in particular on the timorousness of many of those present. (Less than half of the ten thousand men on the hill are thought to have joined the poet in the fighting.) It is difficult to interpret the poem's preference for carnivalesque over heroics in terms other than of repudiation of the United Irish enterprise and tacit acceptance of the Act of Union of 1801.

More generally, however, the Union was met with dismay and even consternation. Section V's epigraph comes from Thomas Moore's 1806 verse epistle 'Corruption'. The vigour and directness with which he denounces the new constitutional arrangements as the final act in the enslavement of Ireland give the lie to caricatures of the leading songwriter of the age as an effete toady. The sense of disempowerment felt by Catholic poets like Moore and James Clarence Mangan was shared by many of their Protestant compatriots, particularly in the south of the country. The Ulster-born Samuel Ferguson embraced the Union, but even his career – as both antiquarian and poet – was based on anxieties about the survival of Irish cultural separateness in the newly combined polity.

Moore may have been an important player in the drama of English romanticism through his friendship with Lord Byron and other figures, and through the popular success of such works as his now virtually unreadable Oriental verse tale *Lalla Rookh* (1817), but with the passing of the years his younger contemporary Mangan (whose twentieth-century admirers included James Joyce and

W. H. Auden) has come to be seen as Ireland's greatest romantic writer and as the most important poet the country produced between Merriman and Yeats. The impoverished, green-cloaked and multi-pseudonymous Mangan, who presented many of his original verses as translations from a range of exotic languages, was as much an early *poète maudit* as a belated romantic. Even when his poems use texts in other languages as their starting point they can transform their sources beyond recognition. The ecstatic nationalist sublime of 'Dark Rosaleen' has no prototype in 'Róisín Dubh', the gentle eighteenth-century *aisling* it 'translates', while the free-verse narrative 'Khidder' is six times longer and far more energetically imagined than 'Chidher', a ballad treatment of a similar theme by the German poet Friedrich Rückert (1788–1866). Mangan's peculiar blend of intensity and abjection takes an autobiographical turn in 'Twenty Golden Years Ago' and 'The Nameless One'. In 'Siberia' he conflates psychological and political vistas in a manner consistent with posterity's view of him as a doomed poet whose sufferings were inseparable from those of his country: in due course he died of malnutrition at the height of the Great Famine.

Mary Tighe and George Darley are minor tributaries to the mainstream of English romanticism. Tighe's *Psyche* was admired by John Keats (1795–1821), whose own erotic poem in Spenserian stanzas, 'The Eve of St Agnes', seems indebted to the lushly sexual account of Cupid's visit to Psyche reproduced here. Darley, a depressive mathematician, won notoriety for his harsh reviews of contemporary poetry and drama in the *Athenaeum* and other periodicals. His antagonists on the London literary scene were quick to identify the exaggerated eloquence of *Nepenthe* and his blank verse plays as a characteristically Irish vice.

Hundreds of poems in comic Hiberno-English were published by writers of both Catholic and Protestant origin throughout the nineteenth century, few of them as witty or lacking in condescension as the relatively early example that represents the mode here, Letter V from Moore's *The Fudges in England* (1835). Patriotic poems were composed in even greater numbers, most of them lachrymose and conventional. 'The Irish Wolf' is atypical in its poise and eschewal of sentimentality. The author, James McCarroll, was a County Longford-born journalist and inventor who in the course of a turbulent career in Canada and the United States gradually shifted his political allegiances from Orangeism to Fenianism: his poem offers a classic statement of Irish nationalism at its most Anglophobic and unreconciled.

Political commentary could take other forms as well. 'In Snow', William Allingham's sonnet on the doubtful wisdom of the 1878–80 British intervention in Afghanistan, has startling resonance more than a century and a quarter later. Yeats's omission of Allingham's name from the list of his literary antecedents – 'Davis, Mangan, Ferguson' – may have done lasting damage to the reputation of a more serious and ambitious poet than Thomas Davis and a more intellectually alert one than Samuel Ferguson. Although Allingham made his career in London, where he was a member of Tennyson's circle, his poetry retained a strong Irish focus. If no poet in the book more clearly exemplifies the distinction between patriotism and nationalism, it is a distinction that has done Allingham few favours where his compatriots' interest in his achievement is concerned.

This is the first section of the book where the Gaelic material – Antoine Ó Raifteirí's good-humoured dialogue with the whiskey and the two examples of keening – comes entirely from the folk realm. The terrible price paid by the rural poor in the 1840s for the dismantling of Gaelic social structures and the *laissez-faire* economic orthodoxies of the day is tallied by Jane Francesca Elgee in 'A Supplication', one of the most impassioned of the many poems elicited by the Famine. James Henry is represented by two characteristically vigorous expressions of his atheism. Composition was something of a sideline for Henry, a philanthropic physician who retired early to devote himself to the study of the manuscripts of *The Aeneid*, in pursuit of which he is said to have crossed the Alps on foot seventeen times.

The Irish Literary Revival that gives its title to **section VI** took place against the background of a larger movement of cultural retrieval involving the Irish language, Gaelic games and traditional lore of various kinds. In its first two decades or so, the Revival's core personnel was drawn from the ranks of a Protestant minority that had been progressively losing its privileges since the Act of Union; its immediate political context was the ongoing shift in power from their ascendancy caste to the majority community. Yeats in 1922 recollected the 'sudden certainty' that came upon him in 'a moment of supernatural insight' in the late 1880s that 'Ireland was to be like soft wax for years to come': the implication was that he and his fellow-Revivalists would set their seal on the wax, offering the inchoate Catholic masses cultural and intellectual guidance and thereby saving the emerging nation from the horrors of mercantile modernity, and their own class from oblivion. History refused to cooperate with these plans. Indeed, throughout the period, the expectations of writers kept being confounded by historical developments. From Ferguson's dramatic monologue on the 1882 Phoenix Park murders at the beginning, to Francis Ledwidge's two poems of mourning for executed Republican leaders at the end, the section is punctuated by responses to overwhelming political events. The most morally urgent of these is undoubtedly Yeats's 'Easter 1916', where the Easter Rising and its turbulent aftermath force the poet to subject his ideas about Ireland, social class and even poetry itself to a series of revisions, and in the process to raise his art to a higher register than it had hitherto achieved. (The poem was withheld from publication until October 1920, when it was included in an issue of the *New Statesman* containing a range of protests against the atrocities authorized by Lloyd George's administration during the War of Independence. It is followed here by 'Reprisals', Yeats's most explicit denunciation of government policy, which was not made public in the poet's lifetime.) The intrusion of history cut short the careers of two of the most promising poets of the era: Thomas MacDonagh was killed by a British firing squad in Kilmainham Jail in Dublin in May 1916; his elegist Francis Ledwidge by a German shell at the Second Battle of Ypres fourteen months later.

History as a thing of the past also features prominently in section VI, in John Todhunter's troubled meditation on state violence during the agrarian disturbances of the Union period; Emily Lawless's dramatization of the departure of the last Catholic aristocrats from Munster ('Clare Coast') a century earlier; and T. W. Rolleston's delicate 'Celtic Twilight' evocation of the immemorial generations of the Gael in 'The Dead at Clonmacnois' (based on a fourteenth-century original). Lawless's 'A Retort' delineates the patrician national feeling shared by many of her rural Anglo-Irish class, a complex loyalty that reconciled love of Ireland and disdain of England with unionist politics.

Yeats's recourse in the 1880s and 1890s to what he called 'Irish scenery' involved neither an eschewal of non-Irish themes nor, as has been alleged by his detractors, a retreat from the difficulties of living. Each of the Celtic poems at the beginning of the selection from his work here explores an ethical or psychological quandary, and the shift towards a more social idiom in the later pieces marks the deepening of an already robust engagement with the contemporary world rather than a sudden onset of consciousness of it. Where the younger poets of the first decades of the new century are concerned, however, everyday language and settings serve an egalitarian political awareness and a repudiation of the social privilege identified with the Revival in its first phase. (J. M. Synge is something of an exception to this rule, albeit his lyrics are more plain-spoken in their realism and more muscular in their physicality than any others in the section.) Joseph Campbell's 'The Newspaper-Seller' and the first two James Stephens poems are as attentive to urban deprivation and injustice as the Padraic Colum pieces are to the economic conditions of life in the countryside. A well-nigh socialist sense of the actuality of manual labour is central even to Stephens's reanimation of the voice of Dáibhí Ó Bruadair.

The title and epigraph of **section VII** are taken from 'Nightwalker', Thomas Kinsella's brooding ambulatory poem from 1967 on the eclipsed idealism of the independent Irish state that had come into being forty-five years earlier. The section opens with Yeats's magisterial 'Meditations in Time of Civil War', an apocalyptic response to the birth in blood of the new constitutional order. Joseph Campbell's excitement about the Easter Rising in the previous section is countered now by his disillusioned prison poems, written during his incarceration by the Free State government for his Republican sympathies. Austin Clarke's 'The Lost Heifer', also composed during the Civil War, laments the descent of nationalist altruism into fratricidal violence.

Yet, initially at least, there was a degree of optimism among the literary classes about the possibilities of hard-won statehood. Yeats was appointed by the governing party to the upper house of the new parliament, and threw his energies into such projects as designing the country's stamps and coinage. His Abbey Theatre became the world's first nationally subsidized theatre in 1925. If the temper of the five decades covered by the section is to be read through the more politically engaged among the poems, however, it was a period of disgruntlement and disaffiliation. The increasingly theocratic nature of the southern state was illustrated by the Censorship of Publications Act of 1929, which implied that literature itself was an enemy of the people. Yeats's 'Crazy Jane Talks with the Bishop', Clarke's 'The Straying Student' and 'Penal Law' and Patrick Kavanagh's *The Great Hunger* protest in different ways against the anti-sexual puritanism of official versions of Irishness. Disaffection was keenest for southern Protestants like Patrick MacDonogh, and half-southern ones like the Belfast-born Louis MacNeice. 'O, Come to the Land' and 'Valediction' bristle with exasperation and despondency at the emerging character of the new state.

For Catholics in Northern Ireland, meanwhile, mere disaffection might have seemed like a luxury. (The institutions of the devolved 'province' – it comprised about two-thirds of Ulster – had been set up a year before those of the Irish Free State.) Doomed to perpetual opposition in the Stormont parliament, the minority community created by the border faced varying degrees of discrimination at local government level and was occasionally subject to abuse by the security machinery of the statelet. Its grievances were sufficient to keep ancient antagonisms alive and set in train the series of events that led to the outbreak of violence in 1969 which sandwiches the poems of the section between the end of one period of 'Troubles' and the beginning of another. John Hewitt's laying bare of the historic Ulster Protestant siege mentality in 'The Colony', from the middle of the period, can be read as a warning to nationalists and others of the consequences of pressuring such a psychology to conform to an identity template it perceives as alien. Derek Mahon's two poems are not so sympathetic to his community of origin: they identify religious fanaticism and lower-middle-class blandness as the poles between which its values can be defined. A politically divided Tyrone landscape is surveyed in John Montague's genial 'What a View' by a less than independently minded seagull (whose parting gift to the flagpole of the British Legion hut at the end of the poem provides the clue to his fealties). The last three poems mentioned were published shortly before the outbreak of the Troubles. If they cannot be said to have predicted the cataclysm (all sides were taken by surprise by the sudden slide into violence) they attest at least to the capacity of poetry to grapple with underlying political realities.

Yeats was the first Irish poet since Moore to have a central impact on literature beyond Ireland. His continuing reputation as one of the great poets of the modern world rests on the work he produced in the 1920s and 30s. A remarkable aspect of his achievement was his ability to make Irish subject matter everybody's business. Of the leading poets of the next generation, only MacNeice made much impression outside Ireland. He is distinguished from his contemporaries Austin Clarke, Patrick Kavanagh and Seán Ó Ríordáin by consistency rather than quality. A higher proportion of his poems retain their interest, perhaps because, conducting his career from England, he operated in a more economically and psychologically sustaining environment than they did. (None of the three enjoyed anything as grand as a career.) Clarke's early work furthers the attempt by William Larminie in the late nineteenth century to accommodate Gaelic metrics in English, and measures the tawdriness of the present against the grandeur of a past that fascinates him as much as it did Samuel Ferguson. His later writing sustains such a campaign against the church-state consensus in the South that he has been seen as a dissident writer on the Soviet model. Kavanagh repudiated the past as a resource and wrote in an idiom based on the day-to-day speech of the community at large, with no agonizing over the loss of Gaelic or the 'foreignness' of English. His matter-of-fact vernacularism was to have a liberating effect on later poets as disparate as Heaney, Durcan and Muldoon. For Ó Ríordáin, born in an Irish-speaking area of West Cork and 'educated' (as he once observed) by tuberculosis, Gaelic had not yet been lost. His lyrics temper a tortured interiority with impish wit, while their idioms and rhythms reflect his reading in anglophone modernism. Along with the poems of Máirtín Ó Direáin and the comparatively traditionalist verse of Máire Mhac an tSaoi, they restored the older language to the forefront of poetry in Ireland for the first time since 1780; a position it retains up to the present.

A brief historical sketch runs the risk of identifying the mood of the times at the expense of the more various moods of the poems themselves. There is little 'disappointment' in some of the strongest writing here: Kavanagh's celebratory 'Kerr's Ass' and 'Innocence', for example, Padraic Fallon's playful 'A Flask of Brandy' or Richard Murphy's rugged recreation of outdoor struggle and achievement, 'Sailing to an Island'. If MacNeice's most brilliant lyrics are obligingly disappointed, the reasons for that are a matter of metaphysics rather than politics. The section ends with short selections from poets whose major work still lay in the future in 1970.

The extract from Austin Clarke's amplification of a sex-change scene from Ovid's *Metamorphoses* that opens **section VIII** sets the signature for a corpus of poetry written during a period which began in great turbulence and witnessed a series of radical social and political transformations in both parts of Ireland. Clarke called 'Tiresias' a 'cheerful' poem, and it is certainly one that treats sexuality in a more carefree manner than did his sometimes morbid earlier work. Sexuality was at the centre of the challenge to the temporal power of the Catholic church in the Republic of Ireland (as the southern polity had been redesignated in 1949). Plebiscites in the 1980s seeking to install and retain Catholic teaching respectively on abortion and divorce in the constitution gave the church victories that proved Pyrrhic a mere decade later when its authority crumbled in the face of clerical and episcopal implication in a series of sex scandals. Women's groups were to the fore in the political resistance to theocracy, and the rise of feminism in Ireland, north and south, is reflected in section VIII's high proportion of women poets. Poetry, too, played a role in the process of liberalization: Brendan Kennelly and Paul Durcan became public figures on the basis of media appearances and packed readings of their libertarian satires, which sold in quantities demonstrative of the art's continuing cultural primacy in Ireland.

The violence that broke out in Northern Ireland in the late 1960s increased in its intensity over the early part of the following decade, and remained a central fact of life there until the ceasefires of 1994. Thousands fell victim to shootings and bombings by Republican and Loyalist paramilitaries; the agents of the state, too, particularly in the first few years of the conflict, were responsible for the deaths of many civilians. Internment without trial in Northern Ireland and high-profile and belatedly rectified miscarriages of justice against Irish people in Britain added to the passions of the day. The burning of the British Embassy in Dublin on 2 February 1972 by members of a crowd protesting against the killings by paratroopers of thirteen civilians at a march in Derry three days earlier brought Anglo-Irish relations back to a point close to where they had been when Yeats wrote 'Reprisals'.

This period of grief and rage provided the unlikely but enabling context for the flowering of poetry by writers born and brought up in Northern Ireland. Seamus Heaney, Michael Longley and Derek Mahon had first become prominent towards the end of the previous decade, but now, under pressure of terrible events, the art of all three grew and developed in diverse and surprising ways. They were soon joined by a second generation of gifted Ulster poets that included Paul Muldoon, Ciaran Carson, Tom Paulin and Medbh McGuckian. Poetry became a space for civility in uncivil times, a forum where traditions locked in vicious antagonism in the political sphere could meet and engage with each other. Some poems ('The Tollund Man', 'The Strand at Lough Beg', 'Wounds', 'The Butchers') dealt directly with the violence, others ('Broagh', 'Courtyards in Delft', 'Dresden', 'Aisling') approached it circumspectly, while others again exercised the prerogative of the art and took their themes as they pleased. If the ambient mayhem added an extra dimension of visibility to the work of the northern writers, the poetry itself was clearly of a moral and aesthetic quality deserving of the attention it attracted.

One unfortunate consequence of the focus on the new category of 'Northern Irish poetry' was the relative lack of interest in developments south of the border, where there was also a significant quickening of poetic energy. Thomas Kinsella's meditative variation on the Big House novel, 'Tao and Unfitness at Inistiogue on the River Nore', and Paul Durcan's exuberant autobiographical narrative 'Give Him Bondi' join such 'northern' pieces as Heaney's 'A Sofa in the Forties', Mahon's 'A Disused Shed in County Wexford' and Muldoon's 'Turkey Buzzards' in challenging comparison with the best poems written anywhere in the anglophone world over the last half century. Purely in terms of poetry, the decades since 1970 are more deserving of the 'renaissance' label than the literary movement led by Yeats nearly a century earlier, which produced only one (admittedly very major) poet of international stature.

The immediately contemporary part of an historical anthology must date more quickly than the others, and must expect to be the subject of controversy. Where poets younger than Paul Muldoon are concerned I have not tried to second-guess posterity but rather to present a selection of work that bears witness to the variety and excellence of current poetic enterprise. Thus 'modernist' poets like Maurice Scully, for whom the art is as much a visual as an aural one, appear alongside writers whose sense of poetry is more consciously rooted in the long traditions of lyric in English or Irish, or both. (Antagonism between champions of 'experimental' poetry and 'well-made' lyrics constitutes a sectarianism as tedious as the religious variety.) Even though the period has been allocated a perhaps disproportionately generous amount of space, it is inevitable that some worthy and promising poets have been omitted and equally inevitable that eyebrows will be raised by one or two inclusions. I have been guided by my sense of the verbal life of the material, and have passed over a good deal of intellectually or otherwise engaging verse that seemed less bracing in its deployment of words than the writing selected.

The award of the Nobel Prize for Literature to Seamus Heaney in 1995 was greeted with joy in Ireland, both for its own sake and because it seemed to mark a new, confident phase in the country's history. The Troubles in the North appeared to be at an end, while the Republic, where the poet had made his home since 1972, had entered a phase of unprecedented economic growth that would be sustained until the global crash of 2008. At the time of writing the Republic is undergoing adjustment to the unwelcome new conditions, adjustment all the more painful because of its own construction bubble and particular form of over-extended credit, and Northern Ireland, too, has been hit hard by the recession. The long tradition of Irish poetry provides a palliative perspective on current difficulties. Indeed, the grim historical realities made available to us by the poems in sections III and V, and also by those in the early part of section VIII, highlight the extraordinary political achievement of the years since Heaney received what Yeats called the bounty of Sweden. Relations between Ireland and Britain have never been so harmonious, and almost all shades of political opinion are represented in the (still somewhat fragile) government of Northern Ireland. How poets will deal with Ireland's loss of the status of 'most distressful country' (conferred by the song 'The Wearing of the Green') remains to be seen.

The songs and ballads of **section IX** have been arranged thematically. An exception is made at the beginning for Thomas Moore, less to indulge the notion of him as National Poet than to acknowledge his historical popularity and the coincidence of his chronology with that of the opening of the section. William Hazlitt's observation in *The Spirit of the Age* (1825) that 'Mr Moore converts the wild harp of Erin into a musical snuff-box' draws attention to a disabling gentility in the songs, certainly, but it misrepresents the weight of their melancholy charm. Moore's lyrics sigh for an unreachable past, whether the historical past of Brian Boru, the mythological one of the Children of Lir, or the autobiographical one of the author's student friendship with Robert Emmet (the 'hero' of 'She is Far from the Land'). Their euphony is beautiful but oppressive, and the experience of moving from them to the love songs of the next subsection is akin to stepping from a stuffy Dublin drawing room into the fresh air of the West.

The two pieces by Antoine Ó Raifteirí certainly range the Connaught outdoors. Notable here also are the spirited Cork song 'I Know My Love' and Gerald Griffin's consummately skilful reconstruction of a Gaelic original, 'Eileen Aroon', a version admired by Tennyson for the delicacy of its vowel music. The Yeats, Campbell and Colum songs at the end are by now part of folk tradition in Ireland and elsewhere, and 'My Lagan Love' has become the anthem of the author's native Belfast. The extent to which any of the three was indebted to oral sources in the first instance is unclear.

Many of the anonymous songs at the head of the 'War, Politics, Prison' subsection share an exuberant anarchism that may be seen as a strategy for dealing with oppression. 'Blarney Castle' – a favourite of James Joyce – and 'The Cow Ate the Piper' hover on the border between the humorous and the grotesque. 'Johnny, I Hardly Knew You' is one of the great anti-war songs of the world. The limbless state of its tragicomic hero might be taken as justification for the direct action against a recruitment party described in the following piece, 'Arthur McBride'. 'The Recruiting Sergeant' demonstrates that resistance to joining the army had taken on a nationalist colouring by the early twentieth century.

The solitary Gaelic song in the group appears to have been written around 1801, when the last remaining woods around the Butler castle in Kilcash, County Tipperary, were felled. James Clarence Mangan's translation is contemporary with the earliest known manuscripts of the lament. The authored songs include two powerful pieces by Patrick MacGill based on his experiences on the Western Front, where he served with the London Irish Rifles. (MacGill is best known for his novel *Children of the Dead End*, 1914.) Brendan Behan's are among the wittiest texts here, even if 'The Captains and the Kings' tells us a good deal more about Irish nationalist fantasy than about the England it purports to describe.

The 'Society' category of the closing subsection avails of a broad definition. Once again, some of the liveliest work comes from the oral tradition. The richest and most extravagant of the 'writerly' songs, James Joyce's 'The Ballad of Persse O'Reilly', draws much of its vigour from that tradition, rather as the author's fiction did in the later phases of its development. (Our extract from *Finnegans Wake* is joined by 'Finnegan's Wake'.) The selections are more or less self-explanatory and, like those in the rest of the book, combine the familiar with the lesser known.

While it is a privilege to end the book with 'Lisdoonvarna', Christy Moore's burlesque on 1980s Irish public life, I should have liked to include more material in contemporary rock and folk idioms. I searched hard for it. I found (or already knew) some good and a few magnificent Irish songs from the post-Beatles era, but none of them had life when reduced to mere print. To say this is no slight. 'Laddie lie near me' is one of the most touching of all the compositions of Robert Burns, but the words are inert without the melody and the power of the song is revealed only in performance. So it is also with some of the best contemporary songs. Mention of omissions affords an opportunity to conclude with the observation that *The Penguin Book of Irish Poetry* constitutes an attempt to represent rather than reproduce the huge wealth of poetry and song that has been Ireland's major contribution to world culture for a millennium and a half. It is a contribution that shows no sign of letting up.

PATRICK CROTTY

# I

# WRITING OUT OF DOORS: EARLIEST TIMES TO 1200

*Dom-farcaí fidbaidæ fál,*
*fom-chain loíd luin – lúad nad cél;*
*húas mo lebrán, ind línech,*
*fom-chain trírech inna n-én.*

*Fomm-chain coí menn – medair mass –*
*hí mbrot glass de dindgnaib doss.*
*Débrad! non-choimmdiu coíma,*
*caín-scríbaimm fo foída ross.*

'Writing Out of Doors'

# THE ARRIVAL OF CHRISTIANITY

## ANONYMOUS

### *Adze-head*

Across the sea will come Adze-head,
crazed in the head,
his cloak with hole for the head,
his stick bent in the head.

He will chant impiety
from a table in the front of his house;
all his people will answer:
'Be it thus. Be it thus.'

*James Carney*

### *I Invoke the Seven Daughters*

I invoke the seven daughters of the sea
Who fashion the threads of the sons of long life.
May three deaths be removed from me,
Three lifetimes granted to me,
Seven waves of good fortune conferred on me!
May phantoms not harm me on my journey

In S. Laserian's corslet without hindrance!
May my name not be pledged in vain!
May old age come to me!
May death not come to me until I am old!

I invoke my Silver Champion
Who dies not, who will not die;
May a time be granted me
Of the excellence of white bronze!
May my form be arranged,
May my right be exalted,
May my strength be increased,
May my tomb not be readied,
May I not die on my journey,
May my return be confirmed!
May the headless serpent not seize me,
Nor the hard grey worm,
Nor the senseless chafer!
May no thief harm me,
Nor band of women,
Nor warrior band!
May increase of time come to me
From the King of the Universe!

I invoke seven-cycled Senach
Whom fairywomen suckled
On the paps of mystic lore.
May my seven candles not be quenched!
I am an invincible fortress,
I am an immovable rock,
I am a precious stone,
I am the symbol of seven treasures.
May my wealth be in hundreds,
My years in hundreds,
Each hundred after the other!

My benefits I call to me;
The grace of the Holy Spirit be upon me!
Wholeness is the Lord's.
Wholeness is Christ's.
Bless, O Lord, Your people!

*P. L. Henry*

## *The Deer's Cry*

Patrick sang this hymn when the ambuscades were laid against him by King Loeguire (Leary) that he might not go to Tara to sow the faith. Then it seemed to those lying in ambush that he and his monks were wild deer with a fawn, even Benen, following them. And its name is 'Deer's Cry'.

I arise today
Through a mighty strength, the invocation of
the Trinity,
Through belief in the threeness,
Through confession of the oneness
Of the Creator of Creation.

I arise today
Through the strength of Christ's birth with
His baptism,
Through the strength of His crucifixion with
His burial,
Through the strength of His resurrection with
His ascension,
Through the strength of His descent for the
judgment of Doom.

I arise today
Through the strength of the love of
Cherubim,
In obedience of angels,

In the service of archangels,
In hope of resurrection to meet with reward,
In prayers of patriarchs,
In predictions of prophets,
In preachings of apostles,
In faiths of confessors,
In innocence of holy virgins,
In deeds of righteous men.

I arise today
Through the strength of heaven:
Light of sun,
Radiance of moon,
Splendour of fire,
Speed of lightning,
Swiftness of wind,
Depth of sea,
Stability of earth,
Firmness of rock.

I arise today
Through God's strength to pilot me:
God's might to uphold me,
God's wisdom to guide me,
God's eye to look before me,
God's ear to hear me,
God's word to speak for me,
God's hand to guard me,
God's way to lie before me,
God's shield to protect me,
God's host to save me
From snares of devils,
From temptations of vices,
From every one who shall wish me ill,
Afar and anear,
Alone and in a multitude.

I summon today all these powers between me and
  those evils,
Against every cruel merciless power that may
  oppose my body and soul,
Against incantations of false prophets,
Against black laws of pagandom,
Against false laws of heretics,
Against craft of idolatry,
Against spells of women and smiths and wizards,
Against every knowledge that corrupts man's
  body and soul.

Christ to shield me today
Against poison, against burning,
Against drowning, against wounding,
So that there may come to me abundance of reward.
Christ with me, Christ before me, Christ behind me,
Christ in me, Christ beneath me, Christ above me,
Christ on my right, Christ on my left,
Christ when I lie down, Christ when I sit down,
  Christ when I arise,
Christ in the heart of every man who thinks of me,
Christ in the mouth of every one who speaks of me,
Christ in every eye that sees me,
Christ in every ear that hears me.

I arise today
Through a mighty strength, the invocation of the
  Trinity,
Through belief in the threeness,
Through confession of the oneness
Of the Creator of Creation.

*Kuno Meyer*

## *from* The Calendar of Oengus

### *The Downfall of Heathendom*

Ailill the king is vanished,
  Vanished Croghan's fort,
Kings to Clonmacnois
  Come to pay their court.

In quiet Clonmacnois
  About Saint Kieran's feet
Everlasting quires
  Raise a concert sweet.

Allen and its lords
  Both are overthrown,
Brigid's house is full,
  Far her fame has flown.

Navan town is shattered,
  Ruins everywhere;
Glendalough remains,
  Half a world is there.

Ferns is a blazing torch,
  Ferns is great and good,
But Beg, son of Owen,
  And his proud hosts are dead.

Old haunts of the heathen
  Filled from ancient days
Are but deserts now
  Where no pilgrim prays.

Little places taken
  First by twos and threes
Are like Rome reborn,
  Peopled sanctuaries.

Heathendom has gone down
  Though it was everywhere;
God the Father's kingdom
  Fills heaven and earth and air.

Sing the kings defeated!
  Sing the Donals down!
Clonmacnois triumphant,
  Cronan with the crown.

All the hills of evil,
  Level now they lie;
All the quiet valleys
  Tossed up to the sky.

*Frank O'Connor*

## *Patrick's Blessing on Munster*

God's blessing upon Munster,
Men, women, children!
A blessing on the land
Which gives them fruit!

A blessing on every wealth
Which is brought forth on their marches!
No one to be in want of help:
God's blessing upon Munster!

A blessing on their peaks,
On their bare flagstones,
A blessing on their glens,
A blessing on their ridges!

Like sand of sea under ships
Be the number of their hearths:
On slopes, on plains,
On mountainsides, on peaks.

*Kuno Meyer*

## *Writing Out of Doors*

A wall of forest looms above
  and sweetly the blackbird sings;
all the birds make melody
  over me and my books and things.

There sings to me the cuckoo
  from bush-citadels in grey hood.
God's doom! May the Lord protect me
  writing well, under the great wood.

*James Carney*

# MONASTICISM

## ANONYMOUS

### *The Hermit's Song (Marbán to Guaire)*

A hiding tuft, a green-barked yew-tree
  Is my roof,
While nearby a great oak keeps me
  Tempest-proof.

I can pick my fruit from an apple
  Like an inn,
Or can fill my fist where hazels
  Shut me in.

A clear well beside me offers
  Best of drink,
And there grows a bed of cresses
  Near its brink.

Pigs and goats, the friendliest neighbours,
  Nestle near,
Wild swine come, or broods of badgers,
  Grazing deer.

All the gentry of the county
  Come to call!
And the foxes come behind them,
  Best of all.

To what meals the woods invite me
   All about!
There are water, herbs and cresses,
   Salmon, trout.

A clutch of eggs, sweet mast and honey
   Are my meat,
Heathberries and whortleberries
   For a sweet.

All that one could ask for comfort
   Round me grows,
There are hips and haws and strawberries,
   Nuts and sloes.

And when summer spreads its mantle
   What a sight!
Marjoram and leeks and pignuts,
   Juicy, bright.

Dainty redbreasts briskly forage
   Every bush,
Round and round my hut there flutter
   Swallow, thrush.

Bees and beetles, music-makers,
   Croon and strum;
Geese pass over, duck in autumn,
   Dark streams hum.

Angry wren, officious linnet
   And black-cap,
All industrious, and the woodpeckers'
   Sturdy tap.

From the sea the gulls and herons
   Flutter in,
While in upland heather rises
   The grey hen.

In the year's most brilliant weather
  Heifers low
Through green fields, not driven nor beaten,
  Tranquil, slow.

In wreathed boughs the wind is whispering,
  Skies are blue,
Swans call, river water falling
  Is calling too.

*Frank O'Connor*

## *The Priest Rediscovers His Psalm-Book*

How good to hear your voice again,
  Old love, no longer young, but true,
As when in Ulster I grew up
  And we were bedmates, I and you.

When first they put us twain to bed,
  My love who speaks the tongue of Heaven,
I was a boy with no bad thoughts,
  A modest youth, and barely seven.

We wandered Ireland over then,
  Our souls and bodies free of blame,
My foolish face aglow with love,
  An idiot without fear of blame.

Yours was the counsel that I sought
  Wherever we went wandering;
Better I found your subtle thought
  Than idle converse with some king.

You slept with four men after that,
  Yet never sinned in leaving me,
And now a virgin you return –
  I say but what all men can see.

For safe within my arms again,
  Weary of wandering many ways,
The face I love is shadowed now
  Though lust attends not its last days.

Faultless my old love seeks me out;
  I welcome her with joyous heart –
My dear, you would not have me lost,
  With you I'll learn that holy art.

Since all the world your praises sings,
  And all acclaim your wanderings past
I have but to heed your counsel sweet
  To find myself with God at last.

You are a token and a sign
  To men of what all men must heed;
Each day your lovers learn anew
  God's praise is all the skill they need.

So may He grant me by your grace
  A quiet end, an easy mind,
And light my pathway with His face
  When the dead flesh is left behind.

*Frank O'Connor*

## *Straying Thoughts*

Shame on these thoughts of mine
  that dart every way
they are piling up trouble
  for Judgement Day

At Psalms they dander
      down unapproved roads
run riot in the face
      of all-seeing God

Through bustling crowds
      through gaggles of girls
through woods through cities
      they swagger and swirl

Along paved highways
      they strut in their pride
down desert tracks in-
      sidiously sidle

Without need of a ship
      they sail the salt seas
with no springboard in sight
      vault to the skies

They follow paths of folly
      to east and west
and when tired stravaiging
      drop home for a rest

Where I try to restrain them
      and hobble their feet
but they run from their shackles
      into the street

There knifeblade and horsewhip
      can't bring them to heel
and they slip through stretched fingers
      like slithering eels

No firmvaulted dungeon
      or lock of hard iron
no fosse or thick fortress
      hampers their run

O dear Christ, my darling
forgiver of the weak
send your sevenfold spirit
render them meek

Take over my mind
dear Lord God of All
til my thoughts serve you duly
obeying your call

Your love is perfection
and that is what I seek,
to be like you, not like me –
straying, fickle, weak.

*PC*

## *Myself and Pangur*

Myself and Pangur, my white cat,
have much the same calling, in that
much as Pangur goes after mice
I go hunting for the precise

word. He and I are much the same
in that I'm gladly 'lost to fame'
when on the *Georgics*, say, I'm bent
while he seems perfectly content

with his lot. Life in the cloister
can't possibly lose its lustre
so long as there's some crucial point
with which we might by leaps and bounds

yet grapple, into which yet sink
our teeth. The bold Pangur will think
through mouse-snagging much as I muse
on something naggingly abstruse,

then fix his clear, unflinching eye
on our lime-white cell wall, while I
focus, in so far as I can,
on the limits of what a man

may know. Something of his rapture
at his most recent mouse-capture
I share when I, too, get to grips
with what has given me the slip.

And so we while away our whiles,
never cramping each other's styles
but practising the noble arts
that so lift and lighten our hearts,

Pangur going in for the kill
with all his customary skill
while I, sharp-witted, swift and sure,
shed light on what had seemed obscure.

*Paul Muldoon*

## *Celibacy*

Little bell,
clinking through the gusty night,
sweeter your call
than a wanton girl's moan of delight.

*PC*

## EARL ROGNVALD OF ORKNEY

(*d.*1158)

### *Irish Monks on a Rocky Island*

Sixteen women tripping on the shore –
I've seen them: forelocks hanging down,
each chin a field shorn
of stubble, smoother than a grey dragon's.

We'll chance a claim
that these insular dames
out west, butt-up to the storm,
are mostly bald as babies' bums.

*Kit Fryatt (Old Norse)*

# DEVOTIONAL POEMS

## ANONYMOUS

### *Eve*

I am Eve, great Adam's wife,
I that wrought my children's loss,
I that wronged Jesus of life,
Mine by right had been the cross.

I a kingly house forsook,
Ill my choice and my disgrace,
Ill the counsel that I took
Withering me and all my race.

I that brought winter in
And the windy glistening sky,
I that brought sorrow and sin,
Hell and pain and terror, I.

*Thomas MacDonagh*

## *The Massacre of the Innocents*

FIRST WOMAN

Why do you tear me from my love,
my body's fruit,
me who brought him into the world?
mine were the breasts he sucked
mine the womb that carried him
mine the bowels that sheltered him
mine the heart he satisfied
mine the life he glorified
mine the death to lose him
mine the strength that faltered
mine the speech that failed
mine the sight blinded with crying.

SECOND WOMAN

You take my son
who did no wrong –
please slaughter me
and not him;
my breasts run dry
my eyes overflow
my hands tremble
my body crumples
my husband heirless
myself senseless
my life my death
my only son (dear God!)
my work unpaid
my travail without issue
unavenged forever
my breasts crushed
my heart tattered.

THIRD WOMAN

Looking for one
you kill all
you slaughter the children
you maim the fathers
you ruin the mothers
you've opened hell
closed heaven
and spilled the blood of the godly without cause.

FOURTH WOMAN

Come to me, Christ
take my life quickly
along with my son's
and come great Mary
mother of God's Son
tell me what
I can do
without a son.

For your Son
my soul and mind have been destroyed;
I am astray in the head
surviving my son;
my heart will stiffen
a drying bloodclot
from the killings today
to the end of all.

*PC*

## BLATHMAC, SON OF CÚ BRETTAN
## (*fl.* 750)

### from *To Mary and Her Son*

May I have from you my three petitions,
beautiful Mary, little white-necked one;
get them, sun amongst women,
from your son who has them in his power.

That I may be in the world till old
serving the Lord who rules starry heaven,
and that then there be a welcome for me
into the eternal, ever-enduring kingdom.

That everyone who uses this as a vigil prayer
at lying down and at rising,
that it may protect him from blemish in the
other world
like a breastplate and helmet.

Everyone of any sort who shall recite it
fasting on Friday night,
provided only that it be with full-flowing tears,
Mary, may he not be for hell.

When your son comes in anger
with his cross on his reddened back,
that then you will save
any friend who shall have keened him.

For you, beautiful Mary,
I shall go as guarantor:
anyone who says the full keen,
he shall have his reward.

I call you with true words,
Mary, beautiful queen,
that we may have talk together
to pity your heart's darling.

So that I may keen the bright Christ
with you in the most heartfelt way,
shining precious jewel,
mother of the great Lord.

Were I rich and honoured
ruling the people of the world to every sea,
they would all come with you and me
to keen your royal son.

There would be beating of hands
by women, children and men,
that they might keen on every hill-top
the king who made every star.

*James Carney*

## ANONYMOUS

### *from* The Metrical Translation of the Gospel of St Thomas

#### *Jesus and the Sparrows*

The little lad, five years of age
– Son of the living God –
Twelve puddles blessed he had just coaxed
From water and from mud.

Twelve statuettes he made then;
'"Sparrows" shall you be named'
He whispered to those perfect shapes
That Sabbath in his game.

'Who plays with toys on the Sabbath Day?'
Spoke out an angry Jew
And marched the boy to Joseph,
His foster-father true.

'What sort of brat have you brought up
That wastes his sacred time
Scrabbling in mud on the Sabbath Day
To make bird-dolls from slime?'

At that the lad clapped two small hands
And with sweet piping words
Called on the dolls before their eyes
To rise as living birds.

No music heard was ever sweeter
Than the music from his mouth
When he told those birds 'Fly to your homes
To east and west and south.'

The story spread throughout the land
And is heard down to this day
And all who hear it still can hear
The sparrows' voices pray.

*PC*

## *St Ite's Song*

Jesukin
stays with me day out, day in;
no loutish priest-spawned lodger he
but my own dear Jesukin.

I did not get this wounded heart
from fostering just anyone;
Jesu and his heavenly gang
curl up with me when day is done.

Jesukin gives me every good
and he gets a just return;
you try praying to any other
and in eternity you'll burn.

No Partholán, Aedh or corner boy
is nurtured in my secret shade
but Jesu, bright angel-headed
son of the Judaean maid.

Sons of puffed-up priests and chiefs
plead for my sweet fostering
but how can I have time for them
when all my care is Jesukin?

You owe your most tuneful praise,
you girls with tender voices,
to Him who reigns in heaven's height
– and under my pierced breast rejoices.

*PC*

## *St Brigit's Housewarming*

What I would like
is the mother of all parties
for the King and his mates
drinking late into eternity;

what I would like
is one pure malt of faith
and to chase it I'd like
a penitential flail;

what I would like
is heaven's men in my kitchen
and to serve them I'd like
casks brimming with patience;

what I would like
is to fill cups with charity
and to wash them down I'd like
bumpers spilling over with mercy;

what I would like
is plenty for all of us
and in our midst I'd like
my own dear Jesus;

what I would like
is the three Maries in my parlour
and friends joining them I'd like
from heaven's every quarter;

what I would like
is to be the vassal of my Lord,
suffering sorrow for his sake,
servant to his living word.

*PC*

## CORMAC, KING BISHOP OF CASHEL
(837–903)

### *The Heavenly Pilot*

Wilt Thou steer my frail black bark
O'er the dark broad ocean's foam?
Wilt Thou come, Lord, to my boat,
Where afloat, my will would roam?
Thine the mighty: Thine the small:
Thine to mark men fall, like rain;
God! wilt Thou grant aid to me
Who come o'er th' upheaving main?

*George Sigerson*

# POEMS RELATING TO COLUM CILLE (COLUMBA) (521–593/7)

## DALLÁN FORGAILL

(*d.*598)

### from *Amra Colm Cille* (*Lament for Colum Cille*)

I

Not newsless is Níall's land.
No slight sigh from one plain,
but great woe, great outcry.
Unbearable the tale this verse tells:
Colum, lifeless, churchless.
How will a fool tell him – even Neire –
the prophet has settled at God's right hand in Sion.
Now he is not, nothing is left to us,
    no relief for a soul, our sage.
For he has died to us, the leader of nations who
    guarded the living,
he has died to us, who was our chief of the needy,
he has died to us, who was our messenger of the Lord;
for we do not have the seer who used to keep fears from us,
for he does not return to us, he who would explain
    the true Word,
for we do not have the teacher who would teach the
    tribes of the Tay.
The whole world, it was his:
It is a harp without a key,
it is a church without an abbot.

II

By the grace of God Colum rose to exalted companionship;
awaiting bright signs, he kept watch while he lived.
His lifetime was short,
scant portions filled him.
He was learning's pillar in every stronghold,
he was foremost at the book of complex Law.
The northern land shone,
the western people blazed,
he lit up the east
with chaste clerics.
Good the legacy of God's angel
when he glorified him.

V

He ran the course which runs past hatred to right action.
The teacher wove the word.
By his wisdom he made glosses clear.
He fixed the Psalms,
he made known the books of Law,
those books Cassian loved.
He won battles with gluttony.
The books of Solomon, he followed them.
Seasons and calculations he set in motion.
He separated the elements according to figures
    among the books of the Law.
He read mysteries and distributed the Scriptures
    among the schools,
and he put together the harmony concerning the
    course of the moon,
the course which it ran with the rayed sun,
and the course of the sea.
He could number the stars of heaven, the one who
    could tell all the rest
which we have heard from Colum Cille.

*Thomas Owen Clancy*

## COLUM CILLE
(attrib.)

### *The Maker on High*

ANCIENT exalted seed-scatterer whom time gave no progenitor:
he knew no moment of creation in his primordial foundation
he is and will be all places in all time and all ages
with Christ his first-born only-born and the holy spirit co-borne
throughout the high eternity of glorious divinity:
three gods we do not promulgate one God we state and intimate
salvific faith victorious: three persons very glorious.

BENEVOLENCE created angels and all the orders of archangels
thrones and principalities powers virtues qualities
denying otiosity to the excellence and majesty
of the not-inactive trinity in all labours of bounty
when it mustered heavenly creatures whose well devised natures
received its lavish proffer through power-word for ever.

CAME down from heaven summit down from angelic limit
dazzling in his brilliance beauty's very likeness
Lucifer downfalling (once woke at heaven's calling)
apostate angels sharing the deadly downfaring
of the author of high arrogance and indurated enviousness
the rest still continuing safe in their dominions.

DAUNTINGLY huge and horrible the dragon ancient and terrible
known as the lubric serpent subtler in his element
than all the beasts and every fierce thing living earthly
dragged a third – so many – stars to his gehenna
down to infernal regions not devoid of dungeons
benighted ones hell's own parasite hurled headlong.

EXCELLENT promethean armoury structuring world harmony
had created earth and heaven and wet acres of ocean
also sprouting vegetation shrubs groves plantations
sun moon stars to ferry fire and all things necessary
birds fish and cattle and every animal imaginable
but lastly the second promethean the protoplast human being.

FAST upon the starry finishing the lights high shimmering
the angels convened and celebrated for the wonders just created
the Lord the only artificer of that enormous vault of matter
with loud and well judged voices unwavering in their praises
an unexampled symphony of gratitude and sympathy
sung not by force of nature but freely lovingly grateful.

GUILTY of assault and seduction of our parents in the garden
the devil has a second falling together with his followers
whose faces set in horror and wingbeats whistling hollow
would petrify frail creatures into stricken fearers
but what men perceive bodily must preclude luckily
those now bound and bundled in dungeons of the underworld.

HE Zabulus was driven by the Lord from mid heaven
and with him the airy spaces were choked like drains with faeces
as the turgid rump of rebels fell but fell invisible
in case the grossest villains became willy-nilly
with neither walls nor fences preventing curious glances
tempters to sin greatly openly emulatingly.

IRRIGATING clouds showering wet winter from sea-fountains
from floods of the abysses three-fourths down through fishes
up to the skyey purlieus in deep blue whirlpools
good rain then for cornfields vineyard-bloom and grain-yields
driven by blasts emerging from their airy treasuring
desiccating not the land-marches but the facing sea-marshes.

KINGS of the world we live in: their glories are uneven
brittle tyrannies disembodied by a frown from God's forehead:
giants too underwater groaning in great horror
forced to burn like torches cut by painful tortures
pounded in the millstones of underworld maelstroms
roughed rubbed out buried in a frenzy of flints and billows.

LETTING the waters be sifted from where the clouds are lifted
the Lord often prevented the flood he once attempted
leaving the conduits utterly full and rich as udders
slowly trickling and panning through the tracts of this planet
freezing if cold was called for warm in the cells of summer
keeping our rivers everywhere running forward for ever.

MAGISTERIAL are his powers as the great God poises
the earth ball encircled by the great deep so firmly
supported by an almighty robust nieve so tightly
that you would think pillar and column held it strong and solemn
the capes and cliffs stationed on solidest foundations
fixed uniquely in their place as if on immovable bases.

NO one needs to show us: a hell lies deep below us
where there is said to be darkness worms beasts carnage
where there are fires of sulphur burning to make us suffer
where men are gnashing roaring weeping wailing deploring
where groans mount from gehennas terrible never-ending
where parched and fiery horror feeds thirst and hunger.

OFTEN on their knees at prayer are many said to be there
under the earth books tell us they do not repel us
though they found it unavailing the scroll not unrolling
whose fixed seals were seven when Christ warning from heaven
unsealed it with the gesture of a resurrected victor
fulfilling the prophets' foreseeing of his coming and his decreeing.

PARADISE was planted primally as God wanted
we read in sublime verses entering into Genesis
its fountain's rich waters feed four flowing rivers
its heart abounds with flowers where the tree of life towers
with foliage never fading for the healing of the nations
and delights indescribable abundantly fruitful.

QUIZ sacred Sinai: who is it has climbed so high?
Who has heard the thunder-cracks vast in the sky-tracts?
Who has heard the enormous bullroaring of the war-horns?
Who has seen the lightning flashing round the night-ring?
Who has seen javelins flambeaus a rock-face in shambles?
Only to Moses is this real only to the judge of Israel.

RUE God's day arriving righteous high king's assizing
dies irae day of the vindex day of cloud and day of cinders
day of the dumbfoundering day of great thundering
day of lamentation of anguish of confusion
with all the love and yearning of women unreturning
as all men's striving and lust for worldly living.

STANDING in fear and trembling with divine judgement
  assembling
we shall stammer what we expended before our life was ended
faced by rolling videos of our crimes however hideous
forced to read the pages of the conscience book of ages
we shall burst out into weeping sobbing bitter and unceasing
now that all means of action have tholed the last retraction.

THE archangelic trumpet-blast is loud and great at every fastness
the hardest vaults spring open the catacombs are broken
the dead of the world are thawing their cold rigor withdrawing
the bones are running and flying to the joints of the undying
their souls hurry to meet them and celestially to greet them
returning both together to be one not one another.

VAGRANT Orion driven from the crucial hinge of heaven
leaves the Pleiades receding most splendidly beneath him
tests the ocean boundaries the oriental quandaries
as Vesper circling steadily returns home readily
the rising Lucifer of the morning after two years mourning:
these things are to be taken as type and trope and token.

X SPIKES and flashes like the Lord's cross marching
down with him from heaven as the last sign is given
moonlight and sunlight are finally murdered
stars fall from dignity like fruits from a fig-tree
the world's whole surface burns like a furnace
armies are crouching in caves in the mountains.

YOU know then the singing of hymns finely ringing
thousands of angels advancing spring up in sacred dances
quartet of beasts gaze from numberless eyes in praise
two dozen elders as happiness compels them
throw all their crowns down to the Lamb who surmounts them
'Holy holy holy' binds the eternal trinity.

ZABULUS burns to ashes all those adversaries
who deny that the Saviour was Son to the Father
but we shall fly to meet him and immediately greet him
and be with him in the dignity of all such diversity
as our deeds make deserved and we without swerve
shall live beyond history in the state of glory.

*Edwin Morgan (Latin)*

## *Colum Cille's Exile*

This were pleasant, O Son of God,
with wondrous coursing
to sail across the swelling torrent
back to Ireland.

To Eólarg's plain, past Benevanagh,
  across Loch Feval,
and there to hear the swans in chorus
  chanting music.

And when my boat, the Derg Drúchtach,
  at last made harbour
in Port na Ferg the joyful Foyle-folk
  would sound a welcome.

I ever long for the land of Ireland
  where I had power,
an exile now in midst of strangers,
  sad and tearful.

Woe that journey forced upon me,
  O King of Secrets;
would to God I'd never gone there,
  to Cooldrevne.

Well it is for son of Dímma
  in his cloister,
and happy I but were I hearing
  with him in Durrow

the wind that ever plays us music
  in the elm-trees,
and sudden cry of startled blackbird,
  wing a-beating.

And listen early in Ros Grencha
  to stags a-belling,
and when cuckoo, at brink of summer,
  joins in chorus.

I have loved the land of Ireland
– I cry for parting;
to sleep at Comgall's, visit Canice,
this were pleasant.

*James Carney*

## *He Sets His Back on Ireland*

A grey eye
will look on Ireland with a sigh;
for never will it see again
Ireland's women or her men.

*PC*

## *He Remembers Derry*

Three reasons I love Derry:
it is calm, it is bright,
it is a thoroughfare for angels
all day and all night.

*PC*

## *'My hand is weary with writing'*

My hand is weary with writing,
My sharp quill is not steady,
My slender-beaked pen juts forth
A black draught of shining dark-blue ink.

A stream of the wisdom of blessed God
Springs from my fair-brown shapely hand:
On the page it squirts its draught
Of ink of the green-skinned holly.

My little dripping pen travels
Across the plain of shining books,
Without ceasing for the wealth of the great –
Whence my hand is weary with writing.

*Kuno Meyer*

## BECCÁN THE HERMIT
## (*d*.677)

### *Last Verses in Praise of Colum Cille*

He brings northward to meet the Lord a bright crowd
of chancels –
Colum Cille, kirks for hundreds, widespread candle.

Wonderful news: a realm with God after the race,
a grand kingdom, since He's set out my life's progress.

He broke passions, brought to ruin secure prisons;
Colum Cille overcame them with bright actions.

Connacht's candle, Britain's candle, splendid ruler;
in scores of curraghs with an army of wretches he
crossed the long-haired sea.

He crossed the wave-strewn wild region, foam-flecked,
seal-filled,
savage, bounding, seething, white-tipped, pleasing, doleful.

Wisdom's champion all round Ireland, he was exalted;
excellent name: Europe is nursed, Britain's sated.

Stout post, milk of meditation, with broad actions,
Colum Cille, perfect customs, fairer than trappings.

On the loud sea he cried to the King who rules thousands,
who rules the plain above cleared fields, kings
and countries.

In the Trinity's care he sought a ship – good his leaving –
on high with God, who always watched him, morning,
evening.

Shepherd of monks, judge of clerics, finer than things,
than kingly gates, than sounds of plagues, than battalions.

Colum Cille, candle brightening legal theory;
the race he ran pierced the midnight of Erc's region.

The skies' kind one, he tends the clouds of harsh heaven;
my soul's shelter, my poetry's fort, Conal's descendant.

Fame with virtues, a good life, his: barque of treasure,
sea of knowledge, Conal's offspring, people's counsellor.

Leafy oak-tree, soul's protection, rock of safety,
the sun of monks, mighty ruler, Colum Cille.

Beloved of God, he lived against a stringent rock,
a rough struggle, the place one could find Colum's bed.

He crucified his body, left behind sleek sides;
he chose learning, embraced stone slabs, gave up bedding.

He gave up beds, abandoned sleep, finest actions;
conquered angers, was ecstatic, sleeping little.

He possessed books, renounced fully claims of kinship:
for love of learning he gave up wars, gave up strongholds.

He left chariots, he loved ships, foe to falsehood;
sun-like exile, sailing, he left fame's steel bindings.

Colum Cille, Colum who was, Colum who will be,
constant Colum, not he a protector to be lamented.

Colum, we sing, until death's tryst, after, before,
by poetry's rules, which gives welcome to him we serve.

I pray a great prayer to Eithne's son – better than treasure –
my soul to his right hand, to heaven, before the
world's people.

He worked for God, kingly prayer, within church ramparts,
with angels' will, Conal's household's child, in vestments.

Triumphant plea: adoring God, nightly, daily,
with hands outstretched, with splendid alms, with
right actions.

Fine his body, Colum Cille, heaven's cleric –
a widowed crowd – well-spoken just one, tongue
triumphant.

*Thomas Owen Clancy*

# EPIGRAMS

## ANONYMOUS

### *The Blackbird of Belfast Lough*

The small bird
chirp-chirruped:
yellow neb,
a note-spurt.

Blackbird over
Lagan water.
Clumps of yellow
whin-burst!

*Seamus Heaney*

### *Bee*

A tremor of yellow from blossom to blossom
the day-shift bee stays out with the sun
then booms across the darkening valley
to his happy date with the honeycomb.

*PC*

## *Parsimony*

Don't expect horses
from him for your verses
 just what befits the louse –
 cows.

*PC*

## *An Ill Wind*

With that fierce storm out there
whipping to frenzy the ocean's hair,
my mind is quiet as the placid sea
the Norseman needs to get to me.

*PC*

## *The King of Connacht*

'Have you seen Hugh,
The Connacht king in the field?'
'All that we saw
Was his shadow under his shield.'

*Frank O'Connor*

## *Sunset*

In Lough Leane
a queen went swimming;
a redgold salmon
flowed into her
at full of evening.

*John Montague*

## *'He is my love'*

He is my love,
    my sweet nutgrove:
a boy he is –
    for him a kiss.

*Michael Hartnett*

# WORLD AND OTHERWORLD

## ANONYMOUS

### *Storm at Sea*

Tempest on the plain of Lir
Bursts its barriers far and near,
  And upon the rising tide
  Wind and noisy winter ride –
Winter throws a shining spear.

When the wind blows from the east
All the billows seem possessed,
  To the west they storm away
  To the farthest, wildest bay
Where the light turns to its rest.

When the wind is from the north
The fierce and shadowy waves go forth,
  Leaping, snarling at the sky,
  To the southern world they fly
And the confines of the earth.

When the wind is from the west
All the waves that cannot rest
  To the east must thunder on
  Where the bright tree of the sun
Is rooted in the ocean's breast.

When the wind is from the south
The waves turn to a devil's broth,
  Crash in foam on Skiddy's beach,
  For Caladnet's summit reach,
Batter Limerick's grey-green mouth.

Ocean's full! The sea's in flood,
Beautiful is the ships' abode;
  In the Bay of the Two Beasts
  The sandy wind in eddies twists,
The rudder holds a shifting road.

Every bay in Ireland booms
When the flood against it comes –
  Winter throws a spear of fire!
  Round Scotland's shores and by Cantyre
A mountainous surging chaos glooms.

God's Son of hosts that none can tell
The fury of the storm repel!
  Dread Lord of the sacrament,
  Save me from the wind's intent,
Spare me from the blast of Hell.

*Frank O'Connor*

## *Summer Has Come*

Summer has come, healthy and free,
Whence the brown wood is aslope;
The slender nimble deer leap,
And the path of seals is smooth.

The cuckoo sings sweet music,
Whence there is smooth restful sleep;
Gentle birds leap upon the hill,
And swift grey stags.

Heat has laid hold of the rest of the deer –
The lovely cry of curly packs!
The white extent of the strand smiles,
There the swift sea is.

A sound of playful breezes in the tops
Of a black oakwood is Drum Daill,
The noble hornless herd runs,
To whom Cuan-wood is a shelter.

Green bursts out on every herb,
The top of the green oakwood is bushy,
Summer has come, winter has gone,
Twisted hollies wound the hound.

The blackbird sings a loud strain,
To him the live wood is a heritage,
The sad angry sea is fallen asleep,
The speckled salmon leaps.

The sun smiles over every land, –
A parting for me from the brood of cares:
Hounds bark, stags tryst,
Ravens flourish, summer has come!

*Kuno Meyer*

## *Gaze North-East*

Gaze north-east
over heaving crest
with sea press
   ceaseless:

seals' road
for sleek sport
the tide run to
fulness.

*John Montague*

## *Winter*

Chill, chill!
All Moylurg is cold and still,
Where can deer a-hungered go
When the snow lies like a hill?

Cold till doom!
All the world obeys its rule,
Every track become a stream,
Every ford become a pool.

Every pool become a lake,
Every lake become a sea,
Even horses cannot cross
The ford at Ross so how can we?

All the fish in Ireland stray
When the cold winds smite the bay,
In the towns no voice is heard,
Bell and bird have had their say.

Even the wolves in Cuan Wood
Cannot find a place to rest
When the small wren of Lon Hill
Is not still within her nest.

The small quire of birds has passed
In cold snow and icy blast,
And the blackbird of Cuan Wood
Finds no shelter that holds fast.

Nothing's easy but our pot,
Our old shack on the hill is not,
For in woodlands crushed with snow
On Ben Bo the trail's forgot.

The old eagle of Glen Rye,
Even he forgets to fly,
With ice crusted on his beak,
He is now too weak to cry.

Best lie still
In wool and feathers, take your fill,
Ice is thick on every ford
And the word I chose is 'chill'.

*Frank O'Connor*

## *World Gone Wrong*

An evil world is now at hand:
In which men shall be in bondage, women free;
Mast wanting, woods smooth, blossom bad;
Winds many, wet summer, green corn;
Much cattle, scant milk;
Dependants burdensome in every country!
Hogs lean, chiefs wicked;
Bad faith, chronic killings:
A world withered, graves in number.

*Standish Hayes O'Grady*

## *from* The Voyage of Bran, Son of Febal, to the Land of the Living

### *The Sea-God's Address To Bran*

Then on the morrow Bran went upon the sea. When he had been at sea two days and two nights, he saw a man in a chariot coming towards him over the sea. It was Manannan, the son of Ler, who sang these quatrains to him.

To Bran in his coracle it seems
A marvellous beauty across the clear sea:
To me in my chariot from afar
It is a flowery plain on which he rides.

What is a clear sea
For the prowed skiff in which Bran is,
That to me in my chariot of two wheels
Is a delightful plain with a wealth of flowers.

Bran sees
A mass of waves beating across the clear sea:
I see myself in the Plain of Sports
Red-headed flowers that have no fault.

Sea-horses glisten in summer
As far as Bran can stretch his glance:
Rivers pour forth a stream of honey
In the land of Manannan, son of Ler.

The sheen of the main on which thou art,
The dazzling white of the sea on which thou
    rowest about –
Yellow and azure are spread out,
It is a light and airy land.

Speckled salmon leap from the womb
Out of the white sea on which thou lookest:
They are calves, they are lambs of fair hue,
With truce, without mutual slaughter.

Though thou seest but one chariot-rider
In the Pleasant Plain of many flowers,
There are many steeds on its surface,
Though them thou seest not.

Large is the plain, numerous is the host,
Colours shine with pure glory,
A white stream of silver, stairs of gold
Afford a welcome with all abundance.

An enchanting game, most delicious,
They play over the luscious wine,
Men and gentle women under a bush,
Without sin, without transgression.

Along the top of a wood
Thy coracle has swum across ridges,
There is a wood laden with beautiful fruit
Under the prow of thy little skiff.

A wood with blossom and with fruit
On which is the vine's veritable fragrance,
A wood without decay, without defect,
On which is a foliage of a golden hue.

We are from the beginning of creation
Without old age, without consummation of clay,
Hence we expect not there might be frailty –
Transgression has not come to us.

Steadily then let Bran row!
It is not far to the Land of Women:
Evna with manifold bounteousness
He will reach before the sun is set.

*Kuno Meyer*

## *The Voyage of Maeldune*

*(Founded on an Irish legend, AD 700)*

I

I was the chief of the race – he had stricken my father dead –
But I gather'd my fellows together, I swore I would strike
off his head.
Each of them look'd like a king, and was noble in birth
as in worth,
And each of them boasted he sprang from the oldest
race upon earth.
Each was as brave in the fight as the bravest hero of song,
And each of them liefer had died than have done one
another a wrong.
*He* lived on an isle in the ocean – we sail'd on a
Friday morn –
He that had slain my father the day before I was born.

II

And we came to the isle in the ocean, and there on the
shore was he.
But a sudden blast blew us out and away thro' a
boundless sea.

III

And we came to the Silent Isle that we never had touch'd
at before,

Where a silent ocean always broke on a silent shore,
And the brooks glitter'd on in the light without sound,
    and the long waterfalls
Pour'd in a thunderless plunge to the base of the
    mountain walls,
And the poplar and cypress unshaken by storm flourish'd
    up beyond sight,
And the pine shot aloft from the crag to an unbelievable
    height,
And high in the heaven above it there flicker'd a
    songless lark,
And the cock couldn't crow, and the bull couldn't low, and
    the dog couldn't bark.
And round it we went, and thro' it, but never a murmur,
    a breath –
It was all of it fair as life, it was all of it quiet as death,
And we hated the beautiful Isle, for whenever we strove
    to speak
Our voices were thinner and fainter than any
    flittermouse-shriek;
And the men that were mighty of tongue and could raise
    such a battle-cry
That a hundred who heard it would rush on a thousand
    lances and die –
O they to be dumb'd by the charm! – so fluster'd with
    anger were they
They almost fell on each other; but after we sail'd away.

IV

And we came to the Isle of Shouting, we landed, a score
    of wild birds
Cried from the topmost summit with human voices
    and words;
Once in an hour they cried, and whenever their voices peal'd
The steer fell down at the plow and the harvest died
    from the field,
And the men dropt dead in the valleys and half of the
    cattle went lame,

And the roof sank in on the hearth, and the dwelling
broke into flame;
And the shouting of these wild birds ran into the hearts
of my crew,
Till they shouted along with the shouting and seized
one another and slew;
But I drew them the one from the other; I saw that
we could not stay,
And we left the dead to the birds and we sail'd with
our wounded away.

V

And we came to the Isle of Flowers: their breath met us
out on the seas,
For the Spring and the middle Summer sat each on the lap
of the breeze;
And the red passion-flower to the cliffs, and the darkblue
clematis clung,
And starr'd with a myriad blossom the long convolvulus
hung;
And the topmost spire of the mountain was lilies in lieu
of snow,
And the lilies like glaciers winded down, running out
below
Thro' the fire of the tulip and poppy, the blaze of gorse,
and the blush
Of millions of roses that sprang without leaf or a thorn
from the bush;
And the whole isle-side flashing down from the peak
without ever a tree
Swept like a torrent of gems from the sky to the blue
of the sea;
And we roll'd upon capes of crocus and vaunted our
kith and our kin,
And we wallow'd in beds of lilies, and chanted the
triumph of Finn,
Till each like a golden image was pollen'd from
head to feet

And each was as dry as a cricket, with thirst in the
middle-day heat.
Blossom and blossom, and promise of blossom, but
never a fruit!
And we hated the Flowering Isle, as we hated the
isle that was mute,
And we tore up the flowers by the million and flung
them in bight and bay,
And we left but a naked rock, and in anger we
sail'd away.

VI

And we came to the Isle of Fruits: all round from the
cliffs and the capes,
Purple or amber, dangled a hundred fathom of grapes,
And the warm melon lay like a little sun on the tawny
sand,
And the fig ran up from the beach and rioted over
the land,
And the mountain arose like a jewell'd throne thro' the
fragrant air,
Glowing with all-colour'd plums and with golden masses
of pear,
And the crimson and scarlet of berries that flamed upon
bine and vine,
But in every berry and fruit was the poisonous pleasure
of wine;
And the peak of the mountain was apples, the hugest
that ever were seen,
And they prest, as they grew, on each other, with hardly
a leaflet between,
And all of them redder than rosiest health or than
utterest shame,
And setting, when Even descended, the very sunset aflame;
And we stay'd three days, and we gorged and we madden'd,
till every one drew
His sword on his fellow to slay him, and ever they struck
and they slew;

And myself, I had eaten but sparely, and fought till I
sunder'd the fray,
Then I bade them remember my father's death, and we
sail'd away.

VII

And we came to the Isle of Fire: we were lured by the light
from afar,
For the peak sent up one league of fire to the Northern Star;
Lured by the glare and the blare, but scarcely could stand
upright,
For the whole isle shudder'd and shook like a man in a
mortal affright;
We were giddy besides with the fruits we had gorged,
and so crazed that at last
There were some leap'd into the fire; and away we sail'd,
and we past
Over that undersea isle, where the water is clearer than air:
Down we look'd: what a garden! O bliss, what a
Paradise there!
Towers of a happier time, low down in a rainbow deep
Silent palaces, quiet fields of eternal sleep!
And three of the gentlest and best of my people, whate'er
I could say,
Plunged head down in the sea, and the Paradise trembled
away.

VIII

And we came to the Bounteous Isle, where the heavens
lean low on the land,
And ever at dawn from the cloud glitter'd o'er us a
sunbright hand,
Then it open'd and dropt at the side of each man, as he
rose from his rest,
Bread enough for his need till the labourless day dipt
under the West;

And we wander'd about it and thro' it. O never was
time so good!
And we sang of the triumphs of Finn, and the boast of
our ancient blood,
And we gazed at the wandering wave as we sat by the
gurgle of springs,
And we chanted the songs of the Bards and the glories
of fairy kings;
But at length we began to be weary, to sigh, and to stretch
and yawn,
Till we hated the Bounteous Isle and the sunbright hand
of the dawn,
For there was not an enemy near, but the whole green Isle
was our own,
And we took to playing at ball, and we took to throwing
the stone,
And we took to playing at battle, but that was a
perilous play,
For the passion of battle was in us, we slew and we
sail'd away.

IX

And we past to the Isle of Witches and heard their
musical cry –
'Come to us, O come, come' in the stormy red
of a sky
Dashing the fires and the shadows of dawn on the
beautiful shapes,
For a wild witch naked as heaven stood on each of
the loftiest capes,
And a hundred ranged on the rock like white seabirds
in a row,
And a hundred gamboll'd and pranced on the wrecks
in the sand below,
And a hundred splash'd from the ledges, and bosom'd
the burst of the spray,
But I knew we should fall on each other, and hastily
sail'd away.

X

And we came in an evil time to the Isle of the Double Towers,
One was of smooth-cut stone, one carved all over with
 flowers,
But an earthquake always moved in the hollows under
 the dells,
And they shock'd on each other and butted each other with
 clashing of bells,
And the daws flew out of the Towers and jangled and
 wrangled in vain,
And the clash and boom of the bells rang into the heart
 and the brain,
Till the passion of battle was on us, and all took sides
 with the Towers,
There were some for the clean-cut stone, there were more
 for the carven flowers,
And the wrathful thunder of God peal'd over us all the day,
For the one half slew the other, and after we sail'd away.

XI

And we came to the Isle of a Saint who had sail'd with
 St Brendan of yore,
He had lived ever since on the Isle and his winters
 were fifteen score,
And his voice was low as from other worlds, and his eyes
 were sweet,
And his white hair sank to his heels and his white beard
 fell to his feet,
And he spake to me, 'O Maeldune, let be this purpose
 of thine!
Remember the words of the Lord when he told us
 "Vengeance is mine!"
His fathers have slain thy fathers in war or in single
 strife,
Thy fathers have slain his fathers, each taken a life
 for a life,

Thy father had slain his father, how long shall the
    murder last?
Go back to the Isle of Finn and suffer the Past to be Past.'
And we kiss'd the fringe of his beard and we pray'd as
    we heard him pray,
And the Holy man he assoil'd us, and sadly we sail'd away.

XII

And we came to the Isle we were blown from, and there
    on the shore was he,
The man that had slain my father. I saw him and
    let him be.
O weary was I of the travel, the trouble, the strife and
    the sin,
When I landed again, with a tithe of my men, on the
    Isle of Finn.

*Alfred Tennyson*

## from *The Vision of Mac Conglinne*

A vision that appeared to me,
An apparition wonderful
  I tell to all:
There was a coracle all of lard
Within a port of New-milk Lake
  Upon the world's smooth sea.

We went into that man-of-war,
'Twas warrior-like to take the road
  O'er ocean's heaving waves.
Our oar-strokes then we pulled
Across the level of the main,
Throwing the sea's harvest up
  Like honey, the sea-soil.

The fort we reached was beautiful,
With works of custards thick,
    Beyond the lake.
Fresh butter was the bridge in front,
The rubble dyke was fair white wheat,
    Bacon the palisade.

Stately, pleasantly it sat,
A compact house and strong.
    Then I went in:
The door of it was hung beef,
The threshold was dry bread,
    Cheese-curds the walls.

Smooth pillars of old cheese
And sappy bacon props
    Alternate ranged;
Stately beams of mellow cream,
White posts of real curds
    Kept up the house.

Behind it was a well of wine,
Beer and bragget in streams,
    Each full pool to the taste.
Malt in smooth wavy sea
Over a lard-spring's brink
    Flowed through the floor.

A lake of juicy pottage
Under a cream of oozy lard
    Lay 'twixt it and the sea.
Hedges of butter fenced it round,
Under a crest of white-mantled lard
    Around the wall outside.

A row of fragrant apple-trees,
An orchard in its pink-tipped bloom,
  Between it and the hill.
A forest tall of real leeks,
Of onions and of carrots, stood
  Behind the house.

Within, a household generous,
A welcome of red, firm-fed men,
  Around the fire:
Seven bead-strings and necklets seven
Of cheeses and of bits of tripe
  Round each man's neck.

The Chief in cloak of beefy fat
Beside his noble wife and fair
  I then beheld.
Below the lofty caldron's spit
Then the Dispenser I beheld,
  His fleshfork on his back.

Wheatlet son of Milklet,
Son of juicy Bacon,
  Is mine own name.
Honeyed Butter-roll
Is the man's name
  That bears my bag.

Haunch of Mutton
Is my dog's name,
  Of lovely leaps.
Lard, my wife,
Sweetly smiles
  Across the brose.

Cheese-curds, my daughter,
Goes round the spit,
  Fair is her fame.
Corned Beef is my son,
Who beams over a cloak,
  Enormous, of fat.

Savour of Savours
Is the name of my wife's maid:
Morning-early
Across New-milk Lake she went.

Beef-lard, my steed,
An excellent stallion
  That increases studs;
A guard against toil
Is the saddle of cheese
  Upon his back.

A large necklace of delicious cheese-curds
  Around his back;
His halter and his traces all
  Of fresh butter.

*Kuno Meyer*

# IRELAND'S WOMEN, AND HER MEN

## ANONYMOUS

### *Créide's Lament for Dínerteach*

These spears that pierce the night
with jags of poisoned light
  are cast by the memory
  of him from near Royny.

Wild love for that great stranger,
that scorner of all danger,
  shrivels heart in breast
  and robs each night of rest.

Hosannas lifted to our Lord
are not as fine as his kind word;
  no fabled warrior ever
  matched in grace my slender lover.

Once, a child, I was pure:
chastity does not endure;
  an adult now, passion's slave
  I grieve and rave.

Here in Aidne's pleasant land
all voices in one sorrow blend
   for on Guaire's bloody plain
   our hero Dínerteach is slain.

O Christ most chaste, that early death
lays me helpless out beneath
   these spears that pierce the night
   with jags of poisoned light.

*PC*

## *The Lament of Baoi, the Nun of Beare Island*

Ebbing always, unlike the sea
Whose ebb will flood tomorrow,
My life, with no tide's turn,
Runs down the strand in sorrow.

I am Baoi, the Nun of Beare;
The plushest gowns I used to wear
Who now am wizened, chaste and thin
– Threadbare habit, mottled skin.

When we lived
It was people we loved
But people today
Care for riches only.

The women and men of these plains
Were a fabled, noble race
Who treated us with courtesy:
Their graces matched our grace.

Much talk today of demanding one's due,
No time for old hospitality;
No talk today of paying one's debts,
Much time for boasting of charity.

Swift coursers then, swift war cars
Winning every prize;
Swifter still the years
Racing past these eyes.

My bitter, dried-up body
Plods towards its last abode –
Called in by the Son of God,
All debts must be repaid.

To think these arms of mine
Now bony and thin
Were draped sumptuously
Round the shoulders of kings!

To think of these arms of mine
So bony and thin
Raised in love's service
Over handsome young men!

When girl-blood stirs for the Maytide
My blood thickens with cold;
Sad though it is to be sapless
It is far sadder to be old.

Sweet honey-breath long since soured
(The wedding lamb escaped the kill!)
Hair lank now and grey and sparse,
My head hangs ready for the veil.

It is no shame to want to hide
Such a head in the white of a veil;
The colours that bedecked that head
The years I sat down to the ale!

To all the old I bear good will
Except wide-pastured Feven
Whose mane though as old as mine
Is sunbright still and golden.

Feven's Stone of the Kings has been battered
By winter's storms time out of mind
But like the Fort of Ronan's in Bregon
Its face is youthful, still unlined.

How great the turmoil of the sea
Stirred up by winter's whips of spray!
Neither nobleman nor bondsman's son
Will cross the strait to me today.

For I know their inclination:
If they row, they row away.
Deeply men sleep among the reeds of Alma
Where water is colder than coldest clay.

Across the wide surface of the sea
Of youth and folly I sail no longer;
The years of beauty I wasted,
The years of my ugliness linger.

And the cold lingers also,
No matter how sultry the weather
I still crave a shawl for my shoulders:
Old age and cold go together.

How swiftly the high summer of youth
To sad autumn descended!
But the winter that now grips my heart
Is a season without ending.

I squandered my youth, yet
– Had I been sober and staid –
Would the cloak of my life not likewise
Have ended up tattered, frayed?

The cloak of my King, though, is seamless
And its green drapes every hill;
The worker who plumps out such cloth
Is the master who never is idle.

But I am a useless poor wretch,
A queen shrivelled, a drone;
After candles and bright laughter at table
The dark oratory here on my own!

Golden mead and rarest red wine
Were our toasts when I feasted with kings;
These nights I feed in a circle of hags
With watery whey for our pledgings.

If I could quaff the whey like ale,
Calling all that pains me the will of God,
I would beseech Him night and day
To quell the anguish in my blood.

This cloak of age wrapped loose about me
Is greying, flaccid, stranger's skin:
Thus an ancient tree prepares for dying,
Its bark all blotched with moss and lichen.

My once sparkling right eye has been taken
As deposit on a small stretch of land
And my left one too has been borrowed
To secure that same patch of ground.

Three floods threaten the fort at Ardree:
A floodhost of men darkening the plain,
A floodherd of horses with hooves thundering,
A floodpack of dogs running, baying.

Flood's wave fills to fullness,
Ebb's drain empties all;
What the rising tide gives you
It takes in its fall.

(Tide's giving
Then taking
Has been my
Unmaking.)

Flood's wave:
Silence of the flooded cellar
Where all who ever visited me
Lie silent under water.

How soundly beneath my roof
Sleeps great Mary's Son!
(I have kept my house always
Open to everyone.)

I pity that creature,
The most wretched of all,
Who watches tide's rising
But misses its fall.

Blessed is the island offshore
That waits for the turn of the tide;
Cursed is the lonely old woman
Whose ebbing will abide.

No face, no house, no feature
She remembers from the past;
Gone is the great flood tide:
Ebb is all at last.

*PC*

## *Liadan*

Gain without gladness
  Is in the bargain I have struck;
One that I loved I wrought to madness.

Mad beyond measure
  But for God's fear that numbed her heart
She that would not do his pleasure.

Was it so great
  My treason? Was I not always kind?
Why should it turn his love to hate?

Liadan,
  That is my name, and Curithir
The man I loved; you know my sin.

Alas too fleet!
  Too brief my pleasure at his side;
With him the passionate hours were sweet.

Woods woke
  About us for a lullaby,
And the blue waves in music spoke.

And now too late
  More than for all my sins I grieve
That I turned his love to hate.

Why should I hide
  That he is still my heart's desire
More than all the world beside?

A furnace blast
  Of love has melted down my heart,
Without his love it cannot last.

*Frank O'Connor*

## *The Wooing of Etain*

Fair lady, will you travel
To the marvellous land of stars?
Pale as snow the body there,
Under a primrose crown of hair.

No one speaks of property
In that glittering community:
White teeth shining, eyebrows black,
The foxglove hue on every cheek.

The landscape bright and speckled
As a wild bird's eggs –
However fair Ireland's Plain,
It is sad after the Great Plain!

Warm, sweet streams water the earth,
And after the choicest of wine and mead,
Those fine and flawless people
Without sin, without guilt, couple.

We can see everyone
Without being seen ourselves:
It is the cloud of Adam's transgression
Conceals us from mortal reckoning.

O woman if you join my strong clan,
Your head will hold a golden crown.
Fresh killed pork, new milk and beer,
We shall share, O Lady Fair!

*John Montague*

## *Advice to Lovers*

The way to get on with a girl
  Is to drift like a man in a mist,
Happy enough to be caught,
  Happy to be dismissed.

Glad to be out of her way,
  Glad to rejoin her in bed,
Equally grieved or gay
  To learn that she's living or dead.

*Frank O'Connor*

## *Speak No Evil*

You want me thrown out of the country, Cinaed,
although I've committed no crime;
why shouldn't I do with a sweetie at court
what I do with my wife all the time?

A jealous old codger's accused me
– God blast him's my solitary wish –
I'd no more eye up his lady-wife's dowry
than a cat would lap milk from a dish,

a buck would jump over high fencing,
a salmon leap up for a fly,
a woman be devilish cunning
or a man call for beer when he's dry.

I'll turn a blind eye to her come-ons
in respect for her husband so dear
till a boar is looked up to by banbhs
and honey proves lure for a bear.

As for evidence that I've been sinning
with Gormlai of Ford-Between-Lips?
it's just that she jiggled her lovely bare thighs
while my hands were caressing her hips.

You surprised me on the grass bank beside her
as I nibbled her ears, lips and throat;
and somehow the sight gave rise to the story
that I have the itch of the goat.

Why ever should you put it about
that your friend is a randy young devil?
if you want to stay pals with me, Cinaed,
you'd better see – and speak – no evil.

*PC*

# HEROES

## ANONYMOUS

### *from* Táin Bó Cuailnge

#### *Fedelm's Vision of Cúchulainn*

I see a battle: a blond man
with much blood about his belt
and a hero-halo round his head.
His brow is full of victories.

Seven hard heroic jewels
are set in the iris of his eye.
His jaws are settled in a snarl.
He wears a looped, red tunic.

A noble countenance I see,
working effect on womenfolk;
a young man of sweet colouring;
a form dragonish in the fray.

His great valour brings to mind
Cúchulainn of Murtheimne,
the hound of Culann, full of fame.
Who he is I cannot tell
but I see, now, the whole host
coloured crimson by his hand.

A giant on the plain I see,
doing battle with the host,
holding in each of his two hands
four short quick swords.

I see him hurling against that host
two *gae bolga* and a spear
and an ivory-hilted sword,
each weapon to its separate task.

He towers on the battlefield
in breastplate and red cloak.
Across the sinister chariot-wheel
the Warped Man deals death
– that fair form I first beheld
melted to a mis-shape.

I see him moving to the fray:
take warning, watch him well,
Cúchulainn, Sualdam's son!
Now I see him in pursuit.

Whole hosts he will destroy,
making dense massacre.
In thousands you will yield your heads.
I am Fedelm. I hide nothing.

The blood starts from warrior's wounds
– total ruin – at his touch:
your warriors dead, the warriors
of Deda mac Sin prowling loose;
torn corpses, women wailing,
because of him – the Forge-Hound.

*Thomas Kinsella*

## *The Morrígan's Chant to the Brown Bull*

restless does the Dark Bull   know death-dealing slaughter
secret that the raven   wrings from writhing soldiers
as the Dark One grazes   on the dark green grasses
waving meadows blossoming   with necks and flowers
lowing cattle of the Badb   the groans of battle
armies ground to dust   the raven struts on corpses
war-clouds raging over   Cúailnge day and night
kith and kin lie down   to join the tribes of dead

*Ciaran Carson*

## *Cuchulainn's Appeal to Ferdiad*

Come not here, nor helmet don,
O Ferdiad, Daman's son;
Worst for thee will be the blow,
Though it bring a world of woe.

Come not here, with wrongful strife,
My hands hold thy last of life;
Why hast not bethought thee well
How my mighty foemen fell?

Art not bought with weapons bright,
Purple belt, and armour light?
She for whom thy weapons shine
Shall not, Daman's son, be thine.

Mave's fair daughter, Findabar,
Brilliant though her beauties are,
Though her form has ev'ry grace,
Her thou never shalt embrace.

King's daughter is Findabar,
Pledged to thee for price of war;
Pledged to other chiefs was she,
Whom she led to death, like thee.

Break our vow of peace not here,
Break not friendship, long and dear;
Break not thou thy plighted word,
Come not hither, with the sword.

They have pledged the peerless maid
Fifty times for battle aid;
Fifty times fit meed I gave
Ev'ry champion found a grave.

Who than Ferbeth was more proud?
Heroes used his court to crowd;
His high rage was soon brought low,
Him I slew with but a blow.

Daré, too, how rude his fate!
Loved by maids of high estate;
Fame afar his name had told,
His robe glowed with threaded gold.

Should she be mine, on whom smiles
All the isle's most valiant youth, –
I would crimson not *thy* breast
East or West, or North or South!

*George Sigerson*

## *Cú Chulainn's Lament over Fer Diad*

It was all play, all sport
till Fer Diad came to the ford.
We were brought up the same,
with the same rights,
the same good foster-mother –
she of the great name.

It was all play, all sport
till Fer Diad came to the ford –
we had the same skills,
the same fire and force.
Scáthach gave two shields,
one to Fer Diad, one to me.

It was all play, all sport
till Fer Diad came to the ford –
Ah, pillar of gold
I cut down in the ford,
you were the fierce bull
that towered above all!

It was all play, all sport
till Fer Diad came to the ford –
ferocious lion, brave
overwhelming wave!

It was all play, all sport
till Fer Diad came to the ford –
I thought beloved Fer Diad
would live forever after me –
yesterday, a mountain-side,
today, nothing but a shade.

Three multitudes on the Táin
I took on board as my foes –
great men, horses and cattle
slaughtered in their countless droves.

As for Crúachan's grand army,
of those incalculable hordes
between a third and a half
were killed in my savage sport.

Never fought on battle-field,
nor sucked at Banba's breast,
nor voyaged over land or sea,
a prince so regally possessed.

*Ciaran Carson*

## POEMS OF THE FIANNA

### *The Praise of Fionn*

Patrick you chatter too loud
  And lift your crozier too high,
Your stick would be kindling soon
  If my son Osgar stood by.

If my son Osgar and God
  Wrestled it out on the hill
And I saw Osgar go down
  I'd say that your God fought well.

But how could the God you praise
  And his mild priests singing a tune
Be better than Fionn the swordsman,
  Generous, faultless Fionn?

Just by the strength of their hands
  The Fenians' battles were fought,
With never a spoken lie,
  Never a lie in thought.

There never sat priest in church
  A tuneful psalm to raise
Better spoken than these
  Scarred in a thousand frays.

Whatever your monks have called
  The law of the King of Grace,
That was the Fenians' law;
  His home is their dwelling-place.

If happier house than Heaven
  There be, above or below,
'Tis there my master Fionn
  And his fighting men will go.

Ah, priest, if you saw the Fenians
  Filling the strand beneath
Or gathered in streamy Naas
  You would praise them with every breath.

Patrick, ask of your God
  Does he remember their might,
Or has he seen east or west
  Better men in a fight?

Or known in his own land
  Above the stars and the moon
For wisdom, courage and strength
  A man the like of Fionn?

*Frank O'Connor*

## *Largesse*

Had the multitudinous leaves been gold
the autumn forests let fall,
and the waves been silver coins –
still Fionn would have given them all.

*PC*

## *The Blackbird of Derrycairn*

Stop, stop and listen for the bough top
Is whistling and the sun is brighter
Than God's own shadow in the cup now!
Forget the hour-bell. Mournful matins
Will sound, Patric, as well at nightfall.

Faintly through mist of broken water
Fionn heard my melody in Norway.
He found the forest track, he brought back
This beak to gild the branch and tell, there,
Why men must welcome in the daylight.

He loved the breeze that warns the black grouse,
The shout of gillies in the morning
When packs are counted and the swans cloud
Loch Erne, but more than all those voices
My throat rejoicing from the hawthorn.

In little cells behind a cashel,
Patric, no handbell gives a glad sound.
But knowledge is found among the branches.
Listen! That song that shakes my feathers
Will thong the leather of your satchels.

*Austin Clarke*

## *Scél Lem Dúib*

Here's a song –
stags give tongue
winter snows
summer goes.

High cold blow
sun is low
brief his day
seas give spray.

Fern clumps redden
shapes are hidden
wildgeese raise
wonted cries.

Cold now girds
wings of birds
icy time –
that's my rime.

*Flann O'Brien*

## *Lullaby and Reply*

GRÁINNE

Sleep just a little, my darling,
you have nothing whatever to fear;
you, the lad I have given my love to,
sleep, sleep, Diarmuid my dear.

Soundly, soundly sleep, Diarmuid,
Clan Duibne's noble heir,
you're more to me than I am to myself
so I shall watch over you here.

Sleep, go on sleep – bless you – sleep
to the hush of the Strong Fields' Spring,
you are the delicate foam thrown up
by strenuous waters meeting.

Sleep the sleep slept in the south
by Fidach of the intricate staves
when he'd spirited Morann's daughter
past Red Branch Conall's love.

Or the sleep slept in the faraway north
by Finnchad of Assaroe
when he'd carried off lovely Sláine
from Fáilbe, his blunt-nosed foe.

Sleep the sleep slept in the west
by Áine, Gáilían's girl,
when she'd crept away by torchlight
with Dubtach, the raven-curled.

Or the sleep slept long ago in the east
by Dedaid, the daring and proud,
when he'd stolen Coinchenn from Deichell
whose sword-tip is darkened with blood.

Dear rampart of old Greek valour
I shall watch over you here;
you know that my heart will break
if you ever slip from my care.

Dear warrior of Carman's lake
to part us two would be
to part children of one womb
or rip the soul from the body.

My dark spell will protect you
from Caoilte's avenging leap:
death and sorrow shall never come near
to leave you in lasting sleep.

DIARMUID:

The antlered stag far off in the east
bells through the night without sleeping;
straying alone through the grove of the blackbirds
he has never the least thought of sleeping.

The hornless hind in search of her fawn
laments through the night without sleeping;
she skitters and noses past brushwood and briar
nervous, alert – and not sleeping.

The bustling linnet that whistles above
the deeply twined leaves is not sleeping;
those leaves are alive with many small thrushes
and not one of those thrushes is sleeping.

The duck that glides on the smooth stream all
night
works two busy paddles, not sleeping;
she never lets up or pauses at all
but swims through the dark without sleeping.

Listen! Tonight the curlew does not sleep
but soars above the storm clouds' gathering;
I hear its strong clear vigilant call
– and I answer that call by not sleeping.

*PC*

## *Caoilte Laments the Passing of the Fianna*

Windswept, untenanted, rises Forad's high hill,
once the look-out of sword-master Fionn;
his war-band has vanished, like the hero himself:
no one hunts now on Allen's wide plain.

The very noblest of households has crumbled,
and who today values high birth?
Illustrious captains who surrounded great Fionn
are ignored now forever in earth.

Roamers over forest and valley, the Fianna
to their deep resting places have gone;
how bitter a fate it is to outlive them
– brave Diarmuid and black-fleeced Conán,

Goll MacMorna from the lowlands of Connaught
and Aillill, whom the hundreds obeyed;
Eogan of the great grey glittering spear
and Conall, ever first into fray.

I mutter their names over and over
and can scarcely believe they are lying,
Dub Drumann among them, covered in clay,
while I am still breathing here, sighing

in grief for my warrior companions
and detesting each minute I live;
I peer out tonight from Fionn's ancient eyrie
and see nothing and no one to love.

*PC*

# DALLÁN MAC MÓIRE

(*fl. c.*900)

## from *The Song of the Sword of Cerball*

Slicing, shuttling sword of Cerball,
weaver through the field of battle,
    blade that knows how to swing
    and decapitate a king,

all hail! Plunder-ready,
in royal fist ever steady,
    sharer of the spoils of war
    with kings, whose one friend you are!

Generations of noblest hands
in Leinster's spreading fruitful lands
    have grasped you; in noisy
    combat you've kept your poise

as, swung by stout unyielding men
you've torn through shield, ribcage, skin
    and sent many a proud young head
    broken to an early bed.

Forty happy years, you boast,
you spent with Eana of the Hosts
    and never met with mishap
    – so sure his grip.

Eana gave you, precious one,
to Dunlang, his warlike son,
    who thirty years looked after you
    until the day you ran him through.

Then to many a well-horsed man
in battle's broils you lent command
    until for sixteen hard fought years
    you stood by Diarmuid – rigid, feared.

At a great feast in Allen once
Diarmuid gave you to a prince
    and you became the trusted ward
    of Murrigan, Mairge's lord.

Two-score years the palm you felt
of Murrigan about your hilt
    and never once had long to wait
    unsheathing for fight.

At last Murrigan of the Gall
in Carman gave you to Cerball
    and Cerball – that wisest man –
    he gave you to no one.

*PC*

## ANONYMOUS

### *from* Buile Shuibhne (The Frenzy of Sweeney)

#### *First Year in the Wilderness*

A year to last night
I have lodged there in branches
from the flood-tide to the ebb-tide
naked.

Bereft of fine women-folk,
the brooklime for a brother –
our choice for a fresh meal
is watercress always.

Without accomplished musicians
without generous women,
no jewel-gift for bards –
respected Christ, it has perished me.

The thorntop that is not gentle
has reduced me, has pierced me,
it has brought me near death
the brown thorn-bush.

Once free, once gentle,
I am banished for ever,
wretch-wretched I have been
a year to last night.

*Flann O'Brien*

## *'Lynchseachan, you are a bother . . .'*

Lynchseachan, you are a bother.
Leave me alone, give me peace.
Is it not enough that Ronan doomed me
to live furtive and suspicious?

When I let fly that fatal spear
at Ronan in the heat of battle
it split his holy breastplate open,
it dented his cleric's bell.

When I nailed him in the battle
with one magnificent spear-cast,
– Let the freedom of the birds be yours!
was how he prayed, Ronan the priest.

And I rebounded off his prayer
up, up and up, flying through air
lighter and nimbler and far higher
than I would ever fly again.

To see me in my morning glory
that Tuesday morning, turn time back;
still in my mind's eye I march out
in rank, in step with my own folk.

But now with my own eyes I see
something more miraculous even:
under the hood of a woman's shawl,
the shifty eyes of Lynchseachan.

*Seamus Heaney*

## *Suibne in the Trees*

When I hear the belling
  of the stag in the glen
my heart begins
  to pine and keen.

Acorns taste
  as sweet as ever
and I still savour
  the hazel's coffer,

but unmet lust
  and unseasoned grief
mar a man's life
  when his home is lost.

Silver birch, waltz
  in the wind that scatters
aspen leaves
  like staves in a battle.

Apple tree, apt
  to be looted by boys,
weather the storm
  with the rowan blossom.

Alder, shield me
  with your pallid branches.
Blackthorn, bless me
  with blood-dark sloes.

Ivy, hold yourself
  close as a halter.
Yew, stand to,
  at odds with the world.

Holly, be a shelter
  from the wind, a barrier.
Ash, be a spear-shaft
  hurled by a warrior.

Dearly it cost me
  to cross you, briar:
a scald of blood money,
  my palm in bloom.

Hateful to me
  as an evil word:
a rootless tree
  holding sway in the wood.

*Paul Batchelor*

## *'I once thought that the quiet speech . . .'*

I once thought that the quiet speech
of people held less melody
than the low throating of doves
that flutter above a pool.

I thought the bell
by my elbow not so sweet
as the fluting of the blackbird to the mountain
or the bellow of a hart in the storm.

I thought the voice
of a lovely woman less melodious
than the dawn-cry
of the mountain grouse.

I thought the yowling
of the wolves more beautiful
than the baa and bleat
of a preaching priest.

Though in your chapel you find melody
in the quiet speech of students,
I prefer the awesome chant
of Glen Bolcain's hounds.

Though you relish salted hams
and the fresh meat of ale-houses,
I would rather taste a spray of cress
in some zone exempt from grief.

I am transfixed; the iron
intrudes on shattered bone.
Tell me, God who sanctions all,
why did I survive Magh Rath?

Though each bed I made
without duplicity was good
I would rather inhabit familiar stone
above Glen Bolcain's wood.

I give thanks to you, Christ,
for partaking of your body;
in my death I truly repent
all my evil deeds.

*Trevor Joyce*

## *from* Njal's Saga

### *A Vision of the Battle of Clontarf, 1014*

On Good-Friday . . . Daurrud . . . went to that bower and looked in through a window . . . and saw that there were women inside, and they had set up a loom. Men's heads were the weights, but men's entrails were the warp and weft, a sword was the shuttle, and the reels were arrows. They sang these songs, and he learnt them by heart:

See how our warp is stretched
for warriors' fall,
how wet in the loom
our weft is with blood;
foreboding the fight,
beneath friends' swift fingers,
our grey woof waxes
with war's alarms,
our warp blood-red,
our weft corpse-blue.

This woof is woven
with men's entrails,
this warp hard-weighted
with heads of the slain,
blood-sprinkled spears
are the spindles we use,
our iron-armoured loom
has arrows for reels;
with swords for shuttles
this war-woof we work;
so we weave, weird sisters,
our war-winning woof.

Now Warwinner walks
to weave in her turn,
Swordswinger steps up,
now Swiftstroke, now Storm;
when they speed up the shuttle
how spear-heads shall flash,
shields crash and helm-gnawer
on harness bite hard!

Wind, we wind swiftly
our war-winning woof,
woof once for a young king
foredoomed like his folk;
forth we will ride,
and rushing through ranks
be busy where friends
exchange their blithe blows.

Wind, we wind swiftly
our war-winning woof,
and after stand steadfast
by the bravest of kings;
then mournful men mark
over gore-spattered shields
how Swordstroke and Spearthrust
stood stout by the prince.

Wind, we wind swiftly
our war-winning woof;
when sword-bearing rangers
rush on to the banners
then, maidens, we spare
no favourite from death,
we corpse-choosing sisters
with charge of the slain.

Now new-coming peoples
that island shall rule,
who on outlying headlands
hid out before battle;
I declare the great King
is now done to death,
and that low beneath spear-point
the Earl bows his head.

Soon over the Irish
sharp sorrow shall fall,
and woe to those warriors
shall nevermore wane;
our woof now is woven,
the battlefield wasted,
over land and wide water
war's tidings will leap.

There is nothing so gruesome
as to gaze all around
when overhead cloud-rack
drives heaven blood-red;
air soon shall be raddled
with dying men's gore
as this spinning forecast
comes swiftly to pass.

So we cheerfully chant
for the young king our charms,
come sisters sing loudly
his war-winning lay;
let him who now listens
believe what his ears tell,
come gladden brave swordsmen
with wild-bursts of war-song.

Now we mount our horses,
and now bare our brands,
and now haste, hard sisters,
to other lands.

*PC, after George W. DaSent*
*(Old Norse)*

## *Hostfinn's News to Earl Gilli*

I have been where warriors wrestled,
High in Erin sang the sword,
Boss to boss met many bucklers,
Steel rung sharp on rattling helm;
I can tell of all their struggle;
Sigurd fell in flight of spears;
Brian fell, but kept his kingdom
Ere he lost one drop of blood.

*George W. DaSent (Old Norse)*

# WISDOM

## ANONYMOUS

### *from* The Instructions of King Cormac mac Airt

'O Cormac, grandson of Conn,' said Carbery, 'what are the dues of a chief and of an ale-house?'

'Not hard to tell,' said Cormac.

'Good behaviour around a good chief,
Lights to lamps,
Exerting oneself for the company,
A proper settlement of seats,
Liberality of dispensers,
A nimble hand at distributing,
Attentive service,
Music in moderation,
Short story-telling,
A joyous countenance,
Welcome to guests,
Silence during recitals,
Harmonious choruses.'

'O Cormac, grandson of Conn,' said Carbery, 'what were your habits when you were a lad?'

'Not hard to tell,' said Cormac.

'I was a listener in woods,
I was a gazer at stars,
I was blind where secrets were concerned,
I was silent in a wilderness,
I was talkative among many,
I was mild in the mead-hall,
I was stern in battle,
I was gentle towards allies,
I was a physician of the sick,
I was weak towards the feeble,
I was strong towards the powerful,
I was not close lest I should be burdensome,
I was not arrogant though I was wise,
I was not given to promising though I was strong,
I was not venturesome though I was swift,
I did not deride the old though I was young,
I was not boastful though I was a good fighter,
I would not speak about anyone in his absence,
I would not reproach, but I would praise,
I would not ask, but I would give, –

for it is through these habits that the young become old and kingly warriors.'

'O Cormac, grandson of Conn,' said Carbery, 'what is the worst thing you have seen?'

'Not hard to tell,' said Cormac. 'Faces of foes in the rout of battle.'

'O Cormac, grandson of Conn,' said Carbery, 'what is the sweetest thing you have heard?'

'Not hard to tell,' said Cormac.

'The shout of triumph after victory,
Praise after wages,
A lady's invitation to her pillow.'

'O Cormac, grandson of Conn,' said Carbery, 'how do you distinguish women?'

'Not hard to tell,' said Cormac. 'I distinguish them, but I make no difference among them.

'They are crabbed as constant companions,
haughty when visited,
lewd when neglected,
silly counsellors,
greedy of increase;
they have tell-tale faces,
they are quarrelsome in company,
steadfast in hate,
forgetful of love,
anxious for alliance,
accustomed to slander,
stubborn in a quarrel,
not to be trusted with a secret,
ever intent on pilfering,
boisterous in their jealousy,
ever ready for an excuse,
on the pursuit of folly,
slanderers of worth,
scamping their work,
stiff when paying a visit,
disdainful of good men,
gloomy and stubborn
viragoes in strife,
sorrowful in an ale-house,
tearful during music,
lustful in bed,
arrogant and disingenuous,
abettors of strife,
niggardly with food,
rejecting wisdom,
eager to make appointments,
sulky on a journey,
troublesome bedfellows,
deaf to instruction,
blind to good advice,
fatuous in society,
craving for delicacies,
chary in their presents,
languid when solicited,

exceeding all bounds in keeping others waiting,
tedious talkers,
close practitioners,
dumb on useful matters,
eloquent on trifles.
Happy he who does not yield to them!
They should be dreaded like fire,
they should be feared like wild beasts.
Woe to him who humours them!
Better to beware of them than to trust them,
better to trample upon them than to fondle them,
better to crush them than to cherish them.
They are waves that drown you,
they are fire that burns you,
they are two-edged weapons that cut you,
they are moths for tenacity,
they are serpents for cunning,
they are darkness in light,
they are bad among the good,
they are worse among the bad.'

'O Cormac, grandson of Conn,' said Carbery, 'what is the worst for the body of man?'

'Not hard to tell,' said Cormac. 'Sitting too long, lying too long, long standing, lifting heavy things, exerting oneself beyond one's strength, running too much, leaping too much, frequent falls, sleeping with one's leg over the bed-rail, gazing at glowing embers, wax, biestings, new ale, bull-flesh, curdles, dry food, bog-water, rising too early, cold, sun, hunger, drinking too much, eating too much, sleeping too much, sinning too much, grief, running up a height, shouting against the wind, drying oneself by a fire, summer-dew, winter-dew, beating ashes, swimming on a full stomach, sleeping on one's back, foolish romping.'

'O Cormac, grandson of Conn,' said Carbery, 'what is the worst pleading and arguing?'

'Not hard to tell,' said Cormac.

'Contending against knowledge,
contending without proofs,
taking refuge in bad language,
a stiff delivery,
a muttering speech,
hair-splitting,
uncertain proofs,
despising books,
turning against custom,
shifting one's pleading,
inciting the mob,
blowing one's own trumpet,
shouting at the top of one's voice.'

'O Cormac, grandson of Conn,' said Carbery, 'who are the worst for whom you have a comparison?'

'Not hard to tell,' said Cormac.

'A man with the impudence of a satirist,
with the pugnacity of a slave-woman,
with the carelessness of a dog,
with the conscience of a hound,
with a robber's hand,
with a bull's strength,
with the dignity of a judge,
with keen ingenious wisdom,
with the speech of a stately man,
with the memory of an historian,
with the behaviour of an abbot,
with the swearing of a horse-thief,

and he wise, lying, grey-haired, violent, swearing, garrulous, when he says "the matter is settled, I swear, you shall swear."'

'O Cormac, grandson of Conn,' said Carbery, 'I desire to know how I shall behave among the wise and the foolish, among friends and strangers, among the old and the young, among the innocent and the wicked.'

'Not hard to tell,' said Cormac.

'Be not too wise, nor too foolish,
be not too conceited, nor too diffident,
be not too haughty, nor too humble,
be not too talkative, nor tdo silent,
be not too hard, nor too feeble.
If you be too wise, one will expect too much of you;
if you be too foolish, you will be deceived;
if you be too conceited, you will be thought vexatious;
if you be too humble, you will be without honour;
if you be too talkative, you will not be heeded;
if you be too silent, you will not be regarded;
if you be too hard, you will be broken;
if you be too feeble, you will be crushed.'

*Kuno Meyer*

## *from* The Triads of Ireland

Three slender things that best support the world: the slender stream of milk from the cow's dug into the pail; the slender blade of green corn upon the ground; the slender thread over the hand of a skilled woman.

The three worst welcomes: a handicraft in the same house with the inmates; scalding water upon your feet; salt food without a drink.

Three rejoicings followed by sorrow: a wooer's, a thief's, a tale-bearer's.

Three rude ones of the world: a youngster mocking an old man; a robust person mocking an invalid; a wise man mocking a fool.

Three fair things that hide ugliness: good manners in the ill-favoured; skill in a serf; wisdom in the misshapen.

Three sparks that kindle love: a face, demeanour, speech.

Three glories of a gathering: a beautiful wife, a good horse, a swift hound.

Three fewnesses that are better than plenty: a fewness of fine words; a fewness of cows in grass; a fewness of friends around good ale.

Three ruins of a tribe: a lying chief, a false judge, a lustful priest.

Three laughing-stocks of the world: an angry man, a jealous man, a niggard.

Three signs of ill-breeding: a long visit, staring, constant questioning.

Three signs of a fop: the track of his comb in his hair; the track of his teeth in his food; the track of his stick behind him.

Three idiots of a bad guest-house: an old hag with a chronic cough; a brainless tartar of a girl; a hobgoblin of a gillie.

Three things that constitute a physician: a complete cure; leaving no blemish behind; a painless examination.

Three things betokening trouble: holding plough-land in common; performing feats together; alliance in marriage.

Three nurses of theft: a wood, a cloak, night.

Three false sisters: 'perhaps', 'maybe', 'I dare say.'

Three timid brothers: 'hush!' 'stop!' 'listen!'

Three sounds of increase: the lowing of a cow in milk; the din of a smithy; the swish of a plough.

Three steadinesses of good womanhood: keeping a steady tongue; a steady chastity; a steady housewifery.

Three excellences of dress: elegance, comfort, lastingness.

Three candles that illume every darkness: truth, nature, knowledge.

Three keys that unlock thoughts: drunkenness, trustfulness, love.

Three youthful sisters: desire, beauty, generosity.

Three aged sisters: groaning, chastity, ugliness.

Three nurses of high spirits: pride, wooing, drunkenness.

Three coffers whose depth is not known: the coffers of a chieftain, of the Church, of a privileged poet.

Three things that ruin wisdom: ignorance, inaccurate knowledge, forgetfulness.

Three things that are best for a chief: justice, peace, an army.

Three things that are worst for a chief: sloth, treachery, evil counsel.

Three services, the worst that a man can serve: serving a bad woman, a bad lord, and bad land.

Three lawful handbreadths: a handbreadth between shoes and hose, between ear and hair, and between the fringe of the tunic and the knee.

Three angry sisters: blasphemy, strife, foul-mouthedness.
Three disrespectful sisters: importunity, frivolity, flightiness.
Three signs of a bad man: bitterness, hatred, cowardice.

*Kuno Meyer*

## *Negative Capability*

When I find myself with the elders
I lay down the law against fun;
when I wind up with the clubbers
I go-go like the youngest one.

*PC*

# LATIN POEMS BY CLERICS

## 'HIBERNICUS EXUL'

(*fl.* late 8th century)

### from *Poet and Muse*

POET

But tell me, great nurse of the venerable bards,
will my praise songs last to the end of time?

MUSE

While the spangled arc of the sky wheels on its hub
and the darkness of night flees before uprising planets
and the day-star surges out of shadows to shine
and strong winds batter the waves of the ocean
and rivers run foaming on towards the sea
and mountaintops threaten to brush against clouds
and valleys lie humble in their dirt tracks
and high hills flaunt their manly prows
and the splendour of kings flares burnished in gold
so long will the gift of the muses remain:
for here become lasting the great deeds of kings
and the things of today are made song for tomorrow
and by the muses' gift is praised the Creator,

radiant with goodness in His heavenly home
and pleased by our ceaseless, well-fitted verses;
so remember to venerate the King with your gift
while I on my pipe add music to your song.

*PC*

## *Teaching Methods*

### (1) THE CARROT

Now is the time for learning, boys; the right age doesn't last
    But flees with the days rotated by the stars.
As the swift stallion gallops reckless across the plain
    So youth speeds by without pausing for breath.
Supple twigs will bend under the gentlest of pressure
    But stout branches snap if they are leaned on.
So while your minds are still responsive, lads,
    Apply them to learning the high ways of God;
Do not waste this lavish gift of childhood,
    For life without learning is not worth living.

### (2) THE STICK

The lazy among you will be punished for their messing;
    No boy is safe, whatever his age:
The older will suffer withdrawal of wine
    And the younger wince at the lash's crack.
I'd prefer, though, you all just did what you're told,
    For those obedient to me have nothing to fear.

*PC*

## COLMAN
## (*fl.* 9th century)

### *St Brigit and the Sunbeam*

One day as rain pelted from the heavens
thunder-clouds gathered out of nowhere in the sky,
water streamed down in rich floods and a girl,
in drenched clothes and as fast as her feet
could carry her, hurried across plains
and saturated pastures to her home, a girl
long since by her old parents christened Brigit.
Going to change her dripping dress she
could find nowhere to hang the blessed thing
when, from the little window as if by chance
into the room glided a sunbright ray
lighting the whole place and settling on her gown.
Then someone there tried to trick
the innocent girl and, nodding towards the ray
as if it were oak, persuaded her
to hang the dress from the tremulous beam.
Though deceit was his aim the tender lass
obeyed and, fitting it along the vibrant ray,
spread the wet dress across the middle of the room;
propped in vacant air by God's will it hung
suspended from the ray, wonderful to see, never
breaking the golden-glowing light
as it stood dripping, airing there
as if stretched on a stout rope. All
were astonished and spread the story round
repeating the girl's name and invoking Christ
who not only held the dress aloft on lightest motes
but by his majesty holds up the heavy world,
who in the beginning of his Father's power

conjured the Earth out of nothing, to whom
the stars submit, who is God's
eternal goodness, who at the Father's right hand
sits, light begotten of unbegotten light.

These few of the many deeds that girl did
through the wonderful gift of Christ
learn from me, readers – the rest
I leave to others after me to write down.

*PC*

## JOHANNES SCOTTUS ÉRIUGENA
(*c.* 815–*c.* 877)

### from *'Homer sang once of his Greeks and his Trojans'*

Homer sang once of his Greeks and his Trojans
and Virgil made poems about the people of Rome:
the deeds sung here were done by the king
to whom earth itself hums endless praise.
Of the flames that levelled high Illium
and boastful champions they loved to speak
but world-vanquishing Christ, the bloodied martyr,
is sole subject of our prayerful epic.
They were skilled in making the false look true
and knew how to delude in Arcadian verse
but candid hymns are what we raise in tribute
to the wisdom and excellence of the father.
The blathering little playlets of the muses
were all folk in the past got to applaud,

but the acts of the prophets come artfully formed now
harmonious out of our hearts, our mouths and our faith.
Therefore let us fix the victories of Christ
as the highest, brightest stars in our minds.
See how the four corners of this earth
are held together by the wood of the cross
where the lord hung of his own accord
once the word of the father had taken on flesh
and become our fitting sacrificial victim.
Consider his pierced palms and feet, his shoulders,
his temples crowned with spiteful thorns;
from his side opens the spring of salvation
and his blood, life's balm, issues in a wave
that cleanses the whole world of its ancient sin,
making even us ungodly mortals godly.

*PC*

## SEDULIUS SCOTTUS
(*fl.* 840–60)

### *Safe Arrival*

Shrinking from the blasts of scowling Boreas,
we shiver under his stinging icy lash:
the ground itself shakes, white-faced & afraid,
ocean moans and hard rocks whimper.

He threatens now the great spaces of the air
with terrifying voice & thunderous roar;
he hides milk-fleeced sky in menacing dark
as earth stands speechless in her gown of snow;

suddenly the hair is whipped from the forests
    and stout oaks tremble like things afraid;
the sun, that once shone bright & resplendent,
    withdraws his rays and hides his face
and terrible it is to see how Boreas
    humbles us scholars and pious priests:
no respecter of rank or station, that wind-eagle
    picks and sorts us with his beak.

Please Hartgar, great prelate, assist the afflicted,
    shine your heart on the scholarly Gael
that blessèd you may stroll in heaven's holy temples,
    Jerusalem the fair and eternal Sion.

The mercy & serenity of that high prelate
    defied Boreas's boasts and beat back his blasts;
opening doors to the drenched & exhausted
    he plucked three scholars from the roaring wind
and clothed and received all three with honour
    making us his grateful, his sheltered sheep.

*PC*

## *He Complains to Bishop Hartgar of Thirst*

The standing corn is green, the wild in flower,
  The vines are swelling, 'tis the sweet o' the year,
Bright-winged the birds, and heaven shrill with song,
  And laughing sea and earth and every star.

But with it all, there's never a drink for me,
  No wine, nor mead, nor even a drop of beer.
Ah, how hath failed that substance manifold,
  Born of the kind earth and the dewy air!

I am a writer, I, a musician, Orpheus the second,
And the ox that treads out the corn, and your well-wisher I,
I am your champion armed with the weapons of wisdom and logic,
Muse, tell my lord bishop and father his servant is dry.

*Helen Waddell*

## *The Hospital*

If you want the gift of health you'd better run
quick as a buck to this stately building;
point your feet towards the hall of healing
& discover secrets hidden from the Greeks.
Once you've knocked back those life-saving draughts
you'll leave in a one-man victory parade.

MOTHER MEDICINE

This great queen comes down from stylish Olympus
& dispenses her gifts to everyone;
three lights shine on her well-bred face,
victorious in battle over armies of pains.
The milk from her breasts is soothing nectar
to nurse to health innumerable crowds.

Receive these gifts from Mother Medicine,
souvenirs of her stay in Paradise:
first, ointments that release incense more
precious than fabled gold or myrrh;
second, antidotes that glitter in rows,
poised to expel injurious spirits

(I hear that Medicine found them years ago
in the gorgeous gardens of the Hesperides);
and third, powders from Mount Olivet,
that, mixed with potions, glow honey-golden.

I bless you, great house, Medicine's ward,
everyone's hope, mankind's gift-hoard.

*PC*

## BISHOP PATRICK
(*d.* 1084)

### *Prologue to the Book of Saintly Patrick the Bishop*

THE INVOCATION OF THE SAINTLY BISHOP PATRICK

Omnipotent God, who fills the recesses of Heaven,
restrain with your oar the hoary waves of the deep.

THE PROLOGUE TO THE BOOK OF THE SAINTLY BISHOP PATRICK BEGINS

Fare forward, boat,
over the wide sea;
Christ on the waves
be your guide,
with his skilful oar,
his blue sky.
Sail swiftly, boat,
through the empty sea,
cut through the wan
& churning flow,
expertly steered
by friendly winds.

Fare forward, little book,
an angel beside you,
through the spreading sea:
visit the kind place
of bishop Wulstan,
find him well who
is worthy of honour
& sweetness in love;
banish his sorrow,
peal out in joy
night & day,
your song lifted
to the sun &
highest stars.
Fare forward, page,
in the sacred strength
of the high cross;
may the sails swell
through clear straits;
learn, boat,
to safely run
across plains
of sea; be like
the deep's monsters
& swim in
bitter waters.

Fare forward, little book:
joyful in wave
& wind will you go,
the scaly hosts
your company;
the helmsman's shout
for you shall sound
from the depths of the sea
with a sweet ring.
Sail swiftly, boat,
in joy through the waves;
may the tops of your sail

be strained full
by wind from the east;
may breezes
cloudlessly
minister to you
& may no
error destroy you
until you are
carried straight
to English fields.
Fare forward, page:
following in thought
I'll be your comrade,
led by love
to visit peace's
dear fosterlings;
to the Christians
of kindly Wulstan
to all of them equally
bring, as is meet,
thrice ten greetings
in lovely sequence.
Fare forward, little book,
with this limping verse,
and from Patrick
of faithful mind,
request, as is right,
for my colleague Aldwin
a thousand crowns
of wholesome life.

THE PROLOGUE ENDS

*PC*

# II

# THERE IS NO LAND ON EARTH ITS PEER: 1201–1600

*Þer nis lond on erþe is pere*

'The Land of Cockayne'

## ANONYMOUS

### *from* The Song of Dermot and the Earl
(early 13th century)

### *Dermot and the Wife of O'Rourke*

In Ireland at the time
No king was more worthy:
Generous and wealthy,
He hated meanness.
Through rude power
He had fought and conquered
O'Neill and Meath,
Bringing into Leinster
Hostages like O'Carroll,
Son of Oriel's king.

In Leath-Chuinn a king,
Called O'Rourke in Irish,
Lived in drab Tirbrun,
A wild, wooded place.
O'Rourke was wealthy,
With a beautiful wife,
Daughter of Melaghlin,
Sprung from the line
Of Melaghlin Boldheart,
Son of Colman, the courteous
And noble king.
But enough about Melaghlin,
I speak of King Dermot.

Dermot, king of Leinster,
Whom this lady loved,
Pretended he loved her,
While not loving her at all,
But wishing, if he could,
To avenge the great shame
Men from Leath-Chuinn brought
On his lands long ago.
King Dermot sent word
To the lady he so loved –
By messenger and letter
He often sent word
That she was without doubt
The love of his life;
Thus he all the time sought
Her true love in secret.
And the lady sent word
Through a private envoy
That she soon would be his:
To the respected king
She sent answer again,
By word of mouth and in writing
That he should come for her
With the army of Leinster
And by violent force
Take her back with him;
She would let him know
Where he would find her
Waiting in hiding
To be carried away . . .

## *The Complaint of O'Rourke*

O'Rourke was bitter
Over the wife he had lost,
And he offered fierce battle
To Leinster's men.
But Dermot, my lords,

Took the lady away
And never ceased marching
Til he reached Kinsellagh.
And the lady a long time
Stayed there, people say:
At Ferns she was placed
As people say, thus.

O'Rourke, much grieving,
To Connaught went hastily.
And to Connaught's king
Related his shame,
How the king of Leinster
Set upon him with force,
Took away his wife
And installed her at Ferns.
To the king of Connaught
He bitterly complained
And earnestly pleaded
For men from that household
To help him avenge
His most bitter shame.

Connaught's king sent word
To the king of Ossory
That he should not fail
To come to their aid.
The two men promised
He'd be king of Leinster
If they first could expel
King Dermot so bold.
Then this man revolted
Against Dermot, his lord,
And Melaghlin, the traitor,
Abandoned him too;
And Mac Torkil of Dublin
Also revolted.
There joined in the treason
One Murrough O'Brien,

Later eaten by dogs
As the song will relate
All in due course
Further on in this story.

## *Dermot before Henry II*

When Dermot the valiant,
Before King Henry
The king of England
At last had come,
He courteously saluted
And finely addressed him:
'May God in Heaven
Save and protect you
And give you also
Courage and will
To avenge the misfortune
My people brought on me;
Hear, great King,
That I was born a lord,
In the country of Ireland
And acknowledged a king;
But my own people wronged me
And took away my kingdom.
To you, Sire, I plead,
Before your barons and lords.
Your liege-man I shall be
All the days of my life,
If you will help me
Not to lose all:
You I shall acknowledge
My sire and my lord,
Right here in front of
Your barons and earls.'

Then the king told him,
That great king of England,
That he would help him
As soon as he could.

## *Richard, Earl of Pembroke at Waterford*

Then before long,
So the old people say,
On St Bartholomew's Eve
The great Earl Richard
And fifteen hundred men
Landed at Waterford.
Ragnald and Sidroc
Were the city's leaders.
On St Bartholomew's Day,
Earl Richard, the prudent,
Assaulted and won
The city of Waterford.
Many were the citizens
Who died in the fighting
Before in the end
Waterford was won.

When the earl by force
Had taken the city,
He straightaway sent
A message to Dermot
Saying he was now
In charge of the place,
And asking the king
To come with his English.
King Dermot speedily
Set out with a will
And in the company
Of many of his barons,
Brought his daughter
To give to the earl.

The earl with honour
Wedded her in public.
King Dermot then gave
To the famous earl
The kingdom of Leinster
With his dear daughter,
Though he asked to retain
Lordship while he lived.
Then the noble earl granted
The king his desire.

*PC, after the version by*
*Goddard Henry Orpen (Norman French)*

## MUIREADHACH ALBANACH Ó DÁLAIGH

(*fl.* early 13th century)

### *A Poem Addressed to the Blessed Virgin*

Listen to me, O great Mary
grant me the pleasure of praying to you;
do not shun your kinsman,
O Mother of the strong King of the elements.

Let me recall the story of your mother,
let me recount and bring to mind
a graceful girl with dark brows
and wavy hair.

That was Anna, God's grandmother,
from whose fair brother a king was born;
she married in turn three husbands,
no woman neared her in dignity.

To each goodman she bore a daughter
this fair bright woman:
three girls, her beautiful children:
with smooth bodies and wavy hair.

An honour to attend them,
the three women, all called Mary.
Each one blue-eyed, a pleasure to behold;
everyone sought their company.

These three Maries from heaven of the saints
took a husband each,
that the three ladies, heavy-haired,
grew gravid and slow of foot.

The three women bore three sons
– magnificent increase.
(What gentle six were greater?)
The youngest of these was God.

The mother of James was one of these women,
shielded from every ordeal,
one was Mary, mother of John,
no one has sung this in poetry.

You are Mary, Mother of God,
none has approached your fame;
the King of true heaven, a royal branch
three-fold, grew in your womb.

Into your good house and your stronghold both,
direct and command me;
O great Mary, O dear one
O yellow gold, O flourishing apple tree.

Food, raiment in your gift,
tressed locks like the field.
Mother, Kinswoman, Love,
direct me well, your poor kinsman.

Your great Son is a kinsman of mine,
O gentle scion, noble Mother,
it is right you should shield a good kinsman,
daughter of your gentle mother.

Until I accepted your Husband's shepherding,
O fair Mary of the thick tressed hair,
my heart was a place of black coals –
today, it is fitting to wash them.

O Mother of God,
hair bright-coloured and deep,
set aside your anger, let us make peace,
O great Mary, red-gold in a vessel of clay.

Have I not sufficient kinship with your Husband
O pure fair woman with the curling hair?
From heaven came his thigh and his fair side,
noble as the river.

O Trinity, O gentle Mary,
every glory passes but yours.
Hear my poem, O Four Persons,
please offer no gold as reward.

Virgin Mary, black brow,
bright garden, great tree,
of women most beloved,
grant me heaven for my humility.

You are descended from David,
great gentle one, no tree compares to you;
from Abraham the fragrant branches
braided on your head.

A Sign of your Husband's wisdom
that You carried him, bright his arm
bright his hand. Your Husband and Father
cradled at your side.

A lovely pair you were, seeking refuge glen to glen:
a dark-browed, white-handed baby,
a woman, heavy-limbed,
slow-moving and comely.

Riding on the ass, you cradled him,
your pure hand caressing
his crown of yellow hair,
his fingers tugging at your locks.

His hand at your white breast:
no need of his was unmet,
you washed the fair branch, kissed
the slender hand and foot.

A yellow-gold splendour on your gentle head
my kind-eyed kinswoman;
Mary of the smooth white heavy breast,
suckling the noble infant.

Woe to him who slanders you –
unslanderable, sinless. Lady,
if your womb is not chaste,
no branch bears a nut in the greenwood.

Vain to mention the clan of thieves,
woman of the fair tresses.
Foolish to doubt you,
soft-haired lady.

The Lord begot Mary's son
with no unholy union,
replete, like the fish's belly
was your full womb.

Because of you, great Mary
it's plain to a man enslaved:
to shun low women is to find peace,
lady of the curled hair.

He resembles you, in his curled hair,
your only son, the slender one –
the same round eyes of the noble scion,
his hands are yours, and the pure red nail.

Your hand is long and bright.
– beneath your sheltering brow,
your face shines, blue-eyed,
– I say the truth, in poetry.

Pure and yellow the curls
wreathed around your head,
pure your slender-fingered hand,
your strong perfect foot.

Your equal has never died,
never will she be born. In truth:
none like you has ever tasted life,
bright womb, God-cradling.

Give me board and ale,
O high head, earth-unsullied,
spare me the endless feast of falsity,
O strong one of the white teeth.

May your dark brow plead
for the love of your soul, O pure love;
your Husband will not be jealous
that I pray to you, bright, white-toothed one.

O Mary of the fine brows,
of the wavy yellow hair,
bear me in your heart,
and forsake me not.

Let us honour together with feasting
your handsome form, O swift one
I offer up my poems, my well-wrought verse,
O noble, O shapely one.

No woman but you in my house,
you its Mistress. Let what is mine
not be led by false women,
nor lured by wealth.

May the drinking-horns of others
be as nought to me, nor their women,
their fine horses and their dogs;
wealth, dogs, horses may I disdain, fair swan.

Lift the dark brow, let me behold
the countenance like calf's blood,
lift and let me witness
the beautiful dark hair.

Lift to me the foot and hand,
the resplendent curls. Raise to me
the clear, blue youthful eye,
that I may revel in your soft locks.

*Kathleen Jamie*

## *Praise of a Dagger*
### *(Before going on Crusade)*

The dagger that goes wherever I go –
She is the woman I love!
Until her master returns home safe
My rapt devotion she'll have.

No thick-ankled peasant girl is she
But a lady – graceful, refined;
The man who gave her as a gift
Is expert in horses and wine.

That deep-browed lord has granted
Ornament for her lip,
All the gold that she can carry
And a blue luxurious slip;

Her point is beautifully keen,
And slender and sleek her side:
A prince has given me royal steel
To wear on my belt with pride.

A fine new plaited scabbard
Holds her in close embrace:
Its gold ridge runs the length of her back
Its carved bough covers her face.

A distinguished southern lady
In otherworld ivory swanked!
A woman of Munster to hang from my waist
With her shapely, clean-edged flank!

Donnchadh Cairbreach of the sleek hounds
From his poet holds nothing back;
I cherish the blade of that golden-haired man
In its covert under my cloak.

And bless Maol Ruanaidh, the craftsman –
May his prestige never fade
Who took no rest but kept working
Until the dagger was made.

*PC*

## *On Cutting His Hair before Going on Crusade*

This hair is for you, Father God.
  A light gift, but a hard one.
Great till tonight my share of sins:
  this hair I give you in their place.

Good its combing and its keeping
  within Ireland's soft-grassed land;
I'm sad for the poor ugly thing.
  This fair hair, Maker, is yours.

I promised to you, Father God,
  My hair shorn from its curling head;
it's right, Father God, to accept it –
  it would have gone on its own.

My hair and my comrade's curled hair
  for your waving hair and soft glance:
this fair hair and the yellow hair –
  I think they'll be too dark for you.

The shearing – small the sacrifice –
  of these two heads for fear of doom;
these two tonight, Son of Mary,
  offer you their fine yellow locks.

Better is your body, wounded
  for our sake – cruel the deed –
better your hair's grace, and purer,
  bluer eye and whiter feet.

Brighter the foot and slender side,
  whiter your breast like trees' flower,
whiter the foot, heart's hazel nut,
  which was pierced, fairer the hand.

Whiter the teeth, browner the brow,
  finer body, gentler face;
lovelier the hue of your curled locks,
  smoother the cheek, softer hair.

Four years has this whole head of hair
  been on me until tonight;
I will shear from me its curved crop:
  my hair will requite my false poems.

*Thomas Owen Clancy*

## *On the Death of His Wife*

I parted from my life last night,
  A woman's body sunk in clay:
The tender bosom that I loved
  Wrapped in a sheet they took away.

The heavy blossom that had lit
  The ancient boughs is tossed and blown;
Hers was the burden of delight
  That long had weighed the old tree down.

And I am left alone tonight
  And desolate is the world I see,
For lovely was that woman's weight
  That even last night had lain on me.

Weeping I look upon the place
  Where she used to rest her head –
For yesterday her body's length
  Reposed upon you too, my bed.

Yesterday that smiling face
  Upon one side of you was laid
That could match the hazel bloom
  In its dark delicate sweet shade.

Maelva of the shadowy brows
  Was the mead-cask at my side;
Fairest of all flowers that grow
  Was the beauty that has died.

My body's self deserts me now,
  The half of me that was her own,
Since all I knew of brightness died
  Half of me lingers, half is gone.

The face that was like hawthorn bloom
  Was my right foot and my right side;
And my right hand and my right eye
  Were no more mine than hers who died.

Poor is the share of me that's left
  Since half of me died with my wife;
I shudder at the words I speak;
  Dear God, that girl was half my life.

And our first look was her first love;
  No man had fondled ere I came
The little breasts so small and firm
  And the long body like a flame.

For twenty years we shared a home,
  Our converse milder with each year;
Eleven children in its time
  Did that tall stately body bear.

It was the King of hosts and roads
  Who snatched her from me in her prime:
Little she wished to leave alone
  The man she loved before her time.

Now King of churches and of bells,
  Though never raised to pledge a lie
That woman's hand – can it be true? –
  No more beneath my head will lie.

*Frank O'Connor*

## GIOLLA BRIGHDE MAC CON MIDHE
(?1210–?72)

### *The Harp that Ransomed*

Bring my King's harp here to me,
That my grief, forgot, may flee;
Full soon shall pass man's sadness
When wakes that voice of gladness.

Noble he, and skilled in all,
Who owned this tree musical;
Many lofty songs he sang
Whilst its soft sweet numbers rang.

Many jewels he bestowed,
Seated, where this fair gem glowed;
Oft he guerdoned the beholder,
Its curved neck on his shoulder.

Dear the hand that smote the chords
Of the slight, smooth, polished boards;
Bright and brave, the tall youth played,
True his hand, for music made.

When his hand o'er this would roam –
Music's meet and perfect home –
Then its great soft tender sigh
Bore away man's misery.

When the curled Dalcassians came,
Guests, within his hall of fame,
Then its deep voice, woke again,
Welcomed Cashel's comely men.

All men admired the Maiden,
Banba with praise was laden:
'Doncad's harp,' they all exclaim,
'The fair, fragrant tree of fame!'

'O'Brian's harp! clear its call
O'er the feast in Gabran's hall;
How the heir of Gabran's Kings
Shook deep music from its strings!'

Son of Gael, of weapon sharp,
Wins not now O'Brian's harp:
Son of stranger shall not gain
From this gem its Spirit's strain.

What woe to come a pleader
For harp of Lim'rick's Leader!
What woe to come a-dreaming
That flocks were thy redeeming!

Sweet thy full melodious voice,
Maid, who wast a Monarch's choice:
Thy blithe voice would woe beguile,
Maiden of my Erinn's isle!

Could I live the yew tree's time
In this deer-loved eastern clime,
I would serve her gladly still, –
The Chief's harp of Brendon Hill.

Dear to me – of right it should –
Alba's ever-winsome wood,
Yet, though strange, more dear I love
This one tree of Erinn's grove!

*George Sigerson*

## *A Response to a Threat against Poetry*

O messenger sent from Rome,
responsible for spreading the word,
speak as the pen has directed,
no lies now, just read what's written!

Out with the ban from Peter's heir,
just as you received it from the chair;
if he gave you a gloomy old bull,
unassailable, let's have it all.

Look after all of the words,
as they were spoken in Rome;
no other voice carries such weight –
burden enough to endure it.

You were not directed in Rome, cleric,
to expel the poets from Erin;
you got this directive's curse
perhaps from some non-Roman source.

Show us where it is written
that the art of poetry needs revision;
make good what you have declared to us
and reveal the contents of your document!

Never have any books insisted
that poetry in its many forms be dismissed;
and it's an ugly and alien idea
that Erin's poets be driven away.

*Donum Dei* is every sweet song,
rooted in traditional learning;
sing it and set out its meaning –
that's God's gift, quite clearly.

To tell good men that songs cost nil,
if lords had poems without a bill,
then none would suffer satire,
cleric, and each would be a noble.

If it be for the sake of wealth
that poets will be denied their due,
doesn't every man have sufficient,
cleric, even after the poet has payment?

Why, when he came from Rome,
did Patrick of the holy religion
not banish our art and song
from the face of gentle Ireland?

And what made Colum Cille,
who knew nothing but truth,
pay for poems as he made his way
to converse with angels each Thursday?

Another decree would have expelled
the poets from the green sod of Fodla;
but in the same year this Colum
made a covenant that saved them.

Blessed Mo-Bhí Clárainech,
though his honour was entirely untarnished,
gave up his life to poets when asked –
a generous gesture, if rather excessive.

And a statue once gave her shoe away
for an eloquent and boisterous lay;
the request itself was inordinate
for it left her with an uncovered foot.

Holy Mary's Son will reward me
with compensation no man would pay;
in return for my songs I'll get heaven,
just like the bard O'Heffernan.

Another proof of the value
of the composers of verse men listen to –
the truth of this has long been told –
freedom for the patron from hell!

The praise of men is praise of Him,
the one who created and shaped them;
there is no praise at all in the world
save praise of His works and miracles.

The rhyme of a stanza, sense of a word,
all redound to the glory of the Lord;
the sound of every tide as it rushes in,
is but praise of the mighty King.

Though falsehood be found in poetry,
they're lasting lies, not transitory;
all is sham, and though shaped from clay,
man himself is a walking lie.

Were a man to act the miser,
his gold and herds would be no greater;
without respect for poetry in the world
there'd be no further need for cattle.

If the poetic art were killed,
no history, no ancient lays retold,
all but the father of each man
would pass away without mention.

If the well of knowledge went dry,
and we did not exist, no nobleman
would hear of his famous forebears,
or know the descent of the Gaels.

A lasting, ill fate and dire
for tender young warriors,
a great loss, leaving them dumb
not knowing the stock from which they come.

Hiding assaults and battles
of the men of Ireland would be useless:
when they died, though courageous they'd been,
interest in prince or nobility gone.

Though he is dead, Guaire lives on;
and the Red-branch hero Cú Chulainn;
as a result of his fame both east and west,
Brian Ború is with us yet.

Since their praise continues to live,
Conall and Conchobar survive;
as his fame remains in place,
Fergus has not yet gone from us.

There's neither flesh nor bone of Lugh,
killed by the hand of Mac Cuill;
but his fame has gone throughout the world,
and thus Lugh lives, his memory preserved.

Had lays not preserved their deeds,
though they were noble men,
a cloak would long since have fallen
on Níall, Cormac, and Conn.

The line of kings of Cashel and Cruachan,
the House of Three Hostels' scions,
Tuathal of Tara and Dath Í:
poets are the roots of those pedigrees.

Were there no poetry sung
to sweet-strung harp or timpan,
none would know of noble passed,
nor his repute nor manly prowess.

Men of high station would never know
their noble past or historical lore;
put all that in poetic composition,
or say goodbye to all man has done.

If they ban the history of Conn's people,
along with songs about you, Donal,
then the children of your keeper of hounds
would enjoy the same status as your own.

If it's the will of men of Ireland, messenger,
to banish the practice of poetry,
then no Gael's birth would merit fanfare,
for each would be but a commoner!

*Patrick K. Ford*

## *Childless*

Blessed Trinity have pity!
  You can give the blind man sight,
Fill the rocks with waving grasses –
  Give my house a child tonight.

You can bend the woods with blossom,
  What is there you cannot do?
All the branches burst with leafage,
  What's a little child to you?

Trout out of a spawning bubble,
  Bird from shell and yolk of an egg,
Hazel from a hazel berry –
  Jesus, for a son I beg!

Corn from shoot and oak from acorn
  Miracles of life awake,
Harvest from a fist of seedlings –
  Is a child so hard to make?

Childless men although they prosper
  Are praised only when they are up,
Sterile grace however lovely
  Is a seed that yields no crop.

There is no hell, no lasting torment
  But to be childless at the end,
A naked stone in grassy places,
  A man who leaves no love behind.

God I ask for two things only,
  Heaven when my life is done,
Payment as befits a poet –
  For my poem pay a son.

Plead with Him O Mother Mary,
  Let Him grant the child I crave,
Womb that spun God's human tissue,
  I no human issue leave.

Brigid after whom they named me,
  Beg a son for my reward,
Let no poet empty-handed
  Leave the dwelling of his lord.

*Frank O'Connor*

## ANONYMOUS

(*c.*1265)

### A Norman French Poem from the Kildare Manuscript

### *from* The Entrenchment of New Ross

#### *A Working Week*

On Monday they began their labours,
Amid the banners, flutes and tabors;
As soon as the noon-hour was come,
These first good people hastened home
Under banners, proudly borne,
And then the youth advanced in turn,
The youth who made the whole town ring
With their merry carolling.
Singing loudly, full of mirth,
They went hard at it, shovelling earth.
Then the priests, once Mass was chanted,
In the wide fosse dug and panted;
Quicker, harder, worked each brother,
Harder, far, than any other;
For both old and young were filled
With empowering holy zeal.
Next came the sailors, line on line,
Quickly marching through the town,
After their banner, held high up,
With its picture of a ship.
Though six hundred they were then,
Full eleven hundred men
Would have gathered by the wall
If they had attended all.

On Tuesday came coat-makers, tailors,
Fullers, cloth-dyers and saddlers;
An expert hand each cheerful lad
Was held to be at his own trade.
They worked as hard as those before,
Though the others numbered more;
If scarce four hundred they did stand
They were a more than worthy band.

On the Wednesday, down there came
Other groups, who worked the same;
Butchers, cordwainers and tanners,
Bearing each their separate banners,
Painted as appropriate
To their craft; among their lot
Many an eligible young man
Big or small, pale or tanned,
Sang, while digging, a working song:
Just three hundred were they strong.

On Thursday came the fishermen
And the hucksters followed then,
Who sell corn and fish: they bore
Many banners, for there were
Four hundred of them; then the crowd
Carolled all and sang aloud;
And the wainwrights, they came too –
But they were only thirty-two;
A single banner went before,
Which a fish and platter bore.
Three hundred and fifty porters came
On the Friday, and some of them
Planted their banners on the side
Of the fosse to vaunt their pride.
On Saturday came the stir
Of blacksmith, mason, carpenter,

Hundreds three with fifty told,
And each one of them true and bold,
Toiling away with main and might
To do what he knew was right.

Then on Sunday there came down
All the dames of that brave town;
Right true good labourers were they,
But their numbers none may say.
In a great mound there were thrown,
By their fair hands, many a stone;
Who had there a gazer been,
Many beauties would have seen.
Many a lovely mantle too,
Of scarlet, green or russet hue;
Many a fair cloak had they,
And robes bedecked with colours gay.
In no land where I have been
Dames work so hard have I seen.
Who had to look on them the power,
Was surely born in a lucky hour.
Many a banner was displayed,
While this work the ladies did;
When their gentle hands had done
Piling up rude heaps of stone,
They walked the finished fosse along,
Singing a sweet cheerful song . . .

*PC, after Mrs George Maclean*
*(Norman French)*

## ANONYMOUS

(late 13th century)

### *Lament for the Children*

Sadly the ousel sings. I know
No less than he a world of woe.
The robbers of his nest have ta'en
His eggs and all his younglings slain.

The grief his sobbing notes would say
I knew it but the other day:
Sad ousel, well I know that tone
Of sorrow for thy nestlings gone!

Some soulless lout of base desire,
Ousel, has turned thy heart to fire;
Empty of birds and eggs thy nest
Touched not the cruel herdboy's breast.

Thy young things in the days gone by
Fluttered in answer to thy cry.
Thy house is desolate. No more
They chirp about the twig-built door.

The heartless herders of the kine
Slew in one day those birds of thine;
I share that bitter fate with thee,
My children too are gone from me.

Till night they hopped among the trees,
Chicks of the bird from overseas,
Till the net's meshes round them fall.
The cruel herdboy took them all.

O God that made the whole world thus,
Alas, thy heavy hand on us!
For all my friends around are gay,
Their wives and children live today.

Out of the fairy hill a flame
To slay my hapless loved ones came:
No wound is on them, but I know
A fairy arrow laid them low.

So in my anguish I complain
All day for wife and young ones slain:
They go not out and in my door,
No marvel my sad heart is sore!

*Robin Flower*

## ANONYMOUS MIDDLE ENGLISH
(early 14th century)

### *Icham of Irlaunde*

Icham of Irlaunde
Ant of the holy londe
Of Irlaunde.

Gode sire, pray ich the,
For of saynte charite,
Come ant daunce wyt me
In Irlaunde.

## ANONYMOUS

### Four Hiberno-English Poems from the Kildare Manuscript
(early 14th century)

#### *The Land of Cockayne*

Out at sea west of Spain
Is a land called Cockayne.
There is no land under the sky
To match it for prosperity.
If Paradise be merry and bright
Cockayne is yet a fairer sight;
What's in Paradise anyway
But flowers, grass and greenery?
Joy and pleasure reign there but
The only thing to eat is fruit;
No hall there, no bower, nor bench
And only water your thirst to quench.
Of humans there are just the two,
Enoch and Elias also;
It must be lonely to wander where
No people live anymore!

In Cockayne are drink and food
And everything to do you good;
The food is fresh, the drink is pure
For lunch, quick bite or full supper.
I want to say it loud and clear:
There is no land on earth its peer
And under heaven nowhere is
Half so full of joy and bliss.
There you'll find many a pleasant sight
And always day but never night;
No conflict in that land nor strife

And no death there but always life.
There is no lack of food or clothing,
And folk there practise love not loathing.
No snake you'll find, no wolf nor fox,
No horse no jade no cow no ox.
No sheep, no pigs, no goats are there,
No dung, God knows, to foul the air.
No horse-raising farm or stud –
The land is full of other good.
Nor is there fly, flea or louse
In any clothing, bed or house.
There is no thunder, sleet or hail
Nor any low vile worm or snail,
No howling storm or rain or wind,
No man or woman there is blind.
There all is pleasure, glee and joy,
Happy the man there as the boy
Where run rivers deep and fine
Of milk and honey, oil and wine.
The water there is used for nothing
But for scenery and washing.
There grows every kind of fruit
And all is comfort and delight.

There you'll find a handsome abbey
Full of monks in white and grey;
On the inside bowers and halls;
Of tasty pies are built the walls,
Of food and fish and rich meat,
The choicest that a man can eat.
Flour cakes are the shingles all
In church and cloister, bower and hall,
The dowels are made of fat puddings,
Tasty food for chiefs and kings.
A man may stuff the whole lot in
And never fear committing sin.
There all is shared by young and old,
By stout and stern, meek and bold.
There is a cloister fair and light

Broad and long, a lovely sight.
The pillars in that cloister's shade
With brightest crystal are inlaid
And each base and capital
Of jasper's made and red coral.
In the garden is a tree
Very beautiful to see,
Of gingered galingale its roots
And pure zedoary its shoots;
Of choicest mace is its flower,
With cinnamon bark of sweet odour.
Its fruit, clove of pleasant flavour,
And bounteous aromatic pepper.
There the reddest roses are
And lilies waving in the air
That never wither day or night,
A wonderfully pleasing sight.
In the abbey are four founts
From which salves and potions mount
And spiced wines and healing balms
Whose constantly replenished streams
Irrigate the earth and mould
With precious stones and shining gold.
There is sapphire and large pearl,
Onyx, topazine and beryl,
Amber, passine and astrion,
Emerald and cut gemstone,
Amethyst and chrysolite,
Chalcedony and hepatite.

There is a bird on every bush,
Throstle, nightingale or thrush,
Golden oriole or lark,
Birds with every kind of mark,
Who never once conserve their might,
But merrily sing all day and night.
I have more to tell you yet:
Geese for roasting on the spit
Fly to that abbey, as God knows,

Crying 'hot geese' with honking voice,
Bringing the garlic so they can be
The best dressed geese a man may see.
The larks fly there from the south
To alight in the eater's mouth
Dressed, as from the stew pot, well
In flour of clove and caramel.
And drinking there is no big deal –
You just top up until you're full.

When the monks go to Mass
All the windows made of glass
Suddenly into crystal brighten
So the monks may have more lighting.
Then when Mass has been said
And the missals laid aside
The crystal turns back into glass
And everything is as it was.
The young monks every day
After meals go out to play.
There is no bird of the sky
Who can fly half so high
As those monks when in the mood
With their streaming sleeves and hoods.
When the abbot sees them fly
He breaks out in jollity
But still he calls the merry throng
Back to earth for evensong.
The monks, refusing to come down,
Fly on towards the setting sun;
When the abbot sees that they
Are about to fly away
He takes a peasant girl to drum
Expertly on her bare bum.
As soon as they see that sight
Instantly the monks alight
And gather round her and set to

Drumming on her bum with gusto
– Thirstier work than you might think,
So they head home for a drink,
Marching off to their collation
In an organized procession.

Another abbey stands nearby,
A very splendid nunnery,
Up a river of sweet milk,
Where there is a wealth of silk.
When the summer day is hot
The young nuns take out a boat
To make their way up that river
With the aid of oars and rudder.
Once clear of the abbey they
Strip bare naked and start to play,
Leaping headfirst into the brim
To show how skilfully they swim.
The young monks, at first hidden, spying,
And then in close formation flying
Come upon the nuns anon
And each of them chooses one;
He quickly carries off his prey
To the safety of his abbey
Where both join in orison
Of rumpy-pumpy, up and down.
The monk who'd like to be a stud
And knows how to arrange his hood
Shall have, without any fear,
Twelve brand-new wives each year,
All by right and not by grace
For his pleasure and solace.
And to the monk who sleeps the best,
Whose favourite pastime is to rest,
Shall surely fall the happy lot
Of being named father abbot.

Whoever to that land would go
He must mortal penance do,
Wading right up to his ears
In pigs' shit for seven years.
My lords, may you never leave
This great world before you give
Yourselves a sporting chance
– By undertaking such penance –
Of seeing that enchanted land
And never coming here again.
We pray to God that this may be,
Amen, *for Saint Charity*.

*PC*

## *Hey!*

Hey, Saint Michael with the long spear!
How pretty are those wings you wear!
The kirtle you've on is as long as it's red
And you're the best angel God ever made.
  This verse is highly wrought,
  Its wisdom widely sought.

Hey, Saint Christopher with the long stake,
Who ferried Baby Jesus over the lake!
Many's the conger eel swims at your feet.
Say, how much does herring now cost to eat?
  This verse is Holy Writ,
  Informed by noble wit.

Saint Mary's bastard, Magdalen's son,
As a natty dresser you're widely known.
You carry a herb box of ingenious device;
If you're so saintly, give us some spice.
  This verse is constructed well
  Of consonant and vowel.

Hey, Saint Dominic with your long staff!
Its upper end is as bent as a gaffe.
That book on your back, I think it's a Bible,
And you're a good cleric, if to pride rather liable.
    A true rhyme, God knows,
    To keep us from prose.

Hey, Saint Francis, the man for the fowls,
Kites and crows and ravens and owls,
Two dozen wild geese, not to mention the peacock –
And hundreds of beggars to bring up your wake!
    This verse is well put,
    Without a stray foot.

Hey, friars with the long white copes!
Whose Drogheda house turns out new ropes.
You wander all over the country like tinkers,
Filching from churches the water sprinklers.
    The master was exceptionally good
    Who this sentence understood.

Hey, hermits with your black gowns!
You abandon the wilderness and fill up the towns.
Beggars without and rich men within,
Your money-grubbing is surely a sin.
    Cleverly this verse is said:
    It would be useless merely read.

Hey, holy monks who cuddle your jugs,
Early and late tanked up to the lugs!
For ale and wine you get a great urge
Whenever you feel Saint Benedict's scourge.
    Pay heed to me
    And my artful ditty.

Hey, nuns of Saint Mary's house,
Each one God's handmaid and his spouse!
You misplace your virtue when tying your shoes
So calling the cobbler is your special ruse.
    You he understood
    Who ensured this poem was good.

Hey, priests with your broad books!
Your crowns are shaved, though curly your locks.
You and your like give alms so meanly
To receive holy bread from you would be unseemly.
    Clearly it was a clerk
    Who made this wily work.

Hey, merchants with your great packs
Of drapery and avoir du poids on your backs,
Precious stones, pounds, marks, gold and silver –
Of which not a groat finds its way to the poor!
    Full of wit he was and fly
    Who said this in poetry.

Hey, tailors with your sharp shears!
To make ill-fitting hoods you cut arse over ears.
Ready for winter, your needles are hot.
Your seams look good but last hardly a jot.
    The clerk who composes verse this deep
    Stays up all night and gets no sleep.

Hey, cobblers with your various lasts,
And treated hides of precious beasts,
Leathers waste, leathers worn, your tools and your awls!
Black are your teeth, and filthy your stalls.
    Is this verse not well set,
    Each word sitting tight?

Hey, skinners with your drenching vat!
That smell would kill a sewer-rat;
During thunder you can shit in it.
Bad luck on your manners, you stink up the street!
    He's worthy to be king
    Who wrote this thing.

Hey, butchers with your woodbole cleavers,
Your leather aprons and foxy ear-hairs!
You stand at the block, thick-set and tough,
Flies follow you everywhere – though you swallow
   enough!
    The best clerk in town
    With skill wrote this down.

Hey, bakers with your loaves so small
Of white bread and black, go set out your stall
Where you stint with the flour against God's law –
May you soon at the pillory stand in awe!
    There's no living tongue can tell
    How this verse was made so well.

Hey, brewers with your measures,
Gallons and quarts and siphoned-off treasures!
Your thumbs in your pint-pots, shame on your guile –
The cucking stool and lake will reform you in style.
    He surely was a clever clerk
    Who so slyly wrought this work.

Hey, hucksters down by the lake,
With candles and bowls and pots of black,
Tripes and cows' feet and sheeps' heads!
With rotten liver may you make your beds.
    He is sorry all his life
    Who is stuck with such a wife.

Fie upon devils, caitiffs who card wool,
The gallows' shameful shadow hangs over your skull!
You raised such a racket outside our homes
That I made one of you sit on a comb.
He was a noble clerk and good
Who this deep lore understood.

Make glad my friends, you sit too still,
Speak now, be happy, drink your fill!
You've heard of men's lives as lived in this land;
Drink deep and be glad, and all will be grand.
This song has been said by me.
Always blessed may you be.

*PC*

## *Christ on the Cross*

Look at your Lord, churl, hanging from the rood
And weep, if you can, tears of real blood.
Look at his head, with spiked thorns crowned,
And his skin besmirched by the sharp spear's wound.
Look! His stripped breast, his bloody side,
His stiffening arms forced open so wide.
His fair cheek palls, his sight fails,
As if tightened on a rack his good body quails.
See how sag there, cold and heavy as stone,
Loins that have lusted after no one.
Look at the nails in his hands and his feet,
And his red blood, streaming precious and sweet.
Cast your gaze from his head to his toe
In one long sweep of anguish and woe.
Turn your dear lover this way and that:
Everything you see is pitiful to look at.

CHRIST SPEAKS

Love, for you my breast shines naked and glistening.
My side sorely stung, my hands ripped and bleeding.

Man, you have brought yourself nearly to Hell.
Turn round, come with me, I will make you well.
First I created and then I forgave you,
Hanging from a tree so I could save you.

Look what I went through up on that tree!
Who ever suffered such pain?
Hear me, who died for you, now cry to you,
Nailed hand and foot for your gain.

Sharp stabs, hard blows, sore wounds,
And the worst pangs of all in my mind:
Such a bitter drink!
Now what thanks

For the love that I gave do I find?

*PC*

## *Age*

Age gelds
and greys me;
when age tries
to cut me
down to size
there is never a No,
though age ever
says Nay
to chatter of May;
when age
wages

war on me
well-being's away;
age loves to cool,
to cling to clay;
must deal with age
to dying day.

Though age blows brave
his bloom soon pales;
if all want growth
unabated
why
is age hated?

Things annoy:
spittle dries
nose runs;
age warps body,
shoulders spindle;
youth dwindles.

I can no more
grope under skirt
though my will, he wants to;
I am yoked to yore,
sin my sole lore,
my sun, set.

So beset with sin
I may not win
to good topic with tongue;
age has me marred,
my soul charred
by longing to be young.

Thus age fore-does me,
tugs out my teeth;
no more loving can I do
but piss on my shoe;
every woman
now a shrew.

My head all hoar,
grey like a mare;
body waxes weak
and eyes dim
to see my shins
so thin;
friends grow rare.

I prattle,
I puff and pout,
shrivel, sob
and snuffle my snout;
I crumble,
grow cold and grumble,
I lean and get lean,
in limb become less;
I pall:
saddle-gelded,
galled
and witless.

I ravel,
wrinkle and rave;
mind roves;
I cling,
croak and cough;
I grow crippled;
I grunt,
groan and girn;
I grouch;

I sneeze,
snap, sniffle
and rage:
all
at behest
of age.

I stint,
stammer and stumble;
bleared,
I go blind;
in bed I snore
ever more;
I spit
and spurn;
I wither
and wane;
I weep that
youth comes
never again.

Spent
is strength;
am feeble
as field that lies fallow,
that once herdsman had
but has since
hollowed.
No one now
follows.

Age
has so hard
taken hold;
look how
he wastes
me, each
twisted tooth
torn out

by the root;
tongue wriggles,
I retch;
listless
in limb,
where age is
I am:
under
his foot.

*PC*

## GEARÓID IARLA MAC GEARAILT
## (1338–98)

### *Dispraise of Women*

Shame, who overleaps his steed,
Rightly rede and understand;
Love with land goes swift behind,
Weigh the worth of Womankind.

Them may malisons enfold,
Though of old we used to mix,
Youth, their tricks are as the wind –
Ware the wiles of Womankind.

He who early looks abroad
Shall a load of ills discern,
Wouldst thou learn the worst to find,
Watch the heart of Womankind.

Married man with witless wife,
Fails in strife with foreign foe;
Bad for hart is belling hind,
Worse the tongue of Womankind.

Dame who hears but does not heed –
Walled indeed her ears with wax,
See her tax her spouse too blind,
Wont to rouse is Womankind.

Show a stranger, – off she trips,
Wreathes her lips with smiles resigned,
Him beguiles with martyred air –
False as fair is Womankind.

Wedded wife from altar rail,
Pious-pale before the priest,
After feast shows bitter rind –
Best beware of Womankind.

Best beware of Womankind,
Meetly mind, this truth proclaim:
He who fails full soon shall find
Bondage blind and bitter shame.

*George Sigerson*

## *Praise of Women*

Woe to him who slanders women.
  Scorning them is no right thing.
All the blame they've ever had
  is undeserved, of that I'm sure.

Sweet their speech and neat their voices.
  They are a sort I dearly love.
Woe to the reckless who revile them.
  Woe to him who slanders women.

Treason, killing, they won't commit
  nor any loathsome, hateful thing.
Church or bell they won't profane.
  Woe to him who slanders women.

But for women we would have,
  for certain, neither kings nor prelates,
prophets mighty, free from fault.
  Woe to him who slanders women.

They are the victims of their hearts.
  They love a sound and slender man
– not soon do they dislike the same.
  Woe to him who slanders women.

Ancient persons, stout and grey,
  they will not choose for company,
but choose a juicy branch, though poor.
  Woe to him who slanders women!

*Thomas F. O'Rahilly*

## *Prayer for His Dead Wife*

I, who saw a vision
in broken sleep,
have known no rest
since soul was ripped

from body by Christ
the peerless one
who took her and left me
to live on alone.

Cruel it was to sunder
two bedfellows pure
in the love and devotion
His sacrament calls for.

Our parting was unwilling
as the King of Heaven knows;
the author of all that is
is author of our woes.

The Trinity placed earth's women
in care of the Virgin's Son;
He had His pick of any
but chose my chosen one.

I beseech Great Mary's Son
who tore her from my arms
let my dear departed soul
meet no eternal harm.

I would shape her elegy
though passion makes me rave
if it would help her more
than this prayer that she be saved.

*PC*

## GOFRAIDH FIONN Ó DÁLAIGH

(*d.* 1387)

### *from* Praise of Maurice Fitz Maurice, Earl of Desmond

#### *The Earl Compared to Lugh*

Just like Maurice, friend to the bard,
was Lugh Longhand:
as great in knowledge, quick with sword,
and as renowned.

When young like Maurice, he gave
      battle and won;
Bladhma's mighty tree, who drove
      the Fomorians down.

At Eamhain in the east he spied
      Tara's ramparts,
who'd scoured the world for such a sight:
      home at last.

But, champion elect, he fails
      to pass: the door is barred.
Striding up to the bare walls
      he raps hard,

and the porter, dander up, asks
      the bright young warrior:
'Who are you and your rosy cheeks
      to pass this barrier?'

No coward soul, Lugh replies:
      'Poet of swan,
of appletree and yewtree I.
      I am of Eamhain.'

'Then there's no welcome here for you,'
      the shout comes back.
'We have a poet and don't need two,
      my bright young buck.

'The house of Miodhchuairt is the fort
      of Ethliu's boys.
Let me tell you a custom honoured
      in this fair house.

'The custom that we keep is, like
      our walls, unbroken:
just one man of each craft we take –
      no second's taken.

'So many skills are practised by
    the Tuatha Dé Danann,
the cloak-weavers, you must supply
    one yet unknown.'

'Among my skills, let word go out,
    is to leap on a bubble
and perch there. Go broadcast that
    around your table.

'To swim beyond all human power,
    to carry a vat
on my elbow. Who has a pair
    of skills like that?

'If my exploits are surpassed
    by a man of yours,
I'll race and best him over grass
    on any horse.

'I trump your men one and all,
    and not in their arts only.
I am master of all arts – my tale
    I tell you calmly.'

Once the youth had had his say
    the porter scurried
off to tell the Tuatha Dé
    every word.

'Matchless is the man at your door,'
    he began,
'Master of every art, the fair
    young red-faced one.'

'If he has come, Ireland's dearest,'
    said Danu's tribe,
'Lugh who gives the rivers rest,
    the hour is ripe.

'Who would not know better than
    to challenge such beauty?
Neither earth nor water's ever seen
    so brave a body.

'Choice are his side, face, and hair:
    like bronze, blood
and lime in colour are
    that triad.

'Sweeter his tongue than lute-strings
    tautened
for the gentle sleep they bring
    at a master's hand.'

'He is come,' the host announced,
    'our love's treasure,
Eithne's son, noble prince,
    never a loser.'

And Danu's tribe: 'Let Tara's porter
    make all haste
and bid the fragrant branch enter,
    Eamhain's guest.'

'If you are Ioldánach of
    the sharp blue skean,'
the porter said, 'greetings, my soft
    young man of the plain.

'Step inside the gates and welcome!'
    'That I won't,'
answered the youth for whom
    all spoils were meant.

'When Art's fort at Tara shuts
    it is forbidden
that you should open up the gates
    til the sun has risen.'

He did not break bloody-weaponed
    Tara's rule,
but stood back, leaped, and hit the ground
    inside the wall.

*David Wheatley*

## *Under Sorrow's Sign*

A pregnant girl, under sorrow's sign,
Condemned to a cell of pain,
Bore, by leave of Creation's Lord,
Her small child in prison.

Swiftly the young lad flourished,
Eager as a bardic novice,
For those first years in prison,
Clear as if we were looking on.

Who would not be moved, alas,
As he darts playful little runs
Within the limit of his walls
While his mother falls into sadness!

For all daylight brought to them –
O sharp plight – was the glimpse
A single augurhole might yield
Of the bright backbone of a field.

Seeing one day on her pale face
A shining tear, the child cried:
'Unfold to me your sorrow
Since I follow its trace.

Does there exist another world
Brighter than where we are:
A home lovelier than this
Source of your heavy weariness?'

'Seeing the narrow track we tread
Between the living and the dead
It would be small wonder if I
Were not sad, heedless boy.

But had you shared my life
Before joining this dark tribe
Then on the tender hobbyhorse
Of your soul, sorrow would ride.

The flame of the wide world
Warmed my days at first;
To be closed in a dark cell
Afterwards: that's the curse.'

Realizing this life's distress
Beyond all balm or sweetness,
The boy's brow did not darken
Before his cold and lonely prison.

This image – this poem's dungeon:
Of those closed in a stern prison
These two stand for the host of living,
Their sentence, life imprisonment.

Against the gaiety of God's son,
Whose kingdom holds eternal sway
Sad every dungeon where earth's hosts
Lie hidden from the light of day.

*John Montague*

## CEARBHALL Ó DÁLAIGH

(late 14th century?)

### *Lover and Echo*

Tell me, Echo fair!
From the air above
Since thou knowest, why
I to sorrow clove?
Echo: Love.

Love! – O no, of course,
That source ceased to flow;
That I knew of yore
Now no more I know.
Echo: No?

Lo, if Fortune hard
Will thy bard oppress,
Is there – tell me sure
Cure for my distress?
Echo: Yes.

Sage and witty Sprite
Rightly now reply,
Since there's healing calm
Choose what balm should I?
Echo: Die.

Die! – if so 'tis so,
Death puts woe away;
Since 'twill cure my ail
Then all hail I say.
Echo: Icy.

I say thrice all hail
  None will wail my fate;
But tell none my tale,
  This I supplicate.
    Echo: Like Kate.

Kate! the devil flee
  With thee, mocking Sprite!
Kate's unkind, and care
  Beareth no respite.
    Echo: Spite!

If Narcissus such
  Jealous touch did wake,
'Tis not strange that he
  Left thee for a lake.
    Echo: Ache!

Aching sobbing sighs
  Still I daily hear;
What can cause thy cries,
  Is not comfort near.
    Echo: Ne'er.

Shall Narcissus hold
  Old Love against the new?
Other fate may fall –
  Always needst not rue.
    Echo: True!

Blessings on thy Voice,
  I rejoice anew!
Since thou far wilt fare,
  Farewell and adieu.
    Echo: Adieu!

*George Sigerson*

# DÁNTA GRÁ (LOVE POEMS)

## ANONYMOUS

### *A History of Love*

This is Love's history
  And how it all began:
As an authority
  I am your foremost man.

Diarmuid the bold and gay,
  Chief of the warrior bands,
With Grania one day
  Invented holding hands.

While Ulster's Hound as well,
  When a Greek girl went by,
Falling beneath her spell,
  Was first with the glad eye.

Naisi, home from the chase,
  Weary, inspired with bliss,
Seeing Deirdre don her trews,
  Endowed us with the kiss.

The son of Conall met
  Their challenges with grace
And left us in his debt
  By figuring the long embrace.

Avartach, king of the fairies,
  Following in their track,
With his arbutus berries
  Put a girl upon her back.

Ceadach, master of trades,
  Seeing them still unversed –
Those white-skinned Irish maids –
  Made women of them first.

And Angus as they say –
  Lord of the Sacred Hill –
First took their clothes away,
  And gave them perfect skill.

Learning that hearts can break
  Under Love's miseries
Beside a Munster lake
  Glas filled the air with sighs.

Lamenting to soft strings
  And moans upon the pipe
Were Mongan's offerings
  To woo some timid wife.

But I, for my own grief,
  First opened Jealousy's door –
This is my tale in brief –
  And now it shuts no more.

*Frank O'Connor*

## *Women*

Every man in Ireland caught
  By some girl with eyes of blue
Dolefully laments his lot
  Unless her hair be golden too.

What has this to do with me?
No fanaticism I share
For blue or black in someone's eye
Or the colour of her hair.

Golden mane or rosy grace
Can never be my whole delight.
Dusky be the woman's face
And her hair as black as night.

Black was the dam of her who brought
Troy into the dust of old,
And the girl for whom they fought,
Helen, was all white and gold.

Beautiful surely were the two
Though one was dark and one was fair.
No one who ever saw them knew
Which was the lovelier of the pair.

In little shells it may befall
The loveliest of pearls is found,
And God created three things small –
The horse, the woman and the hound.

Public confession suits my case,
And all may hear what I would say –
In women, such is my disgrace,
I never found a thing astray.

Though some are small I like them neat
And some are tall of them I sing;
Two long legs to grace the sheet
Are satisfaction for a king.

Foam may be brighter than her skin
Or snow upon the mountain cold,
I'll take what pack I find her in
And think her sweeter for being old.

Nor should I slight a relative
  For someone from outside the state;
Though novelty keep love alive
  Kinsmen love at double rate.

Nor do I ask for intellect:
  A little scholarship will pass;
All that of women I expect
  Is to know water-cress from grass.

I don't require them cold or warm;
  Widows have knowledge and good sense
But there is still a certain charm
  In a young girl's inexperience.

I like them in church, demure and slow,
  Solemn without, relaxed at home;
I like them full of push and go
  When love has left me overcome.

I find no fault in them, by God,
  But being old and gone to waste
Who still are girls at forty odd –
  And every man may suit his taste.

*Frank O'Connor*

## *Aoibhinn, a leabhráin, do thriall*

Delightful, book, your trip
to her of the ringlet head,
a pity it's not you
that's pining, I that sped.

To go, book, where she is
delightful trip in sooth!
the bright mouth red as blood
you'll see, and the white tooth.

You'll see that eye that's grey
the docile palm as well,
with all that beauty you
(not I, alas) will dwell.

You'll see the eyebrow fine
the perfect throat's smooth gleam,
and the sparkling cheek I saw
latterly in a dream.

The lithe good snow-white waist
that won mad love from me –
the handwhite swift neat foot –
these in their grace you'll see.

The soft enchanting voice
that made me each day pine
you'll hear, and well for you –
would that your lot were mine.

*Flann O'Brien*

## *The Dispraise of Absalom*

Veiled in that light amazing,
Lady, your hair soft wavèd
Has cast into dispraising
Absalom son of David.

Your golden locks close clinging,
Like birdflocks of strange seeming,
Silent with no sweet singing
Draw all men into dreaming.

That bright hair idly flowing
Over the keen eyes' brightness,
Like gold rings set with glowing
Jewels of crystal lightness.

Strange loveliness that lingers
From lands that hear the Siren:
No ring enclasps your fingers,
Gold rings your neck environ,

Gold chains of hair that cluster
Round the neck straight and slender,
Which to that shining muster
Yields in a sweet surrender.

*Robin Flower*

## *'O woman, shapely as the swan'*

O woman, shapely as the swan,
On your account I shall not die:
The men you've slain – a trivial clan –
Were less than I.

I ask me shall I die for these –
For blossom teeth and scarlet lips –
And shall that delicate swan-shape
Bring me eclipse?

Well-shaped the breasts and smooth the skin,
The cheeks are fair, the tresses free –
And yet I shall not suffer death,
God over me!

Those even brows, that hair like gold,
Those languorous tones, that virgin way,
The flowing limbs, the rounded heel
Slight men betray!

Thy spirit keen through radiant mien,
Thy shining throat and smiling eye,
Thy little palm, thy side like foam –
I cannot die!

O woman, shapely as the swan,
In a cunning house hard-reared was I:
O bosom white, O well-shaped palm,
I shall not die!

*Padraic Colum*

## *Swift Love*

Swifter than greyhound that none e'er outran
Is the will of my mistress to bed with a man.
Swifter than starling her heart is afire
With inconstant desire.

Swifter than gales in the cold time of spring,
Around the hard crags ceaselessly ravaging,
Is the lust of a heart that is empty and dry,
And a hungry green eye.

By the Lord of Hard Judgment that lives evermore!
By the High King of Heaven, there never before
Was her like among women, for who was afire
With so swift a desire?

*Edward, Lord Longford*

## *Piece Making*

Slaney, daughter of Flanagan
let's make a piece right well,
not the slack work of an innocent
to barter or to sell.

I have a tawny spindle
for a twistless piece is no good
and you have the needed colours,
a skein of black and red.

Stand that tawny spindle
firmly on the piece
and should you want for texture
just move the balls down the crease.

With my two dark balls of wool
your fibres will interlock:
our plaid will look amazing
beside your trim of black.

Make the frame like I said
and I will take the strain,
fulling the piece and plumping it
over and over again.

Slaney, daughter of Flanagan,
you holy church's abbess,
lady from Dun Manannan,
let's make a right good piece!

*Máirin Ní Dhonnchadha and PC*

## *Death and the Maiden*

My girl I say be on your guard
    And put folly from your head,
Take my counsel and be hard,
    Think of me and do not wed.

Though you scorn advice today
    When your cheeks are bright and red
And you do not know my way,
    Think of me and do not wed.

Me? Yourself you do not know,
    Never saw yourself in dread,
Pillared throat and breasts of snow –
    Think of me and do not wed.

Give no man your love or hate,
    Leave the foolish words unsaid,
Spare your kisses, they can wait –
    Think of me and do not wed.

Think of me and do not wed,
    Let the road be smooth or hard,
I shall be there when all are fled –
    My girl, I say be on your guard.

*Frank O'Connor*

## *He Praises His Wife when She Had Gone from Him*

White hands of languorous grace,
Fair feet of stately pace
And snowy-shining knees –
My love was made of these.

Stars glimmered in her hair,
Slim was she, satin-fair;
Dark like seal's fur her brows
Shadowed her cheek's fresh rose.

What words can match its worth,
That beauty closed in earth,
That courteous, stately air
Winsome and shy and fair!

To have known all this and be
Tortured with memory
– Curse on this waking breath –
Makes me in love with death.

Better to sleep than see
This house now dark to me
A lonely shell in place
Of that unrivalled grace.

*Robin Flower*

## *A Jealous Man*

Listen jealous man
    What they say of you
That you watch your wife
    Surely isn't true?

Such an ugly face
    The light loves disown;
Much to your surprise
    Your wife is all your own.

Other men must watch
    Who have wives to shield,
Why should you put up
    A fence without a field?

In a hundred none
    Is as safe as you,
Nobody could think
    Such a thing was true.

Men cry when they're hurt,
    Your cry's out of place,
Who do you think would want
    Such an ugly face?

*Frank O'Connor*

# TWO EPIGRAMS

## ANONYMOUS

### *Jealousy*

Love like heat and cold
    Pierces and then is gone;
Jealousy when it strikes
    Sticks in the marrowbone.

*Frank O'Connor*

### *At Mass*

Ah! light lovely lady with delicate lips aglow,
With breast more white than a branch heavy-laden
    with snow,
When my hand was uplifted at Mass to salute the Host
I looked at you once, and the half of my soul was lost.

*Robin Flower*

## TADHG ÓG Ó HUIGÍNN
### (*d.*1448)

### *A School of Poetry Closes*

Tonight the schools break up,
The beds will be deserted
And we who occupied them
Will weep and separate.

Too bad so many of us
Who bedded down last night
Here in our usual places
Won't close an eye tonight.

My God, how will I bear it?
My home from home abandoned,
And all its past fame cancelled.
What is the sense of it?

Towards Samhain the poetry class
Would reassemble always:
If one man were still with us
This break-up would not happen.

Whoever came here to him
For lodging and art-training
Would come to hate it, once
The cuckoo started calling.

For then the school broke up
And students headed homeward –
But now they won't be back here
For art or training ever.

I would think long when that break came,
I missed my class and master,
But thinking long won't soothe me
For the death of Fearghal Rua.

Since no one can replace him
It is better to disperse now:
Another teacher's lessons
Would be like going to prison.

For thirty years and over –
Let me be the first to say it –
His esteem kept me alive.
Now grief has dug my grave.

My God, how will I bear it?
I have drunk a bitter glassful,
And, God, it is all the sorer
In the aftermath of pleasure.

Without fail, every night,
I was close to him and working:
I shared the hut with Ó hUigínn
Until I was fully fledged.

And if anyone badmouthed me
Behind backs to my tutor
He never deigned to notice.
I basked in his good favour.

From childhood I was party
To his every plan and notion
(Ó hUigínn, God reward you!)
Then next thing we were parted.

Whatever poetry teaching
I give my students now
Was got from Fearghal Rua,
But it cannot match his teaching.

Through his death I realize
How I value poetry:
O hut of our mystery, empty
And isolated always.

Áine's son is dead.
Poetry is daunted.
A stave of the barrel is smashed
And the wall of learning broken.

*Seamus Heaney*

## ANONYMOUS

### Complaints of Gormlaith
(15th century or earlier)

#### *The Empty Fort*

Empty tonight, Dún Cearmna
puts high Tara in danger,
the earth weaves a spell
over pale lonely walls.

Kings unstinting as courageous
made happy use of this fortress.
What a state I'm in –
to be here, with them gone.

Not long now – Tuathal
and Tara will dwindle.
Their emblem and exemplar
the night, and empty Dún Cearmna.

*Kit Fryatt*

## *The Ragged Dress*

Ragged, much-patched scrap!
No one will wonder that
a chatelaine's canny hand
never worked this tawdry tat.

And I was in Tara.
Niall of Emain's green downs
pledged me in joy
our shared cup was his own.

And I was in Limerick
beside kind Niall of Ailech;
I showed off in sumptuous stuff
before the knights of the west.

The sparks of the Uí Néill
loved of old to race foals;
I drank their wine from carved
horn cups, by the skinful.

Seven score waiting-women
assembled on the lawn
and the colts' thundering –
spotless Niall's escutcheon!

I am a woman of Leinster
a daughter of Meath
but those places don't grip me.
Ulster has my heart's truth.

The brambles take hold
of my shoddy rags;
the thorn is my enemy,
the briar a rogue.

*Kit Fryatt*

## *At Niall's Grave*

Monk, back off. Move
away from Niall's grave.
You heap earth on his head;
I shared his bed.

Long time you've piled clods,
monk, on the royal corpse.
Too long already Niall's lain still,
the pit unfilled.

Aed's son liked his booze.
Now he's cold under a cross.
Lay that slab flush enough,
and, monk, back off.

Just as I do Deirdre stood
weeping over Uisnech's lads.
Her heart was great with grief
so, monk, back off.

I am Gormlaith, maker of verses,
my father was Flann of Dún Rois.
Dig my bed here, broad and soft
then, monk, back off.

*Kit Fryatt*

## 3 × 30, 9 × 9

Three thirties, nine times nine
have been lovers of mine
I could take on twenty lads –
or more, the number makes no odds.

I threw them all over for Niall
alone to do his will.
And why not indeed
for my life's liege, that's dead.

Of all the northern champions
Niall was the greatest; he always won.
But considering my troubles,
better I'd married a churl.

He had golden rings and cloaks of purple
the kingdom's best-stocked stable,
but fortune's flood, once full, is turned,
substance wasted and withdrawn.

Between heaven and earth I possess
one black shawl and one grey dress.
In Kells of the hundred kings
no one cares I'm starving.

One holy day I stood with Niall
in the churchyard, by the bell.
In Kells of the high rood
we decided the northern tribute.

I was at his left hand; he gave
me the gentlest little shove
in the small of my back:
'Go to Mass; you'll have all the luck!'

Truth then, we went together
a pack of girls – in walked Mór
ahead of me, flower among the few
she took the buckle from my shoe.

I gave a golden chain and ball
to handsome Abbot Colum's girl.
I gave her the forty cows
that graze the north church close.

I gave her an outlandish blue hood,
a horn-shrine for a holy book,
thirty ounces of gold – and what
did Little Miss Big do? Kept the lot.

Tonight she gave alms to me –
grace matching generosity –
two measures of gritty porridge,
two eggs from her tight clutches.

By Him who brought light to the world!
If Niall Black-knee still walked,
you abbot's drab from Tullylease
could stuff your eggs and oats!

I got from her a comb, a bonnet,
some linen with no dress left in it.
The Slight Red Steed my gift
to her, and sun-gold apples in a dish.

My curse on big spenders,
my curse on misers (hey, Mór!);
before I lost my wealth and looks
all the poets were on my books.

Horses in exchange for verses –
patrons are among God's blessed.
I praise Niall, but I'm an amateur –
the pros would do it nine times better.

*Kit Fryatt*

## *Gormlaith's Last Complaint*

It is time our weeping ceased for Niall,
Aed's son, who brought such steeds to heel.
Pitiful, O Lord, the plight
that I endure between death and life.

For thirty-one years, no word of a lie,
since this righteous chieftain died
the tears for him in which I've foundered
have nightly numbered seven hundred.

After prayers last night I heard
from Niall himself a bitter word:
'Give over, Gormlaith, with your tears
before the Lord's own anger flares',

and all peace routed from my mind.
To the dead man I for once complained:
'Why should the Lord God take offence
at me, whose life is one long penance?'

'But fair Gormlaith, it was God
made heaven and mankind who bade
us share in his delight, not raise
a floodtide to him from our eyes.'

If Niall thought to turn his back
I let out an almighty shriek
at such perversion of our love
from beyond the afterlife

and springing in his wake I threw
myself on a bedpost carved from yew
and pierced my breast and still pressed down
and rent the heart within in twain.

Tonight I ask the Son of God
who formed my flesh to strike me dead,
send me to Niall and let us both,
Lord Jesus, walk the selfsame path.

Hundreds of horses and cows were showered
on me by Cerball of the sword,
and never slow with a generous touch
Cormac gave me twice as much,

but from whom could I conceal
the riches that I had from Niall?
All that I had from that pair ever
I had in a month from him thrice over.

*David Wheatley*

## LOCHLAINN ÓG Ó DÁLAIGH
(*fl.* mid-16th century)

### *Praise for the Young O'Briens*

Proud I am to praise young men,
Three who've won my favour,
The newest sons in Blod's long line,
Comely lads schooled in valour.

Slim boys who came to my chamber
To bind an old allegiance,
Three young males, softly spoken,
Of distinguished countenance.

I have pledged them each a gift,
In accord with their high birth
And destiny as warriors:
A poem well-worked in their honour.

The oldest, Tadg, is Donal's heir,
Chieftain of Tal and its clan.
Trained in the art of warfare,
True branch from the root of Brian.

Conor the sons of Cash will head.
He'll be their chief in Thomond.
I give this pledge under God,
Lest there come an interloper.

The third kernel in this cluster
Is Murty's son, Tadg Junior.
Now a friend to poets in youth,
His fame will grow in men's mouths.

These three will make a fosse
To shield the children of Cash.
No one but a poet shall broach
The triple-fence of thriving oaks.

Three hawks darkening the sky,
Unerring in vengeful flight.
Sprung from our native forest,
Swift birds from the one roost.

Three ruggèd bears in the maul,
Defenders of Maicnia's fort.
Three spearheads in the assault,
A match for Munster's foes.

Three plunderers of Fionn's salmon,
Three seeds from the gold-skinned apple,
Three buds blossoming into verse,
Three mirrors for a girl's kiss.

Three hazels from the nutgrove,
Three streams fresh from granite caves,
Fruit of the ancient vineyard,
Runnels of juice from the orchard.

Before long their javelins
Will whistle throughout Conn's Half.
In fights where wounds are given
Blood will stain their knives.

Soon they'll swap hurling-sticks
For blades with ivory hilts.
It will make a fair exchange,
Bringing concord to the Maigue.

These young men meet at my side,
Three warriors in youth's attire.
Three horsemen from Brian's stable
Who'll ride with golden bridles.

White sparks from the firing-kiln
They'll shoot through Banba's realm.
Men will follow in their steps,
Fearless to join the contest.

It's no flaw in finished gold
To start out molten at the forge.
To be pliable from the fire
Brands them as O'Briens.

Their torsos white as spindrift,
Six strong and supple calves,
Six feet swift and nimble,
Six fine hands to kindle love.

Six cheeks that never blushed,
Six eyes quietly observant.
Not known to spurn suppliants,
Crowds hang upon their words.

Conor with the fair complexion,
Two Tadgs, the poets' patrons,
Each with a royal bard at ease,
Three I've singled out for praise.

The Trinity grant them strength,
Stewardship of our holy ground.
May they bring the people wealth.
To have praised them makes me proud.

*Maurice Riordan*

## RICHARD STANIHURST
## (1547–1618)

### *Upon thee death of thee right honourable* Lord Girald fitz Girald L. Baron *of* Offalye, *who deceased at* S. Albans *in thee yeere 1580. thee last of Iune, thee xxj. yeere of his adge*

Sometyme liv'lye *Girald* in grave now liv'les is harbourd.
A mathchlesse gallant, in byrth and auncestrye nobil.
His nobil linnadge *Kyldaer* with *Mountegue* warrants.
Proper in his person, with gyfts so hym nature adorned.

In valor and in honor wel knowne too no man unequal.
And a true found subject, to his Prince most faythful
abyding.
Theese not with standing his liefe too to hastelye vannisht.
Nipt were thee blossoms, eare fruictful season aproched.
Wherefor his acquayntaunce his death so untymelye
bewayleth.
*Maynoth* lamenteth, *Kilka* and *Rathangan* ar howling.
Nay rather is mated bye this hard hap desolat *Ireland*.
Such claps of batter that seally unfortunat *Island*.
O that I thy prayses could wel decipher in order,
Lyke *Homer* or *Virgil*, lyke *Geffray Chauncer* in English:
Then would thy *Stanyhurst* in pen bee liberal holden.
Thee poet is barrayn, for prayse rich matter is offred.
Heere percase *carpers* wyl twight his iollitye youthful.
Strong reason unstrayned that weake obiection aunswers.
Hee must bee peerlesse who in yong yeers faultes abydeth.
Such byrds flee seldoom, such black swans scantlye
be floating.
In world of mischiefe who finds such glorius angels?
Soom stars passe oothers; al perls doe not equalye luster.
Thee soundest wheatcorne with chaffy filthod is husked.
What shall I say further, this loare divinitye telleth;
Vertuus hee lived, through grace that vertuus eended.
What may be then better, than a godly and gratius upshot?
Too *God* in al pietee, too *Prince* in dutye remayning.
Whearefor (woorthye *Girald*) syth thy eend was hertye
repentaunce,
Thy soul *God* gladdeth with saincts in blessed *Olympus*,
Thogh tumbd bee carcase in towne of martyred *Alban*.

# TADHG DALL Ó HUIGÍNN

(1550–91)

## *Enniskillen*

How sad, seeing Enniskillen –
    its silvery bays and tuneful falls;
Because we cannot let the image go,
    It hurts to gaze on its splendid walls.

Long before I ever came
    to the gleaming hall and grassy knoll,
I knew that if ever I found it
    I'd lack for nothing at all.

The fame had spread, sad to reflect,
    of this otherworld of flawless treasure;
I heard I'd be enchanted, beguiled,
    Nothing would keep me from going there.

What everyone told me was
    That never in Banba was seen
A dwelling the likes of that one,
    Hallowed hall of the lion of Erne.

They also said whoever saw
    the twining wood and dewy plain,
sandy beach and rich green fields,
    would never venture forth again.

Once I'd heard this glowing report,
    Whenever I slept for a while,
No other vision visited me
    But the beauty of that fair domicile.

Off I went, and gained the place –
Enniskillen under gnarled oak,
across the field, through laden boughs,
the sight of it took me aback.

Even before I neared the place,
the sounds were anything but tame:
lively yowls of dogs and hounds
in the woods flushing game.

The shore beside the court,
In the still-watered, fairy bay,
scarcely could any of it be seen
so thick were the masts of ships arrayed.

And beside the court there I could see
a beautiful, gilded plain,
the bright fort's dewy green,
Heaven's domain, or much the same.

This is how I saw the turf –
overturned from horses' hoofs;
plants couldn't grow in the green there,
with herds competing in droves.

The steeds of the court were racing –
I can see them now in their courses,
the hilly terrain completely obscured,
not by mist but by horses.

I kept to my course, straight on,
to the arched fort of the Lia;
those I found inside the fair walls
were a wonderful sort of family.

I found the nobles of Colla's race
in the crowded court giving gifts,
and men who could open the mysteries
of the origins of the Gaels of Greece.

I found, too, throughout the fort,
    its fill of minstrels and poets,
wall to wall one might say;
    happy the house with such talents!

In another part I found maidens,
    fine-lipped and clad in silk,
embroidering fine, golden fringe,
    there in the noble, sportive lodge.

A throng of warriors throughout the house,
    lining the walls within;
their pointed weapons just above them,
    regiment of fruited Drumquin.

A great troop of youth, as if from the *sídh*,
    from Badb's *sídh* or the hostel of Ler,
so shining bright no eye could sight them,
    manned the bright, branched rampart.

A group of artisans making goblets,
    another of smiths forging arms;
craftsmen from many lands about her,
    precious gem of the soft, still water.

Swords being burnished, cloths dyed purple,
    spear heads hammered, horses exercising,
hostages pledged, terms arranged,
    scholars examining lists of kings.

Hostages being taken, others let go,
    warriors recovering, others wounded,
wealth rolling in, gifts handed out
    from this splendid palace, out of this world.

They passed the time part of the day
    recounting deeds and talking conflict;
then for a spate the men of Uisneach
    would drink and dine and listen to music.

And so, till dinner, we passed the day,
    a lovely day that seemed but an hour,
in the shining, bright rampart,
    fertile and grassy enclosure.

Each was set in his proper place,
    on smooth benches in the elegant hall;
rarely would a hostel have seen the likes
    of the throng that filled the long table.

Cú Chonnacht Óg, Cú Chonnacht's son,
    passion's mist clings to him,
when all in the hall were in their seats
    settled into his royal throne.

I sat on the right of the dragon of Tara
    till the drinking had run its course;
and the king did not ignore or snub me,
    though plenty of nobles paid him court.

In a while, when the time came
    for the company to lie and rest,
downy coverlets were all arranged
    for the well-mannered, the very best.

Before dawn broke in the house,
    a crew of them were fitting spears;
horses shod at break of day,
    men rounding up horses.

Barely had I awakened
    there in the bright stone rampart,
when I saw around the hawk of Síoth Truim
    fine warriors armed for conflict.

Before daylight they went from us,
    hardened lads from the king's court;
spear-bearing, solemn, a great brigade;
    suing for peace was not their art.

Not long after, they returned;
 victorious wherever they roamed;
men of Colla with golden bands –
 happy the land they call home!

Many a woman, that day at Loch Erne,
 whose husband did not survive;
and the aftermath of battle,
 saw many a wounded hostage arrive.

There in the house, splendid wealth
 that hadn't been there in the morn,
and cattle grazing close at hand
 that weren't there the night before.

Then came payments to poets
 by the Ó Eochaid who never shunned battle;
their costly verse did little damage,
 though their rewards were more than was due.

I sought my leave of Maguire
 along with the other scholars,
parting from the bright, lofty fort –
 alas that permission was granted!

As I turned to go, he said to me,
 tears coursing down his noble cheek,
that though I might be far away,
 that would not cause our bond to break.

I remember the day I took my leave
 of the palace and all its retainers;
so heavy a pall lay upon them all
 that none saw the grief of the others.

I'm the worse for the loss of the household;
 a pity my own time isn't here
rather than long life after them;
 I fear that I shall long endure.

I never heard of a household so good
as those in that fort, God bless them!
under any of those sprung from Colla –
and so every chief poet will claim.

None would leave, of his own free will,
the bright plain of the hero's haven;
since it lured men from every quarter,
how sad, seeing Enniskillen.

*Patrick K. Ford*

## DIARMAID Ó BRIAIN
(late 16th century?)

### *The Shannon*

Shannon! King Brian's native river,
– Ah! the wide wonder of thy glee –
No more thy waters babble and quiver
As here they join the western sea.

By ancient Borivy thou flowest
And past Kincora rippling by
With sweet unceasing chant thou goest,
For Mary's babe a lullaby.

Born first in Breffney's Iron Mountain
– I hide not thy nativity –
Thou speedest from that northern fountain
Swift through thy lakes, Loch Derg, Loch Ree.

Over Dunass all undelaying
Thy sheer unbridled waters flee;
Past Limerick town they loiter, staying
Their flight into the western sea.

From Limerick, where the tidal welling
Of the swift water comes and goes,
By Scattery, saintly Seanán's dwelling,
Thou goest and whither then who knows?

Thomond is clasped in thy embraces
And all her shores thou lovest well,
Where by Dunass thy cataract races
And where thy seaward waters swell.

Boyne, Siuir and Laune of ancient story,
And Suck's swift flood – these have their fame;
But in the poet's roll of glory
Thine, Shannon, is a nobler name.

*Robin Flower*

## GARRET ('GIRALD') FITZGERALD, BARON OF OFFALY

(1559?–80)

### *A Penitent Sonnet written by thee Lord Girald a litle beefore his death*

By losse in play men oft forget
  Thee duitye they dooe owe,
Too hym that dyd bestow thee same,
  And thowsands millions moe.

I loathe too see theym sweare and stare,
When they the mayne have lost;
Forgetting all thee byes, that weare
With God and holye goast.
By *wounds* and *nayles* they thinck too wyn,
But truely yt is not so:
For al thayre frets and fumes in syn,
They mooniles must goa.
Theare is no wight that usd yt more,
Then *hee* that wrote this verse;
Who cryeth, *peccavi*, now therefore
His othes his hert doe perce.
Therefor example take by *mee*,
That curse thee lucklesse tyme,
That eaver *dice* myne eyes dyd see,
Which bred in mee this *crime*.
Pardon mee for that is past,
I wyl offend no more:
In this moste vile and sinful *cast*,
Which I wyl stil abhore.

## LAOISEACH MAC AN BHAIRD

(*fl.* late 16th century)

### *Brothers*

You who opt for English ways
And crop your curls, your crowning glory,
You, my handsome specimen,
Are no true son of Donncha's.

If you were, you would not switch
To modes in favour with the English;
You, the flower of Fódla's land,
Would never end up barbered.

A full head of long, fair hair
Is not for you; it is your brother
Who scorns the foreigners' close cut.
The pair of you are opposites.

Eoghan Bán won't ape their ways,
Eoghan beloved of noble ladies
Is enemy to English fads
And lives beyond the pale of fashion.

Eoghan Bán is not like you.
Breeches aren't a thing he values.
A clout will do him for a cloak.
Leggings he won't wear, nor greatcoat.

He hates the thought of jewelled spurs
Flashing on his feet and footwear,
And stockings of the English sort,
And being all prinked up and whiskered.

He's Donncha's true son, for sure.
He won't be seen with a rapier
Angled like an awl, out arseways,
As he swanks it to the meeting place.

Sashes worked with threads of gold
And high stiff collars out of Holland
Are not for him, nor satin scarves
That sweep the ground, nor gold rings even.

He has no conceit in feather beds,
Would rather stretch himself on rushes,
Dwell in a bothy than a bawn,
And make the branch his battlement.

Horsemen in the mouth of a glen,
A savage clash, kernes skirmishing –
This man is in his element
Taking on the foreigner.

But you are not like Eoghan Bán.
You're a laughing stock on stepping stones
With your dainty foot: a sad disgrace,
You who opt for English ways.

*Seamus Heaney*

## *The Felling of a Sacred Tree*

My condolence, hill up there!
  Your fall from grace a grievous fate.
A theme for woe your withering Thorn
  that stood out green upon your crest.

That Thorn of Council now means anguish,
  before revered as the meeting-place.
That branch's cutting, my day of grief,
  means the whole nation is despoiled.

My heart is darkened deep within me
  for your sacred tree, my skyline hill.
The prop from which I took my bearings,
  your graceful Thorn, I can see no more.

That bough would always show my way:
  how briefly do directions last! –
All the way west from my northern land
  I would see that branch stand clear for me.

The wind now has savaged its root,
  that tree that stood so long supreme.
Those that it sheltered were not few.
  A sad plague is its destruction.

That graceful branch of sloe-bright hue,
  I mourn its falling under some curse.
Hard not to grieve for Christ's deep passion,
  when I lament so much this tree

that has been taken, and ruined us,
  this lovely Thorntree that screened the birds.
Its equal never grew from earth.
  I will weep for it until I die.

My anguish to the verge of death!
  Alas! That it will rise no more.
When I see the hill and its sapling grove
  the Thorn's fate brings me to tears.

Hill of hilarity, teachers' despair,
  today in the hands of enemies.
That its slopes should cause me pain,
  the graceful hill that stung me to love!

*Bernard O'Donoghue*

## *A Man of Experience*

Really, what a shocking scene!
    A decent girl, a public place!
What the devil do you mean,
    Mooching round with such a face?

Things can't really be so bad,
    Surely someone would have said
If – of course the thing is mad,
    No, your mother isn't dead.

Sighing, sniffling, looking tense,
    Sitting mum the whole day through;
Speaking from experience
    I can guess what's wrong with you.

Roses withering in the cheek,
    Sunlight clouding in the hair,
Heaving breasts and looks so meek –
    You're in love, my girl, I swear.

If love really caused all this
So that looks and grace are gone
Shouldn't you tell me who it is? –
Even if I should be the man.

If I really were the man
You wouldn't find me too severe,
Don't think I'm a Puritan,
I've been through it too my dear.

And if you'd whispered in my ear:
'Darling, I'm in love with you'
I wouldn't have scolded, never fear;
I know just what girls go through.

How does it take you, could you say?
Are you faint when I pass by?
Don't just blush and look away –
Who should know love if not I?

You'll be twice the girl tonight
Once you get it off your chest;
Why – who knows? – you even might
Win me to your snowy breast.

Make love just the way that seems
Fittest to you, 'twill be right.
Think of it! Your wildest dreams
Might come true this very night.

That's enough for once, my dear
Stop that snivelling and begin;
Come now, not another tear –
Lord, look at the state you're in!

*Frank O'Connor*

## ANONYMOUS

### *The Scholar*

Summer delights the scholar
With knowledge and reason.
Who is happy in hedgerow
Or meadow as he is?

Paying no dues to the parish,
He argues in logic
And has no care of cattle
But a satchel and stick.

The showery airs grow softer,
He profits from his ploughland
For the share of the schoolmen
Is a pen in hand.

When midday hides the reaping,
He sleeps by a river
Or comes to the stone plain
Where the saints live.

But in winter by the big fires,
The ignorant hear his fiddle,
And he battles on the chessboard,
As the land lords bid him.

*Austin Clarke*

## *The Curse*

You brindled beast through whom I've lost her!
Out of my sight! the devil take you!
And, 'pon my soul! this is no jest,
This year I'll rest not till I break you.

Satanic Ananias blast you!
Is that the way you learned to carry?
Your master in the mud to hurl
Before the girl he meant to marry.

The everlasting night fiend ride you!
My curse cling closer than your saddle!
Hell's ravens pick your eyes like eggs!
You scarecrow with your legs astraddle!

And it was only yesterday too
I gave the stable-boy a shilling
To stuff your belly full of hay
For fear you'd play this trick, you villain!

I gave you oats, you thankless devil!
And saved your life, you graceless fiend, you!
From ragged mane to scrubby tail
I combed and brushed and scraped and cleaned you.

You brute! the devil scorch and burn you!
You had a decent mare for mother,
And many a pound I've spent on hay
To feed you one day and another.

The best of reins, the finest saddle,
Good crupper and good pad together,
Stout hempen girth – for these I've paid,
And breastplate made of Spanish leather.

What's the excuse? What blindness caused it?
That bias in your indirections
That made a windmill of your legs
And lost for good my Meg's affections.

With my left spur I'll slash and stab you
And run it through the heart within you
And with the right I'll take great lumps
Out of your rumps until I skin you.

If ever again I go a-courting
Across your back – may Hellfire melt you! –
Then may I split my fork in twain
And lose the girl again as well too!

*Robin Flower*

# III

# CIVILIZATIONS: 1601–1800

*Ionmholta malairt bhisigh* ('A turn for the better')

Eochaidh Ó hEodhasa, 'The New Poetry'

## EOCHAIDH Ó HEODHASA

(*c*.1565–1612)

### *O'Hussey's Ode to the Maguire*

Where is my Chief, my Master, this bleak night, *mavrone!*
O, cold, cold, miserably cold is this bleak night for Hugh,
It's showery, arrowy, speary sleet pierceth one through and
 through,
Pierceth one to the very bone!

Rolls real thunder? Or was that red, livid light
Only a meteor? I scarce know; but through the midnight dim
The pitiless ice-wind streams. Except the hate that
 persecutes *him*
Nothing hath crueller venomy might.

An awful, a tremendous night is this, meseems!
The flood-gates of the rivers of heaven, I think, have been
 burst wide –
Down from the overcharged clouds, like unto headlong ocean's
 tide,
Descends grey rain in roaring streams.

Though he were even a wolf ranging the round green woods,
Though he were even a pleasant salmon in the unchainable sea,
Though he were a wild mountain eagle, he could scarce bear, he,
This sharp, sore sleet, these howling floods.

O, mournful is my soul this night for Hugh Maguire!
Darkly, as in a dream, he strays! Before him and behind
Triumphs the tyrannous anger of the wounding wind,
The wounding wind, that burns as fire!

It is my bitter grief – it cuts me to the heart –
That in the country of Clan Darry this should be his fate!
O, woe is me, where is he? Wandering, houseless, desolate,
Alone, without or guide or chart!

Medreams I see just now his face, the strawberry bright,
Uplifted to the blackened heavens, while the tempestuous winds
Blow fiercely over and round him, and the smiting sleet-shower
blinds
The hero of Galang tonight!

Large, large affliction unto me and mine it is,
That one of his majestic bearing, his fair, stately form,
Should thus be tortured and o'erborne – that this unsparing storm
Should wreak its wrath on head like his!

That his great hand, so oft the avenger of the oppressed,
Should this chill, churlish night, perchance, be paralysed
by frost –
While through some icicle-hung thicket – as one lorn and lost –
He walks and wanders without rest.

The tempest-driven torrent deluges the mead,
It overflows the low banks of the rivulets and ponds –
The lawns and pasture-grounds lie locked in icy bonds
So that the cattle cannot feed.

The pale bright margins of the streams are seen by none.
Rushes and sweeps along the untameable flood on every side –
It penetrates and fills the cottagers' dwellings far and wide –
Water and land are blent in one.

Through some dark woods, 'mid bones of monsters, Hugh
now strays,
As he confronts the storm with anguished heart, but manly
brow –
O! what a sword-wound to that tender heart of his were now
A backward glance at peaceful days.

But other thoughts are his – thoughts that can still inspire
With joy and an onward-bounding hope the bosom of MacNee –
Thoughts of his warriors charging like bright billows of the sea,
Borne on the wind's wings, flashing fire!

And though frost glaze tonight the clear dew of his eyes,
And white ice-gauntlets glove his noble fine fair fingers o'er,
A warm dress is to him that lightning-garb he ever wore,
The lightning of the soul, not skies.

Hugh marched forth to the fight – I grieved to see him so depart;
And lo! tonight he wanders frozen, rain-drenched, sad, betrayed –
*But the memory of the lime-white mansions his right hand hath
    laid*
*In ashes warms the hero's heart!*

*James Clarence Mangan*

## *Poem in the Guise of Cú Chonnacht Óg Mág Uidhir to Brighid Chill Dara*

Is it because I'm a stranger, friends,
you all step back in alarm?
An incubus? Or a clay-cold spirit
incapable of harm?

Does it seem when you look closer
I have a body at all?
Or am I just a wraith,
deceiving, ethereal?

I see now there's nothing
I owe to anyone;
true friends, if such you were,
might have grieved to hear I was gone.

And oh what a pity, people,
you lost all you had to give –
what animates my name now
doesn't breathe or truly live.

I am not what you think I am,
see me but do not believe,
a paltry poor ghost best not
crossed – if you want to survive.

Of all the folk who've lived on earth
how few of them have had
two chances at it like I've enjoyed,
your two-timing ghostly lad!

No upright man could claim
I haven't passed away;
it's less a time for telling lies
than a time to kneel and pray

for my soul; the precise instant
it left I remember well
despite the prattle of doubters
who argue I'm alive still.

No wound or sad mishap
undid me, but a rush of joy;
no fit of gloom – is anything worse? –
no plague, no disease laid me low.

If by an angelic creature
in a celestial dream
the soul was snatched from my body
how strange my mourning must seem!

After I'd glimpsed her, Lord,
how could I still desire life?
From one who goes round killing men
only the dead are safe.

No tidal wave of sadness
nor hatred for anyone here
nor no love of earthly thing
killed me, in fact, but terror.

On coming to my senses,
though still consumed by dread,
I soon got wind of the rumour
that said I wasn't dead.

Though I do not know her features
(on them no eye can gaze)
across the front of my mind
her radiant image strays.

I'm enchanted still, a changeling,
at home in perplexity;
let the eye of no ill-willed person
see the human frame you see.

And may God protect me from her
if she try to restore my breath:
what I've endured so far is nothing
to thoughts of a second death.

My name and its meaning were both
well known before I died:
ask for a hound, cunning and swift,
with nowhere left to hide.

*PC*

## *The New Poetry*

Praise be! A turn for the better,
A sudden shift in the weather.
If I don't tap into this new racket
I could end up out of pocket.

Good riddance, then, to the old measures,
To those fussy rules and strictures.
This method's cushier, more enlightened,
And might usher me into the limelight.

Those erstwhile ornamented poems
Fell on deaf ears only – lofty odes
Sailing over the heads of the people,
Like caviar thrown at the general.

If verse of mine from now to the last trump
Perplex the brain of one Ulster dunce
I'll give back – it's a hefty wager –
Every last farthing of my retainer.

Free verse and the open road!
It's what pops the money ball.
I'll soon be paying off my loans
Courtesy of Earl Tyrconnell.

No one's going to best yours truly
When it comes to pap and vacuity.
I'll be out there on the fairground
In all weathers pulling in the crowds.

I've scuppered – what a relief! –
That top-heavy worm-eaten ball-breaking craft.
Though if the Earl gets wind of my drift
He's bound to piss himself laughing.

Let me not ruin a hard-won reputation
For mastery of bardic scholarship and skill.
I'll make sure the Earl (or former Chieftain)
Isn't in town when I give a recital.

The thing is I'm quite a draw,
Flavour of the month in certain quarters.
I'd be gone down that path like a rat from hell,
But I'm wary of the Earl –

Not to mention it was the same Aodh's son
Who once dubbed my strict verse 'easy'.
Thank God he's sojourning with the Saxon.
For the time being, I have a breather.

Those poems I pummelled into shape before
Damn near broke my heart.
The new softer more accessible approach
Will prove a tonic for my health.

And what if the Earl (the ex-Chieftain)
Quibbles now and then with a quatrain –
Aren't there plenty goons about
Who'll shout the pedant down?

*Maurice Riordan*

## ANONYMOUS

### *On the Death of a Poet (composed during the last illness of Eochaidh Ó hEodhasa)*

Poetry is touched by decline:
how can we come to her aid?
She is sure all hope is gone
in her poorly state.

Consider poetry's plight,
fit only for the sickbed
as word of Eochaidh's death is brought
to her who was his bride.

It is hard to witness the honour
once hers turn to scorn:
woeful indignity drawing near,
the cloud of abasement come down.

To Eochaidh above all men she gave
the flower in its prime
of her artistry and love;
and all to nourish him.

The hidden ore of his poet's craft
burned with a gemlike flame
lighting up the art he left;
much died with his name.

Well he knew the schoolmen's work,
who sat among the wise;
poet of the golden cloak,
a great lament shall be his.

He stumbled on the hazel of knowledge
in its secret grove,
and left its branches hung with flesh,
stripping the nutshells off.

Out of words both dark and subtle
the poet makes his art
with perfect ease, and in recital
omits no part.

It is no small help to his work
to add the gold relief
of learning to his every word:
such is the way of the beehive.

Bees all over brim their hoard
with the juice they collect
from the oozings of a milky gourd
or a flower unpacked.

They are examples to the bard
whose craft none can match;
no flower or fruit, soft or hard,
escapes his search.

It is he resolves the doubts
of those already skilled;
he who settles all debates,
he to whom all yield.

Who has not been touched by sorrow
at the master's loss of life?
This disease goes to the marrow
and pierces like a spike.

Like a cow parted from her calf,
my wits are overthrown;
I make melody from my grief,
I am an orphan;

and poetry is a widow unless
Maoilseachlainn's son returns;
no one can make good her loss
but the man she mourns.

*David Wheatley*

# GIOLLA BRIGHDE (BONAVENTURA) Ó HEODHASA

(*c.*1570–1614)

## *In Memoriam Richard Nugent*

It is hard to sleep on a friend's hurt.
Any friend untroubled
by his comrade's wound
is nearer to an enemy.

Who could take his ease
beside a wounded friend? A heart
untainted by another's grief,
uncut, is hardly pure.

For true friends grow of one
unbroken root. Their troubles
and their pains, their joys
and triumphs shared are one.

So could you doubt
my suffering, dear sister,
as your own wound's venom
bites my mind afresh?

Your sighs grow more
than I can bear to hear;
each tear, beloved,
draws my own heart's blood.

Could I displace your sorrow
by my own; with this coin
of my pain earn you relief –
I'd put my care to work.

A horror: to have lost a son.
Your family's dear ambition
and your comfort. Your own
lustrous boy; and only, Janet.

Green with Delvin's hopes,
bright as the hills that bred him,
child of warriors, your champion
and guardian, brave Richard.

Sheltering bloom of the Island
of the Fair, Richard Nugent,
finely formed in heart and deed,
fierce tender of great Marward's line.

So noble was your grown boy,
no one wonders at the fathom
of your loss. He blazed through life;
a fighter, leader, sage.

Who learned all things in their
inner selves, the working parts
of heaven and its deep, moist earth –
and all he cared for flourished.

Don't they tell the stories still
of how he travelled in the stars'
wake, pole to pole, and proved
himself, the world, unshakable?

And though it stings you hard
to hear it, don't resent Him,
who first yielded to your care
the fruits you've lost.

Our father God, old master
who made Richard for himself,
has just reclaimed that pure, bright
hand from your safekeeping.

A man's death is the door to life.
We have no business fretting
over one who dies a blessed death,
whose grace is clear and sure.

Open up your shrouded face,
and dry your gleaming cheek.
I send my prayer to draw
the splinter from your heart, there.

*Tiffany Atkinson*

## RICHARD NUGENT
## (*fl.* 1604)

### *To His Cousin Master Richard Nugent of Dunower*

Mine owne *Dicke Nugent*, if thou list to know
The cause that makes me shun my western home,
And how my tedious time here I bestow,
While angry *Thetis* 'gainst her bounds doth foam,
Wert that to ease that never-healing wound
Which now four summers' heat hath made to fester,
By time, by absence, or by counsel sound,
I flee the soil where my sweet foe doth rest her.
I sojourn here, where I remain so eased,
By this my flight, of the tormenting blow
As doth the dear on whom the shaft hath seized
By late unbending of the deadly bow;
And since, I have this curse ev'n fatal proved,
That I am born to love, and not be loved.

# FEARGHAL ÓG MAC AN BHAIRD

## (*fl.* late 16th/early 17th century)

### *A Letter of Complaint*

Here is a wonder, dear Fr Conry:
I got no respect from people who
should be serving the likes of me.
A wonder of a new, cold kind.

Me to be desolate – isn't this strange? –
and lowly people who rate as nothing
getting the rich juices of Spain
in honour of sweet Brega's plains.

The peasant wives of fools and louts
are over there in finery
and us with nothing: well may we think
that there is something wrong with this.

Against the base-born tribes of Ireland
who have lit the spark of envy in me,
Oh! Fr Fiheal from Eanna's shores,
shine on us your brightest light.

Noblest branch of Tuam city,
reflect how unfitting it is for me
to be remote from noble blood.
Give me some encouragement.

In the west I left my birthright
when I spent my first rich share.
If, Fr Fiheal, you favour me,
it will bode a second fortune.

Your own father would see the outrage,
dear branch from which great riches grew:
my affairs in total ruin
while some pleb's son is coining it.

King Arthur, the whole earth's bulwark,
was a power in this life.
Everyone came under his sway
while he ruled the wide world's plain.

That noblest branch of that other island,
Arthur, would touch neither food nor drink
before he'd hear of some great marvel,
throughout his life as long as he lived.

That leading king of mighty triumphs,
if I'd been around in Arthur's lifetime,
there's little doubt I wouldn't cause him
to go to bed with hunger pangs.

For at the Round Table in his presence
I'd have spoken for my people's sake
of the wonder of my penury
while ignorant pigs are handling gold.

He could eat indeed once he had heard
how robbers' offspring are full of glee
and how great the affront to my Gaelic blood
when I'm not accorded a guest's prestige.

In the court of Louvain of purple hills
I am lodged with people too far east.
It's a hard state for one of my kind,
and less than justice to my forebears.

The Staff of Tuam has an old affection
for the House from which we come.
If that love is still as fervent
it should be extended to me still.

When Fitheal's son the maker Flaithri
was the wise archpoet in that place,
there would have been a local's love
from that shield that stood guard round Loughrea.

That learned star of Uisneach's nobles,
Connacht's Primate, faithful lord,
the sage that every poet praised,
heart of Scholars in the western land.

Salmon of Boyle, great fish of Cong,
branch from the orchard of Tara's Fort,
golden moon that never darkened,
he advanced the cause of the goodly man.

Godlike strain that conquered envy,
crowned prince that defeated greed,
sweet stream flowing down the hillside,
saintly text that will keep its theme.

Descendant of Conn of the Hundred Battles
from high Kildare: Onora's son of endless fame!
Time-honoured tree at the heart of fertile Ireland,
renewing for ever abundant blaze of welcome!

*Bernard O'Donoghue*

## EOGHAN RUA MAC AN BHAIRD
## (*c.*1570–*c.*1630)

### *On Receiving a Letter from Aodh Ó Domhnaill*, aetate 7

Precious the letter unbound here
that took my breath on opening it
  – God keep away bad news –
  it has restored my mind.

Had those Gaels lived, those nobles
I knew at the court of Niall,
  they would have started for joy
  the instant the letter was opened.

The boy that's come over the ocean
though not yet the Ó Domhnaill
  deserves our fervent love: –
  may God protect him forever.

Aodh Ó Domhnaill, my treasure,
still just seven years old!
  heir to my king, my dear one,
  a scholar wrote when you wrote this.

*PC*

## SÉATHRÚN CÉITINN

## (*c.*1580–*c.*1650)

### *Dear Woman, with Your Wiles*

Dear woman, with your wiles,
You'd best remove your hand.
Though you burn with love's fire,
I'm no more an active man.

Look at the grey on my head,
See how my body droops,
Think of my sluggish blood –
What would you have me do?

It's not desire I lack.
Don't bend low like that again.
Love will live without the act
Forever, slender one.

Withdraw your lips from mine,
Strong as the inclination is,
Don't brush against my skin,
It could lead to wantonness.

The intricacy of curls,
Soft eyes clear as dew,
The pale sight of your curves,
Give pleasure to me now.

Bar what the body craves,
And lying with you requires,
I'll do for our love's sake,
Dear woman, with your wiles.

*Maurice Riordan*

## *How Sweet the Tongue of the Gael*

How sweet the tongue of the Gael,
By outside help untainted!
Brightly rings that voice,
A mild mouth's choicest music.

Though Hebrew may be older
And Latin more rich in learning,
Irish owes to neither
A single sound or loanword.

*PC*

## *No Sleep is Mine*

No sleep is mine since the news from the plain of Fál.
Sharp, when I think of our true friends' plight, the pang I feel.
Long they stood, a hedge against the Saxon weeds,
but up through them now, unchecked, the cockle spreads.

Brazen Fódla, shame on you that you close your eyes
to how more fitting it were you suckled Míle's race.
Not a drop of your smooth breast's milk remains,
all drained now by a swinish breed of aliens.

Any worthless shower sailing here with the thought
of seizing Cobhthach the Just's age-old, golden fort
would find our greatest houses all without defence,
like the rich pastures of our lovely-bordered lands.

The race of upstarts teeming over the plain of Lugh
are true-born churls, their pedigrees on show:
Tál's line broken, reeling, of Eoghan's not a trace,
and the youth of Bántsrath scattered overseas.

From Nás's fearsome chieftains not one display of force,
though they in noisy battle-valour once were fierce,
when their roving bands would tweak the English nose;
none now keeps the law, but not theirs the disgrace.

If the high prince of Áine and Drum Daoile lived,
or those lions of the Máigh never without a gift,
not long in the bend of the Bríde would this mob delay,
not a squealing man of them but we'd send on his way.

If the Craftsman of Stars comes not with help when called
against the vengeful foemen ready and bold,
then better gather and sift the finest of our tribe
and set them safe to wander over Clíona's tide.

*David Wheatley*

## BRIGHID CHILL DARA
## (1589–1682)

### *Response to Eochaidh Ó hEodhasa's Poem*

Youngster, who crafted the poem,
emerge from the schoolmen's shade;
the poem that spreads your fame
speaks, though you are tongue-tied.

Those verses that you made,
I'd say, dear chap, don't win
a poet's prize for you
– not that I have one to give.

The poem you recited sweetly
– this is no amateur's verdict –
should earn a hefty reward
for the bard who built it.

Flawless poems are rare
but yours is sheer perfection;
– as green as any novice,
yet a master of implication.

It might have been expected
your poem would be ill-made:
finding it a sure-fire winner
leaves me at a loss for praise.

I swear, dear man, it was you
who spoiled your act in the end,
you should have appeared unschooled
presenting a slipshod attempt.

Mac Con Midhe, Fearghal Óg,
Ó Dálaigh Fionn, lord of poets –
by one such, son of Cú,
was the witty work composed.

Ó hEodhasa, the poets' teacher
who makes swift quatrains well
– it was he devised the lines
or one of the clan Mac Craith.

Yet whatever man of learning
composed that faultless verse
it would be an act of pillage
if the son of Cú took credit.

I won't disclose the name
to a soul, you may believe;
whoever it belongs to
would not die for my love.

My surname will not be heard
until yesterday comes again;
my forename, all may know,
is shared by a saint in Heaven.

*PC*

## RICHARD BELLINGS
## (*c.*1598–1677)

### *The Description of a Tempest*

Bound for my country from the Cambrian shore,
I cut the deep; the Mariners implore,
With whistling prayer, the wind grown too mild,
To hasten to beget their sails with child.
The humble Sea, as of our ship afraid,
Pale, breathless, prostrate at our feet, is laid.
The morn, scarce out of bed, did blush to see
Her rude beholders so unmannerly.
She scarce had blushed, when she began to hide
Her rosy cheeks, like to a tender Bride.
To suit Aurora, all the heavens put on
A mournful veil of black, as she had done,
And gave the garments to the Sea they wore,
Wherewith it grows more blue now than before.
This stage being set, the lightnings tapers were,
The drums such thunder as afright each ear.
Upon this summons great King *Aeolus*,
Attended on by *Nothus* and *Zephirus*,
Enters, and where the King his steps doth place,
The waves do swell, trod with so proud a grace.
He was to speak, but opening of his mouth,
The boisterous wind did blow so hard at South,

I could not hear, but as the rest told me,
He spoke the prologue for a tragedy.
Behold huge mountains in the watery main
That lately was a smooth and liquid plain,
O'er which our Sea-drunk Barque doth reeling ride.
She must obey, but knows not to which tide;
For still she ploughs that rugged mutinous place,
All skillful Pilots call the breaking race.
A while ambition bare her up so high,
Her proud discoloured flag doth touch the sky;
But when the winds these waves do bear away,
She hangs in air, and makes a little stay:
But down again from such presumptuous height
She's headlong borne by her attractive weight
Into the hollow of a gaping grave,
Intomb'd of each side with a stately wave.
Down pour these billows from their height of pride:
Our Barque receives them in at every side,
But when they find no place where to remain,
The scuddle holes do let them out again.
At length, as Castles where no force can find
A conquest, by assault are undermined,
So in our Barque, whose walls no waves could break,
We do discover a most traitorous leak.
To this, though much our hopes do now decline,
We do oppose the Pump, our countermine:
That midway breaks, whereat our Master cries
All hope is past, the Seas must close our eyes;
And to augment death's hideous show the more,
We in the poop can scarse discerne the prore;
Such ugly mists had overcast the air,
That heaven, I thought, had meant we should despair.
But in the last act of this Tragedy,
Behold, our great God's all-discerning eye
Caused in an instant these thick mists disband;
The winds are calmed, and we at Skerries land.

Dread ruler of the floods, whose powerful will
Each thing that hath a being must fulfill,
Whose hand marks forth the end of each man's days
And steers our human ship in unknown ways;
To thee, great guide, the incense I present:
Thou gav'st me time to live, and to repent.

## ANONYMOUS

### *Verse Prophecy about the Irish*

Their days a number small shall make,
Another shall their country take;
Their Children Vagabonds shall be,
Walk up and down most wretchedly;
God shall them put to endless shame,
And quite cut off their hateful name.

## SIR EDMUND BUTLER
## (*fl.* 1648)

### *'Arise, distracted land'*

Arise, distracted land, rouse thee and bring
Timely assistance to thy captive king.
Ormond at length prevailed, time only can
Reveal the Judgment of the Prudent man.
Hadst not thou left us first and then again
Found safety in a shallop through the Main,

Ireland had sunk; the people had not fed,
Wanting an apt hand to dispense the bread.
Through thee (the darling of the Nation) fly
Those beamlings from imprisoned Majesty
Which do enlighten us; these do increase
His bounty, and thy merit, in our Peace.
Expend our substance, sacrifice our blood;
By such a comment 'twill be understood.

The Irish Nation while their King's depressed,
Disclaims in Interest and disdains to rest.

## WILLIAM SMITH
## *(d.1655)*

### *To Ireland*

Hail sacred Island! whom no Threat nor Art
Could tempt to falter in the passive part:
Now be as active, let no Power nor frown
Yoke thy enfranchised thoughts, or pull them down.
Have not thy Altars, where the spotless price
Of Man's Redemption, the true Sacrifice
Was Daily offered, lain too long recluse,
Or, being employed, served to a different use?
Thy sumptuous piles, built for Religious vows
Are the secure retreat of daws and doves;
The owls, the bats, the direful birds of night
Have been preserved before the Sons of light.

Amongst all Realms, it was thy special fate
To have thy sons made illegitimate;
On whom nor place nor profit did descend
Whom neither Judge nor Justice did befriend;
But wallowing in the ill-got spoils of thine,
Others laid up, whiles thou didst dig the mine.

This thou has seen and suffered: yet the sense
Of all these Evils, could find a Patience
Until some Head borne round in Giddiness
Of private Spirits durst so far Transgress
As to dismantle England's crown, and wring
The sap of Honour from so good a King.
Then did the Object of thy sense direct
Thy stupid mind: thou feltst the disrespect
Done unto God by this: thence came the Birth
Of thy fair thoughts: For Kings are Gods on earth.

On, sprightly hearts, you whom the French, the Dutch,
The Pole, the Spaniard, court and love so much.
Let not these blush in your behalf: maintain
That spring of honour, which no war could drain.
He's thoroughly armed, who to the field can bring
Th'interests of his Faith, country, and King.

# PÁDRAIGÍN HAICÉAD

(*c.*1600–54)

## from *Dirge on the Death of Éamon Mac Piarais Buitléir, 1640*

Stand aside you band of keeners,
you've said your fervent verses of bereavement;
leave the tomb of this true leader
to me a while, to recite my grief-song.

It is my right to complete his burial,
it is my right to make known his story;
right for me his career to speak of
since I best know his glorious doings;

From his childhood hard in striving
– though a soldier, he was friendly –
to his death so much lamented
I will look closely at his actions.

I'll not recount the tribes I'm seed of,
not alliances of my people,
nor long lines of hoary numbers
of the pedigree of this leader;

I'll not recount his love so pleasing,
though I saw in public in his features
his constant longing and devotion,
his confidence in me and his affection.

Though I had the best from this regal person
of horses, jewels, riches,
though he did not lord it over my lowness
or even ever leave me quiltless,

it's when I count his superb knowledge –
though his charm was clear as sunlight –
I touch upon his truest mettle,
the stately sun-room of his disposition:

since I have known that griffin's wisdom,
his manners that excelled all others',
'twould be a sin of grave omission
for me, above all, not to lament him.

O people who pity all wretches in bondage,
here is a wretchedness, quite unparalleled,
here, the reckless discordant sorrow;
here, the grief, the most grievious hardship!

Gormfhlaith could not match my grieving
if she left Niall's tomb and she stood beside me;
nor Deirdre with harsh and poignant sighing
in isolation crying for Naoise;

nor beautiful Oisín the spear-man
after sweet-voiced Fionn O Baoisgne,
nor the wife of Hector, son of Priam,
for the death of that shield of the Trojans.

It was no wonder that I'd broadcast
the widespread yearning of the people;
I, among the high and lowly,
who had, of all, most cause for mourning.

His death's caused grief in all the country
of Con, of Flan, of Corc, of Críomhtann,
caused every group to bow in sorrow
to the depths of low anxiety;

caused in lakes an overflowing,
made great stars fierce that once were joyous,
put jet-black drapes on all the heavens,
made planets in the sky look cruel,

his death's made storms come out of calmness,
has quenched the moon and stars at night-time,
has dried up waves, has dried up fountains,
has caused no sun to shine at noonday;

caused tumult in the rattling wind-cry,
has caused lightning to flick through it
like an accomplice – fiery magic –
and fused the elements together.

No salmon stayed in the pleasant rivers,
no tree-top in the wood but withered;
the mountains wore a wet frieze tunic,
a fine black fog was on every hillock.

The rain bears witness to his dying
and grass and flowers that die in forests,
the milk that flows to a dying trickle:
his death fulfills all these conditions.

My lament will get supported
by a hundred other lamentations
and Nature will not grant excuses
if I hide one teardrop for my hero:

for there came a rush of instant grieving
from poets, princes, and from leaders;
the strong, the weak, the fool, the wise man,
the wretch, the sickly and the orphan:

their anxiety is no wonder
since the loss is shared among them;
they lost a chief, a royal one chosen –
clerics their father, art its patron,

the poor its cow, the vagrant shelter,
the widow her steadfast tree of concord,
women their sweetheart and their lover,
the peasants their head, their heart, their promise.

This ruin of all, it digs its way through
every humane and upright nature;
severe chastising, this death of Éamon
who did not return from combat.

(. . .)

The sun, departing west and setting
in pleasant, calm and lovely weather,
is an image of his face most cherished
and the smiling welcome through it.

A forehead broad with manly eyebrows,
brilliant eyes like precious gemstones,
mouth and cheek like glowing embers,
a nose which mocked all snub-noses;

slender neck, breast bright and flaxen,
fairest waistline, broadest shoulders,
strong arms, with each hand perfect,
and fine calves, capable and hose-clad.

Noble hound from kings descended,
of clamorous merry Munster,
of pleasant-rivered Leinster,
of lavish-mansioned Ulster;

Norman blood from royal households –
of the true vine, lasting offshoots:
their best the source of all his breeding –
he has their flower, their chief trophy:

blood of leaders, Tál and Cárthach,
Mac Oilill blood, a griffin's lineage;
blood of Eireamhón, son of Míleadh,
blood of Rógh and of Íth the Golden;

blood of Burkes not crushed by foemen,
blood of Barrys who burned their warship,
blood of Roches of the conquering warbands,
*all* in his blood, gushing vigorously.

(. . .)

He took no submission that was not owed him –
even if he took more than I'm relating –
that Manannán of the Youth of Munster,
Phoenix of fighters, their true flower.

He is a great loss to the people,
many today are poor and naked;
his like's not found except in visions
by Irish people dreaming of him.

Great is the tearful woe for Éamon
in the mind of woman, poet, retainer:
palms ablaze and gravestones polished
and tears of blood poured in a deluge.

'Uch!' aloud's my lasting duty:
but I'll have ready to reproach me
floods of 'uch' and 'uch' said lowly
for my ever-loyal darling.

*Michael Hartnett*

# TWO LATIN POEMS OF CONFEDERATE IRELAND

## WALTER LAWLESS

(*fl.* 1640s)

### *To the most noble Lord, James Marquis of Ormonde . . . his humble servant Walter Lawles wishes happiness and prosperity*

While the turbid waters toss the ark of Noah,
  Its sails are filled and it is driven forward by an angry God.
A human people, cast forth on the harsh soil of Pontus,
  Begs to see once more its native fields.
And it wearies the duke with prayers in submissive voice,
  'Lead us back, so that at last their ancestral lands will nurture us.'
He heard, and sent forth a snow-white dove from the ark,
  Which he asked whether the land they had before was habitable.
She flew off, and brought new olives in her beak,
  A welcome messenger to the wandering ark, approved by Noah.
Great James, these same things accord with your successes;
  Since your land is tossed in the middle of evils.
Jacob's ladder carried a heavenly messenger from the gods
  Downwards to the earth, and carried up prayers from there by turns.
And it is your ladder, James, since you carry back our affairs to the King,
  They can give weight to some things, and make light of others.

While fierce Bellona snarls with sevenfold tempests,
  You are constantly wakeful, the Representative of your
    Fatherland.
You soothe down a contrary King, and like the Dove
  Your promised olive of peace may go about among the *Irish*.
Fleeing from the steep shores of stormy war
  With you as leader, the *Irishman* sought his deserted land.
He sought, and he found it, and the stars promised peace,
  The happy olive of peace in your mouth for everyone:
It grows in eternity, and always flourishes with the *Irish*,
  So that the happy times may applaud your peace:
Thus you will be faithful provider and actor of peace-making
  Confirming the ancient pact of peace with honour.
You bring back your agreeements between the King and God,
  A union of strength and love, a sacred Ark of the love of peace.

*Peter Davidson*

## ANONYMOUS

### *Elegy for Richard Lynch*, d. *Salamanca* 1679

*On the 25th of April, at the fourth hour of the day,*
*Died the reverend Master of Arts, Richard Lynch.*

Logic is only the prelude: now more subtle things call us
Now we stand truly in need of Lynch's lynx-like eyes.
Alas, what will be further allowed to make fine distinctions
Since the slow-moving Fates closed your eyelids, O Lynch.
Where do you go with your pen, since nothing eluded this
    author?
Make your NON PLUS ULTRA here with your pen.

*Peter Davidson*

## ROGER BOYLE, EARL OF ORRERY
(1621–79)

### *Lines Written on the Gates of Bandon Bridge*

Jew, Infidel, or Atheist
May enter here, but not a Papist.

## ANONYMOUS

### *Response Written on the Gates of Bandon Bridge*

Who wrote these words composed them well,
The same are written on the Gates of Hell.

## FAITHFULL TEATE
(1621–?)

### from *Love*

Methinks men's trading with the world might stop
At thought of this who keeps her shop.
Alas! my God, the world is Devil-ridden:
The thing is known and can't be hidden.

Hell hath deflowered the earth, and now I see
  'Twould put its leavings off to me,
Daubing false paint on th'face o'th'wrinkled Creature
  Having worn and spoiled its native feature.

The earth's all *Egypt* now: And *Egypt's* curse
  Is over all the world, or worse:
For *Beelzebub* with his swarming train
  Hath all things fly-blown. To be plain

There is no flesh that's sweet, but Saviour's, now.
  Which Satan tried, but knew not how
To taint. All's dogs-meat else. Lord! teach me choose
  And I shall all the rest refuse,
    And only wish
    For that one dish,

A dish that's wholesome, and 'tis healing too,
  Ah my dear God! what shall I do
To love thy flesh enough that tasted once
  For ever heals my broken bones.

Set thine apart, all other flesh is grass:
  And is my soul an ox or ass?
That it should Love no higher than my beast?
  Or can my soul such fare digest?

Come, Trencher Critics, you that eat by book,
  And in your food for Physic look,
Your Cook must be some small Apothecary
  Will you allow a Verser vary

From your received rules? and be content
  To try a new experiment?
Flesh in a fever's good Divinity,
  Which who most eats, 'scapes best, say I.

Provided that the flesh be sound and good
    (For I would be right understood)
As never did, nor could, corruption see:
    Ah my dear Saviour! I mean thee.

Alas! how low in an high burning Fever
    Of God's displeasure, never never
To have been cured otherwise, did sin
    Once bring me, till I did begin

To fall aboard that sacred flesh? And then
    How soon did I grow well again?
Then welcome, gentle guest, if thou hast not
    To prize and Love thine health forgot,
        Come sit down here
        And Love this Cheer.

## 'PHILO-PHILIPPA'

## (*fl.* 1663)

### from *To the Excellent Orinda*

Let the male Poets their male Phoebus choose,
Thee I invoke, Orinda, for my Muse;
He could but force a Branch, Daphne her Tree
Most freely offers to her Sex and thee,
And says to Verse, so unconstrained as yours,
Her Laurel freely comes, your fame secures:
And men no longer shall with ravished Bays
Crown their forced Poems by as forced a praise.
  Thou glory of our Sex, envy of men,
Who are both pleased and vexed with thy bright Pen:
Its lustre doth entice their eyes to gaze,
But men's sore eyes cannot endure its rays;

It dazzles and surprises so with light,
To find a noon where they expected night:
A Woman Translate Pompey! which the famed
Corneille with such art and labour framed!
To whose close version the Wits club their sense,
And a new Lay poetic SMEC[1] springs thence!
Yes, that bold work a Woman dares Translate,
Not to provoke, nor yet to fear men's hate.
Nature doth find that she hath erred too long,
And now resolves to recompense that wrong:
Phoebus to Cynthia must his beams resign,
The rule of Day and Wit's now Feminine.
  That Sex, which heretofore was not allowed
To understand more than a beast, or crowd;
Of which Problems were made, whether or no
Women had Souls; but to be damned, if so;
Whose highest Contemplation could not pass,
In men's esteem, no higher than the Glass;
And all the painful labours of their Brain,
Was only how to Dress and Entertain:
Or, if they ventured to speak sense, the wise
Made that, and speaking Ox, like Prodigies.
From these thy more than masculine Pen hath reared
Our Sex; first to be praised, next to be feared.
And by the same Pen forced, men now confess,
To keep their greatness, was to make us less.

(. . .)

Pompey, who greater than himself's become,
Now in your Poem, than before in Rome;
And much more lasting in the Poet's Pen,
Great Princes live, than the proud Towers of Men.
He thanks false Egypt for its Treachery,
Since that his Ruin is so sung by thee;
And so again would perish, if withal,
Orinda would but celebrate his Fall.

1. SMEC: from 'Smectymnuus', a work written by several hands.

Thus pleasingly the Bee delights to die,
Foreseeing, he in Amber Tomb shall lie.
If that all Egypt, for to purge its Crime,
Were built into one Pyramid o'er him,
Pompey would lie less stately in that Hearse,
Than he doth now, Orinda, in thy Verse:
This makes Cornelia for her Pompey vow,
Her hand shall plant his Laurel on thy brow:
So equal in their merits were both found,
That the same Wreath Poets and Princes Crowned:
And what on that great Captain's Brow was dead,
She Joys to see re-flourished on thy head.
  In the French Rock Cornelia first did shine,
But shined not like her self till she was thine:
Poems, like Gems, translated from the place
Where they first grew, receive another grace.
Dressed by thy hand, and polished by thy Pen,
She glitters now a Star, but Jewel then:
No flaw remains, no cloud, all now is light,
Transparent as the day, bright parts more bright.
Corneille, now made English, so doth thrive,
As Trees transplanted do much lustier live.
Thus Ore digged forth, and by such hands as thine
Refined and stamped, is richer than the Mine.
Liquors from Vessel into Vessel poured,
Must lose some Spirits, which are scarce restored:
But the French Wines, in their own Vessel rare,
Poured into ours, by thy hand, Spirits are;
So high in taste, and so delicious,
Before his own Corneille thine would chuse.
  He finds himself enlightened here, where shade
Of dark expression his own words had made:
There what he would have said, he sees so writ,
As generously, to just decorum fit.
When in more words than his you please to flow,
Like a spread Flood, enriching all below,
To the advantage of his well meant sense,
He gains by you another excellence.
To render word for word, at the old rate,

Is only but to Construe, not Translate:
In your own fancy free, to his sense true,
We read Corneille, and Orinda too:
And yet ye both are so the very same,
As when two Tapers joined make one bright flame.
And sure the Copier's honour is not small,
When Artists doubt which is Original.
  But if your fettered Muse thus praisèd be,
What great things do you write when it is free?
When it is free to choose both sense and words,
Or any subject the vast World affords?
A gliding Sea of Crystal doth best show
How smooth, clear, full, and rich your Verse doth flow:
Your words are chosen, culled, not by chance writ,
To make the sense, as Anagrams do hit.
Your rich becoming words on the sense wait,
As Maids of Honour on a Queen of State.

## DÁIBHÍ Ó BRUADAIR

(*c.*1623–98)

### *A Glass of Beer*

The lanky hank of a she in the inn over there
Nearly killed me for asking the loan of a glass of beer:
May the devil grip the whey-faced slut by the hair,
And beat bad manners out of her skin for a year.

That parboiled imp, with the hardest jaw you will ever see
On virtue's path, and a voice that would rasp the dead,
Came roaring and raging the minute she looked at me,
And threw me out of the house on the back of my head!

If I asked her master he'd give me a cask a day;
But she, with the beer at hand, not a gill would arrange!
May she marry a ghost and bear him a kitten, and may
The High King of Glory permit her to get the mange.

*James Stephens*

## *Adoramus Te, Christe*

I adore you, spirit of our blood,
  Knight of heaven's fortress,
who for sheer love left your mighty Father,
  through sweet Mary's right, to help us.
As a bolt of sun through glass you came
  to burn through Adam's sins,
and delivered Man and all his hell-bent
  kind, at Easter, with a cross.

Harbour-lamp to calm
  the mortal storms bedevilling
a poor man's soul, I beg you –
  save us, and halt Satan's harm.
For I alone shattered your side;
  with all three nails I tore your skin.
But do not close your lucid eye
  against me. Gather me in.

We cherish all the more, God's own
  – for she was born of David's line –
your maiden nurse: a proof of law,
  with all a mother's graceful bloom
and pride, milk-skinned to cosset you,
  child, in a holy nest.
No womb ever cradled one as pure
  as she, nor will, until time ends.

*Tiffany Atkinson*

## *Éire*

Lady of the bright coils and curlings,
   Intricate turns of your body
Have pleased the foreign churls
   Who kept a bodyguard.
Though middle-aged and long a matron,
   The wife of Nial, the fearless,
You played the harlot with men you hated
   And those who loved you dearly.

You smiled at them, calm stately woman,
   Unsmocked your noble limbs,
Conferred with the Saxon, old in statecraft.
   The wife of Eiver – robed as
A young queen in lime-white mansions –
   Cast modesty in a corner,
Betraying the heroes who were vanquished
   By clatter of hide, war-horn.

You were the wife of Lewy the courageous,
   And never lacked a husband.
Cairbre, Cuchullin, the sage Fionn,
   Felim, no bagman in lust,
Had known the bride of Laery the King,
   And Con the Hundred Fighter.
Too late the gleam of coil and of ringlet,
   Is changed into a sigh.

The Normans went under your mantle,
   Whenever a stronghold burned,
And you pushed back their basinets,
   Cathedral mail, spurning
The meadows inching with dew, the thickets
   At dawn, the river harbours,
Hill-bounding of the hunted prickets,
   For wanton snirt and farding.

### *The Binding*

God soon will humble your pride, pucker your cheeks,
And bring the wife of Fintan and Diarmuid – flaxed
With hair-dye – to the church door, ragged, meekly,
Her placket no longer open to the Saxon.

*Austin Clarke*

### *'To them the state . . .'*

To them the state has doled out nothing –
not a foot of land or a scrap of clothing:
but it will grant them a graceful favour –
let them safe to Spain by proclamations!

And then will come the fat-arsed slaggers
after trampling our culture and our manors,
pewtered, plated, brassy, baggaged,
the crop-head English with their pleasant accents.

All their hags will have beaver-fur mantles
and a dress of silk from head to ankles:
our castles will pass to upstart foragers –
old hands at swallowing cheese and porridge.

This is the gang, though I hate to name them,
who will live in bright motte and bailey:
Goody Hook and Mother Hammer,
Robin Saul and Father Psalm –
selling salt and wearing britches:
Gammer Ruth and Goodman Cabbage,
Mistress Capon, Kate and Anna,
Russell Rake and Master Gaffer!

Where once lived Déirdre the bright-born daughter,
long-haired Eimhear and the Grey of Macha,
where Aoibheall lived in her rocky mansion,
and the elegant ladies of Dé Danann,
there were schools of poets and story-tellers,
intricate dances, gastronomic pleasures,
arm-wrestling and restless soldiers waiting
to pierce with spears the target's framework.

O the going of those soldiers into graveyards
has split the hills of this old nation:
there is no music now but millstones grinding
and fog on the churches of this wife crying.

Humble loving Lamb, who had to carry
that black burden on your back to Calvary,
swiftly send us your help and blessing
and turn to us your bright face henceforth.

O Secret Love, no longer scold it,
the pride of these exhausted soldiers:
give back again the spark of courage
so they can repay their enemies' insults.

Obey the Lord who purchased sorely
peace for you, a heavenly omen:
come with spears and eager standard-bearers
and drive to doom these new-come aliens!

*Michael Hartnett*

## *'To see the art of poetry lost . . .'*

To see the art of poetry lost
with those who honoured it with thought –
its true form lowered to a silly chant,
sought after by the dilettante.

Those who write the Gaelic tongue
just mumble – when they should stay dumb –
the flaw's admired, the lack of passion –
now that doggerel is in fashion.

If one now writes to the proper rule
in the way demanded by the schools,
then some smart-alec Paddy or such
will say that it is obscure as Dutch.

God of Heaven, preserve and keep
the one man who protects from need
the climbers who scale true poetry
and avoid the lovers of English and ease.
*Ámen.*

*Michael Hartnett*

# WENTWORTH DILLON, EARL OF ROSCOMMON (1637–85)

## from *An Essay on Translated Verse*

Words in One Language Elegantly used,
Will hardly in another be excused.
And some that Rome admired in Caesar's Time,
May neither suit Our Genius nor our Clime.
The Genuine Sense, intelligibly Told,
Shows a Translator both Discreet, and Bold.

Excursions are inexpiably Bad,
For 'tis much safer to leave out, than Add.
Be not too fond of a Sonorous Line;
Good Sense will through a plain expression shine.
Few Painters can such Master strokes command,
As are the noblest in a skilful Hand.
In This, your Author will the best advise,
Fall when He falls, and when He Rises, Rise.
Affected Noise is the most wretched Thing,
That to Contempt can Empty Scribblers bring.
Vowels and Accents, Regularly placed
On even Syllables (and still the Last)
Though all imaginable Faults abound,
Will never want the Pageantry of Sound.
Whatever Sister of the learned Nine
Does to your Suit a willing Ear incline,
Urge your success deserve a lasting Name,
She'll Crown a Grateful and a Constant Flame.
But if a wild Uncertainty prevail,
And turn your Veering heart with every Gale,
You lose the Fruits of all your former care,
For the sad Prospect of a Just Despair.

## TADHG Ó RUAIRC
(*fl.* 1684)

### *A Game of Cards and Dice*

I 'take' you, gorgeous adversary,
you of the wavy gold chevelure,
each curl long and provocative
reaching down to the forest floor.

Crazy about you, as you know,
your grey eyes and lingering looks,
your bright cheeks where roses glow,
the eyebrows like twin pen-strokes,

I watch your lips, so rowan-red,
the neat nose, the rounded chin,
your fine teeth as white as chalk,
the swan-white neck that shames the swan.

I listen to the languorous voice
where your superior nature sings,
a finer sound than organ-pipe
or lute, sweeter than harp-strings,

and gaze at your clean limbs, shy hands,
the soft fingers and pink nails
designed to pluck a tremulous note
or draw ink from quivering quills;

the perfect, opalescent breast
no knight or rook has made his own,
the slim body, slender waist:
I yield my heart to you alone.

High time you cornered me, admired
  woman of the skilful palms,
in glistening-sided 'Port of Thighs'
  or 'Groin Fort' of the quiet streams.

I've had my chips if I should glimpse
  a flash of knee or naked side,
the noble ankle, pale instep,
  foot creamy as the incoming tide.

You penetrate my weak defence,
  teasing me with anxious love.
I know the score; my turn to play,
  against your side I make my move.

So put your cards on the table now –
  shuffle the deck, ingenuous face,
and let the dice fall as they will;
  I sacrifice both deuce and ace.

It beats me you can leave erect
  a knight so stricken by desire
unless you're going to let him through:
  it's high stakes we play for here.

Be it tic-tac crooked or tic-tac straight,
  backgammon, checkers, chess, bezique,
strip poker, scrabble, bingo, snap,
  high time you had my man in check.

Above board or in a secret slot,
  sister, quickly make a space
for the poor pawn with whom you toy:
  relieve my vulnerable piece.

Importunately, my darling girl,
  I'm flinging down my double dice
before your beauty, heart and soul,
  aiming at you both ace and deuce.

Blánaid, my dear, my favourite one,
   gentle, fragrant, guileless love,
it's time for you to trump my man
   and 'take' me with a daring move.

Come sit beside me, woman of the wavy hair;
embrace me, bright branch of the cool grey eyes;
resolve my torment, generous-gentle woman,
and 'take' me quickly to your merciful bed.

*Derek Mahon*

## AINDRIAS MAC CRUITÍN
## (*c.*1650–*c.*1738)

### *Praise of the Quim*

A covert there is that won't break you or bruise you,
Where each man in the world wants to hide;
He tenderly shields it before pouring his blessing –
It's as cherished inside as outside.

Like Tuireann's fat porker, in the famous old story,
It can cure any sorrow whatever;
And I firmly believe, if you learn how to score there,
Neither death will get you nor fever.

Its depths and its sides are supple and precious
Its mouth is as soft as a flower;
Its only response, when you try to oppress it,
Is slyly to smile and endure.

Where is the sage who could tally the measure
Of its welcome, its warmth or its worth?
The quickness and glicness of that rich treasure!
(There's no equal of either on earth.)

Ardent, alert, courageous and noble,
Generous, tender and taut:
The power of the kist that engendered all people
Dumbfounds professor and poet.

And even the king who wants to engage it
Must genuflect at its door;
No man alive is higher in station
Than the miner who digs for its ore.

Tunefully, sweetly, those darling new babies,
Hardy, unhurried, refined,
Emerge one by one, bare and unscathed,
From that source of even Caesar's great line.

A clodhopper only, a genuine plonker,
Could fail to come to its call;
So cosy on up and present your endorsement
To the lips that make lords of us all.

*PC*

## SÉAMAS DALL MAC CUARTA

## (*c.*1650–1733)

### *The Drowned Blackbird*

Lovely daughter of Conn O'Neill,
  You are in shock. Sleep a long sleep.
After the loss of what was dearest,
  Don't let your people hear you weep.

The song of the quick-quick flitting bird
  Has fled, sweet girl, left you forlorn.
Always what's dearest is endangered
  So bear up now, no beating of hands.

Instead of keens and beating hands
  Be silent, girl, as dew in air.
Lovely daughter of Conn O'Neill,
  The bird is dead, don't shed a tear.

Child of that high-born kingly Ulster line,
Show what you're made of, don't let yourself go wild
Even though the loveliest bird in the leaf-and-branch scrim
Is drowned, washed white in whitewash: water and lime.

*Seamus Heaney*

## NAHUM TATE

## (1652–1715)

### *Upon the Sight of an Anatomy*

Nay, start not at that *Skeleton*,
'Tis your own Picture which you shun;
Alive it did resemble Thee,
And thou, when dead, like that shalt be:
Converse with it, and you will say,
You cannot better spend the Day;
You little think how you'll admire
The Language of those *Bones* and *Wire*.

The *Tongue* is gone, but yet each Joint
Reads Lectures, and can speak to th' Point.
When all your Moralists are read,
You'll find no Tutors like the Dead.

If in Truth's Paths those *Feet* have trod,
'Tis all one whether bare, or shod:
If used to travel to the Door
Of the Afflicted Sick and Poor,
Though to the Dance they were estranged,
And ne'er their own rude Motion changed;
Those Feet, now winged, may upwards fly,
And tread the Palace of the Sky.

Those *Hands*, if ne'er with Murder stained,
Nor filled with Wealth unjustly gained,
Nor greedily at Honours grasped,
But to the *Poor-Man's* Cry unclasped;
It matters not, if in the Mine
They delved, or did with Rubies shine.

Here grew the *Lips*, and in that Place,
Where now appears a vacant space,
Was fixed the *Tongue*, an Organ, still
Employed extremely well or ill;
I know not if it could retort,
If versed i' th' Language of the Court;
But this I safely can aver,
That if it was no Flatterer;
If it traduced no Man's Repute,
But, where it could not Praise, was Mute:
If no false Promises it made,
If it sung Anthems, if it Prayed,
'Twas a blest *Tongue*, and will prevail
When Wit and Eloquence shall fail.

If Wise as *Socrates*, that *Skull*,
Had ever been 'tis now as dull
As *Midas's*, or if its Wit
To that of *Midas* did submit,
'Tis now as full of Plot and Skill,
As is the Head of *Machiavel:*
Proud Laurels once might shade that Brow,
Where not so much as Hair grows now.

Prime Instances of Nature's Skill,
The *Eyes*, did once those Hollows fill:
Were they quick-sighted, sparkling, clear,
(As those of Hawks and Eagles are.)
Or say they did with Moisture swim,
And were distorted, bleared, and dim;
Yet if they were from Envy free,
Nor loved to gaze on Vanity;
If none with scorn they did behold,
With no lascivious Glances rolled:
Those Eyes, more bright and piercing grown,
Shall view the Great Creator's Throne;
They shall behold th' *Invisible*,
And on Eternal Glories dwell.

See! not the least Remains appear
To show where Nature placed the *Ear!*
Who knows if it were Musical,
Or could not judge of Sounds at all?
Yet if it were to Counsel bent,
To Caution and Reproof attent,
When the shrill Trump shall rouse the Dead,
And others hear their Sentence read;
That *Ear* shall with these Sounds be blest,
*Well done*, and, *Enter into Rest.*

## JONATHAN SWIFT

(1667–1745)

### *Verses Said to be Written on the Union*

The Queen has lately lost a part
Of her entirely English heart,
For want of which by way of botch,
She pieced it up again with Scotch.
Blessed revolution, which creates
Divided hearts, united states.
See how the double nation lies;
Like a rich coat with skirts of frieze:
As if a man in making posies
Should bundle thistles up with roses.
Whoever yet a union saw
Of kingdoms, without faith or law.
Henceforward let no statesman dare,
A kingdom to a ship compare;
Lest he should call our commonweal,
A vessel with a double keel:
Which just like ours, new rigged and manned,
And got about a league from land,

By change of wind to leeward side
The pilot knew not how to guide.
So tossing faction will o'erwhelm
Our crazy double-bottomed realm.

## *A Description of the Morning*

Now hardly here and there a hackney coach
Appearing, showed the ruddy morn's approach.
Now Betty from her master's bed has flown,
And softly stole to discompose her own.
The slipshod prentice from his master's door
Had pared the dirt, and sprinkled round the floor.
Now Moll had whirled her mop with dexterous airs,
Prepared to scrub the entry and the stairs.
The youth with broomy stumps began to trace
The kennel-edge, where wheels had worn the place.
The smallcoal man was heard with cadence deep;
Till drowned in shriller notes of chimney-sweep.
Duns at his Lordship's gate began to meet;
And Brickdust Moll had screamed through half a street.
The turnkey now his flock returning sees,
Duly let out a-nights to steal for fees.
The watchful bailiffs take their silent stands;
And schoolboys lag with satchels in their hands.

## from *Cadenus and Vanessa*

Cadenus many things had writ;
Vanessa much esteemed his wit;
And called for his poetic works;
Meantime the boy in secret lurks,
And while the book was in her hand,
The urchin from his private stand
Took aim, and shot with all his strength
A dart of such prodigious length,
It pierced the feeble volume through,

And deep transfixed her bosom too.
Some lines more moving than the rest,
Stuck to the point that pierced her breast;
And born directly to the heart,
With pains unknown increased her smart.

Vanessa, not in years a score,
Dreams of a gown of forty-four;
Imaginary charms can find,
In eyes with reading almost blind;
Cadenus now no more appears
Declined in health, advanced in years.
She fancies music in his tongue,
Nor further looks, but thinks him young.
What mariner is not afraid,
To venture in a ship decayed?
What planter will attempt to yoke
A sapling with a fallen oak?
As years increase, she brighter shines,
Cadenus with each day declines,
And he must fall a prey to time,
While she continues in her prime.

## *Mary the Cook-Maid's Letter to Dr Sheridan*

Well; if ever I saw such another man since my mother bound
my head,
You a gentleman! marry come up, I wonder where you were bred?
I am sure such words does not become a man of your cloth,
I would not give such language to a dog, faith and troth.
Yes; you called my master a knave; fie Mr Sheridan, 'tis a shame
For a parson, who should know better things, to come out with
such a name.
Knave in your teeth, Mr Sheridan, 'tis both a shame and a sin,
And the Dean my master is an honester man than you and all
your kin:
He has more goodness in his little finger, than you have in your
whole body,

My master is a parsonable man, and not a spindle-shanked
hoddy-doddy.
And now whereby I find you would fain make an excuse,
Because my master one day, in anger, called you goose.
Which, and I am sure I have been his servant four years since
October,
And he never called me worse than 'sweetheart', drunk or sober:
Not that I know his Reverence was ever concerned to my
knowledge,
Though you and your come-rogues keep him out so late in your
wicked college.

You say you will eat grass on his grave: a Christian eat grass!
Whereby you now confess yourself to be a goose or an ass:
But that's as much as to say, that my master should die
before ye;
Well, well, that's as God pleases, and I don't believe that's a true
story,
And so say I told you so, and you may go tell my master; what
care I?
And I don't care who knows it, 'tis all one to Mary.
Everybody knows, that I love to tell truth, and shame the devil;
I am but a poor servant, but I think gentlefolks should be civil.
Besides, you found fault with our victuals one day that you was
here,
I remember it was upon a Tuesday, of all days in the year.
And Saunders the man says, you are always jesting and
mocking,
'Mary' said he, (one day, as I was mending my master's
stocking,)
'My master is so fond of that minister that keeps the school;
I thought my master a wise man, but that man makes him
a fool.'
'Saunders' said I, 'I would rather than a quart of ale,
He would come into our kitchen, and I would pin a dishclout to
his tail.'
And now I must go, and get Saunders to direct this letter,
For I write but a sad scrawl, but sister Marget she writes better.

Well, but I must run and make the bed before my master comes
from prayers,
And see now, it strikes ten, and I hear him coming upstairs:
Whereof I could say more to your verses, if I could write
written hand,
And so I remain in a civil way, your servant to command,

*MARY.*

## *A Satirical Elegy on the Death of a Late Famous General*

His Grace! impossible! what, dead!
Of old age too, and in his bed!
And could that Mighty Warrior fall?
And so inglorious, after all!
Well, since he's gone, no matter how,
The last loud trump must wake him now:
And, trust me, as the noise grows stronger,
He'd wish to sleep a little longer.
And could he be indeed so old
As by the newspapers we're told?
Threescore, I think, is pretty high;
'Twas time in conscience he should die.
This world he cumbered long enough;
He burnt his candle to the snuff;
And that's the reason, some folks think,
He left behind *so great a stink*.
Behold his funeral appears,
Nor widow's sighs, nor orphan's tears,
Wont at such times each heart to pierce,
Attend the progress of his hearse.
But what of that, his friends may say,
He had those honours in his day.
True to his profit and his pride,
He made them weep before he died.

Come hither, all ye empty things,
Ye bubbles raised by breath of kings;
Who float upon the tide of state,
Come hither, and behold your fate.
Let pride be taught by this rebuke,
How very mean a thing's a Duke;
From all his ill-got honours flung,
Turned to that dirt from whence he sprung.

## *Stella at Woodpark*

### *A House of Charles Ford Esq. Eight Miles from Dublin*

*Cuicunque nocere volebat*
*Vestimenta dabat pretiosa.*

Don Carlos in a merry spite,
Did Stella to his house invite:
He entertained her half a year
With generous wines and costly cheer.
Don Carlos made her chief director,
That she might o'er the servants hector.
In half a week the dame grows nice,
Got all things at the highest price.
Now at the table-head she sits,
Presented with the nicest bits:
She looked on partridges with scorn,
Except they tasted of the corn:
A haunch of venison made her sweat,
Unless it had the right *fumette*.
Don Carlos earnestly would beg,
'Dear madam, try this pigeon's leg';
Was happy when he could prevail
To make her only touch a quail.
Through candle-light she viewed the wine,
To see that every glass was fine.
At last grown prouder than the devil,
With feeding high, and treatment civil,
Don Carlos now began to find

His malice work as he designed:
The winter sky began to frown,
Poor Stella must pack off to town.
From purling streams and fountains bubbling,
To Liffey's stinking tide in Dublin:
From wholesome exercise and air
To sossing in an easy chair;
From stomach sharp and hearty feeding,
To piddle like a lady breeding:
From ruling there the household singly,
To be directed here by Dingley:
From every day a lordly banquet,
To half a joint, and God be thank it:
From every meal Pontac in plenty,
To half a pint one day in twenty.
From Ford attending at her call,
To visits of Archdeacon Wall.
From Ford, who thinks of nothing mean,
To the poor doings of the Dean.
From growing richer with good cheer,
To running out by starving here.

But now arrives the dismal day:
She must return to Ormond Quay:
The coachman stopped, she looked, and swore
The rascal had mistook the door:
At coming in you saw her stoop;
The entry brushed against her hoop:
Each moment rising in her airs,
She cursed the narrow winding stairs:
Began a thousand faults to spy;
The ceiling hardly six foot high;
The smutty wainscot full of cracks,
And half the chairs with broken backs:
Her quarter's out at Lady Day,
She vows she will no longer stay,
In lodgings, like a poor *grisette*,
While there are houses to be let.

Howe'er, to keep her spirits up,
She sent for company to sup;
When all the while you might remark,
She strove in vain to ape Woodpark.
Two bottles called for, (half her store;
The cupboard could contain but four;)
A supper worthy of her self,
Five nothings in five plates of Delf.

Thus, for a week the farce went on;
When all her country-savings gone,
She fell into her former scene.
Small beer, a herring, and the Dean.

Thus far in jest. Though now I fear
You think my jesting too severe:
But poets when a hint is new
Regard not whether false or true:
Yet raillery gives no offence,
Where truth has not the least pretence;
Nor can be more securely placed
Than on a nymph of Stella's taste.
I must confess, your wine and victual
I was too hard upon *a little*;
Your table neat, your linen fine;
And, though in miniature, you shine.
Yet, when you sigh to leave Woodpark,
The scene, the welcome, and the spark,
To languish in this odious town,
And pull your haughty stomach down;
We think you quite mistake the case;
The virtue lies not in the place:
For though my raillery were true,
A cottage is Woodpark with you.

## *Verses Occasioned by the Sudden Drying Up of St Patrick's Well near Trinity College, Dublin*

By holy zeal inspired, and led by fame,
To thee, once favourite isle, with joy I came;
What time the Goth, the Vandal, and the Hun,
Had my own native Italy o'errun.
Ierne, to the world's remotest parts,
Renowned for valour, policy and arts.

Hither from Colchus, with the fleecy ore,
Jason arrived two thousand years before.
Thee, happy island, Pallas called her own,
When haughty Britain was a land unknown.
From thee, with pride, the Caledonians trace
The glorious founder of their kingly race:
Thy martial sons, whom now they dare despise,
Did once their land subdue and civilize:
Their dress, their language, and the Scottish name,
Confess the soil from whence the victors came.
Well may they boast that ancient blood, which runs
Within their veins, who are thy younger sons,
A conquest and a colony from thee,
The mother-kingdom left her children free;
From thee no mark of slavery they felt,
Not so with thee thy base invaders dealt;
Invited here to vengeful Morough's aid,
Those whom they could not conquer, they betrayed.
Britain, by thee we fell, ungrateful isle!
Not by thy valour, but superior guile:
Britain, with shame confess, this land of mine
First taught thee human knowledge and divine;
My prelates and my students, sent from hence,
Made your sons converts both to God and sense:
Not like the pastors of thy ravenous breed,
Who come to fleece the flocks, and not to feed.

Wretched Ierne! with what grief I see
The fatal changes time hath made in thee.
The Christian rites I introduced in vain:
Lo! Infidelity returned again.
Freedom and Virtue in thy sons I found,
Who now in Vice and Slavery are drowned.

By faith and prayer, this crozier in my hand,
I drove the venomed serpent from thy land;
The shepherd in his bower might sleep or sing,
Nor dread the adder's tooth, nor scorpion's sting.

With omens oft I strove to warn thy swains,
Omens, the types of thy impending chains.
I sent the magpie from the British soil,
With restless beak thy blooming fruit to spoil,
To din thine ears with unharmonious clack,
And haunt thy holy walls in white and black.
What else are those thou seest in bishop's gear
Who crop the nurseries of learning here?
Aspiring, greedy, full of senseless prate,
Devour the church, and chatter to the state.

As you grew more degenerate and base,
I sent you millions of the croaking race;
Emblems of insects vile, who spread their spawn
Through all thy land, in armour, fur and lawn.
A nauseous brood, that fills your senate walls,
And in the chambers of your Viceroy crawls.

See, where the new-devouring vermin runs,
Sent in my anger from the land of Huns;
With harpy claws it undermines the ground,
And sudden spreads a numerous offspring round;
The amphibious tyrant, with his ravenous band,
Drains all thy lakes of fish, of fruits thy land.

Where is the sacred well, that bore my name?
Fled to the fountain back, from whence it came!
Fair Freedom's emblem once, which smoothly flows,
And blessings equally on all bestows.
Here, from the neighbouring nursery of arts,
The students drinking, raised their wit and parts;
Here, for an age and more, improved their vein,
Their Phoebus I, my spring their Hippocrene.
Discouraged youths, now all their hopes must fail,
Condemned to country cottages and ale;
To foreign prelates make a slavish court,
And by their sweat procure a mean support;
Or, for the classics read the attorney's guide;
Collect excise, or wait upon the tide.

O! had I been apostle to the Swiss,
Or hardy Scot, or any land but this;
Combined in arms, they had their foes defied,
And kept their liberty, or bravely died.
Thou still with tyrants in succession cursed,
The last invaders trampling on the first:
Nor fondly hope for some reverse of fate,
Virtue herself would now return too late.
Not half thy course of misery is run,
Thy greatest evils yet are scarce begun.
Soon shall thy sons, the time is just at hand,
Be all made captives in their native land;
When, for the use of no Hibernian born,
Shall rise one blade of grass, one ear of corn;
When shells and leather shall for money pass,
Nor thy oppressing lords afford thee brass.
But all turn leasers to that mongrel breed,
Who from thee sprung, yet on thy vitals feed;
Who to yon ravenous isle thy treasures bear,
And waste in luxury thy harvests there;
For pride and ignorance a proverb grown,
The jest of wits, and to the courts unknown.

I scorn thy spurious and degenerate line,
And from this hour my patronage resign.

## from *To Dr Delany, on the Libels Writ against Him*

When Jove was, from his teeming head,
Of wit's fair goddess brought to bed,
There followed at his lying-in
For afterbirth, a sooterkin;
Which, as the nurse pursued to kill,
Attained by flight the muses' hill;
There in the soil began to root,
And littered at Parnassus' foot.
From hence the critic-vermin sprung,
With harpy claws, and poisonous tongue,
Who fatten on poetic scraps;
Too cunning to be caught in traps.
Dame Nature, as the learned show,
Provides each animal its foe;
Hounds hunt the hare, the wily fox
Devours your geese, the wolf your flocks:
Thus, envy pleads a natural claim
To persecute the muses' fame;
On poets in all times abusive,
From Homer down to Pope inclusive.

## from *On His Own Deafness*

Deaf, giddy, odious to my friends,
Now all my consolation ends;
No more I hear my church's bell
Than if it rang out for my knell;
At thunder now, no more I start
Than at the rumbling of a cart.

Nay though I know you would not credit –
Although a thousand times I said it:
A scold whom you might hear a mile hence
No more could reach me than her silence.

## from *A Character, Panegyric, and Description of the Legion Club*

As I stroll the city, oft I
Spy a building large and lofty,
Not a bow-shot from the College,
Half a globe from sense and knowledge.
By the prudent architect
Placed against the church direct;
Making good my grandam's jest,
*Near the church* – you know the rest.

Tell us, what this pile contains?
Many a head that holds no brains.
These demoniacs let me dub
With the name of 'Legion Club.'
Such assemblies, you might swear,
Meet when butchers bait a bear;
Such a noise, and such haranguing,
When a brother thief is hanging.
Such a rout and such a rabble
Run to hear jack-pudding gabble;
Such a crowd their ordure throws
On a far less villain's nose.

Could I from the building's top
Hear the rattling thunder drop,
While the devil upon the roof,
If the devil be thunder-proof,
Should with poker fiery red
Crack the stones, and melt the lead;
Drive them down on every skull,
While the den of thieves is full,

Quite destroy that harpies' nest,
How might then our isle be blessed?
For divines allow, that God
Sometimes makes the devil his rod:
And the gospel will inform us,
He can punish sins enormous.

Yet should Swift endow the schools
For his lunatics and fools,
With a rood or two of land,
I allow the pile may stand.
You perhaps will ask me, why so?
But it is with this proviso,
Since the House is like to last,
Let a royal grant be passed,
That the club have right to dwell
Each within his proper cell;
With a passage left to creep in,
And a hole above for peeping.

Let them, when they once get in
Sell the nation for a pin;
While they sit a-picking straws
Let them rave of making laws;
While they never hold their tongue,
Let them dabble in their dung;
Let them form a grand committee,
How to plague and starve the city;
Let them stare and storm and frown,
When they see a clergy-gown.
Let them, 'ere they crack a louse,
Call for the orders of the House;
Let them with their gosling quills,
Scribble senseless heads of bills;
We may, while they strain their throats,
Wipe our arses with their votes.

Let Sir Tom, that rampant ass,
Stuff his guts with flax and grass;
But before the priest he fleeces
Tear the bible all to pieces.
At the parsons, Tom, halloo boy,
Worthy offspring of a shoe-boy,
Footman, traitor, vile seducer,
Perjured rebel, bribed accuser;
Lay the paltry privilege aside,
Sprung from papists and a regicide;
Fall a-working like a mole,
Raise the dirt about your hole.

Come, assist me, muse obedient,
Let us try some new expedient;
Shift the scene for half an hour,
Time and place are in thy power.
Thither, gentle muse, conduct me,
I shall ask, and thou instruct me.

See, the muse unbars the gate;
Hark, the monkeys, how they prate!

All ye gods, who rule the soul;
Styx, through hell whose waters roll!
Let me be allowed to tell
What I heard in yonder hell.

Near the door an entrance gapes,
Crowded round with antic shapes;
Poverty, and Grief, and Care,
Causeless Joy, and true Despair;
Discord periwigged with snakes,
See the dreadful strides she takes.

By this odious crew beset,
I began to rage and fret,
And resolved to break their pates,
Ere we entered at the gates;

Had not Clio in the nick,
Whispered me, 'Let down your stick';
'What,' said I, 'is this the madhouse?'
'These,' she answered, 'are but shadows,
Phantoms, bodiless and vain,
Empty visions of the brain.'

## *An Epigram on Scolding*

Great folks are of a finer mould;
Lord! how politely they can scold;
While a coarse English tongue will itch,
For whore and rogue; and dog and bitch.

# AODHAGÁN Ó RATHAILLE

(*c.*1670–1729)

## *On a Gift of Shoes*

I received jewels of outstanding beauty –
two shoes, supple and finished smoothly;
they came from the south – Barbary leather
brought by the fleet of King Philip hither;

two shoes decorated with neat trimming,
two shoes that will last while tramping hill-tops,
two shoes of well-cut, well-tanned leather,
two shoes that protect me in rough meadows;

two shoes noble, and they're not tight-fitting,
two shoes stalwart, when hurting foe-men,
two shoes narrow, without split or wrinkle,
two shoes well-made, without seam or opening;

two shoes, hardy and brave in high places,
of the hide torn from the white cow's carcass –
the cow that was guarded in the waste-land
and tended with care by a giant watchman.

And a god, he loved her for a season
and saddened and darkened her brother's reason;
till one night she was stolen by a bailiff
from the hundred-eyed head, that ugly doomed creature.

Shoes from her hide the rain cannot soften
nor can heat harden their soles and uppers;
the wind can't destroy their lovely lustre
nor too much heat make them shrink or shrivel.

The soles and uppers were bound with bristles,
feather-like, lovely, belonging to Túis,
brought in a ship by the children of Tuireann
to Lugh the vigorous, the mighty.

Better shoes poets never dreamed of
nor did Achilles get their like for comfort
in his legacy – which brought grief to Ajax;
he did not get them, for all his declaiming.

The awl that pierced the hide I tell ye of
was made of the hardest steel that ever was;
for seven hundred years the demons were
making its spike with Vulcan's connivance.

Black hemp grew on the rim of Acheron
and was spun by hags, companions of Atropos;
by this was sewn my fine shoes' edges,
by the magic power of the Fates most potent.

They were once designed for Darius
till Alexander overcame him;
they were for a time on mighty Caesar
till from his feet were robbed the world's playthings.

They were owned for a time by the gods of Fáilbhe,
by famous Lir, and the plunderer, Lughaidh;
by Bodhbh Dearg, once our supporter,
by battering Balar who throve in slaughter.

Long time in Magh Seanaibh's fairy mansion,
and Aoibheall had them and men of ancient magic;
they do not wear out, or lose their appearance –
from a man of welcomes I received them.

Kind Domhnall, Cathal's son – now, hear me –
he's a luck-bringing chieftain and true hero
of the seed of Glenflesk who knelt to no man,
he presented these shoes to me as a token.

They cure all pain, all problems and all illness,
hoarseness, frenzy, falling sickness;
thirst, starvation, biting hunger,
torment, torture; the stress of going under.

Against enemies, in war and conflict,
with these each breach was charged by Oscar;
though Goll Mac Mórna was great and famous
he wanted a loan of them, like all the nation.

Cúrí had these shoes for a season
and Cúchulainn who was no mean hero;
and the once victorious Maedhbh of Cruachan
and Conall Ceárnach and Niall Glúndubh.

At Clontarf (they were there for certain)
Dúnlaing wore them, very contented –
if he had tied their thongs on him tightly, he would have
brought Murchadh safe from the fighting.

Sacred tree of the sunseed of Fianna Fáilbhe,
of the seers of Cashel kind and manly always,
is the man of great reputation
who gave to me my excellent footwear.

Though he has for some time lived under the foreigners
he did not learn from them to be heartless or sordid;
he has no stingy heart – indeed, he is faultless –
and it grows as he grows, the good gift from his fathers.

A generous man, and kind to the poets,
a virtuous man, who deserted no one;
a man of importance, a giver, bestower,
a steady and merry man and no surly boaster.

It's no false history to broadcast about him
that eighteen kings were in the roots he came from;
they were rulers in the land of Fáilbhe
from Cas of the light to Donnchadh the patron.

There are not many like them, my shoes, like choicest gems;
they are just right on roads of fresh blue stones;
though now sad and sore, I will soon find relief
since Ó Donnchadha chose for me these uppers and soles.

*Michael Hartnett*

## *The Glamoured*

Brightening brightness, alone on the road, she appears,
Crystalline crystal and sparkle of blue in green eyes,
Sweetness of sweetness in her unembittered young voice
And a high colour dawning behind the pearl of her face.

Ringlets and ringlets, a curl in every tress
Of her fair hair trailing and brushing the dew on the grass;
And a gem from her birthplace far in the high universe
Outglittering glass and gracing the groove of her breasts.

News that was secret she whispered to soothe her aloneness,
News of one due to return and reclaim his true place,
News of the ruin of those who had cast him in darkness,
News that was awesome, too awesome to utter in verse.

My head got lighter and lighter but still I approached her,
Enthralled by her thraldom, helplessly held and bewildered,
Choking and calling Christ's name: then she fled in a shimmer
To Luachra Fort where only the glamoured can enter.

I hurtled and hurled myself madly following after
Over keshes and marshes and mosses and treacherous moors
And arrived at that stronghold unsure about how I had got there,
That earthwork of earth the orders of magic once reared.

A gang of thick louts were shouting loud insults and jeering
And a curly-haired coven in fits of sniggers and sneers:
Next thing I was taken and cruelly shackled in fetters
As the breasts of the maiden were groped by a thick-witted boor.

I tried then as hard as I could to make her hear truth,
How wrong she was to be linked to that lazarous swine
When the pride of the pure Scottish stock, a prince of the blood,
Was ardent and eager to wed her and make her his bride.

When she heard me, she started to weep, but pride was the cause
Of those tears that came wetting her cheeks and shone in her
eyes;
Then she sent me a guard to guide me out of the fortress,
Who'd appeared to me, lone on the road, a brightening
brightness.

(. . .)

Calamity, shock, collapse, heartbreak and grief
To think of her sweetness, her beauty, her mildness, her life
Defiled at the hands of a hornmaster sprung from riff-raff,
And no hope of redress till the lions ride back on the wave.

*Seamus Heaney*

## *A Grey Eye Weeping*

That my old bitter heart was pierced in this black doom,
That foreign devils have made our land a tomb,
That the sun that was Munster's glory has gone down
Has made me a beggar before you, Valentine Brown.

That royal Cashel is bare of house and guest,
That Brian's turreted home is the otter's nest,
That the kings of the land have neither land nor crown
Has made me a beggar before you, Valentine Brown.

Garnish away in the west with its master banned,
Hamburg the refuge of him who has lost his land,
An old grey eye, weeping for lost renown,
Have made me a beggar before you, Valentine Brown.

*Frank O'Connor*

## *The Ruin that Befell the Great Families of Ireland*

My pity, that Carthy's heirs are weaklings,
this poor land's people without a leader;
no man to free her, locked up and keyless,
and shieldless now in this land of chieftains.
Land with no prince of her ancient people,
land made helpless from foreigners' beatings;
land stretched out beneath the feet of treason,
land chained down – it is the death of reason.
Land lonely, tortured, broken and beaten,
land sonless, manless, wifeless, and weeping;
land lifeless, soulless, and without hearing,
land where the poor are only ill-treated.
Land without churches, massless and priestless,
land that the wolves have spitefully eaten;
land of misery and obedience
to tyrant robbers, greedy and thieving.

Land that produces nothing of sweetness,
land so sunless, so starless and so streamless;
land stripped naked, left leafless and treeless,
land stripped naked by the English bleaters.
Land in anguish – and drained of its heroes,
land for its children forever weeping;
a widow wounded, crying and keening,
humbled, degraded, and torn to pieces.
The white of her cheeks is never tearless,
and her hair falls down in rainshowers gleaming;
blood from her eyes in torrents comes streaming
and black as coal is her appearance.
Her limbs are shrunken, bound and bleeding;
around her waist is no satin weaving,
but iron from Hades blackly gleaming,
forged by henchmen who are Vulcan's demons.
Red pools are filled by her poor heart's bleeding
and dogs from Bristol lap it up greedily –
her body is being pulled to pieces
by Saxon curs with their bloody teeth full.
Her branches rotten, her forests leafless,
the frosts of Heaven have killed her streams now;
the sunlight shines on her lands but weakly,
the fog of the forge is on her peaks now.
Her quarries, her mines, are exploited freely,
the rape of her trees is pointless, greedy;
her growing plants are all scattered seawards
to foreign countries to seek for freedom.
Griffin and Hedges, the upstart keepers
of the Earl's holdings – it is painful speaking –
Blarney, where only bold wolves are sleeping,
Ráth Luirc is plundered, naked and fearful.
The Laune is taken, has lost its fierceness,
Shannon and Maine and Liffey are bleeding;
Kingly Tara lacks the seed of Niall Dubh,
No Raighleann hero is alive and breathing.
O'Doherty is gone – and his people,
and the Moores are gone, that once were heroes;
O'Flaherty is gone – and his people,

and O'Brien has joined the English cheaters.
Of the brave O'Rourke there is none speaking,
O'Donnell's fame has none to repeat it,
and all the Geraldines, they lie speechless,
and Walsh of the slender ships is needy.

Hear, oh Trinity, my poor beseeching:
take this sorrow from my broken people,
from the seed of Conn and Ír and Eibhear –
restore their lands to my broken people.
They are my tormenting sorrow,
  brave men broken by this rain,
and fat pirates in bed
  in the place of older tribes of fame,
and the tribes that have fled
  and who cared for poets' lives, defamed.
This great crime has me led
  shoeless, bare,
through cold towns crying today.

*Michael Hartnett*

## *He Curses the Wave at the Western Ocean's Edge*

Drearily the drenching night drags; without sleeping or snoring,
Without wealth, without sheep flocks, without fine-horned
  herds;
The waves' onslaught here beside me through my head keeps
  gnawing –
And it's not on winkles, no, nor dogfish that I was reared.

If the shelter-giving king from Laune's banks had lived on,
Ever ready with his war bands to take pity on my want,
Who ruled a warm-sloped region rich in harbours, woods and
  lawns,
It's not destitute in Duibhne's land I'd now find my people
  fawning.

Great MacCarthy, fierce and valorous, to whom all wiles were
hateful,
And MacCarthy of the Lee, brought to slavery and lamed,
MacCarthy, Kanturk's king, in the grave beside his children –
It tears my heart not one of them has left a living name.

My heart it shrivelled up, it curdled all fine feeling,
To see chiefs who never stinted, whose territories once spanned
From Cashel to Tonn Chlíodhna and way on out to Thomond,
Destroyed by Strangers crowding every barony and townland.

Wave below me here, raising high your roaring,
Splitting my head in two with your never-ending shout,
If help just once more could arrive for lovely Ireland
I'd shove your raucous bile straight back down your throat.

*PC*

## THOMAS PARNELL

(1679–1718)

### *Song*

When thy Beauty appears
In its Graces and Airs
All bright as an Angel new dropped from the Sky,
At distance I gaze, and am awed by my Fears:
So strangely you dazzle my Eye!

But when without Art
Your kind Thoughts you impart,
When your Love runs in Blushes through every Vein;
When it darts from your Eyes, when it pants in your Heart,
Then I know you're a Woman again.

There's a Passion and Pride
In our Sex (she replied),
And thus (might I gratify both) I would do:
Still an Angel appear to each Lover beside,
But still be a Woman to you.

## *A Night-Piece on Death*

By the blue Taper's trembling light,
No more I waste the wakeful Night,
Intent with endless view to pore
The Schoolmen and the Sages o'er:
Their books from wisdom widely stray,
Or point at best the longest Way.
I'll seek a readier Path, and go
Where Wisdom's surely taught *below*.

How deep yon Azure dyes the Sky!
Where Orbs of Gold unnumbered lie,
While through their Ranks in silver pride
The nether Crescent seems to glide!
The slumb'ring Breeze forgets to breathe,
The Lake is smooth and clear beneath,
Where once again the spangled Show
Descends to meet our Eyes below.
The Grounds which on the right aspire,
In dimness from the View retire:
The left presents a Place of Graves,
Whose Wall the silent Water laves.
That Steeple guides thy doubtful sight
Among the livid gleams of Night.
There pass with melancholy State,
By all the solemn Heaps of Fate,
And think, as softly-sad you tread
Above the venerable Dead,
*Time was, like thee they Life possessed,*
*And Time shall be, that thou shalt Rest.*

Those Graves, with bending Osier bound,
That nameless heave the crumbled Ground,
Quick to the glancing Thought disclose,
Where *Toil* and *Poverty* repose.

The flat smooth Stones that bear a Name,
The Chisel's slender help to Fame,
(Which ere our Set of Friends decay
Their frequent Steps may wear away,)
A *middle Race* of Mortals own,
Men, half ambitious, all unknown.

The Marble Tombs that rise on high,
Whose Dead in vaulted Arches lie,
Whose Pillars swell with sculptured Stones,
Arms, Angels, Epitaphs, and Bones,
These (all the poor Remains of State)
Adorn the *Rich*, or praise the *Great*;
Who, while on Earth in Fame they live,
Are senseless of the Fame they give.

Ha! while I gaze, pale *Cynthia* fades,
The bursting Earth unveils the Shades!
All slow, and wan, and wrapped with Shrouds
They rise in visionary Crowds,
And all with sober Accent cry,
*Think, mortal, what it is to die.*

Now from yon black and fun'ral Yew,
That bathes the Charnel House with Dew,
Methinks I hear a *Voice* begin;
(Ye Ravens, cease your croaking Din;
Ye tolling Clocks, no Time resound
O'er the long Lake and midnight Ground)
It sends a Peal of hollow Groans
Thus speaking from among the Bones.

*When men my Scythe and Darts supply,*
*How great a* King of Fears *am I!*
*They view me like the last of Things:*
*They make, and then they dread, my Stings.*
*Fools! if you less provoked your Fears,*
*No more my Spectre Form appears.*
*Death's but a Path that must be trod,*
*If Man would ever pass to God;*
*A Port of Calms, a State of Ease*
*From the rough Rage of swelling Seas.*

*Why then thy flowing sable Stoles,*
*Deep pendent Cypress, mourning Poles,*
*Loose Scarfs to fall athwart thy Weeds,*
*Long Palls, drawn Hearses, covered Steeds,*
*And plumes of black, that, as they tread,*
*Nod o'er the 'Scutcheons of the Dead?*

*Nor can the parted Body know,*
*Nor wants the Soul, these Forms of Woe.*
*As men who long in Prison dwell,*
*With Lamps that glimmer round the Cell,*
*Whene'er their suff'ring Years are run,*
*Spring forth to greet the glitt'ring Sun:*
*Such Joy though for transcending Sense,*
*Have pious Souls at parting hence.*
*On Earth, and in the Body placed,*
*A few, and evil Years they waste;*
*But when their Chains are cast aside,*
*See the glad Scene unfolding wide,*
*Clap the glad Wing, and tower away,*
*And mingle with the Blaze of Day.*

# LAURENCE WHYTE

## (*c.*1683–*c.*1753)

## *A Dissertation on Italian and Irish Musick, with some Panegyrick on Carrallan Our Late Irish Orpheus*

### A PRELUDE, OR VOLUNTARY

Begin my *Muse*, with tuneful *Stanzas*
*Concertos*, or *Extravaganzas*,
With something new not sung before,
That shall demand a loud *Encore!*
*Overture*, *Symphony*, or *Solo*,
Goes down with universal *Volo*;
Some brisk *Alegros*, *Fuges*, and *Jiggs*
Will please young *Ladies*, and young *Priggs*,
Your *Echos* may be soft or loud,
With *Gavots* to amuse the *Crowd*;
*Courants* and *Minutes French*, and *Spanish*,
That may our Cares and Sorrows banish.
Play *Voluntaries* smooth and free,
From *E* in *alt* to double *B*,
Spin out your Thoughts on ev'ry Strain,
*Da Capo*, then begin again,
Then some *Adagios* – with your Leave,
To please the sober and the grave;
Some dying Notes, soft and complaining,
Notes full of Energy and Meaning,
Which all the Passions strangely move,
To Joy, or Grief, to Mirth, or Love.
  Sounds elevate the Soul to Prayers,
They mitigate our Toils, and Cares,
Rouse and excite us all to Arms,
Allay our Fury by their Charms,
Compose the Mind, lull us to sleep,
And mollify or make us weep.

### ADAGIO

*Corelly's*, or *Vivaldi's* Style,
Shall from *Corinna* force a Smile,
Which does her Aspect more adorn,
Than all her Cruelty and Scorn,
Thus while you hold her by the Ear,
She catches others in her Snare:
The longer she is kept in Tune,
The more her Charms have Power to ruin.
  Then *Hendal's* Notes shall make her thrill,
When *Raffa* warbles them with Skill,
And if *Dubourg* but touch the String,
To hear him play, and *Raffa* sing,
In Ecstasies – she sounds away,
Revives again to hear him play.

### JIGG

The *Beaus* who watch *Corinna's* Eyes,
*Encore!* and clap them to the Skies,
The Country *Squire* dressed like a *Hero*,
Who'd rather hear *Lill'bolero*,
And having neither Air nor Voice,
Of *Bobbin Joan* would make his Choice,
Now joins in *Chorus* with the rest,
And cries *Encore!* to crown the Jest,
Then out of time he gives a Clap!
Huzzas! and then throws up his Cap!
Cries damn you! play up the *Black Joke*,
Or else you'll get your Fiddles broke,
Then play *Jack Lattin* my dear Honey!
Hey! *Larry Grogan* for my Money!
Then rushes out with seeming Haste,
And leaves that Sample of his Taste.

RECITATIVO

Some *Solo's* Songs, and merry Lays,
These are which will for ever please,
When well performed or sung with Art,
With graces proper for each Part.
Some old ones we have oft revived,
For modern Opera's contrived,
Instead of those *Italian* Airs,
So much in Vogue for many Years;
Poor *Ireland*, like *old England* doats
On Multiplicity of Notes,
And with few *Words* she can dispense,
Sometimes with little or no Sense,
And those spun out so very long,
A *Word* or two would make a *Song*,
Through various *Bars* they rise and fall;
They might as well have none at all;
But to begin with ha, ha, ha,
And to conclude with fa, la, la,
The Words are vanished quite away,
Whilst they in such Meanders stray,
Or swelled so high, so long and loud,
They burst like Thunder from a Cloud,
That from *Olympus* down is cast,
And at the Bottom breathe their last.
  A *Word's* sufficient to the wise,
But *Words* exotic bear the Prize,
Whatever has a *Foreign* Tone,
We like much better than our own,
'Tis often said, *few Words are best*,
To trace their meaning is a Jest,
And such as cannot well be scanned,
What need have we to understand.
  'Tis well the *Vulgar* now of late,
Can relish *Sounds* articulate,
There's scarce a *Forthman* or *Fingallion*,
But sings or whistles in *Italian*,
Instead of good old *Barley Mow*,

With *Tamo tanto* drive the Plough,
They o'er their Cups can sing, *Si caro*,
And dare profane it at the *Harrow*,
There's *Ariadne* crossed the *Shannon*,
She sings in *Gallaway*, *Tuam*, and *Mannin*,
And in her Progress to and fro,
Expels a sweeter Song, *Speak Shoy*,
She travels down to *Portaferry*,
To *Omy* and to *Londonderry*,
Where People hears her with more Pleasure,
Than highland *Lilt*, or *Scottish Measure*,
She, of the *Truagh*, has taken place,
And *Meu Vin Yall*, of *Irish* Race.
She flies to *Munster* for the Air,
To clear her pipes and warble there,
Poor *Cronaan*, being turned out of Play,
With *Rinke Mueenagh* flew away,
To the remotest part of *Kerry*,
In hopes to make the Vulgar merry,
But scarce one Cabbin in their Flight,
Would give them Lodging for a Night,
So taken up with foreign Jingle,
*Tralee* despised them, likewise *Dingle*.
But *Drimin duh* is still in favour,
Since we from *Murphy*, beg, and crave her,
Of him alone we must require
To do her Justice on the Lyre,
She, and old *Eveleen a Rune*,
Are by the *Muses* kept in Tune,
Who many Centuries have thrived,
And doomed by fate to be long lived,
With many others we know well,
Which do in harmony excel.
*Dubourg* improves them in our Days,
And never from the subject strays,
Nor by Extravagance perplext,
Will let them wander from the text.
*MacGowran*, on the *Coal Black Joke*,
(To his great Credit be it spoke)

Has multiplied upon that Strain,
To shew his vast extensive Vein.
  Sweet *Bocchi* thought it worth his while,
In doing honour to our *Isle*,
To build on *Carallan's* Foundation,
Which he performed to Admiration,
On his Pheracas went to work,
With long Divisions on *O'Rowrk*.
  A *Dean* the greatest Judge of Wit,
That ever wrote amongst us yet,
Gave us a Version of the Song,
*Verbatim* from the *Irish* Tongue.
  *Ta me ma choll*, and *Candun dilish*,
For Ages have preserved their Relish,
Together with *Da mihi Manum*,
Which we may reckon an *Arcanum*,
With all the *Plankstys* and *Pleraccas*,
By *Carallan* in his Sonatas,
The greatest *Genius* in his way,
An *Orpheus*, who cou'd sing and play,
So great a *Bard* where can we find,
Like him illiterate, and blind.

## THOMAS SHERIDAN

## (1687–1738)

### *To the Dean, When in England, in 1726*

You will excuse me, I suppose,
For sending rhyme instead of prose,
Because hot weather makes me lazy,
To write in metre is more easy.

While you are trudging London town,
I'm strolling Dublin, up and down;
While you converse with lords and dukes,
I have their betters here, my books:
Fixed in an elbow chair at ease,
I choose companions as I please.
I'd rather have one single shelf,
Than all my friends, except your self;
For after all that can be said,
Our best acquaintance, are the dead.
While you're in raptures with Faustina,
I'm charmed at home, with our Sheelina;
While you are starving there in state,
I'm cramming here with butcher's meat:
You say, when with those Lords you dine,
They treat you with the best of wine;
Burgundy, Cyprus, and Tockay,
Why so can we, as well as they.
No reason, my dear Dean,
But you should travel home again.

What though you mayn't in Ireland hope,
To find such folk as Gay and Pope:
If you with rhymers here would share,
But half the wit, that you can spare;
I'd lay twelve eggs, that in twelve days,
You'd make a doz'n of Popes and Gays.

Our weather's good, our sky is clear,
We've every joy, if you were here;
So lofty, and so bright a sky,
Was never seen by *Ireland's-Eye!*
I think it fit to let you know,
This week I shall to Quilca go;
To see McFayden's horny brothers,
First suck, and after bull their mothers.
To see alas, my withered trees!
To see what all the country sees!
My stunted quicks, my famished beeves,

My servants such a pack of thieves;
My shattered firs, my blasted oaks,
My house in common to all folks:
No cabbage for a single snail,
My turnips, carrots, parsnips, fail;
My no green peas, my few green sprouts,
My mother always in the pouts:
My horses rid, or gone astray,
My fish all stol'n, or run away:
My mutton lean, my pullets old,
My poultry starved, the corn all sold.

A man come now, from Quilca says,
*They've* stolen the locks from all your keys:
But what must fret and vex me more,
He says, they stole the keys before.
They've stol'n the knives from all the forks,
And half the cows from half the sturks;
Nay more, the fellow swears and vows,
They've stol'n the sturks from half the cows.
With many more accounts of woe,
Yet though the devil be there, I'll go:
'Twixt you and me, the reason's clear,
Because, I've more vexation here.

## JAMES WARD

(1691–1736)

### *The Smock Race at Finglas*

Now did the Bagpipe in hoarse Notes begin
Th' expected Signal to the neighb'ring Green;
While the mild Sun, in the Decline of Day,
Shoots from the distant West a cooler Ray.

Alarmed, the sweating Crowds forsake the Town,
Unpeopled Finglas is a Desert grown.
Joan quits her Cows, that with full Udders stand,
And low unheeded for the Milker's Hand.
The joyous Sound the distant Reapers hear,
Their Harvest leave, and to the Sport repair.
The Dublin Prentice, at the welcome Call,
In Hurry rises from his Cakes and Ale;
Handing the flaunting Seamstress o'er the Plains,
He struts a Beau among the homely Swains.

The Butcher's soggy Spouse amid the Throng,
Rubbed clean, and tawdry dressed, puffs slow along:
Her pond'rous Rings the wond'ring Mob behold,
And dwell on every Finger heaped with Gold:
Long to St. Patrick's filthy Shambles bound,
Surprised, she views the rural Scene around;
The distant Ocean there salutes her Eyes,
Here towering Hills in goodly Order rise;
There fruitful Valleys long extended lay,
Here Sheaves of Corn, and Cocks of fragrant Hay.
While whatso'er she hears, she smells, or sees,
Gives her fresh Transports; and she dotes on Trees.
Yet (hapless Wretch) the servile Thirst of Gain,
Can force her to her stinking Stall again.

Nor was the Country Justice wanting there,
To make a Penny of the Rogues that swear;
With supercilious Looks he awes the Green,
'Sirs, keep the Peace – I represent the Queen.'
Poor Paddy swears his whole Week's Gains away,
While my young Squires blaspheme, and nothing pay.
All on the mossy Turf confused were laid,
The jolly Rustic, and the buxom Maid,
Impatient for the Sport, too long delayed.

When lo, old Arbiter amid the Crowd,
Prince of the annual Games, proclaimed aloud,
'Ye Virgins, that intend to try the Race,
The swiftest wins a Smock enriched with Lace:
A Cambric Kerchief shall the next adorn;
And Kidden Gloves shall by the third be worn.'
This said, he high in Air displayed each Prize;
All view the waving Smock with longing Eyes.

Fair Oonah at the Barrier first appears,
Pride of the neighb'ring Mill, in Bloom of Years;
Her native Brightness borrows not one Grace,
Uncultivated Charms adorn her Face,
Her rosy Cheeks with modest Blushes glow,
At once her Innocence and Beauty show:
Oonah the Eyes of each Spectator draws,
What Bosom beats not in fair Oonah's Cause?

Tall as a Pine, Majestic Nora stood,
Her youthful Veins were filled with sprightly Blood,
Inured to Toils, in wholesome Gardens bred,
Exact in every Limb, and formed for Speed.

To thee, O Shevan, next what Praise is due?
Thy Youth and Beauty doubly strike the View,
Fresh as the Plum that keeps the Virgin Blue!
Each well deserves the Smock – but Fates decree
But One must wear it, though deserved by Three.

Now Side by Side the panting Rivals stand,
And fix their Eyes upon th' appointed Hand:
The Signal giv'n, spring forward to the Race;
Not famed Camilla ran with fleeter Pace.
Nora, as Light'ning swift, the rest o'er passed,
While Shevan fleetly ran, yet ran the last.
But Oonah, thou hadst Venus on thy side;
At Norah's Petticoat the Goddess plied,
And in a Trice the fatal String untied.
Quick stopped the Maid, nor would, to win the Prize,

Expose her hidden Charms to vulgar Eyes.
But while to tie the treach'rous Knot she stayed,
Both her glad Rivals pass the weeping Maid.
Now in despair she plies the Race again,
Not wingèd Winds dart swifter o'er the Plain:
She (while chaste Diana aids her hapless Speed)
Shevan outstripped – nor further could succeed.
For with redoubled Haste bright Oonah flies,
Seizes the Goal, and wins the noblest Prize.

Loud Shouts and Acclamations fill the Place,
Though Chance on Oonah had bestowed the Race;
Like Felim none rejoiced – a lovelier Swain
Ne'er fed a Flock on the Fingalian Plain.
Long he with secret Passion loved the Maid,
Now his increasing Flame itself betrayed.
Stripped for the Race how bright did she appear!
No Cov'ring hid her Feet, her Bosom bare,
And to the Wind she gave her flowing Hair.
A thousand Charms he saw, concealed before,
Those, yet concealed, he fancied still were more.

Felim, as Night came on, young Oonah wooed;
Soon willing Beauty was by Truth subdued.
No jarring Settlement their Bliss annoys,
No Licence needed to defer their Joys.
Oonah e'er Morn the Sweets of Wedlock tried;
The Smock she won a Virgin, wore a Bride.

## PEADAR Ó DOIRNÍN

(*c.*1700–*c.*1769)

### *The Mother's Lament for Her Child*

When they came looking for trouble I bared my body
Hoping to appeal to them. Child of the branches,
You smiled at your mother and then at your enemies
And chuckled before they wrenched you from my arms.

When the spear pierced your chest I registered the pain
And watched my own blood spurting. Suicidal now
I struggled with them, happy to die in the skirmish
And lie with you and our friends in unmarked graves.

They tied me to a tree and forced me to witness
Your death-throes, child of the tree of my heart and lungs,
Child of my crucifixion tree, child of the branches,
And then they stuck your screams on the end of a pike.

*Michael Longley*

## MATTHEW PILKINGTON

(1701–74)

### from *The Progress of Music in Ireland*

*Music* henceforward more Domestic grew,
Courts the thronged Towns, and from the Plains withdrew:
The Vagrant *Bard* his circling Visits pays,
And charms the Villages with venal Lays;
The solemn *Harp*, beneath his Shoulder placed,

With both his Arms is earnestly embraced,
Sweetly irregular, now swift, now slow,
With soft Variety his Numbers flow,
The shrill, the deep, the gentle, and the strong,
With pleasing Dissonance adorn his Song;
While through the Chords his Hands unwearied range,
The Music changing as his Fingers change.

The Crowd transported in Attention hung,
Their Breath in Silence sleeps upon the Tongue,
The *Wheels* forget to turn, the Labours cease,
And every Sound but *Music* sinks to Peace.
So when the *Thracian* charmed the Shades below,
And brought down Raptures to the Realms of Woe,
Despairing Ghosts from Labour stand released,
Each Wheel, each Instrument of Torture ceased;
The *Furies* drop their Whips, afflictive Pain
Suspends, with ghastly Smiles, her Iron Reign,
All Groans were stilled, all Sorrow lulled to Rest,
And every Care was hushed in every Breast.

*Joy* spreads her Wings o'er all the raptured *Isle*,
And bids each Face be brightened to a Smile.
Now Nature, pleased, her Gifts profusely pours,
To paint the cheerful Earth with od'rous Flowers:
So changed a Scene she wonders to survey,
And bids ev'n Things inanimate look gay.

## WILLIAM DUNKIN
## (*c*.1709–65)

### *The Poet's Prayer*

If e'er in thy sight I found favour, Apollo,
Defend me from all the disasters, which follow:
From the knaves, and the fools, and the fops of the time,
From the drudges in prose, and the triflers in rhyme:
From the patch-work, and toils of the royal sack-bibber,
Those dead birth-day odes, and the farces of CIBBER:
From servile attendance on men in high places,
Their worships, and honours, and lordships, and graces:
From long dedications to patrons unworthy,
Who hear, and receive, but will do nothing for thee:
From being caress'd, to be left in the lurch,
The tool of a party, in state, or in church:
From dull thinking blockheads, as sober, as Turks,
And petulant bards, who repeat their own works:
From all the gay things of a drawing-room show,
The sight of a Belle, and the smell of a Beau:
From busy back-biters, and tatlers, and carpers,
And scurvy acquaintance with fiddlers, and sharpers:
From old politicians, and coffee-house lectures,
The dreams of a chymist, and schemes of projectors:
From the fears of a jail, and the hopes of a pension,
The tricks of a gamester, and oaths of an ensign:
From shallow free-thinkers, in taverns disputing,
Nor ever confuted, nor ever confuting:
From the constant good fare of another man's board,
My lady's broad hints, and the jests of my lord:
From hearing old chymists prelecting *de oleo*,
And reading of Dutch commentators in folio:
From waiting, like GAY, whole years at Whitehall:
From the pride of great wits, and the envy of small:

From very fine ladies with very fine incomes,
Which they finely lay out on fine toys, and fine trincums:
From the pranks of ridottoes, and court-masquerades,
The snares of young jilts, and the spite of old maids:
From a saucy dull stage, and submitting to share
In an empty third night with a beggarly play'r:
From CURL, and such Printers, as would have me curst
To write second parts, let who will write the first:
From all pious patriots, who would, to their best,
Put on a new tax, and take off an old test:
From the faith of informers, the fangs of the law,
And the great rogues, who keep all the lesser in awe:
From a poor country-cure, that living interment,
With a wife, and no prospect of any preferment:
From scribbling for hire, when my credit is sunk,
To buy a new coat, and to line an old trunk:
From squires, who divert us with jokes at their tables,
Of hounds in their kennels, and nags in their stables:
From the nobles and commons, who bound in strict league are
To subscribe for no book, yet subscribe to Heidegger:
From the cant of fanatics, the jargon of schools,
The censures of wise men, and praises of fools:
From critics, who never read Latin, or Greek,
And pedants, who boast they read both all the week:
From borrowing wit, to repay it like BUDGEL,
Or lending, like POPE, to be paid by a cudgel.
If ever thou didst, or wilt ever befriend me,
From these, and such evils, APOLLO, defend me;
And let me be rather but honest with no-wit,
Than a noisy, nonsensical, half-witted poet.

## from *An Epistle to Robert Nugent, Esquire, with a Picture of Doctor Swift*

Ah! where is now the supple train,
That danced attendance on the Dean?
Say, where are those facetious folks,
Who shook with laughter at his jokes,

And with attentive rapture hung,
On wisdom, dropping from his tongue;
Who looked with high disdainful pride
On all the busy world beside,
And rated his productions more
Than treasures of Peruvian ore?

Good Christians! they with bended knees
Engulfed the wine, but loathe the lees,
Averting, (so the text commands,)
With ardent eyes and upcast hands,
The cup of sorrow from their lips,
And fly, like rats, from sinking ships.
While some, who by his friendship rose
To wealth, in concert with his foes
Run counter to their former track,
Like old Actæon's horrid pack
Of yelling mongrels, in requitals
To riot on their master's vitals,
And, where they cannot blast his laurels,
Attempt to stigmatize his morals,
Through Scandal's magnifying glass
His foibles view, but virtues pass,
And, on the ruins of his fame,
Erect an ignominious name.
So vermin foul, of vile extraction,
The spawn of dirt and putrefaction,
The sounder members traverse o'er,
But fix and fatten on a sore.
Hence! peace, ye wretches, who revile
His wit, his humour, and his style;
Since all the monsters which he drew
Were only meant to copy you;
And, if the colours be not fainter,
Arraign yourselves, and not the painter.

But, O! that He, who gave him breath,
Dread arbiter of life and death,
That He, the moving soul of all,

The sleeping spirit would recall,
And crown him with triumphant meeds,
For all his past heroic deeds,
In mansions of unbroken rest,
The bright republic of the blessed!
Irradiate his benighted mind
With living light of light refined;
And there the blank of thought employ
With objects of immortal joy!

Yet, while he drags the sad remains
Of life, slow-creeping through his veins,
Above the views of private ends,
The tributary Muse attends,
To prop his feeble steps, or shed
The pious tear around his bed.

So pilgrims, with devout complaints,
Frequent the graves of martyred saints,
Inscribe their worth in artless lines,
And, in their stead, embrace their shrines.

## DONNCHADH RUA MAC CON MARA
(1715–1810)

### *Epitaph for Tadgh Gaedhealach Ó Súilleabháin*

Thady is buried here; cast your eye this way, traveller:
This small patch of earth covers the poet in his greatness.
Here, alas, he lies dead; unshakeable fate overcame him,
Leaving the earth, his spirit has sought the high stars.
Who sings Ireland's praises now, who sings the deeds of
her heroes?
Gadelus being silent, the Irish muse sings no more.

Singing a holy song in learned measures he parted,
  As victor he parted to take up his certain reward.
Once he made famous verses in praise of God the Almighty,
  Now in rapture, for ever he sings forth his hymns.
Muses lament, your pupil has left us for ever,
  Eochad's son is now gone, silence falls over all.
Peace was his wish, peace he has sought in the heavens;
  In the realm of the Father, in the blest kingdom above.

*Peter Davidson (Latin)*

## DOROTHEA DUBOIS

(1728–74)

### *The Amazonian Gift*

Is Courage in a Woman's Breast,
  Less pleasing than in Man?
And is a smiling Maid allowed
  No weapon but a Fan?

'Tis true her Tongue, I've heard 'em say,
  Is Woman's chief Defence;
And if you'll b'lieve me, gentle Youths,
  I have no Aid from thence.

And some will say that sparkling Eyes
  More dang'rous are than Swords;
But I ne'er point my Eyes to kill,
  Nor put I trust in words.

Then, since the Arms that Women use,
  Successless are in me,
I'll take the Pistol, Sword or Gun,
  And thus equipped, live free.

The pattern of the *Spartan* Dame
  I'll copy as I can;
To Man, degen'rate Man, I'll give
  That simple Thing, a *Fan*.

## JOHN CUNNINGHAM
## (1729–73)

### *The Ant and Caterpillar: A Fable*

As an Ant, of his talents superiorly vain,
Was trotting, with consequence, over the plain,
A Worm, in his progress remarkably slow,
Cried – 'Bless your good worship wherever you go;
I hope your great mightiness won't take it ill,
I pay my respects with an hearty good-will.'
With a look of contempt and impertinent pride,
'Begone, you vile reptile,' his *Antship* replied;
'Go – go and lament your contemptible state,
But first – look at me – see my limbs how complete;
I guide all my motions with freedom and ease,
Run backward and forward, and turn when I please:
Of nature (grown weary) you shocking essay!
I spurn you thus from me – crawl out of my way.'
The reptile insulted, and vexed to the soul,
Crept onwards, and hid himself close in his hole;
But nature, determined to end his distress,
Soon sent him abroad in a Butterfly's dress.

Ere long the proud Ant, as repassing the road,
(Fatigued from the harvest, and tugging his load)
The beau on a violet bank he beheld,
Whose vesture, in glory, a monarch's excelled;
His plumage expanded – 'twas rare to behold
So lovely a mixture of purple and gold.

The Ant quite amazed at a figure so gay,
Bowed low with respect, and was trudging away.
'Stop, friend,' says the Butterfly – 'don't be surprised,
I once was the reptile you spurned and despised;
But now I can mount, in the sun-beams I play,
While you must, forever, drudge on in your way.'

MORAL

A wretch, though today he's o'er-loaded with sorrow,
May soar above those that oppressed him – tomorrow.

## OLIVER GOLDSMITH
## (1730–74)

### *The Deserted Village*

Sweet Auburn, loveliest village of the plain,
Where health and plenty cheered the labouring swain,
Where smiling spring its earliest visit paid,
And parting summer's lingering blooms delayed;
Dear lovely bowers of innocence and ease,
Seats of my youth, when every sport could please,
How often have I loitered o'er thy green,
Where humble happiness endeared each scene;
How often have I paused on every charm,
The sheltered cot, the cultivated farm,

The never failing brook, the busy mill,
The decent church that topped the neighbouring hill,
The hawthorn bush, with seats beneath the shade,
For talking age and whispering lovers made.
How often have I blessed the coming day,
When toil remitting lent its turn to play,
And all the village train, from labour free,
Led up their sports beneath the spreading tree,
While many a pastime circled in the shade,
The young contending as the old surveyed;
And many a gambol frolicked o'er the ground,
And sleights of art and feats of strength went round.
And still as each repeated pleasure tired,
Succeeding sports the mirthful band inspired;
The dancing pair that simply sought renown,
By holding out to tire each other down;
The swain mistrustless of his smutted face,
While secret laughter tittered round the place,
The bashful virgin's sidelong looks of love,
The matron's glance that would those looks reprove.
These were thy charms, sweet village; sports like these,
With sweet succession, taught even toil to please;
These round thy bowers their cheerful influence shed,
These were thy charms – but all these charms are fled.

Sweet smiling village, loveliest of the lawn,
Thy sports are fled and all thy charms withdrawn;
Amidst thy bowers the tyrant's hand is seen,
And desolation saddens all thy green:
One only master grasps the whole domain,
And half a tillage stints thy smiling plain;
No more thy glassy brook reflects the day,
But, choked with sedges, works its weedy way.
Along thy glades, a solitary guest,
The hollow-sounding bittern guards its nest;
Amidst thy desert walks the lapwing flies,
And tires their echoes with unvaried cries.

Sunk are thy bowers in shapeless ruin all,
And the long grass o'ertops the mouldering wall;
And trembling, shrinking from the spoiler's hand,
Far, far away, thy children leave the land.

Ill fares the land, to hastening ills a prey,
Where wealth accumulates and men decay:
Princes and lords may flourish or may fade;
A breath can make them, as a breath has made;
But a bold peasantry, their country's pride,
When once destroyed, can never be supplied.

A time there was, ere England's griefs began,
When every rood of ground maintained its man:
For him light labour spread her wholesome store,
Just gave what life required, but gave no more;
His best companions, innocence and health;
And his best riches, ignorance of wealth.

But times are altered; trade's unfeeling train
Usurp the land and dispossess the swain;
Along the lawn, where scattered hamlets rose,
Unwieldy wealth and cumbrous pomp repose;
And every want to opulence allied,
And every pang that folly pays to pride.
These gentle hours that plenty bade to bloom,
Those calm desires that asked but little room,
Those healthful sports that graced the peaceful scene,
Lived in each look and brightened all the green;
These, far departing, seek a kinder shore,
And rural mirth and manners are no more.

Sweet Auburn! parent of the blissful hour,
Thy glades forlorn confess the tyrant's power.
Here as I take my solitary rounds,
Amidst thy tangling walks and ruined grounds,
And, many a year elapsed, return to view
Where once the cottage stood, the hawthorn grew,

Here, as with doubtful, pensive steps I range,
Trace every scene, and wonder at the change,
Remembrance wakes with all her busy train,
Swells at my breast and turns the past to pain.

In all my wanderings round this world of care,
In all my griefs – and God has given my share –
I still had hopes my latest hours to crown,
Amidst these humble bowers to lay me down;
To husband out life's taper at the close,
And keep the flame from wasting by repose.
I still had hopes, for pride attends us still,
Amidst the swains to show my book-learned skill,
Around my fire an evening group to draw,
And tell of all I felt and all I saw;
And, as a hare, whom hounds and horns pursue,
Pants to the place from whence at first she flew,
I still had hopes, my long vexations past,
Here to return – and die at home at last.

O blest retirement, friend to life's decline,
Retreats from care, that never must be mine,
How happy he who crowns in shades like these
A youth of labour with an age of ease;
Who quits a world where strong temptations try
And, since 'tis hard to combat, learns to fly.
For him no wretches, born to work and weep,
Explore the mine or tempt the dangerous deep;
No surly porter stands in guilty state
To spurn imploring famine from the gate,
But on he moves to meet his latter end,
Angels around befriending virtue's friend;
Bends to the grave with unperceived decay,
While resignation gently slopes the way;
And, all his prospects brightening to the last,
His Heaven commences ere the world be past!

Sweet was the sound, when oft at evening's close
Up yonder hill the village murmur rose;
There, as I passed with careless steps and slow,
The mingling notes came softened from below;
The swain responsive as the milkmaid sung,
The sober herd that lowed to meet their young;
The noisy geese that gabbled o'er the pool,
The playful children just let loose from school;
The watchdog's voice that bayed the whispering wind,
And the loud laugh that spoke the vacant mind;
These all in sweet confusion sought the shade,
And filled each pause the nightingale had made.
But now the sounds of population fail,
No cheerful murmurs fluctuate in the gale,
No busy steps the grass-grown footway tread,
For all the bloomy flush of life is fled.
All but yon widowed, solitary thing
That feebly bends beside the plashy spring;
She, wretched matron, forced, in age, for bread,
To strip the brook with mantling cresses spread,
To pick her wintry faggot from the thorn,
To seek her nightly shed and weep till morn;
She only left of all the harmless train,
The sad historian of the pensive plain.

Near yonder copse, where once the garden smiled,
And still where many a garden flower grows wild;
There, where a few torn shrubs the place disclose,
The village preacher's modest mansion rose.
A man he was to all the country dear,
And passing rich with forty pounds a year;
Remote from towns he ran his godly race,
Nor e'er had changed, nor wished to change, his place;
Unpractised he to fawn, or seek for power,
By doctrines fashioned to the varying hour;
Far other aims his heart had learned to prize,
More skilled to raise the wretched than to rise.
His house was known to all the vagrant train,
He chid their wanderings, but relieved their pain;

The long-remembered beggar was his guest,
Whose beard descending swept his aged breast;
The ruined spendthrift, now no longer proud,
Claimed kindred there and had his claims allowed;
The broken soldier, kindly bade to stay,
Sat by his fire and talked the night away;
Wept o'er his wounds or tales of sorrow done,
Shouldered his crutch and showed how fields were won.
Pleased with his guests, the good man learned to glow,
And quite forgot their vices in their woe;
Careless their merits or their faults to scan,
His pity gave ere charity began.

Thus to relieve the wretched was his pride,
And even his failings leaned to virtue's side;
But in his duty prompt at every call,
He watched and wept, he prayed and felt, for all.
And, as a bird each fond endearment tries
To tempt its new-fledged offspring to the skies,
He tried each art, reproved each dull delay,
Allured to brighter worlds and led the way.

Beside the bed where parting life was laid,
And sorrow, guilt, and pain by turns dismayed,
The reverend champion stood. At his control,
Despair and anguish fled the struggling soul;
Comfort came down the trembling wretch to raise,
And his last faltering accents whispered praise.

At church, with meek and unaffected grace,
His looks adorned the venerable place;
Truth from his lips prevailed with double sway,
And fools, who came to scoff, remained to pray.
The service past, around the pious man,
With steady zeal, each honest rustic ran;
Even children followed with endearing wile,
And plucked his gown, to share the good man's smile.
His ready smile a parent's warmth expressed,
Their welfare pleased him and their cares distressed;

To them his heart, his love, his griefs were given,
But all his serious thoughts had rest in Heaven.
As some tall cliff, that lifts its awful form,
Swells from the vale and midway leaves the storm,
Though round its breast the rolling clouds are spread,
Eternal sunshine settles on its head.

Beside yon straggling fence that skirts the way,
With blossomed furze unprofitably gay,
There, in his noisy mansion, skilled to rule,
The village master taught his little school;
A man severe he was and stern to view;
I knew him well, and every truant knew;
Well had the boding tremblers learned to trace
The day's disasters in his morning face;
Full well they laughed with counterfeited glee,
At all his jokes, for many a joke had he;
Full well the busy whisper circling round,
Conveyed the dismal tidings when he frowned;
Yet he was kind, or, if severe in aught,
The love he bore to learning was in fault;
The village all declared how much he knew;
'Twas certain he could write and cipher too;
Lands he could measure, terms and tides presage,
And e'en the story ran that he could gauge.
In arguing too, the parson owned his skill,
For even though vanquished, he could argue still;
While words of learned length and thundering sound
Amazed the gazing rustics ranged around,
And still they gazed, and still the wonder grew,
That one small head could carry all he knew.

But past is all his fame. The very spot,
Where many a time he triumphed, is forgot.
Near yonder thorn, that lifts its head on high,
Where once the signpost caught the passing eye,
Low lies that house where nut-brown draughts inspired,
Where greybeard mirth and smiling toil retired,
Where village statesmen talked with looks profound,

And news much older than their ale went round.
Imagination fondly stoops to trace
The parlour splendours of that festive place;
The white-washed wall, the nicely sanded floor,
The varnished clock that clicked behind the door;
The chest contrived a double debt to pay,
A bed by night, a chest of drawers by day;
The pictures placed for ornament and use,
The twelve good rules, the royal game of goose;
The hearth, except when winter chilled the day,
With aspen boughs and flowers and fennel gay;
While broken teacups, wisely kept for show,
Ranged o'er the chimney, glistened in a row.

Vain, transitory splendours! Could not all
Reprieve the tottering mansion from its fall!
Obscure it sinks, nor shall it more impart
An hour's importance to the poor man's heart;
Thither no more the peasant shall repair
To sweet oblivion of his daily care;
No more the farmer's news, the barber's tale,
No more the woodman's ballad shall prevail;
No more the smith his dusky brow shall clear,
Relax his ponderous strength and lean to hear;
The host himself no longer shall be found
Careful to see the mantling bliss go round;
Nor the coy maid, half willing to be pressed,
Shall kiss the cup to pass it to the rest.

Yes! let the rich deride, the proud disdain,
These simple blessings of the lowly train.
To me more dear, congenial to my heart,
One native charm than all the gloss of art;
Spontaneous joys, where nature has its play,
The soul adopts and owns their first-born sway;
Lightly they frolic o'er the vacant mind,
Unenvied, unmolested, unconfined:
But the long pomp, the midnight masquerade,
With all the freaks of wanton wealth arrayed,

In these, ere triflers half their wish obtain,
The toiling pleasure sickens into pain;
And, even while fashion's brightest arts decoy,
The heart distrusting asks, if this be joy.

Ye friends to truth, ye statesmen, who survey
The rich man's joys increase, the poor's decay,
'Tis yours to judge how wide the limits stand
Between a splendid and an happy land.
Proud swells the tide with loads of freighted ore,
And shouting Folly hails them from her shore;
Hoards, even beyond the miser's wish abound,
And rich men flock from all the world around.
Yet count our gains. This wealth is but a name
That leaves our useful products still the same.
Not so the loss. The man of wealth and pride
Takes up a space that many poor supplied;
Space for his lake, his park's extended bounds,
Space for his horses, equipage and hounds;
The robe that wraps his limbs in silken sloth
Has robbed the neighbouring fields of half their growth;
His seat, where solitary sports are seen,
Indignant spurns the cottage from the green;
Around the world each needful product flies,
For all the luxuries the world supplies;
While thus the land, adorned for pleasure all,
In barren splendour feebly waits the fall.

As some fair female unadorned and plain,
Secure to please while youth confirms her reign,
Slights every borrowed charm that dress supplies,
Nor shares with art the triumph of her eyes;
But when those charms are passed, for charms are frail,
When time advances and when lovers fail,
She then shines forth, solicitous to bless,
In all the glaring impotence of dress:
Thus fares the land, by luxury betrayed,
In nature's simplest charms at first arrayed;
But verging to decline, its splendours rise,

Its vistas strike, its palaces surprise;
While scourged by famine from the smiling land,
The mournful peasant leads his humble band;
And while he sinks, without one arm to save,
The country blooms – a garden, and a grave.

Where then, ah where, shall poverty reside,
To 'scape the pressure of contiguous pride?
If to some common's fenceless limits strayed,
He drives his flock to pick the scanty blade,
Those fenceless fields the sons of wealth divide,
And even the bare-worn common is denied.

If to the city sped – what waits him there?
To see profusion that he must not share;
To see ten thousand baneful arts combined
To pamper luxury and thin mankind;
To see those joys the sons of pleasure know
Extorted from his fellow creature's woe.
Here, while the courtier glitters in brocade,
There the pale artist plies the sickly trade;
Here, while the proud their long-drawn pomps display,
There the black gibbet glooms beside the way.
The dome where Pleasure holds her midnight reign
Here, richly decked, admits the gorgeous train;
Tumultuous grandeur crowds the blazing square,
The rattling chariots clash, the torches glare.
Sure scenes like these no troubles e'er annoy!
Sure these denote one universal joy!
Are these thy serious thoughts? – ah, turn thine eyes
Where the poor, houseless, shivering female lies.
She once, perhaps, in village plenty blest,
Has wept at tales of innocence distressed;
Her modest looks the cottage might adorn,
Sweet as the primrose peeps beneath the thorn;
Now lost to all; her friends, her virtue fled,
Near her betrayer's door she lays her head,

And, pinched with cold and shrinking from the shower,
With heavy heart deplores that luckless hour,
When idly first, ambitious of the town,
She left her wheel and robes of country brown.

Do thine, sweet Auburn, thine, the loveliest train,
Do thy fair tribes participate her pain?
Even now, perhaps, by cold and hunger led,
At proud men's doors they ask a little bread!

Ah, no. To distant climes, a dreary scene,
Where half the convex world intrudes between,
Through torrid tracts with fainting steps they go,
Where wild Altama murmurs to their woe.
Far different there from all that charmed before
The various terrors of that horrid shore:
Those blazing suns that dart a downward ray,
And fiercely shed intolerable day;
Those matted woods where birds forget to sing,
But silent bats in drowsy clusters cling;
Those poisonous fields with rank luxuriance crowned,
Where the dark scorpion gathers death around;
Where at each step the stranger fears to wake
The rattling terrors of the vengeful snake;
Where crouching tigers wait their hapless prey,
And savage men more murderous still than they;
While oft in whirls the mad tornado flies,
Mingling the ravaged landscape with the skies.
Far different these from every former scene,
The cooling brook, the grassy-vested green,
The breezy covert of the warbling grove,
That only sheltered thefts of harmless love.

Good Heaven! what sorrows gloomed that parting day,
That called them from their native walks away;
When the poor exiles, every pleasure past,
Hung round their bowers and fondly looked their last,
And took a long farewell and wished in vain
For seats like these beyond the western main;

And shuddering still to face the distant deep,
Returned and wept, and still returned to weep.
The good old sire the first prepared to go
To new found worlds, and wept for others' woe;
But for himself, in conscious virtue brave,
He only wished for worlds beyond the grave.
His lovely daughter, lovelier in her tears,
The fond companion of his helpless years,
Silent went next, neglectful of her charms,
And left a lover's for a father's arms.
With louder plaints the mother spoke her woes,
And blessed the cot where every pleasure rose;
And kissed her thoughtless babes with many a tear,
And clasped them close, in sorrow doubly dear;
Whilst her fond husband strove to lend relief
In all the silent manliness of grief.

O luxury! thou cursed by Heaven's decree,
How ill exchanged are things like these for thee!
How do thy potions with insidious joy
Diffuse their pleasures only to destroy!
Kingdoms, by thee to sickly greatness grown,
Boast of a florid vigour not their own.
At every draught more large and large they grow,
A bloated mass of rank unwieldy woe;
Till sapped their strength and every part unsound,
Down, down they sink and spread a ruin round.

Even now the devastation is begun,
And half the business of destruction done;
Even now, methinks, as pondering here I stand,
I see the rural virtues leave the land.
Down where yon anchoring vessel spreads the sail,
That idly waiting flaps with every gale,
Downward they move, a melancholy band,
Pass from the shore and darken all the strand.
Contented toil and hospitable care,
And kind connubial tenderness are there;
And piety, with wishes placed above,

And steady loyalty and faithful love.
And thou, sweet Poetry, thou loveliest maid,
Still first to fly where sensual joys invade;
Unfit, in these degenerate times of shame,
To catch the heart or strike for honest fame;
Dear charming nymph, neglected and decried,
My shame in crowds, my solitary pride;
Thou source of all my bliss and all my woe,
That found'st me poor at first and keep'st me so;
Thou guide by which the nobler arts excel,
Thou nurse of every virtue, fare thee well!
Farewell, and oh, where'er thy voice be tried,
On Torno's cliffs or Pambamarca's side,
Whether where equinoctial fervours glow,
Or winter wraps the polar world in snow,
Still let thy voice, prevailing over time,
Redress the rigours of the inclement clime;
Aid slighted truth: with thy persuasive strain
Teach erring man to spurn the rage of gain;
Teach him that states of native strength possessed,
Though very poor, may still be very blest;
That trade's proud empire hastes to swift decay,
As ocean sweeps the laboured mole away;
While self-dependent power can time defy,
As rocks resist the billows and the sky.

## from *Retaliation*

Of old, when Scarron his companions invited,
Each guest brought his dish, and the feast was united.
If our landlord supplies us with beef and with fish,
Let each guest bring himself, and he brings the best dish:
Our Dean shall be venison, just fresh from the plains;
Our Burke shall be tongue, with a garnish of brains;
Our Will shall be wild-fowl, of excellent flavour,
And Dick with his pepper shall heighten their savour;
Our Cumberland's sweet-bread its place shall obtain,
And Douglas's pudding, substantial and plain;

Our Garrick's a salad, for in him we see
Oil, vinegar, sugar, and saltness agree;
To make out the dinner, full certain I am
That Ridge is anchovy, and Reynolds is lamb;
That Hickey's a capon, and by the same rule,
Magnanimous Goldsmith a gooseberry fool.
At a dinner so various, at such a repast,
Who'd not be a glutton and stick to the last?
Here, waiter! more wine, let me sit while I'm able,
Till all my companions sink under the table;
Then, with chaos and blunders encircling my head,
Let me ponder, and tell what I think of the dead.

Here lies the good Dean, reunited to earth,
Who mixed reason with pleasure and wisdom with mirth:
If he had any faults, he has left us in doubt:
At least, in six weeks I could not find 'em out;
Yet some have declared, and it can't be denied 'em,
That sly-boots was cursedly cunning to hide 'em.

Here lies our good Edmund, whose genius was such,
We scarcely can praise it or blame it too much;
Who, born for the universe, narrowed his mind,
And to party gave up what was meant for mankind;
Though fraught with all learning, kept straining his throat
To persuade Tommy Townshend to lend him a vote;
Who, too deep for his hearers, still went on refining,
And thought of convincing, while they thought of dining;
Though equal to all things, for all things unfit;
Too nice for a statesman, too proud for a wit;
For a patriot, too cool; for a drudge, disobedient;
And too fond of the *right* to pursue the *expedient*.
In short, 'twas his fate, unemployed or in place, sir,
To eat mutton cold and cut blocks with a razor.

## EOGHAN RUA Ó SÚILLEABHÁIN (c.1748–84)

### *Poet to Blacksmith*

Séamus, make me a side-arm to take on the earth,
A suitable tool for digging and grubbing the ground,
Lightsome and pleasant to lean on or cut with or lift,
Tastily finished and trim and right for the hand.

No trace of the hammer to show on the sheen of the blade,
The thing to have purchase and spring and be fit for the strain,
The shaft to be socketed in dead true and dead straight,
And I'll work with the gang till I drop and never complain.

The plate and the edge of it not to be wrinkly or crooked –
I see it well shaped from the anvil and sharp from the file;
The grain of the wood and the line of the shaft nicely fitted,
And best thing of all, the ring of it, sweet as a bell.

*Seamus Heaney*

### *A Magic Mist*

Through the deep night a magic mist led me
   like a simpleton roaming the land,
no friends of my bosom beside me,
   an outcast in places unknown.
I stretched out dejected and tearful
   in a nut-sheltered wood all alone
and prayed to the bright King of Glory
   with 'Mercy!' alone on my lips.

My heart, I declare, full of turmoil
  in that wood with no human sound nigh,
the thrush's sweet voice the sole pleasure,
  ever singing its tunes on each bough.
Then a noble *sídh*-girl sat beside me
  like a saint in her figure and form:
in her countenance roses contended
  with white – and I know not which lost.

Furrowed thick, yellow-twisting and golden
  was the lady's hair down to her shoes,
her brows without flaw, and like amber
  her luring eye, death to the brave.
Sweet, lovely, delicious – pure music –
  the harp-notes of the *sídh* from her lips,
breasts rounded, smooth, chalk-white, most proper,
  never marred by another, I swear.

Though lost to myself till that moment,
  with love for the lady I throbbed
and I found myself filled with great pleasure
  that she was directed my way.
How it fell, I write out in these verses,
  how I let my lips speak unrestrained,
the sweet things that I told the fair maiden
  as we stretched on the green mountain-slope:

'Are you, languid-eyed lady who pierced me
  with love for your face and your form,
the Fair-One caused hordes to be slaughtered
  as they write in the Battle of Troy?
Or the mild royal girl who let languish
  the chief of Boru and his troop?
Or the queen who decreed that the great prince
  from Howth follow far in pursuit?'

Delicious, sweet, tender, she answered,
  ever shedding tears down in her pain:
'I am none of those women you speak of,
  and I see that you don't know my clan.
I'm the bride wed in bliss for a season,
  under right royal rule, to the King
over Caiseal of Conn and of Eoghan
  who ruled undisputed o'er Fódla.

'Gloomy my state, sad and mournful,
  by horned tyrants daily devoured,
and heavy oppressed by grim blackguards
  while my prince is set sailing abroad.
I look to the great Son of Glory
  to send my lion back to his sway
in his strong native towns, in good order,
  to flay the swarth goats with his blades.'

'Mild, golden-haired, courteous fair lady,
  of true royal blood, and no lie,
I mourn for your plight among blackguards,
  sad and joyless, dark under a pall.
If your King to his strong native mansions
  the Son of Glory should send, in His aid,
those swarth goats – swift, freely and willing –
  with shot would I joyfully flay!

'If our Stuart returned o'er the ocean
  to the lands of Inis Áilge in full course
with a fleet of Louis' men, and the Spaniard's,
  by dint of joy truly I'd be
on a prancing pure steed of swift mettle
  ever sluicing them out with much shot
– after which I'd not injure my spirit
  standing guard for the rest of my life.'

*Thomas Kinsella*

## *Rodney's Glory*

Give ear, ye British hearts of gold,
That e'er disdain to be controlled,
Good news to you I will unfold,
'Tis of brave Rodney's glory,
Who always bore a noble heart,
And from his colours ne'er would start,
But always took his country's part
Against each foe who dared t'oppose
Or blast the bloom of England's Rose,
So now observe my story.

'Twas in the year of Eighty Two,
The Frenchmen know full well 'tis true,
Brave Rodney did their fleet subdue,
Not far from old Fort Royal.
Full early by the morning's light,
The proud De Grasse appeared in sight,
And thought brave Rodney to affright,
With colours spread at each mast-head,
Long pendants, too, both white and red,
A signal for engagement.

Our Admiral then he gave command,
That each should at his station stand,
'Now, for the sake of Old England,
We'll show them British valour.'
Then we the British Flag displayed,
No tortures could our hearts invade,
Both sides began to cannonade,
Their mighty shot we valued not,
We plied our 'Irish pills' so hot,
Which put them in confusion.

This made the Frenchmen to combine,
And draw their shipping in a line,
To sink our fleet was their design,
   But they were far mistaken;
Broadside for broadside we let fly,
Till they in hundreds bleeding lie,
The seas were all of crimson dye,
Full deep we stood in human blood,
Surrounded by a scarlet flood,
   But still we fought courageous.

So loud our cannons that the roar
Re-echoed round the Indian shore,
Both ships and rigging suffered sore,
   We kept such constant firing;
Our guns did roar and smoke did rise,
And clouds of sulphur veiled the skies,
Which filled De Grasse with wild surprise;
Both Rodney's guns and Paddy's sons
Make echo shake where'er they come,
   They fear no French or Spaniards.

From morning's dawn to fall of night,
We did maintain this bloody fight,
Being still regardless of their might,
   We fought like Irish heroes.
Though on the deck did bleeding lie
Many of our men in agony,
We resolved to conquer or die,
To gain the glorious victory,
And would rather suffer to sink or die
   Than offer to surrender.

So well our quarters we maintained,
Five captured ships we have obtained,
And thousands of their men were slain,
   During this hot engagement;
Our British metal flew like hail,
Until at length the French turned tail,

Drew in their colours and made sail
In deep distress, as you may guess,
And when they got in readiness
  They sailed down to Fort Royal.

Now may prosperity attend
Brave Rodney and his Irishmen,
And may he never want a friend
  While he shall reign commander;
Success to our Irish officers,
Seamen bold and jolly tars,
Who like darling sons of Mars
Take delight in the fight
And vindicate bold England's right
  And die for Erin's glory.

## BRIAN MERRIMAN

## (*c.*1749–1805)

### *Cúirt an Mheán-Oíche* (*The Midnight Court*)

'Twas my custom to stroll by a clear winding stream,
With my boots full of dew from the lush meadow green,
Near a neck of the woods where the mountain holds sway,
Without danger or fear at the dawn of the day.
The sight of Lough Graney would dazzle my eyes,
As the countryside sparkled beneath the blue skies;
Uplifting to see how the mountains were stacked,
Each head peeping over a neighbouring back.
It would lighten the heart, be it listless with age,
Enfeebled by folly, or cardiac rage –
Your wherewithal racked by financial disease –
To perceive through a gap in the wood full of trees
A squadron of ducks in a shimmering bay,

Escorting the swan on her elegant way,
The trout on the rise with its mouth to the light,
While the perch swims below like a speckledy sprite,
And the billows of blue become foam as they break
With a thunderous crash on the shores of the lake,
And the birds in the trees whistle bird-songs galore,
The deer gallop lightly though woods dark as yore,
Where trumpeting huntsmen and hounds of the hunt
Chase the shadow of Reynard, who leads from the front.

Yesterday morning, a cloudless blue sky
Bore the signs of another hot day in July;
Bright Phoebus arose from the darkness of night,
And got back to his business of spreading the light.
Around me were branches of trees in full leaf
And glades decked with ferns of a sylvan motif,
With flowers and herbs so profusely in train
It would banish all thoughts of despair from your brain.
Beat out as I was and in need of a doze,
I laid myself down where a grassy bank rose
By the side of a ditch, in arboreal shade,
Where I stretched out my feet, and pillowed my head.
So I shut down my brain, and the lids of my eyes,
With my hat on my face to discourage the flies,
And dropped off to sleep, quite composed and serene,
When I found myself sunk in a horrible dream
That jolted my senses, and grieved my heart sore;
Lying dead to the world, I was shook to the core.

Not long was my slumber when nearby, thought I,
The land rocked and rolled, and a turbulent sky
Brought a storm from the north, an incredible gale
That lit up the harbour as fire fell like hail.
In the blink of an eyelid – a thing I still see –
A female approached from the side of the quay,
Broad-arsed and big-bellied, built like a tank,
And angry as thunder from shoulder to shank.
Of her stature I made an intelligent guess
Of some twenty-one feet, while the hem of her dress

Trailed five yards behind, through the mire and the muck,
And her mantle was slobbered with horrible guck.
Majestic and mighty to gaze on her brow,
Which was furrowed and gullied as if by a plough;
Formidable, fearsome the leer of her grin,
Purple-gummed, ulcered, with no teeth within.
Dear God! how she waved like a wand in her fist
A flagpole, so fiercely as not to be missed,
With a brazen plaque stuck to the top of a spike,
On which were inscribed a bum-bailiff's rights.

Then gruffly and roughly she uttered this spake:
'Rouse yourself, stir yourself, sluggard, awake!
Shame on you, blame on you, slumped on your ear,
While the court is convened and the thousands draw near!
Not a court without standing, or statute, or code,
Nor an imported court of the plundering mode,
But a court that is ruled by a civilized throng,
Where the weak are empowered and women are strong;
And the people of Ireland can hold their heads high
That the fairy host gathers from far and from nigh
To argue the case for two days and two nights
In the many roomed mansion on Moygraney's heights.
And great is the grief on the mien of their king,
And his fairy assembly, ranged ring on ring,
And all of those others collectively there,
That the nation has suffered such great disrepair –
An old race indeed, without freedom or land,
Without rights to its rent, and its leaders all banned,
The rich farmlands ruined, their bounty replaced
By brambles and nettles and fields full of waste.
The nobles we had are all scattered abroad,
And upstarts and gangsters now take up the rod,
Their sport to deceive, and to rob without shame,
To exploit the blind and the halt and the lame.
O bleak is the prospect and black is the day,
When Justice lies shackled, her laws disarrayed,
The weak so enfeebled, infallibly tied
To a future of fraud where no fairness abides;

Duplicitous lawyers, and crooks on the bench,
Hush money, slush funds, and all conscience quenched,
Where backhanders buy you a piece of the judge,
And everyone knows that the law is a fudge.

*Ciaran Carson*

To add to which, the whole assembly
Decreed on the Bible this very day:
The youth has failed, declined, gone fallow –
Bad news and bad marks, sir, for you.
In living memory, with birth rates fallen
And marriage in Ireland on the wane,
The country's life has been dissipated,
Pillage and death have combined to waste it.
Blame arrogant kings, blame emigration,
But it's you and your spunkless generation.
You're a source blocked off that won't refill.
You have failed your women, one and all.

Think of the way they're made and moulded,
The flush and zest in their flesh and blood –
Those easy ladies half on offer
And the big strait-laced ones, all ignored.
Why aren't they all consoled and gravid,
In full proud sail with their breasts in bud?
Say but the word and the clustered fruit
Will be piled like windfalls round your feet.

So the meeting pondered the country's crisis
And the best opinions agreed on this:
That one of their own should be deputed
To come back here to adjudicate.
Then Aoibheall rises, as Munster's guardian
And Craglee's peerless fairy queen
And offers to leave the fairy palace
And go to Thomond to hear the case.
And, honest princess, she makes a promise
To come down hard on the law's abuse.

Might without right to be defeated
And right as right reinstated straight.
So hereinafter, greasing the palm
Of pimp or madam or sycophant
Won't work or avail, for it's not an inch
Now that Her Grace is boss of the bench.
Already at Feakle the court's in session
That you must answer. The pressure's on
For you to appear. So move. And fast.
Move or I'll make you move, you bast—.'

With that she crooked her staff in my cape
And hooked me behind and hauled me up
And we went like hell over glen and hill
To Moinmoy Church, by the gable wall.

And there (I am sure) lit torches showed
A handsome, grand, well-built abode,
A stately, steadfast, glittering space,
Accessible and commodious.
And I saw a lovely vision woman
Ensconced on the bench of law and freedom,
And saw her fierce, fleet guard of honour
Rank upon rank in throngs around her.
I saw then too rooms filling full,
Crowding with women from wall to wall,
And saw this other heavenly beauty
With her lazy eye, on her dignity,
Seductive, pouting, with curling locks,
Biding her time in the witness box.
Her hair spilled down, loosed tress on tress,
And a hurt expression marked her face;
She was full of fight, with a glinting eye,
Hot on the boil, ill-set and angry –
Yet for all her spasms, she couldn't speak
For her hefts and huffing had made her weak.
She looked like death or a living death wish
She was so cried out; but straight as a rush,
She stood to the fore as a witness stands

Flailing and wailing and wringing hands.
And she kept it up; she raved and screeched
Till sighing restored her powers of speech.
Then her downlook went, her colour rose,
She dried her eyes and commenced as follows:

'A thousand welcomes! And bless Your Highness!
Aoibheall of Crag, our prophetess!
Our daylight's light, our moon forever,
Our hope of life when the weeping's over!
O head of all the hosted sisters,
Thomond can thole no more! Assist us!
My cause, my case, the reason why
My plea's prolonged so endlessly
Until I'm raving and round the twist
Like a maenad whirled in a swirl of mist –
The reason why is the unattached
And unprovided for, unmatched
Women I know, like flowers in a bed
Nobody's dibbled or mulched or weeded
Or trimmed or watered or ever tended;
So here they are, unhusbanded,
Unasked, untouched, beyond conception –
And, needless to say, I'm no exception.
I'm scorched and tossed, a sorry case
Of nerves and drives and neediness,
Depressed, obsessed, awake at night,
Unused, unsoothed, disconsolate,
A throbbing ache, a dumb discord,
My mind and bed like a kneading board.
O Warden of the Crag, incline!
Observe the plight of Ireland's women,
For if things go on like this, then fuck it!
The men will have to be abducted!

*Seamus Heaney*

'By the time it strikes them to take a partner
there isn't a person left would have them
– limp, sucked dry, exhausted ancients.
If it happens at all, in the heat of youth,
that a man out of seven, on feeling his beard,
goes out with a girl, it's never some mild one
nicely settled in seed and breed,
well-mannered, gentle, soft, and shapely,
who can seat herself or make an entrance,
but an icy dullard or woeful ghost
with an ill-fitting dowry gathered in pain.
It's a scald to my heart and drives me wild
with my brain worn out and all its broodings
ill, at an ebb, in pain, exhausted,
lamenting and wailing – a pitiful leavings –
when I see a courageous, cordial man,
busy and bouncing, alive and alert,
knowing and skilful, sturdy and warm,
sweet-cheeked, laughing, loving and fine,
or a firm-footed boy, well-balanced and brisk,
commanding and proper, well-fashioned and fair,
bargained and bought and in wedlock bound
to a worm or a fool, a hag or a half-wit
slovenly slut of an indolent girl,
sullen and sulky, a whinge and a shame,
ignorant, fussy, a gossipy nag,
nosy and nasty, ill-tempered, inert.
Destruction and ruin! Some ignorant sulk,
some trollop all feet, with her hair unfixed,
is being bound this night, and it burns me sore
– for where is my fault I'm not chosen first?

'Where is the cause I remain unloved
and I so slender, fine and shy?
My mouth so good, and my teeth and smile?
I've a glowing complexion, a tender brow.
I have delicate eyes and a forelock fine,
curled and plaited and looped and twined.

My features, free from dirt or grime,
are fine-drawn, shapely, timid and bright.
My throat and bosom, hands and fingers,
seize between them beauty's prize.
Observe my waist! How slight the bones.
No baldness here. Am I bent, or stiff?
Bum, body and limbs: no cause for shame.
And safe under cover my nameless gem.
I'm no slut of a girl, no slug of a woman,
but handsome and good, delightful and fair,
no sloven or slattern or streel in a mess,
no ill-mannered heap you can't ease or please,
no useless hussy or festering mope,
but a maiden as choice as choice can be!

'If my spirits were sagging like some of the neighbours,
stupid and slow, without wisdom or wit
or vision or verve in the use of my looks,
I'd have cause to be crying, and fall in despair.
But I never went out in the public gaze,
at weddings or wakes, with old or young,
off at the sports or a dance or the races,
mixing with people all over the plain,
but I dressed at my ease and with never a flaw
in the finest of garments from head to foot,
my hair wound round, with its share of powder,
the back of my bonnet starched and set,
with a shiny hood and no shortage of ribbons,
a gown all speckled and finished with frills;
and never was missing an airy facing,
handsome and fine, on my crimson cloak,
or flowers and fruits and birds in plenty
on my striped and queenly cambric slip,
or shaped and slender dainty heels,
shiny and high, screwed under my shoes,
or buckles and rings and silken gloves,
bracelets and hoops or the dearest lace.

'Careful, then; I'm not fearful or shy,
a sheepish child or a witless fool,
lonely and worried or crying in fear,
feeble or touched, unbalanced or blind.
I won't be dodging the people's gaze;
my face and my brow are proud and high.
And I'm certainly always on display
at every field where the game's fought hard,
at dances, hurling, races, courting,
bone-fires, gossip and dissipation,
at fairs and markets and Sunday Mass
to see and be seen, and choose a man.
But I've wasted my sense in the hopeless hunt;
they deceived me ever and wrung my guts
after my wooing and lapse and love
and all I've suffered of awful anguish,
and all I spent on tossing the cups,
on muttering women, and hags with cards!

'There isn't a trick you can hear or read of
when the moon is new, or reaches the full,
at Shrovetide, Samhain – the whole year through –
but I've found it silly to seek for sense in it.
I never could settle me down to sleep
without fruit in a sock beneath my ear;
I found it no trouble to fast devoutly
– three vigils I'd swallow no bite or sup;
I'd rinse my shift against the stream
for a whisper in dream from my future spouse;
many a time I have swept the corn-stack,
I've left my nails and my hair in the ash,
I'd place the flail behind the fork
and quietly under my pillow, a spade;
in the kiln by the ford, I'd place my distaff,
in Raghnall's lime-kiln, my ball of thread,
out in the street, a seed of flax,
and under my bedding a head of cabbage.
There isn't a trick I have just related
but I prayed of the Devil and all his brethren!

But the point and purpose of my tale
is I've done my best and I've still no man;
hence, alas, my long recital!
In the knot of the years I am tangled tight,
I am heading hard for my days of grey
and I fear that I'll die without anyone asking.

'O Pearl of Heaven! I call and cry,
I beg and beseech! My soul upon you!
Don't let me wander and streel about,
a slovenly hag without vigour or bloom,
stale and unwanted at stingy hearths,
without family, friends, relief or rest.
Thunder and lightning! Jesus' blood!
I was fooled – an idiot: whole, entire –
while the pick of the worst and the fools of Fódla
got their hands on the goods before my eyes:
Sadhbh has a rich and restful brute,
Muireann is merry, her face to her mate,
Mór and Marcella are buried in comfort,
jeering between them and joking about me.
Sláine and Síle are skittish and easy
and Áine and Cecily, their litters around them;
and more, likewise, of the nation's women,
and me as I am, without issue or milk,
a long time useless, worn by weakness.

'But grant me time – the cure is at hand:
a matter of herbs decayed and devilish
and magical charms, to gain me yet
a handsome boy, some elegant heir,
and win me over his love and affection.
A lot of the kind I have seen employed
and I could make use of the same devices . . .
A sterling aid in arranging pairs
is the bite of an apple, or powdered herbs
– little Balls-of-Joy or Lumps-of-Dung,
the Shining Splicer, or Hammer-the-Hole,
Nannygoat's-Bait or Maiden's Dart,

Goldenlove – all lustful spells,
the burning up of leaves in secret,
and more of the like that shouldn't be learned.
It's a thing of great wonder, Thomond over,
that the maiden yonder obtained a spouse
– but she told me at Shrove, in confidence
(and the wedding occurred on the verge of Samhain!)
that she ate and drank, this lady fair,
nothing but bog-flies burnt in ale!
I'm a long time waiting. I need release.
Enough delay. Spur on with speed!
If your circuit-round can't cure my colic
serious measures I'll have to take!'

*Thomas Kinsella*

Then up there jumps from a neighbouring chair
A little old man with a spiteful air,
Staggering legs and panting breath,
And a look in his eye like poison and death;
And this apparition stumps up the hall
And says to the girl in the hearing of all:
'Damnation take you, you bastard's bitch,
Got by a tinkerman under a ditch!
No wonder the seasons are all upsot,
Nor every beating Ireland got;
Decline in decency and manners,
And the cows gone dry and the price of bonhams!
Mavrone! what more can we expect
With Doll and Moll and the way they're decked?
You slut of ill-fame, allow your betters
To tell the court how you learned your letters!
Your seed and breed for all your brag
Were tramps to a man with rag and bag;
I knew your da and what passed for his wife,
And he shouldered his traps to the end of his life,
An aimless lout without friend or neighbour,
Knowledge or niceness, wit or favour:
The breeches he wore were riddled with holes

And his boots without a tack of the soles.
Believe me, friends, if you sold at a fair,
Himself and his wife, his kids and gear,
When the costs were met, by the Holy Martyr,
You'd still go short for a glass of porter.
But the devil's child has the devil's cheek –
You that never owned cow nor sheep,
With buckles and brogues and rings to order –
You that were reared in the reek of solder!
However the rest of the world is gypped
I knew you when you went half-stripped;
And I'd venture a guess that in what you lack
A shift would still astonish your back;
And, shy as you seem, an inquisitive gent
Might study the same with your full consent.
Bosom and back are tightly laced,
Or is it the stays that gives you the waist?
Oh, all can see the way you shine,
But your looks are no concern of mine.
Now tell us the truth and don't be shy
How long are you eating your dinner dry?
A meal of spuds without butter or milk,
And dirt in layers beneath the silk.
Bragging and gab are yours by right,
But I know too where you sleep at night,
And blanket or quilt you never saw
But a strip of old mat and a bundle of straw,
In a hovel of mud without a seat,
And slime that settles about your feet,
A carpet of weeds from door to wall
And hens inscribing their tracks on all;
The rafters in with a broken back
And brown rain lashing through every crack –
'Twas there you learned to look so nice,
But now may we ask how you came by the price?
We all admired the way you spoke,
But whisper, treasure, who paid for the cloak?
A sparrow with you would die of hunger –
How did you come by all the grandeur,

All the tassels and all the lace –
Would you have us believe they were got in grace?
The frock made a hole in somebody's pocket,
And it wasn't you that paid for the jacket;
But assuming that and the rest no news,
How the hell did you come by the shoes?

'Your worship, 'tis women's sinful pride
And that alone has the world destroyed.
Every young man that's ripe for marriage
Is hooked like this by some tricky baggage,
And no one is secure, for a friend of my own,
As nice a boy as ever I've known
That lives from me only a perch or two –
God help him! – married misfortune too.
It breaks my heart when she passes by
With her saucy looks and head held high,
Cows to pasture and fields of wheat,
And money to spare – and all deceit!
Well-fitted to rear a tinker's clan,
She waggles her hips at every man,
With her brazen face and bullock's hide,
And such airs and graces, and mad with pride.
And – that God may judge me! – only I hate
A scandalous tongue, I could relate
Things of that woman's previous state
As one with whom every man could mate
In any convenient field or gate
As the chance might come to him early or late!
But now, of course, we must all forget
Her galloping days and the pace she set;
The race she ran in Ibrackane,
In Manishmore and Teermaclane,
With young and old of the meanest rabble
Of Ennis, Clareabbey and Quin astraddle!
Toughs from Tradree out on a fling,
And Cratlee cutthroats sure to swing;
But still I'd say 'twas the neighbours' spite,

And the girl did nothing but what was right,
But the devil take her and all she showed!
I found her myself on the public road,
On the naked earth with a bare backside
And a Garus turf-cutter astride!
Is it any wonder my heart is failing,
That I feel that the end of the world is nearing,
When, ploughed and sown to all men's knowledge,
She can manage the child to arrive with marriage,
And even then, put to the pinch,
Begrudges Charity an inch;
For, counting from the final prayer
With the candles quenched and the altar bare
To the day when her offspring takes the air
Is a full nine months with a week to spare?

'But you see the troubles a man takes on!
From the minute he marries his peace is gone;
Forever in fear of a neighbour's sneer –
And my own experience cost me dear.
I lived alone as happy as Larry
Till I took it into my head to marry,
Tilling my fields with an easy mind,
Going wherever I felt inclined,
Welcomed by all as a man of price,
Always ready with good advice.
The neighbours listened – they couldn't refuse
For I'd money and stock to uphold my views –
Everything came at my beck and call
Till a woman appeared and destroyed it all:
A beautiful girl with ripening bosom,
Cheeks as bright as apple-blossom,
Hair that glimmered and foamed in the wind,
And a face that blazed with the light behind;
A tinkling laugh and a modest carriage
And a twinkling eye that was ripe for marriage.
I goggled and gaped like one born mindless
Till I took her face for a form of kindness,

Though that wasn't quite what the Lord intended
For He marked me down like a man offended
For a vengeance that wouldn't be easy mended
With my folly exposed and my comfort ended.

'Not to detain you here all day
I married the girl without more delay,
And took my share in the fun that followed.
There was plenty for all and nothing borrowed.
Be fair to me now! There was no one slighted;
The beggarmen took the road delighted;
The clerk and mummers were elated;
The priest went home with his pocket weighted.
The lamps were lit, the guests arrived;
The supper was ready, the drink was plied;
The fiddles were flayed, and, the night advancing,
The neighbours joined in the sport and dancing.

'A pity to God I didn't smother
When first I took the milk from my mother,
Or any day I ever broke bread
Before I brought that woman to bed!
For though everyone talked of her carouses
As a scratching post of the publichouses
That as sure as ever the glasses would jingle
Flattened herself to married and single,
Admitting no modesty to mention,
I never believed but 'twas all invention.
They added, in view of the life she led,
I might take to the roads and beg my bread,
But I took it for talk and hardly minded –
Sure, a man like me could never be blinded! –
And I smiled and nodded and off I tripped
Till my wedding night when I saw her stripped,
And knew too late that this was no libel
Spread in the pub by some jealous rival –
By God, 'twas a fact, and well-supported:
I was a father before I started!

'So there I was in the cold daylight,
A family man after one short night!
The women around me, scolding, preaching,
The wife in bed and the baby screeching.
I stirred the milk as the kettle boiled
Making a bottle to give the child;
All the old hags at the hob were cooing
As if they believed it was all my doing –
Flattery worse than ever you heard:
"Glory and praise to our blessed Lord,
Though he came in a hurry, the poor little creature,
He's the spit of his da in every feature.
Sal, will you look at the cut of that lip!
There's fingers for you! Feel his grip!
Would you measure the legs and the rolls of fat!
Was there ever a seven month child like that?"
And they traced away with great preciseness
My matchless face in the baby's likeness;
The same snub nose and frolicsome air,
And the way I laugh and the way I stare;
And they swore that never from head to toe
Was a child that resembled his father so.
But they wouldn't let me go near the wonder –
"Sure, a draught would blow the poor child asunder!"
All of them out to blind me further –
"The least little breath would be noonday murder!"
Malice and lies! So I took the floor,
Mad with rage and I cursed and swore,
And bade them all to leave my sight.
They shrank away with faces white,
And moaned as they handed me the baby:
"Don't crush him now! Can't you handle him easy?
The least thing hurts them. Treat him kindly!
Some fall she got brought it on untimely.
Don't lift his head but leave him lying!
Poor innocent scrap, and to think he's dying!
If he lives at all till the end of day
Till the priest can come 'tis the most we'll pray!"

'I off with the rags and set him free,
And studied him well as he lay on my knee.
That too, by God, was nothing but lies
For he staggered myself with his kicks and cries.
A pair of shoulders like my own,
Legs like sausages, hair fullgrown;
His ears stuck out and his nails were long,
His hands and wrists and elbows strong;
His eyes were bright, his nostrils wide,
And the knee-caps showing beneath his hide –
A champion, begod, a powerful whelp,
As healthy and hearty as myself!

'Young woman, I've made my case entire.
Justice is all that I require.
Once consider the terrible life
We lead from the minute we take a wife,
And you'll find and see that marriage must stop
And the men unmarried must be let off.
And, child of grace, don't think of the race;
Plenty will follow to take our place;
There are ways and means to make lovers agree
Without making a show of men like me.
There's no excuse for all the exploiters;
Cornerboys, clerks and priests and pipers –
Idle fellows that leave you broke
With the jars of malt and the beer they soak,
When the Mother of God herself could breed
Without asking the views of clerk of creed.
Healthy and happy, wholesome and sound,
The come-by-twilight sort abound;
No one assumes but their lungs are ample,
And their hearts as sound as the best example.
When did Nature display unkindness
To the bastard child in disease or blindness?
Are they not handsomer, better-bred
Than many that come of a lawful bed?

'I needn't go far to look for proof
For I've one of the sort beneath my roof –
Let him come here for all to view!
Look at him now! You see 'tis true.
Agreed, we don't know his father's name,
But his mother admires him just the same,
And if in all things else he shines
Who cares for his baptismal lines?
He isn't a dwarf or an old man's error,
A paralytic or walking terror,
He isn't a hunchback or a cripple
But a lightsome, laughing gay young divil.
'Tis easy to see he's no flash in the pan;
No sleepy, good-natured, respectable man,
Without sinew or bone or belly or bust,
Or venom or vice or love or lust,
Buckled and braced in every limb
Spouted the seed that flowered in him:
For back and leg and chest and height
Prove him to all in the teeth of spite
A child begotten in fear and wonder
In the blood's millrace and the body's thunder.

'Down with marriage! It's out of date;
It exhausts the stock and cripples the state.
The priest has failed with whip and blinker
Now give a chance to Tom the Tinker,
And mix and mash in Nature's can
The tinker and the gentleman!
Let lovers in every lane extended
Struggle and strain as God intended
And locked in frenzy bring to birth
The morning glory of the earth;
The starry litter, girl and boy
Who'll see the world once more with joy.

Clouds will break and skies will brighten,
Mountains bloom and spirits lighten,
And men and women praise your might,
You who restore the old delight.'

*Frank O'Connor*

The girl having listened to this peroration,
She jumped to her feet with no little impatience,
And glared at the geezer with eyes full of fire,
And gave him an earful of feminine ire:

'By the crown of Craglee, if I didn't admit
That you're doting, decrepit, and feeble of wit –
And to treat this assembly with all due respect –
I'd rip off your head from its scrawny wee neck,
And I'd knock it for six with the toe of my boot,
And I'd give the remainder no end of abuse,
And I'd pluck such a tune from the strings of your heart,
I'd consign you to Hell without halo or harp.
It's beneath me to answer your cretinous case –
You snivelling creep, you're a bloody disgrace!
But I want to reveal to the court and the judge
How you made a true lady a miserable drudge.

'She was poor, and alone, without cattle or land,
With no roof, and no hearth, and no family at hand;
Bewildered by life, and as pale as a ghost,
Homeless she wandered from pillar to post,
Without respite or comfort by day and by night,
Of necessity begging the odd sup or bite.
He promised her this and he promised her that,
This wretch promised all, with his plausible chat –
Her fair share of wealth, and a field of good cows,
Her nights to be spent in a bed of soft down,
A brightly tiled hearth, an abundance of peat,
A kitchen, a parlour, an elegant suite,
Lamb's wool and linen to weave into clothes,

And a well-slated roof on this cosy abode.
It's well known to most of the girls in the town
It wasn't for love that she married this clown,
But that all things being equal, 'twas better to wed
Than to walk the dark roads, and to beg for her bread.

'What pleasure she had when she got into bed
With this manky old geezer left much to be said –
Sharp were his shanks, and bony his shoulders;
Icy his thighs, and his knees even colder;
His feet bore the pong of a fire of damp turf;
His body was shrivelled, and covered in scurf.
What jewel alive could endure such a fate,
Without going as grey as her doddering mate,
Who rarely, if ever, was struck by the wish
To determine her sex, whether boy, flesh or fish?
As flaccid and bony beside her he lay –
Huffy and surly, with no urge for play.
And oh! how she longed for her conjugal right,
A jolly good tumble at least once a night!
Don't think for a minute that she was to blame,
Too modest or frigid to kindle a flame!
Attractive and bright, with an amiable heart,
This lady was skilled in the amorous art;
She'd work through the night, and she liked it a lot,
For she'd give the right fellow as good as she got,
And, urging him on with her murmurs and sighs,
She would stretch at her ease, with a gleam in her eyes.
She wouldn't retreat in a sulk at his touch,
Or assault like a wildcat, with sideswipe and scratch,
But slither and slide in a mutual embrace,
Her legs round his body, her face to his face,
Exchanging sweet nothings, and stroking his skin,
Her mouth on his mouth, and their tongues going in,
Caressing his back with the ball of her heel,
And rubbing her brush from his waist to his knee.
As for the old sluggard, she'd snatch off the quilt
And try to arouse what lay under his kilt,

But for all that she nuzzled and nibbled and squeezed,
The more that she snuggled, and tickled and teased –
Well, I hate to relate how she spent the whole night,
Despairingly wrapped in her amorous plight;
Tossing and turning with bedclothes awry,
She'd shiver and shake till she thought she would die,
From sunset to dawn neither waking nor sleeping,
But hugging her bosom, and sobbing and weeping.

'How dare this old dirt-bird discuss womankind,
When a proof of his manhood no woman can find!
And were he a blade who'd got no satisfaction,
I might go along with his angry reaction.
Take a fox on the prowl, or a fish in the mere,
An eagle on wing or a wandering deer –
Would any dumb beast, for a day or a year,
Go hungry for grub when its lunch is so near?
And where in the world would you find such a case,
Of a brute so perverse, with a brain so debased,
That it grazed stony pastures, or fields of bare clay,
When under its nose was a fine feed of hay?
Answer me now, you despicable leech,
And I'll fathom the depths of your floundering speech!
When you sit down to dinner, what matter to you,
If the lady's been feasting for one month or two?
Would your acre of spuds be less likely to yield,
If five million Playboys had ploughed the same field?
Do you breathe? Do you feel? Do you shrink at a touch?
Do you think you might want if you want it too much?
And how many gulps do you think it might take,
To empty the Shannon, and drain all its lakes?
How many cupfuls to bail out the ocean?
How deep down its bed, do you have any notion?
Now, don't be so headstrong, the next time you chat;
As for the two horns, keep them under your hat.
And don't throw a fit, or fall out of your tree,
At the thought of a girl who is easy and free;

If she spent the day serving a jolly fine crew,
There still would be plenty left over for you.
Bejasus! such jealousy might be allowed
In a stud of some standing, a man well endowed
With panache and pizzazz, full of gusto and go,
With good shots in his locker, and strings to his bow –
A rollicking rover, a noble explorer,
A foraging forward, a dashing top scorer –
But not in a doddering, cack-handed clod,
A grumpy old runt with no bone in his rod!

'It's time that I mentioned a puzzle I've pondered,
A thorny conundrum that fills me with wonder –
Why priests when ordained in the clerical life
Are enjoined not to join or engage with a wife.
I chafe and I fret, like a bird in a cage;
Great is the patience that tempers my rage
That given the number of girls without men,
From the fellows in black we are forced to abstain.
O pity the maid of an amorous bent,
When she sees such a rosy-cheeked clerical gent,
Of classic proportions, handsome and tall,
Broad-shouldered, slim-waisted, bum nice and small,
Fresh-faced and smiling, his muscles well toned,
In the bloom of his youth, with firm flesh on his bones,
Solidly built, with an upstanding back,
Well able for pleasure, and up for the *craic*.
At the highest of tables they're welcome to dine,
With Waterford crystal, the finest of wine;
Downy their pillows, and ample their beds;
Provided with dainties, they're always well fed,
Most of them young, with their spunk at full flood,
For as we girls can tell you, they're real flesh and blood.
Were they tittering pansies, or poxy old gets,
Or young whippersnappers, I'd not be upset,
But they're sporty young fellows with shot in their guns,
Asleep on the job when there's work to be done!

'And some, I believe, might well chance their arm
For a wee bit of fun, and if so, what's the harm?
There's good and there's bad, and to give them their due,
You don't hang the many because of the few,
And to blame the whole order, it just wouldn't do;
You don't sink the ship to drown one of the crew.
Now some, it's well known, have always been rakes,
And others have broken what rules they could break,
And there's cranky old buggers – they're not hard to find –
Full of ranting and raving, who hate womankind.
But others unlike them are kindly disposed,
And are touched by the love from which charity flows:
And many's the girl who had set out her stall
Found it heaving with goods, from a clerical call.
It's well I remember their members being praised
For the wonderful families their efforts have raised;
It's often I've heard through the breadth of the land
Appreciative words for their principled stand;
It's often I've seen the results of their labours
Being given false names, and brought up by the neighbours.
But it sickens my heart, when they spend all their time
With widows and wives who are well past their prime,
While the maidens of Ireland cry out in their need –
Such a terrible waste of the sanctified seed!
Such woe that is caused to the whole of the nation,
By clerical orders of no propagation!
O Kernel of Knowledge, I want to submit
That the celibate state is a baneful remit,
And that most who endure it have entered it blind.
And if blind I might be, draw the veil from my mind,
Recite, as you can, what the Prophets affirmed,
That same teaching of love the Apostle confirmed –
For where is it written, by what Word Divine,
That the joys of the flesh should in jail be confined?
I don't think St Paul ever said to a soul
Not to marry, but told us to go out and sow,
To part from our parents, and cleave to a wife,
Two bodies as close as the haft to the knife.

I know it's presumptuous of me, a mere girl,
To quote scripture to you, O Heavenly Pearl!
For Your Grace can remember the Biblical text,
Every twist, every turn, from each word to the next,
Every pith, every gist, every meaning unfold,
Of the stories that Christ to the multitudes told:
God's Mother Herself was espoused to a man,
And Woman is big in the Biblical plan.

'I beg and implore you, O All-knowing Vision!
Descended from heaven, give us a decision!
O Glorious Light! O Queen of the Nation!
Incline to my pleading, and further our station;
Weigh in your mind all our feminine needs,
The thousands of fields without husband or seed,
For the number of females is on the increase,
Falling over each other like flocks of young geese.
And the urchins you see running wild on the street –
Skinny wee lassies with dirty wee feet –
Will be healthy and fat in a month and a day
Should you feed them with greens and big mugfuls of whey,
Till they put on a spurt of unstoppable force,
And they blossom and bud as their blood takes its course.
It sickens my happiness! Look for a mate?
When I have to contend with a river in spate?
Hope for a tumble, a wee bit of fun,
When the girls are outnumbered by men three to one?
The province of Munster is utterly sunk,
And the wastrels of Munster are wasting their spunk;
The weeds are increasing, the country is spent,
Its youth growing feeble and agèd and bent.
Unmarried, impatient, deprived of coition,
I'm looking to you to improve my position:
So get me a man, and like birds of a feather
We'll make a fine couplet in harness together!'

*Ciaran Carson*

Bathed in an aura of morning light,
Her Grace on the bench got up to her feet;
Beautiful, youthful, full of poise,
She cleared her throat and raised her voice,
Then clenched her fists with definite menace
And ordered the bailiff to call for silence.
The court complied; they sat entranced
As her lovely fluent lips pronounced:

'To my mind, girl, you've stated your case
With point and force. You deserve redress.
So I here enact a law for women:
Unmated men turned twenty-one
To be sought, pursued, and hunted down,
Tied to this tree beside the headstone,
Their vests stripped off, their jackets ripped,
Their backs and asses scourged and whipped.
But the long-in-the-tooth and the dry-in-marrow,
The ones whose harrow-pins won't harrow,
Who pen the pent and lock away
The ram that's rampant in their body,
Keeping in hand what should go the rounds
And fencing off the pleasure grounds –
Their nemesis I leave to you
Whose hearths they'd neither fan nor blow.
Dear natural sexual women, think!
Consult your gender, mind and instinct.
Take cognizance. Co-operate.
For I here invest you with the right
(To be exercised to the breaking point)
And powers of violent punishment.

'Yet who gives a damn in the end of all
For them and their dribbling stroup and fall?
With forks collapsed and the feeling gone,
Their hardest part is a pubic bone.
So let them connive, sing dumb and smile
If ever a young man rings their bell
For it seems to me that the best solution

For men past making a contribution
Is not to resent their conjugal plight
But stand by their wives when they put it about,
Facilitate their womanly drives
And lend their name when the baby arrives.
And that, for the moment, will have to do.
I'm on the circuit, and overdue
In another part of Munster. So:
My verdict's short because I go.
But I'll be back, and God help then
Recalcitrant, male-bonded men.'

She stopped, but still her starry gaze
Transfixed me in a kind of daze
I couldn't shake off. My head went light,
I suffered cramps and a fainting fit.
The whole earth seemed to tilt and swing,
My two ears sang from the tongue-lashing
And then the awful targe who'd brought me,
The plank-armed bailiff, reached and caught me
Up by the ears and scruff of the neck
And dragged me struggling into the dock.
Where next comes skipping, clapping hands,
The lass who had aired her love-demands
And says to my face, 'You hardened chaw,
I've waited long, now I'll curry you raw!
You've had your warnings, you cold-rifed blirt.
But now you're caught in a woman's court
And nobody's here to plead your case.
Where is the credit you've earned with us?
Is there anyone here your action's eased?
One that your input's roused or pleased?
Observe him closely, Madam Judge.
From head to toe, he's your average
Passable male – no paragon
But nothing a woman wouldn't take on.
Unshapely, yes, and off the plumb,
But with all his kit of tools about him.
A shade whey-faced and pale and wan,

But what about it? There's bone and brawn.
For it's him and his likes with their humps and stoops
Can shoulder doors and flutter the coops;
As long as a man is randy and game,
Who gives a damn if he's bandy or lame?
So why is he single? Some secret wound
Or problem back in the family background?
And him the quality's darling boy,
All smiles and friends with everybody,
Playing his tunes, on sprees and batters
With his intellectual and social betters.
Wining and dining, day in, day out –
The creep, I can see why they think he's great!
A star bucklepper, the very man
You'd be apt to nickname "merry man",
But the kind of man I would sweep away,
The virgin merry, going grey.
It bothers me deeply. I've come to hate
His plausible, capable, charming note
And his beaming, bland, unfurrowed forehead:
Thirty years old, and never bedded.

'So hear me now, long-suffering judge!
My own long hurt and ingrown grudge
Have me desolated. I hereby claim
A woman's right to punish him.
And you, dear women, you must assist.
So rope him, Una, and all the rest –
Anna, Maura – take hold and bind him.
Double twist his arms behind him.
Remember all the sentence called for
And execute it to the letter.
Maeve and Sive and Sheila! Maureen!
Knot the rope till it tears the skin.
Let Mr Brian take what we give,
Let him have it. Flay him alive
And don't draw back when you're drawing blood.
Test all of your whips against his manhood.

Cut deep. No mercy. Make him squeal.
Leave him in strips from head to heel
Until every single mother's son
In the land of Ireland learns the lesson.

'And it only seems both right and fitting
To note the date of this special sitting
So calm your nerves and start computing:
A thousand minus a hundred and ten –
Take what that gives you, double it, then
Your product's the year.' She'd lifted her pen
And her hand was poised to ratify
The fate that was looking me straight in the eye.
She was writing it down, the household guard
Sat at attention, staring hard
As I stared back. Then my dreaming ceased
And I started up, awake, released.

*Seamus Heaney*

## WILLIAM DRENNAN
## (1754–1820)

### *The Wake of William Orr*

Here our murdered brother lies:
Wake him not with women's cries;
Mourn the way that manhood ought;
Sit in silent trance of thought.

Write his merits on your mind:
Morals pure and manners kind;
In his head, as on a hill,
Virtue placed her citadel.

Why cut off in palmy youth?
Truth he spoke, and acted truth:
'Countrymen, unite!' he cried,
And died – for what his Saviour died.

God of Peace, and God of Love,
Let it not thy vengeance move,
Let it not thy lightnings draw –
A nation guillotined by law!

Hapless nation! rent and torn,
Thou wert early taught to mourn,
Warfare of six hundred years –
Epochs marked with blood and tears!

Hunted through thy native grounds,
Or flung reward to human hounds;
Each one pulled and tore his share,
Heedless of thy deep despair.

Hapless nation – hapless land,
Heap of uncementing sand
Crumbled by a foreign weight;
And by worse – domestic hate.

God of mercy! God of peace!
Make the mad confusion cease;
O'er the mental chaos move,
Through it speak the light of love.

Monstrous and unhappy sight!
Brothers' blood will not unite;
Holy oil and holy water
Mix, and fill the world with slaughter.

Who is she with aspect wild?
The widowed mother with her child,
Child new stirring in the womb,
Husband waiting for the tomb!

Angel of this sacred place,
Calm her soul and whisper peace;
Cord, or axe, or guillotine
Make the sentence – not the sin.

Here we watch our brother's sleep:
Watch with us, but do not weep;
Watch with us through dead of night,
But expect the morning light.

Conquer fortune – persevere! –
Lo! it breaks, the morning clear!
The cheerful cock awakes the skies,
The day is come – arise! – arise!

## PAT O'KELLY

## (1754–*c.*1812)

### *The Litany for Doneraile*

Alas! how dismal is my Tale,
I lost my Watch in Doneraile.
My Dublin Watch, my Chain and Seal,
Pilfered at once in Doneraile.
May Fire and Brimstone never fail
To fall in Showers on Doneraile.
May all the leading Fiends assail
The thieving Town of Doneraile.
As Light'ning's Flash across the vale,
So down to Hell with Doneraile.
The fate of Pompey at Pharsale,
Be that the Curse for Doneraile.
May Beef or Mutton, Lamb or Veal,
Be never found in Doneraile,

But Garlic Soup and scurvy Cale
Be still the food for Doneraile.
And forward as the creeping Snail
Th'Industry be of Doneraile.
May Heav'n a chosen Curse entail
On rigid, rotten Doneraile.
May Sun and Moon for ever fail
To beam their lights on Doneraile.
May every pestilential Gale
Blast that cursed spot called Doneraile.
May no Cuckoo, Thrush or Quail,
Be ever heard in Doneraile.
May Patriots, Kings, and Commonweal
Despise and harass Doneraile.
May every Post, Gazette and Mail,
Sad Tidings bring of Doneraile.
May loudest Thunders ring a Peal
To blind and deafen Doneraile.
May vengeance fall at head and tail
From North to South at Doneraile.
May Profit light and tardy Sale
Still damp the Trade of Doneraile.
May Egypt's plagues at once prevail
To thin the Knaves at Doneraile.
May Frost and Snow, and Sleet and Hail
Benumb each joint in Doneraile.
May Wolves and Bloodhounds trace and trail
The cursed Crew of Doneraile.
May Oscar with his fiery Flail
To Atoms thresh all Doneraile.
May every Mischief fresh and stale
Abide henceforth in Doneraile.
May all from Belfast to Kinsale
Scoff, curse, and damn you, Doneraile.
May neither Flour nor Oatmeal

Be found or known in Doneraile.
May Want and Woe each Joy curtail
That e'er was known in Doneraile.
May not one Coffin want a Nail
That wraps a Rogue in Doneraile.
May all the Sons of Granuwale
Blush at the thieves of Doneraile.
May Mischief big as Norway Whale
O'erwhelm the Knaves of Doneraile.
May Curses wholesale and retail
Pour with full force on Doneraile.
May every Transport wont to Sail
A Convict bring from Doneraile.
May every Churn and milking Pail
Fall dry to staves in Doneraile.
May Cold and Hunger still congeal
The stagnant Blood of Doneraile.
May every Hour new Woes reveal
That Hell reserves for Doneraile.
May every chosen Ill prevail
O'er all the Imps of Doneraile.
May not one Wish or Prayer avail
To soothe the Woes of Doneraile.
May th'Inquisition straight impale
The Rapparees of Doneraile.
May Curse of Sodom now prevail
And sink to Ashes Doneraile.
May Charon's Boat triumphant sail
Completely manned from Doneraile;
And may grim Pluto's inner Jail
Forever groan with Doneraile;
And may my Couplets never fail
To find new Curses for Doneraile!

## SAMUEL THOMSON

(1766–1816)

### *To a Hedge-Hog*

*Unguarded beauty is disgrace.*
Broome

While youthful poets, thro' the grove,
Chaunt saft their canny lays o' love,
And a' their skill exert to move
The darling object;
I chuse, as ye may shortly prove,
A rougher subject.

What fairs[1] to bother us in sonnet,
'Bout chin an' cheek, an' brow an' bonnet?
Just chirlin[2] like a widow'd linnet,
Thro' bushes lurchin;
Love's stangs[3] are ill to thole, I own it,
But to my hurchin.[4]

Thou grimest far o' grusome tykes,[5]
Grubbing thy food by thorny dykes,
Gudefaith *thou* disna want for *pikes*,
Baith sharp an' rauckle;[6]
Thou looks (L—d save's) array'd in spikes,
A creepin heckle![7]

1. *fairs*: young women 2. *chirlin*: chirping 3. *stangs*: stings 4. *hurchin*: hedgehog
5. *tykes*: curs, ill-conditioned animals 6. *rauckle*: rash, rough 7. *heckle*: flax-comb

Some say thou'rt sib[8] kin to the sow,
But sibber to the deil,[9] I trow;
An' what thy use can be, there's few
That can explain;
But naithing, as the learn'd allow,
Was made in vain.

Sure Nick begat thee, at the first,
On some auld *whin*[10] or thorn accurst;
An' some horn-finger'd harpie nurst
The ugly urchin;
Then Belzie,[11] laughin, like to burst
First ca'd thee *Hurchin.*

Fok tell how thou, sae far frae daft,
Whar wind fa'n fruit lie scatter'd saft,
Will row thysel, wi' cunning craft,
An' bear awa
Upon thy back, what fairs[12] thee aft
A day or twa.

But whether this account be true,
Is mair than I will here avow;
If that thou stribs[13] the outler[14] cow,
As some assert,
A pretty milkmaid, I allow,
Forsooth thou art.

I've heard the superstitious say,
To meet thee on our morning way,
Portends some dire misluck that day –
Some black mischance;
Sic fools, howe'er, are far astray
Frae common sense.

8. *sib*: related to 9. *deil*: devil 10. *whin*: gorse bush 11. *Belzie*: Beelzebub
12. *fairs*: provides for 13 *stribs*: milks 14. *outler*: an animal that remains outside all winter

Right monie a hurchin I hae seen,
At early morn, and eke[15] at e'en,
Baith setting off, an' whan I've been
Returning hame;
But Fate, indifferent, I ween,
Was much the same.

How lang will mortals nonsense blether,
And sauls to superstition tether!
For witchcraft, omens, altogether,
Are damn'd hotch-potch mock,[16]
That now obtain sma credit either
Frae us or Scotch fok.

Now creep awa the way ye came,
And tend your squeakin pups at hame;
Gin Colley should o'erhear the same,
It might be fatal,
For you, wi' a' the pikes ye claim,
Wi' him to battle.

## THOMAS DERMODY

(1775–1802)

### *Tam to Rab: An Odaic Epistle*

Hail, brither Rab, thou genuine Bard,
May laurels be thy grand reward!
Laurels, with gold and siller hard,
To fill the purse,
For else, they are not worth a card,
Or Beldame's curse.

15. *eke*: also 16. *mock*: foolish talk

*Arcades ambo!*[1] baith are ready,
T'invoke, and woo, each tunefu' Lady,
But thou, sweet friend, hast got a trade, I
        Ken no such thing,
Thou can'st e'en drive the ploughshare steady;
        I can but sing.

Yet, would I glad gang out with thee,
To strew my barley on the lea;
Wow! we would gloriously agree,
        Poetics gabbling,
Ne, ever, o'er the dram, would we
        Be squabbling.

Keen as thy wit, the scythe we'd wield,
Culling each flower the wild woods yield,
Together, urge our team afield;
        Together rhyme,
And mark the Sun yon mountain gild
        Till supper time.

Allan's braw lilts we'd rehearse,
And laugh and weep and talk in verse;
While grey-eyed Judgment, sapient nurse,
        Our thoughts would prune,
And Fancy roseate bands disperse,
        Our brows to crown.

Yes, Rab, I love thee in my heart,
Thy simple notes, uncurbed by art;
That bid the tear of passion start,
        And, sure I am,
Ere from this wicked world we part,
        You'll jostle Tam.

1. *Arcades ambo*: Arcadians both (i.e., two rascals)

And if you do, by Peter's keys,
We'll quaff stout whiskey at our ease;
Drive fools before our verse, like geese,
And clink the can,
Till we shall rise, by twelve degrees,
'Bove reptile Man.

## *The Simile*

'Tis like a hat without a head,
'Tis like a house without a shed,
'Tis like a gun without a lock,
'Tis like a swain without a flock,
'Tis like a town without a school,
'Tis like a King without a fool,
'Tis like a dog without a tail,
'Tis like a barn without a flail,
'Tis like a goose without a spit,
'Tis like a brain without a wit,
'Tis like a cap without a border,
'Tis like a bill without an order,
'Tis like a shop without a clerk,
'Tis like a flint without a spark,
'Tis like a knave without a place,
'Tis like a knife without a case,
'Tis like a lawyer without Latin,
'Tis like a meeting without 'G' –
In short, at once to stop my mouthing,
'Tis like – what is it like? – like nothing.

## *The Poet's Inventory*

A broken stool, two legs demolished,
A board, by constant friction polished;
A bottle-neck, for ink or candle;
A battered jug, without a handle;
A dozen pens, the worse for scribbling;

A trap, to keep the mice from nibbling;
A box for coals, the bottom out;
A teapot, lacking top and spout;
A tott'ring chair, the back long missing;
A screen, which wants a woundy piecing;
A bed, without a sheet or blanket;
A pint of beer, if no one drank it;
A Fielding's *Works*, Volume the Second;
And thus the whole estate is reckoned.

## ROBERT EMMET

(1778–1803)

### *Arbour Hill*

No rising column marks this spot,
    Where many a victim lies;
But oh! the blood that here has streamed,
    To heaven for justice cries.

It claims it on the oppressor's head,
    Who joys in human woe,
Who drinks the tears by misery shed,
    And mocks them as they flow.

It claims it on the callous judge,
    Whose hands in blood are dyed,
Who arms injustice with the sword,
    The balance throws aside.

It claims it for his ruined isle,
    Her wretched children's grave;
Where withered Freedom droops her head,
    And man exists – a slave.

O sacred justice! free this land
From tyranny abhorred;
Resume thy balance and thy seat –
Resume – but sheathe thy sword.

No retribution should we seek –
Too long has horror reigned;
By mercy marked may freedom rise,
By cruelty unstained.

Nor shall the tyrant's ashes mix
With those our martyred dead;
This is the place where Erin's sons
In Erin's cause have bled.

And those who here are laid at rest,
Oh! hallowed be each name;
Their memories are forever blest –
Consigned to endless fame.

Unconsecrated is this ground,
Unblest by holy hands;
No bell here tolls its solemn sound,
No monument here stands.

But here the patriot's tears are shed,
The poor man's blessing given;
These consecrate the virtuous dead,
These waft their fame to heaven.

# IV

# SONG TO 1800

*Upon a fair morning for soft recreation . . .*

'The Blackbird'

# OLD IRISH

## DALLÁN FORGAILL
(attrib.)

### *Be Thou My Vision*

Be Thou my vision, O Lord of my heart,
be all else but naught to me, save that thou art;
be Thou my best thought in the day and the night,
both waking and sleeping, Thy presence my light.

Be Thou my wisdom, be Thou my true word,
be Thou ever with me, and I with Thee Lord;
be Thou my great Father, and I Thy true son;
be Thou in me dwelling, and I with Thee one.

Be Thou my breastplate, my sword for the fight;
be Thou my whole armour, be Thou my true might;
be Thou my soul's shelter, be Thou my strong tower:
O raise Thou me heavenward, great Power of my power.

Riches I heed not, nor man's empty praise:
be Thou mine inheritance now and always;
be Thou and Thou only the first in my heart;
O Sovereign of heaven, my treasure Thou art.

High King of heaven, thou heaven's bright sun,
O grant me its joys after victory is won;
great Heart of my own heart, whatever befall,
still be Thou my vision, O Ruler of all.

*Mary Elizabeth Byrne and Eleanor Hull*

## ULTÁN OF ARDBRACCAN
(*fl. c.*660)

### *Hymn to St Brigit*

Brigit, dazzling flame,
ever steady woman,
draw us to eternity,
be our sparkling sun.

Lead us safely through
jostling crowds of devils;
rout before our eyes
every tempting evil.

The snares that plague all flesh
may she destroy within us,
Brigit the flowering branch,
mother, too, of Jesus.

Loved and honest virgin,
maid of immense honour,
vigilant protectress,
saint of local Leinster.

She and holy Patrick,
twin pillars of this kingdom,
she the fragrant blossom
and personage most queenly.

When we reach old age
in penitential sackcloth,
please still give us shelter,
grace-dispensing Brigit.

*Máirín Ní Dhonnchadha*
*and PC*

# LATIN

## COLUMBANUS

(*c.*543–615)

### *Hymn to the Trinity*

This to the Father
king of might
Christ Jesus
and the Holy Ghost.

One God
whole substance
trefoil person
single essence.

Bright effluence
increate
pure ethereal
lightfont.

Equinox springing
Son-like shone
on worldstuff
from Heaven.

Firstword firstflesh
one light ever
into worldmatter
sent by the Father.

He stripped power
from Chaos
banished Night
at once.

Old foes down,
He untied
the firmament's
deathbonds.

What before
was darkgulch
this day of days
light drenched.

The very day
light revealing
a pendent chain
ignorance concealing.

This same day
it is said
Israel freed,
parted the Red Sea.

Thus we learn
put no value
on worldly deed –
cleave to virtue.

Cruel Pharaoh drowned
eager voices hymn
God's renown
their beacon.

Saved from straits
we likewise
should offer God
our praise.

He
initiates light
He
ordains salvation.

First
in diurnal turning
second
in faith's fever.

At worldsend
clearing mystery
He will come
in clemency.

This much
is elementary
prophets proclaim –
most celebratory!

Born a man
fleshly making;
heaven-present,
Trinity-partaking.

Swaddled, He mewls
as mages kneel down
shining among stars
adored in heaven.

Bounded in
a mere cradle
His fist
girdles the world.

First portent
His disciples saw
water changed
to wine's nectar.

He brought to pass
words of the prophet:
*the cripple shall*
*bound as the hart.*

The mute speaks
tonguechain
unlinked at
His command.

Deaf hear, blind see,
lepers take cure
borne corpse
steps from bier.

Five thousand
men, five loaves;
it is true
none starved.

Such stock
of mercy,
(spurred by spite
the Adversary

thwarts as he
hates and envies)
His sacrifice
made for enemies.

A criminal
charge against
Him, who
is all grace.

They came for
Him armed, as if
He were a robber
hell-bound thief.

He stood before
man's doom,
the Eternal judged
by mortal tribune.

Nailed to rood
He made heaven
quake; the third hour
quenched the sun.

Rocks racked
holy veil rent
tombs open
dead awake.

He tore through rusted
teeth of hell
that which kept us
long in thrall.

Adam Firstmade
his sad generations
flung to death's wild
maw by sin.

Man who lived once
in Paradise
by mercy's work
home at last.

The head is raised of
a catholic corps
founded in Father,
Son and Holy Ghost.

Heaven-sent pillars
of the Church; gates
point to eternity
with God's confederates.

He hoists
the stray lamb
bears it
to the pen.

We look forward
to judgement
returning to Him
our talent.

What recompense
when He gives
at such high rate
so generous!

How can mortal
stammerers
speak of such
great mysteries?

We can but pray,
eternally pray,
O Lord hear
our *miserere*.

*Kit Fryatt*

## *Rowing Song*

Though hewn from the forests, our little boat now glides
Up the twin-horned Rhine as if born to the task.
*Heave, men, heave, let echo shout back Heave!*

Winds may get blowy and rain drive at us hard
But strength of men combined can conquer any storm.
*Heave, men, heave, let echo shout back Heave!*

Clouds will give way, the tempest will surrender
To all-taming toil when labour wins the spoils.
*Heave, men, heave, let echo shout back Heave!*

Bear up and we'll get through – for has the Lord not
plucked us
Safe and sound before from fixes worse than this?
*Heave, men, heave, let echo shout back Heave!*

Our Enemy lies in wait for the quailing of our hearts,
Ready with temptation to shake us to the core.
*Think of Christ, men, with thinking minds cry Heave!*

So stick to the oar-work, and scorn his ancient wiles,
Protected head to foot in virtue's gleaming armour.
*Think of Christ, men, with thinking minds cry Heave!*

Firm faith and blessed zeal will overcome anything: –
The Old One is retreating; see! his darts are broken.
*Think of Christ, men, with thinking minds cry Heave!*

The King of virtues, height of power, fount of all,
Offers prizes to the striver, rewards the victor always.
*Think of Christ, men, with thinking minds cry Heave!*

*PC*

## ANONYMOUS

### *The Good Rule of Bangor*

The rule we keep is good
In the monastery at Bangor,
A sight that pleases God,
A just, exalted wonder.

Bangor's monks are blessed
With faith firm and certain;
By charity possessed,
Cloaked in hope of heaven.

A ship that never lurched
When assailed by deadly storm,
A pure bride come to church
To wed her very Lord.

The one true stock
From the land of Moses;
Founded on a rock,
House of holy joys.

A town to withstand war,
With wall and citadel,
A marvel seen from far,
Set upon a hill.

Ark with sculpted angels
And gold enamelling,
Fit for sacred treasure
That four men carry in.

For Christ a lovely queen
Clothed in rays of sun;
A simple, learned mind
Not to be undone.

A true royal stronghold
With precious stones aglitter;
Christ's own sheepfold
Protected by the Father.

Virgin full and fertile,
Unviolated mother;
Trembling and yet joyful,
Waiting on the Word;

Her whole life sanctified
By dear God our Father;
Her soul will reside
In a perfect future.

*PC*

## CÚ CHUIMNE OF IONA

(*fl. c.*740)

### *Hymn to the Virgin Mary*

Let us sing daily
  and our measures vary
  as we raise to God
  a hymn of Our Lady.

Our two-part chorus
praises Mary together
one note strikes one ear
the next the other.

Mary, sprung of Judah
mother of Lord Jesus
held out a cure
for mankind's sickness.

Gabriel brought the Word
down from God's bosom
it quickened and grew
in Mary's womb.

She is high, she is holy
venerable maiden
she did not step back
but embraced her burden.

Never before, never after
was such a one
and never of woman
came such as her Son.

For a tree and a woman
the world first was lost
another woman's virtue
restores it to us.

Brave new mother
delivered of her father
who – baptism over –
we believe our Saviour.

She nourished a pearl
(no phantom was this)
for which good Christians
trade all they possess.

She wove a coat
 without any seam
 which at His death
 fell prize to a game.

Raise weapons of light
 the shield and the spear
 perfect us for God
 through Mary's prayer.

Our repeated amens
 through Christ's noble bearer
 ask reprieve from the flame
 of the funeral pyre.

We call on Christ's name
 and the angels aver it
 may we thrive, written down
 in heavenly script!

COLLECT:

Holy Mary, we implore
 your merit and dignity
 may we be fit
 to dwell in glory.

*Kit Fryatt*

# MIDDLE IRISH

## MAELÍSA Ó BROLCHÁIN
(*c.*970–1038)

### *Deus Meus*

*Deus meus adiuva me,*[1]
Give me Thy love, O Christ, I pray,
Give me Thy love, O Christ, I pray,
*Deus meus adiuva me.*

*In meum cor ut sanum sit,*[2]
Pour loving King, Thy love in it,
Pour loving King, Thy love in it,
*In meum cor ut sanum sit.*

*Domine, da ut peto a te,*[3]
O, pure bright sun, give, give today,
O, pure bright sun, give, give today,
*Domine, da ut peto a te.*

*Hanc spero rem et quæro quam*[4]
Thy love to have where'er I am,
Thy love to have where'er I am,
*Hanc spero rem et quæro quam.*

1. My God, assist Thou me 2. Into my heart that it sound may be
3. Lord, grant Thou what I ask of Thee 4. This thing I hope and seek of Thee

*Tuum amorem sicut uis,*[5]
Give to me swiftly, strongly, this,
Give to me swiftly, strongly, this,
*Tuum amorem sicut uis.*

*Quæro, postulo, peto a te*[6]
That I in heaven, dear Christ, may stay,
That I in heaven, dear Christ, may stay,
*Quæro, postulo, peto a te.*

*Domine, Domine, exaudi me,*[7]
Fill my soul, Lord, with Thy love's ray,
Fill my soul, Lord, with Thy love's ray,
*Domine, Domine, exaudi me.*
*Deus meus adiuva me,*
*Deus meus adiuva me.*

*George Sigerson*

5. Thy love as Thou mayst will 6. I seek, I claim, I ask of Thee 7. Lord, Lord, hearken to me

# IRISH

## ANONYMOUS

### *Donal Óg*

I

It is late last night the dog was speaking of you;
the snipe was speaking of you in her deep marsh.
It is you are the lonely bird through the woods;
and that you may be without a mate until you find me.

You promised me, and you said a lie to me,
that you would be before me where the sheep are flocked;
I gave a whistle and three hundred cries to you,
and I found nothing there but a bleating lamb.

You promised me a thing that was hard for you,
a ship of gold under a silver mast;
twelve towns with a market in all of them,
and a fine white court by the side of the sea.

You promised me a thing that is not possible,
that you would give me gloves of the skin of a fish;
that you would give me shoes of the skin of a bird;
and a suit of the dearest silk in Ireland.

When I go by myself to the Well of Loneliness,
I sit down and I go through my trouble;
when I see the world and do not see my boy,
he that has an amber shade in his hair.

It was on that Sunday I gave my love to you;
the Sunday that is last before Easter Sunday.
And myself on my knees reading the Passion;
and my two eyes giving love to you for ever.

My mother said to me not to be talking with you today,
or tomorrow, or on the Sunday;
it was a bad time she took for telling me that;
it was shutting the door after the house was robbed.

My heart is as black as the blackness of the sloe,
or as the black coal that is on the smith's forge;
or as the sole of a shoe left in white halls;
it was you put that darkness over my life.

You have taken the east from me; you have taken the west
    from me;
you have taken what is before me and what is behind me;
you have taken the moon, you have taken the sun from me;
and my fear is great that you have taken God from me!

*Lady Augusta Gregory*

## *The Stars Stand Up in the Air*

The stars stand up in the air,
    The sun and the moon are gone,
The strand of its waters is bare,
    And her sway is swept from the swan.

The cuckoo was calling all day,
    Hid in the branches above,
How my stóirín is fled far away –
    'Tis my grief that I give her my love!

Three things through love I see,
  Sorrow and sin and death –
And my mind reminding me
  That this doom I breathe with my breath.

But sweeter than violin or lute
  Is my love, and she left me behind –
I wish that all music were mute,
  And I to my beauty were blind.

She's more shapely than swan by the strand,
  She's more radiant than grass after dew,
She's more fair than the stars where they stand –
  'Tis my grief that her ever I knew!

*Thomas MacDonagh*

## *From the Cold Sod that's o'er You*

From the cold sod that's o'er you
  I never shall sever;
Were my hands twined in yours, Love,
  I'd hold them for ever.
My fondest, my fairest,
  We may now sleep together!
I've the cold earth's damp odour,
  And I'm worn from the weather.

This heart filled with fondness
  Is wounded and weary;
A dark gulf beneath it
  Yawns jet-black and dreary.
When death comes, a victor,
  In mercy to greet me,
On the wings of the whirlwind
  In the wild wastes you'll meet me.

When the folk of my household
  Suppose I am sleeping,
On your cold grave till morning
  The lone watch I'm keeping.
My grief to the night wind
  For the mild maid to render,
Who was my betrothed
  Since infancy tender.

Remember the lone night
  I last spent with you, Love,
Beneath the dark sloe-tree
  When the icy wind blew, Love.
High praise to thy Saviour
  No sin-stain had found you,
That your virginal glory
  Shines brightly around you.

The priests and the friars
  Are ceaselessly chiding,
That I love a young maiden
  In life not abiding.
O ! I'd shelter and shield you
  If wild storms were swelling!
And O, my wrecked hope,
  That the cold earth's your dwelling!

*Edward Walsh*

## *Dear Dark Head*

Put your head, darling, darling, darling,
  Your darling black head my heart above;
Oh, mouth of honey, with the thyme for fragrance,
  Who, with heart in breast, could deny you love?
Oh, many and many a young girl for me is pining,
  Letting her locks of gold to the cold wind free,

For me, the foremost of our gay young fellows;
  But I'd leave a hundred, pure love, for thee!
Then put your head, darling, darling, darling,
  Your darling black head my heart above;
Oh, mouth of honey, with the thyme for fragrance,
  Who, with heart in breast, could deny you love?

*Samuel Ferguson*

## *Cashel of Munster*

I'd wed you without herds, without money, or rich array,
And I'd wed you on a dewy morning at day-dawn grey;
My bitter woe it is, love, that we are not far away
In Cashel town, though the bare deal board were our
  marriage-bed this day!

Oh, fair maid, remember the green hill side,
Remember how I hunted about the valleys wide;
Time now has worn me; my locks are turn'd to grey,
The year is scarce and I am poor, but send me not, love, away!

Oh, deem not my blood is of base strain, my girl,
Oh, deem not my birth was as the birth of the churl;
Marry me, and prove me, and say soon you will,
That noble blood is written on my right side still!

My purse holds no red gold, no coin of the silver white,
No herds are mine to drive through the long twilight!
But the pretty girl that would take me, all bare though
  I be and lone,
Oh, I'd take her with me kindly to the county Tyrone.

Oh, my girl, I can see 'tis in trouble you are,
And, oh, my girl, I see 'tis your people's reproach you bear:
'I am a girl in trouble for his sake with whom I fly,
And, oh, may no other maiden know such reproach as I!'

*Samuel Ferguson*

## *My Grief on the Sea*

My grief on the sea,
  How the waves of it roll!
For they heave between me
  And the love of my soul!

Abandoned, forsaken,
  To grief and to care,
Will the sea ever waken
  Relief from despair?

My grief and my trouble!
  Would he and I were
In the province of Leinster,
  Or county of Clare!

Were I and my darling –
  Oh, heart-bitter wound! –
On board of the ship
  For America bound!

On a green bed of rushes
  All last night I lay,
And I flung it abroad
  With the heat of the day.

And my love came behind me –
  He came from the South;
His breast to my bosom,
  His mouth to my mouth.

*Douglas Hyde*

## TOMÁS Ó FLANNGHAILE
(*fl.* mid-17th century)

### *The County of Mayo*

On the deck of Patrick Lynch's boat I sat in woeful plight,
Through my sighing all the weary day and weeping all the night.
Were it not that full of sorrow from my people forth I go,
By the blessed sun, 'tis royally I'd sing thy praise, Mayo.

When I dwelt at home in plenty, and my gold did much abound,
In the company of fair young maids the Spanish ale went round.
'Tis a bitter change from those gay days that now I'm forced
  to go,
And must leave my bones in Santa Cruz, far from my own
  Mayo.

They're altered girls in Irrul now; 'tis proud they're grown and
  high,
With their hair-bags and their top-knots – for I pass their
  buckles by.
But it's little now I heed their airs, for God will have it so,
That I must depart for foreign lands, and leave my sweet Mayo.

'Tis my grief that Patrick Loughlin is not Earl in Irrul still,
And that Brian Duff no longer rules as Lord upon the Hill;
And that Colonel Hugh MacGrady should be lying dead and
    low,
And I sailing, sailing swiftly from the county of Mayo.

*George Fox*

## ANONYMOUS

### *Shaun O'Dwyer of the Glen*

AD 1651

Oft, at pleasant morning,
Sunshine all adorning,
I've heard the horn give warning
    With bird's mellow call –
Badgers flee before us,
Woodcocks startle o'er us,
Guns make ringing chorus,
    'Mid the echoes all;
The fox run higher and higher,
Horsemen shouting nigher,
The maiden mourning by her
    Fowl he left in gore.
Now, they fell the wild-wood:
Farewell, home of childhood,
Ah, Shaun O'Dwyer a' Glanna, –
    Thy day is o'er!

It is my sorrow sorest,
Woe, – the falling forest!
The north wind gives me no rest,
    And Death's in the sky:

My faithful hound's tied tightly,
Never sporting brightly,
Who'd make a child laugh lightly,
  With tears in his eye.
The antlered, noble-hearted
Stags are never started,
Never chased nor parted
  From the furzy hills.
If peace came, but a small way,
I'd journey down on Galway,
And leave, tho' not for alway,
  My Erinn of Ills.

The land of streamy valleys
Hath no head nor rallies –
In city, camp, or palace,
  They never toast her name.
Alas, no warrior column, –
From Cloyne to peaks of Colum,
O'er wasted fields and solemn,
  The shy hares grow tame:
O! when shall come the routing,
The flight of churls and flouting?
We hear no joyous shouting
  From the blackbird brave;
More warlike is the omen,
Justice comes to no men,
Priests must flee the foemen
  To the mountain cave.

It is my woe and ruin
That sinless death's undoing
Came not, ere the strewing
  Of all my bright hopes.
How oft, at sunny morning,
I've watched the Spring returning,
The Autumn apples burning,
  And dew on woodland slopes!
Now my lands are plunder,

Far my friends asunder,
I must hide me under
    Branch and bramble screen –
If soon I cannot save me
By flight from foes who crave me,
O Death, at last I'll brave thee
    My bitter foes between!

*George Sigerson*

## *Patrick Sarsfield, Lord Lucan*

Farewell Patrick Sarsfield wherever you may roam,
You crossed the sea to France and left empty camps at home,
To plead our cause before many a foreign throne
Though you left ourselves and poor Ireland overthrown.

Good luck Patrick Sarsfield you were sent to us by God,
And holy forever is the earth that you trod;
May the sun and the white moon light your way,
You trounced King Billy and won the day.

With you Patrick Sarsfield goes the prayer of everyone,
My own prayer too, and the prayer of Mary's Son,
You rode through Birr, the Narrow Ford you passed,
You beat them at Cullen and took Limerick at last.

I'll climb the mountain a lonely man,
And I'll go east again if I can,
'Twas there I saw the Irish ready for the fight,
The lousy crowd that wouldn't unite!

Who's that I see now yonder on Howth Head?
'One of Jamie's soldiers sir, now the king has fled,
Last year with gun and knapsack I marched with joyous tread,
But this year sir I'm begging my bread.'

And God when I think how Diarmuid went under,
His standard broken and his limbs pulled asunder,
And God Himself couldn't fight a way through
When they chopped off his head and held it in our view.

The corn tumbled soon as the scythes went through,
The twelve Kilkenny men were the first that they slew,
My two brothers died and I held my breath,
But the death that broke me was Diarmuid's death.

At the Boyne bridge we took our first beating,
From the bridge at Slane we were soon retreating,
And then we were beaten at Aughrim too –
Ah, fragrant Ireland, that was goodbye to you.

The fumes were choking as the house went alight,
And Black Billy's heroes were warming to the fight,
And every shell that came, wherever it lit,
Colonel Mitchell asked was Lord Lucan hit.

So goodbye Limerick and your homes so fair,
And all the good friends that quartered with us there,
And the cards we played by the watchfires' glare
And the priests that called us all night to prayer.

But on you Londonderry may misfortune come
Like the smoke that lit with every bursting gun
For all the fine soldiers you gathered together
By your walls without shelter from wind or weather.

Many and many a good lad, all proud and gay,
Seven weeks ago they were passing this way,
With guns and swords and pikes on show,
And now in Aughrim they're lying low.

Aughrim has manure that's neither lime nor sand
But sturdy young soldiers to nourish the land,
The men we left behind on the battlefield that day
Torn like horsemeat by the dogs where they lay.

And over the seas are Ireland's best,
The Dukes and the Burkes, Prince Charlie and the rest,
And Captain Talbot their ranks adorning,
And Patrick Sarsfield, Ireland's darling.

*Frank O'Connor*

## *Mairgréad ni Chealleadh*

At the dance in the village
  Thy white foot was fleetest;
Thy voice 'mid the concert
  Of maidens was sweetest;
The swell of thy white breast
  Made rich lovers follow;
And thy raven hair bound them,
  Young Mairgréad ni Chealleadh.

Thy neck was, lost maid,
  Than the ceanabhan whiter,
And the glow of thy cheek
  Than the monadan brighter;
But death's chain hath bound thee,
  Thine eye's glazed and hollow,
That shone like a sunburst,
  Young Mairgréad ni Chealleadh.

No more shall mine ear drink
  Thy melody swelling;
Nor thy beamy eye brighten
  The outlaw's dark dwelling;
Or thy soft heaving bosom
  My destiny hallow,
When thine arms twine around me,
  Young Mairgréad ni Chealleadh.

The moss couch I brought thee
  Today from the mountain,
Has drank the last drop
  Of thy young heart's red fountain –
For this good skian beside me
  Struck deep and rung hollow
In thy bosom of treason,
  Young Mairgréad ni Chealleadh.

With strings of rich pearls
  Thy white neck was laden,
And thy fingers with spoils
  Of the Sassanach maiden:
Such rich silks enrob'd not
  The proud dames of Mallow –
Such pure gold they wore not
  As Mairgréad ni Chealleadh.

Alas! that my loved one
  Her outlaw would injure –
Alas! that he e'er proved
  Her treason's avenger!
That this right hand should make thee
  A bed cold and hollow,
When in death's sleep it laid thee,
  Young Mairgréad ni Chealleadh.

And while to this lone cave
  My deep grief I'm venting,
The Saxon's keen bandog
  My footsteps is scenting;
But true men await me
  Afar in Duhallow.
Farewell, cave of slaughter,
  And Mairgréad ni Chealleadh.

*Edward Walsh*

## *The Dirge of O'Sullivan Bear*

The sun on Ivera
  No longer shines brightly,
The voice of her music
  No longer is sprightly,
No more to her maidens
  The light dance is dear,
Since the death of our darling
  O'Sullivan Bear.

Scully! thou false one,
  You basely betrayed him,
In his strong hour of need,
  When thy right hand should aid him;
He fed thee – he clad thee –
  You had all could delight thee:
You left him – you sold him –
  May Heaven requite thee!

Scully! may all kinds
  Of evil attend thee!
On thy dark road of life
  May no kind one befriend thee!
May fevers long burn thee,
  And agues long freeze thee!
May the strong hand of God
  In His red anger seize thee!

Had he died calmly
  I would not deplore him,
Or if the wild strife
  Of the sea-war closed o'er him;
But with ropes round his white limbs
  Through ocean to trail him,
Like a fish after slaughter –
  'Tis therefore I wail him.

Long may the curse
  Of his people pursue them:
Scully that sold him,
  And soldier that slew him!
One glimpse of heaven's light
  May they see never!
May the hearthstone of hell
  Be their best bed for ever!

In the hole which the vile hands
  Of soldiers had made thee,
Unhonour'd, unshrouded,
  And headless they laid thee;
No sigh to regret thee,
  No eye to rain o'er thee,
No dirge to lament thee,
  No friend to deplore thee!

Dear head of my darling,
  How gory and pale
These aged eyes see thee,
  High spiked on their gaol!
That cheek in the summer sun
  Ne'er shall grow warm;
Nor that eye e'er catch light,
  But the flash of the storm.

A curse, blessed ocean,
  Is on thy green water,
From the haven of Cork
  To Ivera of slaughter:
Since thy billows were dyed
  With the red wounds of fear,
Of Muiertach Oge,
  Our O'Sullivan Bear!

*Jeremiah Joseph Callanan*

## *The Convict of Clonmel*

How hard is my fortune,
  And vain my repining!
The strong rope of fate
  For this young neck is twining.
My strength is departed,
  My cheek sunk and sallow,
While I languish in chains
  In the gaol of Clonmala.

No boy in the village
  Was ever yet milder.
I'd play with a child,
  And my sport would be wilder;
I'd dance without tiring
  From morning till even,
And the goal-ball I'd strike
  To the lightning of heaven.

At my bed-foot decaying,
  My hurlbat is lying;
Thro' the boys of the village
  My goal-ball is flying;
My horse 'mong the neighbours
  Neglected may fallow,
While I pine in my chains
  In the gaol of Clonmala.

Next Sunday the patron
  At home will be keeping,
And the young active hurlers
  The field will be sweeping;
With the dance of fair maidens
  The evening they'll hallow,
While this heart, once so gay,
  Shall be cold in Clonmala.

*Jeremiah Joseph Callanan*

## SEÁN Ó NEACHTAIN
(*c.*1650–1729)

### *Proposal to Úna Ní Bhroin*

Glad I'd go to the wood with you, girl of the gold curls
and see the birds there in sweet-throated session:
the nightingale will play fiddle, the thrush a whistle
the blackbird accompany himself on the harp,

his dun mate on the organ, the wren wake a lute
the laverock and titmouse on tabor and snare.
Parked on a green bough, the trumpeter sparrow
will strike up a hot number all for your love.

Woodpigeon and turtle will chortle together
starling and fieldfare trotting nearby
the cuckoo will seek just one shy keek
of you, and the corncrake's your boon friend.

Echoes at our shoulders relay merry laughter
women from the raths and the mounds ply their strings
everything you could think to wish for, my minx,
is yours, and my love will never depart you.

Daylight will drench us, down through the branches
orient drops upon them sparkle and play
you the chattering music of water, while the otter
and the fish writhe together, intricately.

*Kit Fryatt*

## ÚNA NÍ BHROIN
(*d.c.*1706)

### *Reply to Seán Ó Neachtain's Proposal*

From the time that I gave you my hand and my promise
And my love, too, forever, young Seán of the Neachtains
The advice of my friends could never divide us
– For you I'd abandon the halls of the angels.

Oh, love, a whole year I could go, I declare,
Without one bite of food or one round drop of drink,
My mouth on your mouth, love, and my hands in your hair
– Your love-talk would soon have us both in the pink.

I will leave with you now and will make no excuses
But lie down and listen to the small birds at play
– One hundred times better than feasting in castles –
My firm love, my darling, how can I say Nay?

*PC*

## TOIRDHEALBHACH Ó CEARBHALLÁIN (1670–1738)

### *Mabel Kelly*

Lucky the husband
Who puts his hand beneath her head.
They kiss without scandal
Happiest two near feather-bed.
He sees the tumble of brown hair
Unplait, the breasts, pointed and bare
When nightdress shows
From dimple to toe-nail,
All Mabel glowing in it, here, there, everywhere.

Music might listen
To her least whisper,
Learn every note, for all are true.
While she is speaking,
Her voice goes sweetly
To charm the herons in their musing.
Her eyes are modest, blue, their darkness
Small rooms of thought, but when they sparkle
Upon a feast-day,
Glasses are meeting,
Each raised to Mabel Kelly, our toast and darling.

Gone now are many Irish ladies
Who kissed and fondled, their very pet-names
Forgotten, their tibia degraded.
She takes their sky. Her smile is famed.
Her praise is scored by quill and pencil.
Harp and spinet
Are in her debt
And when she plays or sings, melody is content.

No man who sees her
Will feel uneasy.
He goes his way, head high, however tired.
Lamp loses light
When placed beside her.
She is the pearl and being of all Ireland:
Foot, hand, eye, mouth, breast, thigh and instep, all that
we desire.
Tresses that pass small curls as if to touch the ground;
So many prizes
Are not divided.
Her beauty is her own and she is not proud.

*Austin Clarke*

## *Peggy Browne*

The dark-haired girl, who holds my thought entirely
Yet keeps me from her arms and what I desire,
Will never take my word for she is proud
And none may have his way with Peggy Browne.

Often I dream that I am in the woods
At Westport House. She strays alone, blue-hooded,
Then lifts her flounces, hurries from a shower,
But sunlight stays all day with Peggy Browne.

Her voice is music, every little echo
My pleasure and O her shapely breasts, I know,
Are white as her own milk, when taffeta gown
Is let out, inch by inch, for Peggy Browne.

A lawless dream comes to me in the night-time,
That we are stretching together side by side,
Nothing I want to do can make her frown.
I wake alone, sighing for Peggy Browne.

*Austin Clarke*

# CATHAL BUÍ MAC GIOLLA GHUNNA
## (c.1680–1756)

### *The Yellow Bittern*

Yellow bittern, I'm sad it's over.
  Your bones are frozen and all caved in.
It wasn't hunger but thirst and craving
  That left you foundering on the shore.
What odds is it now about Troy's destruction
  With you on the flagstones upside down,
Who never injured or hurt a creature
  And preferred bog-water to any wine?

Bittern, bittern, your end was awful,
  Your perished skull there on the road,
You that would call me every morning
  With your gargler's song as you guzzled mud.
And that's what's ahead of your brother Cahal
  (You know what they say about me and the stuff),
But they've got it wrong, and the truth is simple:
  A drop would have saved that croaker's life.

I am saddened, bittern, and broken-hearted
  To find you in scrags in the rushy tufts
And the big rats scampering down the ratpaths
  To wake your carcass and have their fun.
If you could have got word to me in time, bird,
  That you were in trouble and craved a sup
I'd have struck the fetters off those lough waters
  And have wet your thrapple with the blow I struck.

Your common birds do not concern me,
  The blackbird, say, or the thrush or crane,
But the yellow bittern, my heartsome namesake
  With my looks and locks, he's the one I mourn.
Constantly he was drinking, drinking,
  And by all accounts I am just the same,
But every drop I get I'll down it
  For fear I might get my end from drouth.

The woman I love says to give it up now
  Or else I'll go to an early grave,
But I say no and keep resisting
  For taking drink's what prolongs your days.
You saw for yourselves a while ago
  What happened the bird when its throat went dry;
So, my friends and neighbours, let it flow:
  You'll be stood no rounds in eternity.

*Seamus Heaney*

## PEADAR Ó DOIRNÍN

### *The Green Hill of Cian, Son of Cáinte*

Flower of maidens of fairest face,
Famed for human splendour;
Head of curls, beloved of poets
Enhances warmth and welcome;
Face as the sun each bright new dawn,
Banishes grief with laughter;
It is my sad woe, love, that we're not alone,
In that fort of Cian, son of Cáinte.

I'm deep now in pain, sleepless, awake,
Longing for you, fairest maiden;
It's you I prefer in all of Éireann,
I deny not one whit, for that reason;
If you were to walk with me, unblemished star,
My health would be light and carefree,
You'll get flower and mead and the fruit of trees,
In the fort of Cian, son of Cáinte.

The call of the hounds you will hear as they chase
The wide-haunched, swift-legged hare;
The cuckoo's sweet voice and sound of thrush
Joyful on boughs in the dales;
In the pond, calm and cool, you will see fish in shoals,
Swimming and chasing each other,
And beyond you can see in the distance, the bay,
From the fort of Cian, son of Cáinte.

My gentle sweet girl, it is better you'd fare,
To spend your young life with me there,
Than sad in a corner with a miserly boor,
At your spinning-wheel and carders;
You'll have sweet music played nimbly on harpstrings
To awake you, and love poems, thereafter;
There's no fort on earth as airy and bright
As the hill of Cian, son of Cáinte.

Charming sweet lass of the pearled curling tresses,
Come out later on in the night,
When the people and clergy are deep in slumber
Asleep beneath linens white;
Far north we will both be, away from them all,
At the break of tomorrow's new dawn,
Together and fearless in sweet isolation
In the cave of Cian, son of Cáinte.

'Away with your pleading – though much you have
stated –
A habit of interest to many;
And the finest of gifts, than a great many jewels,
I have never heard you relating;
Free holdings there of cows and sheep
And hoards of pearls in palaces,
Its worth I receive not without a device
Used at night time, for making children.'

*Pádraigín Ní Uallacháin*

## DONNCHADH RUA MAC CON MARA

### *The Fair Hills of Ireland*

A plenteous place is Ireland for hospitable cheer,
*Uileacan dubh*[1] *O!*
Where the wholesome fruit is bursting from the yellow
barley ear;
*Uileacan dubh O!*
There is honey in the trees where her misty vales expand,
And her forest paths, in summer, are by falling waters fann'd,
There is dew at high noontide there, and springs i' the
yellow sand,
On the fair hills of holy Ireland.

1. *Uileacan dubh*: black lament

Curl'd he is and ringletted, and plaited to the knee,
*Uileacan dubh O!*
Each captain who comes sailing across the Irish sea,
*Uileacan dubh O!*
And I will make my journey, if life and health but stand,
Unto that pleasant country, that fresh and fragrant strand,
And leave your boasted braveries, your wealth and high
command,
For the fair hills of holy Ireland.

Large and profitable are the stacks upon the ground,
*Uileacan dubh O!*
The butter and the cream do wondrously abound,
*Uileacan dubh O!*
The cresses on the water and the sorrels are at hand,
And the cuckoo's calling daily his note of music bland,
And the bold thrush sings so bravely his song i' the
forests grand,
On the fair hills of holy Ireland.

*Samuel Ferguson*

## ART MAC CUMHAIGH

(*c.*1738–73)

### *The Churchyard of Creggan*

HE

By the Churchyard of Creggan I lay last night in misery,
And at dawn a fair queenly one up and saluted me.
Her hair it shone golden, her cheeks blushed fiery:
'Twas a tonic for mankind just to look on her beauty.

SHE

Kind sir, don't loiter with your mind in a mist,
But get up, keep me company on the road to the west,
Through sweet lands never gripped by the outlander's fist,
Be fêted in great halls, and by music caressed.

HE

Honey queen, are you Helen, who wrought such distress,
Or one of the nine Parnassians, decked out in fleshly dress?
Where on earth were you reared, a star all so cloudless,
That you ask me to pipe as you make stately progress?

SHE

Enough questions there! I don't couch this side of Boyne,
I was fostered by Gráinne Óg since a halfling bairn,
Among the schools of poets, I'm liberal with song,
At twilight in Tara or at daybreak in Tyrone.

HE

Great pity the loss of the Gaels of Tyrone,
The heirs of the Fews lie in grief under stone,
They never forsook music, Niall Frasach's pure scions,
But at Christmas gave us coats in exchange for praise-poems.

SHE

The tribes fell at Aughrim, at Boyne were low laid,
The crowned sons of Ír, the shelter of the priesthood.
Wouldn't you sooner be in my green hill each noontide,
Than have Bully's Orange shaft ever lodged in your side?

HE

I'd not refuse you, not for an emperor's ransom,
Except for the friends that I'd leave here at home,
And the wife I wooed with promises handsome,
If I left her now, she would grieve me and groan.

SHE

I don't think your friends are true friends at all,
To leave you thus ragged, poor and distressful,
Better to come along now – take my hand smooth and small –
Than to have your verses met with sneers and catcalls.

HE

My heart, what destiny decrees, I can't but obey,
But vouchsafe me this, as we set out on our way,
If I die by Shannon, on Manannaun's shore, or in grand
  Egypt, say
That you'll bury me, Gael with Gael, in Creggan's cold clay.

*Kit Fryatt*

## EOGHAN RUA Ó SÚILLEABHÁIN

### *The Volatile Kerryman*

OWEN

I travelled the land from Leap to Corbally
From bright Glandore to sweet Roscarbery,
    Oh-roh! and to Cashel of sloes.
Fairs twice a week there on Thursday and Saturday,
High and low Masses there sung by the clergy,
Tankards and quarts full of wine and brandy,
Fine young women to keep you handy,
    Oh-roh! 'tis Heaven below.

GIRL

That would be the poor day if I ran away with you,
'Tis a rake of your like that would make me play with you,
        Oh-roh! 'Twould be madness to go!
Oh, my father won't mind if you say you'll marry me,
But he'll murder us both if to Kerry you carry me,
        Oh-roh! with a terrible blow.
But if you give your oath that you'll never stray from me
I'll buy you strong drink that will coax you to stay with me.
Make up your mind and say you'll come home with me,
  *(Coaxing)*
Make up your mind and say you'll come home with me,
        Oh-roh! And my fortune you'll own.

OWEN

Oh, there's no place on earth that I wouldn't go with you,
And I'd fit out a ship if I thought 'twould pleasure you,
        Oh-roh! O'er the ocean we'd go.
I would carry you with me across to Germany,
In Venice or Rome we'd have wine and company,
Come and be brave! Don't be afraid of me!
  *(Coaxing)*
Come and be nice, and travel away with me.
        Oh-roh! my darling, my own.

GIRL

Oh, I'd travel the world and Newfoundland with you,
And to see foreign countries would surely be grand
  with you,
        Oh-roh! 'tis happy I'd go.
But to wed me your promise I must be certain of,
And to live out our lives in sweet contentment, love,
        Oh-roh! 'tis you I adore.

OWEN

Here is my hand in your hand to hold with you,
To bind us for life so that I'll grow old with you,
Our engagement is made now, and love in my heart for you,
There's a half of my soul that will never part from you.
        Oh-roh! while the world shall roll.

GIRL

If I follow you close to the slopes of Carbery,
My senses I'll lose if you don't come home with me,
        Oh-roh! the teardrops will flow.

OWEN

Bring a purseful of gold for the road along with you,
For money's no load when 'tis golden sovereigns,
        Oh-roh! to spend as we roam.

GIRL

Your hands will be soft without trace of work on them
No digging potatoes or cutting turf with them,

OWEN

There'll be dancing all night, and drinking and devilment;

GIRL

Music and whiskey,

OWEN

                    For money makes merriment,

BOTH

        Oh-roh! 'tis the Devil's own sport.

GIRL

But you're telling me lies, you don't mean the half of it,
Coaxing me now, and in a while you'll laugh at it,
        Oh-roh! 'Twould make me a show.

OWEN

Oh love of my heart, my dear, pay heed to me,
I wouldn't deceive you for Ireland free to me.
For fear it would lead me to Hell's black deanery,
Sweet and dear will you always be to me,
        Oh-roh! 'til in the coffin I go.

GIRL

Don't mention the coffin, bad luck to speak of it,
But talk of fine sport for 'tis we'll be seeking it,
        Oh-roh! and adventures galore!
Call in the neighbours, there's barrels of porter full
And we'll make a great noise will be heard in Waterford.
        Oh-roh! while the world shall roll!
Oh, I'd rather your love than the riches of Solomon,
Acres of cattle or valleys of singing birds,
I've made up my mind, and the Pope couldn't change it now,
I'd give you the world if I could arrange it now.
        Oh-roh! my darling, my own!

OWEN

A fortnight spent travelling far and wide with her,
Making up songs for her, telling lies to her,
        Oh-roh! to keep her aglow,
'Til the last golden sovereign I winkled out of her,
Sweetly and easily, never a shout from her,
        Oh-roh! indeed money's no load!
Oh, 'twas smartly I settled my beaver hat on me,
The blackthorn stick and the coat that flattered me,
And over the ditches I fled like a bat from her,
Home to Kerry, like a scalded cat from her,
        Oh-roh! while she trotted below.

As nightfall came on, she was most astonished
To see that her darling had totally vanished –
        Oh-roh! with a great hullagone!
She tore at her hair like a raving lunatic,
She swore I betrayed her and fairly ruined her,

# OLIVER GOLDSMITH

## *from* She Stoops to Conquer

### *Song*

Let schoolmasters puzzle their brain,
  With grammar and nonsense and learning;
Good liquor, I stoutly maintain,
  Gives genius a better discerning.
Let them brag of their heathenish gods,
  Their Lethes, their Styxes and Stygians,
Their Quis and their Quaes and their Quods –
  They're all but a parcel of pigeons.
    *Toroddle, toroddle, toroll.*

When Methodist preachers come down
  A-preaching that drinking is sinful,
I'll wager the rascals a crown
  They always preach best with a skinful.
But when you come down with your pence
  For a slice of their scurvy religion,
I'll leave it to all men of sense –
  But you, my good friend, are the pigeon.
    *Toroddle, toroddle, toroll.*

Then come, put the jorum about,
  And let us be merry and clever;
Our hearts and our liquors are stout:
  Here's the Three Jolly Pigeons forever.
Let some cry up woodcock or hare,
  Your bustards, your ducks and your widgeons;
But of all the birds in the air,
  Here's a health to the Three Jolly Pigeons.
    *Toroddle, toroddle, toroll.*

# JOHN O'KEEFFE

(1747–1833)

## Amo, Amas, *I Love a Lass*

*Amo, amas,*
I love a lass
As a cedar tall and slender;
Sweet cowslips' grace
Is her Nominative Case,
And she's of the Feminine Gender.
*Rorum, corum, sunt Divorum,*
*Harum, scarum Divo!*
Tag rag, merry derry, periwig and hatband,
*Hic hac, horum Genetivo!*

Can I decline
A nymph divine?
Her voice as a flute is *dulcis,*
Her *oculi* bright,
Her *manus* white,
And soft, when I *tacto*, her pulse is!
*Rorum, corum, sunt Divorum,*
*Harum scarum Divo!*
Tag rag, merry derry, periwig and hatband,
*Hic hac, horum Genetivo!*

O, how *bella*
Is my *Puella!*
I'll kiss *sæculorum!*
If I've luck, Sir,
She's my *Uxor* –
*O, dies benedictorum!*
*Rorum, corum, sunt Divorum,*
*Harum scarum Divo!*
Tag rag, merry derry, periwig and hatband,
*Hic, hac, horum Genetivo!*

## JOHN PHILPOTT CURRAN
## (1750–1817)

### *The Deserter's Meditation*

If sadly thinking, with spirits sinking,
  Could, more than drinking, my cares compose,
A cure for sorrow from sighs I'd borrow,
  And hope tomorrow would end my woes.
But as in wailing there's nought availing,
  And Death unfailing will strike the blow,
Then for that reason, and for a season,
  Let us be merry before we go!

To joy a stranger, a wayworn ranger,
  In ev'ry danger my course I've run;
Now hope all ending, and death befriending,
  His last aid lending, my cares are done.
No more a rover, or hapless lover,
  My griefs are over – my glass runs low;
Then for that reason, and for a season,
  Let us be merry before we go!

## RICHARD ALFRED MILLIKEN
## (1767–1815)

### *The Groves of Blarney*

The groves of Blarney
  They look so charming,
Down by the purling
  Of sweet, silent brooks,

Being banked with posies
That spontaneous grow there,
Planted in order
  By the sweet 'Rock Close'.
'Tis there the daisy
And the sweet carnation,
The blooming pink
  And the rose so fair.
The daffodowndilly,
Likewise the lily,
All flowers that scent
  The sweet, fragrant air.

'Tis Lady Jeffers
That owns this station;
Like Alexander,
  Or Queen Helen fair,
There's no commander
In all the nation,
For emulation,
  Can with her compare.
Such walls surround her,
That no nine-pounder
Could dare to plunder
  Her place of strength;
But Oliver Cromwell
Her he did pommell,
And made a breach
  In her battlement.

There's gravel walks there
For speculation
And conversation
  In sweet solitude.
'Tis there the lover
May hear the dove, or
The gentle plover
  In the afternoon;

And if a lady
Would be so engaging
As to walk alone in
   Those shady bowers,
'Tis there the courtier
He may transport her
Into some fort, or
   All under ground.

For 'tis there's a cave where
No daylight enters,
But cats and badgers
   Are for ever bred;
Being mossed by nature,
That makes it sweeter
Than a coach-and-six or
   A feather bed.
'Tis there the lake is,
Well stored with perches,
And comely eels in
   The verdant mud;
Besides the leeches,
And groves of beeches,
Standing in order
   For to guard the flood.

There's statues gracing
This noble place in –
All heathen gods
   And nymphs so fair;
Bold Neptune, Plutarch,
And Nicodemus,
All standing naked
   In the open air!
So now to finish
This brave narration,
Which my poor genii
   Could not entwine;

But were I Homer,
Or Nebuchadnezzar,
'Tis in every feature
  I would make it shine.

## ANONYMOUS

### *The Boyne Water*

July the first, of a morning clear, one thousand six hundred
  and ninety,
King William did his men prepare, of thousands he had thirty,
To fight King James and all his foes, encamped near the Boyne
  Water;
He little feared, though two to one, their multitude to scatter.

King William called his officers, saying, 'Gentlemen, mind
  your station,
And let your valour here be shown before this Irish nation;
My brazen walls let no man break, and your subtle foes you'll
  scatter,
Be sure you show them good English play as you go over the
  water.'

Both foot and horse they marched on, intending them to batter,
But the brave Duke Schomberg he was shot as he crossed over
  the water.
When that King William did observe the brave Duke
  Schomberg falling,
He reined his horse with a heavy heart, on the Enniskilleners
  calling:

'What will you do for me, brave boys see yonder men
retreating?
Our enemies encouraged are, and English drums are beating.'
He says, 'My boys feel no dismay at the losing of one
commander,
For God shall be our King this day, and I'll be general under.'

Within four yards of our forefront, before a shot was fired,
A sudden snuff they got that day, which little they desired;
For horse and man fell to the ground, and some hung on their
saddle:
Others turned up their forked ends, which we call *coup
de ladle*.

Prince Eugene's regiment was the next, on our right hand
advanced
Into a field of standing wheat, where Irish horses pranced;
But the brandy ran so in their heads, their senses all did
scatter,
They little thought to leave their bones that day at the Boyne
Water.

Both men and horse lay on the ground, and many lay there
bleeding,
I saw no sickles there that day but, sure, there was sharp
shearing.
Now, praise God, all true Protestants, and heaven's and
earth's Creator,
For the deliverance he sent our enemies to scatter.
The Church's foes will pine away, like churlish-hearted Nabal,
For our deliverer came this day like the great Zorobabal.

So praise God, all true Protestants, and I will say no further,
But had the Papists gained that day, there would have been
open murder.
Although King James and many more were ne'er that way
inclined,
It was not in their power to stop what the rabble they
designed.

## *Shule Aroon*

I would I were on yonder hill,
'Tis there I'd sit and cry my fill,
And every tear would turn a mill,
*Is go d-teidh tu, a mhúrnín, slán!*
*Siubhail, siubhail, siubhail, a rúin!*
*Siubhail go socair, agus siubhail go ciúin,*
*Siubhail go d-ti an doras agus eulaigh liom,*
*Is go d-teidh tu, a mhúrnín, slán!*[1]

I'll sell my rock, I'll sell my reel,
I'll sell my only spinning-wheel,
To buy for my love a sword of steel,
*Is go d-teidh tu, a mhúrnín, slán!*
*Siubhail, siubhail, siubhail, a rúin!*
*Siubhail go socair, agus siubhail go ciúin,*
*Siubhail go d-ti an doras agus eulaigh liom,*
*Is go d-teidh tu, a mhúrnín, slán!*

I'll dye my petticoats, I'll dye them red,
And round the world I'll beg my bread,
Until my parents shall wish me dead,
*Is go d-teidh tu, a mhúrnín, slán!*
*Siubhail, siubhail, siubhail, a rúin!*
*Siubhail go socair, agus siubhail go ciúin,*
*Siubhail go d-ti an doras agus eulaigh liom,*
*Is go d-teidh tu, a mhúrnín, slán!*

I wish, I wish, I wish in vain,
I wish I had my heart again,
And vainly think I'd not complain,
*Is go d-teidh tu, a mhúrnín, slán!*

1. Come, come, come, O Love!
Quickly come to me, softly move;
Come to the door, and away we'll flee,
And safe for aye may my darling be! (tr. George Sigerson)

*Siubhail, siubhail, siubhail, a rúin!*
*Siubhail go socair, agus siubhail go ciúin,*
*Siubhail go d-ti an doras agus eulaigh liom,*
*Is go d-teidh tu, a mhúrnín, slán!*

But now my love has gone to France,
To try his fortune to advance;
If he e'er come back, 'tis but a chance,
*Is go d-teidh tu, a mhúrnín, slán!*
*Siubhail, siubhail, siubhail, a rúin!*
*Siubhail go socair, agus siubhail go ciúin,*
*Siubhail go d-ti an doras agus eulaigh liom,*
*Is go d-teidh tu, a mhúrnín, slán!*

## *My Love is Like the Sun*

The winter is past,
And the summer's come at last
And the blackbirds sing in every tree;
The hearts of these are glad
But my poor heart is sad,
For my true love is parted from me.

The rose upon the briar
By the water running clear
Gives joy to the linnet and the bee;
Their little hearts are blest
But mine is not at rest,
Since my true love is absent from me.

A livery I'll wear
And I'll comb out my hair,
And in velvet so green I will appear,
And straight I will repair
To the Curragh of Kildare
For it's there I'll find tidings of my dear.

I'll wear a cap of black
With a frill around my neck,
Gold rings on my fingers I will wear:
And this I'll undertake
All for my true love's sake,
Who resides at the Curragh of Kildare.

I would not think it strange
The whole wide world to range
In search of tidings of my dear;
But here in Cupid's chain
I am bound to remain,
And to spend my whole life in despair.

My love is like the sun
That in the firmament does run,
And always proves constant and true;
But he is like the moon
That wanders up and down,
The moon that every month is new.

All ye that are in love
And cannot it remove,
I pity the pains you endure;
For experience lets me know
That your hearts are full of woe,
A woe that no mortal can cure.

## *The Blackbird*

Upon a fair morning for soft recreation,
I heard a fair lady making her moan,
With sighing and sobbing and sad lamentation,
Saying, my Blackbird most royal is flown;
My thoughts they deceive me,
Reflections do grieve me,

And I am over-burdened with sad misery,
Yet if death it should blind me,
As true love inclines me,
My Blackbird I'll seek out wherever he be.

Once in fair England my Blackbird did flourish,
He was the chief flower that in it did spring –
Prime ladies of honour his person did nourish,
Because he was the true son of a king.
But this false fortune,
Which still is uncertain,
Has caused this parting between him and me,
His name I'll advance
In Spain and in France,
And seek out my Blackbird, wherever he be.

The birds of the forest they all met together –
The turtle was chosen to dwell with the dove,
And I am resolved in fair or foul weather
To seek out until I find my true love;
He's all my heart's treasure,
My joy and my pleasure
And justly, my love, my heart will follow thee,
Who is constant and kind,
And courageous of mind,
All bliss to my Blackbird wherever he be.

In England my Blackbird and I were together,
Where he was still noble and generous of heart,
And woe to the time that he first went thither,
Alas, he was forced from thence to depart.
In Scotland he is deemed,
And highly esteemed,
In England he seemed a stranger to be,
Yet his name shall remain
In France and in Spain,
All bliss to my Blackbird, wherever he be.

What if the fowler my Blackbird has taken?
  Then sighing and sobbing shall be all my tune;
But if he is safe, I will not be forsaken,
  And hope yet to see him in May or in June.
    For him through the fire,
    Through mud and through mire
  I'll go, for I love him to such a degree,
    Who is generous and kind,
    And noble of mind,
  Deserving all blessings wherever he be.

It is not the ocean can fright me with danger,
  For though like a pilgrim I wander forlorn
I may meet with friendship from one that's a stranger
  More than from one that in England was born.
    Oh! Heaven so spacious,
    To Britain be gracious,
  Though some there be odious both to him and me,
    Yet joy and renown
    And laurel shall crown
My Blackbird with honour wherever he be.

## *The Night before Larry was Stretched*

The night before Larry was stretched,
  The boys they all paid him a visit;
A bait in their sacks, too, they fetched;
  They sweated their duds till they riz it:
For Larry was ever the lad,
  When a boy was condemned to the squeezer,
Would fence all the duds that he had
  To help a poor friend to a sneezer,
    And warm his gob 'fore he died.

The boys they came crowding in fast,
  They drew all their stools round about him,
Six glims round his trap-case were placed,
  He couldn't be well waked without 'em.

When one of us asked could he die
  Without having duly repented,
Says Larry, 'That's all in my eye;
  And first by the clargy invented,
    To get a fat bit for themselves.'

'I'm sorry, dear Larry,' says I,
  'To see you in this situation;
And, blister my limbs if I lie,
  I'd as lieve it had been my own station.'
'Ochone! it's all over,' says he,
  'For the neckcloth I'll be forced to put on,
And by this time tomorrow you'll see
  Your poor Larry as dead as a mutton,
    Because, why, his courage was good.

'And I'll be cut up like a pie,
  And my nob from my body be parted.'
'You're in the wrong box, then,' says I,
  'For blast me if they're so hard-hearted:
A chalk on the back of your neck
  Is all that Jack Ketch dares to give you;
Then mind not such trifles a feck,
  For why should the likes of them grieve you?
    And now, boys, come tip us the deck.'

The cards being called for, they played,
  Till Larry found one of them cheated;
A dart at his napper he made
  (The boy being easily heated):
'Oh, by the hokey, you thief,
  I'll scuttle your nob with my daddle!
You cheat me because I'm in grief,
  But soon I'll demolish your noddle,
    And leave you your claret to drink.'

Then the clergy came in with his book,
  He spoke him so smooth and so civil;
Larry tipped him a Kilmainham look,
  And pitched his big wig to the devil;
Then sighing, he threw back his head
  To get a sweet drop of the bottle,
And pitiful sighing, he said:
  'Oh, the hemp will be soon round my throttle
    And choke my poor windpipe to death.

'Though sure it's the best way to die,
  Oh, the devil a better a-livin'!
For, sure, when the gallows is high
  Your journey is shorter to Heaven:
But what harasses Larry the most,
  And makes his poor soul melancholy,
Is to think of the time when his ghost
  Will come in a sheet to sweet Molly –
    Oh, sure it will kill her alive!'

So moving these last words he spoke,
  We all vented our tears in a shower;
For my part, I thought my heart broke,
  To see him cut down like a flower.
On his travels we watched him next day;
  Oh, the throttler! I thought I could kill him;
But Larry not one word did say,
  Nor changed till he come to 'King William' –
    Then, *musha!* his colour grew white.

When he came to the nubbling chit,
  He was tucked up so neat and so pretty,
The rumbler jogged off from his feet,
  And he died with his face to the city;
He kicked, too – but that was all pride,
  For soon you might see 'twas all over;
Soon after the noose was untied,
  And at darky we waked him in clover,
    And sent him to take a ground sweat.

## *Willy Reilly*

'Oh! rise up, Willy Reilly, and come along with me,
I mean for to go with you and leave this counterie,
To leave my father's dwelling, his houses and free land.'
And away goes Willy Reilly and his dear *Coolen Ban*.

They go by hills and mountains, and by yon lonesome plain,
Through shady groves and valleys, all dangers to refrain;
But her father followed after with a well-armed band,
And taken was poor Reilly and his dear *Coolen Ban*.

It's home then she was taken, and in her closet bound;
Poor Reilly all in Sligo jail lay on the stony ground,
Till at the bar of justice, before the Judge he'd stand,
For nothing but the stealing of his dear *Coolen Ban*.

'Now in the cold, cold iron my hands and feet are bound,
I'm handcuffed like a murderer, and tied unto the ground.
But all the toil and slavery I'm willing for to stand,
Still hoping to be succoured by my dear *Coolen Ban*.'

The jailor's son to Reilly goes, and thus to him did say:
'Oh! get up, Willy Reilly, you must appear this day,
For great Squire Foillard's anger you never can withstand,
I'm afeer'd you'll suffer sorely for your dear *Coolen Ban*.

'This is the news, young Reilly, last night that I did hear:
The lady's oath will hang you or else will set you clear.'
'If that be so,' says Reilly, 'her pleasure I will stand,
Still hoping to be succoured by my dear *Coolen Ban*.'

Now Willy's drest from top to toe all in a suit of green,
His hair hangs o'er his shoulders most glorious to be seen;
He's tall and straight, and comely as any could be found;
He's fit for Foillard's daughter, was she heiress to a crown.

The Judge he said: 'This lady being in her tender youth,
If Reilly has deluded her she will declare the truth.'
Then, like a moving beauty bright, before him she did stand,
'You're welcome there, my heart's delight and dear
*Coolen Ban*.'

'Oh, gentlemen,' Squire Foillard said, 'with pity look on me,
This villain came amongst us to disgrace our family,
And by his base contrivances this villainy was planned;
If I don't get satisfaction I'll quit this Irish land.'

The lady with a tear began, and thus replied she:
'The fault is none of Reilly's, the blame lies all on me;
I forced him for to leave his place and come along with me;
I loved him out of measure, which wrought our destiny.'

Out bespoke the noble Fox, at the table he stood by:
'Oh, gentlemen, consider on this extremity;
To hang a man for love is a murder, you may see:
So spare the life of Reilly, let him leave this counterie.'

'Good my lord, he stole from her her diamonds and her rings,
Gold watch and silver buckles, and many precious things,
Which cost me in bright guineas more than five hundred
pounds,
I'll have the life of Reilly should I lose ten thousand pounds.'

'Good my lord, I gave them him as tokens of true love,
And when we are a-parting I will them all remove;
If you have got them, Reilly, pray send them home to me.'
'I will, my loving lady, with many thanks to thee.'

'There is a ring among them I allow yourself to wear,
With thirty locket diamonds well set in silver fair,
And as a true-love token wear it on your right hand,
That you'll think on my poor broken heart when you're
in foreign land.'

Then out spoke noble Fox: 'You may let the prisoner go;
The lady's oath has cleared him, as the Jury all may know.
She has released her own true love, she has renewed his
name;
May her honour bright gain high estate, and her offspring
rise to fame!'

## *The Irish Phœnix*

Once more kind Muses it is your duty, for to infuse me with verse
sublime,
My subject surely is now amusing, as you have chose me for to
repine;
Ye mangling poets don't dare oppose me, for now my notions are
raised on high,
Kind Gods support me through these my posies, in you I glory
and still rely.

One pleasant evening for recreation, as I was ranging down by
the shore,
I spied a maiden a lovely fair one, I thought her Venus sprung
from the foam,
In admiration on her I gazed, in deep amazement I stood to view,
This second Phœnix exceeding nature and for to praise her it is
my due.

To you fair Sabra in all her charms or chaste Diana can't equalize,
Nor she whom Paris as is recorded was pleased to order the
Golden Prize;
The bright Aurora in all her glory or Goddess Flora you far
outvie,
My brain is roving in sad emotions I must adore you until I die.

You are an angel, your good and pleasing, your fine behaviour
enchanted me,
Your chains are really, I'm doomed to wear them, I wish sincerely
for liberty.

These wounds you gave me, say will you heal them, you have enslaved me, now set me free,
It's you can ease me, from bonds release me, and let me gain my tranquility.

My jewel and darling, more fair than morning, or orient radiant you far outshine,
Your eyes transparent has me alarmed, I wish, my charmer, that you were mine;
Your swan-like bosom, your neck including, your cheeks are blooming vermillion red,
Sure every feature new beauty graces, and auburn tresses flow from your head.

My breast is loaded with discomposure, in love sick motion I now complain,
Sly Cupid sporting at my corrodings, that brat he glories in giving pain;
Will you relieve me, from death reprieve me, your captive bleeder I now remain,
I'm always weeping and still am grieving, but it's when sleeping of you I dream.

All recreations I'll now renege them, in silent places I mean to rove,
My prayers compleatly I'll offer daily, in adoration near Willow Grove,
Ye Supreme Deities say will I gain her, will I obtain her, can I intrude,
On you my fairest what shall I say love, but that I'm almost crazy for Mary Booth?

# ANONYMOUS SONGS OF THE 1798 REBELLION

## IRISH

### *Slievenamon*

It is my sorrow that this day's troubles
    Poor Irishmen so sore did strike,
Because our tyrants are laughing at us,
    And say they fear neither fork nor pike;
Our Major never came to lead us,
    We had no orders and drifted on
As you'd send a drover with a cow to the fair
    On the sunny side of Slievenamon.

Ross was the place we were defeated,
    There we left many a pikeman dead,
Little children burned to ashes,
    Women in holes and ditches hid.
But I promise you the men that slew them
    We'll meet them yet with pike and gun,
And we'll drive the yeomen in flight before us
    When we pay them back on Slievenamon.

The sturdy Frenchman with ships in order
    Beneath sharp masts is long at sea;
They're always saying they will come to Ireland,
    And they will set the Irish free.

Light as a blackbird on a green bough swinging
Would be my heart if the French would come –
O the broken ranks and the trumpets ringing
On the sunny side of Slievenamon!

*Frank O'Connor*

## ENGLISH

### *The Star of Liberty*

O'er the vine-cover'd hills and gay regions of FRANCE,
See the day Star of LIBERTY rise;
Thro' the clouds of detraction, unwearied, advance,
And hold its new course thro' the skies.
An effulgence so mild, with a lustre so bright,
All Europe, with wonder, surveys;
And from desarts of darkness, and dungeons of night,
Contends for a share of the blaze.

Let BURKE, like a Bat, from its splendour retire,
A splendour too strong for his eyes,
Let pedants and fools his effusions admire,
Intrapt in his cobwebs, like flies:
Shall frenzy and sophistry hope to prevail
Where reason opposes her weight –
When the welfare of millions is hung in the scale,
And the balance yet trembles with fate?

Ah! who 'midst the horrors of night wou'd abide,
That can taste the pure breezes of morn;
Or who, that has drunk of the chrystalline tide,
To the feculent flood would return?

When the bosom of beauty the throbbing heart meets,
Ah! who can the transport decline?
Or who that has tasted of Liberty's sweets,
The prize, but with life, wou'd resign?

But 'tis over; – high Heav'n the decision approves –
Oppression has struggled in vain:
To the hell she has form'd, superstition removes;
And tyranny bites its own chain.
In the records of time a new æra unfolds, –
All nature exults in its birth –
His creation, benign, the CREATOR beholds,
And gives a new charter to earth.

O catch its high import, ye winds, as ye blow!
O hear it, ye waves, as ye roll!
From regions that feel the sun's vertical glow,
To the farthest extremes of the pole.
*Equal rights* – *equal laws* – to the nations around,
*Peace* and *friendship*, its precepts impart –
And wherever the footsteps of *man* shall be found,
May he bind the DECREE ON HIS HEART.

## *The Shan Van Vocht*

'Oh! the French are on the say,'
Says the Shan Van Vocht;
'The French are on the say,'
Says the Shan Van Vocht;
'Oh! the French are in the Bay,
They'll be here without delay,
And the Orange will decay,'
Says the Shan Van Vocht.
'Oh ! the French are in the Bay,
They'll be here by break of day
And the Orange will decay,'
Says the Shan Van Vocht.

'And where will they have their camp?'
Says the Shan Van Vocht;
'Where will they have their camp?'
Says the Shan Van Vocht;
'On the Curragh of Kildare,
The boys they will be there,
With their pikes in good repair,'
Says the Shan Van Vocht.
'To the Curragh of Kildare
The boys they will repair
And Lord Edward will be there,'
Says the Shan Van Vocht.

'Then what will the yeomen do?'
Says the Shan Van Vocht;
'What should the yeomen do?'
Says the Shan Van Vocht;
'What should the yeomen do,
But throw off the red and blue,
And swear that they'll be true
To the Shan Van Vocht?
What should the yeomen do,
But throw off the red and blue,
And swear that they'll be true
To the Shan Van Vocht?'

'And what colour will they wear?'
Says the Shan Van Vocht;
'What colour will they wear?'
Says the Shan Van Vocht;
'What colours should be seen
Where their father's homes have been
But their own immortal green?'
Says the Shan Van Vocht.

'And will Ireland then be free?'
Says the Shan Van Vocht;
'Will Ireland then be free?'
Says the Shan Van Vocht;

'Yes! Ireland shall be free,
From the centre to the sea;
Then hurrah for Liberty!'
        Says the Shan Van Vocht;
'Yes! Ireland shall be free,
From the centre to the sea;
Then hurrah for Liberty!'
        Says the Shan Van Vocht.

## *The Croppy Boy*

'Twas early, early in the spring,
The birds did whistle and sweetly sing,
Changing their notes from tree to tree,
And the song they sang was Old Ireland free.

'Twas early, early in the night,
The yeoman cavalry gave me a fright;
The yeoman cavalry was my downfall
And taken was I by Lord Cornwall.

'Twas in the guard-house that I was laid
And in a parlour that I was tried;
My sentence passed and my courage low
To New Geneva I was forced to go.

As I was passing by my father's door,
My brother William stood on the floor;
My aged father stood at the door,
And my tender mother her hair she tore.

As I was walking up Wexford Street
My own first cousin I chanced to meet;
My own first cousin did me betray,
And for one bare guinea swore my life away.

My sister Mary heard the express,
She ran downstairs in her morning-dress,
'Five hundred guineas I will lay down,
To see my brother safe in Wexford Town.'

As I was walking up Wexford Hill,
Who could blame me if I cried my fill?
I looked behind and I looked before,
But my tender mother I could see no more.

As I was mounted on the platform high,
My aged father was standing by;
My aged father did me deny,
And the name he gave me was the Croppy Boy.

It was in Geneva this young man died,
And in Geneva his body lies;
And you good Christians that do pass by
Shed just one tear for the Croppy Boy.

## *General Wonder*

General Wonder in our land,
And General Consternation;
General Gale on Bantry strand,
For General Preservation.

General Rich he shook with awe
At General Insurrection;
General Poor his sword did draw,
With General Disaffection.

General Blood was just at hand,
As General Hoche appeared;
General Woe fled through our land,
And General Want was feared.

General Gale our fears dispersed,
  He conquered General Dread;
General Joy each heart has swelled,
      As General Hoche has fled.

General Love no blood has shed,
  He left us General Ease;
General Horror he has fled,
      Let God get General Praise.

To that great General of the skies
  That sent us General Gale,
With General Love our voices rise
      In one great General Peal.

# V

# UNION AND DISSENSION: 1801–80

*Thy struggling nation still retains her pride*

Thomas Moore, 'Corruption: An Epistle'

## JAMES ORR
## (1770–1816)

### *Donegore Hill*

*Ephie's base bairntime, trail-pike brood,*
*Were arm'd as weel as tribes that stood;*
*Yet on the battle iika cauf*[1]
*Turn'd his backside, an' scamper'd aff.*
Psalm 78:9

The dew-draps wat[2] the fiels o' braird,[3]
That soon the war-horse thortur'd;[4]
An falds[5] were op'd by monie a herd
Wha lang ere night lay tortur'd;
Whan chiels[6] wha grudg'd to be sae tax'd
An tyth'd by rack-rent blauth'ry,[7]
Turn'd out *en masse*, as soon as ax'd –
An unco[8] throuither[9] squath'ry[10]
Were we, that day.

While close-leagu'd crappies rais'd the hoards
O' pikes, pike-shafts, forks, firelocks,
Some melted lead – some saw'd deal-boards –
Some hade, like hens in byre-neuks;[11]
Wives baket bonnocks[12] for their men,
Wi' tears instead o' water;
An' lasses made cockades o' green
For chaps wha us'd to flatter
Their pride ilk day.

1. *cauf*: calf 2. *wat*: wet 3. *braird*: first shoots of grain 4. *thortur'd*: crossed
5. *falds*: folds 6. *chiels*: fellows 7. *blauth'ry*: nonsense 8. *unco*: exceedingly
9. *throuither*: confusedly mingled 10. *squath'ry*: something scattered into pieces
11. *byre-neuks*: corners of byres 12. *bonnocks*: oatmeal cakes

A brave man firmly leain'[13] hame
I ay was proud to think on;
The wife-obeyin' son o' shame
Wi' kindlin e'e I blink on:
'Peace, peace be wi' ye! – ah! return
Ere lang and lea the daft anes' –
'Please guid,' quo he, 'before the morn
In spite o' a' our chieftains,
An' guards, this day.'

But when the pokes[14] o' provender
Were slung on ilka shou'der,
Hags, wha to henpeck didna spare,
Loot out the yells the louder. –
Had they, whan blood about their heart
Cauld fear made cake,[15] an' crudle,[16]
Ta'en twa rash gills frae Herdman's quart,
'Twad rous'd the calm, slow puddle
I' their veins that day.

Now *Leaders*, laith[17] to lea the rigs
Whase leash they fear'd was broken
An' *Privates*, cursin' purse-proud prigs,
Wha brought 'em balls to sloken;
Repentant Painites at their pray'rs,
An' dastards crousely craikin',[18]
Move on, heroic, to the wars
They meant na to partake in,
By night, or day.

Some fastin' yet, now strave to eat
The piece, that butter yellow'd;
An' some, in flocks, drank out cream crocks,
That wives but little valu'd:
Some lettin' on their burn to mak',

13. *leain'*: leaving 14. *pokes*: bags 15. *cake*: quake 16. *crudle*: curdle
17. *laith*: loath 18. *crousely craikin'*: coarsely croaking

The rear-guard, goadin', hasten'd;
Some hunk'rin' at a lee dyke back,
Boost houghel[19] on, ere fasten'd
Their breeks, that day.

The truly brave, as journeyin' on
They pass by *weans* an' *mithers*,
Think on red fiel's, whare soon may groan,
The *husbands*, an' the *fathers*:
They think how soon thae bonie things
May lose the youths they're true to;
An' see the rabble, strife ay brings,
Ravage their mansions, new to
Sic[20] scenes, that day.

When to the tap o' DONEGORE
Braid-islan' corps cam' postin',
The red-wud, warpin, wild uproar,
Was like a bee scap castin';[21]
For ******* ***** took ragweed farms,
(Fears e'e has ay the jaundice)
For *Nugent's* red-coats, bright in arms,
An' rush! the pale-fac'd randies[22]
Took leg, that day.

The *camp's* brak up. Owre braes, an' bogs,
The *patriots* seek their *sections*;
Arms, ammunition, bread-bags, brogues,
Lye skail'd[23] in a' directions:
Ane half, alas! wad fear'd to face
Auld Fogies, faps,[24] or women;
Tho' strong, untried, they swore in pride,
'Moilie[25] wad dunch[26] the yeomen,'
Some wiss'd-for day.

19. *houghel*: coughing (?) 20. *sic*: such 21. *bee scap castin'*: beehive opening 22. *randies*: beggars 23. *skail'd*: scattered 24. *faps*: fops 25. *Moilie*: a harmless person 26. *dunch*: knock over, defeat

Come back, ye dastards! – Can ye ought
Except at your returnin',
But wives an' weans stript, cattle hought,
An' cots, an' claughins[27] burnin'?
Na, haste ye hame; ye ken ye'll 'scape,
'Cause *martial worth* ye're clear o';
The nine-tail'd cat, or choakin' rape,
Is maistly for some hero,
On sic a day.

*Saunt Paul* (auld Knacksie!)[28] counsels weel –
*Pope*, somewhere, does the samen,
That, 'first o' a', folk sud themsel's
Impartially examine';
Gif that's na done, whate'er ilk[29] loun[30]
May swear to, never swith'rin',[31]
In ev'ry pinch, he'll basely flinch –
'Guidbye to ye, my brethren,'
He'll cry, that day.

The leuks[32] o' wheens[33] wha stay'd behin',
Were mark'd by monie a passion;
By dread to staun, by shame to rin,
By scorn an' consternation:
Wi' spite they curse, wi' grief they pray,
Now move, now pause a bit ay;
''Tis mad to gang, 'tis death to stay,'
An unco dolefu' ditty,
On sic a day.

What joy at hame our entrance gave!
'Guid God! is't you? fair fa' ye! –
'Twas wise, tho' fools may ca't no' brave,
To rin or e'er they saw ye.' –

27. *claughins*: hamlets 28. *Knacksie*: ingenious person 29. *ilk*: each 30. *loun*: boy, fellow 31. *swith'rin'*: hesitating 32. *leuks*: looks 33. *wheens*: small numbers

'Aye wife, that's true without dispute,
But lest saunts[34] fail in Zion,
I'll hae to swear *** forc'd me out;
Better he swing than I, on
Some hangin' day.'

My story's done, an' to be free,
Owre sair,[35] I doubt,[36] they smarted,
Wha wad hae bell'd the cat awee,
Had they no been deserted:
Thae warks pat skill, tho' in my min'
That ne'er was in't before, mon,
In tryin' times, maist folk, you'll fin',
Will act like Donegore men
On onie day.

## *Written in Winter*

The green warl's[1] awa, but the white ane[2] can charm them
What skait on the burn,[3] or wi' settin' dogs rin:
The hind's[4] dinlin'[5] han's, numb't wi' snaw-baws, to warm them,
He claps[6] on his hard sides, whase doublets[7] are thin.

How dark the hail show'r mak's yon vale, aince sae pleasing!
How laigh[8] stoops the bush that's ower-burden't[9] wi' drift!
The icicles dreep[10] at the half-thow't[11] house-easin',[12]
When blunt[13] the sun beams frae the verge o' the lift.[14]

34. *saunts*: saints 35. *owre sair*: too sure 36 *doubt*: suspect

1. *warl*: world 2. *ane*: one 3. *burn*: brook, stream 4. *hind*: farm worker
5. *dinlin'*: tingling 6. *claps*: pats 7. *doublets*: clothes 8. *laigh*: low
9. *ower-burden't*: overburdened 10. *dreep*: drip 11. *half-thow't*: half-thawed
12. *easin'*: eaves 13. *blunt*: weakly 14. *lift*: sky

The hedge-hauntin' blackbird, on ae fit whiles[15] restin',
Wad fain[16] heat the tither[17] in storm-rufflet wing;
The silly[18] sweel't[19] sheep, aye[20] the stifflin'[21] storm breastin',
Are glad o' green piles[22] at the side o' the spring.

What coof[23] fir'd that shot? were you no far to blame, man,
To pierce the poor Hare that was starvin' before?
Gif she wham ye court were like ane I'll no name, man,
Her fine han' wad spurn ye, distin't[24] sae[25] wi' gore.

The night wi' the lass that I hope will be kin' soon,
Wi' Sylvia, wha charms me, a wee while I'll stap:
He e'e is as clear as the ice the moon shines on,
As gentle her smile as the snaw-flakes that drap.

Perhaps she's now plannin', to pit a restriction
Upon my profusion on neist[26] new-year's night,
To help some poor fam'lie on bed's o' affliction,
Without food or fuel, attendants or light.

Perhaps, singin' noo the dirge I tak' pride in,
She thinks on the last storm, wi' pity and dread –
How the spait[27] crush't the cots, how Tam brak his leg slidin'
An' herds in the muir[28] fand[29] the poor pedlar dead.

'Tis guidness mak's beauty: the face ne'er was lo'esome[30]
That weepsna whaur woe is, and smilesna wi' glee;
If Sympathy's strange to the saft female bosom
It's want's no made up by a bright cheek, or e'e.

15. *ae fit whiles*: one foot sometimes 16. *fain*: gladly, eagerly 17. *tither*: other
18. *silly*: hapless 19. *sweel't*: soaked, drenched 20. *aye*: continually
21. *stifflin'*: conducive to coughing or bronchitis 22. *piles*: blades, stalks
23. *coof*: fool 24. *distin't*: characterized by 25. *sae*: so 26. *neist*: next
27. *spait*: spate, flood 28. *muir*: moor 29. *fand*: found 30. *lo'esome*: lovable

# MARY TIGHE

(1772–1810)

## *from* Psyche or The Legend of Love

### from *Canto I*

Wrapped in a cloud unseen by mortal eye,
He sought the chamber of the royal maid;
There, lulled by careless soft security,
Of the impending mischief nought afraid,
Upon her purple couch was Psyche laid,
Her radiant eyes a downy slumber sealed;
In light transparent veil alone arrayed,
Her bosom's opening charms were half revealed,
And scarce the lucid folds her polished limbs concealed.

A placid smile plays o'er each roseate lip,
Sweet severed lips, while thus your pearls disclose,
That slumbering thus unconscious she may sip
The cruel presage of her future woes!
Lightly, as fall the dews upon the rose,
Upon the coral gates of that sweet cell
The fatal drops he pours; nor yet he knows,
Nor, though a God, can he presaging tell
How he himself shall mourn the ills of that sad spell!

Nor yet content, he from his quiver drew,
Sharpened with skill divine, a shining dart:
No need had he for bow, since thus too true
His hand might wound her all-exposèd heart;
Yet her fair side he touched with gentlest art,

And half relenting on her beauties gazed;
Just then awaking with a sudden start
Her opening eye in humid lustre blazed,
Unseen he still remained, enchanted and amazed.

The dart which in his hand now trembling stood,
As o'er the couch he bent with ravished eye,
Drew with its daring point celestial blood
From his smooth neck's unblemished ivory;
Heedless of this, but with a pitying sigh
The evil done now anxious to repair,
He shed in haste the balmy drops of joy
O'er all the silky ringlets of her hair;
Then stretched his plumes divine, and breathed celestial air.

## THOMAS MOORE

(1779–1852)

### from *Corruption: An Epistle*

Boast on, my friend – though stripped of all beside,
Thy struggling nation still retains her pride:
That pride, which once in genuine glory woke
When Marlborough fought, and brilliant St John spoke;
That pride which still, by time and shame unstung,
Outlives even Wh–tel–cke's sword and H–wk–sb'ry's tongue!
Boast on, my friend, while in this humbled isle
Where Honour mourns and Freedom fears to smile,
Where the bright light of England's fame is known
But by the shadow o'er our fortunes thrown;
Where, doomed ourselves to nought but wrongs and slights,
We hear you boast of Britain's glorious rights,
As wretched slaves, that under hatches lie,
Hear those on deck extol the sun and sky!

Boast on, while wandering through my native haunts,
I coldly listen to thy patriot vaunts;
And feel, though close our wedded countries twine,
More sorrow for my own than pride from thine.

(. . .)

See that smooth lord, whom nature's plastic pains
Would seem to've fashion'd for those Eastern reigns
When eunuchs flourished, and such nerveless things
As men rejected were the chosen of kings; –
Even *he*, forsooth, (oh mockery accurst)
Dared to assume the patriot's name at first –
Thus Pitt began, and thus begin his apes;
Thus devils, when *first* raised, take pleasing shapes.
But oh, poor Ireland! if revenge be sweet
For centuries of wrong, for dark deceit
And withering insult – for the Union thrown
Into thy bitter cup, when that alone
Of slavery's draught was wanting – if for this
Revenge be sweet, thou *hast* that dæmon's bliss;
For, oh, 'tis more than hell's revenge to see
That England trusts the men who've ruined thee; –
That, in these awful days, when every hour
Creates some new or blasts some ancient power,
When proud Napoleon, like th' enchanted shield
Whose light compelled each wondering foe to yield,
With baleful lustre blinds the brave and free,
And dazzles Europe into slavery –
That, in this hour, when patriot zeal should guide,
When Mind should rule, and – Fox should *not* have died,
All that devoted England can oppose
To enemies made friends and friends made foes,
Is the rank refuse, the despised remains
Of that unpitying power, whose whips and chains
Drove Ireland first, in wild and wicked trance,
Turn false to England – give her hand to France,
Those hacked and tainted tools, so foully fit
For the grand artisan of mischief, P–tt,

So useless ever but in vile employ,
So weak to save, so vigorous to destroy –
Such are the men that guard thy threatened shore,
Oh England! sinking England! boast no more.

## *from* The Fudges in England

### from *Letter V: From Larry O'Branigan, in England, to his wife Judy, at Mullinafad*

Dear Judy, I sind you this bit of a letther,
By mail-coach conveyance, – for want of a betther, –
To tell you what luck in this world I have had
Since I left the sweet cabin, at Mullinafad.
Och, Judy, that night! – when the pig which we meant
To dry-nurse in the parlour to pay off the rent,
Julianna, the craythur, – that name was the death of her, –
Gave us the shlip and we saw the last breath of her!
And *there* were the childher, six innocent sowls,
For their nate little play-fellow tuning up howls;
While yourself, my dear Judy, (though grievin's a folly),
Stud over Julianna's remains, melancholy, –
Cryin', half for the craythur, and half for the money,
'Arrah, why did ye die till we'd sowld you, my honey?'
But God's will be done! – and then, faith, sure enough,
As the pig was decaised, 'twas high time to be off.
So we gother'd up all the poor duds we could catch,
Locked the owld cabin-door, put the kay in the thatch,
Then tuk lave of each other's sweet lips in the dark,
And set off, like the Chrishtians turn'd out of the Ark;
The six childher with you, my dear Judy, ochone!
And poor I wid myself, left condolin' alone.
How I came to this England, o'er say and o'er lands,
And what cruel hard walkin' I've had on my hands,

Is, at this present writin', too tadious to speak,
So I'll mintion it all in a postscript, next week: –
Only starved I was, surely, as thin as a lath,
Till I came to an up-and-down place they call Bath,
Where, as luck was, I managed to make a meal's meat,
By dhraggin owld ladies all day through the street, –
Which their docthors, (who pocket, like fun, the pound
    starlins),
Have brought into fashion to plase the owld darlins.
Div'l a boy in all Bath, though *I* say it, could carry
The grannies up hill half so handy as Larry;
And the higher they lived, like owld crows, in the air,
The more *I* was wanted to lug them up there.
But luck has two handles, dear Judy, they say,
And mine has *both* handles put on the wrong way.
For, pondherin', one morn, on a drame I'd just had
Of yourself and the babbies at Mullinafad,
Och, there came o'er my sinses so plasin' a flutther,
That I spilt an owld Countess right clane in the gutther,
Muff, feathers and all! – the descint was most awful,
And – what was still worse, faith – I knew 'twas unlawful:
For, though, with mere *women*, no very great evil,
T'upset an owld *Countess* in Bath is the divil!
So, liftin' the chair, with herself safe upon it,
(For nothin' about her was *kilt*, but her bonnet,)
Without even mentionin' 'By your lave, ma'am,'
I tuk to my heels and – here, Judy, I am!

## ANTOINE Ó RAIFTEIRÍ
## (1784–1835)

### *Raftery's Dialogue with the Whiskey*

RAFTERY

If you shortened many a road and put a halo
On every thought that was growing in my head
Have I not been to you as the brown nut to the hazel?
Your fruit, O my comrade?
And in many a lonely bed have I not praised you
With sleepy words no virgin ever heard?
And after all this, O the spite of it, here in Kilcreest
You topple a tallow candle and burn my beard.

Troy in its tall sticks never burned with a blaze
As bright as Raftery's hairs when that evil spark
Leaped on his skull and from that holy rooftree
Pitchforked his spluttering thatch;
Shame on you! not even Mercury who rose
Out of the cradle to fall on evil ways,
Stealing cattle, would hobble my wits and roast them
Hide and hair like that in the fire of my face.

O I was the sight then and the great commotion;
Wells running dry and poor people peeling their legs
With barrels and pails, and the fish flying down to the ocean;
And look at me now! a mere plaster of white of eggs!
Look at me! a bonfire to folly! but no man
Was ever saint till he was a sinner first;
And I'll break with you now though it cost me the mannerly
company
Of the gay talkers who follow a thirst.

So I dismiss you. Here! Take your mouth from my mouth!

I have weighed you, O creature of air, and the weighman cries,
'Here's nothing will balance a holding of land in the south,
Beef on the hoof there and grass climbing up to the skies;
What's whiskey to hanging bacon?
To a glittering hearth and blue delphware?
Will it put a Sunday coat on any man,
I ask you, or leave him to walk bare?'

Ah, sweet whisperer, my dear wanton, I
Have followed you, shawled in your warmth, since I left the breast
Been toady for you and pet bully
And a woeful heartscald to the parish priest;
And look! If I took the mint by storm and spent it,
Heaping on you in one wild night the dazzle of a king's whore,
And returned next morning with no money for a curer,
Your Publican would throw me out of the door.

THE WHISKEY

You blow hot and cold, grumbling,
The privilege of the woman and the poet.
Now let me advise you, Man of fancy stomach,
Carry a can and milk a nanny goat!
Drink milk! for I am not for you – as I am not indeed
For your brother the miser; but, ah, when the miser's heir
Grows into manhood and squanders I'll walk through the company
And call that man my dear.

I grow too heady now for your grey blood;
And you do little good to my reputation
With your knock-knees and tremulous jowls – for God's sake
Pay the tailor to press your pelt and tuck it in!
What can I be to you now but a young wife to an old man?
Leave me to the roarers in the great universities,
The masters of Latin with the big ferrules
Who know what use strong whiskey is!

Hush, now! I'll speak or burst. You have no pith,
And I pity the botch of a carpenter who planed you down.
You are maudlin at table ere the company is lit,
And among clowns, the heaviest clown.
I have given you pleasure, yet you round on me like a lackey
Who will swear he was overworked and underpaid;
And tomorrow, O most grievous insult of all, you'll repent
    of me
That the priest may help you into a holy grave.

### RAFTERY

Ah, that tongue was sharpened in many a bad house
Where candles are hooded on the black quays of the world;
Many is the sailor it stripped to the bleak hose
And the Light Dragoon with his feather furled;
I hear it now and I pray that a great bishop
Will rise with a golden crook and rout you out of the land
Yourself and the rising family of your sins,
As Patrick drove the worms out of Ireland.

You're an illness, a cancer, a canker, a poison,
Galloping consumption, broken breath,
Indiaman's liver, thin diseases of the person,
Cholera Morbus and the yellow death;
You're the two sour women who wait here by my mattress
With Christian charity and broken hen-eggs
To mess my only features, but if I live to denounce you
I'll empty every tavern when I get upon my legs.

### THE WHISKEY

If hard words broke bones every sad rascal
With a bleached tongue who turns on me of a morning
Would have done for me long ago, yet I rise again like the
    pasch
Quietly, brightly, in their minds and they return.

RAFTERY

Who returns but the shiftless drifters, the moon's men?
Stray calves who'd suck at any udder?
Waifs, bagmen, beggars, and an odd fool of a lord
Crazy enough not to know better?

THE WHISKEY

Men of merriment, the wide girthed men
Whose eyes pen cattle, and slender men who hold
The curves of a filly together with one finger
While the other strips an heiress of her gold;
Equal those, O Fiddler, men of the great gay world
Who can dance a stately figure or bow prettily to a queen
And keep fine manners though the blood be rearing
Like a red stallion on the fair green.

RAFTERY

Blackguards, rakes, who rise up from cards
Only when the sun is trumped there on the table
Like the red ace of hearts, take them, the gamblers
Who wouldn't pay their debts were they able;
Dicers, procurers, who'll give you an I.O.U.
On the honour or dishonour of a wife or daughter,
Take them, the lot of them, hog, devil, or dog,
And drown them in a bucket of bog water.

THE WHISKEY

Poets and musicians –

RAFTERY

and absentee landlords,
Militiamen on hayfeet-strawfeet who burn
Brightly as red lamps in a lanewife's back parlour,
Taking, as always, the wrong turn;
I leave you to them and to the landlord's agent
Who shivers beside you day-in day-out
Walled in by the hostile murmurs of the rainy grasslands
In an old windy house.

THE WHISKEY

For a homespun poet whose pride I nursed
When doors were shut on him and dogs barked at his heels,
Your gratitude is such I'll swear a cutpurse was your father.
And your mother the lady who tied eels.
Desert me, indeed? You windy bag of old words,
You wan wizened weasel with one worn tooth!
If I whistled tomorrow you'd hobble to me on your sores;
And that's the truth.

RAFTERY

Whistle then!

THE WHISKEY

I'll whistle when
I'm in the mood.

RAFTERY

Whistle! Whistle!

THE WHISKEY

Maybe when you've money and can spend,
When you're a farmer slaughtering the poor thistle,
Stoning crows or coaxing cows,
Counting your corn grain by grain,
With thirteen bonhams to every one of your sows,
And you carrying a big purse at the fair.

RAFTERY

Goodbye for ever then!

THE WHISKEY

Goodbye Raftery.

RAFTERY

I'll never be a farmer.

THE WHISKEY

And where is the need?
Poetry and whiskey have lived always on the country.
Why wouldn't they indeed?

RAFTERY

You're right. Why shouldn't I tax the heavy farmer?
I give him wit. And you? You give him – what?

THE WHISKEY

No matter. We are two necessary luxuries.

RAFTERY

Listen! I'll drink to that.

*Padraic Fallon*

## JEREMIAH JOSEPH CALLANAN
## (1795–1829)

### *The Outlaw of Loch Lene*

O many a day have I made good ale in the glen,
That came not of stream, or malt, like the brewing of men.
My bed was the ground, my roof the greenwood above,
And the wealth that I sought – one far kind glance from my love.

Alas! on that night when the horses I drove from the field,
That I was not near from terror my angel to shield.
She stretched forth her arms – her mantle she flung to the wind,
And swam o'er Loch Lene, her outlawed lover to find.

O would that a freezing sleet-winged tempest did sweep,
And I and my love were alone far off on the deep!
I'd ask not a ship, or a bark, or pinnace to save, –
With her hand round my waist, I'd fear not the wind or the wave.

'Tis down by the lake where the wild tree fringes its sides,
The maid of my heart, the fair one of Heaven resides –
I think as at eve she wanders its mazes along,
The birds go to sleep by the sweet wild twist of her song.

## *Gougane Barra*

There is a green island in lone Gougane Barra,
Where Allua of songs rushes forth as an arrow;
In deep-valleyed Desmond – a thousand wild fountains
Come down to that lake, from their home in the mountains.
There grows the wild ash, and a time-stricken willow
Looks chidingly down on the mirth of the billow;
As, like some gay child, that sad monitor scorning,
It lightly laughs back to the laugh of the morning.

And its zone of dark hills – oh! to see them all bright'ning.
When the tempest flings out its red banner of lightning;
And the waters rush down, 'mid the thunder's deep rattle,
Like clans from their hills at the voice of the battle;
And brightly the fire-crested billows are gleaming,
And wildly from Mullagh the eagles are screaming.
Oh! where is the dwelling in valley, or highland,
So meet for a bard as this lone little island!

How oft when the summer sun rested on Clara,
And lit the dark heath on the hills of Ivera,
Have I sought thee, sweet spot, from my home by the ocean,
And trod all thy wilds with a minstrel's devotion,
And thought of thy bards, when assembling together,
In the cleft of thy rocks, or the depth of thy heather,
They fled from the Saxon's dark bondage and slaughter,
And waked their last song by the rush of thy water.

High sons of the lyre, oh! how proud was the feeling,
To think while alone through that solitude stealing,
Though loftier Minstrels green Erin can number,
I only awoke your wild harp from its slumber,
And mingled once more with the voice of those fountains
The songs even Echo forgot on her mountains;
And gleaned each grey legend, that darkly was sleeping
Where the mist and the rain o'er their beauty were creeping.

Least bard of the hills! were it mine to inherit
The fire of thy harp, and the wing of thy spirit,
With the wrongs which like thee to our country has bound me,
Did your mantle of song fling its radiance around me,
Still, still in those wilds may young Liberty rally,
And send her strong shout over mountain and valley,
The star of the west may yet rise in its glory,
And the land that was darkest be brighest in story.

I too shall be gone; – but my name shall be spoken
When Erin awakes, and her fetters are broken;
Some minstrel will come, in the summer eve's gleaming,
When Freedom's young light on his spirit is beaming,
And bend o'er my grave with a tear of emotion,
Where calm Avon Buee seeks the kisses of ocean,
Or plant a wild wreath, from the banks of that river,
The heart, and the harp, that are sleeping for ever.

# GEORGE DARLEY
## (1795–1846)

## *from* Nepenthe

### from *Canto I*

Hurry me, Nymphs! O, hurry me
Far above the grovelling sea,
Which, with blind weakness and base roar
Casting his white age on the shore,
Wallows along that slimy floor;
With his widespread webbed hands
Seeking to climb the level sands,
But rejected still to rave
Alive in his uncovered grave.

Light-skirt dancers, blithe and boon
With high hosen and low shoon,
'Twixt sandal bordure and kirtle rim
Showing one pure wave of limb,
And frequent to the cestus fine
Lavish beauty's undulous line,
Till like roses veiled in snow
Neath the gauze your blushes glow;
Nymphs, with tresses which the wind
Sleekly tosses to its mind,
More deliriously dishevelled
Than when the Naxian widow revelled
With her flush bridegroom on the ooze,
Hurry me, Sisters! where ye choose,
Up the meadowy mountains wild,
Aye by the broad sun oversmiled,
Up the rocky paths of gray
Shaded all my hawthorn way,

Past the very turban crown
Feathered with pine and aspen spray,
Darkening like a soldan's down
O'er the mute stoopers to his sway,
Meek willows, daisies, brambles brown,
Grasses and reeds in green array,
Sighing what he in storm doth say –
Hurry me, hurry me, Nymphs, away!

Here on the mountain's sunburnt side
Trip we round our steepy slide,
With tinsel moss, dry-woven pall,
Minist'ring many a frolic fall;
Now, sweet Nymphs, with ankle trim
Foot we around this fountain brim,
Where even the delicate lilies show
Transgressing bosoms in bright row
(More lustrous-sweet than yours, I trow!)
Above their deep green bodices.
Shall you be charier still than these?
Garments are only good to inspire
Warmer, wantoner desire;
For those beauties make more riot
In our hearts, themselves at quiet
Under veils and vapoury lawns
Thro' which their moon-cold lustre dawns,
And might perchance if full revealed
Seem less wondrous than concealed,
Greater defeat of Virtue made
When Love shoots from an ambuscade,
Than with naked front and fair.
Who the loose Grace in flowing hair
Hath ever sought with so much care,
As the crape-enshrouded nun
Scarce warmed by touches of the sun?
Nathless, whatsoe'er your tire,
Hurry me, sweet Nymphs, higher, higher!
Till the broad seas shrink to streams,
Or, beneath my lofty eye,

Ocean a broken mirror seems,
Whose fragments 'tween the lands do lie,
Glancing me from its hollow sky,
Till my cheated vision deems
My place in heaven twice as high!

## from *Canto II*

Welcome! Before my bloodshot eyes,
Steed of the East, a camel stands,
Mourning his fallen lord that dies.
Now, as forth his spirit flies,
Ship of the Desert! bear me on,
O'er this wavy-bosomed lea,
That solid seemed and staid anon,
But now looks surging like a sea. –
On she bore me, as the blast
Whirling a leaf, to where in calm
A little fount poured dropping-fast
On dying Nature's heart its balm.
Deep we sucked the spongy moss,
And cropt for dates the sheltering palm,
Then with fleetest amble cross
Like desert, fed upon like alm.
That most vital beverage still,
Tho' near exhaust, preserved me till
Now the broad Barbaric shore
Spread its havens to my view,
And mine ear rung with ocean's roar,
And mine eye glistened with its blue!
Till I found me once again
By the ever-murmuring main,
Listening across the distant foam
My native church bells ring me home.
Alas! why leave I not this toil
Thro' stranger lands, for mine own soil?
Far from ambition's worthless coil,
From all this wide world's wearying moil, –

Why leave I not this busy broil,
For mine own clime, for mine own soil,
My calm, dear, humble, native soil!
There to lay me down at peace
In my own first nothingness?

## JAMES HENRY
## (1798–1876)

### *The Lord and Adam in the Garden of Eden*

THE LORD
– For, dust thou art, and shalt to dust return.

ADAM
If dust I am, and shall to dust return,
All's right. I shall return to what I am.

THE LORD
Thou'rt quite too literal; I love a trope.

ADAM
That's more than I do. I must fairly own
I don't like to have sand thrown in mine eyes.
Why make that harder still to understand,
Which, in itself, is hard? The plainest speech
Pleases me most.

THE LORD
He'll not make a bad Quaker. *[aside]*
– And for thy sake the serpent too is cursed,
Shall on his belly go, and eat the dust.

ADAM

That's a trope too, no doubt.

THE LORD

Why, half and half;
Trope, he shall eat the dust; but literal
And matter of fact, he shall go on his belly.

ADAM

Excuse me – on his back; for on his belly
He goes at present and has always gone.

THE LORD

Belly or back, 's small difference in a serpent;
From either he'll know how to bruise thy heel.

ADAM

But I'll go in a carriage, ride on horseback,
Or, if I go on foot, wear leather boots.

THE LORD

Literal again! It would have saved some trouble,
To have put a few grains more of poetry
Into the dull prose of thy composition.

ADAM

It can't be helped now; but next time you're making
A thing, like me, with an immortal soul
– For I'm none of your dust, I'm bold to tell you,
But an ethereal spirit in a case –
'Twere well you'd make him with sufficient wit
To understand your flights of poetry,
Or, if not, that you'd talk to him in prose.

## *'Another and another and another . . .'*

Another and another and another
And still another sunset and sunrise,
The same yet different, different yet the same,
Seen by me now in my declining years
As in my early childhood, youth and manhood;
And by my parents and my parents' parents,
And by the parents of my parents' parents,
And by their parents counted back for ever,
Seen, all their lives long, even as now by me;
And by my children and my children's children
And by the children of my children's children
And by their children counted on for ever
Still to be seen as even now seen by me;
Clear and bright sometimes, sometimes dark and clouded
But still the same sunsetting and sunrise;
The same for ever to the never ending
Line of observers, to the same observer
Through all the changes of his life the same:
Sunsetting and sunrising and sunsetting,
And then again sunrising and sunsetting,
Sunrising and sunsetting evermore.

# JAMES CLARENCE MANGAN

(1803–49)

## *The Young Parson's Dream*

In the lone stillness of the new-year's night,
   A Bishop at his window stood, and turned
His dim eyes to the firmament, where bright
   And pure a million rolling planets burned,

And then upon the earth all cold and white, –
  And felt that moment that, of all who mourned
And groaned upon its bosom, none there were
With his hypocrisy and great despair.

For near him lay his grave; concealed from view,
  Not by the flowers of youth, but by the snows
Of age alone: in torturing thought he flew
  Over the past, and on his memory rose
That picture of his life which memory drew
  With all its fruits, diseases, sins, and woes:
A ruined frame, a blighted soul, dark years
Of agony, remorse, and withering fears!

Like spectres now his days of youth came back,
  And that cross-road of life where, when a boy,
His father placed him first; its right hand track
  Leads to a land of glory, peace and joy,
Its left to wilderness, waste and black,
  Where snakes and plagues and poisonous blasts
      destroy.
Where was he now? alas! the serpents hung
Coiled round his heart, their venom on his tongue.

Choaked with unutterable grief, he cried –
  'Restore to me my youth! oh Heaven! restore
My morn of life! oh father! be my guide,
  And let me, let me choose my path once more!'
But on the wide waste air his ravings died
  Away, and all was silent as before.
His youth had glided by, swift as the wave;
His father came not; he was in his grave.

Wild lights went flickering by; a star was falling;
  Down to the miry marsh he saw it rush.
'Myself,' he said, and oh! the thought was galling,
  And hot and heart-wrung tears began to gush:

Sleepwalkers crossed his glance in shapes appalling,
  Huge windmills lifted up their arms to crush,
And death-like faces started from the dim
Depths of the charnel-house and glared on him.

Amid these overboiling bursts of feeling,
  Rich music, heralding the young year's birth,
Flowed from a distant STEEPLE, like the pealing
  Of some celestial organ o'er the earth.
Milder emotions over him came stealing;
  He felt the spirit's awful, priceless worth –
'Return' – again he cried imploringly,
'Oh my lost youth! return, return to me!'

*And youth returned*, and age withdrew his terrors,
  Still was he young, for he had dreamed the whole:
But faithful is the picture conscience mirrors,
  Whenever PARSON avarice gluts the soul.
Alas! too real were his sins and errors.
  Too truly had he made the earth his goal:
He wept and blessed his God that with the will
He had the power to choose the right path still.

Here, youthful curate, ponder – and if thou,
  Like him, art reeling over the abyss
Of church hypocrisy and mammon, now,
  This ghastly dream may be thy guide to bliss.
But should age once bring MITRES to thy brow,
  Its wrinkles will not leave a dream like this –
Thy tears may then flow vainly o'er the urn
Of innocence, that never can return!

## *'My heart is a monk'*

*— Rahaki*

My heart is a monk, and thy bosom his cloister:
So sleeps the bright pearl in the shell of the oyster.

## *Relic of Prince Bayazeed, Son of Suleiman (d.1561)*

Slow through my bosom's veins their last cold blood is flowing,
Above my heart even now I feel the rank grass growing.
Hence to the Land of Nought! The caravan is starting –
Its bell already tolls the signal for departing.

Rejoice, my soul! Poor bird, thou art at last delivered!
Thy cage is crumbling fast; its bars will soon be shivered.
Farewell, thou troubled world, where Sin and Crime run riot,
For SHAHI henceforth rests in GOD's own House of Quiet.

## *Twenty Golden Years Ago*

*— Selber*

O, the rain, the weary, dreary rain,
    How it plashes on the window-sill!
Night, I guess too, must be on the wane,
    Strass and Gass around are grown so still.
Here I sit, with coffee in my cup –
    Ah! 'twas rarely I beheld it flow
In the taverns where I loved to sup
        Twenty golden years ago!

Twenty years ago, alas! – but stay –
  On my life 'tis half-past twelve o'clock!
After all, the hours *do* slip away –
  Come, here goes to burn another block!
For the night, or morn, is wet and cold,
  And my fire is dwindling rather low –
I had fire enough, when young and bold,
    Twenty golden years ago!

Dear! I don't feel well at all, somehow:
  Few in Weimar dream how bad I am;
Floods of tears grow common with me now,
  High-Dutch floods, that Reason cannot dam,
Doctors think I'll neither live nor thrive
  If I mope at home so – I don't know –
*Am* I living *now?* I *was* alive
    Twenty golden years ago.

Wifeless, friendless, flaggonless, alone,
  Not quite bookless, though, unless I chuse,
Left with nought to do, except to groan,
  Not a soul to woo, except the Muse –
O! this, this is hard for *me* to bear,
  Me, who whilome lived so much *en haut*,
Me, who broke all hearts like chinaware
    Twenty golden years ago!

P'rhaps 'tis better – Time's defacing waves
  Long have quenched the radiance of my brow –
They who curse me nightly from their graves
  Scarce could love me were they living now;
But my loneliness hath darker ills –
  Such dun duns as Conscience, Thought and Co,
Awful Gorgons! worse than tailors' bills
    Twenty golden years ago!

Did I paint a fifth of what I feel,
  O, how plaintive you would ween I was!
But I won't, albeit I have a deal
  More to wail about than Kerner has!
Kerner's tears are wept for withered flowers,
  Mine for withered hopes; my Scroll of Woe
Dates, alas! from Youth's deserted bowers,
    Twenty golden years ago!

Yet, may Deutschland's bardlings flourish long!
  Me, I tweak no beak among them – hawks
Must not pounce on hawks; besides, in song
  I could once beat all of them by chalks.
Though you find me, as I near my goal,
  Sentimentalizing like Rousseau,
O! I had a grand Byronian soul
    Twenty golden years ago!

Tick-tick, tick-tick! – Not a sound save Time's,
  And the windgust, as it drives the rain –
Tortured torturer of reluctant rhymes,
  Go to bed, and rest thine aching brain!
Sleep! – no more the dupe of hopes or schemes;
  Soon thou sleepest where the thistles blow –
Curious anticlimax to thy dreams
    Twenty golden years ago!

## *The Ride Round the Parapet*

— *Rückert*
*'Sie sprach: ich will nicht sitzen*
*im stillen Kämmerlein.'*

She said, I was not born to mope at home in loneliness –
The Lady Eleanora von Alleyne.
She said, I was not born to mope at home in loneliness,
When the heart is throbbing sorest, there is balsam in the forest;
There is balsam in the forest for its pain,
Said the Lady Eleanora,
Said the Lady Eleanora von Alleyne.

She doffed her silks and pearls, and donned instead her
hunting-gear,
The Lady Eleanora von Alleyne.
She doffed her silks and pearls, and donned instead her
hunting-gear,
And, till Summertime was over, as a huntress and a rover
Did she couch upon the mountain or the plain,
She, the Lady Eleanora,
Noble Lady Eleanora von Alleyne.

Returning home agen, she viewed with scorn the tournaments –
The Lady Eleanora von Alleyne.
Returning home agen, she viewed with scorn the tournaments;
She saw the morions cloven and the crowning chaplets woven,
And the sight awakened only the disdain
Of the Lady Eleanora,
Of the Lady Eleanora von Alleyne.

My feeling towards Man is one of utter scornfulness,
Said Lady Eleanora von Alleyne.
My feeling towards Man is one of utter scornfulness,
And he that would o'ercome it, let him ride around the summit
Of my battlemented Castle by the Maine,
Said the Lady Eleanora,
Said the Lady Eleanora von Alleyne.

So came a knight anon to ride around the parapet,
For Lady Eleanora von Alleyne.
So came a knight anon to ride around the parapet.
Man and horse were hurled together o'er the crags that beetled nether.
Said the Lady, There, I fancy, they'll remain!
Said the Lady Eleanora,
Queenly Lady Eleanora von Alleyne!

Then came another knight to ride around the parapet,
For Lady Eleanora von Alleyne!
Then came another knight to ride around the parapet.
Man and horse fell down, asunder, o'er the crags that beetled under.
Said the Lady, They'll not leap the leap again!
Said the Lady Eleanora,
Lovely Lady Eleanora von Alleyne!

Came other knights anon to ride around the parapet,
For Lady Eleanora von Alleyne.
Came other knights anon to ride around the parapet,
Till six and thirty corses of both mangled men and horses
Had been sacrificed as victims at the fane
Of the Lady Eleanora,
Stately Lady Eleanora von Alleyne!

That woeful year was by, and Ritter none came afterwards
To Lady Eleanora von Alleyne.
That woeful year was by, and Ritter none came afterwards.
The castle's lonely basscourt looked a wild o'ergrown-with-
grasscourt;
'Twas abandoned by the Ritters and their train
To the Lady Eleanora,
Haughty Lady Eleanora von Alleyne!

She clomb the silent wall, she gazed around her sovranlike,
The Lady Eleanora von Alleyne.
She clomb the silent wall, she gazed around her sovranlike;
And wherefore have departed all the Brave, the Lionhearted,
Who have left me here to play the Castellain?
Said the Lady Eleanora,
Said the Lady Eleanora von Alleyne.

And is it fled for aye, the palmy time of Chivalry?
Cried Lady Eleanora von Alleyne.
And is it fled for aye, the palmy time of Chivalry?
Shame light upon the cravens! May their corpses gorge the
ravens,
Since they tremble thus to wear a woman's chain!
Said the Lady Eleanora,
Said the Lady Eleanora von Alleyne.

The story reached at Gratz the gallant Margrave Gondibert
Of Lady Eleanora von Alleyne.
The story reached at Gratz the gallant Margrave Gondibert.
Quoth he, I trow the woman must be more or less than human;
She is worth a little peaceable campaign,
Is the Lady Eleanora,
Is the Lady Eleanora von Alleyne!

He trained a horse to pace round narrow stones laid merlonwise,
For Lady Eleanora von Alleyne.
He trained a horse to pace round narrow stones laid merlonwise.
Good Grey! Do thou thy duty, and this rocky-bosomed beauty
Shall be taught that all the vauntings are in vain
Of the Lady Eleanora,
Of the Lady Eleanora von Alleyne!

He left his castle-halls, he came to Lady Eleanor's,
The Lady Eleanora von Alleyne.
He left his castle-halls, he came to Lady Eleanor's.
O, Lady, best and fairest! Here am I – and, if thou carest,
I will gallop round the parapet amain,
Noble Lady Eleanora,
Noble Lady Eleanora von Alleyne!

She saw him spring to horse, that gallant Margrave Gondibert,
The Lady Eleanora von Alleyne.
She saw him spring to horse, that gallant Margrave Gondibert.
O, bitter, bitter sorrow! I shall weep for this tomorrow!
It were better that in battle he were slain,
Said the Lady Eleanora,
Said the Lady Eleanora von Alleyne.

Then rode he round and round the battlemented parapet,
For Lady Eleanora von Alleyne.
Then rode he round and round the battlemented parapet.
The Lady wept and trembled, and her paly face resembled,
As she looked away, a lily wet with rain;
Hapless Lady Eleanora,
Hapless Lady Eleanora von Alleyne!

So rode he round and round the battlemented parapet,
For Lady Eleanora von Alleyne.
So rode he round and round the battlemented parapet.
Accurst be my ambition! He but rideth to perdition,
He but rideth to perdition without rein!
Wept the Lady Eleanora,
Wept the Lady Eleanora von Alleyne.

Yet rode he round and round the battlemented parapet,
For Lady Eleanora von Alleyne.
Yet rode he round and round the battlemented parapet.
Meanwhile her terror shook her – yea, her breath well nigh
forsook her;
Fire was burning in the bosom and the brain
Of the Lady Eleanora,
Of the Lady Eleanora von Alleyne!

Then rode he round and off the battlemented parapet
To Lady Eleanora von Alleyne.
Then rode he round and off the battlemented parapet.
Now blest be GOD for ever! This is marvellous! I never
Cherished hope of laying eyes on thee agayne,
Cried the Lady Eleanora,
Joyous Lady Eleanora von Alleyne!

The Man of Men thou art, for thou hast fairly conquered me,
The Lady Eleanora von Alleyne!
The Man of Men thou art, for thou hast fairly conquered me.
I greet thee as my lover, and, ere many days be over,
Thou shalt wed me and be Lord of my domain,
Said the Lady Eleanora,
Said the Lady Eleanora von Alleyne.

Then bowed that graceful knight, the gallant Margrave
Gondibert,
To Lady Eleanora von Alleyne.
Then bowed that graceful knight, the gallant Margrave
Gondibert,
And thus he answered coldly, there be many who as boldly
Will adventure an achievement they disdain,
For the Lady Eleanora,
For the Lady Eleanora von Alleyne.

Mayest bide until they come, O, stately Lady Eleanor!
    O, Lady Eleanora von Alleyne!
Mayest bide until they come, O, stately Lady Eleanor!
And thou and they may marry, but, for me, I must not tarry,
    I have won a wife already out of Spain,
        Virgin Lady Eleanora,
    Virgin Lady Eleanora von Alleyne!

Thereon he rode away, the gallant Margrave Gondibert,
    From Lady Eleanora von Alleyne.
Thereon he rode away, the gallant Margrave Gondibert,
And long in shame and anguish did that haughty Lady languish,
    Did she languish without pity for her pain,
        She the Lady Eleanora,
    She the Lady Eleanora von Alleyne.

And year went after year, and still in barren maidenhood
    Lived Lady Eleanora von Alleyne.
And wrinkled Eld crept on, and still her lot was maidenhood,
And, woe! her end was tragic; she was changed, at length, by
        magic,
    To an ugly wooden image, they maintain;
        She, the Lady Eleanora,
    She, the Lady Eleanora von Alleyne!

And now, before the Gate, in sight of all, transmogrified,
    Stands Lady Eleanora von Alleyne.
Before her castle-gate, in sight of all, transmogrified,
And he that won't salute her must be fined in foaming pewter,
    If a boor – but, if a burgher, in champagne,
        For the Lady Eleanora,
    Wooden Lady Eleanora von Alleyne!

## *Khidder*

Thus said or sung
Khidder, the ever young.
Journeying, I passed an ancient town –
Of lindens green its battlements bore a crown,
And at its turreted gates, on either hand,
Did fountains stand,
In marble white of rarest chiselling,
The which on high did fling
Water, that then like rain went twinkling down
With a rainbow glancing in the spray
As it wreathed in the sunny ray.
I marked where, 'neath the frown
Of the dark rampart, smiled a garden fair;
And an old man was there,
That gathered fruit. 'Good father,' I began,
'Since when, I pray you, standeth here
This goodly city with its fountains clear?'
To which that agèd man
Made answer – 'Ever stood
The city where it stands today,
And as it stands so shall it stand for aye,
Come evil days or good.'

Him gathering fruit I left, and journeyed on;
But when a thousand years were come and gone
Again I passed that way, and lo!
There was no city, there were no
Fountains of chiselling rare,
No garden fair;
Only
A lonely
Shepherd was piping there,
Whose little flock seemed less
In that wide pasture of the wilderness.

'Good friend,' quoth I,
'How long hath the fair city passed away,
That stood with gates so high,
With fountains bright, and gardens gay,
Where now these sheep do stray?'
And he replied, 'What withers makes but room
For what springs up in verdurous bloom –
Sheep have grazed ever here, and here will graze
for aye.'

Him piping there I left, and journeyed on –
But when a thousand years were come and gone,
Again I passed
That way, and see! there was a lake
That darkened in the blast,
And waves that brake
With a melancholy roar
Along that lonely shore.
And on a shingly point that ran
Far out into the lake, a fisherman
Was hauling in his net. To him I said,
'Good friend,
I fain would know
Since when it is that here these waters flow.'
Whereat he shook his head,
And answer made, 'Heaven lend
Thee better wit, good brother! Ever here
These waters flowed, and so
Will ever flow;
And aye in this dark rolling mere
Men fished, and still fish,
And ever will fish,
Until fish
No more in water swim.'

Him
Hauling his net I left, and journeyed on,
But when a thousand years were come and gone,
Again I passed that way, and lo! there stood,
Where waves had rolled, a green and flourishing wood –
Flourishing in youth it seemed, and yet was old,
And there it stood where deep blue waves had rolled.

A place of pleasant shade!
A wandering wind among the branches played,
And birds were now where fish had been;
And through the depth of green,
In many a gush the golden sunshine streamed;
And small flowers gleamed
About the brown and mossy
Roots of the ancient trees,
And the cushioned sward so glossy,
That compassed these.

Here as I passed, there met
Me, on the border of that forest wide,
One with an axe, whom when I spied,
Quoth I, 'Good neighbour, let
Me ask, I pray you, *how* long hath the wood
Stood,
Spreading its covert, broad and green,
Here, where mine eyes have seen
A royal city stand, whose battlements
Were like the ancient rocks;
And then a place for shepherds' tents,
And pasturage of flocks;
And then,
Roughening beneath the blast,
A vast
Dark mere – a haunt of fishermen?'

There was a cold surprise
In the man's eyes
While thus I spake, and, as I made an end,
This was his dry
Reply –
'Facetious friend,
This wood
Hath ever stood
Even where it stands today;
And as it stands, so shall it stand for aye.
And here men catch no fish – here tend
No sheep – to no town-markets wend;
But aye in these
Green shades men felled, and still fell,
And ever will fell
Trees.'

Him with his axe I left, and journeyed on,
But when a thousand years were come and gone,
Again I passed
That way, and lo! a town –
And spires, and domes, and towers looked proudly
 down
Upon a vast
And sounding tide of life,
That flowed through many a street, and surged
In many a market-place, and urged
Its way in many a wheeling current, hither
And thither.
How rose the strife
Of sounds! the ceaseless beat
Of feet!
The noise of carts, of whips – the roll
Of chariots, coaches, cabs, *gigs* – all
Who keep the last-named vehicle we call
*Respectable* – horse-trampings, and the toll

Of bells; the whirl, the clash, the hubbub-mingling
Of voices, deep and shrill; the clattering, jingling,
The indescribable, indefinable roar;
The grating, creaking, booming, clanking, thumping,
And bumping;
The stumping,
Of folks with wooden legs; the gabbling,
And babbling,
And many more
Quite nameless helpings
To the general effect; dog-yelpings,
Laughter, and shout, and cry; all sounds of gladness,
Of sadness,
And madness –
For there were people marrying,
And others carrying
The dead they would have died for, to the grave –
(Sadly the church bell tolled
When the young were burying the old,
More sadly spake that bodeful tongue
When the old were burying the young.)
Thus did the tumult rave
Through that fair city – nor were wanting there
Or dancing dogs or bear,
Or needy knife-
Grinder, or man with dismal wife,
That sang deplorably of '*purling groves*
*And verdant streams, all where young Damon roves*
*With tender Phillida, the nymph he loves,*
*And softly breathe*
*The balmy moonbeam's wreathe,*
*And amorous turtle-doves*';
Or other doleful men, that blew
The melancholiest tunes – the which they only knew –
On flutes, and other instruments of wind;
Or small dark imp, with hurdy-
Gurdy,
And marmoset, that grinned
For nuts, and might have been his brother,

They were so like each other;
Or man,
That danced like the god Pan,
Twitching
A spasmy face
From side to side with a grace
Bewitching,
The while he whistled
In sorted pipes, all at his chin that bristled;
Or fiddler, fiddling much
For little profit, and a many such
Street musics most forlorn,
In that too pitiless rout quite overborne.

Now, when as I beheld
The stir, and heard the din of life once more
Swell, as it swelled
In that same place four thousand years before,
I asked of them that passed me in the throng,
How long
The city thereabouts had stood,
And what was gone with pasture, lake, and wood.
But at such questions most men did but stare,
And so pass on; and some did laugh and shake
Their heads, me deeming mad; but none would spare
The time, or take
The pains to answer me, for there
All were in haste – all busy – bent to make
The most of every minute,
And do, an' if they might, an hour's work in it.

Yet as I gave not o'er, but pertinaciously
Plied with my question every passer-by,
A dozen voices did at length reply
Ungraciously –
'What ravest thou
Of pasture, lake, and wood? As it is now,

So was it always here, and so will be for aye.'
Them, hurrying there, I left, and journeyed on –
But when a thousand years are come and gone,
Again I'll pass that way.

## *Siberia*

In Siberia's wastes
  The Ice-wind's breath
Woundeth like the toothèd steel.
Lost Siberia doth reveal
  Only blight and death.

Blight and death alone.
  No Summer shines.
Night is interblent with Day.
In Siberia's wastes alway
  The blood blackens, the heart pines.

In Siberia's wastes
  No tears are shed,
For they freeze within the brain.
Nought is felt but dullest pain,
  Pain acute, yet dead;

Pain as in a dream,
  When years go by
Funeral-paced, yet fugitive,
When man lives, and doth not live,
  Doth not live – nor die.

In Siberia's wastes
  Are sands and rocks.
Nothing blooms of green or soft,
But the snowpeaks rise aloft
  And the gaunt ice-blocks.

And the exile there
  Is one with those;
They are part, and he is part,
For the sands are in his heart,
  And the killing snows.

Therefore, in those wastes
  None curse the Czar.
Each man's tongue is cloven by
The North Blast, who heweth nigh
  With sharp scymitar.

And such doom each drees,
  Till, hunger-gnawn,
And cold-slain, he at length sinks there,
Yet scarce more a corpse than ere
  His last breath was drawn.

## *Dark Rosaleen*

O, my Dark Rosaleen,
  Do not sigh, do not weep!
The priests are on the ocean green,
  They march along the Deep.
There's wine . . . from the royal Pope,
  Upon the ocean green;
And Spanish ale shall give you hope,
  My Dark Rosaleen!
  My own Rosaleen!
Shall glad your heart, shall give you hope,
Shall give you health, and help, and hope,
  My Dark Rosaleen!

Over hills, and through dales,
  Have I roamed for your sake;
All yesterday I sailed with sails
  On river and on lake.

The Erne . . . at its highest flood,
  I dashed across unseen,
For there was lightning in my blood,
  My Dark Rosaleen!
  My own Rosaleen!
Oh! there was lightning in my blood,
Red lightning lightened through my blood,
  My Dark Rosaleen!

All day long, in unrest,
  To and fro, do I move.
The very soul within my breast
  Is wasted for you, love!
The heart . . . in my bosom faints
  To think of you, my Queen,
My life of life, my saint of saints,
  My Dark Rosaleen!
  My own Rosaleen!
To hear your sweet and sad complaints,
My life, my love, my saint of saints,
  My Dark Rosaleen!

Woe and pain, pain and woe,
  Are my lot, night and noon,
To see your bright face clouded so,
  Like to the mournful moon.
But yet . . . will I rear your throne
  Again in golden sheen;
'Tis you shall reign, shall reign alone,
  My Dark Rosaleen!
  My own Rosaleen!
'Tis you shall have the golden throne,
'Tis you shall reign, and reign alone,
  My Dark Rosaleen!

Over dews, over sands,
  Will I fly, for your weal;
Your holy delicate white hands
  Shall girdle me with steel.

At home . . . in your emerald bowers,
  From morning's dawn till e'en,
You'll pray for me, my flower of flowers,
  My Dark Rosaleen!
  My fond Rosaleen!
You'll think of me through Daylight's hours,
My virgin flower, my flower of flowers,
  My Dark Rosaleen!

I could scale the blue air,
  I could plough the high hills,
Oh, I could kneel all night in prayer,
  To heal your many ills!
And one . . . beamy smile from you
  Would float like light between
My toils and me, my own, my true,
  My Dark Rosaleen!
  My fond Rosaleen!
Would give me life and soul anew,
A second life, a soul anew,
  My Dark Rosaleen!

O! the Erne shall run red
  With redundance of blood,
The earth shall rock beneath our tread,
  And flames wrap hill and wood,
And gun-peal, and slogan cry,
  Wake many a glen serene,
Ere you shall fade, ere you shall die,
  My Dark Rosaleen!
  My own Rosaleen!
The Judgement Hour must first be nigh,
Ere you can fade, ere you can die,
  My Dark Rosaleen!

## *The Nameless One*

Roll forth, my song, like the rushing river
That sweeps along to the mighty sea;
God will inspire me while I deliver
My soul of thee!

Tell thou the world, when my bones lie whitening
Amid the last homes of youth and eld,
That there was once one whose veins ran lightning
No eye beheld.

Tell how his boyhood was one drear night-hour,
How shone for *him*, through his griefs and gloom,
No star of all Heaven sends to light our
Path to the tomb.

Roll on, my song, and to after-ages
Tell how, disdaining all earth can give,
He would have taught Men, from Wisdom's pages,
The way to live.

And tell how, trampled, derided, hated,
And worn by Weakness, Disease, and Wrong,
He fled for shelter to God, who mated
His soul with song –

With song which alway, sublime or vapid,
Flowed like a rill in the morning-beam,
Perchance not deep, but intense and rapid –
A mountain-stream.

Tell how this Nameless, condemned for years long
To herd with demons from Hell beneath,
Saw things that made him, with groans and tears, long
For even Death.

Go on to tell how, with genius wasted,
Betrayed in Friendship, befooled in Love,
With spirit shipwrecked, and young hopes blasted,
He still, still strove –

Till, spent with Toil, dreeing Death for others,
And some whose hands should have wrought for *him*
(If children live not for sires and mothers),
His mind grew dim;

And he fell far through that pit abysmal,
The gulf and grave of Maginn and Burns,
And pawned his soul for the Devil's dismal
Stock of returns –

But yet redeemed it in days of darkness,
And shapes and signs of the Final Wrath,
When Death, in hideous and ghastly starkness,
Stood on his path.

And tell how now, amid Wreck and Sorrow,
And Want, and Sickness, and houseless nights,
He bides in calmness the Silent Morrow
That no ray lights.

And lives he still, then? Yes! Old and hoary
At thirty-nine, from Despair and Woe,
He lives, enduring what future Story
Will never know.

Him grant a grave to, ye pitying Noble,
Deep in your bosoms! There let him dwell!
He, too, had tears for all souls in trouble,
Here and in Hell.

# SAMUEL FERGUSON
## (1810–86)

### *The Forging of the Anchor*

Come, see the Dolphin's anchor forged – 'tis at a white heat
now:
The bellows ceased, the flames decreased though on the forge's
brow
The little flames still fitfully play through the sable mound,
And fitfully you still may see the grim smiths ranking round,
All clad in leathern panoply, their broad hands only bare:
Some rest upon their sledges here, some work the windlass
there.

The windlass strains the tackle chains, the black mound heaves
below,
And red and deep a hundred veins burst out at every throe:
It rises, roars, rends all outright – O, Vulcan, what a glow!
'Tis blinding white, 'tis blasting bright – the high sun shines not
so!
The high sun sees not, on the earth, such fiery fearful show,
The roof-ribs swarth, the candent hearth, the ruddy lurid row
Of smiths that stand, an ardent band, like men before the foe,
As, quivering through his fleece of flame, the sailing monster,
slow
Sinks on the anvil: – all about the faces fiery grow;
'Hurrah!' they shout, 'leap out – leap out'; bang, bang the
sledges go:
Hurrah! the jetted lightnings are hissing high and low –
A hailing fount of fire is struck at every squashing blow;
The leathern mail rebounds the hail, the rattling cinders strow
The ground around; at every bound the sweltering fountains
flow,
And thick and loud the swinking crowd at every stroke pant
'ho!'

Leap out, leap out, my masters; leap out and lay on load!
Let's forge a goodly anchor – a bower thick and broad;
For a heart of oak is hanging on every blow, I bode;
I see the good ship riding all in a perilous road –
The low reef roaring on her lee – the roll of ocean pour'd
From stem to stern, sea after sea, the mainmast by the board,
The bulwarks down, the rudder gone, the boats stove at the
chains!
But courage still, brave mariners – the bower yet remains,
And not an inch to flinch he deigns, save when ye pitch sky
high;
Then moves his head, as though he said, 'Fear nothing – here
am I.'
Swing in your strokes in order, let foot and hand keep time;
Your blows make music sweeter far than any steeple's chime:
But, while you sling your sledges, sing – and let the burthen be,
The anchor is the anvil-king, and royal craftsmen we!

Strike in, strike in – the sparks begin to dull their rustling red;
Our hammers ring with sharper din, our work will soon be sped.
Our anchor soon must change his bed of fiery rich array,
For a hammock at the roaring bows, or an oozy couch of clay;
Our anchor soon must change the lay of merry craftsmen here,
For the yeo-heave-o', and the heave-away, and the sighing
seaman's cheer;
When, weighing slow, at eve they go – far, far from love and
home;
And sobbing sweethearts, in a row, wail o'er the ocean foam.

In livid and obdurate gloom he darkens down at last:
A shapely one he is, and strong, as e'er from cat was cast:
O trusted and trustworthy guard, if thou hadst life like me,
What pleasures would thy toils reward beneath the deep green
sea!
O deep-Sea-diver, who might then behold such sights as thou?
The hoary monster's palaces! methinks what joy 'twere now
To go plumb plunging down amid the assembly of the whales,
And feel the churn'd sea round me boil beneath their scourging
tails!

Then deep in tangle-woods to fight the fierce sea unicorn,
And send him foil'd and bellowing back, for all his ivory horn;
To leave the subtle sworder-fish of bony blade forlorn;
And for the ghastly-grinning shark, to laugh his jaws to scorn:
To leap down on the kraken's back, where 'mid Norwegian isles
He lies, a lubber anchorage for sudden shallow'd miles;
Till snorting, like an under-sea volcano, off he rolls;
Meanwhile to swing, a-buffeting the far astonished shoals
Of his back-browsing ocean-calves; or, haply, in a cove,
Shell-strown, and consecrate of old to some Undiné's love,
To find the long-hair'd mermaidens; or, hard by icy lands,
To wrestle with the Sea-serpent, upon cerulean sands.

O broad-arm'd Fisher of the deep, whose sports can equal
thine?
The Dolphin weighs a thousand tons, that tugs thy cable line;
And night by night, 'tis thy delight, thy glory day by day,
Through sable sea and breaker white the giant game to play –
But shamer of our little sports! forgive the name I gave –
A fisher's job is to destroy – thine office is to save.
O lodger in the sea-kings' halls, couldst thou but understand
Whose be the white bones by thy side, or whose that dripping
band,
Slow swaying in the heaving waves, that round about thee bend,
With sounds like breakers in a dream blessing their ancient
friend –
Oh, couldst thou know what heroes glide with larger steps
round thee,
Thine iron side would swell with pride; thou'dst leap within the
sea!

Give honour to their memories who left the pleasant strand,
To shed their blood so freely for the love of Fatherland –
Who left their chance of quiet age and grassy churchyard grave,
So freely, for a restless bed amid the tossing wave –
Oh, though our anchor may not be all I have fondly sung,
Honour him for their memory, whose bones he goes among!

## *Lament for Thomas Davis*

I walked through Ballinderry in the spring-time,
  When the bud was on the tree;
And I said, in every fresh-ploughed field beholding
  The sowers striding free,
Scattering broadcast forth the corn in golden plenty
  On the quick seed-clasping soil,
'Even such, this day, among the fresh-stirred hearts of Erin,
  Thomas Davis, is thy toil!'

I sat by Ballyshannon in the summer,
  And saw the salmon leap;
And I said, as I beheld the gallant creatures
  Spring glittering from the deep,
Thro' the spray, and thro' the prone heaps striving onward
  To the calm clear streams above,
'So seekest thou thy native founts of freedom, Thomas Davis,
  In thy brightness of strength and love!'

I stood on Derrybawn in the autumn,
  And I heard the eagle call,
With a clangorous cry of wrath and lamentation
  That filled the wide mountain hall,
O'er the bare deserted place of his plundered eyrie;
  And I said, as he screamed and soared,
'So callest thou, thou wrathful-soaring Thomas Davis,
  For a nation's rights restored!'

And, alas! to think but now, and thou art lying,
  Dear Davis, dead at thy mother's knee;
And I, no mother near, on my own sick-bed,
  That face on earth shall never see:
I may lie and try to feel that I am not dreaming,
  I may lie and try to say, 'Thy will be done' –
But a hundred such as I will never comfort Erin
  For the loss of the noble son!

Young husbandman of Erin's fruitful seed-time,
  In the fresh track of danger's plough!
Who will walk the heavy, toilsome, perilous furrow
  Girt with freedom's seed-sheets now?
Who will banish with the wholesome crop of knowledge
  The flaunting weed and the bitter thorn,
Now that thou thyself art but a seed for hopeful planting
  Against the Resurrection morn?

Young salmon of the flood-tide of freedom
  That swells round Erin's shore!
Thou wilt leap against their loud oppressive torrent
  Of bigotry and hate no more:
Drawn downward by their prone material instinct,
  Let them thunder on their rocks and foam –
Thou hast leapt, aspiring soul, to founts beyond their raging
  Where troubled waters never come!

But I grieve not, eagle of the empty eyrie,
  That thy wrathful cry is still;
And that the songs alone of peaceful mourners
  Are heard today on Erin's hill;
Better far, if brothers' war be destined for us
  (God avert that horrid day, I pray!),
That ere, our hands be stained with slaughter fratricidal
  Thy warm heart should be cold in clay.

But my trust is strong in God, who made us brothers,
  That He will not suffer those right hands
Which thou hast joined in holier rites than wedlock
  To draw opposing brands.
Oh, many a tuneful tongue that thou mad'st vocal
  Would lie cold and silent then;
And songless long once more, should often-widowed Erin
  Mourn the loss of her brave young men.

Oh, brave young men, my love, my pride, my promise,
  'Tis on you my hopes are set,
In manliness, in kindliness, in justice,
  To make Erin a nation yet:
Self-respecting, self-relying, self-advancing,
  In union or in severance, free and strong –
And if God grant this, then, under God, to Thomas Davis
  Let the greater praise belong.

## *The Burial of King Cormac*

'Crom Cruach and his sub-gods twelve'
  Said Cormac, 'are but carven treene;
The axe that made them, haft or helve,
  Had worthier of our worship been.

'But He who made the tree to grow
  And hid in earth the iron-stone,
And made the man with mind to know
  The axe's use, is God alone.'

Anon to priests of Crom was brought –
  Where, girded in their service dread,
They minister'd on red Moy Slaught –
  Word of the words King Cormac said.

They loosed their curse against the King –
  They cursed him in his flesh and bones –
And daily in their mystic ring
  They turn'd the maledictive stones,

Till, where at meat the monarch sate,
  Amid the revel and the wine,
He choked upon the food he ate,
  At Sletty, southward of the Boyne.

High vaunted then the priestly throng,
  And far and wide they noised abroad,
With trump and loud liturgic song,
  The praise of their avenging god.

But ere the voice was wholly spent
  That priest and prince should still obey,
To awed attendants o'er him bent
  Great Cormac gather'd breath to say:

'Spread not the beds of Brugh for me
  When restless death-bed's use is done;
But bury me at Rosnaree,
  And face me to the rising sun.

'For all the Kings who lie in Brugh
  Put trust in gods of wood and stone;
And 'twas at Ross that first I knew
  One, Unseen, who is God alone.

'His glory lightens from the East;
  His message soon shall reach our shore;
And idol-god and cursing priest,
  Shall plague us from Moy Slaught no more.'

Dead Cormac on his bier they laid.
  'He reign'd a king for forty years,
And shame it were,' his captains said,
  'He lay not with his royal peers.

'His grandsire, Hundred-Battle, sleeps
  Serene in Brugh; and all around
Dead kings in stone sepulchral keeps
  Protect the sacred burial ground.

'What though a dying man should rave
  Of changes o'er the Eastern sea?
In Brugh of Boyne shall be his grave,
  And not in noteless Rosnaree.'

Then northward forth they bore the bier
  And down from Sletty side they drew,
With horseman and with charioteer,
  To cross the fords of Boyne to Brugh.

There came a breath of finer air,
  That touch'd the Boyne with ruffling wings;
It stirr'd him in his sedgy lair,
  And in his mossy moorland springs.

And as the burial train came down
  With dirge and savage dolorous shows,
Across their pathway, broad and brown,
  The deep full-hearted river rose;

From bank to bank through all his fords,
  'Neath blackening squalls he swell'd and boil'd,
And thrice the wondering Gentile lords
  Essay'd to cross, and thrice recoil'd.

Then forth stepp'd grey-hair'd warriors four;
  They said: 'Through angrier floods than these
On link'd shields once our King we bore
  From Dread-Spear and the hosts of Deece.

'And long as loyal will holds good,
  And limbs respond with helpful thews,
Nor flood, nor fiend within the flood,
  Shall bar him of his burial dues.'

With slanted necks they stoop'd to lift;
  They heaved him up to neck and chin;
And, pair and pair, with footsteps swift,
  Lock'd arm and shoulder, bore him in.

'Twas brave to see them leave the shore;
  To mark the deep'ning surges rise,
And fall subdued in foam before
  The tension of their striding thighs.

'Twas brave, when now a spear-cast out,
  Breast-high the battling surges ran;
For weight was great, and limbs were stout
  And loyal man put trust in man.

But ere they reach'd the middle deep,
  Nor steadying weight of clay they bore,
Nor strain of sinewy limbs could keep
  Their feet beneath the swerving four.

And now they slide, and now they swim,
  And now, amid the blackening squall,
Grey locks afloat, with clutchings grim,
  They plunge around the floating pall;

While as a youth with practised spear
  Through justling crowds bears off the ring,
Boyne from their shoulders caught the bier
  And proudly bore away the king.

At morning, on the grassy marge
  Of Rosnaree, the corpse was found;
And shepherds at their early charge
  Entomb'd it in the peaceful ground.

A tranquil spot – a hopeful sound
  Comes from the ever youthful stream,
And still on daisied mead and mound
  The dawn delays with tenderer beam.

Round Cormac Spring renews her buds;
  In march perpetual by his side,
Down come the earth-fresh April floods,
  And up the sea-fresh salmon glide.

And life and time rejoicing run
  From age to age their wonted way;
But still he waits the risen Sun,
  For still 'tis only dawning Day.

## *Deirdre's Lament for the Sons of Usnach*

The lions of the hill are gone,
And I am left alone – alone –
Dig the grave both wide and deep,
For I am sick, and fain would sleep!

The falcons of the wood are flown,
And I am left alone – alone –
Dig the grave both deep and wide,
And let us slumber side by side.

The dragons of the rock are sleeping,
Sleep that wakes not for our weeping:
Dig the grave and make it ready;
Lay me on my true Love's body.

Lay their spears and bucklers bright
By the warriors' sides aright;
Many a day the Three before me
On their linkèd bucklers bore me.

Lay upon the low grave floor,
'Neath each head, the blue claymore;
Many a time the noble Three
Redden'd those blue blades for me.

Lay the collars, as is meet,
Of their greyhounds at their feet;
Many a time for me have they
Brought the tall red deer to bay.

Oh! to hear my true Love singing,
Sweet as sound of trumpets ringing:
Like the sway of ocean swelling
Roll'd his deep voice round our dwelling.

Oh! to hear the echoes pealing
Round our green and fairy sheeling,
When the Three, with soaring chorus,
Pass'd the silent skylark o'er us.

Echo now, sleep, morn and even –
Lark alone enchant the heaven! –
Ardan's lips are scant of breath, –
Neesa's tongue is cold in death.

Stag, exult on glen and mountain –
Salmon, leap from loch to fountain –
Heron, in the free air warm ye –
Usnach's Sons no more will harm ye!

Erin's stay no more you are,
Rulers of the ridge of war;
Never more 'twill be your fate
To keep the beam of battle straight.

Woe is me! by fraud and wrong –
Traitors false and tyrants strong –
Fell Clan Usnach, bought and sold,
For Barach's feast and Conor's gold!

Woe to Eman, roof and wall! –
Woe to Red Branch, hearth and hall! –
Tenfold woe and black dishonour
To the false and foul Clan Conor!

Dig the grave both wide and deep,
Sick I am, and fain would sleep!
Dig the grave and make it ready,
Lay me on my true Love's body.

## *Willy Gilliland: An Ulster Ballad*

Up in the mountain solitudes, and in a rebel ring,
He has worshipped God upon the hill, in spite of church and king;
And sealed his treason with his blood on Bothwell Bridge he hath;
So he must fly his father's land, or he must die the death;
For comely Claverhouse has come along with grim Dalzell,
And his smoking rooftree testifies they've done their errand well.

In vain to fly his enemies he fled his native land;
Hot persecution waited him upon the Carrick strand;
His name was on the Carrick cross, a price was on his head,
A fortune to the man that brings him in alive or dead!
And so on moor and mountain, from the Lagan to the Bann,
From house to house, and hill to hill, he lurked an out-lawed
man.

At last, when in false company he might no longer bide,
He stayed his houseless wanderings upon the Collon side,
There in a cave all underground he laired his heathy den,
Ah, many a gentleman was fain to earth like hill fox then!
With hound and fishing-rod he lived on hill and stream by day;
At night, betwixt his fleet greyhound and his bonny mare he lay.

It was a summer evening, and, mellowing and still,
Glenwhirry to the setting sun lay bare from hill to hill;
For all that valley pastoral held neither house nor tree,
But spread abroad and open all, a full fair sight to see,
From Slemish foot to Collon top lay one unbroken green,
Save where in many a silver coil the river glanced between.

And on the river's grassy bank, even from the morning grey,
He at the angler's pleasant sport had spent the summer day;
Ah! many a time and oft I've spent the summer day from dawn,
And wondered, when the sunset came, where time and care
had gone,
Along the reaches curling fresh, the wimpling pools and streams,
Where he that day his cares forgot in those delightful dreams.

His blithe work done, upon a bank the outlaw rested now,
And laid the basket from his back, the bonnet from his brow;
And there, his hand upon the Book, his knee upon the sod,
He filled the lonely valley with the gladsome word of God;
And for a persecuted kirk, and for her martyrs dear,
And against a godless church and king he spoke up loud and
clear.

And now upon his homeward way, he crossed the Collon high,
And over bush and bank and brae he sent abroad his eye;
But all was darkening peacefully in grey and purple haze,
The thrush was silent in the banks, the lark upon the braes –
When suddenly shot up a blaze, from the cave's mouth it came;
And troopers' steeds and troopers' caps are glancing in the same!

He couched among the heather, and he saw them, as he lay,
With three long yells at parting, ride lightly east away:
Then down with heavy heart he came, to sorry cheer came he,
For ashes black were crackling where the green whins used to be,
And stretched among the prickly comb, his heart's blood smoking
round,
From slender nose to breast-bone cleft, lay dead his good
greyhound!

'They've slain my dog, the Philistines! They've ta'en my bonny
mare!'
He plunged into the smoking hole; no bonny beast was there –
He groped beneath his burning bed (it burned him to the bone,)
Where his good weapon used to be, but broadsword there was
none;
He reeled out of the stifling den, and sat down on a stone,
And in the shadows of the night 'twas thus he made his moan –

'I am a houseless outcast: I have neither bed nor board,
Nor living thing to look upon, nor comfort save the Lord:
Yet many a time were better men in worse extremity;
Who succoured them in their distress, He now will succour me, –
He now will succour me, I know; and, by His holy Name,
I'll make the doers of this deed right dearly rue the same!

'My bonny mare! I've ridden you when Claver'se rode behind,
And from the thumbscrew and the boot you bore me like the
wind;
And, while I have the life you saved, on your sleek flank I swear,
Episcopalian rowel shall never ruffle hair!
Though sword to wield they've left me none – yet Wallace wight,
I wis,
Good battle did on Irvine side wi' waur weapon than this.' –

His fishing-rod with both his hands he griped it as he spoke,
And, where the butt and top were spliced, in pieces twain he
broke;
The limber top he cast away, with all its gear abroad,
But, grasping the thick hickory butt, with spike of iron shod,
He ground the sharp spear to a point; then pulled his bonnet
down,
And, meditating black revenge, set forth for Carrick town.

The sun shines bright on Carrick wall and Carrick Castle grey,
And up thine aisle, St. Nicholas, has ta'en his morning way,
And to the North-Gate sentinel displayeth far and near
Sea, hill, and tower, and all thereon, in dewy freshness clear,
Save where, behind a ruined wall, himself alone to view,
Is peering from the ivy green a bonnet of the blue.

The sun shines red on Carrick wall and Carrick Castle old,
And all the western buttresses have changed their grey for gold;
And from thy shrine, Saint Nicholas, the pilgrim of the sky
Has gone in rich farewell, as fits such royal votary;
But, as his last red glance he takes down past black Slieve-a-true,
He leaveth where he found it first, the bonnet of the blue.

Again he makes the turrets grey stand out before the hill;
Constant as their foundation rock, there is the bonnet still!
And now the gates are open'd, and forth in gallant show
Prick jeering grooms and burghers blythe, and troopers in a row;
But one has little care for jest, so hard bested is he,
To ride the outlaw's bonny mare, for this at last is she!

Down comes her master with a roar, her rider with a groan,
The iron and the hickory are through and through him gone!
He lies a corpse; and where he sat, the outlaw sits again,
And once more to his bonny mare he gives the spur and rein;
Then some with sword, and some with gun, they ride and run
amain!
But sword and gun, and whip and spur, that day they plied in
vain!

Ah! little thought Willy Gilliland, when he on Skerry side
Drew bridle first, and wiped his brow after that weary ride,
That where he lay like hunted brute, a caverned outlaw lone,
Broad lands and yeoman tenantry should yet be there his own:
Yet so it was; and still from him descendants not a few
Draw birth and lands, and, let me trust, draw love of Freedom
too.

## AUBREY DE VERE

(1814–1902)

### *The Little Black Rose*

The Little Black Rose shall be red at last;
What made it black but the March wind dry,
And the tear of the widow that fell on it fast?
It shall redden the hills when June is nigh!

The Silk of the Kine shall rest at last;
What drove her forth but the dragon fly?
In the golden vale she shall feed full fast,
With her mild gold horn and her slow, dark eye.

The wounded wood-dove lies dead at last!
  The pine long-bleeding, it shall not die!
This song is secret. Mine ear it passed
  In a wind o'er the plains at Athenry.

## SHERIDAN LE FANU
## (1814–73)

### from *The Legend of the Glaive*

Through the woods of Morrua and over its root-knotted flooring,
The hero speeds onward, alone, on his terrible message;
When faint and far-off, like the gathering gallop of battle,
The hoofs of the hurricane louder and louder come leaping,
There's a gasp and a silence around him, a swooning of nature,
And the forest trees moan, and complain with a presage of evil.
And nearer, like great organ's wailing, high-piping through
  thunder,
Subsiding, then lifted again to a thousand-tongued tumult,
And crashing, and deafening and yelling in clangorous uproar.
Soaring onward, down-riding, and rending the wreck of its
  conquest,
The tempest swoops on: all the branches before it bend, singing
Like cordage in shipwreck; before it sear leaves fly like vapour;
Before it bow down like wide armies, plumed heads of the forest,
In frenzy dark-rolling, up-tossing their scathed arms like
  Mænads.
Dizzy lightnings split this way and that in the blind void above
  him;
For a moment long passages reeling and wild with the tempest,

In the blue map and dazzle of lightning, throb vivid and vanish;
And white glare the wrinkles and knots of the oaktrees beside
him,
While close overhead clap the quick mocking palms of the
Storm-Fiend.

## THOMAS DAVIS
(1814–45)

### *Fontenoy, 1745*

Thrice, at the huts of Fontenoy, the English column failed,
And, twice, the lines of Saint Antoine, the Dutch in vain assailed;
For town and slope were filled with fort and flanking battery,
And well they swept the English ranks, and Dutch auxiliary.
As vainly, through De Barri's wood, the British soldiers burst,
The French artillery drove them back, diminished, and dispersed.
The bloody Duke of Cumberland beheld with anxious eye,
And ordered up his last reserve, his latest chance to try,
On Fontenoy, on Fontenoy, how fast his generals ride!
And mustering come his chosen troops, like clouds at eventide.

Six thousand English veterans in stately column tread,
Their cannon blaze in front and flank, Lord Hay is at their head;
Steady they step a-down the slope – steady they climb the hill;
Steady they load – steady they fire, moving right onward still,
Betwixt the wood and Fontenoy, as through a furnace blast,
Through rampart, trench, and palisade, and bullets showering
fast;

And on the open plain above they rose, and kept their course,
With ready fire and grim resolve, that mocked at hostile force:
Past Fontenoy, past Fontenoy, while thinner grow their ranks –
They break, as broke the Zuyder Zee through Holland's ocean
  banks.

More idly than the summer flies, French tirailleurs rush round;
As stubble to the lava tide, French squadrons strew the ground;
Bomb-shell, and grape, and round-shot tore, still on they
  marched and fired –
Fast, from each volley, grenadier and voltigeur retired.
'Push on, my household cavalry!' King Louis madly cried:
To death they rush, but rude their shock – not unavenged they
  died.
On through the camp the column trod – King Louis turns his rein:
'Not yet, my liege,' Saxe interposed, 'the Irish troops remain';
And Fontenoy, famed Fontenoy, had been a Waterloo,
Were not these exiles ready then, fresh, vehement, and true.

'Lord Clare,' he says, 'you have your wish; there are your
  Saxon foes!'
The Marshal almost smiles to see, so furiously he goes!
How fierce the look these exiles wear, who're wont to be so gay,
The treasured wrongs of fifty years are in their hearts today –
The treaty broken, ere the ink wherewith 'twas writ could dry,
Their plundered homes, their ruined shrines, their women's
  parting cry,
Their priesthood hunted down like wolves, their country
  overthrown –
Each looks as if revenge for all were staked on him alone.
On Fontenoy, on Fontenoy, nor ever yet elsewhere,
Rushed on to fight a nobler band than these proud exiles were.

O'Brien's voice is hoarse with joy, as, halting, he commands,
'Fix bay'nets! – charge!' Like mountain storm, rush on these fiery
  bands!
Thin is the English column now, and faint their volleys grow,
Yet, must'ring all the strength they have, they make a gallant
  show.

They dress their ranks upon the hill to face that battle-wind –
Their bayonets the breakers' foam; like rocks, the men behind!
One volley crashes from their line, when, through the surging smoke,
With empty guns clutched in their hands, the head-long Irish broke.
On Fontenoy, on Fontenoy, hark to that fierce huzza!
'Revenge! remember Limerick! dash down the Sacsanach!'

Like lions leaping at a fold, when mad with hunger's pang,
Right up against the English line the Irish exiles sprang:
Bright was their steel, 'tis bloody now, their guns are filled with gore;
Through shattered ranks, and severed files, the trampled flags they tore;
The English strove with desperate strength, paused, rallied, staggered, fled –
The green hill-side is matted close with dying and with dead.
Across the plain, and far away passed on that hideous wrack,
While cavalier and fantassin dash in upon their track.
On Fontenoy, on Fontenoy, like eagles in the sun,
With bloody plumes, the Irish stand – the field is fought and won!

## *O'Connell's Statue*

Chisel the likeness of The Chief,
Not in gaiety, nor grief;
Change not by your art to stone,
Ireland's laugh, or Ireland's moan.
Dark her tale, and none can tell
Its fearful chronicle so well.
Her frame is bent – her wounds are deep –
Who, like him, her woes can weep?
He can be gentle as a bride,
While none can rule with kinglier pride;
Calm to hear, and wise to prove,
Yet gay as lark in soaring love.

Well it were, posterity
Should have some image of his glee;
That easy humour, blossoming
Like the thousand flowers of spring!
Glorious the marble which could show
His bursting sympathy for woe:
Could catch the pathos, flowing wild,
Like mother's milk to craving child.

And oh! how princely were the art
Could mould his mien, or tell his heart
When sitting sole on Tara's hill,
While hung a million on his will!
Yet, not in gaiety, nor grief,
Chisel the image of our Chief;
Nor even in that haughty hour
When a nation owned his power.

But would you by your art unroll
His own and Ireland's secret soul,
And give to other times to scan
The greatest greatness of the man?
Fierce defiance let him be
Hurling at our enemy. –
From a base as fair and sure,
As our love is true and pure,
Let his statue rise as tall
And firm as a castle wall;
On his broad brow let there be
A type of Ireland's history;
Pious, generous, deep, and warm,
Strong and changeful as a storm;
Let whole centuries of wrong
Upon his recollection throng –
Strongbow's force, and Henry's wile,
Tudor's wrath, and Stuart's guile,
And iron Strafford's tiger jaws,

And brutal Brunswick's penal laws;
Not forgetting Saxon faith,
Not forgetting Norman scath,
Not forgetting William's word,
Not forgetting Cromwell's sword.
Let the Union's fetter vile –
The shame and ruin of our isle –
Let the blood of 'Ninety-Eight
And our present blighting fate –
Let the poor mechanic's lot,
And the peasant's ruined cot,
Plundered wealth and glory flown,
Ancient honours overthrown –
Let trampled altar, rifled urn,
Knit his look to purpose stern.
Mould all this into one thought,
Like wizard cloud with thunder fraught;
Still let our glories through it gleam,
Like fair flowers through a flooded stream,
Or like a flashing wave at night,
Bright, – 'mid the solemn darkness, bright.
Let the memory of old days
Shine through the statesman's anxious face –
Dathi's power, and Brian's fame,
And headlong Sarsfield's sword of flame;
And the spirit of Red Hugh,
And the pride of 'Eighty-Two,
And the victories he won,
And the hope that leads him on!

Let whole armies seem to fly
From his threatening hand and eye;
Be the strength of all the land
Like a falchion in his hand,
And be his gesture sternly grand.
A braggart tyrant swore to smite

A people struggling for their right;
O'Connell dared him to the field,
Content to die, but never yield.
Fancy such a soul as his,
In a moment such as this,
Like cataract, or foaming tide,
Or army charging in its pride.
Thus he spoke, and thus he stood,
Proffering in our cause his blood.
Thus his country loves him best –
To image this is your behest.
Chisel thus, and thus alone,
If to man you'd change the stone.

## JAMES MCCARROLL
## (1814–91)

### *The Irish Wolf*

The Times *once used this term to designate the Irish people.*

Seek music in the wolf's fierce howl
  Or pity in his blood-shot eye,
When hunger drives him out to prowl
  Beneath a rayless northern sky:

But seek not that we should forgive
  The hand that strikes us to the heart,
And yet in mockery bids us live
  To count our stars as they depart.

We've fed the tyrant with our blood;
 Won all his battles – built his throne –
Established him on land and flood,
 And sought his glory next our own.

We raised him from his low estate;
 We plucked his pagan soul from hell,
And led him pure to heaven's gate,
 Till he, for gold, like Judas fell.

And when in one long, soulless night
 He lay unknown to wealth or fame,
We gave him empire – riches – light,
 And taught him how to spell his name.

But now, ungenerous and unjust,
 Forgetful of our old renown,
He bows us to the very dust;
 But wears our jewels in his crown.

## MOTHER OF DIARMAID MAC CÁRTHAIGH
(*fl.* 1850)

### *A Lament for Diarmaid Mac Cárthaigh of Ráth Dubháin, Who Was a Butter-Merchant in Cork*

Dear friend and darling,
If you were at home,
Neither worsted or spinning,
Nor the socks they were knitting
Would be their concern,
But the roads too narrow
For the roaring men
And the screaming women
Coming to see you,
Dear grey-eyed horseman.

Dear love and sweetheart,
Your downfall was there,
At the Knight's Paling,
Where the men used to gather
When they hunted the deer –
May God not protect them;
They hadn't half your energy,
Dear iron-stirruped horseman.

Dear love and treasure,
The young women wonder
That the likes of me reared you:
If they'd walked over Mushera
And the short-cut through the Curraghs,
And all the paths I've taken,
I'd be very surprised if
They didn't look as rough.

My love and my dear one,
I had great hopes for you:
That roads would be cleared for you,
That walls would be whitewashed,
Swards spread before you,
As you brought a woman home;
Not like this, surrounded
By boors from England
And the children of merchants,
Carried by four men
Out of the city –
But my thanks to all of you,
Since I've come among you
For I needed help –
Dear King of Bounty.

Dear love and dear treasure,
If I had a messenger,
Or a spirited runner
To go west along the Maine
Many a fine sturdy woman,
Many a proud stately horseman,
With their saddles all crimson
And their horse-bits of silver,
Would be galloping towards you,
Knocking sparks from the rocks,
As they left the city.

Dear love and dear treasure,
If you're going to bed,
Take the quickest way home,
And don't forget Tig na Croise:
Call the two lovely girls,
And Diarmaid, son of Eoghan na Toinne.
Their messenger told me
Their new clothes weren't ready;
That their bridles were broken,
And their saddles lacked girths;
That their horses had run away

Wild in the hills, and
No blacksmith was there
Who could get them all ready
For the hunt or the chase.

Dear love and precious one,
Sweet Máire, daughter of Eoghan,
Who was neither small nor big,
But perfectly shaped;
Who would halt the men from work,
Or the children from their play,
Or the horses in the field,
Listening to your song,
On a lovely autumn morning,
As you milked the cows outdoors.

Dear love and beloved,
Dear little calf's calf,
Dear delicious crumbs of bacon,
Dear juice of the butter,
Whom I never criticized
(Or if I did, didn't realize),
Till you left me, and settled
Below in Cloghboley,
With Maití Sín na Circe,
Who would curb your heart's blood,
With his fussing and organizing,
And harnessing his plough-team;
All you got for your trouble
Was the baby's leftovers.
He'd take the butter from the churn
While you sat at the fire;
He'd shut the hens in at night.

My friend and my dear one,
He beat you with the bridle,
With the nine-thonged whip,
And then with a stick;
But you never told me,
Till I found the marks on you
In bed a year later.

Dear love and dear treasure,
I gave you twenty milking cows
Along with a bull, and
A trough to knead bread in –
But now instead I curse you,
Not your livestock or harvest;
Not the fire on your hearth,
But your heart and your veins,
To leave you maimed,
You bilious lout!

My love and my precious,
You wrote to the King's parliament,
And to Cork of the sailing ships.
Where they wined and dined your messenger,
And enjoyed your conversation,
Dearest child and precious one.

Dear love and precious,
I could name your townlands
All the way to lovely Kerry,
And all the way back
To the parish of Cullen:
Áthán with its smooth saplings,
Drishane with its high castle,

Far Prothus with its elder-tree,
Rathcoole for good company,
Gortbrack with its headstones,
And Booleymore beside it,
And one I forgot to mention,
So I turn and go back
To the Black Cow's Ridge.

Dear love and pet,
You'll come with me
To limewashed Drishane
With its dazzling castle,
The finest in Ireland,
If it only had a harbour.
But even without one,
It has honey and beeswax,
Wheat in thick swathes
Overlapping on the ground,
And besides all that,
The place is a holy one!

My friend and my darling,
I'll take you with me
To fragrant Drishane
With its four-cornered castle –
With sweet-smelling berries,
Beech-nuts knee high,
Gentle cows lowing
On a fine dewy morning,
Ready for milking.

My love and my dear!
I very much fear
That a low stony cell
In the graveyard's east side
Is where you've chosen to lie.

*Angela Bourke*

## MORIAN SHEHONE

(*fl. c.*1850?)

### *Lament of Morian Shehone for Miss Mary Bourke*

*from an Irish keen*

'There's darkness in thy dwelling-place, and silence reigns above,
And Mary's voice is heard no more, like the soft voice of love.
Yes! thou art gone, my Mary dear! and Morian Shehone
Is left to sing his song of woe, and wail for thee alone.
O! snow-white were thy virtues – the beautiful, the young,
The old with pleasure bent to hear the music of thy tongue:
The young with rapture gazed on thee, and their hearts in love were bound,
For thou wast brighter than the sun that sheds its light around.
My soul is dark, O Mary dear! thy sun of beauty's set;
The sorrowful are dumb for thee – the grieved their tears forget;
And I am left to pour my woe above thy grave alone;
For dear wert thou to the fond heart of Morian Shehone.
Fast-flowing tears above the grave of the rich man are shed,
But they are dried when the cold stone shuts in his narrow bed;
Not so with my heart's faithful love – the dark grave cannot hide
From Morian's eyes thy form of grace, of loveliness, and pride.
Thou didst not fall like the sere leaf, when autumn's chill winds blow –
'Twas a tempest and a storm-blast that has laid my Mary low.
Hadst thou not friends that loved thee well? hadst thou not garments rare?
Wast thou not happy, Mary? wast thou not young and fair?
Then why should the dread spoiler come, my heart's peace to destroy,
Or the grim tyrant tear from me my all of earthly joy?
O! am I left to pour my woes above thy grave alone?
Thou idol of the faithful heart of Morian Shehone!

Sweet were thy looks and sweet thy smiles, and kind wast thou
to all;
The withering scowl of envy on thy fortunes dared not fall;
For thee thy friends lament and mourn, and never cease to
weep –
O! that their lamentations could awake thee from thy sleep!
O! that thy peerless form again could meet my loving clasp!
O! that the cold damp hand of Death could loose his iron grasp!
Yet, when the valley's daughters meet beneath the tall elm tree,
And talk of Mary as a dream that never more shall be,
Then may thy spirit float around, like music in the air,
And pour upon their virgin souls a blessing and a prayer.
O! am I left to pour my wail above thy grave alone?'
Then sinks in silence the lament of Morian Shehone!

*Anonymous*

## WILLIAM ALLINGHAM
## (1824–89)

### from *Invitation to a Painter (Sent from the West of Ireland)*

I

Flee from London, good my Walter! boundless jail of bricks
and gas,
Weary purgatorial flagstones, dreary parks of burnt-up grass,
Exhibitions, evening parties, dust and swelter, glare and crush,
Fashion's costly idle pomp, Mammon's furious race and rush;
Leave your hot tumultuous city for the breaker's rival roar,
Quit your small suburban garden for the rude hills by the shore,
Leagues of smoke for morning vapour lifted off a mountain-
range,

Silk and lace for barefoot beauty, and for 'something new and
strange'
All your towny wit and gossip. You shall both in field and fair,
Paddy's cunning and politeness with the Cockney ways compare,
Catch those lilts and old-world tunes maidens at their needle sing,
Peep at dancers, from an outskirt of the blithe applausive ring,
See our petty Court of Justice, where the swearing's very strong,
See our little plain St Peter's with its kneeling peasant throng;
Hear the brogue and Gaelic round you; sketch a hundred Irish
scenes
(Not mere whisky and shillelagh) – wedding banquets, funeral
*keens*;
Rove at pleasure, noon or midnight; change a word with all you
meet;
Ten times safer than in England, far less trammelled in your feet.
Here, the only danger known
Is walking where the land's your own.
Landscape-lords are left alone.

V

Now I've thought of something! mind me, for no artist's clever
sake,
Merely artist, should I dare to sit his comrade at a Wake;
You're at home with tears and laughter, friend of mine, and bear
a heart
Full of sympathetic kindness, taking every brother's part.
Through the mob that fills the kitchen, clouded with tobacco-
fume,
Joking, singing – we have cross'd the threshold of that inside
room
Where the seniors and relations sitting gravely by the wall
Speak in murmurs; on a table, lighted candles thick and tall;
Straight the bed-quilt and the curtains; on the pillow calm within
A moveless Face with close-shut eyelids and a cloth about the
chin,
Under a crucifix. You see: and sideways through the open door
Laughing looks and odd grimaces, and you hear a blithe uproar
From the youthful merrymakers. Kneeling silent by the bed

Prays a woman; weeps a woman, rocking, sobbing, at its head,
Nigh the Face, which spoke this morning, unregarding,
undiscerning.
Louder bursts the lively voices; wearily the candles burning;
Elders gravely on the whisper; Time for ever slowly turning;
Bringing round the book and spade,
Another hillock duly made,
The cottage swept, the grief allayed.

VI

Ere we part at winter's portal, I shall row you of a night
On a swirling Stygian river, to a ghostly yellow light.
When the nights are black and gusty, then do eels in myriads glide
Through the pools and down the rapids, hurrying to the ocean-
tide,
(But they fear the frost or moonshine, in their mud beds coiling
close)
And the wearmen, on the platform of that pigmy water-house
Built among the river-currents, with a dam to either bank,
Pull the purse-net's heavy end to swing across their wooden tank,
Ere they loose the cord about it, then a slimy wriggling heap
Falls with splashing, where a thousand fellow-prisoners heave
and creep.
Chill winds roar above the wearmen, darkling rush the floods
below;
There they watch and work their eel-nets, till the late dawn lets
them go.
There we'll join their eely supper, bearing smoke the best we can,
(House's furniture a salt-box, truss of straw, and frying-pan),
Hearken Con's astounding stories, how a mythologic eel
Chased a man o'er miles of country, swallowed two dogs at a
meal,
To the hissing, bubbling music of the pan and *pratie*-pot.
Denser grows the reek around us, each like Mussulman a-squat,
Each with victuals in his fingers, we devour them hot and hot;
Smoky rays our lantern throwing,
Ruddy peat-fire warmly glowing,
Noisily the river flowing.

## *The Abbot of Inisfalen (A Killarney Legend)*

I

The Abbot of Inisfalen awoke ere dawn of day;
Under the dewy green leaves went he forth to pray.
The lake around his island lay smooth and dark and deep,
And wrapt in a misty stillness the mountains were all asleep.
Low kneeled the Abbot Cormac when the dawn was dim and
gray;
The prayers of his holy office he faithfully 'gan say.
Low kneeled the Abbot Cormac while the dawn was waxing red;
And for his sins' forgiveness a solemn prayer he said:
Low kneeled that holy Abbot while the dawn was waxing clear;
And he prayed with loving-kindness for his convent-brethren
dear.
Low kneeled that blessed Abbot while the dawn was waxing
bright;
He prayed a great prayer for Ireland, he prayed with all his
might.
Low kneeled that good old Father while the sun began to dart;
He prayed a prayer for all men, he prayed it from his heart.
His blissful soul was in Heaven, though a breathing man was he;
He was out of time's dominion, so far as the living may be.

II

The Abbot of Inisfalen arose upon his feet;
He heard a small bird singing, and O but it sung sweet!
It sung upon a holly-bush, this little snow-white bird;
A song so full of gladness he never before had heard.
It sung upon a hazel, it sung upon a thorn;
He had never heard such music since the hour that he was born.
It sung upon a sycamore, it sung upon a briar;
To follow the song and hearken this Abbot could never tire.
Till at last he well bethought him; he might no longer stay;
So he blessed the little white singing-bird, and gladly went his way.

III

But, when he came to his Abbey, he found a wondrous wondrous
 change;
He saw no friendly faces there, for every face was strange.
The strange men spoke unto him; and he heard from all and each
The foreign tongue of the Sassenach, not wholesome Irish speech.
Then the oldest monk came forward, in Irish tongue spake he:
'Thou wearest the holy Augustine's dress, and who hath given it
 to thee?'
'I wear the holy Augustine's dress, and Cormac is my name,
The Abbot of this good Abbey by grace of God I am.
I went forth to pray, at the dawn of day; and when my prayers
 were said,
I hearkened awhile to a little bird, that sung above my head.'
The monks to him made answer, 'Two hundred years have gone
 o'er,
Since our Abbot Cormac went through the gate, and never was
 heard of more.
Matthias now is our Abbot, and twenty have passed away.
The stranger is lord of Ireland; we live in an evil day.'
'Days will come and go,' he said, 'and the world will pass away,
In Heaven a day is a thousand years, a thousand years are a day.'

IV

'Now give me absolution; for my time is come,' said he.
And they gave him absolution, as speedily as might be.
Then, close outside the window, the sweetest song they heard
That ever yet since the world began was uttered by any bird.
The monks looked out and saw the bird, its feathers all white
 and clean;
And there in a moment, beside it, another white bird was seen.
Those two they sang together, waved their white wings, and fled;
Flew aloft, and vanished; but the good old man was dead.
They buried his blessed body where lake and green-sward meet;
A carven cross above his head, a holly-bush at his feet;
Where spreads the beautiful water to gay or cloudy skies,
And the purple peaks of Killarney from ancient woods arise.

# *from* Laurence Bloomfield in Ireland

## from *Chapter II: Neighbouring Landlords*

Unlike this careful management (between
The two, Sir Ulick's townlands intervene)
Is that of Termon on the river-side,
Domain and mansion of insolvent pride,
Where Dysart, drawing from ancestral ground
One sterling penny for each phantom pound
Of rent-roll, lives, when all the truth is known,
Mere factor in the place he calls his own;
Through mortgages and bonds, one wide-spread maze,
Steps, dances, doubles round by devious ways,
While creditor, to creditor a foe,
Hangs dubious o'er the vast imbroglio.
And thus, minute in bargain where he can,
There, closing quick with ready-money man,
Despised for cunning, and for malice feared,
Yet still by custom and old name endeared
To Celtic minds, who also better like
A rule of thumb than Gough's arithmetic, –
Dysart has shuffled on, to this good day,
Let creditors and courts do what they may.
The house is wondrous large, and wondrous mean;
Its likeness year by year more rarely seen;
A ragged billiard-table decks the hall,
Abandoned long ago of cue and ball,
With whips and tools and garments littered o'er,
And lurking dogs possess the dangerous floor.
Ghost, from Proconsul Rutland's time, show in
To this great shabby room, which heard the din
Of bet and handicap, oath, toast, and song,
From squires and younger sons, a vanished throng,
Who drank much wine, who many foxes slew,
Hunted themselves by creditors all through,
And caught at last, or fairly run to earth;

A cold and ghastly room of bygone mirth.
Above the dusty fox's-brush see hung
Our grandpapa the Major, spruce and young,
In faded scarlet; on that other side
The needy Viscount's daughter, his fair bride;
And many portraits with once-famous names,
Of ancestors and horses, dogs and dames,
Now damp, or smutched, or dropping from their frames.
Big doleful house it is, with many a leak;
With dingy passages and bedrooms bleak;
With broken window-panes and mildewed walls;
With grass-grown courtyard and deserted stalls
That proudly echoed to the hunting-stud,
Where still one stable shows its 'bit of blood'.
Tom is not wed; long wed is brother Hugh;
They seldom meet, and quarrel when they do.
Tom is a staunch good Protestant by creed,
But half a Mormon, judged by act and deed;
A dozen wives he has, but underhand,
*Sub rosa*, not confessed, you understand,
And this makes all the difference, of course.
His pretty little babes, except perforce,
He never knows, and never wants to know;
Yet, clippings of his purse must that way go.

## from *Chapter V: Ballytullagh*

Old Father Flynn and his plain chapel walls
Are both no more; from a great steeple calls
A bell that dins the rival church to shame,
And pseudo-gothic art asserts its claim
For pence and wonder in the unfinished pile,
A dull burlesque on mediaeval style,
Stone nightmare, lumpish, set with eye and horn,
Of architectural indigestion born.
Roofless and ruined each old stately fane,
Or if a living voice in some remain,
The rich usurper's – now on Irish skies

These new-born proofs of ancient faith arise.
Adair, the zealous, careful parish priest,
Is gentle, smooth, and mild to man and beast,
With comely presence and colloquial skill,
Of secret thoughts, and cool tenacious will;
An Irish mitre is perhaps his hope;
A proper man for cardinal or pope.
Outside the Church, all teaching is a crime,
All strength diabolism: he bides his time
To gain at last the public purse for schools
In strict accordancy with holy rules;
The dark unlawful oath he blames no less
Than Pigot; all must One Great Power confess.
(What Power? – enough! each wandering thought suppress.)
Likes not England's rule, nor will he curse;
The Church's children's oft times please him worse;
Dark oaths and alien bonds are things of sin;
Yet agitation doth concession win;
He favours loyalty of much that kind
Which in a doubtful-tempered dog you find,
That fawns and growls, obeys and shows his teeth, –
Servility with danger underneath;
For so must selfish England understand
That Ireland is not wholly in her hand,
Yet want that old excuse to knit a frown,
Cry 'rebel!' and with fury smite her down.
Irish Republic? – Irish Kingdom? – none
Could less desire such thing beneath the sun
Than Father John Adair: your ship may roll,
But will you run her straight on rock or shoal
For mere impatience? Of all men that live,
Such clerics are the most conservative;
Perusing somewhat bitterly, no less,
Their map and daily roll-call of distress,
When scores around them, with the name of land,
Staring on hungry wife and children stand,
Unused by beggars' art to seek and shift,
And dreading from their only hold to drift.

## from *Chapter VII: Tenants at Will*

But Pigot's ruddy cheek and sharp black eye
Display no softer hint, as months go by;
And now the trembling tenants whisper sad, –
'O Queen of Heaven! and would he be so bad?
And will they send us begging, young and old,
And seize the fields, and make the firesides cold,
Where, God's our witness, poor enough we live,
But still content with what the Lord may give,
Our hearts with love and veneration tied
To where our fathers' fathers lived and died?'
Or else more fiercely, – ''Tis our native land!
But cruel tyrants have us at command,
To let us grow, if best it serves their needs,
Or tear and cast us forth like poison-weeds.
The law's their implement: who make the law?
The rich men for the rich, and leave no flaw.
And what's the poor man's part? to drudge and sweat
For food and shelter. Does the poor man get
Bare food and shelter? – praties, cabin, rags.
Now fling him out to famish – or he drags
His weary body to that gaol and grave
The Poorhouse; – he must live and die a slave,
Toil, starve, and suffer, creep, and crouch, and crawl,
Be cursed and trampled, and submit to all,
Without one murmur, one rebellious trace
Among the marks of misery on his face!'

Each tongue around old Oona feared to tell
The great misfortune, worse than yet befell
In all her length of journey. When they tried
To move her – 'Would they take her life?' she cried;
At which it rested, hap what happen might.
And scarcely one, in truth, prepared for flight;

Contempt of prudence, anger, and despair,
And *vis inertiæ*, kept them as they were;
'God and the world will see it,' – so they said,
'Let all the wrong be on the doer's head!'

In early morning twilight, raw and chill,
Damp vapours brooding on the barren hill,
Through miles of mire in steady grave array
Threescore well-arm'd police pursue their way;
Each tall and bearded man a rifle swings,
And under each greatcoat a bayonet clings;
The Sheriff on his sturdy cob astride
Talks with the Chief, who marches by their side,
And, creeping on behind them, Paudeen Dhu
Pretends his needful duty much to rue.
Six big-boned labourers, clad in common frieze,
Walk in the midst, the Sheriff's staunch allies;
Six crow-bar-men, from distant county brought, –
Orange, and glorying in their work, 'tis thought,
But wrongly, – churls of Catholics are they,
And merely hired at half-a-crown a day.

The Hamlet clustering on its hill is seen,
A score of petty homesteads, dark and mean;
Poor always, not despairing until now;
Long used, as well as poverty knows how,
With life's oppressive trifles to contend.
This day will bring its history to an end.
Moveless and grim against the cottage walls
Lean a few silent men: but some one calls
Far off; and then a child 'without a stitch'
Runs out of doors, flies back with piercing screech,
And soon from house to house is heard the cry
Of female sorrow, swelling loud and high,
Which makes the men blaspheme between their teeth.
Meanwhile, o'er fence and watery field beneath,
The little army moves through drizzling rain;
A 'Crowbar' leads the Sheriff's nag; the lane

Is entered, and their plashing tramp draws near;
One instant, outcry holds its breath to hear;
'Halt!' – at the doors they form in double line,
And ranks of polished rifles wetly shine.

The Sheriff's painful duty must be done;
He begs for quiet – and the work's begun.
The strong stand ready; now appear the rest,
Girl, matron, grandsire, baby on the breast,
And Rosy's thin face on a pallet borne;
A motley concourse, feeble and forlorn.
One old man, tears upon his wrinkled cheek,
Stands trembling on a threshold, tries to speak,
But, in defect of any word for this,
Mutely upon the doorpost prints a kiss,
Then passes out for ever. Through the crowd
The children run bewildered, wailing loud;
Where needed most, the men combine their aid;
And, last of all, is Oona forth conveyed,
Reclined in her accustomed strawen chair,
Her aged eyelids closed, her thick white hair
Escaping from her cap; she feels the chill,
Looks round and murmurs, then again is still.
Now bring the remnants of each household fire;
On the wet ground the hissing coals expire;
And Paudeen Dhu, with meekly dismal face,
Receives the full possession of the place.

## from *Chapter IX: The Fair*

Crowds push through Lisnamoy, shop, street, and lane,
Archway, and yard, corn-store, and butter-crane.
Say, as we push, could anywhere be found
A Town more ugly, ev'n on Irish ground? –
With dwellings meanly low or meanly tall,
With ragged roads, and harsh straight workhouse wall,
With foul decrepit huts, and here and there
A roof half-stripped and smoky rafters bare;

With churches that on rival mounts encamp,
One praised for neatness, one admired for pomp;
*This*, which combines the gaudy and the mean,
(Alas! the white old chapel on its green)
With misplaced ornament that leads your eye
To note the baldness, like a wig awry;
*That*, less prodigious, odious not the less,
All prim and trim in tidy ugliness,
A square box with a tall box at the end,
While through the wall a stove-pipe's arms extend.
What more? *these* gates are wide, the passing prayer
Finds when it will a solemn welcome there;
*Those* gates are locked, the sexton lets you through,
And shows for sixpence every empty pew;
Here climbs a gilded cross above the roof,
There turns a glittering weathercock aloof;
Here, every day, the watchful power of Rome,
The English rite on Sundays there at home.
Clean police-barrack perched a-top the hill,
At foot the dusty slating of a mill,
Town hall betwixt, with many a broken pane,
A squat Wesleyan chapel down a lane,
Make up the total – which, though you despise,
Kindles admiring awe in rustic eyes.
Mud hovels fringe the 'Fair-green' of this town,
A spot misnamed, at every season brown,
O'erspread with countless man and beast today,
Which bellow, squeak, and shout, bleat, bray, and neigh.
The 'jobbers' there, each more or less a rogue,
Noisy or smooth, with each his various brogue,
Cool wiry Dublin, Connaught's golden mouth,
Blunt Northern, plaintive sing-song of the South,
Feel cattle's ribs, or jaws of horses try
For truth, since men's are very sure to lie,
And shun with parrying blow and practised heed
The rushing horns, the wildly prancing steed.
The moistened penny greets with sounding smack
The rugged palm, which smites the greeting back;
Oaths fly, the bargain like a quarrel burns,

And oft the buyer turns, and oft returns;
Now mingle Sassenach and Gaelic tongue;
On either side are slow concessions wrung;
An anxious audience interfere; at last
The sale is closed, and whiskey binds it fast,
In cave of quilting upon oziers bent,
With many an ancient patch and breezy rent.

## *In Snow*

O English mother, in the ruddy glow
Hugging your baby closer when outside
You see the silent, soft, and cruel snow
Falling again, and think what ills betide
Unsheltered creatures – your sad thoughts may go
Where War and Winter now, two spectre-wolves,
Hunt in the freezing vapour that involves
Those Asian peaks of ice and gulfs below.
Does this young soldier heed the snow that fills
His mouth and open eyes? or mind, in truth,
Tonight, *his* mother's parting syllables?
Ha! Is't a red coat? – Merely blood. Keep ruth
For others; this is but an Afghan youth
Shot by the stranger on his native hills.

## from *Blackberries*

Not men and women in an Irish street,
But Catholics and Protestants you meet.

(...)

The Poet launched a stately fleet: it sank.
His fame was rescued on a single plank.

# JANE FRANCESCA ELGEE (LADY WILDE) (1826–96)

## *A Supplication*

*De profundis clamavi ad te Domine*

By our looks of mute despair,
By the sighs that rend the air,
From lips too faint to utter prayer,
*Kyrie Eleison.*

By the last groans of our dying,
Echoed by the cold wind's sighing
On the wayside as they're lying,
*Kyrie Eleison.*

By our fever-stricken bands
Lifting up their wasted hands
For bread throughout the far-off lands,
*Kyrie Eleison.*

Miserable outcasts we,
Pariahs of humanity,
Shunned by all where'er we flee,
*Kyrie Eleison.*

For our dead no bell is ringing,
Round their forms no shroud is clinging,
Save the rank grass newly springing,
*Kyrie Eleison.*

Golden harvests we are reaping,
With golden grain our barns heaping,
But for us our bread is weeping,
*Kyrie Eleison.*

Death-devoted in our home,
Sad we cross the salt sea's foam,
But death we bring where'er we roam,
*Kyrie Eleison.*

Whereso'er our steps are led,
They can track us by our dead,
Lying on their cold earth bed,
*Kyrie Eleison.*

We have sinned – in vain each warning –
Brother lived his brother scorning,
Now in ashes see us mourning,
*Kyrie Eleison.*

Heeding not our country's state,
Trodden down and desolate,
While we strove in senseless hate,
*Kyrie Eleison.*

We have sinned, but holier zeal
May we Christian patriots feel,
Oh! for our dear country's weal,
*Kyrie Eleison.*

Let us lift our streaming eyes
To God's throne above the skies,
He will hear our anguish cries,
*Kyrie Eleison.*

Kneel beside me, oh! my brother,
Let us pray each with the other,
For Ireland, our mourning mother,
*Kyrie Eleison.*

## JOHN BOYLE O'REILLY
## (1844–90)

### *A White Rose*

The red rose whispers of passion,
  And the white rose breathes of love;
Oh, the red rose is a falcon,
  And the white rose is a dove.

But I send you a cream-white rosebud
  With a flush on its petal tips;
For the love that is purest and sweetest
  Has a kiss of desire on the lips.

# VI

# REVIVAL: 1881–1921

*I see her in those coming days,*
*Still young, still gay; her unbound hair*
*Crowned with a crown of starlike rays,*
*Serenely fair.*

Emily Lawless, 'A Retort'

## SAMUEL FERGUSON

### *At the Polo-Ground*

*6th May 1882*

Not yet in sight. 'Twere well to step aside,
Beyond the common eye-shot, till he comes.
He – I've no quarrel under heaven with him:
I'd rather it were Forster; rather still
One higher up than either; but since Fate
Or Chance has so determined, be it he.
How cool I feel; and all my wits about
And vigilant; and such a work in hand!
Yes: loitering here, unoccupied, may draw
Remark and question. How came such a one there?
Oh; I've strolled out to see the polo-players:
I'll step across to them; but keep an eye
On who comes up the highway.
                                        Here I am
Beside the hurdles fencing off the ground
They've taken from us who have the right to it,
For these select young gentry and their sport.
Curse them! I would they all might break their necks!
Young fops and lordlings of the garrison
Kept up by England here to keep us down:
All rich young fellows not content to own
Their chargers, hacks, and hunters for the field,
But also special ponies for their game;
And doubtless, as they dash along, regard
Us who stand outside as a beggarly crew. –
'Tis half-past six. Not yet. No, that's not he. –
Well, but 'tis pretty, sure, to see them stoop
And take the ball, full gallop; and when I

In gown and cocked hat once drove up Cork Hill,
Perhaps myself have eyed the common crowd,
Lining the footway, with a similar sense
Of higher station, just as these do me,
And as the man next door no doubt does them.
'Tis very sure that grades and differences
Of rich and poor and small men and grandees
Have all along existed, and still will, –
Though many a man has risen and thriven well
By promising the Poor to make them rich
By taking from the Rich their overplus,
And putting all on a level: beggars all.
Yet still the old seize-ace comes round again;
And though my friends upon the pathway there –
No. Not he neither. That's a taller man –
Look for a general scramble and divide,
Such a partition, were it possible,
Would not by any means suit me. My share
Already earned and saved would equal ten
Such millionth quotients and sub-multiples.
No: they may follow Davitt. 'Tis Parnell
And property – in proper hands – will win.
But, say the Mob's the Master; and who knows
But some o' these days the ruffians may have votes
As good as mine or his, and pass their Act
For every man his share, and equal all?
No doubt they'd have a slice from me. What then?
I'm not afraid. I'll float. Allow the scums
Rise to the surface, something rises too
Not scum, but Carey; and will yet rise higher.
No place too high but he may look for it.
Member for Dublin, Speaker, President,
Lord Mayor for life – why not? One gentleman,
Who when he comes to deal with this day's work –
No: not in sight. That man is not so tall –
Will find, to his surprise, a stronger hand
Than his controls the rudder, sat three years
And hangs his medal on the sheriff's chain.

Yes; say Lord Mayor: my liveries green and gold,
My secretary with me in my coach,
And chaplain duly seated by my side.
My boy shall have his hack, and pony too,
And play at polo with the best of them;
Such as will then be best. He need not blush
To think his father was a bricklayer;
For laying bricks is work as reputable
As filling noggins or appraising pawns,
Or other offices of those designed
For fathers of our Dublin swells to be.
'Tis twenty minutes now to seven o'clock.
What if he should not come at all? 'Twere then
Another – oh – *fiasco* as they call it,
Not pleasant to repeat to Number One,
But, for myself, perhaps not wholly bad.
For, if he comes, there will be consequences
Will make a stir; and in that stir my name
May come in play – well, one must run some risk
Who takes a lead and keeps and thrives by it
As I have done. But sure the risk is small.
I know those cut-throats on the pathway there
May be relied on. Theirs is work that shuts
The door against approval of both sorts.
But he who drives them, I've remarked in him
A flighty indecision in the eye,
Such as, indeed, had I a looking-glass,
I might perhaps discover in my own
When thoughts have crossed me how I should behave
In this or that conjuncture of the affair.
Him I distrust. But not from him or them
Or any present have I aught to fear.
For never have I talked to more than one
Of these executive agents at a time,
Nor let a scrap of writing leave my hand
Could compromise myself with anyone.
And should I – though I don't expect I shall –
Be brought, at any time, to book for this,

'Twill not be – or I much mistake – because
Of any indiscretion hitherto.
But, somehow, these reflections make me pause
And set me inly questioning myself,
Is it worth while – the crime itself apart –
To pull this settled civil state of life
To pieces, for another just the same,
Only with rawer actors for the posts
Of Judges, Landlords, Masters, Capitalists?
And then, the innocent blood. I've half a mind
To trip across this elm-root at my foot,
And turn my ankle.
Oh, he comes at last!
No time for thinking now. My own life pays
Unless I play my part. I see he brings
Another with him, and, I think, the same
I heard them call Lord – something – Cavendish.
If one; two, likely. That can't now be helped.
Up. Drive on straight, – if I blow my nose
And show my handkerchief in front of them,
And then turn back, what's that to anyone?
No further, driver. Back to Island Bridge.
No haste. If some acquaintance chanced to pass,
He must not think that we are running away.
I don't like, but I can't help looking back.
They meet: my villains pass them. Gracious Powers,
Another failure! No, they turn again
And overtake; and Brady lifts his arm –
I'll see no more. On – by the Monument.
On – brisker, brisker – but yet leisurely.
By this time all is over with them both.
Ten minutes more, the Castle has the news,
And haughty Downing Street in half an hour
Is struck with palsy. For a moment there,
Among the trees, I wavered. Brady's knife
Has cut the knot of my perplexities;
Despite myself, my fortune mounts again.
The English rule will soon be overthrown,
And ours established in the place of it.

I'm free again to look, as long as I please,
In Fortune's show-box. Yes; I see the chain,
I see the gilded coach. God send the boy
May take the polish! There's but one thing now
That troubles me. These cursed knives at home
That woman brought me, what had best be done
To put them out o' the way? I have it. Yes,
That old Fitzsimon's roof's in need of repairs.
I'll leave them in his cock-loft. Still in time
To catch the tram, I'll take a seat a-top –
For no one must suppose I've anything
To hide – and show myself in Grafton Street.

## JOHN TODHUNTER
## (1839–1916)

### *Under the Whiteboy Acts, 1800: An Old Rector's Story*

Ay, I was once a soldier, as you've heard,
A cornet in the Irish Yeomanry.
To say what that meant fifty years ago
Would seem, thank God! to young fellows like you,
Like telling tales about some foreign land
In the dark ages. Yes, my memory
Has its black chamber, where, whene'er I look,
There flicker out, shining with ghastly fire,
Some ugly pictures painted on the wall –
Bad sights!
 Now here's a sample: I was once
Riding at night along a country road,
Patrolling with my troop – one August night.
The moon was full, and surely bright and fair
As when she rose on Eden's innocence
The night before the Fall. What brought us there,

Out of our beds? Well, in the peasants' phrase,
'The Boys was out.' The Whiteboy scare, in fact,
Was in full cry, and Ireland in the grip,
Under the Whiteboy Acts, of martial law:
Nothing new, mind; the district was proclaimed,
And we patrolled it, to repress the crime
Of being out of doors between the hours
Of sunset and sunrise.
                                        Well, there I sat,
Loose in my saddle, in a kind of dream,
Thinking, I fancy, of the County Ball,
A pretty face – I was a youngster then –
Had made for me a chapter of romance,
To be re-read by that romantic moon.
Oh! but 'twas wonderful, that moonlight, mixed
With woodbine scents, and gusts of meadowsweet.
An Irish boy's first love, a cornet's pride
In his new soldiership and uniform!
Why, 'twas sheer ecstasy – I feel it still,
As I remember how, athwart my mood,
The martial noise of our accoutrements,
Clanking and jingling to the chargers' tramp,
Chimed in a sort of music.
                                        The road turned,
And a stream crossed it. On the further side
There was a man, a scared look in his face,
White in that great moonlight. And there he stood,
And never ran – the creature never ran,
But quavered out some question: 'tis my guess
He said: 'Is that the sogers?' Then I saw,
Like a bad dream, the captain of our troop,
(Whom I'll here name 'Lord Blank') ride at him straight,
And cut him down. You, maybe, never saw
A man cut down? Nor I, till that bad hour.
Well, 'twas an ugly sight – a brutal sight.
The strangest thing was that the man seemed dazed,
Made no attempt to run, or dodge the sword,
Shrank rather from the wind of the horse, I thought,
His hands held out in a groping sort of way;

But never raised, I saw, to guard his head,
Till the blow sent him reeling, with a shriek:
'O Lord have mercy!' Then he plunged, face down,
Clutching and wallowing in a pool of blood.
He spoke no more – just moaned. 'Twas horrible,
And all the more for something half grotesque;
You'd never think a man's last agony
Could look so like a joker's antics, played
To raise a laugh. Yet no one laughed, I think.
We had pushed across the stream. I saw them lift
His head, with long grey hair dabbled with blood.
The sword had caught him under the right ear,
And through the gash his poor, scared, struggling heart
Simply pumped out his life. 'Twas over soon.
They laid him down, stone dead, with staring eyes;
And then I saw it all – the man was blind.
Then someone said: 'Lord save us! Sure it's Tom –
It's ould blind Tom, the fiddler! Sure enough,
He lives just here in the boreen beyant.'
Another said: 'He's due to play today
In Ballintogher Fair. He must ha' thought
'Twas mornin', an' come here to clane himself,
Here in the sthrame. Poor Tom! 'Twas just your luck,
Misfort'nate craythur that ye always wor!
Well, you'll chune up no more; God rest your sowl!'
We found his stick, indeed, beside the stream.
Then we rode on and left him lying there
Upon a grassy tussock by the road.
An ugly business that. I never knew
How My Lord felt about that sad mistake:
Such things will happen under martial law,
And ill-judged deeds, done through excess of zeal,
The King's Commission covers in such times.
We heard no more of it. But all that night
I felt myself next door to a murderer,
And rode with a sick chill about my heart.
No more pride in my uniform; no more
Delight under that ghastly, glaring moon

That showed me Tom's dead face.
Perhaps you'll think
This made me sick of soldiering? Well, not quite.
The young mistrust their instinct, sir, when first
Thrust forth new fledged into the great rough world.
I was shocked, surely; but was half ashamed
To be so shocked.
Then I saw other things
My conscience quite convinced me went beyond
The necessary horrors of this life. For me I felt
From that time forth the uniform I wore
Smother my soul in shame. I changed it soon
For this poor cassock, which, though not so smart,
I find more comfortable every way.

## EMILY LAWLESS
## (1845–1913)

### *Clare Coast*

*c.1720*

See, cold island, we stand
Here tonight on your shore,
Tonight, but never again;
Lingering a moment more.
See, beneath us our boat
Tugs at its tightening chain,
Holds out its sail to the breeze,
Pants to be gone again.
Off then with shouts and mirth,
Off with laughter and jests,
Mirth and song on our lips,
Hearts like lead in our breasts.

Death and the grave behind,
Death and a traitor's bier;
Honour and fame before,
Why do we linger here?
Why do we stand and gaze,
Fools, whom fools despise,
Fools untaught by the years,
Fools renounced by the wise?
Heartsick, a moment more,
Heartsick, sorry, fierce,
Lingering, lingering on,
Dreaming the dreams of yore;
Dreaming the dreams of our youth,
Dreaming the days when we stood
Joyous, expectant, serene,
Glad, exultant of mood,
Singing with hearts afire,
Singing with joyous strain,
Singing aloud in our pride,
'We shall redeem her again!'
Ah, not tonight that strain, –
Silent tonight we stand,
A scanty, a toil-worn crew,
Strangers, foes in the land!
Gone the light of our youth,
Gone for ever, and gone
Hope with the beautiful eyes,
Who laughed as she lured us on;
Lured us to danger and death,
To honour, perchance to fame, –
Empty fame at the best,
Glory half dimmed with shame.
War-battered dogs are we,
Fighters in every clime,
Fillers of trench and of grave,
Mockers, bemocked by time.

War-dogs, hungry and grey,
Gnawing a naked bone,
Fighters in every clime,
Every cause but our own.

See us, cold isle of our love!
Coldest, saddest of isles –
Cold as the hopes of our youth,
Cold as your own wan smiles.
Coldly your streams outpour,
Each apart on the height,
Trickling, indifferent, slow,
Lost in the hush of the night.
Colder, sadder the clouds,
Comfortless bringers of rain;
Desolate daughters of air,
Sweep o'er your sad grey plain
Hiding the form of your hills,
Hiding your low sand dunes;
But coldest, saddest, oh isle!
Are the homeless hearts of your sons.

Coldest, and saddest there,
In yon sun-lit land of the south,
Where we sicken, and sorrow, and pine,
And the jest flies from mouth to mouth,
And the church bells crash overhead,
And the idle hours flit by,
And the beaded wine-cups clink.
And the sun burns fierce in the sky;
And your exiles, the merry of heart,
Laugh and boast with the best, –
Boast, and extol their part,
Boast, till some lifted brow,
Crossed with a line severe,
Seems with displeasure to ask,
'Are these loud braggarts we hear,

Are they the sons of the West,
The wept-for, the theme of songs,
The exiled, the injured, the banned,
The men of a thousand wrongs?'

Fool, did you never hear
Of sunshine which broke through rain?
Sunshine which came with storm?
Laughter that rang of pain?
Boastings begotten of grief,
Vauntings to hide a smart,
Braggings with trembling lip,
Tricks of a broken heart?

Sudden some wayward gleam,
Sudden some passing sound, –
The careless splash of an oar,
The idle bark of a hound,
A shadow crossing the sun,
An unknown step in the hall,
A nothing, a folly, a straw! –
Back it returns – all – all!
Back with the rush of a storm,
Back the old anguish and ill,
The sad, green landscape of home,
The small grey house by the hill,
The wide grey shores of the lake,
The low sky, seeming to weave
Its tender pitiful arms
Round the sick lone landscape at eve.
Back with its pains and its wrongs,
Back with its toils and its strife,
Back with its struggle and woe,
Back flows the stream of our life.
Darkened with treason and wrong,
Darkened with anguish and ruth,
Bitter, tumultuous, fierce,
Yet glad in the light of our youth.

So, cold island, we stand
Here tonight on your shore, –
Tonight, but never again,
Lingering a moment more.
See, beneath us our boat
Tugs at its tightening chain,
Holds out its sail to the breeze,
Pants to be gone again.
Off then with shouts and mirth,
Off with laughter and jests,
Jests and song on our lips,
Hearts like lead in our breasts.

## *A Retort*

Not hers your vast imperial mart,
Where myriad hopes on fears are hurled,
Where furious rivals meet and part
To woo a world.

Not hers your vast imperial town,
Your mighty mammoth piles of gain,
Your loaded vessels sweeping down
To glut the main.

Unused, unseen, *her* rivers flow,
From mountain tarn to ocean tide;
Wide vacant leagues the sunbeams show,
The rain-clouds hide.

*You* swept them vacant! Your decree
Bid all her budding commerce cease;
*You* drove her from your subject sea,
To starve in peace!

Well, be it peace! Resigned they flow,
No laden fleet adown them glides,
But wheeling salmon sometimes show
Their silvered sides.

And sometimes through the long still day
The breeding herons slowly rise,
Lifting grey tranquil wings away,
To tranquil skies.

Stud all your shores with prosperous towns!
Blacken your hill-sides, mile on mile!
Redden with bricks your patient downs!
And proudly smile!

A day will come before you guess,
A day when men, with clearer light,
Will rue that deed beyond redress,
Will loathe that sight.

And, loathing, fly the hateful place,
And, shuddering, quit the hideous thing,
For where unblackened rivers race,
And skylarks sing.

For where, remote from smoke and noise,
Old Leisure sits knee-deep in grass;
Where simple days bring simple joys,
And lovers pass.

I see her in those coming days,
Still young, still gay; her unbound hair
Crowned with a crown of starlike rays,
Serenely fair.

I see an envied haunt of peace,
Calm and untouched; remote from roar,
Where wearied men may from their burdens cease
On a still shore.

# WILLIAM LARMINIE
(1849–1900)

## from *Fand*

*(Emer warns Cuhoolin against Fand)*

Heed her not, O Cuhoolin, husband mine;
Delusive is the bliss she offers thee –
Bliss that will to torment turn,
Like one bright colour for ever before thine eyes,
Since of mortal race thou art.
Man is the shadow of a changing world;
As the image of a tree
By the breeze swayed to and fro
On the grass, so changeth he;
Night and day are in his breast;
Winter and summer, all the change
Of light and darkness and the seasons marching;
Flowers that bud and fade,
Tides that rise and fall.
Even with the waxing and the waning moon
His being beats in tune;
The air that is his life
Inhales he with alternate heaving breath;
Joyous to him is effort, sweet is rest;
Life he hath and death.

Then seek not thou too soon that permanence
Of changeless joy that suits unchanging gods,
In whom no tides of being ebb and flow.
Out of the flux and reflux of the world
Slowly man's soul doth gather to itself,
Atom by atom, the hard elements –
Firm, incorruptible, indestructible –
Whereof, when all his being is compact,

No more it wastes nor hungers, but endures,
Needing not any food of changing things,
But fit among like-natured gods to live,
Amongst whom, entering too soon, he perishes,
Unable to endure their fervid gaze.
Though now thy young, heroic soul
Be mate for her immortal might,
Yet think: thy being is still but as a lake
That, by the help of friendly streams unfed,
Full soon the sun drinks up.
Wait till thou hast sea-depths –
Till all the tides of life and deed,
Of action and of meditation,
Of service unto others and their love,
Shall pour into the caverns of thy being
The might of their unconquerable floods.
Then canst thou bear the glow of eyes divine,
And like the sea beneath the sun at noon
Shalt shine in splendour inexhaustible.
Therefore be no more tempted by her lures –
Not that way lies thine immortality:
But thou shalt find it in the ways of men,
Where many a task remains for thee to do,
And shall remain for many after thee,
Till all the storm-winds of the world be bound.

## THOMAS GIVEN
## (1850–1917)

### *A Song for February*

Day in an' day oot on his auld farrant[1] loom,
Time lengthens the wab o' the past;
Dame Nature steps in like a lamp tae the room,
Hir e'e[2] tae the simmer o' life geein' bloom.
So winter slips by, wi' its mirth an' its gloom,
As spring is appearin' at last.

The robin gets up an' he lauchs in his glee,
In view o' the prospect so braw;
Sets his heid tae the side, wi' its feathers agee,[3]
As he spies a bit snaw drop at fit[4] o' the tree,
An' says tae himsel' a'll hae denties[5] tae pree[6]
By an' by when the splash is awa.

The blackbird keeks[7] oot frae the fog[8] at the broo,[9]
Gees his neb[10] a bit dicht[11] on a stane;
His eye caught the primrose appearin' in view,
An' the tiny wee violet o' Nature's ain blue;
He sung them a sang o' the auld an' the new –
A sang we may a' let alane.

The thrush cuff't[12] the leaves 'neath the skep[13] o' the bee,
An' he tirrl't[14] them aside wae a zest;
I maun hurry awa tae rehearsal, quo he,
This work fits the sparrow far better than me;
His sang pleased the ear frae the tap o' the tree
As he fell intae tune wae the rest.

1. *auld farrant*: old-fashioned 2. *e'e*: eye 3. *agee*: awry 4. *fit*: foot 5. *denties*: dainties 6. *pree*: try out 7. *keeks*: peeks 8. *fog*: long stems of last year's grass 9. *broo*: higher side of a ditch 10. *neb*: beak 11. *dicht*: wipe 12. cuff't: hit 13. *skep*: hive 14. *tirrl't*: elbowed

Thus Nature provides for hir hoose an' hir wanes,[15]
  An' we may rejoice in the plan;
The wren tae the bluebonnet sings his refrain
On causey[16] o' cottier or lordly domain;
The wagtail looks on withoot shade o' disdain,
  May we aye say the same o' the man.

## OSCAR WILDE

(1854–1900)

### *from* Poems in Prose

#### *The Artist*

One evening there came into his soul the desire to fashion an image of *The Pleasure that abideth for a Moment*. And he went forth into the world to look for bronze. For he could only think in bronze.

But all the bronze of the whole world had disappeared, nor anywhere in the whole world was there any bronze to be found, save only the bronze of the image of *The Sorrow that endureth for Ever*.

Now this image he had himself, and with his own hands, fashioned, and had set it on the tomb of the one thing he had loved in life. On the tomb of the dead thing he had most loved had he set this image of his own fashioning, that it might serve as a sign of the love of man that dieth not, and a symbol of the sorrow of man that endureth for ever. And in the whole world there was no other bronze save the bronze of this image.

And he took the image he had fashioned, and set it in a great furnace, and gave it to the fire.

And out of the bronze of the image of *The Sorrow that endureth for Ever* he fashioned an image of *The Pleasure that abideth for a Moment*.

15. *wanes*: young ones 16. *causey*: cobbled path

## *The Disciple*

When Narcissus died the pool of his pleasure changed from a cup of sweet waters into a cup of salt tears, and the Oreads came weeping through the woodland that they might sing to the pool and give it comfort.

And when they saw that the pool had changed from a cup of sweet waters into a cup of salt tears, they loosened the green tresses of their hair and cried to the pool and said, 'We do not wonder that you should mourn in this manner for Narcissus, so beautiful was he.'

'But was Narcissus beautiful?' said the pool.

'Who should know that better than you?' answered the Oreads. 'Us did he ever pass by, but you he sought for, and would lie on your banks and look down at you, and in the mirror of your waters he would mirror his own beauty.'

And the pool answered, 'But I loved Narcissus because, as he lay on my banks and looked down at me, in the mirror of his eyes I saw ever my own beauty mirrored.'

# T. W. ROLLESTON

(1857–1920)

## *The Dead at Clonmacnois*

In a quiet water'd land, a land of roses,
    Stands Saint Kieran's city fair:
And the warriors of Erin in their famous generations
    Slumber there.

There beneath the dewy hillside sleep the noblest
  Of the clan of Conn,
Each below his stone with name in branching Ogham
  And the sacred knot thereon.

There they laid to rest the seven Kings of Tara,
  There the sons of Cairbré sleep –
Battle-banners of the Gael, that in Kieran's plain of crosses
  Now their final hosting keep.

And in Clonmacnois they laid the men of Teffia,
  And right many a lord of Breagh;
Deep the sod above Clan Creidé and Clan Conaill,
  Kind in hall and fierce in fray.

Many and many a son of Conn, the Hundred-Fighter,
  In the red earth lies at rest;
Many a blue eye of Clan Colman the turf covers,
  Many a swan-white breast.

## KATHARINE TYNAN
## (1861–1931)

### *Sheep and Lambs*

All in the April evening,
    April airs were abroad;
The sheep with their little lambs
    Passed me by on the road.

The sheep with their little lambs
    Passed me by on the road;
All in an April evening,
    I thought on the Lamb of God.

The lambs were weary, and crying
    With a weak, human cry.
I thought on the Lamb of God
    Going meekly to die.

Up in the blue, blue mountains
    Dewy pastures are sweet;
Rest for the little bodies,
    Rest for the little feet.

But for the Lamb of God
    Up on the hill-top green,
Only a Cross of shame,
    Two stark crosses between.

All in the April evening,
    April airs were abroad;
I saw the sheep with their lambs,
    And thought of the Lamb of God.

## *Waiting*

In a grey cave, where comes no glimpse of sky,
    Set in the blue hill's heart full many a mile,
Having the dripping stone for canopy,
    Missing the wind's laugh and the good sun's smile,
I, Fionn, with all my sleeping warriors lie.

In the great outer cave our horses are,
    Carved of grey stone, with heads erect, amazed,
Purple their trappings, gold each bolt and bar,
    One fore-foot poised, the quivering thin ears raised:
Methinks they scent the battle from afar.

A frozen hound lies by each warrior's feet –
  Ah, Bran, my jewel! Bran, my king of hounds!
Deep-throated art thou, mighty-flanked, and fleet;
  Dost thou remember how with giant bounds
Didst chase the red deer in the noontide heat?

I was a king in ages long ago,
  A mighty warrior, and a seer likewise,
Still mine eyes look with solemn gaze of woe
  From stony lids adown the centuries,
And in my frozen heart I know, I know.

A giant I, of a primeval race,
  These, great-limbed, bearing helm and shield and sword,
My good knights are, and each still, awful face
  Will one day wake to knowledge at a word –
O'erhead the groaning years turn round apace.

Here with the peaceful dead we keep our state;
  Some day a cry shall ring adown the lands:
'The hour is come, the hour grown large with fate.'
  He knows who hath the centuries in His hands
When that shall be – till then we watch and wait.

The queens that loved us, whither be they gone,
  The sweet, large women with the hair as gold,
As though one drew long threads from out the sun?
  Ages ago, grown tired, and very cold,
They fell asleep beneath the daisies wan.

The waving woods are gone that once we knew,
  And towns grown grey with years are in their place:
A little lake, as innocent and blue
  As my queen's eyes were, lifts a baby face
Where once my palace towers were fair to view.

The fierce old gods we hailed with worshipping,
   The blind old gods, waxed mad with sin and blood,
Laid down their godhead as an idle thing
   At a God's feet, whose throne was but a Rood;
His crown, wrought thorns; His joy, long travailing.

Here in the gloom I see it all again,
   As ages since in visions mystical
I saw the swaying crowds of fierce-eyed men,
   And heard the murmurs in the judgment hall.
Oh, for one charge of my dark warriors then!

Nay, if He willed, His Father presently
   Twelve star-girt legions unto Him had given.
I traced the blood-stained path to Calvary,
   And heard far off the angels weep in heaven;
Then the Rood's arms against an awful sky.

I saw Him when they pierced Him, hands and feet,
   And one came by and smote Him, this new King,
So pale and harmless, on the tired face sweet;
   He was so lovely and so pitying,
The icy heart in me began to beat.

Then a strong cry – the mountain heaved and swayed
   That held us in its heart, the groaning world
Was reft with lightning and in ruins laid,
   His Father's awful hand the red bolts hurled,
And He was dead – I trembled, sore afraid.

Then I upraised myself with mighty strain
   In the gloom, I heard the tumult rage without,
I saw those large dead faces glimmer plain,
   The life just stirred within them and went out,
And I fell back, and grew to stone again.

So the years went – on earth how fleet they be!
  Here in this cave their feet are slow of pace,
And I grow old, and tired exceedingly,
  I would the sweet earth were my dwelling-place –
Shamrocks and little daisies wrapping me!

There I should lie, and feel the silence sweet
  As a meadow at noon, where birds sing in the trees;
To mine ears should come the patter of little feet,
  And baby cries, and croon of summer seas,
And the wind's laughter in the upland wheat.

Meantime o'erhead the years were full and bright,
  With a kind sun, and gold wide fields of corn;
The happy children sang from morn to night,
  The blessed church bells rang, new arts were born,
Strong towns rose up and glimmered fair and white.

Once came a wind of conflict, fierce as hail,
  And beat about my brows: on the eastward shore,
Where never since the Vikings' dark ships sail,
  All day the battle raged with mighty roar;
At night the Victor's fair dead face was pale.

Ah! the dark years since then, the anguished cry
  That pierced my deaf ears, made my hard eyes weep,
From Erin wrestling in her agony,
  While we, her strongest, in a helpless sleep,
Lay, as the blood-stained years trailed slowly by.

And often in those years the East was drest
  In phantom fires, that mocked the distant dawn,
Then blackest night – her bravest and her best
  Were led to die, while I slept dumbly on,
With the whole mountain's weight upon my breast.

Once in my time it chanced a peasant hind
  Strayed to this cave. I heard, and burst my chain,
And raised my awful face stone-dead and blind,
  Cried, 'Is it time?' and so fell back again.
I heard his wild cry borne adown the wind.

Some hearts wait with us. Owen Roe O'Neill,
  The kingliest king that ever went uncrowned,
Sleeps in his panoply of gold and steel
  Ready to wake, and in the kindly ground
A many another's death-wounds close and heal.

Great Hugh O'Neill, far off in purple Rome,
  And Hugh O'Donnell, in their stately tombs
Lie, with their grand fair faces turned to home.
  Some day a voice will ring adown the glooms:
'Arise, ye Princes, for the hour is come!'

And these will rise, and we will wait them here,
  In this blue hill-heart in fair Donegal;
That hour shall sound the clash of sword and spear,
  The steeds shall neigh to hear their masters' call,
And the hounds' cry shall echo shrill and clear.

## WILLIAM BUTLER YEATS
## (1865–1939)

### *The Madness of King Goll*

I sat on cushioned otter-skin:
My word was law from Ith to Emain,
And shook at Inver Amergin
The hearts of the world-troubling seamen,

And drove tumult and war away
From girl and boy and man and beast;
The fields grew fatter day by day,
The wild fowl of the air increased;
And every ancient Ollave said,
While he bent down his fading head,
'He drives away the Northern cold.'
*They will not hush, the leaves a-flutter round me, the beech leaves old.*

I sat and mused and drank sweet wine;
A herdsman came from inland valleys,
Crying, the pirates drove his swine
To fill their dark-beaked hollow galleys.
I called my battle-breaking men
And my loud brazen battle-cars
From rolling vale and rivery glen;
And under the blinking of the stars
Fell on the pirates by the deep,
And hurled them in the gulph of sleep:
These hands won many a torque of gold.
*They will not hush, the leaves a-flutter round me, the beech leaves old.*

But slowly, as I shouting slew
And trampled in the bubbling mire,
In my most secret spirit grew
A whirling and a wandering fire:
I stood: keen stars above me shone,
Around me shone keen eyes of men:
I laughed aloud and hurried on
By rocky shore and rushy fen;
I laughed because birds fluttered by,
And starlight gleamed, and clouds flew high,
And rushes waved and waters rolled.
*They will not hush, the leaves a-flutter round me, the beech leaves old.*

And now I wander in the woods
When summer gluts the golden bees,
Or in autumnal solitudes
Arise the leopard-coloured trees;
Or when along the wintry strands
The cormorants shiver on their rocks;
I wander on, and wave my hands,
And sing, and shake my heavy locks.
The grey wolf knows me; by one ear
I lead along the woodland deer;
The hares run by me growing bold.
*They will not hush, the leaves a-flutter round me, the*
*beech leaves old.*

I came upon a little town
That slumbered in the harvest moon,
And passed a-tiptoe up and down,
Murmuring, to a fitful tune,
How I have followed, night and day,
A tramping of tremendous feet,
And saw where this old tympan lay
Deserted on a doorway seat,
And bore it to the woods with me;
Of some inhuman misery
Our married voices wildly trolled.
*They will not hush, the leaves a-flutter round me, the*
*beech leaves old.*

I sang how, when day's toil is done,
Orchil shakes out her long dark hair
That hides away the dying sun
And sheds faint odours through the air:
When my hand passed from wire to wire
It quenched, with sound like falling dew,
The whirling and the wandering fire;
But lift a mournful ulalu,

For the kind wires are torn and still,
And I must wander wood and hill
Through summer's heat and winter's cold.
*They will not hush, the leaves a-flutter round me, the beech leaves old.*

## *Fergus and the Druid*

*Fergus.* This whole day have I followed in the rocks,
And you have changed and flowed from shape to shape,
First as a raven on whose ancient wings
Scarcely a feather lingered, then you seemed
A weasel moving on from stone to stone,
And now at last you wear a human shape,
A thin grey man half lost in gathering night.
*Druid.* What would you, king of the proud Red Branch kings?
*Fergus.* This would I say, most wise of living souls;
Young subtle Conchubar sat close by me
When I gave judgment, and his words were wise,
And what to me was burden without end,
To him seemed easy, so I laid the crown
Upon his head to cast away my sorrow.
*Druid.* What would you, king of the proud Red Branch kings?
*Fergus.* A king and proud! and that is my despair.
I feast amid my people on the hill,
And pace the woods, and drive my chariot-wheels
In the white border of the murmuring sea;
And still I feel the crown upon my head.
*Druid.* What would you, Fergus?
*Fergus.* Be no more a king
But learn the dreaming wisdom that is yours.
*Druid.* Look on my thin grey hair and hollow cheeks
And on these hands that may not lift the sword,
This body trembling like a wind-blown reed.
No woman's loved me, no man sought my help.
*Fergus.* A king is but a foolish labourer
Who wastes his blood to be another's dream.

*Druid.* Take, if you must, this little bag of dreams;
Unloose the cord, and they will wrap you round.
*Fergus.* I see my life go drifting like a river
From change to change; I have been many things –
A green drop in the surge, a gleam of light
Upon a sword, a fir-tree on a hill,
An old slave grinding at a heavy quern,
A king sitting upon a chair of gold –
And all these things were wonderful and great;
But now I have grown nothing, knowing all.
Ah! Druid, Druid, how great webs of sorrow
Lay hidden in the small slate-coloured thing!

## *The Man who Dreamed of Faeryland*

He stood among a crowd at Dromahair;
His heart hung all upon a silken dress,
And he had known at last some tenderness,
Before earth took him to her stony care;
But when a man poured fish into a pile,
It seemed they raised their little silver heads,
And sang what gold morning or evening sheds
Upon a woven world-forgotten isle
Where people love beside the ravelled seas;
That Time can never mar a lover's vows
Under that woven changeless roof of boughs:
The singing shook him out of his new ease.

He wandered by the sands of Lissadell;
His mind ran all on money cares and fears,
And he had known at last some prudent years
Before they heaped his grave under the hill;
But while he passed before a plashy place,
A lug-worm with its grey and muddy mouth
Sang that somewhere to north or west or south
There dwelt a gay, exulting, gentle race

Under the golden or the silver skies;
That if a dancer stayed his hungry foot
It seemed the sun and moon were in the fruit:
And at that singing he was no more wise.

He mused beside the well of Scanavin,
He mused upon his mockers: without fail
His sudden vengeance were a country tale,
When earthy night had drunk his body in;
But one small knot-grass growing by the pool
Sang where – unnecessary cruel voice –
Old silence bids its chosen race rejoice,
Whatever ravelled waters rise and fall
Or stormy silver fret the gold of day,
And midnight there enfold them like a fleece
And lover there by lover be at peace.
The tale drove his fine angry mood away.

He slept under the hill of Lugnagall;
And might have known at last unhaunted sleep
Under that cold and vapour-turbaned steep,
Now that the earth had taken man and all:
Did not the worms that spired about his bones
Proclaim with that unwearied, reedy cry
That God has laid His fingers on the sky,
That from those fingers glittering summer runs
Upon the dancer by the dreamless wave.
Why should those lovers that no lovers miss
Dream, until God burn Nature with a kiss?
The man has found no comfort in the grave.

## *The Song of Wandering Aengus*

I went out to the hazel wood,
Because a fire was in my head,
And cut and peeled a hazel wand,
And hooked a berry to a thread;

And when white moths were on the wing,
And moth-like stars were flickering out,
I dropped the berry in a stream
And caught a little silver trout.

When I had laid it on the floor
I went to blow the fire aflame,
But something rustled on the floor,
And some one called me by my name:
It had become a glimmering girl
With apple blossom in her hair
Who called me by my name and ran
And faded through the brightening air.

Though I am old with wandering
Through hollow lands and hilly lands,
I will find out where she has gone,
And kiss her lips and take her hands;
And walk among long dappled grass,
And pluck till time and times are done
The silver apples of the moon,
The golden apples of the sun.

## *Adam's Curse*

We sat together at one summer's end,
That beautiful mild woman, your close friend,
And you and I, and talked of poetry.
I said, 'A line will take us hours maybe;
Yet if it does not seem a moment's thought,
Our stitching and unstitching has been naught.
Better go down upon your marrow-bones
And scrub a kitchen pavement, or break stones
Like an old pauper, in all kinds of weather;
For to articulate sweet sounds together

Is to work harder than all these, and yet
Be thought an idler by the noisy set
Of bankers, schoolmasters, and clergymen
The martyrs call the world.'

And thereupon
That beautiful mild woman for whose sake
There's many a one shall find out all heartache
On finding that her voice is sweet and low
Replied, 'To be born woman is to know –
Although they do not talk of it at school –
That we must labour to be beautiful.'

I said, 'It's certain there is no fine thing
Since Adam's fall but needs much labouring.
There have been lovers who thought love should be
So much compounded of high courtesy
That they would sigh and quote with learned looks
Precedents out of beautiful old books;
Yet now it seems an idle trade enough.'

We sat grown quiet at the name of love;
We saw the last embers of daylight die,
And in the trembling blue-green of the sky
A moon, worn as if it had been a shell
Washed by time's waters as they rose and fell
About the stars and broke in days and years.

I had a thought for no one's but your ears:
That you were beautiful, and that I strove
To love you in the old high way of love;
That it had all seemed happy, and yet we'd grown
As weary-hearted as that hollow moon.

## *A Drinking Song*

Wine comes in at the mouth
And love comes in at the eye;
That's all we shall know for truth
Before we grow old and die.
I lift the glass to my mouth,
I look at you, and I sigh.

## *Introductory Rhymes to* Responsibilities

Pardon, old fathers, if you still remain
Somewhere in ear-shot for the story's end,
Old Dublin merchant 'free of the ten and four'
Or trading out of Galway into Spain;
Old country scholar, Robert Emmet's friend,
A hundred-year-old memory to the poor;
Merchant and scholar who have left me blood
That has not passed through any huckster's loin,
Soldiers that gave, whatever die was cast:
A Butler or an Armstrong that withstood
Beside the brackish waters of the Boyne
James and his Irish when the Dutchman crossed;
Old merchant skipper that leaped overboard
After a ragged hat in Biscay Bay;
You most of all, silent and fierce old man,
Because the daily spectacle that stirred
My fancy, and set my boyish lips to say,
'Only the wasteful virtues earn the sun';
Pardon that for a barren passion's sake,
Although I have come close on forty-nine,
I have no child, I have nothing but a book,
Nothing but that to prove your blood and mine.

*January 1914*

## *Her Praise*

She is foremost of those that I would hear praised.
I have gone about the house, gone up and down
As a man does who has published a new book,
Or a young girl dressed out in her new gown,
And though I have turned the talk by hook or crook
Until her praise should be the uppermost theme,
A woman spoke of some new tale she had read,
A man confusedly in a half dream
As though some other name ran in his head.
She is foremost of those that I would hear praised.
I will talk no more of books or the long war
But walk by the dry thorn until I have found
Some beggar sheltering from the wind, and there
Manage the talk until her name come round.
If there be rags enough he will know her name
And be well pleased remembering it, for in the old days,
Though she had young men's praise and old men's blame,
Among the poor both old and young gave her praise.

## *Easter 1916*

I have met them at close of day
Coming with vivid faces
From counter or desk among grey
Eighteenth-century houses.
I have passed with a nod of the head
Or polite meaningless words,
Or have lingered awhile and said
Polite meaningless words,
And thought before I had done
Of a mocking tale or a gibe
To please a companion
Around the fire at the club,

Being certain that they and I
But lived where motley is worn:
All changed, changed utterly:
A terrible beauty is born.

That woman's days were spent
In ignorant good-will,
Her nights in argument
Until her voice grew shrill.
What voice more sweet than hers
When, young and beautiful,
She rode to harriers?
This man had kept a school
And rode our wingèd horse;
This other his helper and friend
Was coming into his force;
He might have won fame in the end,
So sensitive his nature seemed,
So daring and sweet his thought.
This other man I had dreamed
A drunken, vainglorious lout.
He had done most bitter wrong
To some who are near my heart,
Yet I number him in the song;
He, too, has resigned his part
In the casual comedy;
He, too, has been changed in his turn,
Transformed utterly:
A terrible beauty is born.

Hearts with one purpose alone
Through summer and winter seem
Enchanted to a stone
To trouble the living stream.
The horse that comes from the road,
The rider, the birds that range
From cloud to tumbling cloud,
Minute by minute they change;
A shadow of cloud on the stream

Changes minute by minute;
A horse-hoof slides on the brim,
And a horse plashes within it;
The long-legged moor-hens dive,
And hens to moor-cocks call;
Minute by minute they live:
The stone's in the midst of all.

Too long a sacrifice
Can make a stone of the heart.
O when may it suffice?
That is Heaven's part, our part
To murmur name upon name,
As a mother names her child
When sleep at last has come
On limbs that had run wild.
What is it but nightfall?
No, no, not night but death;
Was it needless death after all?
For England may keep faith
For all that is done and said.
We know their dream; enough
To know they dreamed and are dead;
And what if excess of love
Bewildered them till they died?
I write it out in a verse –
MacDonagh and MacBride
And Connolly and Pearse
Now and in time to be,
Wherever green is worn,
Are changed, changed utterly:
A terrible beauty is born.

*September 25, 1916*

## *Reprisals*

Some nineteen German planes, they say,
You had brought down before you died.
We called it a good death. Today
Can ghost or man be satisfied?
Although your last exciting year
Outweighed all other years, you said,
Though battle joy may be so dear
A memory, even to the dead,
It chases other thought away,
Yet rise from your Italian tomb,
Flit to Kiltartan cross and stay
Till certain second thoughts have come
Upon the cause you served, that we
Imagined such a fine affair:
Half-drunk or whole-mad soldiery
Are murdering your tenants there.
Men that revere your father yet
Are shot at on the open plain.
Where may new-married women sit
And suckle children now? Armed men
May murder them in passing by
Nor law nor parliament take heed.
Then close your ears with dust and lie
Among the other cheated dead.

# JOHN MILLINGTON SYNGE
## (1871–1909)

### *Queens*

Seven dog-days we let pass
Naming Queens in Glenmacnass,
All the rare and royal names
Wormy sheepskin yet retains,
Etain, Helen, Maeve, and Fand,
Golden Deirdre's tender hand,
Bert, the big-foot, sung by Villon,
Cassandra, Ronsard found in Lyon.
Queens of Sheba, Meath and Connaught,
Coifed with crown, or gaudy bonnet,
Queens whose finger once did stir men,
Queens were eaten of fleas and vermin,
Queens men drew like Monna Lisa,
Or slew with drugs in Rome and Pisa,
We named Lucrezia Crivelli,
And Titian's lady with amber belly,
Queens acquainted in learned sin,
Jane of Jewry's slender shin:
Queens who cut the bogs of Glanna,
Judith of Scripture, and Gloriana,
Queens who wasted the East by proxy,
Or drove the ass-cart, a tinker's doxy,
Yet these are rotten – I ask their pardon –
And we've the sun on rock and garden,
These are rotten, so you're the Queen
Of all are living, or have been.

## *Patch-Shaneen*

Shaneen and Maurya Prendergast
Lived west in Carnareagh,
And they'd a cur-dog, cabbage plot,
A goat, and cock of hay.

He was five foot one or two,
Herself was four foot ten,
And he went travelling asking meal
Above through Caragh Glen.

She'd pick her bag of carrageen
Or perries through the surf,
Or loan an ass of Foxy Jim
To fetch her creel of turf.

Till on one windy Samhain night,
When there's stir among the dead,
He found her perished, stiff and stark,
Beside him in the bed.

And now when Shaneen travels far
From Droum to Ballyhyre
The women lay him sacks or straw,
Beside the seed of fire.

And when the grey cocks crow and flap,
And winds are in the sky,
'Oh, Maurya, Maurya, are you dead?'
You'll hear Patch-Shaneen cry.

### *In Kerry*

We heard the thrushes by the shore and sea,
And saw the golden stars' nativity,
Then round we went the lane by Thomas Flynn,
Across the church where bones lie out and in;
And there I asked beneath a lonely cloud
Of strange delight, with one bird singing loud,
What change you'd wrought in graveyard, rock and sea,
This new wild paradise to wake for me . . .
Yet knew no more than knew these merry sins
Had built this stack of thigh-bones, jaws and shins.

## THOMAS MACDONAGH

## (1878–1916)

### *Dublin Tramcars*

A sailor sitting in a tram –
A face that winces in the wind –
That sees and knows me what I am,
That looks through courtesy and sham
And sees the good and bad behind –
He is not God to save or damn,
Thank God, I need not wish him blind!

Calvin and Chaucer I saw today
Come into the Terenure car:
Certain I am that it was they,
Though someone may know them here and say
What different men they are,
I know their pictures – and there they sat,

And passing the Catholic church at Rathgar
Calvin took off his hat
And blessed himself, and Chaucer at that
Chuckled and looked away.

## *The Night Hunt*

In the morning, in the dark,
When the stars begin to blunt,
By the wall of Barna Park
Dogs I heard and saw them hunt.
All the parish dogs were there,
All the dogs for miles around,
Teeming up behind a hare,
In the dark, without a sound.

How I heard I scarce can tell –
'Twas a patter in the grass –
And I did not see them well
Come across the dark and pass;
Yet I saw them and I knew
Spearman's dog and Spellman's dog
And, beside my own dog too,
Leamy's from the Island Bog.

In the morning when the sun
Burnished all the green to gorse,
I went out to take a run
Round the bog upon my horse;
And my dog that had been sleeping
In the heat beside the door
Left his yawning and went leaping
On a hundred yards before.

Through the village street we passed –
Not a dog there raised a snout –
Through the street and out at last
On the white bog road and out

Over Barna Park full pace,
Over to the Silver Stream,
Horse and dog in happy race,
Rider between thought and dream.

By the stream, at Leamy's house,
Lay a dog – my pace I curbed –
But our coming did not rouse
Him from drowsing undisturbed;
And my dog, as unaware
Of the other, dropped beside
And went running by me there
With my horse's slackened stride.

Yet by something, by a twitch
Of the sleeper's eye, a look
From the runner, something which
Little chords of feeling shook,
I was conscious that a thought
Shuddered through the silent deep
Of a secret – I had caught
Something I had known in sleep.

## *The Man Upright*

I once spent an evening in a village
Where the people are all taken up with tillage,
Or do some business in a small way
Among themselves, and all the day
Go crooked, doubled to half their size,
Both working and loafing, with their eyes
Stuck in the ground or in a board, –
For some of them tailor, and some of them hoard
Pence in a till in their little shops,
And some of them shoe-soles – they get the tops
Ready-made from England, and they die cobblers –
All bent up double, a village of hobblers
And slouchers and squatters, whether they straggle

Up and down, or bend to haggle
Over a counter, or bend at a plough,
Or to dig with a spade, or to milk a cow,
Or to shove the goose-iron stiffly along
The stuff on the sleeve-board, or lace the fong
In the boot on the last, or to draw the wax-end
Tight cross-ways – and so to make or to mend
What will soon be worn out by the crooked people.
The only thing straight in the place was the steeple,
I thought at first. I was wrong in that;
For there past the window at which I sat
Watching the crooked little men
Go slouching, and with the gait of a hen
An odd little woman go pattering past,
And the cobbler crouching over his last
In the window opposite, and next door
The tailor squatting inside on the floor –
While I watched them, as I have said before,
And thought that only the steeple was straight,
There came a man of a different gait –
A man who neither slouched nor pattered,
But planted his steps as if each step mattered;
Yet walked down the middle of the street
Not like a policeman on his beat,
But like a man with nothing to do
Except walk straight upright like me and you.

## JOSEPH CAMPBELL
## (1879–1944)

### *The Newspaper-Seller*

*(Times Square, New York, about two o'clock on a winter's morning)*

And how is Cabey's Lane?
I'm forty years left Ennis, sir,
And never like to see the place again.
'Twas out of there I married her –
The first one – Mattha Twomey's daughter.
The 'bit o' paint', they called her.
She was young, tall as a birch-tree, pale,
With blushes in her cheeks,
And eyes as brown as Burren water.
Faith, and there was lavish drinking
At her wedding. Now, as I'm thinking –
Four half-barrels of ale,
Old whisky, cordial and wine;
And eating fine.

I'd ten by her;
Ten topping childer, sir,
Like apples, red and sweet.
In fair-meadow or street
You wouldn't see the likes of 'em . . .
And then she died.

You can't live by the dead,
Leastways, when you have hungry mouths to fill
That's what my people said.
And so inside a year I wed again –
This time, to Mary Quill,

A Limerick girl was lodging in the lane
West of Cabey's. The first was quiet and wise,
The second had laughing eyes:
I put a charm on them, and married her.

Says she on the wedding night,
'You're in a sorry plight
With me and the little ones. Let's go away.'
'Where to?' says I. 'To America,'
Says she. 'This country is too poor and small
For us, and over there there's work and bread for all.'

She was an eager kind, you see –
Far different to Sibby.
Well, by dint of slaving night and day
We made the passage out, and Boston Quay
Saw me and her in Eighteen Seventy-Three,
The Blizzard Year. That's four decades ago;
But even now I feel the bitter snow –
I feel it in my marrow, sir – the snow
And the high, driving wind.
We left our clan behind
In Cabey's Lane with neighbours
Till such times as I could find
The cash to fetch 'em after us.
And God was kind –
Kinder than I thought He'd be
In a strange land.
For work came rolling to my hand, sir,
And I wrought for constant pay
In a bakehouse. He was German, sir,
The boss; and Germans, mostly, mixed the dough,
And watched the fires. That's how I came to know
The Deutsch. I speak it better than I used to do
The Gaelic at home.

I'd twelve by Mary, sir –
Ten living and two dead.
I'd ten by Sibby. Twenty childer, sir –
Twelve daughters and eight sons . . .
And better for myself I ne'er had one!
My curse on Matt and Ned
That let old age come down on my grey head,
And left me selling *Worlds*!
My curse on Shaun!
My curse on Meehaul Ban,
The fair-haired boy, the gentleman,
That wouldn't look the road I doddered on!
My seven curses on him,
And the flaming curse of God!
My curse on Peter!
My blessing on poor Joe, who's now in quod
For housebreaking – the white lamb of the flock
He helped me when my right hand was a crock
With blood-poison, and paid the rent for me.
My curse on all my daughters!
On Sibby Ann, who's married west,
And has her auto, while I creep on limbs
All crookened with the pains!
My curse on Peg and Fan!
My curse on Angeline!
My curse on Ceely, and the rest!
I don't know half their names:
The devil's brood, but no brood of mine.
And Cabey's Lane, sir? I was happy there,
In Ennis town in Clare,
When I was young. Ah, young, not old . . .
God help us, isn't it bitter cold!

## *Raven's Rock*

The line of the hills is a song.
Abhna, Aa-na-craebhi,
Places of trees and rivers,
Praise God with their sweetness.
The lake shines, darker than a hound's eye.

On the stones
The shadows of fern-stalks
Write secretly in ogham.
The rainbows build their towers,
And pull them down again.
A cloud comes,
And out of it a sun-stained man.

Who is it that is coming?

*Cumhall's son, of the sídh of Almhain.*
*The Red Spears are no more:*
*They have gone from the bright world.*

Who is the grey head that follows?

*I came over sea;*
*I freed Fál from her bondage;*
*I blessed the fountain;*
*I walk now bodiless.*

Who passes, crowned with a crown?

*A knitter of warring rules,*
*A maker of circuits,*
*A giver of gold;*
*Slain at last on the still edge of battle.*

Who is the boy on horseback?

*No stranger to this glen.*
*Through snowdrifts they hunted me,*
*As the lame wolf is hunted.*

Who is he, pale and bloody from a wound?

*When the wild geese cry, the west listens.*
*I died not for my own,*
*But my own love me.*

Who is the young man with sad dreams?

*The weavers of green cloth,*
*The beaters of pikes may tell you.*
*You will not see my name cut on a grave.*

Who is the proud, bearded man?

*Shorn by a woman of kingship,*
*Thus far have I led you,*
*But set no mark to your journey.*

Who are the marching fianna?

*Ask the spring,*
*The summer torrent that wept us.*
*If we are dead, it is for the great love*
*We bore the Gael.*

Who is the tall prisoner?

*I go to the rope and the quicklime.*
*They have no hands that would deliver me –*
*O Christ of Nazareth! no hands.*

The cloud lightens:
The vision is gone.
Dúas, like a woman's nipple,
Bares itself in beauty.
The lake shines, whiter than honey-comb.

On the stones
The ferns, with moveless strokes,
Write the saga of time.
The rainbow-branches bud,
And flower, and wither again.
Silent, the earth waits the hour of her travail.

## JAMES STEPHENS

## (1880?–1950)

### *The Red-haired Man's Wife*

I have taken that vow!
And you were my friend
But yesterday – Now
All that's at an end;
And you are my husband, and claim me, and
  I must depend!

Yesterday I was free!
Now you, as I stand,
Walk over to me
And take hold of my hand;
You look at my lips! Your eyes are too
  bold, your smile is too bland!

My old name is lost;
My distinction of race!
Now, the line has been crossed,
Must I step to your pace?
Must I walk as you list, and obey,
  and smile up in your face?

All the white and the red
Of my cheeks you have won!
All the hair of my head!
And my feet, tho' they run,
Are yours, and you own me and end me,
  just as I begun!

Must I bow when you speak!
Be silent and hear;
Inclining my cheek
And incredulous ear
To your voice, and command, and behest;
  hold your lightest wish dear!

I am woman! But still
Am alive, and can feel
Every intimate thrill
That is woe or is weal:
I, aloof, and divided, apart, standing far,
  can I kneel?

Oh, if kneeling were right,
I should kneel nor be sad!
And abase in your sight
All the pride that I had!
I should come to you, hold to you, cling to
  you, call to you, glad!

If not, I shall know,
I shall surely find out!
And your world will throw
In disaster and rout!
I am woman, and glory, and beauty; I,
  mystery, terror and doubt!

I am separate still!
I am I and not you!
And my mind and my will,
As in secret they grew,
Still are secret; unreached, and untouched,
  and not subject to you.

## *The Street Behind Yours*

The night droops down upon the street,
Shade after shade! A solemn frown
Is pressing to
A deeper hue
The houses drab and brown;
Till all in blackness touch and meet,
Are mixed and melted down.

All is so silent! Not a sound
Comes through the dark! The gas-lamps throw,
From here and there,
A feeble glare
On the pavement cracked below;
On the greasy, muddy ground;
On the houses in a row.

Those rigid houses, black and sour!
Each dark thin building stretching high;
Rank upon rank
Of windows blank
Stare from a sullen eye;
With doleful aspect scowl and glower
At the timid passer-by.

And down between those spectre files
The narrow roadway, thick with mud,
Doth crouch and hide!
While close beside
The gutter churns a flood
Of noisome water through the piles
Of garbage, thick as blood!

And tho' 'tis silent! Tho' no sound
Crawls from the blackness thickly spread!
Yet darkness brings
Grim, noiseless things
That walk as they were dead!
They glide, and peer, and steal around,
With stealthy, silent tread!

You dare not walk! That awful crew
Might speak or laugh as you pass by!
Might touch and paw
With a formless claw,
Or leer from a sodden eye!
Might whisper awful things they knew!
– Or wring their hands and cry!

There is the doorway mean and low!
And there are the houses drab and brown!
And the night's black pall!
And the hours that crawl!
And the forms that peer and frown!
And the lamps' dim flare on the slush below!
And the gutter grumbling down!

## *O Bruadair*

I will sing no more songs! The pride of my country I sang
Through forty long years of good rhyme, without any avail;
And no one cared even the half of the half of a hang
For the song or the singer – so, here is an end to the tale!

If you say, if you think, I complain, and have not got a cause,
Let you come to me here, let you look at the state of my hand!
Let you say if a goose-quill has calloused these horny old paws,
Or the spade that I grip on, and dig with, out there in the land?

When our nobles were safe and renowned and were rooted and
tough,
Though my thought went to them and had joy in the fortune of
those,
And pride that was proud of their pride – they gave little
enough!
Not as much as two boots for my feet, or an old suit of clothes!

I ask of the Craftsman that fashioned the fly and the bird;
Of the Champion whose passion will lift me from death in a
time;
Of the Spirit that melts icy hearts with the wind of a word,
That my people be worthy, and get, better singing than mine.

I had hoped to live decent, when Ireland was quit of her care,
As a poet or steward, perhaps, in a house of degree,
But my end of the tale is – old brogues and old breeches to wear!
So I'll sing no more songs for the men that care nothing for me.

## PADRAIC COLUM
## (1881–1972)

### *A Drover*

To Meath of the pastures,
From wet hills by the sea,
Through Leitrim and Longford,
Go my cattle and me.

I hear in the darkness
Their slipping and breathing –
I name them the by-ways
They're to pass without heeding;

Then the wet, winding roads,
Brown bogs with black water,
And my thoughts on white ships
And the King o' Spain's daughter.

O farmer, strong farmer!
You can spend at the fair,
But your face you must turn
To your crops and your care;

And soldiers, red soldiers!
You've seen many lands,
But you walk two by two,
And by captain's commands!

O the smell of the beasts,
The wet wind in the morn,
And the proud and hard earth
Never broken for corn!

And the crowds at the fair,
The herds loosened and blind,
Loud words and dark faces,
And the wild blood behind!

(O strong men with your best
I would strive breast to breast,
I could quiet your herds
With my words, with my words!)

I will bring you, my kine,
Where there's grass to the knee,
But you'll think of scant croppings
Harsh with salt of the sea.

## *The Poor Girl's Meditation*

I am sitting here
Since the moon rose in the night,
Kindling a fire,
And striving to keep it alight;
The folk of the house are lying
In slumber deep;
The geese will be gabbling soon:
The whole of the land is asleep.

May I never leave this world
Until my ill-luck is gone;
Till I have cows and sheep,
And the lad that I love for my own;
I would not think it long,
The night I would lie at his breast,
And the daughters of spite, after that,
Might say the thing they liked best.

Love takes the place of hate,
If a girl have beauty at all:
On a bed that was narrow and high,
A three-month I lay by the wall:
When I bethought on the lad
That I left on the brow of the hill,
I wept from dark until dark,
And my cheeks have the tear-tracks still.

And, O young lad that I love,
I am no mark for your scorn;
All you can say of me is
Undowered I was born:
And if I've no fortune in hand,
Nor cattle and sheep of my own,
This I can say, O lad,
I am fitted to lie my lone!

## *The Poet*

'The blackbird's in the briar,
The seagull's on the ground –
They are nests, and they're more than nests,' he said,
'They are tokens I have found.

There, where the rain-dashed briar
Marks an empty glade,
The blackbird's nest is seen,' he said,
'Clay-rimmed, uncunningly made.

By shore of the inland lake,
Where surgeless water shoves,
The seagulls have their nests,' he said,
'As low as cattles' hooves.'

I heard a poet say it,
The sojourner of a night;
His head was up to the rafter
Where he stood in candles' light.

'Your houses are like the seagulls'
Nests – they are scattered and low;
Like the backbirds' nests in briars,' he said,
'Uncunningly made – even so:

But close to the ground are reared
The wings that have widest sway,
And the birds that sing best in the wood,' he said,
'Were reared with breasts to the clay.

You've wildness – I've turned it to song;
You've strength – I've turned it to wings;
The welkin's for your conquest then,
The wood to your music rings.'

I heard a poet say it,
The sojourner of a night;
His head was up to the rafter,
Where he stood in candles' light.

## JAMES JOYCE
## (1882–1941)

### *from* Chamber Music

#### XXXVI: *I hear an army charging upon the land*

I hear an army charging upon the land,
  And the thunder of horses plunging, foam about their knees:
Arrogant, in black armour, behind them stand,
  Disdaining the reins, with fluttering whips, the charioteers.

They cry unto the night their battle-name:
  I moan in sleep when I hear afar their whirling laughter.
They cleave the gloom of dreams, a blinding flame,
  Clanging, clanging upon the heart as upon an anvil.

They come shaking in triumph their long, green hair:
  They come out of the sea and run shouting by the shore.
My heart, have you no wisdom thus to despair?
  My love, my love, my love, why have you left me alone?

## *Watching the Needleboats at San Sabba*

I heard their young hearts crying
Loveward above the glancing oar
And heard the prairie grasses sighing:
*No more, return no more!*

O hearts, O sighing grasses,
Vainly your loveblown bannerets mourn!
No more will the wild wind that passes
Return, no more return.

*Trieste, 1912*

# FRANCIS LEDWIDGE

(1887–1917)

## *The Death of Ailill*

When there was heard no more the war's loud sound
And only the rough corn-crake filled hours,
And hill winds in the furze and drowsy flowers,
Maeve in her chamber with her white head bowed

On Ailill's heart was sobbing: 'I have found
The way to love you now,' she said, and he
Winked an old tear away and said: 'The proud
Unyielding heart loves never.' And then she:
'I love you now, tho' once when we were young
We walked apart like two who were estranged
Because I loved you not, now all is changed.'
And he who loved her always called her name
And said: 'You do not love me, 'tis your tongue
Talks in the dusk; you love the blazing gold
Won in the battles, and the soldier's fame.
You love the stories that are often told
By poets in the hall.' Then Maeve arose
And sought her daughter Findebar: 'O child,
Go tell your father that my love went wild
With all my wars in youth, and say that now
I love him stronger than I hate my foes . . .'
And Findebar unto her father sped
And touched him gently on the rugged brow,
And knew by the cold touch that he was dead.

## *The Wife of Llew*

And Gwydion said to Math, when it was Spring:
'Come now and let us make a wife for Llew.'
And so they broke broad boughs yet moist with dew,
And in a shadow made a magic ring:
They took the violet and the meadowsweet
To form her pretty face, and for her feet
They built a mound of daisies on a wing,
And for her voice they made a linnet sing
In the wide poppy blowing for her mouth.
And over all they chanted twenty hours.
And Llew came singing from the azure south
And bore away his wife of birds and flowers.

## *Thomas MacDonagh*

He shall not hear the bittern cry
In the wild sky, where he is lain,
Nor voices of the sweeter birds
Above the wailing of the rain.

Nor shall he know when loud March blows
Thro' slanting snows her fanfare shrill,
Blowing to flame the golden cup
Of many an upset daffodil.

And when the Dark Cow leaves the moor,
And pastures poor with greedy weeds,
Perhaps he'll hear her low at morn
Lifting her horn in pleasant meads.

## *The Blackbirds*

I heard the Poor Old Woman say:
'At break of day the fowler came,
And took my blackbirds from their songs
Who loved me well thro' shame and blame.

No more from lovely distances
Their songs shall bless me mile by mile,
Nor to white Ashbourne call me down
To wear my crown another while.

When bended flowers the angels mark
For the skylark the place they lie,
From there its little family
Shall dip their wings first in the sky.

And when the first surprise of flight
Sweet songs excite, from the far dawn
Shall there come blackbirds loud with love,
Sweet echoes of the singers gone.

But in the lonely hush of eve
Weeping I grieve the silent bills.'
I heard the Poor Old Woman say
In Derry of the little hills.

# VII

# THE SEA OF DISAPPOINTMENT: 1922–70

*I think*
*This is the Sea of Disappointment.*

Thomas Kinsella, 'Nightwalker'

## WILLIAM BUTLER YEATS

### *Meditations in Time of Civil War*

I

*Ancestral Houses*

Surely among a rich man's flowering lawns,
Amid the rustle of his planted hills,
Life overflows without ambitious pains;
And rains down life until the basin spills,
And mounts more dizzy high the more it rains
As though to choose whatever shape it wills
And never stoop to a mechanical
Or servile shape, at others' beck and call.

Mere dreams, mere dreams! Yet Homer had not sung
Had he not found it certain beyond dreams
That out of life's own self-delight had sprung
The abounding glittering jet; though now it seems
As if some marvellous empty sea-shell flung
Out of the obscure dark of the rich streams,
And not a fountain, were the symbol which
Shadows the inherited glory of the rich.

Some violent bitter man, some powerful man
Called architect and artist in, that they,
Bitter and violent men, might rear in stone
The sweetness that all longed for night and day,
The gentleness none there had ever known;
But when the master's buried mice can play,
And maybe the great-grandson of that house,
For all its bronze and marble, 's but a mouse.

O what if gardens where the peacock strays
With delicate feet upon old terraces,
Or else all Juno from an urn displays
Before the indifferent garden deities;
O what if levelled lawns and gravelled ways
Where slippered Contemplation finds his ease
And Childhood a delight for every sense,
But take our greatness with our violence?

What if the glory of escutcheoned doors,
And buildings that a haughtier age designed,
The pacing to and fro on polished floors
Amid great chambers and long galleries, lined
With famous portraits of our ancestors;
What if those things the greatest of mankind
Consider most to magnify, or to bless,
But take our greatness with our bitterness?

II

*My House*

An ancient bridge, and a more ancient tower,
A farmhouse that is sheltered by its wall,
An acre of stony ground,
Where the symbolic rose can break in flower,
Old ragged elms, old thorns innumerable,
The sound of the rain or sound
Of every wind that blows;
The stilted water-hen
Crossing stream again
Scared by the splashing of a dozen cows;

A winding stair, a chamber arched with stone,
A grey stone fireplace with an open hearth,
A candle and written page.
*Il Penseroso*'s Platonist toiled on
In some like chamber, shadowing forth
How the daemonic rage

Imagined everything.
Benighted travellers
From markets and from fairs
Have seen his midnight candle glimmering.

Two men have founded here. A man-at-arms
Gathered a score of horse and spent his days
In this tumultuous spot,
Where through long wars and sudden night alarms
His dwindling score and he seemed castaways
Forgetting and forgot;
And I, that after me
My bodily heirs may find,
To exalt a lonely mind,
Befitting emblems of adversity.

III

*My Table*

Two heavy trestles, and a board
Where Sato's gift, a changeless sword,
By pen and paper lies,
That it may moralize
My days out of their aimlessness.
A bit of an embroidered dress
Covers its wooden sheath.
Chaucer had not drawn breath
When it was forged. In Sato's house,
Curved like new moon, moon-luminous,
It lay five hundred years.
Yet if no change appears
No moon; only an aching heart
Conceives a changeless work of art.
Our learned men have urged
That when and where 'twas forged
A marvellous accomplishment,
In painting or in pottery, went
From father unto son

And through the centuries ran
And seemed unchanging like the sword.
Soul's beauty being most adored,
Men and their business took
The soul's unchanging look;
For the most rich inheritor,
Knowing that none could pass Heaven's door
That loved inferior art,
Had such an aching heart
That he, although a country's talk
For silken clothes and stately walk,
Had waking wits; it seemed
Juno's peacock screamed.

## IV

### *My Descendants*

Having inherited a vigorous mind
From my old fathers, I must nourish dreams
And leave a woman and a man behind
As vigorous of mind, and yet it seems
Life scarce can cast a fragrance on the wind,
Scarce spread a glory to the morning beams,
But the torn petals strew the garden plot;
And there's but common greenness after that.

And what if my descendants lose the flower
Through natural declension of the soul,
Through too much business with the passing hour,
Through too much play, or marriage with a fool?
May this laborious stair and this stark tower
Become a roofless ruin that the owl
May build in the cracked masonry and cry
Her desolation to the desolate sky.

The Primum Mobile that fashioned us
Has made the very owls in circles move;
And I, that count myself most prosperous,
Seeing that love and friendship are enough,

For an old neighbour's friendship chose the house
And decked and altered it for a girl's love,
And know whatever flourish and decline
These stones remain their monument and mine.

V

*The Road at My Door*

An affable Irregular,
A heavily-built Falstaffian man,
Comes cracking jokes of civil war
As though to die by gunshot were
The finest play under the sun.

A brown Lieutenant and his men,
Half dressed in national uniform,
Stand at my door, and I complain
Of the foul weather, hail and rain,
A pear-tree broken by the storm.

I count those feathered balls of soot
The moor-hen guides upon the stream,
To silence the envy in my thought;
And turn towards my chamber, caught
In the cold snows of a dream.

VI

*The Stare's Nest by My Window*

The bees build in the crevices
Of loosening masonry, and there
The mother birds bring grubs and flies.
My wall is loosening; honey-bees,
Come build in the empty house of the stare.

We are closed in, and the key is turned
On our uncertainty; somewhere
A man is killed, or a house burned,
Yet no clear fact to be discerned:
Come build in the empty house of the stare.

A barricade of stone or of wood;
Some fourteen days of civil war;
Last night they trundled down the road
That dead young soldier in his blood:
Come build in the empty house of the stare.

We had fed the heart on fantasies,
The heart's grown brutal from the fare;
More substance in our enmities
Than in our love; O honey-bees,
Come build in the empty house of the stare.

VII

*I see Phantoms of Hatred and of the Heart's*
*Fullness and of the Coming Emptiness*

I climb to the tower-top and lean upon broken stone,
A mist that is like blown snow is sweeping over all,
Valley, river, and elms, under the light of a moon
That seems unlike itself, that seems unchangeable,
A glittering sword out of the east. A puff of wind
And those white glimmering fragments of the mist sweep by.
Frenzies bewilder, reveries perturb the mind;
Monstrous familiar images swim to the mind's eye.

'Vengeance upon the murderers,' the cry goes up,
'Vengeance for Jacques Molay.' In cloud-pale rags, or in lace,
The rage-driven, rage-tormented, and rage-hungry troop,
Trooper belabouring trooper, biting at arm or at face,
Plunges towards nothing, arms and fingers spreading wide
For the embrace of nothing; and I, my wits astray
Because of all that senseless tumult, all but cried
For vengeance on the murderers of Jacques Molay.

Their legs long, delicate and slender, aquamarine their eyes,
Magical unicorns bear ladies on their backs.
The ladies close their musing eyes. No prophecies,
Remembered out of Babylonian almanacs,
Have closed the ladies' eyes, their minds are but a pool
Where even longing drowns under its own excess;
Nothing but stillness can remain when hearts are full
Of their own sweetness, bodies of their loveliness.

The cloud-pale unicorns, the eyes of aquamarine,
The quivering half-closed eyelids, the rags of cloud or of lace,
Or eyes that rage has brightened, arms it has made lean,
Give place to an indifferent multitude, give place
To brazen hawks. Nor self-delighting reverie,
Nor hate of what's to come, nor pity for what's gone,
Nothing but grip of claw, and the eye's complacency,
The innumerable clanging wings that have put out the moon.

I turn away and shut the door, and on the stair
Wonder how many times I could have proved my worth
In something that all others understand or share;
But O! ambitious heart, had such a proof drawn forth
A company of friends, a conscience set at ease,
It had but made us pine the more. The abstract joy,
The half-read wisdom of daemonic images,
Suffice the ageing man as once the growing boy.

*1923*

## *In Memory of Eva Gore-Booth and Con Markiewicz*

The light of evening, Lissadell,
Great windows open to the south,
Two girls in silk kimonos, both
Beautiful, one a gazelle.
But a raving autumn shears
Blossom from the summer's wreath:
The older is condemned to death,

Pardoned, drags out lonely years
Conspiring among the ignorant.
I know not what the younger dreams –
Some vague Utopia – and she seems,
When withered old and skeleton-gaunt,
An image of such politics.
Many a time I think to seek
One or the other out and speak
Of that old Georgian mansion, mix
Pictures of the mind, recall
That table and the talk of youth,
Two girls in silk kimonos, both
Beautiful, one a gazelle.

Dear shadows, now you know it all,
All the folly of a fight
With a common wrong or right.
The innocent and the beautiful
Have no enemy but time;
Arise and bid me strike a match
And strike another till time catch;
Should the conflagration climb,
Run till all the sages know.
We the great gazebo built,
They convicted us of guilt;
Bid me strike a match and blow.

*October 1927*

## *Coole Park and Ballylee, 1931*

Under my window-ledge the waters race,
Otters below and moor-hens on the top,
Run for a mile undimmed in Heaven's face
Then darkening through 'dark' Raftery's 'cellar' drop,

Run underground, rise in a rocky place
In Coole demesne, and there to finish up
Spread to a lake and drop into a hole.
What's water but the generated soul?

Upon the border of that lake's a wood
Now all dry sticks under a wintry sun,
And in a copse of beeches there I stood,
For Nature's pulled her tragic buskin on
And all the rant's a mirror of my mood:
At sudden thunder of the mounting swan
I turned about and looked where branches break
The glittering reaches of the flooded lake.

Another emblem there! That stormy white
But seems a concentration of the sky;
And, like the soul, it sails into the sight
And in the morning's gone, no man knows why;
And is so lovely that it sets to right
What knowledge or its lack had set awry,
So arrogantly pure, a child might think
It can be murdered with a spot of ink.

Sound of a stick upon the floor, a sound
From somebody that toils from chair to chair;
Beloved books that famous hands have bound,
Old marble heads, old pictures everywhere;
Great rooms where travelled men and children found
Content or joy; a last inheritor
Where none has reigned that lacked a name and fame
Or out of folly into folly came.

A spot whereon the founders lived and died
Seemed once more dear than life; ancestral trees,
Or gardens rich in memory glorified
Marriages, alliances and families

And every bride's ambition satisfied.
Where fashion or mere fantasy decrees
We shift about – all that great glory spent –
Like some poor Arab tribesman and his tent.

We were the last romantics – chose for theme
Traditional sanctity and loveliness;
Whatever's written in what poets name
The book of the people; whatever most can bless
The mind of man or elevate a rhyme;
But all is changed, that high horse riderless,
Though mounted in that saddle Homer rode
Where the swan drifts upon a darkening flood.

## from *Words for Music Perhaps*

### VI

### *Crazy Jane Talks with the Bishop*

I met the Bishop on the road
And much said he and I.
'Those breasts are flat and fallen now,
Those veins must soon be dry;
Live in a heavenly mansion,
Not in some foul sty.'

'Fair and foul are near of kin,
And fair needs foul,' I cried.
'My friends are gone, but that's a truth
Nor grave nor bed denied,
Learned in bodily lowliness
And in the heart's pride.

'A woman can be proud and stiff
When on love intent;
But Love has pitched his mansion in
The place of excrement;
For nothing can be sole or whole
That has not been rent.'

XX

*'I am of Ireland'*

*'I am of Ireland,*
*And the Holy Land of Ireland,*
*And time runs on,' cried she.*
*'Come out of charity,*
*Come dance with me in Ireland.'*

One man, one man alone
In that outlandish gear,
One solitary man
Of all that rambled there
Had turned his stately head.
'That is a long way off,
And time runs on,' he said,
'And the night grows rough.'

*'I am of Ireland,*
*And the Holy Land of Ireland,*
*And time runs on,' cried she.*
*'Come out of charity*
*And dance with me in Ireland.'*

'The fiddlers are all thumbs,
Or the fiddle-string accursed,
The drums and the kettledrums
And the trumpets all are burst,
And the trombone,' cried he,

'The trumpet and trombone,'
And cocked a malicious eye,
'But time runs on, runs on.'

*'I am of Ireland,*
*And the Holy Land of Ireland,*
*And time runs on,' cried she.*
*'Come out of charity*
*And dance with me in Ireland.'*

## *Lapis Lazuli*

*For Harry Clifton*

I have heard that hysterical women say
They are sick of the palette and fiddle-bow,
Of poets that are always gay,
For everybody knows or else should know
That if nothing drastic is done
Aeroplane and Zeppelin will come out,
Pitch like King Billy bomb-balls in
Until the town lie beaten flat.

All perform their tragic play,
There struts Hamlet, there is Lear,
That's Ophelia, that Cordelia;
Yet they, should the last scene be there,
The great stage curtain about to drop,
If worthy their prominent part in the play,
Do not break up their lines to weep.
They know that Hamlet and Lear are gay;
Gaiety transfiguring all that dread.
All men have aimed at, found and lost;
Black out; Heaven blazing into the head:
Tragedy wrought to its uttermost.
Though Hamlet rambles and Lear rages,

And all the drop-scenes drop at once
Upon a hundred thousand stages,
It cannot grow by an inch or an ounce.

On their own feet they came, or on shipboard,
Camel-back, horse-back, ass-back, mule-back,
Old civilizations put to the sword.
Then they and their wisdom went to rack:
No handiwork of Callimachus,
Who handled marble as if it were bronze,
Made draperies that seemed to rise
When sea-wind swept the corner, stands;
His long lamp-chimney shaped like the stem
Of a slender palm, stood but a day;
All things fall and are built again,
And those that build them again are gay.

Two Chinamen, behind them a third,
Are carved in lapis lazuli,
Over them flies a long-legged bird,
A symbol of longevity;
The third, doubtless a serving-man,
Carries a musical instrument.

Every discoloration of the stone,
Every accidental crack or dent,
Seems a water-course or an avalanche,
Or lofty slope where it still snows
Though doubtless plum or cherry-branch
Sweetens the little half-way house
Those Chinamen climb towards, and I
Delight to imagine them seated there;
There, on the mountain and the sky,
On all the tragic scene they stare.
One asks for mournful melodies;
Accomplished fingers begin to play.
Their eyes mid many wrinkles, their eyes,
Their ancient, glittering eyes, are gay.

## *High Talk*

Processions that lack high stilts have nothing that catches
the eye.
What if my great-granddad had a pair that were twenty foot
high,
And mine were but fifteen foot, no modern stalks upon higher,
Some rogue of the world stole them to patch up a fence or a fire.
Because piebald ponies, led bears, caged lions, make but poor
shows,
Because children demand Daddy-long-legs upon his timber toes,
Because women in the upper storeys demand a face at the pane,
That patching old heels they may shriek, I take to chisel and
plane.

Malachi Stilt-Jack am I, whatever I learned has run wild,
From collar to collar, from stilt to stilt, from father to child.
All metaphor, Malachi, stilts and all. A barnacle goose
Far up in the stretches of night; night splits and the dawn breaks
loose;
I, through the terrible novelty of light, stalk on, stalk on;
Those great sea-horses bare their teeth and laugh at the dawn.

## *Cuchulain Comforted*

A man that had six mortal wounds, a man
Violent and famous, strode among the dead;
Eyes stared out of the branches and were gone.

Then certain Shrouds that muttered head to head
Came and were gone. He leant upon a tree
As though to meditate on wounds and blood.

A Shroud that seemed to have authority
Among those bird-like things came, and let fall
A bundle of linen. Shrouds by two and three

Came creeping up because the man was still.
And thereupon that linen-carrier said:
'Your life can grow much sweeter if you will

'Obey our ancient rule and make a shroud;
Mainly because of what we only know
The rattle of those arms makes us afraid.

'We thread the needles' eyes, and all we do
All must together do.' That done, the man
Took up the nearest and began to sew.

'Now must we sing and sing the best we can,
But first you must be told our character:
Convicted cowards all, by kindred slain

'Or driven from home and left to die in fear.'
They sang, but had nor human tunes nor words,
Though all was done in common as before;

They had changed their throats and had the throats of
birds.

*January 13, 1939*

## JOSEPH CAMPBELL

### *from* Prison Poems

### *Chesspieces*

It was a time of trouble – executions,
Dearth, searches, nightly firing, balked escapes –
And I sat silent, while my cellmate figured

Ruy Lopez' Gambit from the 'Praxis'. Silence
Best fitted with our mood: we seldom spoke.
'I have a thought,' he said, tilting his stool.
'We prisoners are so many pieces taken,
Swept from the chessboard, only used again
When a new game is started.' 'There's that hope,'
I said, 'the hope of being used again.
Some day of strength, when ploughs are out in March,
The Dogs of Fionn will slip their iron chains,
And, heedless of torn wounds and failing wind,
Will run the old grey Wolf to death at last.'
He smiled. 'I like the image. My fat Kings,
And painted Queens, and purple-cassocked Bishops
Are tame, indeed, beside your angry Dogs!'

## *New Year, 1923*

Lying awake at midnight in the prison,
I heard a sudden crash of chiming bells,
Bronze bass and silver tenor, tone on tone.
– 'The church,' thought I, 'rings in another year.'
Then through the jangled bells the wail of horns
(Ship's sirens blowing from the river walls)
Smote, like a trumpet blast in sea-born 'Tristan.'
– 'Commerce,' thought I, 'rings in another year.'
And, as if stricken with the night's wild fever,
The prison shook in peals of Fenian cheers;
Mugs rattled, chambers clanked, old songs were sung.
– 'The Law,' thought I, 'rings in another year.'
Ear-surfeited, I turned to sleep; but sleep
Fled fearfully before a Thompson gun
Making new music at the prison gate.
– 'War,' pondered I, 'rings in another year!'

## *Country Sorrow*

In quiet dawn
Across small farms cold with shadow
A cock answers another:
Lonelier than lakewash,
Sadder than lightrise.
– Ai-ai, ai-oa, ai-ee!

In golden noon
From the thorned briars of the pasture
A lamb bleats to the ewe:
Lonelier than scythewhet,
Sadder than sawsound.

In set of sun
Somewhere along the mountain
A fluteplayer plays his flute:
Lonelier than grassbreath,
Sadder than girlsong.

In blueing dusk
On the road to the lighted hamlet
A cart's axle clacks:
Lonelier than dogbark,
Sadder than deadbell.

In midmost night
Over the sleeping doors and haggards
A goatowl passes:
Lonelier than cronecough,
Sadder than childsigh.
– Ai-ai, ai-oa, ai-ee!

## *Ad Limina*

The ewes and lambs, loving the far hillplaces,
Cropping by choice the succulent tops of heather,
Drinking the pure water of cloudborn lochlands,
Resting under erratics fostered with Abel –
Come to my haggard gate, my very doorstep.

The birds of freest will and strongest wingbeat,
Sad curlew, garrulous stonechat, hawk and coaltit,
Haunting lone bog or scalp or broken ruin,
Poising the rough thrust of air's excesses –
Come to my haggard gate, my very doorstep.

The trout in the river, below the hanging marllot,
Swift, with ancestral fear of hook and shadow,
The elvers of cold drain and slough, remembering
The warm tangles of Caribbee and Sargasso –
Come to my haggard gate, my very doorstep.

Even the stoats and rats, who know a possessor
Of the rare sixth sense, the bardic insight,
Match, and more, for their devilish perversions,
And the deer, shyest of shy at autumn rutting –
Come to my haggard gate, my very doorstep.

Am I not a lucky man, trusted, Franciscan,
That these spacious things, gentle or hostile,
Following God's urge, denying their nature,
Harbingers of high thoughts and fathers of poems –
Come to my haggard gate, my very doorstep.

## BLANAID SALKELD
## (1880–1959)

### *Role*

I am become tired warder of the days:
Each greets me, risen, with a sulphur glare,
Since I prolong time's wrong, time's useless care –
The dry routine – though I am loth to raise
Dead eyes to window, nor can ever praise
The grudging slave that peddles my despair
About the parish. I uptie my hair,
And jolt the jolly mirror with my face,
Then patter in and out of airless rooms;
Trip stairs; slam door; and stamp along the street,
Slapping the solid reticence of day.
Tomorrow forgotten, in the often gay
Visit of night, I thankfully retreat
Into a gloomy hazard, like the tomb's.

### *Art*

Imagination is off paddling among rocks
while thought is pulling on its morning socks
or rummaging for words in drawer and box.

Give over. Art is easy. All awards –
(out of the fog, the bog, and the slaughter yards) –
no going back to those masks, those muddy discards;
finished the novitiate in dank jungles of terrestrial
fevers, where lightnings mocked what thunder guessed at.

Crazed, self-entangled, whither have I not fled –
In dark tumble-down ablution houses of the dead
at wild sudden recognitions hung my head.

But art has escaped – to holy colour, close music, power –
to grace and virtue,
to the far-come dew
on the precise flower.

## JAMES JOYCE

### *Buy a book in brown paper*

Buy a book in brown paper
From Faber and Faber
To see Annie Liffey trip, tumble and caper.
Sevensinns in her singthings,
Plurabells on her prose,
Seashell ebb music wayriver she flows.

### *from* Finnegans Wake

### *The Ondt and the Gracehoper*

He larved ond he larved on he merd such a nauses
The Gracehoper feared he would mixplace his fauces.
I forgive you, grondt Ondt, said the Gracehoper, weeping,
For their sukes of the sakes you are safe in whose keeping.
Teach Floh and Luse polkas, show Bienie where's sweet

And be sure Vespatilla fines fat ones to heat.
As I once played the piper I must now pay the count
So saida to Moyhammlet and marhaba to your Mount!
Let who likes lump above so what flies be a full 'un;
I could not feel moregruggy if this was prompollen.
I pick up your reproof, the horsegift of a friend,
For the prize of your save is the price of my spend.
Can castwhores pulladeftkiss if oldpollocks forsake 'em
Or Culex feel etchy if Pulex don't wake him?
A locus to loue, a term it t'embarass,
These twain are the twins that tick *Homo Vulgaris*.
Has Aquileone nort winged to go syf
Since the Gwyfyn we were in his farrest drewbryf
And that Accident Man not beseeked where his story ends
Since longsephyring sighs sought heartseast for their orience?
We are Wastenot with Want, precondamned, two and true,
Till Nolans go volants and Bruneyes come blue.
Ere those gidflirts now gadding you quit your mocks for my
gropes
An extense must impull, an elapse must elopes,
Of my tectucs takestock, tinktact, and ail's weal;
As I view by your farlook hale yourself to my heal.
Partiprise my thinwhins whiles my blink points unbroken on
Your whole's whercabroads with Tout's trightyright token on.
My in risible universe youdly haud find
Sulch oxtrabeeforeness meat soveal behind.
Your feats end enormous, your volumes immense,
(May the Graces I hoped for sing your Ondtship song sense!),
Your genus its worldwide, your spacest sublime!
But, Holy Saltmartin, why can't you beat time?

## AUSTIN CLARKE
## (1896–1974)

### *The Lost Heifer*

When the black herds of the rain were grazing
In the gap of the pure cold wind
And the watery hazes of the hazel
Brought her into my mind,
I thought of the last honey by the water
That no hive can find.

Brightness was drenching through the branches
When she wandered again,
Turning the silver out of dark grasses
Where the skylark had lain,
And her voice coming softly over the meadow
Was the mist becoming rain.

### *The Planter's Daughter*

When night stirred at sea
And the fire brought a crowd in,
They say that her beauty
Was music in mouth
And few in the candlelight
Thought her too proud,
For the house of the planter
Is known by the trees.

Men that had seen her
Drank deep and were silent,
The women were speaking
Wherever she went –

As a bell that is rung
Or a wonder told shyly,
And O she was the Sunday
In every week.

## *The Straying Student*

On a holy day when sails were blowing southward,
A bishop sang the Mass at Inishmore,
Men took one side, their wives were on the other
But I heard the woman coming from the shore:
And wild in despair my parents cried aloud
For they saw the vision draw me to the doorway.

Long had she lived in Rome when Popes were bad,
The wealth of every age she makes her own,
Yet smiled on me in eager admiration,
And for a summer taught me all I know,
Banishing shame with her great laugh that rang
As if a pillar caught it back alone.

I learned the prouder counsel of her throat,
My mind was growing bold as light in Greece;
And when in sleep her stirring limbs were shown,
I blessed the noonday rock that knew no tree:
And for an hour the mountain was her throne,
Although her eyes were bright with mockery.

They say I was sent back from Salamanca
And failed in logic, but I wrote her praise
Nine times upon a college wall in France.
She laid her hand at darkfall on my page
That I might read the heavens in a glance
And I knew every star the Moors have named.

Awake or in my sleep, I have no peace now,
Before the ball is struck, my breath has gone,
And yet I tremble lest she may deceive me
And leave me in this land, where every woman's son
Must carry his own coffin and believe,
In dread, all that the clergy teach the young.

## *Penal Law*

Burn Ovid with the rest. Lovers will find
A hedge-school for themselves and learn by heart
All that the clergy banish from the mind,
When hands are joined and head bows in the dark.

## *Martha Blake at Fifty-one*

Early, each morning, Martha Blake
  Walked, angeling the road,
To Mass in the Church of the Three Patrons.
  Sanctuary lamp glowed
And the clerk halo'ed the candles
  On the High Altar. She knelt
Illumined. In gold-hemmed alb,
  The priest intoned. Wax melted.

Waiting for daily Communion, bowed head
  At rail, she hears a murmur.
Latin is near. In a sweet cloud
  That cherub'd, all occurred.
The voice went by. To her pure thought,
  Body was a distress
And soul, a sigh. Behind her denture,
  Love lay, a helplessness.

Then, slowly walking after Mass
  Down Rathgar Road, she took out
Her Yale key, put a match to gas-ring,
  Half filled a saucepan, cooked
A fresh egg lightly, with tea, brown bread,
  Soon, taking off her blouse
And skirt, she rested, pressing the Crown
  Of Thorns until she drowsed.

In her black hat, stockings, she passed
  Nylons to a nearby shop
And purchased, daily, with downcast eyes,
  Fillet of steak or a chop.
She simmered it on a low jet,
  Having a poor appetite,
Yet never for an hour felt better
  From dilatation, tightness.

She suffered from dropped stomach, heartburn
  Scalding, water-brash
And when she brought her wind up, turning
  Red with the weight of mashed
Potato, mint could not relieve her.
  In vain her many belches,
For all below was swelling, heaving
  Wamble, gurgle, squelch.

She lay on the sofa with legs up,
  A decade on her lip,
At four o'clock, taking a cup
  Of lukewarm water, sip
By sip, but still her daily food
  Repeated and the bile
Tormented her. In a blue hood,
  The Virgin sadly smiled.

When she looked up, the Saviour showed
  His Heart, daggered with flame
And, from the mantle-shelf, St Joseph
  Bent, disapproving. Vainly
She prayed, for in the whatnot corner,
  The new Pope was frowning. Night
And day, dull pain, as in her corns,
  Recounted every bite.

She thought of St Teresa, floating
  On motes of a sunbeam,
Carmelite with scatterful robes,
  Surrounded by demons,
Small black boys in their skin. She gaped
  At Hell: a muddy passage
That led to nothing, queer in shape,
  A cupboard closely fastened.

Sometimes, the walls of the parlour
  Would fade away. No plod
Of feet, rattle of van, in Garville
  Road. Soul now gone abroad
Where saints, like medieval serfs,
  Had laboured. Great sun-flower shone.
Our Lady's Chapel was borne by seraphs,
  Three leagues beyond Ancona.

High towns of Italy, the plain
  Of France, were known to Martha
As she read in a holy book. The sky-blaze
  Nooned at Padua,
Marble grotto of Bernadette.
  Rose-scatterers. New saints
In tropical Africa where the tsetse
  Fly probes, the forest taints.

Teresa had heard the Lutherans
  Howling on red-hot spit,
And grill, men who had searched for truth
  Alone in Holy Writ.
So Martha, fearful of flame lashing
  Those heretics, each instant,
Never dealt in the haberdashery
  Shop, owned by two Protestants.

In ambush of night, an angel wounded
  The Spaniard to the heart
With iron tip on fire. Swooning
  With pain and bliss as a dart
Moved up and down within her bowels
  Quicker, quicker, each cell
Sweating as if rubbed up with towels,
  Her spirit rose and fell.

St John of the Cross, her friend, in prison
  Awaits the bridal night,
Paler than lilies, his wizened skin
  Flowers. In fifths of flight,
Senses beyond seraphic thought,
  In that divinest clasp,
Enfolding of kisses that cauterize,
  Yield to the soul-spasm.

Cunning in body had come to hate
  All this and stirred by mischief
Haled Martha from heaven. Heart palpitates
  And terror in her stiffens.
Heart misses one beat, two . . . flutters . . . stops.
  Her ears are full of sound.
Half fainting, she stares at the grandfather clock
  As if it were overwound.

The fit had come. Ill-natured flesh
  Despised her soul. No bending
Could ease rib. Around her heart, pressure
  Of wind grew worse. Again,
Again, armchaired without relief,
  She eructated, phelgm
In mouth, forgot the woe, the grief,
  Foretold at Bethlehem.

Tired of the same faces, side-altars,
  She went to the Carmelite Church
At Johnson's Court, confessed her faults,
  There, once a week, purchased
Tea, butter in Chatham St. The pond
  In St Stephen's Green was grand.
She watched the seagulls, ducks, black swan,
  Went home by the 15 tram.

Her beads in hand, Martha became
  A member of the Third Order,
Saved from long purgatorial pain,
  Brown habit and white cord
Her own when cerges had been lit
  Around her coffin. She got
Ninety-five pounds on loan for her bit
  Of clay in the common plot.

Often she thought of a quiet sick-ward,
  Nuns, with delicious ways,
Consoling the miserable: quick
  Tea, toast on trays. Wishing
To rid themselves of her, kind neighbours
  Sent for the ambulance,
Before her brother and sister could hurry
  To help her. Big gate clanged.

No medical examination
  For the new patient. Doctor
Had gone to Cork on holidays.
  Telephone sprang. Hall-lock
Proclaimed the quarters. Clatter of heels
  On tiles. Corridor, ward,
A-whirr with the electric cleaner,
  The creak of window cord.

She could not sleep at night. Feeble
  And old, two women raved
And cried to God. She held her beads.
  O how could she be saved?
The hospital had this and that rule.
  Day-chill unshuttered. Nun, with
Thermometer in reticule,
  Went by. The women mumbled.

Mother Superior believed
  That she was obstinate, self-willed.
Sisters ignored her, hands-in-sleeves,
  Beside a pantry shelf
Or counting pillow-case, soiled sheet.
  They gave her purgatives.
Soul-less, she tottered to the toilet.
  Only her body lived.

Wasted by colitis, refused
  The daily sacrament
By regulation, forbidden use
  Of bed-pan, when meals were sent up,
Behind a screen, she lay, shivering,
  Unable to eat. The soup
Was greasy, mutton, beef or liver,
  Cold. Kitchen has no scruples.

The Nuns had let the field in front
  As an Amusement Park,
Merry-go-round, a noisy month, all
  Heltering-skeltering at darkfall,
Mechanical music, dipper, hold-tights,
  Rifle-crack, crash of dodgems.
The ward, godless with shadow, lights,
  How could she pray to God?

Unpitied, wasting with diarrhea
  And the constant strain,
Poor Child of Mary with one idea,
  She ruptured a small vein,
Bled inwardly to jazz. No priest
  Came. She had been anointed
Two days before, yet knew no peace:
  Her last breath, disappointed.

## *A Strong Wind*

All day a strong wind blew
Across the green and brown from Kerry.
The leaves hurrying, two
By three, over the road, collected
In chattering groups. New berry
Dipped with old branch. Careful insects
Flew low behind their hedges.
Held back by her pretty petticoat,
Butterfly struggled. A bit of
Paper, on which a schoolgirl had written
'Máire loves Jimmy', jumped up
Into a tree. Tapping in haste,
The wind was telegraphing, hundreds
Of miles. All Ireland raced.

## *New Liberty Hall*

Higher than county lark
Can fly, a speck that sings,
Sixteen-floored Liberty Hall
Goes up through scaffoldings
In memory of Larkin,
Shot Connolly. With cap
On simple head, hallmark
Of sweat, new capitalists
Rent out expensive suites
Of glassier offices,
Babel'd above our streets,
The unemployed may scoff, but
Workers must skimp and scrape
To own so fine a skyscraper,
Beyond the dream of Gandon,
Shaming the Custom House
The giant crane, the gantries.
Labour is now accustomed
To higher living. Railing
Is gone that I leaned against
To watch that figure, tall and lean,
Jim Larkin, shouting, railing.
Why should he give a damn
That day for English grammar,
Arm-waving, eloquent?
On top, a green pagoda
Has glorified cement,
Umbrella'd the sun. Go, da,
And shiver in your tenement.

## F. R. HIGGINS

(1896–1941)

### *Song for the Clatter-bones*

God rest that Jewy woman,
Queen Jezebel, the bitch
Who peeled the clothes from her shoulder-bones
Down to her spent teats
As she stretched out of the window
Among the geraniums, where
She chaffed and laughed like one half daft
Titivating her painted hair –

King Jehu he drove to her,
She tipped him a fancy beck;
But he from his knacky side-car spoke,
'Who'll break that dewlapped neck?'
And so she was thrown from the window;
Like Lucifer she fell
Beneath the feet of the horses and they beat
The light out of Jezebel.

That corpse wasn't planted in clover;
Ah, nothing of her was found
Save those grey bones that Hare-foot Mike
Gave me for their lovely sound;
And as once her dancing body
Made star-lit princes sweat,
So I'll just clack: though her ghost lacks a back
There's music in the old bones yet.

## PATRICK MACDONOGH

(1902–61)

### *No Mean City*

Though naughty flesh will multiply
Our chief delight is in division;
Whatever of Divinity
We all are Doctors of Derision.
Content to risk a far salvation
For the quick coinage of a laugh
We cut, to make wit's reputation,
Our total of two friends by half.

### *O, Come to the Land*

O, come to the land of the saint and the scholar
Where learning and piety live without quarrel,
Where the coinage of mind outvalues the dollar
And God is the immanent shaper of thought and behaviour;
Where old ceremonious usage survives as the moral
And actual pattern of grace, where the blood of our Saviour
Is real as our sin, and replenishes spirit and brain
Till they blossom in pity and love as our fields in the rain.

*No, but come to a land where the secret censor*
*Snouts in the dark, where authority smothers*
*The infant conscience and shadows a denser*
*Darkness on ignorant minds in their tortuous groping*
*For spectreless day: a land where austerity mothers*
*The coldly deliberate sins, where harsh masters are roping*
*The heels of the heavenly horse and blinding the bright*
*Incorruptible eye that dares open in passionless light.*

O, come to the land where man is yet master
Of tyrannous time and will pause for the pleasure
Of speech or of sport though worldly disaster
Pluck at torn sleeves; a land where soft voices
Meet answering laughter, where the business of living is leisure,
Where there's no heart so poor but it's kindly and quick
   and rejoices
In horse or in hound or the mettlesome boy with a ball,
Where a jibe's for the proud, but a hand's for the helpless
   from all.

*No, but come to a land where the mediaeval*
*Dread of the woman mutters in corners,*
*Thunders from pulpits, where the only evil*
*Lacking forgiveness is love; a land where the spirit*
*Withers the flowering flesh, where whispering mourners*
*Crowd to the grave of romance and expect to inherit*
*Great scandalous wealth to lighten long evenings and bring*
*A venomous joy to harsh lips whose kiss is a sting.*

O, come to the land where imagination
Fashions the speech of the common people
Rich as a tenement's shattered mouldings
Where the wrong of defeat has bequeathed to a nation
Ironic traditional wit, like a polished steeple
Rising precise and clear from the huddled holdings
Of intricate minds that, in face of Eternity, know
Harsh humour and absolute faith their sole strongholds below.

*No, but come to a land where the dying eagle*
*Is mocked by the crow and the patient vulture,*
*Where nobility fails and the ancient regal*
*Pride of inheritance yields to the last invaders –*
*Image and hare-brained song, the scum of an alien culture*
*Bubbling in village and street, where unmannerly traders*
*And politic slaves have supplanted the gentle and brave,*
*Where the hero will never have honour except in the grave.*

# PATRICK KAVANAGH
## (1904–67)

### *Inniskeen Road: July Evening*

The bicycles go by in twos and threes –
There's a dance in Billy Brennan's barn tonight,
And there's the half-talk code of mysteries
And the wink-and-elbow language of delight.
Half-past eight and there is not a spot
Upon a mile of road, no shadow thrown
That might turn out a man or woman, not
A footfall tapping secrecies of stone.

I have what every poet hates in spite
Of all the solemn talk of contemplation.
Oh, Alexander Selkirk knew the plight
Of being king and government and nation.
A road, a mile of kingdom, I am king
Of banks and stones and every blooming thing.

### *A Christmas Childhood*

I

One side of the potato-pits was white with frost –
How wonderful that was, how wonderful!
And when we put our ears to the paling-post
The music that came out was magical.

The light between the ricks of hay and straw
Was a hole in Heaven's gable. An apple tree
With its December-glinting fruit we saw –
O you, Eve, were the world that tempted me

To eat the knowledge that grew in clay
And death the germ within it! Now and then
I can remember something of the gay
Garden that was childhood's. Again

The tracks of cattle to a drinking-place,
A green stone lying sideways in a ditch,
Or any common sight, the transfigured face
Of a beauty that the world did not touch.

II

My father played the melodion
Outside at our gate;
There were stars in the morning east
And they danced to his music.

Across the wild bogs his melodion called
To Lennons and Callans.
As I pulled on my trousers in a hurry
I knew some strange thing had happened.

Outside in the cow-house my mother
Made the music of milking;
The light of her stable-lamp was a star
And the frost of Bethlehem made it twinkle.

A water-hen screeched in the bog,
Mass-going feet
Crunched the wafer-ice on the pot-holes,
Somebody wistfully twisted the bellows wheel.

My child poet picked out the letters
On the grey stone,
In silver the wonder of a Christmas townland,
The winking glitter of a frosty dawn.

Cassiopeia was over
Cassidy's hanging hill,
I looked and three whin bushes rode across
The horizon – the Three Wise Kings.

An old man passing said:
'Can't he make it talk –
The melodion.' I hid in the doorway
And tightened the belt of my box-pleated coat.

I nicked six nicks on the door-post
With my penknife's big blade –
There was a little one for cutting tobacco.
And I was six Christmases of age.

My father played the melodion,
My mother milked the cows,
And I had a prayer like a white rose pinned
On the Virgin Mary's blouse.

## from *The Great Hunger*

I

Clay is the word and clay is the flesh
Where the potato-gatherers like mechanized scare-crows move
Along the side-fall of the hill – Maguire and his men.
If we watch them an hour is there anything we can prove
Of life as it is broken-backed over the Book
Of Death? Here crows gabble over worms and frogs
And the gulls like old newspapers are blown clear of the hedges,
  luckily.
Is there some light of imagination in these wet clods?
Or why do we stand here shivering?
                                        Which of these men
Loved the light and the queen
Too long virgin? Yesterday was summer. Who was it promised
  marriage to himself

Before apples were hung from the ceilings for Hallowe'en?
We will wait and watch the tragedy to the last curtain,
Till the last soul passively like a bag of wet clay
Rolls down the side of the hill, diverted by the angles
Where the plough missed or a spade stands, straitening the way.

A dog lying on a torn jacket under a heeled-up cart,
A horse nosing along the posied headland, trailing
A rusty plough. Three heads hanging between wide-apart
Legs. October playing a symphony on a slack wire paling.
Maguire watches the drills flattened out
And the flints that lit a candle for him on a June altar
Flameless. The drills slipped by and the days slipped by
And he trembled his head away and ran free from the world's
    halter,
And thought himself wiser than any man in the townland
When he laughed over pints of porter
Of how he came free from every net spread
In the gaps of experience. He shook a knowing head
And pretended to his soul
That children are tedious in hurrying fields of April
Where men are spanging across wide furrows,
Lost in the passion that never needs a wife –
The pricks that pricked were the pointed pins of harrows.
Children scream so loud that the crows could bring
The seed of an acre away with crow-rude jeers.
Patrick Maguire, he called his dog and he flung a stone in the air
And hallooed the birds away that were the birds of the years.
Turn over the weedy clods and tease out the tangled skeins.
What is he looking for there?
He thinks it is a potato, but we know better
Than his mud-gloved fingers probe in this insensitive hair.

'Move forward the basket and balance it steady
In this hollow. Pull down the shafts of that cart, Joe,
And straddle the horse,' Maguire calls.
'The wind's over Brannagan's, now that means rain.
Graip up some withered stalks and see that no potato falls

Over the tail-board going down the ruckety pass –
And *that's* a job we'll have to do in December,
Gravel it and build a kerb on the bog-side. Is that Cassidy's ass
Out in my clover? Curse o' God –
Where is that dog?
Never where he's wanted.' Maguire grunts and spits
Through a clay-wattled moustache and stares about him from the height.
His dream changes again like the cloud-swung wind
And he is not so sure now if his mother was right
When she praised the man who made a field his bride.

Watch him, watch him, that man on a hill whose spirit
Is a wet sack flapping about the knees of time.
He lives that his little fields may stay fertile when his own body
Is spread in the bottom of a ditch under two coulters crossed in Christ's Name.

He was suspicious in his youth as a rat near strange bread
When girls laughed; when they screamed he knew that meant
The cry of fillies in season. He could not walk
The easy road to his destiny. He dreamt
The innocence of young brambles to hooked treachery.
O the grip, O the grip of irregular fields! No man escapes.
It could not be that back of the hills love was free
And ditches straight.
No monster hand lifted up children and put down apes
As here.
'O God if I had been wiser!'
That was his sigh like the brown breeze in the thistles.
He looks towards his house and haggard. 'O God if I had been wiser!'
But now a crumpled leaf from the whitethorn bushes
Darts like a frightened robin, and the fence
Shows the green of after-grass through a little window,
And he knows that his own heart is calling his mother a liar.
God's truth is life – even the grotesque shapes of its foulest fire.

The horse lifts its head and cranes
Through the whins and stones
To lip late passion in the crawling clover.
In the gap there's a bush weighted with boulders like morality,
The fools of life bleed if they climb over.

The wind leans from Brady's, and the coltsfoot leaves are holed
with rust,
Rain fills the cart-tracks and the sole-plate grooves;
A yellow sun reflects in Donaghmoyne
The poignant light in puddles shaped by hooves.

Come with me, Imagination, into this iron house
And we will watch from the doorway the years run back,
And we will know what a peasant's left hand wrote on the page.
Be easy, October. No cackle hen, horse neigh, tree sough, duck
quack.

II

Maguire was faithful to death:
He stayed with his mother till she died
At the age of ninety-one.
She stayed too long,
Wife and mother in one.
When she died
The knuckle-bones were cutting the skin of her son's backside
And he was sixty-five.

O he loved his mother
Above all others.
O he loved his ploughs
And he loved his cows
And his happiest dream
Was to clean his arse
With perennial grass
On the bank of some summer stream;
To smoke his pipe
In a sheltered gripe

In the middle of July –
His face in a mist
And two stones in his fist
And an impotent worm on his thigh.

But his passion became a plague
For he grew feeble bringing the vague
Women of his mind to lust nearness,
Once a week at least flesh must make an appearance.

So Maguire got tired
Of the no-target gun fired
And returned to his headlands of carrots and cabbage,
To the fields once again
Where eunuchs can be men
And life is more lousy than savage.

XIII

The world looks on
And talks of the peasant:
The peasant has no worries;
In his little lyrical fields
He ploughs and sows;
He eats fresh food.
He loves fresh women,
He is his own master;
As it was in the Beginning,
The simpleness of peasant life.
The birds that sing for him are eternal choirs,
Everywhere he walks there are flowers.
His heart is pure,
His mind is clear,
He can talk to God as Moses and Isaiah talked –
The peasant who is only one remove from the beasts he drives.
The travellers stop their cars to gape over the green bank into
his fields: –

*There* is the source from which all cultures rise,
And all religions,
*There* is the pool in which the poet dips
And the musician.
Without the peasant base civilization must die,
Unless the clay is in the mouth the singer's singing is useless.
The travellers touch the roots of the grass and feel renewed
When they grasp the steering wheels again.
The peasant is the unspoiled child of Prophecy,
The peasant is all virtues – let us salute him without irony –
The peasant ploughman who is half a vegetable,
Who can react to sun and rain and sometimes even
Regret that the Maker of Light had not touched him more
    intensely,
Brought him up from the sub-soil to an existence
Of conscious joy. He was not born blind.
He is not always blind: sometimes the cataract yields
To sudden stone-falling or the desire to breed.

The girls pass along the roads
And he can remember what man is,
But there is nothing he can do.
Is there nothing he can do?
Is there no escape?
No escape, no escape.

The cows and horses breed,
And the potato-seed
Gives a bud and a root and rots
In the good mother's way with her sons;
The fledged bird is thrown
From the nest – on its own.
But the peasant in his little acres is tied
To a mother's womb by the wind-toughened navel-cord
Like a goat tethered to the stump of a tree –
He circles around and around wondering why it should be.
No crash,
No drama.

That was how his life happened.
No mad hooves galloping in the sky,
But the weak, washy way of true tragedy –
A sick horse nosing around the meadow for a clean place
to die.

XIV

We may come out into the October reality, Imagination,
The sleety wind no longer slants to the black hill where Maguire
And his men are now collecting the scattered harness and
baskets.
The dog sitting on a wisp of dry stalks
Watches them through the shadows.
'Back in, back in.' One talks to the horse as to a brother.
Maguire himself is patting a potato-pit against the weather –
An old man fondling a new-piled grave:
'Joe, I hope you didn't forget to hide the spade
For there's rogues in the townland. Hide it flat in a furrow.
I think we ought to be finished by tomorrow.'
Their voices through the darkness sound like voices from a cave,
A dull thudding far away, futile, feeble, far away,
First cousins to the ghosts of the townland.

A light stands in a window. Mary Anne
Has the table set and the tea-pot waiting in the ashes.
She goes to the door and listens and then she calls
From the top of the haggard-wall:
'What's keeping you
And the cows to be milked and all the other work there's to do?'
'All right, all right,
We'll not stay here all night.'

Applause, applause,
The curtain falls.
Applause, applause
From the homing carts and the trees
And the bawling cows at the gates.

From the screeching water-hens
And the mill-race heavy with the Lammas floods curving
over the weir.
A train at the station blowing off steam
And the hysterical laughter of the defeated everywhere.
Night, and the futile cards are shuffled again.
Maguire spreads his legs over the impotent cinders that wake no
manhood now
And he hardly looks to see which card is trump.
His sister tightens her legs and her lips and frizzles up
Like the wick of an oil-less lamp.
The curtain falls –
Applause, applause.

Maguire is not afraid of death, the Church will light him a
candle
To see his way through the vaults and he'll understand the
Quality of the clay that dribbles over his coffin.
He'll know the names of the roots that climb down to tickle his
feet.
And he will feel no different than when he walked through
Donaghmoyne.
If he stretches out a hand – a wet clod,
If he opens his nostrils – a dungy smell;
If he opens his eyes once in a million years –
Through a crack in the crust of the earth he may see a face
nodding in
Or a woman's legs. Shut them again for that sight is sin.

He will hardly remember that life happened to him –
Something was brighter a moment. Somebody sang in the
distance.
A procession passed down a mesmerized street.
He remembers names like Easter and Christmas
By the colour his fields were.
Maybe he will be born again, a bird of an angel's conceit
To sing the gospel of life
To a music as flightily tangent
As a tune on an oboe.

And the serious look of the fields will have changed to the leer
of a hobo
Swaggering celestially home to his three wishes granted.
Will that be? will that be?
Or is the earth right that laughs, haw haw,
And does not believe
In an unearthly law.
The earth that says:
Patrick Maguire, the old peasant, can neither be damned nor
glorified;
The graveyard in which he will lie will be just a deep-drilled
potato-field
Where the seed gets no chance to come through
To the fun of the sun.
The tongue in his mouth is the root of a yew.
Silence, silence. The story is done.

He stands in the doorway of his house
A ragged sculpture of the wind,
October creaks the rotted mattress,
The bedposts fall. No hope. No lust.
The hungry fiend
Screams the apocalypse of clay
In every corner of this land.

## *Threshing Morning*

On an apple-ripe September morning
Through the mist-chill fields I went
With a pitchfork on my shoulder
Less for use than for devilment.

The threshing mill was set-up, I knew,
In Cassidy's haggard last night,
And we owed them a day at the threshing
Since last year. O it was delight

To be paying bills of laughter
And chaffy gossip in kind
With work thrown in to ballast
The fantasy-soaring mind.

As I crossed the wooden bridge I wondered,
As I looked into the drain,
If ever a summer morning should find me
Shovelling up eels again.

And I thought of the wasps' nest in the bank
And how I got chased one day
Leaving the drag and the scraw-knife behind,
How I covered my face with hay.

The wet leaves of the cocksfoot
Polished my boots as I
Went round by the glistening bog-holes
Lost in unthinking joy.

I'll be carrying bags today, I mused,
The best job at the mill,
With plenty of time to talk of our loves
As we wait for the bags to fill . . .

Maybe Mary might call round . . .
And then I came to the haggard gate,
And I knew as I entered that I had come
Through fields that were part of no earthly estate.

## *Kerr's Ass*

We borrowed the loan of Kerr's big ass
To go to Dundalk with butter,
Brought him home the evening before the market
An exile that night in Mucker.

We heeled up the cart before the door,
We took the harness inside –
The straw-stuffed straddle, the broken breeching
With bits of bull-wire tied;

The winkers that had no choke-band,
The collar and the reins . . .
In Ealing Broadway, London Town,
I name their several names

Until a world comes to life –
Morning, the silent bog,
And the god of imagination waking
In a Mucker fog.

## *Innocence*

They laughed at one I loved –
The triangular hill that hung
Under the Big Forth. They said
That I was bounded by the whitethorn hedges
Of the little farm and did not know the world.
But I knew that love's doorway to life
Is the same doorway everywhere.

Ashamed of what I loved
I flung her from me and called her a ditch
Although she was smiling at me with violets.

But now I am back in her briary arms;
The dew of an Indian Summer morning lies
On bleached potato-stalks –
What age am I?

I do not know what age I am,
I am no mortal age;
I know nothing of women,
Nothing of cities,
I cannot die
Unless I walk outside these whitethorn hedges.

## *Come Dance with Kitty Stobling*

No, no, no, I know I was not important as I moved
Through the colourful country, I was but a single
Item in the picture, the namer not the beloved.
O tedious man with whom no gods commingle.
Beauty, who has described beauty? Once upon a time
I had a myth that was a lie but it served:
Trees walking across the crests of hills and my rhyme
Cavorting on mile-high stilts and the unnerved
Crowds looking up with terror in their rational faces.
O dance with Kitty Stobling, I outrageously
Cried out-of-sense to them, while their timorous paces
Stumbled behind Jove's page boy paging me.
I had a very pleasant journey, thank you sincerely
For giving me my madness back, or nearly.

## *The Hospital*

A year ago I fell in love with the functional ward
Of a chest hospital: square cubicles in a row,
Plain concrete, wash basins – an art lover's woe,
Not counting how the fellow in the next bed snored.
But nothing whatever is by love debarred,
The common and banal her heat can know.
The corridor led to a stairway and below
Was the inexhaustible adventure of a gravelled yard.

This is what love does to things: the Rialto Bridge,
The main gate that was bent by a heavy lorry,
The seat at the back of a shed that was a suntrap.
Naming these things is the love-act and its pledge;
For we must record love's mystery without claptrap,
Snatch out of time the passionate transitory.

### *The One*

Green, blue, yellow and red –
God is down in the swamps and marshes,
Sensational as April and almost incred-
    ible the flowering of our catharsis.
A humble scene in a backward place
Where no one important ever looked;
The raving flowers looked up in the face
Of the One and the Endless, the Mind that has baulked
The profoundest of mortals. A primrose, a violet,
A violent wild iris – but mostly anonymous performers,
Yet an important occasion as the Muse at her toilet
Prepared to inform the local farmers
That beautiful, beautiful, beautiful God
Was breathing His love by a cut-away bog.

## PADRAIC FALLON

(1905–74)

### *A Flask of Brandy*

You, said the Lionwoman,
Pliz, this errand, a snipe of brandy
From the first shop. Here's money;
And for you this penny.

And on my way I saw:
Item, a clown who waltzed on stilts;
A bear saluting with a paw;
Two pairs of dancing dogs in kilts;
Eight midget ponies in a single file,
A very piccolo of ponies;
Then the princess far off in her smile;
And the seven beautiful distant ladies:
And then –

Facing after the big bandwagon, he
The boy in spangles, lonely and profound:
Behind him the Ringmaster, a redfaced man,
Followed by silence heavy as a wound,
And empty.

Quickly as two feet can did I come back
To the Lionwoman with her cognac.

You, said the Lionwoman;
Pliz to the window, said foreign gutterals in
The cave of the caravan.
I waited, errand done.

And waiting on one foot saw:
Item: a twitching coloured chintz
Moved by a lemontaloned claw:
And after a woman with her face in paints,
A throat thickened in its round of tan
On shoulders sick and white with nature;
Behind was a pair of bloomers on a line,
Blue; a table with a tin platter:
More else:

A black electric cat, a stove, a pot
Purring, and a wild Red Indian blanket
Crouching sidewise on a bunk;
And some exciting smell that stunk
Till the Lionwoman rising blotted out
All but a breast as heavy as a sigh
That stared at me from one bruised eye.

## SAMUEL BECKETT

## (1906–89)

### from *Six Poèmes 1947–1949*

my way is in the sand flowing
between the shingle and the dune
the summer rain rains on my life
on me my life harrying fleeing
to its beginning to its end

my peace is there in the receding mist
when I may cease from treading these long shifting
thresholds
and live the space of a door
that opens and shuts

*

what would I do without this world faceless incurious
where to be lasts but an instant where every instant
spills in the void the ignorance of having been
without this wave where in the end
body and shadow together are engulfed

what would I do without this silence where the murmurs die
the pantings the frenzies towards succour towards love
without this sky that soars
above its ballast dust

what would I do what I did yesterday and the day before
peering out of my deadlight looking for another
wandering like me eddying far from all the living
in a convulsive space
among the voices voiceless
that throng my hiddenness

*

I would like my love to die
and the rain to be raining on the graveyard
and on me walking the streets
mourning her who thought she loved me

## JOHN HEWITT

(1907–87)

### *The Colony*

First came the legions, then the colonists,
provincials, landless citizens, and some
camp-followers of restless generals
content now only with the least of wars.
Among this rabble, some to feel more free
beyond the ready whim of Caesar's fist;
for conscience' sake the best of these, but others
because their debts had tongues, one reckless man,
a tax absconder with a sack of coin.

With these, young lawclerks skilled with chart and stylus,
their boxes crammed with lease-scrolls duly marked
with distances and names, to be defined
when all was mapped.
When they'd surveyed the land,
they gave the richer tillage, tract by tract,
from the great captains down to men-at-arms,
some of the sprawling rents to be retained
by Caesar's mistresses in their far villas.

We planted little towns to garrison
the heaving country, heaping walls of earth
and keeping all our cattle close at hand;
then, thrusting north and west, we felled the trees,
selling them off the foot hills, at a stroke
making quick profits, smoking out the nests
of the barbarian tribesmen, clan by clan,
who hunkered in their blankets, biding chance,
till, unobserved, they slither down and run
with torch and blade among the frontier huts
when guards were nodding, or when shining corn
bade sword-hand grip the sickle. There was once
a terrible year when, huddled in our towns,
my people trembled as the beacons ran
from hill to hill across the countryside,
calling the dispossessed to lift their standards.
There was great slaughter then, man, woman, child,
with fire and pillage of our timbered houses;
we had to build in stone for ever after.

That terror dogs us; back of all our thought
the threat behind the dream, those beacons flare,
and we run headlong screaming in our fear;
fear quickened by the memory of guilt
for we began the plunder – naked men
still have their household gods and holy places,

and what a people loves it will defend.
We took their temples from them and forbade them,
for many years, to worship their strange idols.
They gathered secret, deep in the dripping glens,
chanting their prayers before a lichened rock.

We took the kindlier soils. It had been theirs,
this patient, temperate, slow, indifferent,
crop-yielding, crop-denying, in-neglect-
quickly-returning-to-the-nettle-and-bracken,
sodden and friendly land. We took it from them.
We laboured hard and stubborn, draining, planting,
till half the country took its shape from us.

Only among the hills with hare and kestrel,
will you observe what once this land was like
before we made it fat for human use –
all but the forests, all but the tall trees –
I could invent a legend of those trees,
and how their creatures, dryads, hamadryads,
fled from the copses, hid in thorny bushes,
and grew a crooked and malignant folk,
plotting and waiting for a bitter revenge
on their despoilers. So our troubled thought
is from enchantments of the old tree magic,
but I am not a sick and haunted man . . .

Teams of the tamer natives we employed
to hew and draw, but did not call them slaves.
Some say this was our error. Others claim
we were too slow to make them citizens;
we might have made them Caesar's bravest legions.
This is a matter for historians,
or old beards in the Senate to wag over,
not pertinent to us these many years.

But here and there the land was poor and starved,
which, though we mapped, we did not occupy,
leaving the natives, out of laziness
in our demanding it, to hold unleased
the marshy quarters, fens, the broken hills,
and all the rougher places where the whin
still thrust from limestone with its cracking pods.

They multiplied and came with open hands,
begging a crust because their land was poor,
and they were many; squatting at our gates,
till our towns grew and threw them hovelled lanes
which they inhabit still. You may distinguish,
if you were schooled with us, by pigmentation,
by cast of features or by turn of phrase,
or by the clan-names on them which are they,
among the faces moving in the street.

They worship Heaven strangely, having rites
we snigger at, are known as superstitious,
cunning by nature, never to be trusted,
given to dancing and a kind of song
seductive to the ear, a whining sorrow.
Also they breed like flies. The danger's there;
when Caesar's old and lays his sceptre down,
we'll be a little people, well-outnumbered.

Some of us think our leases have run out
but dig square heels in, keep the roads repaired;
and one or two loud voices would restore
the rack, the yellow patch, the curfewed ghetto.
Most try to ignore the question, going their way,
glad to be living, sure that Caesar's word
is Caesar's bond for legions in our need.
Among us, some, beguiled by their sad music,

make common cause with the natives, in their hearts
hoping to win a truce when the tribes assert
their ancient right and take what once was theirs.
Already from other lands the legions ebb
and men no longer know the Roman peace.

Alone, I have a harder row to hoe:
I think these natives human, think their code,
though strange to us, and farther from the truth,
only a little so – to be redeemed
if they themselves rise up against the spells
and fears their celibates surround them with.
I find their symbols good, as such, for me,
when I walk in dark places of the heart;
but name them not to be misunderstood.
I know no vices they monopolize,
if we allow the forms by hunger bred,
the sores of old oppression, the deep skill
in all evasive acts, the swaddled minds,
admit our load of guilt – I mourn the trees
more than as symbol – and would make amends
by fraternizing, by small friendly gestures,
hoping by patient words I may convince
my people and this people we are changed
from the raw levies which usurped the land,
if not to kin, to co-inhabitants,
as goat and ox may graze in the same field
and each gain something from proximity;
for we have rights drawn from the soil and sky;
the use, the pace, the patient years of labour,
the rain against the lips, the changing light,
the heavy clay-sucked stride, have altered us;
we would be strangers in the Capitol;
this is our country also, nowhere else;
and we shall not be outcast on the world.

## LOUIS MACNEICE
## (1907–63)

### *A Cataract Conceived as the March of Corpses*

The river falls and over the walls the coffins of cold funerals
Slide deep and sleep there in the close tomb of the pool,
And yellow waters lave the grave and pebbles pave its mortuary
And the river horses vault and plunge with their assault and
battery,
And helter-skelter the coffins come and the drums beat and the
waters flow.
And the panther horses lift their hooves and paw and shift and
draw the bier,
The corpses blink in the rush of the river, and out of the water
their chins they tip
And quaff the gush and lip the draught and crook their heads
and crow,
Drowned and drunk with the cataract that carries them and
buries them
And silts them over and covers them and lilts and chuckles over
their bones;
The organ-tones that the winds raise will never pierce the water
ways,
So all they will hear is the fall of hooves and the distant shake
of harness,
And the beat of the bells on the horses' heads and the
undertaker's laughter,
And the murmur that will lose its strength and blur at length to
quietness,
And afterwards the minute heard descending, never ending
heard,
And then the minute after and the minute after the minute after.

## *Valediction*

Their verdure dare not show . . . their verdure dare not show . . .
Cant and randy – the seals' heads bobbing in the tide-flow
Between the islands, sleek and black and irrelevant
They cannot depose logically what they want:
Died by gunshot under borrowed pennons,
Sniped from the wet gorse and taken by the limp fins
And slung like a dead seal in a boghole, beaten up
By peasants with long lips and the whisky-drinker's cough.
Park your car in the city of Dublin, see Sackville Street
Without the sandbags in the old photos, meet
The statues of the patriots, history never dies,
At any rate in Ireland, arson and murder are legacies
Like old rings hollow-eyed without their stones
Dumb talismans.
See Belfast, devout and profane and hard,
Built on reclaimed mud, hammers playing in the shipyard,
Time punched with holes like a steel sheet, time
Hardening the faces, veneering with a grey and speckled rime
The faces under the shawls and caps:
This was my mother-city, these my paps.
Country of callous lava cooled to stone,
Of minute sodden haycocks, of ship-sirens' moan,
Of falling intonations – I would call you to book
I would say to you, Look;
I would say, This is what you have given me
Indifference and sentimentality
A metallic giggle, a fumbling hand,
A heart that leaps to a fife band:
Set these against your water-shafted air
Of amethyst and moonstone, the horses' feet like bells of hair
Shambling beneath the orange cart, the beer-brown spring
Guzzling between the heather, the green gush of Irish spring.
Cursèd be he that curses his mother. I cannot be
Anyone else than what this land engendered me:

In the back of my mind are snips of white, the sails
Of the Lough's fishing-boats, the bellropes lash their tails
When I would peal my thoughts, the bells pull free –
Memory in apostasy.
I would tot up my factors
But who can stand in the way of his soul's steam-tractors?
I can say Ireland is hooey, Ireland is
A gallery of fake tapestries,
But I cannot deny my past to which my self is wed,
The woven figure cannot undo its thread.
On a cardboard lid I saw when I was four
Was the trade-mark of a hound and a round tower,
And that was Irish glamour, and in the cemetery
Sham Celtic crosses claimed our individuality,
And my father talked about the West where years back
He played hurley on the sands with a stick of wrack.
Park your car in Killarney, buy a souvenir
Of green marble or black bog-oak, run up to Clare,
Climb the cliff in the postcard, visit Galway city,
Romanticize on our Spanish blood, leave ten per cent of pity
Under your plate for the emigrant,
Take credit for our sanctity, our heroism and our sterile want
Columba Kevin and briny Brandan the accepted names,
Wolfe Tone and Grattan and Michael Collins the accepted
names,
Admire the suavity with which the architect
Is rebuilding the burnt mansion, recollect
The palmy days of the Horse Show, swank your fill,
But take the Holyhead boat before you pay the bill;
Before you face the consequence
Of inbred soul and climatic maleficence
And pay for the trick beauty of a prism
In drug-dull fatalism.
I will exorcize my blood
And not to have my baby-clothes my shroud
I will acquire an attitude not yours
And become as one of your holiday visitors,
And however often I may come

Farewell, my country, and in perpetuum;
Whatever desire I catch when your wind scours my face
I will take home and put in a glass case
And merely look on
At each new fantasy of badge and gun.
Frost will not touch the hedge of fuchsias,
The land will remain as it was,
But no abiding content can grow out of these minds
Fuddled with blood, always caught by blinds;
The eels go up the Shannon over the great dam;
You cannot change a response by giving it a new name.
Fountain of green and blue curling in the wind
I must go east and stay, not looking behind,
Not knowing on which day the mist is blanket-thick
Nor when sun quilts the valley and quick
Winging shadows of white clouds pass
Over the long hills like a fiddle's phrase.
If I were a dog of sunlight I would bound
From Phoenix Park to Achill Sound,
Picking up the scent of a hundred fugitives
That have broken the mesh of ordinary lives,
But being ordinary too I must in course discuss
What we mean to Ireland or Ireland to us;
I have to observe milestone and curio
The beaten buried gold of an old king's bravado,
Falsetto antiquities, I have to gesture,
Take part in, or renounce, each imposture;
Therefore I resign, good-bye the chequered and the quiet hills
The gaudily-striped Atlantic, the linen-mills
That swallow the shawled file, the black moor where half
A turf-stack stands like a ruined cenotaph;
Good-bye your hens running in and out of the white house
Your absent-minded goats along the road, your black cows
Your greyhounds and your hunters beautifully bred
Your drums and your dolled-up Virgins and your ignorant dead.

## from *Autumn Journal*

### IX

Now we are back to normal, now the mind is
  Back to the even tenor of the usual day
Skidding no longer across the uneasy camber
  Of the nightmare way.
*We* are safe though others have crashed the railings
  Over the river ravine; their wheel-tracks carve the bank
But after the event all we can do is argue
  And count the widening ripples where they sank.
October comes with rain whipping around the ankles
  In waves of white at night
And filling the raw clay trenches (the parks of London
  Are a nasty sight).
In a week I return to work, lecturing, coaching,
  As impresario of the Ancient Greeks
Who wore the chiton and lived on fish and olives
  And talked philosophy or smut in cliques;
Who believed in youth and did not gloze the unpleasant
  Consequences of age;
What is life, one said, or what is pleasant
  Once you have turned the page
Of love? The days grow worse, the dice are loaded
  Against the living man who pays in tears for breath;
Never to be born was the best, call no man happy
  This side death.
Conscious – long before Engels – of necessity
  And therein free
They plotted out their life with truism and humour
  Between the jealous heaven and the callous sea.
And Pindar sang the garland of wild olive
  And Alcibiades lived from hand to mouth

Double-crossing Athens, Persia, Sparta,
  And many died in the city of plague, and many of drouth
In Sicilian quarries, and many by the spear and arrow
  And many more who told their lies too late
Caught in the eternal factions and reactions
  Of the city-state.
And free speech shivered on the pikes of Macedonia
  And later on the swords of Rome
And Athens became a mere university city
  And the goddess born of the foam
Became the kept hetaera, heroine of Menander,
  And the philosopher narrowed his focus, confined
His efforts to putting his own soul in order
  And keeping a quiet mind.
And for a thousand years they went on talking,
  Making such apt remarks,
A race no longer of heroes but of professors
  And crooked business men and secretaries and clerks;
Who turned out dapper little elegiac verses
  On the ironies of fate, the transience of all
Affections, carefully shunning an over-statement
  But working the dying fall.
The Glory that was Greece: put it in a syllabus, grade it
  Page by page
To train the mind or even to point a moral
  For the present age:
Models of logic and lucidity, dignity, sanity,
  The golden mean between opposing ills
Though there were exceptions of course but only
    exceptions –
  The bloody Bacchanals on the Thracian hills.
So the humanist in his room with Jacobean panels
  Chewing his pipe and looking on a lazy quad
Chops the Ancient World to turn a sermon
  To the greater glory of God.
But I can do nothing so useful or so simple;
  These dead are dead

And when I should remember the paragons of Hellas
  I think instead
Of the crooks, the adventurers, the opportunists,
  The careless athletes and the fancy boys,
The hair-splitters, the pedants, the hard-boiled sceptics
  And the Agora and the noise
Of the demagogues and the quacks; and the women pouring
  Libations over graves
And the trimmers at Delphi and the dummies at Sparta and
    lastly
  I think of the slaves.
And how one can imagine oneself among them
  I do not know;
It was all so unimaginably different
  And all so long ago.

## *Autobiography*

In my childhood trees were green
And there was plenty to be seen.

*Come back early or never come.*

My father made the walls resound,
He wore his collar the wrong way round.

*Come back early or never come.*

My mother wore a yellow dress;
Gently, gently, gentleness.

*Come back early or never come.*

When I was five the black dreams came;
Nothing after was quite the same.

*Come back early or never come.*

The dark was talking to the dead;
The lamp was dark beside my bed.

*Come back early or never come.*

When I woke they did not care;
Nobody, nobody was there.

*Come back early or never come.*

When my silent terror cried,
Nobody, nobody replied.

*Come back early or never come.*

I got up; the chilly sun
Saw me walk away alone.

*Come back early or never come.*

## *Neutrality*

The neutral island facing the Atlantic,
The neutral island in the heart of man,
Are bitterly soft reminders of the beginnings
That ended before the end began.

Look into your heart, you will find a County Sligo,
A Knocknarea with for navel a cairn of stones,
You will find the shadow and sheen of a moleskin mountain
And a litter of chronicles and bones.

Look into your heart, you will find fermenting rivers,
Intricacies of gloom and glint,
You will find such ducats of dream and great doubloons of ceremony
As nobody today would mint.

But then look eastward from your heart, there bulks
A continent, close, dark, as archetypal sin,
While to the west off your own shores the mackerel
Are fat – on the flesh of your kin.

## *Soap Suds*

This brand of soap has the same smell as once in the big
House he visited when he was eight: the walls of the bathroom
    open
To reveal a lawn where a great yellow ball rolls back through a
    hoop
To rest at the head of a mallet held in the hands of a child.

And these were the joys of that house: a tower with a telescope;
Two great faded globes, one of the earth, one of the stars;
A stuffed black dog in the hall; a walled garden with bees;
A rabbit warren; a rockery; a vine under glass; the sea.

To which he has now returned. The day of course is fine
And a grown-up voice cries Play! The mallet slowly swings,
Then crack, a great gong booms from the dog-dark hall and the
    ball
Skims forward through the hoop and then through the next and
    then

Through hoops where no hoops were and each dissolves in turn
And the grass has grown head-high and an angry voice cries Play!
But the ball is lost and the mallet slipped long since from the
    hands
Under the running tap that are not the hands of a child.

## *The Taxis*

In the first taxi he was alone tra-la,
No extras on the clock. He tipped ninepence
But the cabby, while he thanked him, looked askance
As though to suggest someone had bummed a ride.

In the second taxi he was alone tra-la
But the clock showed sixpence extra; he tipped according
And the cabby from out his muffler said: 'Make sure
You have left nothing behind tra-la between you.'

In the third taxi he was alone tra-la
But the tip-up seats were down and there was an extra
Charge of one-and-sixpence and an odd
Scent that reminded him of a trip to Cannes.

As for the fourth taxi, he was alone
Tra-la when he hailed it but the cabby looked
Through him and said: 'I can't tra-la well take
So many people, not to speak of the dog.'

## *Charon*

The conductor's hands were black with money:
Hold on to your ticket, he said, the inspector's
Mind is black with suspicion, and hold on to
That dissolving map. We moved through London,
We could see the pigeons through the glass but failed
To hear their rumours of wars, we could see
The lost dog barking but never knew
That his bark was as shrill as a cock crowing,
We just jogged on, at each request
Stop there was a crowd of aggressively vacant
Faces, we just jogged on, eternity
Gave itself airs in revolving lights
And then we came to the Thames and all

The bridges were down, the further shore
Was lost in fog, so we asked the conductor
What we should do. He said: Take the ferry
Faute de mieux. We flicked the flashlight
And there was the ferryman just as Virgil
And Dante had seen him. He looked at us coldly
And his eyes were dead and his hands on the oar
Were black with obols and varicose veins
Marbled his calves and he said to us coldly:
If you want to die you will have to pay for it.

## *The Introduction*

They were introduced in a grave glade
And she frightened him because she was young
And thus too late. Crawly crawly
Went the twigs above their heads and beneath
The grass beneath their feet the larvae
Split themselves laughing. Crawly crawly
Went the cloud above the treetops reaching
For a sun that lacked the nerve to set
And he frightened her because he was old
And thus too early. Crawly crawly
Went the string quartet that was tuning up
In the back of the mind. You two should have met
Long since, he said, or else not now.
The string quartet in the back of the mind
Was all tuned up with nowhere to go.
They were introduced in a green grave.

## W. R. RODGERS
(1909–69)

### *The Net*

Quick, woman, in your net
Catch the silver I fling!
O I am deep in your debt,
Draw tight, skin-tight, the string,
And rake the silver in.
No fisher ever yet
Drew such a cunning ring.

Ah, shifty as the fin
Of any fish this flesh
That, shaken to the shin,
Now shoals into your mesh,
Bursting to be held in;
Purse-proud and pebble-hard,
Its pence like shingle showered.

Open the haul, and shake
The fill of shillings free,
Let all the satchels break
And leap about the knee
In shoals of ecstasy.
Guineas and gills will flake
At each gull-plunge of me.

Though all the Angels, and
Saint Michael at their head,
Nightly contrive to stand
On guard about your bed,
Yet none dare take a hand,
But each can only spread
His eagle-eye instead.

But I, being man, can kiss
And bed-spread-eagle too;
All flesh shall come to this,
Being less than angel is,
Yet higher far in bliss
As it entwines with you.

Come, make no sound, my sweet;
Turn down the candid lamp
And draw the equal quilt
Over our naked guilt.

## MÁIRTÍN Ó DIREÁIN

(1910–88)

### *End of an Era*

My grief on the men of the stories
And the death that fells them!
The shawled women following
And I still alive
Anonymous amid the throng,
Without 'Who's he?' on their lips
Or knowledge of my surname.

Never again will I try
To press friendship on grey stones!
There's no welcome for me on the rock,
Hunting my youth on the way
Like Oisín on the crags,
Nor again along the foreshore
Lamenting the host of the dead.

*PC*

## *Sunday Memory*

I see the Sunday sun beating
Down on the face of the ground
In the beloved island all afternoon;
Much stone, little clay
That's the bleak island's testimony,
The wretched inheritance of my people.

I see how the stone has cast each man,
And bruised him into its own shape.
And I see the crowd who forsook forever
Stone and clay and wretched inheritance,
And I see too each put-upon mother
Composing her brood like a poem to memorize.

*PC*

## *Strong Beams*

Stand your ground, soul:
Hold fast to everything that's rooted,
And don't react like some pubescent boy
When your friends let you down.

Often you've seen a redshank
Lonely on a wet rock;
If he won no spoil from the wave
That was no cause for complaint.

You brought from your dark kingdom
No lucky caul on your head
But protective beams were placed
Firmly round your cradle.

Withered beams they placed round you,
Iron tongs above you,
A piece of your father's clothes beside you
And a poker in the fire below.

Put your weight to your strong oar-beams
Against neap-tide and low water;
Preserve the spark of your vision –
Lose that and you're finished.

*PC*

## SEÁN Ó RÍORDÁIN

(1917–77)

### *Switch*

'Come here,' said Turnbull, 'till you see the sadness
In the horse's eyes,
If you had such big hooves under you there'd be sadness
In your eyes too.'

It was clear that he understood so well the sadness
In the horse's eyes,
And had pondered it so long that in the end he'd plunged
Into the horse's mind.

I looked at the horse to see the sadness
Obvious in its eyes,
And saw Turnbull's eyes looking in my direction
From the horse's head.

I looked at Turnbull one last time
  And saw on his face
Outsize eyes that were dumb with sadness –
  The horse's eyes.

*PC*

## *Despair*

No dead men will leave the tomb
to seek out the confines of night or day.
Abandon your designs on them;
humble your bare head to the clay.

Don't think you can put flesh on a wraith.
The beautiful was never true.
I know that My Redeemer lieth.
No pennies will fall from heaven for you.

You want a pooka to breathe down your neck,
and all the heavenly lies he'd spin.
You've settled for the hump on your back;
don't let it spread to your brain.

Amidst your pooka shadowmancy
find the pooka truth and way.
Cast a hunchshadow all can see
and humble your bare head to the clay.

Make a show of yourself. The critic rates
the hunchshadowself you hide in
that once was laid between the sheets
to kiss while deafness blew from heaven.

And a gentle hand entombed and rotting,
a dream in a separate tomb imprisoned,
the dearest dream, the rarest thing,
in a deep tomb inside the mind,

and the black chalice of night drained low,
and a crooked sleep, tossed left and right,
while Veronica mopped His brow,
while the hunchback stripped bare in the night.

*Hypocrite lecteur* who read
the poem I beget on sickness,
try judging *that* and then decide
what failure is and what success.

*David Wheatley*

## *Claustrophobia*

Next to the wine
Stand a candle and terror,
The statue of my Lord
Bereft of its power;
What's left of the night
Is massing in the yard,
Night's empire
Is outside the window;
If my candle fails
Despite my efforts
The night will leap
Right into my lungs,
My mind will collapse
And terror engulf me,
Taken over by night,
I'll be darkness alive:
  But if my candle lasts
  Just this one night
  I'll be a republic of light
  Until dawn.

*PC*

## *Fever*

The mountains of the bed are high,
The sick-valley sultry with heat,
It's a long way down to the floor,
  And miles and miles further
  To a world of work and leisure.

We're in a land of sheets
Where chairs have no meaning,
But there was a time before this levelled time,
  A walking time long ago,
  When we were high as a window.

The picture on the wall is heaving,
The frame has liquefied,
Without faith I can't hold it at bay,
  Everything's driving at me
  And I feel the world falling away.

A whole district's arriving from the sky,
A neighbourhood's set up on my finger,
Easy now to grab a church –
  There are cows on the northern road
  And the cows of eternity are not so quiet.

*PC*

## MÁIRE MHAC AN TSAOI
## (*b.*1922)

### *Mary Hogan's Quatrains*

I

If I once got free of this net –
And God grant that won't take too long –
I could maybe live on the memory
Of the ease I found in your arms.

When I learn again how to pray,
Hear Mass and go to Communion,
Who'll say then it's not right
To storm heaven for you and for me?

But a bit of advice in the meantime –
Don't get too fondly attached;
For I am intent on breaking
Every bond there could ever be between us.

II

A fig for people's opinions,
A fig for the priest's interdictions,
For everything but lying stretched
Between you and the wall –

The freezing night is nothing,
And nothing the driving rain
To the secret world of warmth that spans
From one side of the bed to the other.

No need to think of the future
Nor of what has gone before –
Now is the hour, dear heart:
It will last until morning.

III

A whole year now I've spent
Stretched beneath your quilt,
It's difficult at this stage to say
What I was hoping to gain!

Your feet trod all over
What was given so freely at first,
While you had never a thought for
What trampled flesh must endure.

And still the body submits
For the sake of an ancient promise,
But now that the song has been stilled in my heart
Delight ebbs from our love-making.

IV

The child of jealousy is suckling my breast
– He demands it by day and by night –
He's an ugly whelp and he's cutting his teeth,
Their grip fills my veins with poison.

Don't let the little wretch divide us, love,
So wholesome and healthy was our mating;
Skin to skin our union's guarantee,
Its seal a hand granted every freedom.

Look, I've no wish to deny affection,
Even if doubt's roots have driven deep;
Don't force a reliable mare, and she'll
Serve you well in the future.

V

Pain is a wonderful thing!
How it wears out the rib-cage,
And gives no relief nor respite
By day or night –

The person in pain like me
Can never be solitary,
Carrying an eternal companion
Like a mother carrying her unborn child.

VI

'I don't sleep at night' –
An easy boast, but who can measure
The weight of the night
On open eyes?

VII

How long tonight is!
There was once a night
We did not think long –
If I dare to remember.

The road I'd follow
Would be no hard road –
If return were permitted
After repentance.

Lying down for pleasure
And rising with delight
Such was our practice –
If I could only resume it.

*PC*

## PEARSE HUTCHINSON

(*b*.1927)

### *Petition to Release*

*for Bert Achong*

And they all go winding assiduously watches –
tiny, jewelled informers, time-jailers
(for time walked round, whipped round a prison-yard,
must find it hard, never achieving oblivion,
telling the world: Wait! and patting pillows).

And they all go winding deciduously watches –
for every twist of the wrist is a leaf loosened,
a life lessened, a lesson learnt, a letter burnt;
the tick-talk may gloss across the losing,
but not the loss. Who can fasten back the leaf?
relive the life? or forget the lesson?
or look at the letter unsigned as it puzzled the anguish
of the angry or penitent lover, while his watch
muttered warnings of late mornings, the witch?

I don't know who the hell could get me to work,
a black boy goes boasting beside Mayaro Bay.
They may all go winding aciduously watches,
but I don't know who the hell could get me to work,
for I'm sweet, not bitter – nor the sea to work,
for it's strong, not petty. But the princess-pretty
thoughts you wear, singer, in your soft blue hair
we share behind our chained wrists and
our winding, assiduous, bitter, brittle days.
For someone stupid like a station-master,
a competent rebel, or a duck-faced emperor,
invented once in a wicked whoopee

espionage and prison against our friend –
el tiempo: amigo mio, nuestro amado.
And all the little ingredients went winding
themselves assiduously up, and finding fun.

Tempus Tyrannus, Tempus Rex,
only wears a crown upon his soft blue hair
(to hide it, so that wise-men declare him decrepit)
when the glass dungeons close out the sun
and the river and the white white girl with a rose
in her soft gold hair and the grinning beggar;
and they all go (the jewelled and brainless jailers),
winding
        assiduously
                watches
                        deciduously
                                chuckling.

## RICHARD MURPHY

## (*b.*1927)

### *Sailing to an Island*

The boom above my knees lifts, and the boat
Drops, and the surge departs, departs, my cheek
Kissed and rejected, kissed, as the gaff sways
A tangent, cuts the infinite sky to red
Maps, and the mast draws eight and eight across
Measureless blue, the boatmen sing or sleep.

We point all day for our chosen island,
Clare, with its crags purpled by legend:
There under castles the hot O'Malleys,
Daughters of Granuaile, the pirate queen

Who boarded a Turk with a blunderbuss,
Comb red hair and assemble cattle.
Across the shelved Atlantic groundswell
Plumbed by the sun's kingfisher rod,
We sail to locate in sea, earth and stone
The myth of a shrewd and brutal swordswoman
Who piously endowed an abbey.
Seven hours we try against wind and tide,
Tack and return, making no headway.
The north wind sticks like a gag in our teeth.

Encased in a mirage, steam on the water,
Loosely we coast where hideous rocks jag,
An acropolis of cormorants, an extinct
Volcano where spiders spin, a purgatory
Guarded by hags and bristled with breakers.

The breeze as we plunge slowly stiffens:
There are hills of sea between us and land,
Between our hopes and the island harbour.
A child vomits. The boat veers and bucks.
There is no refuge on the gannet's cliff.
We are far, far out: the hull is rotten,
The spars are splitting, the rigging is frayed,
And our helmsman laughs uncautiously.
What of those who must earn their living
On the ribald face of a mad mistress?
We in holiday fashion know
This is the boat that belched its crew
Dead on the shingle in the Cleggan disaster.

Now she dips, and the sail hits the water.
She luffs to a squall; is struck; and shudders.
Someone is shouting. The boom, weak as scissors,
Has snapped. The boatman is praying.
Orders thunder and canvas cannonades.
She smothers in spray. We still have a mast;
The oar makes a boom. I am told to cut
Cords out of fishing-lines, fasten the jib.

Ropes lash my cheeks. Ease! Ease at last:
She swings to leeward, we can safely run.
Washed over rails our Clare Island dreams,
With storm behind us we straddle the wakeful
Waters that draw us headfast to Inishbofin.

The bows rock as she overtakes the surge.
We neither sleep nor sing nor talk,
But look to the land where the men are mowing.
What will the islanders think of our folly?

The whispering spontaneous reception committee
Nods and smokes by the calm jetty.
Am I jealous of these courteous fishermen
Who hand us ashore, for knowing the sea
Intimately, for respecting the storm
That took nine of their men on one bad night
And five from Rossadillisk in this very boat?
Their harbour is sheltered. They are slow to tell
The story again. There is local pride
In their home-built ships.
We are advised to return next day by the mail.

But tonight we stay, drinking with people
Happy in the monotony of boats,
Bringing the catch to the Cleggan market,
Cultivating fields, or retiring from America
With enough to soak till morning or old age.

The bench below my knees lifts, and the floor
Drops, and words depart, depart, with faces
Blurred by the smoke. An old man grips my arm,
His shot eyes twitch, quietly dissatisfied.
He has lost his watch, an American gold
From Boston gas-works. He treats the company

To the secretive surge, the sea of his sadness.
I slip outside, fall among stones and nettles,
Crackling dry twigs on an elder tree,
While an accordion drones above the hill.

Later, I reach a room, where the moon stares
Through a cobwebbed window. The tide has ebbed,
Boats are careened in the harbour. Here is a bed.

## *Girl at the Seaside*

I lean on a lighthouse rock
Where the seagowns flow,
A trawler slips from the dock
Sailing years ago.

Wine, tobacco and seamen
Cloud the green air,
A head of snakes in the rain
Talks away desire.

A sailor kisses me
Tasting of mackerel,
I analyse misery
Till Mass bells peal.

I wait for clogs on the cobbles,
Dead feet at night,
Only a tempest blows
Darkness on sealight.

I've argued myself here
To the blue cliff-tops:
I'll drop through the sea-air
Till everything stops.

## THOMAS KINSELLA
(*b*.1928)

### *Chrysalides*

Our last free summer we mooned about at odd hours
Pedalling slowly through country towns, stopping to eat
Chocolate and fruit, tracing our vagaries on the map.

At night we watched in the barn, to the lurch of melodeon music,
The crunching boots of countrymen – huge and weightless
As their shadows – twirling and leaping over the yellow concrete.

Sleeping too little or too much, we awoke at noon
And were received with womanly mockery into the kitchen,
Like calves poking our faces in with enormous hunger.

Daily we strapped our saddlebags and went to experience
A tolerance we shall never know again, confusing
For the last time, for example, the licit and the familiar.

Our instincts blurred with change; a strange wakefulness
Sapped our energies and dulled our slow-beating hearts
To the extremes of feeling – insensitive alike

To the unique succession of our youthful midnights,
When by a window ablaze softly with the virgin moon
Dry scones and jugs of milk awaited us in the dark,

Or to lasting horror, a wedding flight of ants
Spawning to its death, a mute perspiration
Glistening like drops of copper, agonized, in our path.

## *First Light*

A prone couple still sleeps.
Light ascends like a pale gas
Out of the sea: dawn-light
Reaching across the hill
To the dark garden. The grass
Emerges, soaking with grey dew.

Inside, in silence, an empty
Kitchen takes form, tidied and swept,
Blank with marriage – where shrill
Lover and beloved have kept
Another vigil far
Into the night, and raved and wept.

Upstairs a whimper or sigh
Comes from an open bedroom door
And lengthens to an ugly wail
– A child enduring a dream
That grows, at the first touch of day,
Unendurable.

## from *Nightwalker*

2

The human taste grows faint, leaving a taste
Of self and laurel leaves and rotted salt.
And gardens smelling of half-stripped rocks in the dark.

A cast-iron lamp standard on the sea wall
Sheds yellow light on a page of the day's paper
Turning in the gutter:
Our new young minister
Glares in his hunting suit, white haunch on haunch.

Other lamps are lighting along a terrace
Of high Victorian houses, toward the tower
Rising into the dark at the Forty Foot.
The tide drawing back from the promenade
Far as the lamplight can reach, into a dark
Alive with signals. Little bells clonk in the channel
Beyond the rocks; Howth twinkling across the Bay;
Ships' lights moving along invisible sea lanes;
The Bailey light sweeping the middle distance,
Flickering on something.

*

Watcher in the tower,
Be with me now. Turn your milky spectacles
On the sea, unblinking.

A dripping cylinder
Pokes up into sight, picked out by the moon.
Two blazing eyes. Two tough shoulders of muscle
Lit from within by joints and bones of light.
Another head: animal, with nostrils
Straining open, red as embers. Google eyes.
A phantom whinny. Forehooves scrape at the night.
A spectral stink of horse and rider's sweat.
The rider grunts and urges.

Father of Authors!
It is himself! In silk hat, accoutred
In stern jodhpurs. The Sonhusband
Coming in his power, climbing the dark
To his mansion in the sky, to take his place
In the influential circle, mounting to glory
On his big white harse!

A new sign: Foxhunter.
Subjects will find the going hard but rewarding.
You may give offence, but this should pass.
Marry the Boss's daughter.

*

The soiled paper settles back in the gutter.
THE NEW IRELAND . . .

Awkward in the saddle

But able and willing for the foul ditch,
And sitting as well as any at the kill,
Whatever iron Faust opens the gate.

It is begun: curs mill and yelp at your heel,
Backsnapping and grinning. They eye your back.
Beware the smile of the dog.

But you know the breed,
And all it takes to turn them
To a pack of lickspittles running as one.

5

A pulse hisses in my ear.
I am an arrow piercing the void, unevenly
As I correct and correct. But swift as thought.

I arrive enveloped in quiet.
A true desert,
Sterile and odourless. Naked to every peril.

A bluish light beats down,

To kill every bodily thing.
But the shadows are alive.

They scuttle and flicker across the surface,
Searching for any sick spirits,
To suck at the dry juices.

If I stoop down and touch the dust
It has a human taste:
                                        massed human wills.

I believe
                  I have heard of this place. I think
This is the Sea of Disappointment.

*

It is time I turned for home.

Her dear shadow on the blind.
The breadknife. She was slicing and buttering
A loaf of bread. My heart stopped. I starved for speech.

I believe now that love is half persistence,
A medium in which from change to change
Understanding may be gathered.

Hesitant, cogitating, exit.

## JOHN MONTAGUE

(*b.*1929)

### *The Trout*

*for Barrie Cooke*

Flat on the bank I parted
Rushes to ease my hands
In the water without a ripple
And tilt them slowly downstream
To where he lay, tendril-light,
In his fluid sensual dream.

Bodiless lord of creation,
I hung briefly above him
Savouring my own absence,
Senses expanding in the slow
Motion, the photographic calm
That grows before action.

As the curve of my hands
Swung under his body
He surged, with visible pleasure.
I was so preternaturally close
I could count every stipple
But still cast no shadow, until

The two palms crossed in a cage
Under the lightly pulsing gills.
Then (entering my own enlarged
Shape, which rode on the water)
I gripped. To this day I can
Taste his terror on my hands.

## *All Legendary Obstacles*

All legendary obstacles lay between
Us, the long imaginary plain,
The monstrous ruck of mountains
And, swinging across the night,
Flooding the Sacramento, San Joaquin,
The hissing drift of winter rain.

All day I waited, shifting
Nervously from station to bar
As I saw another train sail
By, the San Francisco Chief or
Golden Gate, water dripping
From great flanged wheels.

At midnight you came, pale
Above the negro porter's lamp.
I was too blind with rain
And doubt to speak, but
Reached from the platform
Until our chilled hands met.

You had been travelling for days
With an old lady, who marked
A neat circle on the glass
With her glove, to watch us
Move into the wet darkness
Kissing, still unable to speak.

## *What a View*

*What a view he has*
*of our town, riding*
*inland, the seagull!*

*Rows of shining roofs*
*and cars, the dome of*
*a church, or a bald-*

*headed farmer, and*
*a thousand gutters*
*flowing under the*

*black assembly*
*of chimneys! If*
*he misses anything*

*it might be history*
*(the ivy-strangled*
*O'Neill Tower only*

*a warm shelter to*
*come to roost if*
*crows don't land*

*first, squabbling;*
*and a Planter's*
*late Georgian house*

*with its artificial*
*lake, and avenue of*
*poplars, less than*

*the green cloth of*
*our golf-course where*
*fat worms hide from*

*the sensible shoes*
*of lady golfers).*
*Or religion. He may*

*not recognize who*
*is driving to Mass*
*with his army of*

*freckled children –*
*my second brother –*
*or hear Eustace*

*hammer and plane*
*a new coffin for*
*an old citizen,*

*swearing there is*
*no one God as the*
*chips fly downward!*

*He would be lost,*
*my seagull, to see*
*why the names on*

*one side of the street*
*(MacAteer, Carney)*
*are Irish and ours*

*and the names across*
*(Carnew, MacCrea)*
*are British and theirs*

*but he would understand*
*the charred, sad stump*
*of the factory chimney*

*which will never burn*
*his tail feathers as*
*he perches on it*

*and if a procession,*
Orange *or* Hibernian,
*came stepping through*

*he would hear the*
*same thin, scrannel*
*note, under the drums.*

*And when my mother*
*pokes her nose out*
*once, up and down*

*the narrow street,*
*and retires inside,*
*like the lady in*

*the weather clock,*
*he might well see*
*her point. There are*

*few pickings here,*
*for a seagull, so*
*far inland. A last*

*salute on the flag*
*pole of the British*
*Legion hut, and he*

*flaps away, the*
*small town sinking*
*into its caul*

*of wet, too well-*
*hedged, hillocky*
*Tyrone grassland.*

# SEAMUS HEANEY

## (*b.*1939)

### *Death of a Naturalist*

All year the flax-dam festered in the heart
Of the townland; green and heavy-headed
Flax had rotted there, weighted down by huge sods.
Daily it sweltered in the punishing sun.
Bubbles gargled delicately, bluebottles
Wove a strong gauze of sound around the smell.
There were dragonflies, spotted butterflies,
But best of all was the warm thick slobber
Of frogspawn that grew like clotted water
In the shade of the banks. Here, every spring
I would fill jampotfuls of the jellied
Specks to range on window-sills at home,
On shelves at school, and wait and watch until
The fattening dots burst into nimble-
Swimming tadpoles. Miss Walls would tell us how
The daddy frog was called a bullfrog
And how he croaked and how the mammy frog
Laid hundreds of little eggs and this was
Frogspawn. You could tell the weather by frogs too
For they were yellow in the sun and brown
In rain.

Then one hot day when fields were rank
With cowdung in the grass the angry frogs
Invaded the flax-dam; I ducked through hedges
To a coarse croaking that I had not heard
Before. The air was thick with a bass chorus.
Right down the dam gross-bellied frogs were cocked
On sods; their loose necks pulsed like sails. Some hopped:
The slap and plop were obscene threats. Some sat

Poised like mud grenades, their blunt heads farting.
I sickened, turned, and ran. The great slime kings
Were gathered there for vengeance and I knew
That if I dipped my hand the spawn would clutch it.

## *The Peninsula*

When you have nothing more to say, just drive
For a day all round the peninsula.
The sky is tall as over a runway,
The land without marks, so you will not arrive

But pass through, though always skirting landfall.
At dusk, horizons drink down sea and hill,
The ploughed field swallows the whitewashed gable
And you're in the dark again. Now recall

The glazed foreshore and silhouetted log,
That rock where breakers shredded into rags,
The leggy birds stilted on their own legs,
Islands riding themselves out into the fog,

And drive back home, still with nothing to say
Except that now you will uncode all landscapes
By this: things founded clean on their own shapes,
Water and ground in their extremity.

## *Requiem for the Croppies*

The pockets of our greatcoats full of barley –
No kitchens on the run, no striking camp –
We moved quick and sudden in our own country.
The priest lay behind ditches with the tramp.
A people, hardly marching – on the hike –
We found new tactics happening each day:

We'd cut through reins and rider with the pike
And stampede cattle into infantry,
Then retreat through hedges where cavalry must be
  thrown.
Until, on Vinegar Hill, the fatal conclave.
Terraced thousands died, shaking scythes at cannon.
The hillside blushed, soaked in our broken wave.
They buried us without shroud or coffin
And in August the barley grew up out of the grave.

## *Bogland*

*for T. P. Flanagan*

We have no prairies
To slice a big sun at evening –
Everywhere the eye concedes to
Encroaching horizon,

Is wooed into the cyclops' eye
Of a tarn. Our unfenced country
Is bog that keeps crusting
Between the sights of the sun.

They've taken the skeleton
Of the Great Irish Elk
Out of the peat, set it up,
An astounding crate full of air.

Butter sunk under
More than a hundred years
Was recovered salty and white.
The ground itself is kind, black butter

Melting and opening underfoot,
Missing its last definition
By millions of years.
They'll never dig coal here,

Only the waterlogged trunks
Of great firs, soft as pulp.
Our pioneers keep striking
Inwards and downwards,

Every layer they strip
Seems camped on before.
The bogholes might be Atlantic seepage.
The wet centre is bottomless.

## MICHAEL LONGLEY
## (*b*.1939)

### *In Memoriam*

My father, let no similes eclipse
Where crosses like some forest simplified
Sink roots into my mind; the slow sands
Of your history delay till through your eyes
I read you like a book. Before you died,
Re-enlisting with all the broken soldiers
You bent beneath your rucksack, near collapse,
In anecdote rehearsed and summarized
These words I write in memory. Let yours
And other heartbreaks play into my hands.

Now I see in close-up, in my mind's eye,
The cracked and splintered dead for pity's sake
Each dismal evening predecease the sun,
You, looking death and nightmare in the face
With your kilt, harmonica and gun,
Grow older in a flash, but none the wiser

(Who, following the wrong queue at The Palace,
Have joined the London Scottish by mistake),
Your nineteen years uncertain if and why
Belgium put the kibosh on the Kaiser.

Between the corpses and the soup canteens
You swooned away, watching your future spill.
But, as it was, your proper funeral urn
Had mercifully smashed to smithereens,
To shrapnel shards that sliced your testicle.
That instant I, your most unlikely son,
In No Man's Land was surely left for dead,
Blotted out from your far horizon.
As your voice now is locked inside my head,
I yet was held secure, waiting my turn.

Finally, that lousy war was over.
Stranded in France and in need of proof
You hunted down experimental lovers,
Persuading chorus girls and countesses:
This, father, the last confidence you spoke.
In my twentieth year your old wounds woke
As cancer. Lodging under the same roof
Death was a visitor who hung about,
Strewing the house with pills and bandages,
Till he chose to put your spirit out.

Though they overslept the sequence of events
Which ended with the ambulance outside,
You lingering in the hall, your bowels on fire,
Tears in your eyes, and all your medals spent,
I summon girls who packed at last and went
Underground with you. Their souls again on hire,
Now those lost wives as recreated brides
Take shape before me, materialize.
On the verge of light and happy legend
They lift their skirts like blinds across your eyes.

## MICHAEL HARTNETT
## (1941–99)

### *For My Grandmother, Bridget Halpin*

Maybe morning lightens over
the coldest time in all the day,
but not for you. A bird's hover,
seabird, blackbird, or bird of prey,
was rain, or death, or lost cattle.
The day's warning, like red plovers
so etched and small the clouded sky,
was book to you, and true bible.
You died in utter loneliness,
your acres left to the childless.
You never saw the animals
of God, and the flower under
your feet; and the trees change a leaf;
and the red fur of a fox on
a quiet evening; and the long
birches falling down the hillside.

### *Bread*

Her iron beats
the smell of bread
from damp linen,
silver, crystal,
and warm white things.
Whatever bird
I used to be,
hawk or lapwing,
tern, or something
wild, fierce or shy,

these birds are dead,
and I come here
on tiring wings.
Odours of bread . . .

## *from* Notes on My Contemporaries

### 1 *The Poet Down*

*for Patrick Kavanagh*

He sits between the doctor and the law.
Neither can help. Barbiturate in paw
one, whiskey in paw two, a dying man:
the poet down, and his fell caravan.
They laugh and they mistake the lash that lurks
in his tongue for the honey of his works.
The poet is at bay, the hounds baying,
dig his grave with careful kindness, saying:
'Another whiskey, and make it a large one!'
Priests within, acolytes at the margin
the red impaled bull's roar must fascinate –
they love the dead, the living man they hate.
They were designing monuments – in case –
and making furtive sketches of his face,
and he could hear, above their straining laughs,
the rustling foolscap of their epitaphs.

## DEREK MAHON

## (*b*.1941)

### *Glengormley*

Wonders are many and none is more wonderful than man
Who has tamed the terrier, trimmed the hedge
And grasped the principle of the watering can.
Clothes-pegs litter the window-ledge
And the long ships lie in clover; washing lines
Shake out white linen over the chalk thanes.

Now we are safe from monsters, and the giants
Who tore up sods twelve miles by six
And hurled them out to sea to become islands
Can worry us no more. The sticks
And stones that once broke bones will not now harm
A generation of such sense and charm.

Only words hurt us now. No saint or hero,
Landing at night from the conspiring seas,
Brings dangerous tokens to the new era –
Their sad names linger in the histories.
The unreconciled, in their metaphysical pain,
Dangle from lamp-posts in the dawn rain;

And much dies with them. I should rather praise
A worldly time under this worldly sky –
The terrier-taming, garden-watering days
Those heroes pictured as they struggled through
The quick noose of their finite being. By
Necessity, if not choice, I live here too.

## *Ecclesiastes*

God, you could grow to love it, God-fearing, God-
  chosen purist little puritan that,
for all your wiles and smiles, you are (the
  dank churches, the empty streets,
the shipyard silence, the tied-up swings) and
  shelter your cold heart from the heat
of the world, from woman-inquisition, from the
  bright eyes of children. Yes, you could
wear black, drink water, nourish a fierce zeal
  with locusts and wild honey, and not
feel called upon to understand and forgive
  but only to speak with a bleak
afflatus, and love the January rains when they
  darken the dark doors and sink hard
into the Antrim hills, the bog meadows, the heaped
  graves of your fathers. Bury that red
bandana and stick, that banjo; this is your
  country, close one eye and be king.
Your people await you, their heavy washing
  flaps for you in the housing estates –
a credulous people. God, you could do it, God
  help you, stand on a corner stiff
with rhetoric, promising nothing under the sun.

## EAVAN BOLAND

## (*b.*1944)

### *From the Painting* Back from Market *by Chardin*

Dressed in the colours of a country day –
Grey-blue, blue-grey, the white of seagulls' bodies –
Chardin's peasant woman
Is to be found at all times in her short delay
Of dreams, her eyes mixed
Between love and market, empty flagons of wine
At her feet, bread under her arm. He has fixed
Her limbs in colour and her heart in line.

In her right hand the hindlegs of a hare
Peep from a cloth sack. Through the door
Another woman moves
In painted daylight. Nothing in this bare
Closet has been lost
Or changed. I think of what great art removes:
Hazard and death. The future and the past.
A woman's secret history and her loves –

And even the dawn market from whose bargaining
She has just come back, where men and women
Congregate and go
Among the produce, learning to live from morning
To next day, linked
By a common impulse to survive, although
In surging light they are single and distinct
Like birds in the accumulating snow.

# VIII

# TRANSFORMATIONS: 1971–2009

*Another day when they were sitting on the headland in the Small Fields, the men discussed the changes they had seen and a debate arose about what was the greatest change had happened in their lifetime.*
*'What do you think?' my father asked Dan-Jo.*

Maurice Riordan, 'Idyll 2'

## AUSTIN CLARKE

### from *Tiresias*

#### *from* II

'Strolling one day, beyond the Kalends, on Mount Cyllene,
What should I spy near the dusty track but a couple of
    sun-spotted
Snakes – writhen together – flashen as they copulated,
Dreamily! Curious about the origin of species, I touched them.
Tunic shrank. I felt in alarm two ugly tumours
Swell from my chest. Juno, our universal mother, you
Know how easily a child wets the bed at night. Pardon
Frankness in saying that my enlarged bladder let go.
    "Gods," it
Lamented, "has he become an unfortunate woman, humbled by
Fate, yes, forced twice a day, to crouch down on her hunkers?
Leaf-cutting bee affrights me, Ariadne within her web-rounds."
Timidly hidden as hamadryad against her oak-bark,
I dared to pull up resisting tunic, expose my new breasts –
Saw they were beautiful. Lightly I fingered the nipples
And as they cherried, I felt below the burning answer;
Still drenched, I glanced down, but only a modesty of auburn
Curlets was there. If a man whose limb has been amputated
Still feels the throb of cut arteries, could I forget now
Prickle of pintel? Hour-long I grieved until full moonlight,
Entering the forestry, silvered my breasts. They rose up so
    calmly,
So proud, that peace – taking my hand in gladness – led me
Home, escorted by lucciole.
                                        My mother wept loudly,

Crying, "Forgive me, Tiresias, the fault is
Mine alone for when I carried you in my womb, I
Prayed at the local temple that Our Lady Lucina
Might bestow on me a daughter." Tear-in-smile, she hugged me,
Kissing my lips and breasts, stood back with little starts of
Admiration, hugged me again, spread out our late supper:
Cake, sweet resin'd wine, put me to bed, whispered:
"Twenty-five years ago, I chose the name of Pyrrha
For you. Now I can use it at last." She tucked me in, murmured
"Pyrrha, my latecome Pyrrha, sleep better than I shall."
Next morning
Gaily she said:
"I must instruct you in domestic
Economy, show you, dear daughter, how to make your
own bed, lay
Table, wash up, tidy the house, cook every sort of
Meal, sew, darn, mend, do your hair, then find a well-off
Husband for you. As a young man you have spent too many
Hours in the study of history and science, never frequented
Dance-hall, bull-ring, hurried, I fear, too often to the stews."
Laughter-in-sigh, she handed me a duster.
One fine day
During siesta I gazed in reverence at my naked
Body, slim as a nespoli tree, dared to place my shaving
Mirror of polished silver – a birthday gift from my mother –
Between my legs, inspected this way and that, the fleshy
Folds guarding the shortcut, red as my real lips, to Pleasure
Pass. Next day I awoke in alarm, felt a trickle of blood half-
Way down my thigh.
"Mother," I sobbed.
"Our bold Penates
Pricked me during sleep."
"Let me look at it, Pyrrha."
She laughed, then
Said:
"Why it's nothing to worry about, my pet, all women
Suffer this shame every month."
"What does it mean?"
"That you are

Ready for nuptial bliss."
And saying this, she cleansed, bandaged,
Bound my flowers.
When I recovered, a burning sensation
Stayed. Restless at night, lying on my belly, I longed for
Mortal or centaur to surprise me.
One day during
Siesta, I put on my tanagra dress, tightly
Belted, with flouncy skirt, and carrying a blue mantle,
Tiptoed from our home by shuttered window, barred shop-
front,
Local temple, took the second turn at the trivium,
Reached a sultriness of hills.
I went up a mule-track
Through a high wood beyond the pasturage: a shepherd's
Bothy was there before me. I peeped, saw a bed of bracken
Covered with a worn sheep-skin. I ventured in: listened,
Heard far away *clink-clank*, *clink-clank* as a bell-wether
Grazed with his flock while master and dog were myrtled
Somewhere in the coolness. By now I had almost forgotten
Much of my past, yet remembered the love-songs that
shepherds
Piped among rock-roses to pretty boy or shy goat-girl.
Was it a pastoral air that had led me to this bothy?
Surely I was mistaken. Paper-knife, pumice, goose-quill,
Manuscripts, had been piled untidily together,
Inkstand, wax tablets, small paint-brushes on a rustic
Table.
"A student lives here,"
I thought,
and half-undressing,
Wearily spreading my cloak along the sheepskin,
Lay on blueness, wondered as I closed my eyelids,
"What will he do when he sees me in my déshabillé?"
Soon
Morpheus hid me in undreaming sleep until dusk. I woke up –
Not in the arms of softness but underneath the gentle
Weight of a naked youth.
Vainly I called out, "Almighty

Jove," struggled against his rigid will-power.'
'And yielded?'
'Yes, for how could I stop him when I burned as he did?
In what seemed less than a minute, I had been deflowered
Without pleasure or pang. Once more, the young man
mounted.
Determined by every goddess in high heaven to share his
Spilling, I twined, but just as I was about to . . .'
'What happened?'
'He spent.
O why should the spurren pleasure of expectant
Woman be snaffled within a yard of the grand stand?
While he was resting, I asked him:
"What is your name?"
"Chelos,
Third-year student in Egyptology. Later
I'll show you rolled papyri, hieroglyphics,
Tinted lettering, sand-yellow, Nilus-brown, reed-green,
Outlined with hawk, horn, lotus-bud, sceptre, sun-circles,
Crescent."
He told me of foreign wonders, the Colossus
Guarding the harbour of Rhodes, his cod bulkier than a
Well-filled freighter passing his shins, unfloodable
Temples beyond Assuan, rock-treasuries, the Mountains
Of the Moon, Alexandria and the Pharos –
Night-light of shipping.
Soon in a grotto-spring under fern-drip,
Knee-deep, we sponged one another, back and side, laughing.
Chelos faggoted, tricked the brazier from smoke to flame,
while I
Found in a cupboard cut of ibex, stewed it with carob
Beans, sliced apple, onion, thyme-sprig. And so we had supper,
Sharing a skin of Aetnian wine until the midnight
Hour, then tiptoed tipsily back to our mantled love-bed.
Drowsily entwined, we moved slowly, softly, withholding
Ourselves in sweet delays until at last we yielded,
Mingling our natural flow, feeling it almost linger
Into our sleep.
Stirred by the melilot daylight, I woke up.

Chelos lay asprawl and I knew that he must be dreaming of me
For he murmured "Pyrrha". I fondled his ithyphallus, uncapped it,
Saw for the first time the knob, a purply-red plum, yet firmer.
Covering him like a man, I moved until he gripped:
Faster, yet faster, we sped, determined down-thrust rivalling
Up-thrust – succus glissading us – exquisite spasm
Contracting, dilating, changed into minute preparatory
Orgasms, a pleasure unknown to man, that culminated
Within their narrowing circles into the great orgasmos.'

## RICHARD MURPHY

### *Seals at High Island*

The calamity of seals begins with jaws.
Born in caverns that reverberate
With endless malice of the sea's tongue
Clacking on shingle, they learn to bark back
In fear and sadness and celebration.
The ocean's mouth opens forty feet wide
And closes on a morsel of their rock.

Swayed by the thrust and backfall of the tide,
A dappled grey bull and a brindled cow
Copulate in the green water of a cove.
I watch from a cliff-top, trying not to move.
Sometimes they sink and merge into black shoals;
Then rise for air, his muzzle on her neck,
Their winged feet intertwined as a fishtail.

She opens her fierce mouth like a scarlet flower
Full of white seeds; she holds it open long
At the sunburst in the music of their loving;
And cries a little. But I must remember
How far their feelings are from mine marooned.
If there are tears at this holy ceremony
Theirs are caused by brine and mine by breeze.

When the great bull withdraws his rod, it glows
Like a carnelian candle set in jade.
The cow ripples ashore to feed her calf;
While an old rival, eyeing the deed with hate,
Swims to attack the tired triumphant god.
They rear their heads above the boiling surf,
Their terrible jaws open, jetting blood.

At nightfall they haul out, and mourn the drowned,
Playing to the sea sadly their last quartet,
An improvised requiem that ravishes
Reason, while ripping scale up like a net:
Brings pity trembling down the rocky spine
Of headlands, till the bitter ocean's tongue
Swells in their cove, and smothers their sweet song.

## *Stormpetrel*

Gypsy of the sea
In winter wambling over scurvy whaleroads,
Jooking in the wake of ships,
A sailor hooks you
And carves his girl's name on your beak.

Guest of the storm
Who sweeps you off to party after party,
You flit in a sooty grey coat
Smelling of must
Barefoot across a sea of broken glass.

Waif of the afterglow
On summer nights to meet your mate you jink
Over sea-cliff and graveyard,
Creeping underground
To hatch an egg in a hermit's skull.

Pulse of the rock
You throb till daybreak on your cryptic nest
A song older than fossils,
Ephemeral as thrift.
It ends with a gasp.

## *Morning Call*

Up from trawlers in the fishdock they walk to my house
On high-soled clogs, stepping like fillies back from a forge
Newly shod, to wake me at sunrise from a single bed
With laughter peeling skin from a dream ripening on mossy
Branches of my head – 'Let us in quick!' – and half naked
I stumble over books on the floor to open my glass door
To a flood that crosses the threshold, little blue waves

Nudging each other, dodging rocks they've got to leap over,
Freshening my brackish pools, to tell me of 'O such a night
Below in the boats!' 'We can't go home! What *will* they say?'
Can I think of a lie to protect them from God only knows
What trouble this will cause, what rows? 'We'll run away
And never come back!' – till they flop into black armchairs,
Two beautiful teenage girls from a tribe of tinkers,

Lovely as seals wet from fishing, hauled out on a rock
To dry their dark brown fur glinting with scales of salmon
When the spring tide ebbs. This is their everlasting day
Of being young. They bring to my room the sea's iodine odour
On a breeze of voices ruffling my calm as they comb their long
Hair tangled as weed in a rockpool beginning to settle clear.
Give me the sea-breath from your mouths to breathe a while!

# THOMAS KINSELLA

## *38 Phoenix Street*

Look.
        I was lifted up
past rotten bricks weeds
to look over the wall.
A mammy lifted up a baby on the other side.
Dusty smells. Cat. Flower bells
hanging down purple red.

Look.
        The other. Looking.
My finger picked at a bit of dirt
on top of the wall and a quick
wiry redgolden thing
ran back down a little hole.

*

We knelt up on our chairs in the lamplight
and leaned on the brown plush, watching the gramophone.
The turning record shone and hissed
under the needle, liftfalling, liftfalling.
John McCormack chattered in his box.

Two little tongues of flame burned
in the lamp chimney, wavering
their tips. On the glass belly
little drawnout images quivered.
Jimmy's mammy was drying the delph in the shadows.

*

Mister Cummins always hunched down
sad and still beside the stove,
with his face turned away toward the bars.
His mouth so calm, and always set so sadly.
A black rubbery scar stuck on his white forehead.

Sealed in his sad cave. Hisshorror erecting
slowly out of its rock nests, nosing the air.
He was buried for three days under a hill of dead,
the faces congested down all round him
grinning *Dardanelles!* in the dark.

They noticed him by a thread of blood
glistening among the black crusts on his forehead.
His heart gathered all its weakness, to beat.

A worm hanging down, its little round
black mouth open. Sad father.

*

I spent the night there once
in a strange room, tucked in against the wallpaper
on the other side of our own bedroom wall.

Up in the corner of the darkness the Sacred Heart
leaned down in his long clothes over a red oil lamp
with his women's black hair and his eyes lit up in red,
hurt and blaming. He held out the Heart
with his women's fingers, like a toy.

The lamp-wick, with a tiny head
of red fire, wriggled in its pool.
The shadows flickered: the Heart beat!

## *His Father's Hands*

I drank firmly
and set the glass down between us firmly.
You were saying.

My father
Was saying.

His finger prodded and prodded,
marring his point. Emphas-
emphasemphasis.

I have watched
his father's hands before him

            cupped, and tightening the black Plug
between knife and thumb,
carving off little curlicues
to rub them in the dark of his palms,

or cutting into new leather at his bench,
levering a groove open with his thumb,
insinuating wet sprigs for the hammer.

He kept the sprigs in mouthfuls
and brought them out in silvery
units between his lips.

I took a pinch out of their hole
and knocked them one by one into the wood,
bright points among hundreds gone black,
other children's – cousins and others, grown up.

Or his bow hand scarcely moving,
scraping in the dark corner near the fire,
his plump fingers shifting on the strings.

To his deaf, inclined head
he hugged the fiddle's body
whispering with the tune

with breaking heart
whene'er I hear
in privacy, across a blocked void,

the wind that shakes the barley.
The wind . . .
round her grave . . .

on my breast in blood she died . . .
But blood for blood without remorse
I've ta'en . . .

Beyond that.

*

Your family, Thomas, met with and helped
many of the Croppies in hiding from the Yeos
or on their way home after the defeat
in south Wexford. They sheltered the Laceys
who were later hanged on the Bridge in Ballinglen
between Tinahely and Anacorra.

From hearsay, as far as I can tell
the Men Folk were either Stone Cutters
or masons or probably both.
In the 18
and late 1700s even the farmers
had some other trade to make a living.

They lived in Farnese among a Colony
of North of Ireland or Scotch settlers left there
in some of the dispersals or migrations
which occurred in this Area of Wicklow and Wexford
and Carlow. And some years before that time
the Family came from somewhere around Tullow.

Beyond that.

*

Littered uplands. Dense grass. Rocks everywhere,
wet underneath, retaining memory of the long cold.

First, a prow of land
chosen, and wedged with tracks;
then boulders chosen
and sloped together, stabilized in menace.

I do not like this place.
I do not think the people who lived here
were ever happy. It feels evil.
Terrible things happened.
I feel afraid here when I am on my own.

*

Dispersals or migrations.
Through what evolutions or accidents
toward that peace and patience
by the fireside, that blocked gentleness . . .

That serene pause, with the slashing knife,
in kindly mockery,
as I busy myself with my little nails
at the rude block, his bench.

The blood advancing
– gorging vessel after vessel –
and altering in them
one by one.

Behold, that gentleness already
modulated twice, in others:
to earnestness and iteration;
to an offhandedness, repressing various impulses.

*

Extraordinary . . . The big block – I found it
years afterward in a corner of the yard
in sunlight after rain
and stood it up, wet and black:
it turned under my hands, an axis
of light flashing down its length,
and the wood's soft flesh broke open,
countless little nails
squirming and dropping out of it.

## *Tao and Unfitness at Inistiogue on the River Nore*

### *Noon*

The black flies kept nagging in the heat.
Swarms of them, at every step, snarled
off pats of cow dung spattered in the grass.

Move, if you move, like water.

The punts were knocking by the boathouse, at full tide.
Volumes of water turned the river curve
hushed under an insect haze.

Slips of white,
trout bellies, flicked in the corner of the eye
and dropped back onto the deep mirror.

Respond. Do not interfere. Echo.

Thick green woods along the opposite bank
climbed up from a root-dark recess
eaved with mud-whitened leaves.

*

In a matter of hours all that water is gone,
except for a channel near the far side.
Muck and shingle and pools where the children
wade, stabbing flatfish.

*Afternoon*

Inistiogue itself is perfectly lovely,
like a typical English village, but a bit sullen.
Our voices echoed in sunny corners
among the old houses; we admired
the stonework and gateways, the interplay
of roofs and angled streets.

The square, with its 'village green', lay empty.
The little shops had hardly anything.
The Protestant church was guarded by a woman
of about forty, a retainer, spastic
and indistinct, who drove us out.

An obelisk to the Brownsfoords and a Victorian
Celto-Gothic drinking fountain, erected
by a Tighe widow for the villagers,
'erected' in the centre. An astronomical-looking
sundial stood sentry on a platform
on the corner where High Street went up out of the square.

We drove up, past a long-handled water pump
placed at the turn, with an eye to the effect,
then out of the town for a quarter of a mile
above the valley, and came to the dead gate
of Woodstock, once home of the Tighes.

*

The great ruin presented its flat front
at us, sunstruck. The children disappeared.
Eleanor picked her way around a big fallen branch
and away along the face toward the outbuildings.
I took the grassy front steps and was gathered up
in a brick-red stillness. A rook clattered out of the dining
room.

A sapling, hooked thirty feet up
in a cracked corner, held out a ghost-green
cirrus of leaves. Cavities
of collapsed fireplaces connected silently
about the walls. Deserted spaces, complicated
by door-openings everywhere.

There was a path up among bushes and nettles
over the beaten debris, then a drop, where bricks
and plaster and rafters had fallen into the kitchens.
A line of small choked arches . . . The pantries, possibly.

Be still, as though pure.

A brick, and its dust, fell.

*Nightfall*

The trees we drove under in the dusk
as we threaded back along the river through the woods
were no mere dark growth, but a flitting-place
for ragged feeling, old angers and rumours.

Black and Tan ghosts up there, at home
on the Woodstock heights: an iron mouth
scanning the Kilkenny road: the house
gutted by the townspeople and burned to ruins.

The little Ford we met, and inched past, full of men
we had noticed along the river bank during the week,
disappeared behind us into a fifty-year-old night.
Even their caps and raincoats . . .

Sons, or grandsons. Poachers.
                                        Mud-tasted salmon
slithering in a plastic bag around the boot,
bloodied muscles, disputed since King John.

The ghosts of daughters of the family
waited in the uncut grass as we drove
down to our mock-Austrian lodge and stopped.

*

We untied the punt in the half-light, and pushed out
to take a last hour on the river, until night.
We drifted, but stayed almost still.
The current underneath us
and the tide coming back to the full
cancelled in a gleaming calm, punctuated
by the plop of fish.

Down on the water . . . at eye level . . . in the little light
remaining overhead . . . the mayfly passed in a loose drift,
thick and frail, a hatch slow with sex,
separate morsels trailing their slack filaments,
olive, pale evening dun, imagoes, unseen eggs
dropping from the air, subimagoes, the river filled
with their nymphs ascending and excited trout.

Be subtle, as though not there.

We were near the island – no more than a dark mass
on a sheet of silver – when a man appeared in mid-river
quickly and with scarcely a sound, his paddle touching
left and right of the prow, with a sack behind him.
The flat cot's long body slid past effortless
as a fish, sinewing from side to side,
as he passed us and vanished.

## *At the Western Ocean's Edge*

Hero as liberator. There is also
the warrior marked by Fate, who overmasters
every enemy in the known world
until the elements reveal themselves.
And one, finding the foe inside his head,
who turned the struggle outward, against the sea.

Yeats discovered him through Lady Gregory,
and found him helpful as a second shadow
in his own sour duel with the middle classes.
He grew to know him well in his own right
– mental strife; renewal in reverse;
emotional response; the revelation.

Aogan O Rathaille felt their forces meeting
at the Western ocean's edge
– the energy of chaos and a shaping
counter-energy in throes of balance;
the gale wailing inland off the water
arousing a voice responding in his head,

storming back at the waves with their own force
in a posture of refusal, beggar rags
in tatters in a tempest of particulars.
A battered figure. Setting his face
beyond the ninth shadow, into dead calm.
The stranger waiting on the steel horizon.

### *The Design*

Goodness is required.
It is part of the design.
Badness is understood.
It is a lapse, and part of the design.

Acknowledgment of the good
and condemnation of the bad
are required. Lapses
are not understood.

## JOHN MONTAGUE

### *Windharp*

*for Patrick Collins*

The sounds of Ireland,
that restless whispering
you never get away
from, seeping out of
low bushes and grass,
heatherbells and fern,
wrinkling bog pools,
scraping tree branches,
light hunting cloud,
sound hounding sight,
a hand ceaselessly
combing and stroking
the landscape, till
the valley gleams
like the pile upon
a mountain pony's coat.

## *Herbert Street Revisited*

*for Madeleine*

I

A light is burning late
in this Georgian Dublin street:
someone is leading our old lives!

And our black cat scampers again
through the wet grass of the convent garden
upon his masculine errands.

The pubs shut: a released bull,
Behan shoulders up the street,
topples into our basement, roaring 'John!'

A pony and donkey cropped flank
by flank under the trees opposite;
short neck up, long neck down,

as Nurse Mullen knelt by her bedside
to pray for her lost Mayo hills,
the bruised bodies of Easter Volunteers.

Animals, neighbours, treading the pattern
of one time and place into history,
like our early marriage, while

tall windows looked down upon us
from walls flushed light pink or salmon
watching and enduring succession.

II

As I leave, you whisper,
'Don't betray our truth,'
and like a ghost dancer,
invoking a lost tribal strength,
I halt in tree-fed darkness

to summon back our past,
and celebrate a love that eased
so kindly, the dying bone,
enabling the spirit to sing
of old happiness, when alone.

III

So put the leaves back on the tree,
put the tree back in the ground,
let Brendan trundle his corpse down
the street singing, like Molly Malone.

Let the black cat, tiny emissary
of our happiness, streak again
through the darkness, to fall soft
clawed into a landlord's dustbin.

Let Nurse Mullen take the last
train to Westport, and die upright
in her chair, facing a window
warm with the blue slopes of Nephin.

And let the pony and donkey come –
look, someone has left the gate open –
like hobbyhorses linked in
the slow motion of a dream

parading side by side, down
the length of Herbert Street,
rising and falling, lifting
their hooves through the moonlight.

## *Mount Eagle*

I

The eagle looked at this changing world;
sighed and disappeared into the mountain.

Before he left he had a last reconnoitre:
the multi-coloured boats in the harbour

nodded their masts and a sandy white
crescent of strand smiled back at him.

How he liked the slight, drunk lurch
of the fishing fleet, the tide hoist-

ing them a little, at their ropes' end.
Beyond, wrack, and the jutting rocks

emerging, slowly, monsters stained
and slimed with strands of seaweed.

Ashore, beached boats and lobster-
pots, settled as hens in the sand.

II

Content was life in its easiest form;
another was the sudden growling storm

which the brooding eagle preferred,
bending his huge wings into the winds'

wild buffeting, or thrusting down along
the wide sky, at an angle, slideways

to survey the boats, scurrying homewards,
tacking against the now contrary winds,

all of whom he knew by their names.
To be angry in the morning, calmed

by midday, but brooding again in
the evening was all in a day's quirk

with lengthy intervals for silence,
gliding along, like a blessing, while

the fleet toiled on earnestly beneath
him, bulging with a fine day's catch.

III

But now he had to enter the mountain.
Why? Because a cliff had asked him?

The whole world was changing, with one
language dying; and another encroaching,

bright with buckets, cries of children.
There seemed to be no end to them,

and the region needed a guardian –
so the mountain had told him. And

a different destiny lay before him:
to be the spirit of that mountain.

Everyone would stand in awe of him.
When he was wrapped in the mist's caul

they would withdraw because of him,
peer from behind blind or curtain.

When he lifted his wide forehead
bold with light, in the morning,

they would all laugh and smile with him.
It was a greater task than an eagle's

aloofness, but sometimes, under his oilskin
of coiled mist, he sighs for lost freedom.

## *She Cries*

She puts her face against the wall
and cries, crying for herself,
crying for our children, crying
for all of us
                    in this strange age
of shrinking space, with the needle
of Concorde saluting Mount Gabriel
with its supersonic boom, soaring
from London or Paris to Washington,
a slender, metallic, flying swan

and all the other paraphernalia, hidden
missiles hoarded in silos, bloated
astronauts striding the dusty moon,
and far beyond, our lonely message,
that long probe towards Venus

but most of all for her husband
she cries, against the wall,
the poet at his wooden desk,
that toad with a jewel in his head,
no longer privileged, but still
trying to crash, without faltering,
the sound barrier, the dying word.

## BRENDAN KENNELLY

(*b.* 1936)

### *from* The Book of Judas

#### *prades*

ozzie is stonemad about prades
so he say kummon ta belfast
for de 12th an we see de orangemen
beatin de shit outa de drums
beltin em as if dey was katliks' heads

so we set out from dublin
an landed in belfast for de fun
it was brill
dere was colour an music an everyone
was havin a go at sumtin i dunno

what but i'll never forget ozzie in
de middul of all de excitement
pickin pockets right left and centre

on de train back to dublin he was laffin his head
off, dere shud be more fukken prades he said

### from *The Man Made of Rain*

#### 21

There's no edge, only a new place with
one side veering away into nothing and
Mary Moroney is kindness itself, all care
loving care, turns over that body anytime
day or night.

Colours of the left leg, cut from ankle to groin
or groin to ankle if you prefer, I like
ankle to groin for reasons I'll not go into here,
invade the head and capture
three major cities
with the convinced skill of Oliver Cromwell
my old foepal for whom I received
a whack on the jaw on O'Connell Bridge
the night after I mentioned to Gaybo
Oliver had a lot going for him
and we could do with a visit now.
He'd show the killers how to behave so he would,
he'd take the shine off their bliss,
he'd lay down the law, the Lugs Branigan.

Black yellow red brown and
a vaguely disgusting white
are the colours of my left leg.
They hurtle into each other like dirty footballers,
you'd swear my colours wanted to knock each other out,
I was white once, or as white as the next Paddy,
the only thing to do when you're backward is
let yourself fly, I'm blueredblackyellowbrown
                                and I don't mind it at all
so don't give it a thought if you see me cry.

I never thought I'd see the day
when I'd cry like the rain
and not begin to know why.

Truth is the tears I can never explain.

Say I'm buried, say I'm on show somewhere,
on exhibition in Merrion Square,
a postmodern explosion of latent rebellions,
Handy Andy from New York would enjoy me
and I haven't even been bombed
or expelled from my province
to become a sly colonizing refugee

with a genius for eliciting sympathy.
I haven't cut off my ear
or jumped off a bridge
or distinguished between essential and obvious
because here you could take these labels
turn them upside down for a laugh
and find the battle of the colours
going on in my skin
in that room in the Gallery
where they hang masterpieces
like Judas moving in for the kiss
discovered in old Jesuits' bedrooms
or Big Houses down the country
the IRA forgot to burn
or was it the other lads?
Someone will burn them some day,
                    don't worry your head.

Black yellow brown red
blood on the pillow

a woman in my bed
where did she come from?

It was like a tractor going over your body,
says Shirley Love
with the angeltouch.

Massey Ferguson was my favourite tractor,
treacherous bastards tractors are,
plough you into the ground in no time at all
when you wouldn't be looking
with nothing but the green green
grass of home for company
and a trickle of red, you wonder
a moment what is the source of red,
red red who called it red,
woman nowoman in my bed?

Eyelids fall.

The colours are even clearer now
and a few new ones
have joined the company.
These new ones were born in the mind of snow
but they never honoured me till now.

O the colours of pain
are enough to make me dance
at a feis in a field
between Asdee and Ballybunion.

Dance, sing the colours, dance
till he comes, man of rain
whose colours the rainbow envies.

He looks at the colours of my left leg,
touches them, they start to change
into the colours of each other,
Jews into Arabs, Arabs into Jews,
Ulster Protestants into Ulster Catholics
and vice versa, making new colours,
no words for them, not yet, no words
needed they flow
like trout like eels in the Feale,
there is no edge, only this new place

where I am real, real

as my colours
in late October
with leaves falling

and Dermot Gillespie
in the next bed
breathing,

against all the evidence

breathing.

## SEAMUS HEANEY

### *Broagh*

Riverbank, the long rigs
ending in broad docken
and a canopied pad
down to the ford.

The garden mould
bruised easily, the shower
gathering in your heelmark
was the black O

in *Broagh*,
its low tattoo
among the windy boortrees
and rhubarb-blades

ended almost
suddenly, like that last
*gh* the strangers found
difficult to manage.

### *The Tollund Man*

I

Some day I will go to Aarhus
To see his peat-brown head,
The mild pods of his eyelids,
His pointed skin cap.

In the flat country nearby
Where they dug him out,
His last gruel of winter seeds
Caked in his stomach,

Naked except for
The cap, noose and girdle,
I will stand a long time.
Bridegroom to the goddess,

She tightened her torc on him
And opened her fen,
Those dark juices working
Him to a saint's kept body,

Trove of the turfcutters'
Honeycombed workings.
Now his stained face
Reposes at Aarhus.

II

I could risk blasphemy,
Consecrate the cauldron bog
Our holy ground and pray
Him to make germinate

The scattered, ambushed
Flesh of labourers,
Stockinged corpses
Laid out in the farmyards,

Tell-tale skin and teeth
Flecking the sleepers
Of four young brothers, trailed
For miles along the lines.

III

Something of his sad freedom
As he rode the tumbril
Should come to me, driving,
Saying the names

Tollund, Grauballe, Nebelgard,
Watching the pointing hands
Of country people,
Not knowing their tongue.

Out there in Jutland
In the old man-killing parishes
I will feel lost,
Unhappy and at home.

## *The Strand at Lough Beg*

*in memory of Colum McCartney*

*All round this little island, on the strand*
*Far down below there, where the breakers strive,*
*Grow the tall rushes from the oozy sand.*
Dante, *Purgatorio*, I, 100–103

Leaving the white glow of filling stations
And a few lonely streetlamps among fields
You climbed the hills towards Newtownhamilton
Past the Fews Forest, out beneath the stars –
Along that road, a high, bare pilgrim's track
Where Sweeney fled before the bloodied heads,
Goat-beards and dogs' eyes in a demon pack
Blazing out of the ground, snapping and squealing.
What blazed ahead of you? A faked roadblock?
The red lamp swung, the sudden brakes and stalling
Engine, voices, heads hooded and the cold-nosed gun?
Or in your driving mirror, tailing headlights

That pulled out suddenly and flagged you down
Where you weren't known and far from what you knew:
The lowland clays and waters of Lough Beg,
Church Island's spire, its soft treeline of yew.

There you once heard guns fired behind the house
Long before rising time, when duck shooters
Haunted the marigolds and bulrushes,
But still were scared to find spent cartridges,
Acrid, brassy, genital, ejected,
On your way across the strand to fetch the cows.
For you and yours and yours and mine fought shy,
Spoke an old language of conspirators
And could not crack the whip or seize the day:
Big-voiced scullions, herders, feelers round
Haycocks and hindquarters, talkers in byres,
Slow arbitrators of the burial ground.

Across that strand of yours the cattle graze
Up to their bellies in an early mist
And now they turn their unbewildered gaze
To where we work our way through squeaking sedge
Drowning in dew. Like a dull blade with its edge
Honed bright, Lough Beg half-shines under the haze.
I turn because the sweeping of your feet
Has stopped behind me, to find you on your knees
With blood and roadside muck in your hair and eyes,
Then kneel in front of you in brimming grass
And gather up cold handfuls of the dew
To wash you, cousin. I dab you clean with moss
Fine as the drizzle out of a low cloud.
I lift you under the arms and lay you flat.
With rushes that shoot green again, I plait
Green scapulars to wear over your shroud.

## *Song*

A rowan like a lipsticked girl.
Between the by-road and the main road
Alder trees at a wet and dripping distance
Stand off among the rushes.

There are the mud-flowers of dialect
And the immortelles of perfect pitch
And that moment when the bird sings very close
To the music of what happens.

## *The Harvest Bow*

As you plaited the harvest bow
You implicated the mellowed silence in you
In wheat that does not rust
But brightens as it tightens twist by twist
Into a knowable corona,
A throwaway love-knot of straw.

Hands that aged round ashplants and cane sticks
And lapped the spurs on a lifetime of gamecocks
Harked to their gift and worked with fine intent
Until your fingers moved somnambulant:
I tell and finger it like braille,
Gleaning the unsaid off the palpable,

And if I spy into its golden loops
I see us walk between the railway slopes
Into an evening of long grass and midges,
Blue smoke straight up, old beds and ploughs in hedges,
An auction notice on an outhouse wall –
You with a harvest bow in your lapel,

Me with the fishing rod, already homesick
For the big lift of these evenings, as your stick
Whacking the tips off weeds and bushes
Beats out of time, and beats, but flushes
Nothing: that original townland
Still tongue-tied in the straw tied by your hand.

*The end of art is peace*
Could be the motto of this frail device
That I have pinned up on our deal dresser –
Like a drawn snare
Slipped lately by the spirit of the corn
Yet burnished by its passage, and still warm.

## *from* Sweeney Redivivus

### *The Cleric*

I heard new words prayed at cows
in the byre, found his sign
on the crock and the hidden still,

smelled fumes from his censer
in the first smokes of morning.
Next thing he was making a progress

through gaps, stepping out sites,
sinking his crozier deep
in the fort-hearth.

If he had stuck to his own
cramp-jawed abbesses and intoners
dibbling round the enclosure,

his Latin and blather of love,
his parchments and scheming
in letters shipped over water –

but no, he overbore
with his unctions and orders,
he had to get in on the ground.

History that planted its standards
on his gables and spires
ousted me to the marches

of skulking and whingeing.
Or did I desert?
Give him his due, in the end

he opened my path to a kingdom
of such scope and neuter allegiance
my emptiness reigns at its whim.

## *The Scribes*

I never warmed to them.
If they were excellent they were petulant
and jaggy as the holly tree
they rendered down for ink.
And if I never belonged among them,
they could never deny me my place.

In the hush of the scriptorium
a black pearl kept gathering in them
like the old dry glut inside their quills.
In the margin of texts of praise
they scratched and clawed.
They snarled if the day was dark
or too much chalk had made the vellum bland
or too little left it oily.

Under the rumps of lettering
they herded myopic angers.
Resentment seeded in the uncurling
fernheads of their capitals.

Now and again I started up
miles away and saw in my absence
the sloped cursive of each back and felt them
perfect themselves against me page by page.

Let them remember this not inconsiderable
contribution to their jealous art.

## *Hailstones*

I

My cheek was hit and hit:
sudden hailstones
pelted and bounced on the road.

When it cleared again
something whipped and knowledgeable
had withdrawn

and left me there with my chances.
I made a small hard ball
of burning water running from my hand

just as I make this now
out of the melt of the real thing
smarting into its absence.

II

To be reckoned with, all the same,
those brats of showers.
The way they refused permission,

rattling the classroom window
like a ruler across the knuckles,
the way they were perfect first

and then in no time dirty slush.
Thomas Traherne had his orient wheat
for proof and wonder

but for us, it was the sting of hailstones
and the unstingable hands of Eddie Diamond
foraging in the nettles.

III

Nipple and hive, bite-lumps,
small acorns of the almost pleasurable
intimated and disallowed

when the shower ended
and everything said *wait*.
For what? For forty years

to say there, there you had
the truest foretaste of your aftermath –
in that dilation

when the light opened in silence
and a car with wipers going still
laid perfect tracks in the slush.

## from *Settings*

### XIV

One afternoon I was seraph on gold leaf.
I stood on the railway sleepers hearing larks,
Grasshoppers, cuckoos, dog-barks, trainer planes

Cutting and modulating and drawing off.
Heat wavered on the immaculate line
And shine of the cogged rails. On either side,

Dog daisies stood like vestals, the hot stones
Were clover-meshed and streaked with engine oil.
Air spanned, passage waited, the balance rode,

Nothing prevailed, whatever was in store
Witnessed itself already taking place
In a time marked by assent and by hiatus.

### XV

And strike this scene in gold too, in relief,
So that a greedy eye cannot exhaust it:
Stable straw, Rembrandt-gleam and burnish

Where my father bends to a tea-chest packed with salt,
The hurricane lamp held up at eye-level
In his bunched left fist, his right hand foraging

For the unbleeding, vivid-fleshed bacon,
Home-cured hocks pulled up into the light
For pondering a while and putting back.

That night I owned the piled grain of Egypt.
I watched the sentry's torchlight on the hoard.
I stood in the door, unseen and blazed upon.

## *A Sofa in the Forties*

All of us on the sofa in a line, kneeling
Behind each other, eldest down to youngest,
Elbows going like pistons, for this was a train

And between the jamb-wall and the bedroom door
Our speed and distance were inestimable.
First we shunted, then we whistled, then

Somebody collected the invisible
For tickets and very gravely punched it
As carriage after carriage under us

Moved faster, *chooka-chook*, the sofa legs
Went giddy and the unreachable ones
Far out on the kitchen floor began to wave.

*

Ghost-train? Death-gondola? The carved, curved ends,
Black leatherette and ornate gauntness of it
Made it seem the sofa had achieved

Flotation. Its castors on tiptoe,
Its braid and fluent backboard gave it airs
Of superannuated pageantry:

When visitors endured it, straight-backed,
When it stood off in its own remoteness,
When the insufficient toys appeared on it

On Christmas mornings, it held out as itself,
Potentially heavenbound, earthbound for sure,
Among things that might add up or let you down.

*

We entered history and ignorance
Under the wireless shelf. *Yippee-i-ay*,
Sang 'The Riders of the Range'. HERE IS THE NEWS

Said the absolute speaker. Between him and us
A great gulf was fixed where pronunciation
Reigned tyrannically. The aerial wire

Swept from a treetop down in through a hole
Bored in the windowframe. When it moved in wind
The sway of language and its furtherings

Swept and swayed in us like nets in water
Or the abstract, lonely curve of distant trains
As we entered history and ignorance.

*

We occupied our seats with all our might,
Fit for the uncomfortableness.
Constancy was its own reward already.

Out in front, on the big upholstered arm,
Somebody craned to the side, driver or
Fireman, wiping his dry brow with the air

Of one who had run the gauntlet. We were
The last thing on his mind, it seemed; we sensed
A tunnel coming up where we'd pour through

Like unlit carriages through fields at night,
Our only job to sit, eyes straight ahead,
And be transported and make engine noise.

## *Postscript*

And some time make the time to drive out west
Into County Clare, along the Flaggy Shore,
In September or October, when the wind
And the light are working off each other
So that the ocean on one side is wild
With foam and glitter, and inland among stones
The surface of a slate-grey lake is lit
By the earthed lightning of a flock of swans,
Their feathers roughed and ruffling, white on white,
Their fully grown headstrong-looking heads
Tucked or cresting or busy underwater.
Useless to think you'll park and capture it
More thoroughly. You are neither here nor there,
A hurry through which known and strange things pass
As big soft buffetings come at the car sideways
And catch the heart off guard and blow it open.

## *Perch*

Perch on their water-perch hung in the clear Bann River
Near the clay bank in alder-dapple and waver,

Perch we called 'grunts', little flood-slubs, runty and ready,
I saw and I see in the river's glorified body

That is passable through, but they're bluntly holding the pass,
Under the water-roof, over the bottom, adoze,

Guzzling the current, against it, all muscle and slur
In the finland of perch, the fenland of alder, on air

That is water, on carpets of Bann stream, on hold
In the everything flows and steady go of the world.

## *The Blackbird of Glanmore*

On the grass when I arrive,
Filling the stillness with life,
But ready to scare off
At the very first wrong move.
In the ivy when I leave.

It's you, blackbird, I love.

I park, pause, take heed.
Breathe. Just breathe and sit
And lines I once translated
Come back: 'I want away
To the house of death, to my father

Under the low clay roof.'

And I think of one gone to him,
A little stillness dancer –
Haunter-son, lost brother –
Cavorting through the yard,
So glad to see me home,

My homesick first term over.

And think of a neighbour's words
Long after the accident:
'Yon bird on the shed roof,
Up on the ridge for weeks –
I said nothing at the time

But I never liked yon bird.'

The automatic lock
Clunks shut, the blackbird's panic
Is shortlived, for a second
I've a bird's eye view of myself,
A shadow on raked gravel

In front of my house of life.

Hedge-hop, I am absolute
For you, your ready talkback,
Your each stand-offish comeback,
Your picky, nervy goldbeak –
On the grass when I arrive,

In the ivy when I leave.

## MICHAEL LONGLEY

### *Wounds*

Here are two pictures from my father's head –
I have kept them like secrets until now:
First, the Ulster Division at the Somme
Going over the top with 'Fuck the Pope!'
'No Surrender!': a boy about to die,
Screaming 'Give 'em one for the Shankill!'
'Wilder than Gurkhas' were my father's words
Of admiration and bewilderment.
Next comes the London-Scottish padre
Resettling kilts with his swagger-stick,
With a stylish backhand and a prayer.
Over a landscape of dead buttocks
My father followed him for fifty years.
At last, a belated casualty,

He said – lead traces flaring till they hurt –
'I am dying for King and Country, slowly.'
I touched his hand, his thin head I touched.

Now, with military honours of a kind,
With his badges, his medals like rainbows,
His spinning compass, I bury beside him
Three teenage soldiers, bellies full of
Bullets and Irish beer, their flies undone.
A packet of Woodbines I throw in,
A lucifer, the Sacred Heart of Jesus
Paralysed as heavy guns put out
The night-light in a nursery for ever;
Also a bus-conductor's uniform –
He collapsed beside his carpet-slippers
Without a murmur, shot through the head
By a shivering boy who wandered in
Before they could turn the television down
Or tidy away the supper dishes.
To the children, to a bewildered wife,
I think 'Sorry Missus' was what he said.

## *The Linen Industry*

Pulling up flax after the blue flowers have fallen
And laying our handfuls in the peaty water
To rot those grasses to the bone, or building stooks
That recall the skirts of an invisible dancer,

We become a part of the linen industry
And follow its processes to the grubby town
Where fields are compacted into window-boxes
And there is little room among the big machines.

But even in our attic under the skylight
We make love on a bleach green, the whole meadow
Draped with material turning white in the sun
As though snow reluctant to melt were our attire.

What's passion but a battering of stubborn stalks,
Then a gentle combing out of fibres like hair
And a weaving of these into christening robes,
Into garments for a marriage or funeral?

Since it's like a bereavement once the labour's done
To find ourselves last workers in a dying trade,
Let flax be our matchmaker, our undertaker,
The provider of sheets for whatever the bed –

And be shy of your breasts in the presence of death,
Say that you look more beautiful in linen
Wearing white petticoats, the bow on your bodice
A butterfly attending the embroidered flowers.

## *Between Hovers*

*in memory of Joe O'Toole*

And not even when we ran over the badger
Did he tell me he had cancer, Joe O'Toole
Who was psychic about carburettor and clutch
And knew a folk cure for the starter-engine.
Backing into the dark we floodlit each hair
Like a filament of light our lights had put out
Somewhere between Kinnadoohy and Thallabaun.
I dragged it by two gritty paws into the ditch.
Joe spotted a ruby where the canines touched.
His way of seeing me safely across the duach
Was to leave his porch light burning, its sparkle
Shifting from widgeon to teal on Corragaun Lake.
I missed his funeral. Close to the stony roads
He lies in Killeen Churchyard over the hill.

This morning on the burial mound at Templedoomore
Encircled by a spring tide and taking in
Cloonaghmanagh and Claggan and Carrigskeewaun,
The townlands he'd wandered tending cows and sheep,
I watched a dying otter gaze right through me
At the islands in Clew Bay, as though it were only
Between hovers and not too far from the holt.

## *The Butchers*

When he had made sure there were no survivors in his house
And that all the suitors were dead, heaped in blood and dust
Like fish that fishermen with fine-meshed nets have hauled
Up gasping for salt water, evaporating in the sunshine,
Odysseus, spattered with muck and like a lion dripping blood
From his chest and cheeks after devouring a farmer's bullock,
Ordered the disloyal housemaids to sponge down the armchairs
And tables, while Telemachos, the oxherd and the swineherd
Scraped the floor with shovels, and then between the portico
And the roundhouse stretched a hawser and hanged the women
So none touched the ground with her toes, like long-winged thrushes
Or doves trapped in a mist-net across the thicket where they roost,
Their heads bobbing in a row, their feet twitching but not for long,
And when they had dragged Melanthios's corpse into the haggard
And cut off his nose and ears and cock and balls, a dog's dinner,
Odysseus, seeing the need for whitewash and disinfectant,
Fumigated the house and the outhouses, so that Hermes
Like a clergyman might wave the supernatural baton
With which he resurrects or hypnotizes those he chooses,
And waken and round up the suitors' souls, and the housemaids',
Like bats gibbering in the nooks of their mysterious cave
When out of the clusters that dangle from the rocky ceiling
One of them drops and squeaks, so their souls were bat-squeaks

As they flittered after Hermes, their deliverer, who led them
Along the clammy sheughs, then past the oceanic streams
And the white rock, the sun's gatepost in that dreamy region,
Until they came to a bog-meadow full of bog-asphodels
Where the residents are ghosts or images of the dead.

## *Form*

Trying to tell it all to you and cover everything
Is like awakening from its grassy form the hare:
In that make-shift shelter your hand, then my hand
Mislays the hare and the warmth it leaves behind.

## *The Campfires*

All night crackling campfires boosted their morale
As they dozed in no man's land and the killing fields.
(There are balmy nights – not a breath, constellations
Resplendent in the sky around a dazzling moon –
When a clearance high in the atmosphere unveils
The boundlessness of space, and all the stars are out
Lighting up hilltops, glens, headlands, vantage
Points like Tonakeera and Allaran where the tide
Turns into Killary, where salmon run from the sea,
Where the shepherd smiles on his luminous townland.
That many camp-fires sparkled in front of Ilium
Between the river and the ships, a thousand fires,
Round each one fifty men relaxing in the fire-light.)
Shuffling next to the chariots, munching shiny oats
And barley, their horses waited for the sunrise.

## *Ceasefire*

I

Put in mind of his own father and moved to tears
Achilles took him by the hand and pushed the old king
Gently away, but Priam curled up at his feet and
Wept with him until their sadness filled the building.

II

Taking Hector's corpse into his own hands Achilles
Made sure it was washed and, for the old king's sake,
Laid out in uniform, ready for Priam to carry
Wrapped like a present home to Troy at daybreak.

III

When they had eaten together, it pleased them both
To stare at each other's beauty as lovers might,
Achilles built like a god, Priam good-looking still
And full of conversation, who earlier had sighed:

IV

'I get down on my knees and do what must be done
And kiss Achilles' hand, the killer of my son.'

## *The Evening Star*

*in memory of Catherine Mercer, 1994–96*

The day we buried your two years and two months
So many crocuses and snowdrops came out for you
I tried to isolate from those galaxies one flower:
A snowdrop appeared in the sky at dayligone,

The evening star, the star in Sappho's epigram
Which brings back everything that shiny daybreak
Scatters, which brings the sheep and brings the goat
And brings the wean back home to her mammy.

## *Overhead*

The beech tree looks circular from overhead
With its own little cumulus of exhalations.
Can you spot my skull under the nearby roof,
Its bald patch, the poem-cloud hanging there?

## *Above Dooaghtry*

Where the duach rises to a small plateau
That overlooks the sand dunes from Dooaghtry
To Roonkeel, and just beyond the cottage's
Higgledy perimeter fence-posts
At Carrigskeewaun, bury my ashes,

For the burial mound at Templedoomore
Has been erased by wind and sea, the same
Old stone-age sea that came as far inland
As Cloonaghmanagh and chose the place
That I choose as a promontory, a fort:

Let boulders at the top encircle me,
Neither a drystone wall nor a cairn, space
For the otter to die and the mountain hare
To lick snow stains from her underside,
A table for the peregrine and ravens,

A prickly double-bed as well, nettles
And carline-thistles, a sheeps' wool pillow,
So that, should she decide to join me there,
Our sandy dander to Allaran Point
Or Tonakeera will take for ever.

## *Sleep & Death*

Zeus the cloud-gatherer said to sunny Apollo:
'Sponge the congealed blood from Sarpedon's corpse,
Take him far away from here, out of the line of fire,
Wash him properly in a stream, in running water,
And rub supernatural preservative over him
And wrap him up in imperishable fabrics,
Then hand him over to those speedy chaperons,
Sleep and his twin brother Death, who will bring him
In no time at all to Lycia's abundant farmland
Where his family will bury him with grave-mound
And grave-stone, the entitlement of the dead.'
And Apollo did exactly as he was told:
He carried Sarpedon out of the line of fire,
Washed him properly in a stream, in running water,
And rubbed supernatural preservative over him
And wrapped him up in imperishable fabrics
And handed him over to the speedy chaperons,
Sleep and his twin brother Death, who brought him
In no time at all to Lycia's abundant farmland.

## *Whalsay*

He fitted all of the island
Inside a fisherman's float – his
Cosmology of sea breezes
Cooling the seabirds' eggs
Or filling otter prints with sand:

For such phenomena, for
Sea lavender and spindrift, he –
Ravenous, insomniac – beach-
Combed the exact dialect words
Under a sky of green glass.

## MICHAEL HARTNETT

### *Lament for Tadhg Cronin's Children*

*based on a poem by Aodhagán Ó Rathaille, c.1670–1729*

That day the sails of the ship were torn
and a fog obscured the lawns.
In the whitewashed house the music stopped.
A spark jumped up at the gables
and the silk quilts on the bed caught fire.
They cry without tears –
their hearts cry –
for the three dead children.

Christ God neglect them not
nor leave them in the ground!

They were ears of corn!
They were apples!
They were three harpstrings!
And now their limbs lie underground
and the black beetle walks across their faces.
I, too, cry without tears –
my heart cries –
for the three dead children.

### from *Inchicore Haiku*

8

My English dam bursts
and out stroll all my bastards.
Irish shakes its head.

18

I push in a plug.
Mozart comes into the room
riding a cello.

37

What do bishops take
when the price of bread goes up?
A vow of silence.

78

On Tyrconnell Road,
Catholic Emancipation –
thirteen milk-bottles.

## EAMON GRENNAN

(*b*.1941)

### from *The Quick of It*

*because the body stops here because you can only reach out so*
*far because the pointed*
*blade of the headache maps the landscape inside the skull and*
*the rising peaks with*
*their roots behind your eyes their summits among the wrinkles*
*of your brow because*
*the sweat comes weeping from your hands and knotted*
*nipples because your tears keep*
*kissing your cheek and your cheek feels the tip of another's*
*tongue testing your tears*

*because the feel of a beard along the back of a neck is enough to melt the windows in a*
*little room because the toes the thighs the eyes the penis the vagina and the heart are*
*what they are and all they are (orphan, bride, pheasant or fox, freshwater glintfish of*
*simple touch) we have to be at home here no matter what no matter what the shivering*
*belly says or the dry-salted larynx no matter the frantic pulse no matter what happens*

(. . .)

When I see the quick ripple of a groundhog's back above the grass, its earth-
brown pelt vanishing into a hedgerow which for a minute or two is a shaken
screen of greens and then again still, the creature melted into nature's mouth
and sending back no sign of itself though I know it's in there and I can sense
how its breath and broadly distributed embrace of its gaze have become so fully
what it inhabits it will even winter there, curled round its own heart beating
at quarter speed, at ease in the sphere of its own immediate knowings – then
for some reason Avon's native comes to mind, quill-end tipping his tongue
as he takes a breath and disappears into the leaves and lavish music of another
turbulent little word-shiver for a minute, and he is all alone there, listening.

(. . .)

Casual, prodigal, these piss-poor opportunists, the weeds
in their gladrags and millennial hand-me-downs
of yellow and purple and pale green, are everywhere
along the highway, on every inch of waste ground
in our cultivated suburbs where they raise their families

and squinny in through lace-curtained windows, wagging
their heads at us, flaunting their speechless force, their
eager teeming in themselves, the irresistible fact that
theirs is the kingdom, the power, and the glory
of the real world smiling full and frightful in our faces.

(. . .)

Even under the rain that casts a fine white blanket over
mountain and lake
and smothers green islands and soaks grass and makes a solid
slow dripping
trickle in the sycamore; even under the rain that's general all
over the valley;
even under the steady rain measuring my life perched beside
the big window;
even under the blank remorseless grind and colonizing
hegemony of rain –

the bees are out among the furled or flapping scarlets of
fuchsia bells, seeking
till they find a fresh one, then settling and entering,
gathering what they need
in deliberate slow shudderings of the whole body shaking
suddenly the honey-core,
then extracting themselves in silence, a little heavier, limb
filaments glinty,
to go on cruising through this dust-fine deliquescence of
damp the falling rain is.

## DEREK MAHON

### *An Image from Beckett*

In that instant
There was a sea, far off,
As bright as lettuce,

A northern landscape
And a huddle
Of houses along the shore.

Also, I think, a white
Flicker of gulls
And washing hung to dry –

The poignancy of those
Back yards – and the gravedigger
Putting aside his forceps.

Then the hard boards
And darkness once again.
But in that instant

I was struck by the
Sweetness and light,
The sweetness and light,

Imagining what grave
Cities, what lasting monuments,
Given the time.

They will have buried
Our great-grandchildren, and theirs,
Beside us by now

With a subliminal batsqueak
Of reflex lamentation.
Our knuckle bones

Litter the rich earth
Changing, second by second,
To civilizations.

It was good while it lasted,
And if it only lasted
The Biblical span

Required to drop six feet
Through a glitter of wintry light,
There is No One to blame.

Still, I am haunted
By that landscape,
The soft rush of its winds,

The uprightness of its
Utilities and schoolchildren –
To whom in my will,

This, I have left my will.
I hope they have time,
And light enough, to read it.

## A Disused Shed in Co. Wexford

*Let them not forget us, the weak souls among the asphodels.*

—Seferis, *Mythistorema*

*(for J. G. Farrell)*

Even now there are places where a thought might grow –
Peruvian mines, worked out and abandoned
To a slow clock of condensation,
An echo trapped for ever, and a flutter
Of wild flowers in the lift-shaft,
Indian compounds where the wind dances
And a door bangs with diminished confidence,
Lime crevices behind rippling rain-barrels,
Dog corners for bone burials;
And in a disused shed in Co. Wexford,

Deep in the grounds of a burnt-out hotel,
Among the bathtubs and the washbasins
A thousand mushrooms crowd to a keyhole.
This is the one star in their firmament
Or frames a star within a star.
What should they do there but desire?
So many days beyond the rhododendrons
With the world waltzing in its bowl of cloud,
They have learnt patience and silence
Listening to the rooks querulous in the high wood.

They have been waiting for us in a foetor
Of vegetable sweat since civil war days,
Since the gravel-crunching, interminable departure
Of the expropriated mycologist.
He never came back, and light since then
Is a keyhole rusting gently after rain.

Spiders have spun, flies dusted to mildew
And once a day, perhaps, they have heard something –
A trickle of masonry, a shout from the blue
Or a lorry changing gear at the end of the lane.

There have been deaths, the pale flesh flaking
Into the earth that nourished it;
And nightmares, born of these and the grim
Dominion of stale air and rank moisture.
Those nearest the door grow strong –
'Elbow room! Elbow room!'
The rest, dim in a twilight of crumbling
Utensils and broken pitchers, groaning
For their deliverance, have been so long
Expectant that there is left only the posture.

A half century, without visitors, in the dark –
Poor preparation for the cracking lock
And creak of hinges; magi, moonmen,
Powdery prisoners of the old regime,
Web-throated, stalked like triffids, racked by drought
And insomnia, only the ghost of a scream
At the flash-bulb firing-squad we wake them with
Shows there is life yet in their feverish forms.
Grown beyond nature now, soft food for worms,
They lift frail heads in gravity and good faith.

They are begging us, you see, in their wordless way,
To do something, to speak on their behalf
Or at least not to close the door again.
Lost people of Treblinka and Pompeii!
'Save us, save us,' they seem to say,
'Let the god not abandon us
Who have come so far in darkness and in pain.
We too had our lives to live.
You with your light meter and relaxed itinerary,
Let not our naive labours have been in vain!'

## *Courtyards in Delft*

*—Pieter de Hooch, 1659*

*for Gordon Woods*

Oblique light on the trite, on brick and tile –
Immaculate masonry, and everywhere that
Water tap, that broom and wooden pail
To keep it so. House-proud, the wives
Of artisans pursue their thrifty lives
Among scrubbed yards, modest but adequate.
Foliage is sparse, and clings; no breeze
Ruffles the trim composure of those trees.

No spinet-playing emblematic of
The harmonies and disharmonies of love,
No lewd fish, no fruit, no wide-eyed bird
About to fly its cage while a virgin
Listens to her seducer, mars the chaste
Perfection of the thing and the thing made.
Nothing is random, nothing goes to waste.
We miss the dirty dog, the fiery gin.

That girl with her back to us who waits
For her man to come home for his tea
Will wait till the paint disintegrates
And ruined dikes admit the esurient sea;
Yet this is life too, and the cracked
Outhouse door a verifiable fact
As vividly mnemonic as the sunlit
Railings that front the houses opposite.

I lived there as a boy and know the coal
Glittering in its shed, late-afternoon
Lambency informing the deal table,
The ceiling cradled in a radiant spoon.

I must be lying low in a room there,
A strange child with a taste for verse,
While my hard-nosed companions dream of fire
And sword upon parched veldt and fields of rain-swept
 gorse.

## *from* The Yellow Book

### *VII: An Bonnán Buí*

*A heron-like species, rare visitors, most recent records referring to winter months . . . very active at dusk.*
—Guide to Irish Birds

A sobering thought, the idea of you stretched there,
bittern, under a dark sky, your exposed bones
yellow too in a ditch among cold stones,
ice glittering everywhere on bog and river,
the whole unfortunate country frozen over
and your voice stilled by enforced sobriety –
a thought more wrenching than the fall of Troy
because more intimate; for we'd hear your shout
of delight from a pale patch of watery sunlight
out on the mud there as you took your first
drink of the day and now, destroyed by thirst,
you lie in brambles while the rats rotate.
I'd've broken the ice for you, given an inkling;
now, had I known it, we might both be drinking
and singing too; for ours is the same story.
Others have perished – heron, blackbird, thrushes –
and lie shivering like you under whin-bushes;
but I mourn only the bittern, withdrawn and solitary,
who used to carouse alone among the rushes
and sleep rough in the star-glimmering bog-drain.
It used to be, with characters like us,

they'd let us wander the roads in wind and rain
or lock us up and throw away the key –
but now they have a cure for these psychoses
as indeed they do for most social diseases
and, rich at last, we can forget our pain.
She says I'm done for if I drink again;
so now, relieved of dangerous stimuli,
at peace with my plastic bottle of $H_2O$
and the slack strings of insouciance, I sit
with bronze Kavanagh on his canal-bank seat,
not in 'the tremendous silence of mid-July'
but the fast bright zing of a winter afternoon
dizzy with head-set, flash-bulb and digifone,
to learn the *tao* he once claimed as his own
and share with him the moor-hen and the swan,
the thoughtless lyric of a cloud in the sky
and the play of light and shadow on the slow
commemorative waters; relax, go with the flow.

## *'Things'*

*for Jane*

It rained for years when I was young.
I sat there as in the old pop song
and stared at a lonely avenue
like everybody else I knew
until, one day, the sun came out.
I too came out, to shout and sing
and see what it was all about.
Oh yes, I remember everything.

## *Biographia Literaria*

*(Samuel Taylor Coleridge, 1772–1834)*

A spoilt child shivers at the river's edge –
night-hiding yes but anxious to be found,
a troubled soul torn between fear and rage.
Sun, moon and star on the sky-blue clock face
in the south transept of St. Mary's mind
the autumn dark, and shadows have changed place
obscurely, each tick an 'articulate sound',
as he dozes off under a rustic bridge.

When he wakes at dawn to a slow-waning moon,
frozen and scared, curled up like the unborn,
the sun blinking behind an owl-eyed barn,
frost in the fields and winter coming on,
a frigate flutters on a glittering sea.
A great cold has gripped the heart already
with signs of witchery in an ivy tree:
now nothing will ever be the same again.

Genie, taper and paper, long solitary cliff walks,
cloud thoughts unfolding over the Quantocks
sheer to shore beneath high, feathery springs.
The cottage shines its light above the rocks,
the world's oceans tear in from the west
and an Aeolian harp the size of a snuff-box
sings in a casement where its tingling strings
record the faintest whisper, the loudest blast.

Receptive, tense, adrift in a breezy trance,
the frame is seized as if in a nightmare
by some quotation, fugue, some fugitive air,
some distant echo of the primal scream.

Silence, dead calm, no worldly circumstance;
the words form figures and begin to dance –
and then the miracle, the pleasure dome,
the caves of ice, the vibrant dulcimer.

Stowey to Göttingen, philosophy in a mist,
wide-eyed sublimities of ghost and *Geist*,
wild wind-and-rain effects of Greta Hall,
the rattling windows and the icy lake,
babbling excursions and the perpetual
white roaring rose of a close waterfall;
finally Highgate Grove and table talk,
a 'destined harbour' for the afflicted soul.

Asra and Christabel in confused opium dreams,
heartbroken whimpers and nocturnal screams
grow ever fainter as he becomes 'a sage
escaped from the inanity', aghast
at furious London and its rising smoke,
the sinister finance of a dark new age.
Dunn's pharmacy is only a short walk;
his grown-up daughter visits him there at last.

## EILÉAN NÍ CHUILLEANÁIN
(*b.*1942)

### *Deaths and Engines*

We came down above the houses
In a stiff curve, and
At the edge of Paris airport
Saw an empty tunnel
– The back half of a plane, black
On the snow, nobody near it,
Tubular, burnt-out and frozen.

When we faced again
The snow-white runways in the dark
No sound came over
The loudspeakers, except the sighs
Of the lonely pilot.

The cold of metal wings is contagious:
Soon you will need wings of your own,
Cornered in the angle where
Time and life like a knife and fork
Cross, and the lifeline in your palm
Breaks, and the curve of an aeroplane's track
Meets the straight skyline.

The images of relief:
Hospital pyjamas, screens round a bed
A man with a bloody face
Sitting up in bed, conversing cheerfully
Through cut lips:
These will fail you some time.

You will find yourself alone
Accelerating down a blind
Alley, too late to stop
And know how light your death is;
You will be scattered like wreckage,
The pieces every one a different shape
Will spin and lodge in the hearts
Of all who love you.

## *MacMoransbridge*

Although the whole house creaks from their footsteps
The sisters, when he died,
Never hung up his dropped dressing-gown,
Took the ash from the grate, or opened his desk. His will,
Clearly marked, and left in the top drawer,
Is a litany of objects lost like itself.
The tarnished silver teapot, to be sold
And the money given to a niece for her music-lessons,
Is polished and used on Sundays. The rings and pendants
Devised by name to each dear sister are still
Tucked between silk scarves in his wardrobe, where he found
And hid them again, the day they buried his grandmother.
And his posthumous plan of slights and surprises
Has failed – though his bank account's frozen – to dam up time.

He had wanted it all to stop,
As he stopped moving between that room
With its diaries and letters posted abroad
And the cold office over the chemist's
Where he went to register deaths and births,

While the sisters went on as they do now, never
All resting at once – one of them would be
Boiling up mutton-shanks for broth, or washing out blankets,
Dipping her black clothes in boiled vitriol and oak-gall
(He used to see from his leafy window
Shoulders bobbing at the pump like pistons).

And still the youngest goes down at night to the stream,
Tending the salmon-nets at the weir,
And comes home to bed as the oldest of all
Can already be heard adding up small change with the servant.

## *Fireman's Lift*

I was standing beside you looking up
Through the big tree of the cupola
Where the church splits wide open to admit
Celestial choirs, the fall-out of brightness.

The Virgin was spiralling to heaven,
Hauled up in stages. Past mist and shining,
Teams of angelic arms were heaving,
Supporting, crowding her, and we stepped

Back, as the painter longed to
While his arm swept in the large strokes.
We saw the work entire, and how the light

Melted and faded bodies so that
Loose feet and elbows and staring eyes
Floated in the wide stone petticoat
Clear and free as weeds.

This is what love sees, that angle:
The crick in the branch loaded with fruit,
A jaw defining itself, a shoulder yoked,

The back making itself a roof
The legs a bridge, the hands
A crane and a cradle.

Their heads bowed over to reflect on her
Fair face and hair so like their own
As she passed through their hands. We saw them
Lifting her, the pillars of their arms

(Her face a capital leaning into an arch)
As the muscles clung and shifted
For a final purchase together
Under her weight as she came to the edge of the cloud.

*Parma 1963–Dublin 1994*

## *The Real Thing*

The Book of Exits, miraculously copied
Here in this convent by an angel's hand,
Stands open on a lectern, grooved
Like the breast of a martyred deacon.

The bishop has ordered the windows bricked up on this side
Facing the fields beyond the city.
Lit by the glow from the cloister yard at noon
On Palm Sunday, Sister Custos
Exposes her major relic, the longest
Known fragment of the Brazen Serpent.

True stories wind and hang like this
Shuddering loop wreathed on a lapis lazuli
Frame. She says, this is the real thing.
She veils it again and locks up.
On the shelves behind her the treasures are lined.
The episcopal seal repeats every coil,
Stamped on all closures of each reliquary
Where the labels read: *Bones*
*Of Different Saints. Unknown.*

Her history is a blank sheet,
Her vows a folded paper locked like a well.
The torn end of the serpent
Tilts the lace edge of the veil.
The real thing, the one free foot kicking
Under the white sheet of history.

## *A Capitulary*

Now in my sleep I can hear them beyond the wall,
A chapterhouse growl, gently continuous:
The sound the child heard, waking and dozing again
All the long night she was tucked up in the library
While her father told his story to the chaplain
And then repeated it before the bishop.

She heard his flat accent, always askew
Responding to the Maynooth semitones,
A pause, and then the whisper of the scribe
Sweeping up the Latin like dust before a brush,
Lining up the ablatives, a refined
Countrywoman's hiss, and the neuter scrape of the pen.

I feel the ticking of their voices and remember how
My sister before she was born listened for hours
To my mother practising scales on the cello;
A grumble of thick string, and then climbing
To a high note that lifted
        that lifted its head
                like a seal –
To a high note that lifted its head like a seal in the water.

## *Gloss/Clós/Glas*

Look at the scholar, he has still not gone to bed,
Raking the dictionaries, darting at locked presses,
Hunting for keys. He stacks the books to his oxter,
Walks across the room as stiff as a shelf.

His nightwork, to make the price of his release:
Two words, as opposite as *his* and *hers*
Which yet must be as close
As the word *clós* to its meaning in a Scots courtyard
Close to the spailpín ships, or as close as the note

On the uilleann pipe to the same note on the fiddle –
As close as the grain in the polished wood, as the finger
Bitten by the string, as the hairs of the bow
Bent by the repeated note –
                                        Two words
Closer to the bone than the words I was so proud of,
*Embrace* and *strict* to describe the twining of bone and flesh.

The rags of language are streaming like weathervanes,
Like weeds in water they turn with the tide, as he turns
Back and forth the looking-glass pages, the words
Pouring and slippery like the silk thighs of the tomcat
Pouring through the slit in the fence, lightly,
Until he reaches the language that has no word for *his*,
No word for *hers*, and is brought up sudden
Like a boy in a story faced with a small locked door.
Who is that he can hear panting on the other side?
The steam of her breath is turning the locked lock green.

## DOROTHY MOLLOY

(1942–2004)

### *Ghost Train*

I pay sixpence to go round the loop. Slide the coin
with the greyhound and harp from my red pillar-box.
Slip it into the hand of the garlicky carnival-man.

He whispers, as always: 'That's grand.' But this time
his face is too close to my cheek. There's a shag
of thick hair on his chest. He half-jests in my ear: 'Not a word

to your folks and the next ride's on me.' He follows
my spark as I clickety-clack round the track.
Skeletons hang in the dark, lighting up, as we pass.

I pretend he's a friendly old dog when he jumps in
beside me and rests his white head on my knee.
But I find I can't slap him away when he opens his flippety

-flap, takes the blanket-pin out of my pleats, leaves a
slobber all over my lap.

### *Gethsemane Day*

They've taken my liver down to the lab,
left the rest of me here on the bed;
the blood I am sweating rubs off on the sheet,
but I'm still holding on to my head.

What cocktail is Daddy preparing for me?
What ferments in pathology's sink?
Tonight they will tell me, will proffer the cup,
and, like it or not, I must drink.

## JOHN F. DEANE

(*b.*1943)

### *The Instruments of Art*

*Edvard Munch*

We move in draughty, barn-like spaces, swallows
busy round the beams, like images. There is room
for larger canvases to be displayed, there are storing-places
for our weaker efforts; hold

to warm clothing, to surreptitious nips of spirits
hidden behind the instruments of art. It is all, ultimately,
a series of bleak self-portraits, of measured-out
reasons for living. Sketches

of heaven and hell. Self-portrait with computer;
self-portrait, nude, with blanching flesh; self
as Lazarus, mid-summons, as Job, mid-scream.
There is outward

dignity, white shirt, black tie, a black hat
held before the crotch; within, the turmoil, and advanced
decay. Each work achieved and signed announcing itself
the last. The barn door slammed shut.

*

There was a pungency of remedies on the air, the house
hushed for weeks, attending. A constant focus
on the sick-room. When I went in, fingers reached for me,
like crayfish bones; saliva

hung in the cave of the mouth like a web. Later,
with sheets and eiderdown spirited away, flowers stood
fragrant in a vase in the purged room. Still life. Leaving
a recurring sensation of dread, a greyness

like a dye, darkening the page; that *Dies Irae*, a slow
fretsaw wailing of black-vested priests. It was Ireland
subservient, relishing its purgatory. Books, indexed,
locked in glass cases. Night

I could hear the muted rhythms in the dance-hall; bicycles
slack against a gable-wall; bicycle-clips, minerals, the raffle;
words hesitant, ill-used, like groping. In me the dark bloom
of fascination, an instilled withdrawal.

*

He had a long earth-rake and he drew lines
like copy-book pages on which he could write
seeds, meaning – love; and can you love, be loved, and never
say 'love', never hear 'love'?

The uncollected apples underneath the trees
moved with legged things and a chocolate-coloured rust;
if you speak out flesh and heart's desire will the naming of it
canker it? She cut hydrangeas,

placed them in a pewter bowl (allowing herself at times
to cry) close by the tabernacle door; patience in pain
mirroring creation's order. The boy, suffering puberty, sensed
in his flesh a small revulsion, and held

*

hands against his crotch in fear. Paint the skin
a secret-linen white with a smart stubble of dirt. The first
fountain-pen, the paint-box, pristine tablets of Prussian Blue,
of Burnt Sienna – words

sounding in the soul like organ-music, Celeste and Diapason –
and that brush-tip, its animated bristles; he began at once
painting the dark night of grief, as if the squirrel's tail
could empty the ocean onto sand. Life-

drawing, with naked girl, half-light of inherited faith,
colour it in, and rhyme it, blue. In the long library, stooped
over the desks, we read cosmology, the reasoning
of Aquinas; we would hold

the knowledge of the whole world within us. The dawn
chorus: *laudetur Jesus Christus*; and the smothered,
smothering answer: *in aeternum. Amen.* Loneliness
hanging about our frames, like cassocks. New

*

world, new day. It is hard to shake off darkness, the black
habit. The sky at sunset – fire-red, opening its mouth
to scream; questions of adulthood, exploration of the
belly-flesh
of a lover. It was like

the rubbling of revered buildings, the moulding of words
into new shapes. In the cramped cab of a truck she, first time,
fleshed
across his knees; the kiss, two separate, not singular,
alive. It was death already, prowling

at the dark edge of the wood, fangs bared, saliva-white.
Sometimes you fear insanity, the bridge humming to your
scream
(oil, casein, pastel) but there is nobody to hear, the streaming
river
only, and the streaming sky; soon

on a dark night, the woman tearing dumbly at her hair while
you
gaze uselessly onto ashes. Helpless again you fear
woman: saint and whore and hapless devotee. Paint your words
deep violet, pale yellow,

*

the fear, *Winter in Meath, Fugue, the Apotheosis of Desire.*
The terror is not to be able to write. Naked and virginal
she embraced the skeleton and was gone. What, now,
is the colour of *God is love*

when they draw the artificial grass over the hole, the rains
hold steady, and the diggers wait impatiently under trees?
Too long
disturbing presences were shadowing the page, the bleak
ego-walls, like old galvanize

round the festering; that artificial mess collapsing
down on her, releasing a small, essential spirit, secular
bone-structure, the fingers reaching out of *need*, no longer *will*.
Visceral edge of ocean,

wading things, the agitated ooze, women on the jetty
watching out to sea; at last, I, too, could look
out into the world again. The woman, dressed in blue, broke
from the group on the jetty and came

*

purposefully towards us, I watched through stained glass
of the door,
and loved her. Mine the religion of poetry, the poetry
of religion, the worthy Academicians unwilling to realize
we don't live off neglect. Is there

a way to understand the chaos of the human heart? our
slaughters, our carelessness, our unimaginable wars?
Without a God can we win some grace? Will our canvases,
their patterns and forms, their

rhymes and rhythms, supply a modicum of worth?
The old man dragged himself up the altar steps,
beginning the old rites; the thurible clashed against its chain;
we rose, dutifully, though they

have let us down again, holding their forts
against new hordes; I had hoped the canvas would be filled
with radiant colours, but the word God became a word
of scorn, easiest to ignore. We

*

came out again, our heartache unassuaged.
The high corral of the Academy, too, is loud with gossipers,
the ego-traffickers, nothing to be expected there. Self-
portrait, with grief

and darkening sky. Soon it will be the winter studio; a small room, enclosed; you will sit, stilled, on a wooden chair, tweed heavy about your frame, eyes focused inwards, where there is no past, no future; you sit alone,

your papers in an ordered disarray; images stilled, like nests emptied; the phone beside you will not ring; nor will the light come on; everything depends on where your eyes
focus; when

the darkness comes, drawing its black
drape across the window, there will remain
the stillness of paint, words on the page, the laid down
instruments of your art.

## EAVAN BOLAND

### *Mise Eire*

I won't go back to it –

my nation displaced
into old dactyls,
oaths made
by the animal tallows
of the candle –

land of the Gulf Stream,
the small farm,
the scalded memory,
the songs
that bandage up the history,
the words
that make a rhythm of the crime

where time is time past.
A palsy of regrets.
No. I won't go back.
My roots are brutal:

I am the woman –
a sloven's mix
of silk at the wrists,
a sort of dove-strut
in the precincts of the garrison –

who practises
the quick frictions,
the rictus of delight
and gets cambric for it,
rice-coloured silks.

I am the woman
in the gansy-coat
on board the 'Mary Belle',
in the huddling cold,

holding her half-dead baby to her
as the wind shifts East
and North over the dirty
waters of the wharf

mingling the immigrant
guttural with the vowels
of homesickness who neither
knows nor cares that

a new language
is a kind of scar
and heals after a while
into a passable imitation
of what went before.

## PAUL DURCAN
(*b.*1944)

### *Ireland 1972*

Next to the fresh grave of my belovèd grandmother
The grave of my first love murdered by my brother.

### *Ireland 1977*

'I've become so lonely, I could die' – he writes,
The native who is an exile in his native land:
'Do you hear me whispering to you across the Golden Vale?
Do you hear me bawling to you across the hearthrug?'

### *Give Him Bondi*

Gerard enquires: 'Is there anything you'd like to do
On your last day in Sydney?'
I reply: 'I'd like to go to Bondi Beach.'
Too cautious to confess:
I'd like to swim at Bondi Beach.
Cautious not for fear of drowning in the sea
(I have been swimming since aged seven –
I've never thought of myself drowning –
*Unseen, only other people drown*)
But for fear of drowning in my own mortification –
An off-white northman in a sea of bronze loin-clothed men
With their bronze loin-clothed women.

As I step down onto the quartz sand of Bondi
I have to step around a young, topless virgin
Lying flat out on her back, eyes shut,
Each breast strewn askew her chest

Like a cone of cream gimleted with a currant
In a shock of its own slack:
Primeval Still Life awaiting the two Chardins,
Teilhard, Jean-Baptiste.

Will she one day
At the age of twenty-two
Not knowing she is not alone
With her infant twins in her arms
Commit suicide
On the newly carpeted staircase
Of her showcase home?
Please God open her closed eyes.

In our black slacks and long-sleeved white shirts
Gerard and I tip-toe up and down Bondi Beach
Like two corkscrewed, avid seminarians
On a day trip to the seaside.
Only that I, in a spasm of morning optimism,
Instead of underpants donned swimming briefs.
I feel – Gerard must also feel –
Estranged from our surroundings;
Teetering loners
Amid flocks of lovers,
Boys and girls
Skating precipices of surf.

In wistful exuberance resuscitating lives
Of priests, nuns, writers we have known –
*Solvitur ambulando* –
We promenade for an hour before
Gerard cries: 'It's nearly time to go.'
I am booked to recite to the pupils of his old school –
Robert Hughes's old school, too –
And Mick Scott's and Charlie Fraser's –
St Ignatius's at Riverview in North Sydney.
I gasp: 'To hell with it – this is idiocy:
To be standing here at Bondi, not swimming.'

I yank down my trousers to expose black briefs –
Too brief, really –
*Body-Glory* briefs –
And Gerard coughs, smiles, splutters:
'Well played, old chap –
Swim between the flags.'
He'll stand guard over my little cache of manhood:
My wristwatch – my twentieth-century tag;
My white shirt folded in a sandwich;
My black slacks curled up in a chaste ball;
My black nylon socks twinned back to back;
My black leather slip-ons with fake gold studs.

I tumble out into the shallows where maybe twenty-five
Youths and maidens gay frolic
And I chin-dive and become a boy again –
A curly-headed blue-eyed fourteen year old
Leaping and whooping in the surf,
Romping into the rollers,
Somersaulting into the dumpers,
A surf-flirt in my element,
In the spray of the foliage of the sea.
Gerard patrols on the fringes of the foam
With his pants rolled up, snapping me
With a disposable Instamatic I've handed him.

I essay a breaststroke, but desist –
Being unfit, overweight, dead-beat.
Yesterday I flew in from Ayers Rock;
The day before alone in the low 30s
Humping five litres of water,
I trekked five miles in the Olgas.
Again I strike out, this time with an overarm
But after six or seven strokes flail up against
A barrage of exhaustion.
I spin over self-cossetingly on my spine,
My pudgy vertebrae,
And float, watching my toes:
Inspecting my toes

Strutting their stuff
On a catwalk of silver faucets,
Toenails pared and gleaming,
Their parings littering
A hotel bathroom floor
In the Northern Territory;
All ten toes of mine present and correct,
Pristine, pink, erect, perky,
Bouncing on a trampoline
Such is the buoyancy of Bondi.

This is my Theory of Floating
Which has served me well,
My Theory of Daydreaming.
If one may speak well of oneself
I may say I have not craved
Conquest or complacency
But exclusively
The existence of existence,
The survival of survival,
The dreaming of the day.
I did not climb Ayers Rock,
Not out of an excess of virtue
But out of a modicum of attention
To the signposts of the local people:
*Please do not climb our sacred mountain.*
It would have been a sin
Against the genetics
Of all the chromosomes of ethics
To have climbed Ayers Rock.

To float is to be on the whale's back.
Gurgling to myself:
There she blows!
Only three weeks ago
In the company of Mary Clare Power
And Nicholas Shakespeare
On a motorboat off Fraser Island
In Queensland

From fifty yards away
I saw two humpback whales
Steeplechasing the waves, courting;
Rising up, cresting, plunging;
Flaunting their tattooed tails.
Toe-gazing, I go on chatting to myself:
Amn't I a humpback too?
Mother shrieking at me: 'Straighten up
Or you'll get curvature of the spine
And you'll be a humpback!'
She meant the Hunchback of Notre Dame.
Guy de Maupassant
Was *her* mother's idol.
Why did *my* mother eat me?
*Her* mother minded me.
In my prime I could scoff
Back in one gulp
15,000 gallons of salt water
While continuing to speak
Ten to the dozen
About anything under the sun.
Never mind, this day is Elysium!
Alone to own and range
The bush of the sea.
How fortunate I am
Who in spite of all my loss and failure –
All my defeats quadrupling daily –
I find myself here floating at Bondi Beach –
A little, pale saffron, five-and-a-half dollar boomerang
In a black penis-purse.
I flip over my gaze upon the hard blue sky.

But I must not keep Gerard waiting.
Time to swim ashore, go on
With life's obligation.
I flip over on my belly to swim
To see that I am twice as far out
As I should be! Pulled out to sea
While floating! Out of sight

Of the flags! But I'm an old hand
At swimming. Didn't Uncle Mick
Teach all of us to swim
At the age of seven
Off the famine pier
At Enniscrone of the Seaweed Baths?
Out of our depth
On the deep, steep steps
And not, not, not
To be afraid?
By God he did!
I strike out for home.
Only to find myself swimming backwards!
Christ O Lord the sea
Is kidnapping me!
Like that man in the back lane
When I was nine
On my way home from school!
He asked me to climb over a wall
With him and I did. No!
I decline to believe it! No!
                    I go
Into denial!
                    Stop, sea, stop!
Into hysteria!
                    Stop it, stop it!
O save me, save me!
                    No! No!
O God, O God!
                    O save me, save me.
Of what use be these now –
All thy litanies of ejaculations?
All these cries aeons ago
Airbrushed into extinction.

Pounding forwards I am surging backwards.
Instead of me catching the waves,
The waves are dumping me backwards!
I who presume myself a porpoise

With fifty years of Floating Theory
Chalked up on my flippers
Am now a mouse being toyed with
By the tom-cat of the sea!
In this drifting micromoment
The stopwatch stops:
I behold my death eyeball me
Like a sadistic schoolmaster
Cornering me at the blackboard.

I wave, but no one sees me
And, as I wave, I begin to sink.
I'm being eaten alive.
Save me, O Christ, save me!
Your what? Your own death?
Your own end? Your own oblivion?
Death by drowning?
                    The fury of it!
The remorseless deep closing o'er your head!
Alone, alone, all, all alone!
Within seconds, to be but a swab –
A trace in water –
That scarcely decipherable but tell-tale trace
In the sea after a substance has sunk.
Fear frying your bones.
I thought I had known fear –
Oceans of fear – but I had not:
Not until now
This micromoment of 100-carat fear;
My body incapable of coping
But my psyche clear with fear
Not muddled or mesmerized,
But clarifed – a seer
Of the final second, seeing
The sea about to snatch,
Suck, swallow me.

The sea! Oh, the sea!
That stunning, wholly together She –
The one with her Mountain Passes
In all the right places.
You've flirted with her all your life
Having it both ways as always;
Your wife your mistress not your wife;
Your mistress your wife not your mistress;
Solitude your company;
Being mortal claiming immortality;
Every single time without exception
That the air hostess models the life jacket
You insouciantly ignore her,
Flaunting yourself a superior stoic
Who plumbs the secret of the voyage.
Voyager your voyage about to end
Faster than an airliner plummeting
How goes your voyaging?

Why are you standing in water
Out of your depth dying?
Far from your own bed?
Naught now between your legs
But disdainful water?
Being buried alive?
Dying, Durcan, dying
In your own standing?
Hanging on by one hand
From the sky's yardarm
About to plop
Down into Davy Jones's locker?
Where be your swashbuckling now?
Your hip-hop-hip mating?
Your waistcoated machismo?
Where be all your cheek-to-cheek glowing?
Your eyebrow-to-eyebrow acrobatics?
Where be all your toe-to-toe conniving?
You are being struck down,
Having glowed, having connived.

Neither being seen nor being heard
But tomorrow in a scrap of newscasting
On ABC:
'Irish poet trapped in rips,
Washed up between the Heads
Of Sydney Harbour.'

Ocean – compleat ocean – clenches me
In its JCB claws,
Hissing at me that this time there'll be no pause
And my brains gape down upon my own terror.
In the vice of drowning I know
I have no power, my fate
Decided, all I can
Be said to be doing is lingering;
Out of my depth, flailing
Legs, arms, caterwauling
In my kitty
And meekly screaming – I am lingering;
*Fresh blows the breeze from off the bow;*
*My Irish boy, where lingerest thou?*
This fling in which you're lingering
Will last but seconds and after
You will be but a thing
Flung against the automatic sliding doors
Of the sea's casino.
My father and mother
Each a wowser
Resenting one another,
Resented me
Because I was a bother.
How so much better
It would have been
Not to have given birth
To such a bother.
All presumption walloped o'er the horizon,
All my naïveté, all my toxic pride,
All my vanity, all my conceit.
There is nothing I can do – I realize –

Except shout, bawl, cry, whimper.
In the cot of the sea,
On the rails of the waves
I bang my little knuckles.
The sea seethes:
Paul Durcan, you are
The epitome of futility.

I cry out 'Help! Help!'
But no one hears me.
A cry? I –
Did I ever reply
To a cry?
A cry of a tiny, frail Scotsman
In a damp basement bedsit
In Buckingham Palace Road
Choking on his own loneliness?
Aye! A cry!
Nobody hears me, the dead man!
I cry out again with all my ego.
The about-to-be-overtaken sprinter
At the finishing line,
Lunging one last futile fingertipslength.
The ocean is the mighty woman
You have hunted all your life.
But now that she has got you
In the palm of her hand –
In her thimble of no reprieve! –
You are crying out 'Help!'
She is moulding her knuckles around you.
You are her prey.
This is the yarn you will not live to spin,
The blackest yarn,
A groundswell is spinning out your life
At once slowly, speedily –
A groundswell no longer a cliché
But a mother of death!
You are a puppet out of your depth
And your legs are diced dancers

Dangling from deadwood,
Thrashing in their throes
Out of sight slipping.
The sea is a headless goddess
All flesh sans eyes sans mouth.
Paul Durcan, this is one lady
Through whose eyes and mouth,
Through whose free looks
You will not talk your way.

HELP!
My teensy-weensy voicette fetches
Over the uncut surf and the sealed ocean
To two young men who shout back –
Their seal heads bobbing a quarter-mile off –
Something like 'Hold on! Hold on!'
And blubbering I pant for breath
As my head slides beneath the waves,
My shoulders caving in,
My paunch of guts dragging me down,
My kidneys wincing,
My crimson ankles skipping,
My snow-white fetlocks like faulty pistons
Halting for the last time.

I can hear myself sobbing 'O God, O God!'
Floating downwards with every surge;
Hurtling upwards with every heave.
'O Christ, I don't want to die!
After all that church-going and hymn-singing
This is not the only life I know
But it's the only life I want!
I WANT TO LIVE!'
They clutch me round the neck
And flail and thrash to lug me shorewards.
A third joins them – an off-duty lifeguard
Called Brian who happens to be doing
A stint of training – but the breaking rollers
At each crash uppercut me.

Each other roller clubs me on the head.
Not once of course, but again again
Clubbing, clubbing, clubbing,
Such stuffing as is in me goes limp.
My rescuers scream: 'Keep your lips tight shut!'
As each wave crashes I writhe for consciousness –
A newborn baby pawing air;
My lungs spewing up bladders of salt water –
The rash smart sloggering brine.
Wrenching me they fling me shorewards –
These three fierce young men –
Until they lash me to a surfboard
And sail me in facedown the final furlong,
The final rumble strips of foam,
Racing the shoreline, beaching me,
Dumping me on wet sand bereft of ocean,
Raising me up by the armpits, hauling me.
On my hands and knees
In amber froth
I crawl the final metre.
On the keel of an upturned boat I sat down
And wept and shivered and stretched to vomit.
Sat retching there like a shredded parsnip,
The cowering genius of the shore.
Another Bondi casualty bent forlorn
Upon the tourist shingles
Of New South Wales.

When I am able to look up
My three midwives have gone
Whose names I do not know,
Only Brian. The two together
Were English boys. They waddled off
Into the anonymity of selflessness –
'All part of the lifesaver's ethos'
It is explained to me weeks later by
The North Bondi Surf Life-Saving Club.
Drowning and trying to wave
And not being seen

But being heard in the nick of time.
On the instructions of Brian,
With Gerard's help,
I present myself
At the Bondi Medical Centre,
34 Campbell Parade.
A young Chinese doctor who cannot help
In spite of his instinctive etiquette
Smirking at my ludicrous appearance –
Trouserless in a green blazer –
Applies a stethoscope to my spine
And chimes: 'Sir, you're fine.'
Dr C. Chin.
35 Australian dollars.
Cash payment.

Gerard drives me to St Ignatius's school
Where for half-an-hour
I play the serious fool
To waves of applause.
That night I do not dare to sleep
But keep on the bedside light
Listening to my own breathing,
The possum in the wainscotting.
Instead of being a cold cod
On a slab in Sydney morgue
I am a warm fish in bed –
How can this be?
What sort of justice is this?
The crab of luck?

May I when I get home,
If I get home,
Chatter less cant
Especially when it comes
To life and death
Or to other people's lives;

May I be
Less glib, less cocky;
May I be
Never righteous.
If I conclude
I ever have the right
To call Ayers Rock 'Uluru'
May I be
Not smug about it –
Remember I'm only a white man.
May I take to heart
What the Aboriginal people
Of Brisbane, Alice Springs, Canberra,
Said and did not say to me.
May I never romanticize
The lives of Aboriginal people.
May I never write trite
Codswallop about indigenousness;
May I begin to listen.
May I decipher next time
Silences under gum trees:
'Give him Bondi!'

Don't think I will swim
Again in any sea.
Doubt if I will walk
Again by any sea.
But if I do –
If ever again I should have
The cheek to walk
The strand at Keel
In Achill Island –
To walk those three
Skies-in-the-sands miles
By those riding-stable half-doors
Of the Sheik of Inishturk,
With their herds of white horses

Leaning out at me fuming –
I will make that long walk
In nausea as well as awe:
The wings of the butterflies in my stomach
Weighed down by salt for evermore.

Next day I board a Boeing 747
From Sydney to Bangkok
Not caring – glancing over
My shoulder on the tarmac
At Mascot, not caring.
Not caring about anything.
Not about Egypt.
Not about Mayo.
Not about Ireland.
Not even longing for home.
*Not even longing for home.*
Praying once for all
I am gutted of ego;
That I have at last learnt
The necessity of being nothing,
The *XYZ* of being nobody.
In so far as I care
May I care nothing for myself,
Care everything for you –
Young mother of two
In the next seat;
A boy and a girl.
Thumbs in their mouths,
Helplessly asleep.
Back in Dublin
One person in whom
I can confide: Colm,
In that brusque,
Anti-sentimental,
Staccato-magnanimous,
Shooting-self-pity-in-the-eye
Tongue of his whispers
On the telephone at noon:

'I swam in Rottnest
Off the coast of Perth,
Nearly lost my . . .
The sea is different in Australia, Paul,
A different pull.'

A year later
I cannot sleep
For thinking of Bondi;
Nightly re-enactment
Of being eaten alive
Under bottomless ceilings,
Pillows sprinting above me,
The bedroom window
Declining to open,
A schoolyard of faces
Pressing their noses
Against double-glazed glass
Waving at me
Hail or Farewell? –
I cannot know.
I am come into deep waters
Where the floods overflow me.

## *Ireland 2001*

Where's my bikini?
We'll be late for Mass.

## *Ireland 2002*

Do you ever take a holiday abroad?
No, we always go to America.

# BERNARD O'DONOGHUE

(*b.*1945)

## *Casement on Banna*

In this dawn waking, he is Oisin
Stretching down for the boulder
That will break his girth and plunge
Him into age; he's Columcille
Waiting for foreign soil to leak
From his sandals and bring him death
In Ireland. He can't be roused
By any fear of danger once he's started
His own laying-out on this white sand.

Watching the usual landmarks in the sky,
He can no longer place them. Is that
Pegasus? Where's Orion? Surer of
The wash and whisper from the Maharees,
He spots the oyster-catcher going off
To raise the alarm: an insane Orpheus
Craving a past he'd never had. His quest
Beached here that started in mutilation
And manacled rubber-harvesters.

Suddenly it has thrown him on the ground,
A man sick with his past, middled-aged,
Mad, more or less, who waits to be lifted
High, kicking in mid-air, gurgling
For breath, swaying, while Banna's lonely sand
Drips for the last time from his shoe. So:
Was this the idea? The cure for every woe,
Injustice, brutishness? In this ecstasy
Larks rising everywhere, as he'd forgotten.

## *Ter Conatus*

Sister and brother, nearly sixty years
They'd farmed together, never touching once.
Of late she had been coping with a pain
In her back, realization dawning slowly
That it grew differently from the warm ache
That resulted periodically
From heaving churns on to the milking-stand.

She wondered about the doctor. When,
Finally, she went, it was too late,
Even for chemotherapy. And still
She wouldn't have got round to telling him,
Except that one night, watching television,
It got so bad she gasped, and struggled up,
Holding her waist. 'D'you want a hand?' he asked,

Taking a step towards her. 'I can manage,'
She answered, feeling for the stairs.
Three times, like that, he tried to reach her.
But, being so little practised in such gestures,
Three times the hand fell back, and took its place,
Unmoving at his side. After the burial,
He let things take their course. The neighbours watched

In pity the rolled-up bales, standing
Silent in the fields, with the aftergrass
Growing into them, and wondered what he could
Be thinking of: which was that evening when,
Almost breaking with a lifetime of
Taking real things for shadows,
He might have embraced her with a brother's arms.

# TREVOR JOYCE

(*b.*1947)

## *all that is the case*

take first a crux take any crossing say take noon or ten to five
from it subtract the gravity the drag the I am not in pain

the year which passes and today and once before
the one who is about to get here just before the give to me
the house which we shall see exactly three days
afterwards the which the how the very book thou gavest

as while about to fall I saw thee while about to fall I saw
then the she who came here yesterday who will approach

tomorrow that that red box see it still is empty and so too
the green that tomorrow I will go away again and stay
with numeral intensifier and frequentative
the feverish am I intermittent fevers hold me tell

what now is left say can you play do you thirst very very much
in darkness the some days the street is sky and nothing else

## *now then*

this room is empty      all
noise is the day everywhere
i haven't stopped remembering
being unsure      & the day is high
& warm outside      to say there is nothing
happening here would be
to exaggerate      it's
a slack one today said the sun
to the glass      let's us just say

that time encompasses the walls
here        (o flare of morning!)
that something is about
to happen        who are you?

## FRANK ORMSBY

(*b*.1947)

### *The Gate*

I

There's a gate in the middle of the field.
It leads into the middle of the field and out of it.
We lean on the gate in the hedge that leads into the field
and stare at the gate in the middle.

II

Travellers point to the gate in the middle of the field.
They approach and investigate. They invest the gate
with mysterious purpose. They want to interrogate
whoever put it there. They admire a gate
that has gatecrashed the middle of a field.
Let all gates have such freedom, they think, bar none.

III

We swing on the thought of a gate in the middle of a field,
Where it has no business, long after the gate has gone.
'Remember the gate?' we say and at night in our dreams
we head for the space in the middle.
We pass in file through the space in the middle of the field
and close, always, reverently, the gate behind us.

### *The Whooper Swan*

When you croon your impression of a whooper swan,
at lunchtime, *sotto voce*, in Flanagan's Bar,
the notes are beyond language, you are living that sound
by tidal shallows a hundred miles away
in a season part-voiceless until the swan's return.
A moment's silence. I imagine each dolorous yomp
as a bid for the true pitch, as though it defers
to a lough's memory of winter or the last
death on an island, yet even in autumn lifts
a bronchial trump of resurrection.
When dawn was a soundless birth and sunset mimed
the idea of loss, the whooper happened in
with the vowel to suit October in these parts,
a tone that made somehow bearable the wind's
insistent dismissals, its miserly null-and-void.
Though earthbound, land-locked, I never lacked till now
the gift of a coastal childhood, or missed a life
edged with Atlantic: sea-self, sky-self, land-self
among the dunes in late autumn, balance restored
by the rich plaint, the vibrant ochone of the whooper swan.

## CIARAN CARSON
(*b*.1948)

### *Dresden*

Horse Boyle was called Horse Boyle because of his brother
    Mule;
Though why Mule was called Mule is anybody's guess. I stayed
    there once,
Or rather, I nearly stayed there once. But that's another story.

At any rate they lived in this decrepit caravan, not two miles out of Carrick,
Encroached upon by baroque pyramids of empty baked bean tins, rusts
And ochres, hints of autumn merging into twilight. Horse believed
They were as good as a watchdog, and to tell you the truth
You couldn't go near the place without something falling over:
A minor avalanche would ensue – more like a shop bell, really,

The old-fashioned ones on string, connected to the latch, I think,
And as you entered in, the bell would tinkle in the empty shop, a musk
Of soap and turf and sweets would hit you from the gloom. Tobacco.
Baling wire. Twine. And, of course, shelves and pyramids of tins.
An old woman would appear from the back – there was a sizzling pan in there,
Somewhere, a whiff of eggs and bacon – and ask you what you wanted;
Or rather, she wouldn't ask; she would talk about the weather. It had rained
That day, but it was looking better. They had just put in the spuds.
I had only come to pass the time of day, so I bought a token packet of Gold Leaf.

All this time the fry was frying away. Maybe she'd a daughter in there
Somewhere, though I hadn't heard the neighbours talk of it; if anybody knew,
It would be Horse. Horse kept his ears to the ground.
And he was a great man for current affairs; he owned the only TV in the place.
Come dusk he'd set off on his rounds, to tell the whole townland the latest
Situation in the Middle East, a mortar bomb attack in Mullaghbawn –

The damn things never worked, of course – and so he'd tell the story
How in his young day it was very different. Take young Flynn, for instance,
Who was ordered to take this bus and smuggle some sticks of gelignite

Across the border, into Derry, when the RUC – or was it the RIC? –
Got wind of it. The bus was stopped, the peeler stepped on. Young Flynn
Took it like a man, of course: he owned up right away. He opened the bag
And produced the bomb, his rank and serial number. For all the world
Like a pound of sausages. Of course, the thing was, the peeler's bike
Had got a puncture, and he didn't know young Flynn from Adam. All he wanted
Was to get home for his tea. Flynn was in for seven years and learned to speak
The best of Irish. He had thirteen words for a cow in heat;
A word for the third thwart in a boat, the wake of a boat on the ebb tide.

He knew the extinct names of insects, flowers, why this place was called
Whatever: *Carrick*, for example, was a *rock*. He was damn right there –
As the man said, *When you buy meat you buy bones, when you buy land you buy stones.*
You'd be hard put to find a square foot in the whole bloody parish
That wasn't thick with flints and pebbles. To this day he could hear the grate
And scrape as the spade struck home, for it reminded him of broken bones:
Digging a graveyard, maybe – or better still, trying to dig a reclaimed tip

Of broken delft and crockery ware – you know that sound that sets your teeth on edge
When the chalk squeaks on the blackboard, or you shovel ashes from the stove?

Master McGinty – he'd be on about McGinty then, and discipline, the capitals
Of South America, Moore's *Melodies*, the Battle of Clontarf, and
*Tell me this, an educated man like you: What goes on four legs when it's young,*
*Two legs when it's grown up, and three legs when it's old?* I'd pretend
I didn't know. McGinty's leather strap would come up then, stuffed
With threepenny bits to give it weight and sting. Of course, it never did him
Any harm: *You could take a horse to water but you couldn't make him drink.*
He himself was nearly going on to be a priest.
*And many's the young cub left the school as wise as when he came.*

Carrowkeel was where McGinty came from – *Narrow Quarter*, Flynn explained –
Back before the Troubles, a place that was so mean and crabbed,
Horse would have it, men were known to eat their dinner from a drawer.
Which they'd slide shut the minute you'd walk in.
He'd demonstrate this at the kitchen table, hunched and furtive, squinting
Out the window – past the teetering minarets of rust, down the hedge-dark aisle –
To where a stranger might appear, a passer-by, or what was maybe worse,
Someone he knew. Someone who wanted something. Someone who was hungry.

Of course who should come tottering up the lane that
instant but his brother

Mule. I forgot to mention they were twins. They were as like
two –
No, not peas in a pod, for this is not the time nor the place
to go into
Comparisons, and this is really Horse's story, Horse who –
now I'm getting
Round to it – flew over Dresden in the war. He'd emigrated
first, to
Manchester. Something to do with scrap – redundant mill
machinery,
Giant flywheels, broken looms that would, eventually, be
ships, or aeroplanes.
He said he wore his fingers to the bone.
And so, on impulse, he had joined the RAF. He became a rear
gunner.
Of all the missions, Dresden broke his heart. It reminded him
of china.

As he remembered it, long afterwards, he could hear, or
almost hear
Between the rapid desultory thunderclaps, a thousand tinkling
echoes –
All across the map of Dresden, storerooms full of china
shivered, teetered
And collapsed, an avalanche of porcelain, slushing and
cascading: cherubs,
Shepherdesses, figurines of Hope and Peace and Victory,
delicate bone fragments.
He recalled in particular a figure from his childhood, a milkmaid
Standing on the mantelpiece. Each night as they knelt down
for the Rosary,
His eyes would wander up to where she seemed to beckon to
him, smiling,
Offering him, eternally, her pitcher of milk, her mouth of
rose and cream.

One day, reaching up to hold her yet again, his fingers
stumbled, and she fell.
He lifted down a biscuit tin, and opened it.
It breathed an antique incense: things like pencils, snuff, tobacco.
His war medals. A broken rosary. And there, the milkmaid's
creamy hand, the outstretched
Pitcher of milk, all that survived. Outside, there was a scraping
And a tittering; I knew Mule's step by now, his careful
drunken weaving
Through the tin-stacks. I might have stayed the night, but there's
no time
To go back to that now; I could hardly, at any rate, pick up
the thread.
I wandered out through the steeples of rust, the gate that was
a broken bed.

## *A Date Called* Eat Me

The American Fruit Company had genetically engineered a new
variety of designer apple,
Nameless as yet, which explored the various Platonic ideals of
the 'apple' synapse.

Outside the greengrocer's lighted awning it is dusky
Hallowe'en. It is
Snowing on a box of green apples, crinkly falling on the tissue
paper. It is

Melting on the green, unbitten, glistening apples, attracted by
their gravity.
I yawned my teeth and bit into the dark, mnemonic cavity.

That apple-box was my first book-case. I covered it in wood-
grain Fablon –
You know that Sixties stick-on plastic stuff? I thought it
looked dead-on:

Blue Pelicans and orange Penguins, *The Pocket Oxford*
 *English Dictionary*;
Holmes and Poe, *The Universe*, the fading aura of an apple
 named Discovery –

I tried to extricate its itsy-bitsy tick of rind between one tooth
 and another tooth,
The way you try to winkle out the 'facts' between one truth
 and another truth.

Try to imagine the apple talking to you, tempting you like
 something out of Aesop,
Clenched about its navel like a fist or face, all pith and pips and
 sap

Or millions of them, hailing from the heavens, going *pom,*
 *pom, pom, pom, pom*
On the roof of the American Fruit Company, whose computer
 banks are going *ohm* and *om*.

They were trying to get down to the nitty-gritty, sixty-four-
 thousand dollar question of whether the stalk
Is apple or branch or what. The programme was stuck.

The juice of it explodes against the roof and tongue, the cheek
 of it.
I lied about the Fablon, by the way. It was really midnight
 black with stars on it.

## *from* The Twelfth of Never

### *The Rising Sun*

As I was driven into smoky Tokyo
The yen declined again. It had been going down
All day against the buoyant Hibernian Pound.
Black rain descended like a harp arpeggio.

The Professor took me to a bonsai garden
To imbibe some thimblefuls of Japanese poteen.
We wandered through the forest of the books of Arden.
The number of their syllables was seventeen.

I met a maiden of Hiroshima who played
The hammer dulcimer like psychedelic rain.
The rising sun was hid behind a cloud of jade.

She sang to me of Fujiyama and of Zen,
Of yin and yang, and politics, and crack cocaine,
And Plato's caverns, which are measureless to men.

## *from* Breaking News

### *Trap*

backpack radio
antenna

twitching
rifle

headphones
cocked

I don't
read you

what the

over

## *Wake*

near dawn

boom

the window
trembled

bomb

I thought

then in
the lull

a blackbird
whistled in

a chink
of light

between
that world

and this

## *from* For All We Know

### from *Part One: The Fetch*

To see one's own doppelgänger is an omen of death.
The doppelgänger casts no reflection in a mirror.

Shelley saw himself swimming towards himself before he
drowned.
Lincoln met his fetch at the stage door before he was shot.

It puts me in mind of prisoners interrogated,
of one telling his story so well he could see himself

performing in it, speaking the very words he spoke now,
seeing the face of the accomplice he had invented.

When all is said and done there is nothing more to be said.
No need for handcuffs, or any other restraint. They take

a swab of his sweat from the vinyl chair in which he sat.
Should he ever escape his prison the dogs shall be loosed.

Your death stands always in the background, but don't be
afraid.
For he will only come to fetch you when your time has
come.

## from *Part Two: The Fetch*

I woke. You were lying beside me in the double bed,
prone, your long dark hair fanned out over the downy
pillow.

I'd been dreaming we stood on a beach an ocean away
watching the waves purl into their troughs and tumble over.

Knit one, purl two, you said. Something in your voice
made me think
of women knitting by the guillotine. Your eyes met mine.

The fetch of a wave is the distance it travels, you said,
from where it is born at sea to where it founders to shore.

I must go back to where it all began. You waded in
thigh-deep, waist-deep, breast-deep, head-deep, until you
disappeared.

I lay there and thought how glad I was to find you again.
You stirred in the bed and moaned something. I heard a
footfall

on the landing, the rasp of a man's cough. He put his head
around the door. He had my face. I woke. You were not
there.

## TOM PAULIN
## (*b.*1949)

### *A Written Answer*

This poem by Rupert Brookeborough
is all about fishing and the stout B-men
(they live for always in our hearts,
their only crime was being loyal),
there is a lough in it and stacks of rivers,
also a brave wee hymn to the sten-gun.
The poet describes Gough of the Curragh
and by his use of many metric arts
he designs a fictionary universe
which has its own laws and isn't quite
the same as this place that we call real.
His use of metonymy is pretty desperate
and the green symbolism's a contradiction,
but I like his image of the elm and chestnut,
for to me this author is a fly man
and the critics yonder say his work is alright.

## *The Road to Inver*
(Pessoa)

*for Xon de Ros and Jamie McKendrick*

I left a village called Tempo
oh maybe an hour back
and now I'm driving to Inver
in an old beatup gunked Toyota
I've borrowed from a mate in Belfast
(there was a poet down south
who blessed all the new Toyotas in Ireland
– everyone else was driving in circles
but he came out with a firm line
and drove it straight home)

cold as a hub cap
there's a full moon shining
over the pine plantation
that belongs here really
no more than I do
though man and boy I've watched it grow
from naked wee saplings
to mature slightly sinister trees
just as I've watched them bed
two salmon farms and an oyster
farm out there in the bay
(if it was daylight I'd point to
a spot on the ocean that's corrugated
and rusted like scrap metal or
– same thing – a tank trap at high tide)
but it looks like I'm on another journey
in another time
where I go on – go on and on –
without ever having left Belfast
or having to go to Inver
– in Irish it means *river
mouth* – which is a bit like not having read

– I don't know the language –
like not having read
that book – is it a novel or memoir? –
called *The House at Inver*
which stood somewhere on the shelves
in our house in Belfast
which reminds me my grandmother's house
in Belfast was called *Invergowrie*
after the village in the Lowlands she was born in
or maybe that her family came from
(they brought the bronze nameplate with them
when they moved from Glasgow
and settled – more or less – in Ireland)

I'm going to spend the night in Inver
– check in to some B&B
because I can't stay in Belfast
but when I get to Inver I'll be sorry
I didn't stay behind in Belfast
– always this disquiet – I'm anxious
– anxious to no purpose –
always always always
and always too much – over the top –
and all for nothing
on the road to Inver
it's a dream road this
the same road that leads
to the Elver Inn on Lough Neagh
– 's just a phrase *dream road*
like *the rood of time*
or *the long road to nowhere*
or *big fat pursy toad*

the wheel of my borrowed car
is taut like a fishing line
or like reins
and the wheels they go smoothly
over the tired the humpy
old road

that feels a bit like a bog road
– I smile at this symbol as I recall it
and make a right turn
– how many borrowed things do
I go about in or use all day?
but the things that are lent I take
them over and make them mine
– one day way back they even loaned me me
– I'd stake my life on that
though the idea cuts me like a knife
(I feel like – well
a double agent who might be triple)

there's a mobile home by the roadside
– one with no wheels I often used dream of
when my heart and my spirit they
felt cut to pieces as I worried
what would happen my children
– the headlights catch its fence
that's new gardencentre wattle
an open field and the moon
making it cold like bare metal
for the car in which – leaving Tempo –
I felt like a freedom rider
has boxed me in
it's like I'm trapped inside her
and can only control – well the thing –
if I'm locked in it
and feel the car's part of me
I guess they're happy in that stretched
caravan but if they saw me driving past
they'd say *there goes a happy fella*
*he doesn't give a damn what his car looks like*
*no one's ever asked him to write a poem*
*in praise of its make and makers*
– they'd say that of course
if they could see the state this
what they call a *cyar* is in
but none of them would know

that on the road to Inver
in moonlight in my own so
deepdown sadness driving this borrowed
Toyota disconsolately
I'm losing myself in the road in front of me
I'm adding myself to the distance
and then suddenly
out of some terrible desire
I put my foot down and wham forward
but my heart stays with that pile of stones
I swerved past without seeing
– it stood at the wattle gate
a pile of road metal
– yes my heart is empty
my unsatisfied heart
my heart more human than I am and so
much more exact than life is
on the road to Inver near midnight
at the wheel under the moon's light
on the road to Inver – oh
how tiring one's imagination is
on the road to Inver always closer
to Inver – I want to reach out and touch it
like the rocks round Bantry Bay
on the road to Inver
craving peace its slow so slow
drop into our laps but as far
from it and myself as ever

## MEDBH MCGUCKIAN
## (*b.*1950)

### *The Seed-Picture*

This is my portrait of Joanna – since the split
The children come to me like a dumb-waiter,
And I wonder where to put them, beautiful seeds
With no immediate application . . . the clairvoyance
Of seed-work has opened up
New spectrums of activity, beyond a second home.
The seeds dictate their own vocabulary,
Their dusty colours capture
More than we can plan,
The mould on walls, or jumbled garages,
Dead flower heads where insects shack . . .
I only guide them not by guesswork
In their necessary numbers,
And attach them by the spine to a perfect bedding,
Woody orange pips, and tear-drop apple,
The banana of the caraway, wrinkled peppercorns,
The pocked peach, or waterlily honesty,
The seamed cherry stone so hard to break.

Was it such self-indulgence to enclose her
In the border of a grandmother's sampler,
Bonding all the seeds in one continuous skin,
The sky resolved to a cloud the length of a man?
To use tan linseed for the trees, spiky
Sunflower for leaves, bright lentils
For the window, patna stars
For the floral blouse? Her hair
Is made of hook-shaped marigold, gold
Of pleasure for her lips, like raspberry grain.
The eyelids oatmeal, the irises
Of Dutch blue maw, black rape

For the pupils, millet
For the vicious beige circles underneath.
The single pearl barley
That sleeps around her dullness
Till it catches light, makes women
Feel their age, and sigh for liberation.

## *The Sitting*

My half-sister comes to me to be painted:
She is posing furtively, like a letter being
Pushed under a door, making a tunnel with her
Hands over her dull-rose dress. Yet her coppery
Head is as bright as a net of lemons. I am
Painting it hair by hair as if she had not
Disowned it, or forsaken those unsparkling
Eyes as blue may be sifted from the surface
Of a cloud; and she questions my brisk
Brushwork, the note of positive red
In the kissed mouth I have given her,
As a woman's touch makes curtains blossom
Permanently in a house: she calls it
Wishfulness, the failure of the tampering rain
To go right into the mountain, she prefers
My sea-studies, and will not sit for me
Again, something half-opened, rarer
Than railroads, a soiled red-letter day.

## *Monody for Aghas*

You won't be a voice to me any more,
the weather of my own creation
repeating the highest possible shared
symptoms of the day. You were born

in a leap year, just as one day
was ending and the next beginning,
in a new time zone where landscape
has become language . . . blue bloom

of the faultless month of May,
with its heart set on conquering
every green glen . . . springtime
in action, springtime unfolding

into words, a literature of spring,
spring in place, time and eternity,
she-bird in its velvet dress
of soft blackbird colour,

maroon seed dashed from the hand.
Let me taste the whole of it,
my favourite tomb, the barbarity
and vividness of the route,

my due feet standing all night
in the sea of your pale goldfish
skin without body, its glimmering
sponged out by a tall white storm:

the red flag could not have made you
less Irish, your once-red lips before
and after folded together and left down
quietly, never to be parted,

that were forced open, strapped open,
by a sort of meal of a fixed gag,
a three-foot tube previously
used on ten others,

dipped in hot water, and withdrawn
and inserted, clogged and withdrawn,
and cleansed . . . your broad heart
became broader as you opened

to the Bridewell and the Curragh,
Mountjoy and Ship Street.
It was fifty hours without
plank bed or covering

while Max Green, Sir Arthur Chance,
Dr Lowe and the JP
almost wept, then attended
a banquet, before you smashed

the cell window for want of air,
and the Sisters of Charity
at the Mater Hospital
painted your mouth with brandy:

like a high-mettled horse,
soothing and coaxing him
with a sieve of provender in one hand
and a bridle in the other,

ready to slip it over his head
while he is snuffling at the food.
Today the fairest wreath is an inscape
mixed of strength and grace –

the ash tree trim above your grave.

## *She is in the Past, She has this Grace*

My mother looks at her watch,
as if to look back over the curve
of her life, her slackening rhythms:
nobody can know her, how she lost herself
evening after evening in that after,
her hourly feelings, the repetition,
delay and failure of her labour
of mourning. The steps space themselves
out, the steps pass, in the mists

and hesitations of the summer,
and within a space which is doubled
one of us has passed through the other,
though one must count oneself three,
to figure out which of us
has let herself be traversed.

Nothing advances, we don't move,
we don't address one another.
I haven't opened my mouth
except for one remark,
and what remark was that?
A word which appeases the menace
of time in us, reading as if
I were stripping the words
of their ever-mortal high meaning.

She is in dark light, or an openness
that leads to a darkness,
embedded in the wall
her mono-landscape
stays facing the sea
and the harbour activity,
her sea-conscience being ground up
with the smooth time of the deep,
her mourning silhouetted against
the splendour of the sea
which is now to your left,
as violent as it is distant
from all aggressive powers
or any embassies.

And she actively dreams
in the very long ending of this moment,
she is back in her lapping marshes,
still walking with the infinite
step of a prisoner, that former dimension
in which her gaze spreads itself
as a stroke without regarding you,
making you lower your own gaze.

Who will be there,
at that moment, beside her,
when time becomes sacred,
and her voice becomes an opera,
and the solitude is removed
from her body, as if my hand
had been held in some invisible place?

## PETER FALLON

## (*b.*1951)

### *The Company of Horses*

They are flesh on the bones
of the wind, going full gallop,
the loan of freedom.
But the company of broken

horses is a quiet blessing.
Just to walk in the paddock;
to stand by their stall.
Left to their own devices

they graze or doze, hock to fetlock
crooked at ease, or – head to tail –
nibble withers, hips and flanks.
They fit themselves flat

to the ground. They roll.
But the mere sound or smell
of us – and they're all neighs
and nickerings, their snorts

the splinters of the waves.
And growing out of morning
mists the ghosts of night
form silhouettes along the ridge,

a dun, two chestnuts,
and a bay. A shy colt stares
and shivers – a trembling like
fine feathers in a sudden breeze

around the hooves of heavy
horses. And the dam,
with foal to foot, steadies herself
to find her bearings,

her ears antennae of attention.
Put your hand towards her head-
collar, whispering your *Ohs* and *Whoa*,
*Oh the boy* and *Oh the girl*,

close your eyes and lean
your head towards
her quiet head, the way
the old grey mare,

hearing that her hero
joined the sleep
of death, spread her mane
across his breast and began to wail and weep.

## PAUL MULDOON

(*b.*1951)

### *The Electric Orchard*

The early electric people had domesticated the wild ass.
They knew all about falling off.
Occasionally, they would have fallen out of the trees.
Climbing again, they had something to prove
To their neighbours. And they did have neighbours.
The electric people lived in villages
Out of their need of security and their constant hunger.
Together they would divert their energies

To neutral places. Anger to the banging door,
Passion to the kiss.
And electricity to earth. Having stolen his thunder
From an angry god, through the trees
They had learned to string his lightning.
The women gathered random sparks into their aprons,
A child discovered the swing
Among the electric poles. Taking everything as given,

The electric people were confident, hardly proud.
They kept fire in a bucket,
Boiled water and dry leaves in a kettle, watched the lid
By the blue steam lifted and lifted.
So that, where one of the electric people happened to fall,
It was accepted as an occupational hazard.
There was something necessary about the thing. The North Wall

Of the Eiger was notorious for blizzards,
If one fell there his neighbour might remark, Bloody fool.
All that would have been inappropriate,
Applied to the experienced climber of electric poles.
I have achieved this great height?

No electric person could have been that proud,
Thirty or forty feet. Perhaps not that,
If the fall happened to be broken by the roof of a shed.
The belt would burst, the call be made,

The ambulance arrive and carry the faller away
To hospital with a scream.
There and then the electric people might invent the railway,
Just watching the lid lifted by the steam.
Or decide that all laws should be based on that of gravity,
Just thinking of the faller fallen.
Even then they were running out of things to do and see.
Gradually, they introduced legislation

Whereby they nailed a plaque to every last electric pole.
They would prosecute any trespassers.
The high up, singing and live fruit liable to shock or kill
Were forbidden. Deciding that their neighbours
And their neighbours' innocent children ought to be stopped
For their own good, they threw a fence
Of barbed wire round the electric poles. None could describe
Electrocution, falling, the age of innocence.

## *Cuba*

My eldest sister arrived home that morning
In her white muslin evening dress.
'Who the hell do you think you are,
Running out to dances in next to nothing?
As though we hadn't enough bother
With the world at war, if not at an end.'
My father was pounding the breakfast-table.

'Those Yankees were touch and go as it was –
If you'd heard Patton in Armagh –
But this Kennedy's nearly an Irishman
So he's not much better than ourselves.
And him with only to say the word.
If you've got anything on your mind
Maybe you should make your peace with God.'

I could hear May from beyond the curtain.
'Bless me, Father, for I have sinned.
I told a lie once, I was disobedient once.
And, Father, a boy touched me once.'
'Tell me, child. Was this touch immodest?
Did he touch your breast, for example?'
'He brushed against me, Father. Very gently.'

## *Anseo*

When the Master was calling the roll
At the primary school in Collegelands,
You were meant to call back *Anseo*
And raise your hand
As your name occurred.
*Anseo,* meaning here, here and now,
All present and correct,
Was the first word of Irish I spoke.
The last name on the ledger
Belonged to Joseph Mary Plunkett Ward
And was followed, as often as not,
By silence, knowing looks,
A nod and a wink, the Master's droll
'And where's our little Ward-of-court?'

I remember the first time he came back
The Master had sent him out
Along the hedges
To weigh up for himself and cut
A stick with which he would be beaten.

After a while, nothing was spoken;
He would arrive as a matter of course
With an ash-plant, a salley-rod.
Or, finally, the hazel-wand
He had whittled down to a whip-lash,
Its twist of red and yellow lacquers
Sanded and polished,
And altogether so delicately wrought
That he had engraved his initials on it.

I last met Joseph Mary Plunkett Ward
In a pub just over the Irish border.
He was living in the open,
In a secret camp
On the other side of the mountain.
He was fighting for Ireland,
Making things happen.
And he told me, Joe Ward,
Of how he had risen through the ranks
To Quartermaster, Commandant:
How every morning at parade
His volunteers would call back *Anseo*
And raise their hands
As their names occurred.

## from *Immram*

I was just about getting things into perspective
When a mile-long white Cadillac
Came sweeping out of the distant past
Like a wayward Bay mist,
A transport of joy. There was that chauffeur
From the 1931 Sears Roebuck catalogue,
Susannah, as you guessed,
And this refugee from F. Scott Fitzgerald
Who looked as if he might indeed own the world.
His name was James Earl Caulfield III.

This was how it was. My father had been a mule.
He had flown down to Rio
Time and time again. But he courted disaster.
He tried to smuggle a wooden statue
Through the airport at Lima.
The Christ of the Andes. The statue was hollow.
He stumbled. It went and shattered.
And he had to stand idly by
As a cool fifty or sixty thousand dollars worth
Was trampled back into the good earth.

He would flee, to La Paz, then to Buenos Aires,
From alias to alias.
I imagined him sitting outside a hacienda
Somewhere in the Argentine.
He would peer for hours
Into the vastness of the pampas.
Or he might be pointing out the constellations
Of the Southern hemisphere
To the open-mouthed child at his elbow.
He sleeps with a loaded pistol under his pillow.

The mile-long white Cadillac had now wrapped
Itself round the Park Hotel.
We were spirited to the nineteenth floor
Where Caulfield located a secret door.
We climbed two perilous flights of steps
To the exclusive penthouse suite.
A moment later I was ushered
Into a chamber sealed with black drapes.
As I grew accustomed to the gloom
I realized there was someone else in the room.

He was huddled on an old orthopaedic mattress,
The makings of a skeleton,
Naked but for a pair of draw-string shorts.
His hair was waistlength, as was his beard.
He was covered in bedsores.
He raised one talon.

'I forgive you,' he croaked. 'And I forget.
On your way out, you tell that bastard
To bring me a dish of ice-cream.
I want Baskin-Robbins banana-nut ice-cream.'

I shimmied about the cavernous lobby.
Mr and Mrs Alfred Tennyson
Were ahead of me through the revolving door.
She tipped the bell-hop five dollars.
There was a steady stream of people
That flowed in one direction,
Faster and deeper,
That I would go along with, happily,
As I made my way back, like any other pilgrim,
To Main Street, to Foster's pool-room.

## *Aisling*

I was making my way home late one night
this summer, when I staggered
into a snow drift.

Her eyes spoke of a sloe-year,
her mouth a year of haws.

Was she Aurora, or the goddess Flora,
Artemidora, or Venus bright,
or Anorexia, who left
a lemon stain on my flannel sheet?

It's all much of a muchness.

In Belfast's Royal Victoria Hospital
a kidney machine
supports the latest hunger-striker
to have called off his fast, a saline
drip into his bag of brine.

A lick and a promise. Cuckoo spittle.
I hand my sample to Doctor Maw.
She gives me back a confident *All Clear*.

## *They that Wash on Thursday*

She was such a dab hand, my mother. Such a dab hand
at raising her hand
to a child. At bringing a cane down across my hand
in such a seemingly offhand
manner I almost have to hand
it to her. 'Many hands,'
she would say, 'spoil the broth.' My father took no hand
in this. He washed his hands
of the matter. He sat on his hands.
So I learned firsthand
to deal in the off-, the under-, the sleight-of-hand,
writing now in that great, open hand
yet never quite showing my hand.
I poured myself a drink with a heavy hand.
As for the women with whom I sat hand-in-hand
in the Four-in-Hand,
as soon as they were eating out of my hand
I dismissed them out of hand.
Then one would play into my hands –
or did she force my hand? –
whose lily-white hand
I took in marriage. I should have known beforehand
it wouldn't work. 'When will you ever take yourself in hand?'
'And give you the upper hand?'
For things were by now completely out of hand.
The show of hands
on a moonlit hill under the Red Hand.
The Armalite in one hand
and the ballot box in the other. Men dying at hand.
Throughout all of which I would hand
back to continuity as the second hand
came up to noon. 'On the one hand . . .

On the other . . .' The much-vaunted even hand
of the BBC. Though they'd pretty much given me a free hand
I decided at length to throw in my hand
and tendered my resignation 'by hand'.
I was now quite reconciled to living from hand
to mouth. (Give that man a big, big hand.)
My father was gone. My mother long gone. Into Thy hands,
O Lord . . . Gone, too, the ink-stained hands
of Mary Powers. Now I'd taken another lily-white hand
put in by the hole of the door. A hand
no bigger than a cloud. Now she and I and the child of my
    right hand
stand hand in hand,
brave Americans all, and I know ('The bird in the hand
is the early bird . . .') that the time is at hand
for me to set my hand
to my daughter's still-wet, freehand
version of the Muldoon 'coat of arms' that came to hand
in a heraldry shop on Nassau Street – on a green field a white
    hand.

## *Third Epistle to Timothy*

*You made some mistake when you intended to favor me with some of the new valuable grass seed . . . for what you gave me . . . proves mere timothy.*

—A letter from Benjamin Franklin to Jared Eliot, July 16, 1747

I

Midnight. June 1923. Not a stir except for the brough and
    brouhaha
surrounding the taper or link
in which a louse
flares up and a shadow, my da's,
clatters against a wall of the six-by-eight-by-six-foot room

he sleeps in, eleven years old, a servant boy at Hardys of
Carnteel.
There's a boot-polish lid filled with turps
or paraffin oil
under each cast-iron bed leg, a little barrier
against bedbugs under each bed foot.

II

That knocking's the knocking against their stalls of a team
of six black Clydesdales mined in Coalisland
he's only just helped to unhitch from the cumbersome
star of a hay rake. Decently and in order
he brought each whitewashed nose
to its nosebag of corn, to its galvanized bucket.
One of the six black Clydesdale mares
he helped all day to hitch and unhitch
was showing, on the near hock, what might be a bud of farcy
picked up, no doubt, while on loan to Wesley Cummins.

III

'Decently and in order,' Cummins would proclaim, 'let all
Inniskillings
be done.' A week ago my da helped him limber up
the team to a mowing machine as if to a gun carriage. 'For no
Dragoon
can function without his measure of char.'
He patted his bellyband. 'A measure, that is, against
dysentery.'
This was my da's signal to rush
into the deep shade of the hedge to fetch such little tea as
might remain
in the tea urn. 'Man does not live,' Cummins would snort,
'only by scraps
of wheaten farls and tea dregs.
You watch your step or I'll see you're shipped back to
Killeter.'

IV

'Kill*eeshill*,' my da says, 'I'm from Killeeshill.' Along the
cast-iron
rainbow of his bed end
comes a line
of chafers or cheeselips that have scaled the bed legs
despite the boot-polish lids. Eleven years of age. A servant boy
on the point of falling asleep. The reek of paraffin
or the pinewoods reek
of turpentine
good against roundworm in horses. That knocking against
their stalls
of six Clydesdales, each standing at sixteen hands.

V

Building hay even now, even now drawing level with the
team's headbrass,
buoyed up by nothing more than the ballast
of hay – meadow cat's-tail, lucerne, the leaf upon trodden leaf
of white clover and red –
drawing level now with the taper blooms of a horse chestnut.
Already light in the head.
'Though you speak, young Muldoon . . .' Cummins calls up
from trimming the skirt
of the haycock, 'though you speak with the tongue
of an angel, I see you for what you are . . . Malevolent.
Not only a member of the church malignant but a *malevolent*
spirit.'

VI

Even now borne aloft by bearing down on lap cocks and
shake cocks
from under one of which a ruddy face
suddenly twists and turns upward as if itself carried
on a pitchfork and, meeting its gaze

he sees himself, a servant boy still, still ten or eleven,
breathing upon a Clydesdale's near hock and finding a farcy bud
like a tiny glow in a strut of charcoal.
'I see you,' Cummins points at him with the pitchfork, 'you
    little byblow,
I see you casting your spells, your sorceries,
I see you coming as a thief in the night to stab us in the back.'

VII

A year since they kidnapped Anketell Moutray from his home
    at Favour Royal,
dragging him, blindfolded, the length of his own gravel path,
eighty years old, the Orange County grand master. Four A
    Specials shot on a train
in Clones. The Clogher valley
a blaze of flax mills and haysheds. Memories of the Land
    League. Davitt and Biggar.
Breaking the boycott at Lough Mask.
The Land Leaguers beaten
at the second battle of Saintfield. It shall be revealed . . .
A year since they cut out the clapper of a collabor . . .
    a collabor . . .
a collaborator from Maguiresbridge.

VIII

That knocking's the team's near-distant knocking on wood
while my da breathes upon
the blue-yellow flame on a fetlock, on a deep-feathered pastern
of one of six black Shires . . . 'Because it shall be revealed by fire,'
Cummins's last pitchfork is laden
with thistles, 'as the sparks fly upward
man is born into trouble. For the tongue may yet be cut
from an angel.' The line of cheeselips and chafers
along the bed end. 'Just wait till you come back down and I
    get a hold
of you, young Muldoon . . . We'll see what spells you'll cast.'

IX

For an instant it seems no one else might scale
such a parapet of meadow cat's-tail, lucerne, red and white
    clovers,
not even the line of chafers and cheeselips
that overthrow as they undermine
when, light in the head, unsteady on his pegs as Anketell
    Moutray,
he squints through a blindfold of clegs
from his grass-capped, thistle-strewn vantage point,
the point where two hay ropes cross,
where Cummins and his crew have left him, in a straw hat
    with a fraying brim,
while they've moved on to mark out the next haycock.

X

That next haycock already summoning itself from windrow
    after wind-weary windrow
while yet another brings itself to mind in the acrid stink
of turpentine. There the image of Lizzie,
Hardy's last servant girl, reaches out from her dais
of salt hay, stretches out an unsunburned arm
half in bestowal, half beseechingly, then turns away to appeal
to all that spirit troop
of hay treaders as far as the eye can see, the coil on coil
of hay from which, in the taper's mild uproar,
they float out across the dark face of the earth, an earth
    without form, and void.

## *The Breather*

Think of this gravestone
as a long, low chair
strategically placed
at a turn in the stair.

## *Turkey Buzzards*

They've been so long above it all,
    those two petals
so steeped in style they seem to stall
    in the kettle

simmering over the town dump
    or, better still,
the neon-flashed, X-rated rump
    of fresh roadkill

courtesy of the interstate
    that Eisenhower
would overtake in the home straight
    by one horsepower,

the kettle where it all boils down
    to the thick scent
of death, a scent of such renown
    it's given vent

to the idea buzzards can spot
    a deer carcass
a mile away, smelling the rot
    as, once, Marcus

Aurelius wrinkled his nose
    at a gas leak
from the Great Sewer that ran through Rome
    to the Tiber

then went searching out, through the gloam,
    one subscriber
to the other view that the rose,
    full-blown, antique,

its no-frills ruff, the six-foot shrug
    of its swing-wings,
the theologian's and the thug's
    twin triumphings

in a buzzard's shaved head and snood,
    buzz-buzz-buzzy,
its logic in all likelihood
    somewhat fuzzy,

would ever come into focus,
    it ever deign
to dispense its hocus-pocus
    in that same vein

as runs along an inner thigh
    to where, too right,
the buzzard vouchsafes not to shy
    away from shite,

its mission not to give a miss
    to a bête noire,
all roly-poly, full of piss
    and vinegar,

trying rather to get to grips
    with the grommet
of the gut, setting its tinsnips
    to that grommet

in the spray-painted hind's hindgut
    and making a
sweeping, too right, a sweeping cut
    that's so blasé

it's hard to imagine, dear Sis,
    why others shrink
from this sight of a soul in bliss,
    so in the pink

from another month in the red
 of the shambles,
like a rose in over its head
 among brambles,

unflappable in its belief
 it's Ararat
on which the Ark would come to grief,
 abjuring that

Marcus Aurelius humbug
 about what springs
from earth succumbing to the tug
 at its heartstrings,

reported to live past fifty,
 as you yet may,
dear Sis, perhaps growing your hair
 in requital,

though briefly, of whatever tears
 at your vitals,
learning, perhaps, from the nifty,
 nay *thrifty*, way

these buzzards are given to stoop
 and take their ease
by letting their time-chastened poop
 fall to their knees

till they're almost as bright with lime
 as their night roost,
their poop containing an enzyme
 that's known to boost

their immune systems, should they prong
 themselves on small
bones in a cerebral cortex,
 at no small cost

to their well-being, sinking fast
  in a deer crypt,
buzzards getting the hang at last
  of being stripped

of their command of the vortex
  while having lost
their common touch, they've been so long
  above it all.

## KERRY HARDIE
## (*b.*1951)

### *Ship of Death*

*for my mother*

Watching you, for the first time,
turn to prepare your boat, my mother;
making it clear you have other business now –
the business of your future –
I was washed-through with anger.

It was a first survey,
an eye thrown
over sails, oars, timbers,
as many a time I'd seen that practised eye
scan a laden table.

How can you plan going off like this
when we stand at last, close enough, if the wind is right,
to hear what the other is saying?
I never thought you'd do this, turning away,
mid-sentence, your hand testing a rope,

your ear tuned
to the small thunder of the curling wave
on the edge of the great-night sea,
neither regretful nor afraid –
anxious only for the tide.

## *Seal Morning*

The small seal, laid on the greyish sand
like a bolster – the same off-white colour –
its smooth, tight, belly-ticking holed by a crow,
one thick thread of blackened entrail
pulled out and looped loosely over its body.
And the crow – standing off – waiting.

Like those old stories of the Vikings,
how they'd prick a man's belly and hook out
a coil of his gut. Then they'd nail it to a tree
and make him crawl round and around,
unwinding himself, the tree taking his entrails,
as a bobbin draws thread from a spool.

The sea mist was a blowing whiteness,
the small seal lay on its back in a curve,
one flipper folded across its body,
the other outstretched. Like a sunbather
lying in easy abandon, asleep. Too private really;
too like someone at rest in their own bed.

The pale-grey spots of its markings
just showed through the white belly-bristle,
and on the sands were blooms of flattened weed
and gutted crabs and broken shells
and the long line
of the small, low waves, running in.

It was like those Impressionist views
of beaches in Northern France
in the white, morning light –
the people strolling in pale clothes,
the navy ribbons on the boaters flapping,
the sun, trying to break through.

The crow stood on the tide-stretched strand,
surveying its handiwork.
Attentive, but also indifferent.
Like the Vikings.
Like the painter
when the whitish light is in the painting.

## NUALA NÍ DHOMHNAILL
(*b.*1952)

### *The Shannon Estuary Welcomes the Fish*

The salmon's leap
In the darkness –
Bare blade
Silver shield;
And me welcoming, net-
Draped and slippery
Full of seaweed
Of quiet eddies
And eel-tails.

All meat
Is this fish
Almost nothing of bone
Less of entrail

Twenty packed pounds
Of tensed muscle
Straining
Towards its nest among the neat mosses.

And I sing a lullaby
To my darling
Wave on wave
Verse after verse,
My phosphorescence a sheet beneath him
My chosen one, drawn from afar.

*PC*

## *The Language Issue*

I place my hope on the water
in this little boat
of the language, the way a body might put
an infant

in a basket of intertwined
iris leaves,
its underside proofed
with bitumen and pitch,

then set the whole thing down amidst
the sedge
and bulrushes by the edge
of a river

only to have it borne hither and thither,
not knowing where it might end up;
in the lap, perhaps,
of some Pharaoh's daughter.

*Paul Muldoon*

## *My Father's People*

I am still with you, my father's people,
On the cold flags of the kitchen before dawn of day,
Waiting for the cock's first cry, barefoot on the cold stone,
Waiting for the ghosts to scatter so you can go out and start
working
Earth too poor to feed you, a living fit for snipe –
But what choice have you but to go on hammering at it,
What keeps you going but a taste for work and the sharp edge of
struggle,
The proverb your war cry, 'Rent for a landlord or food for a
child.'

Mickey the Skinner was put out on the side of the road
During the Land War. The neighbours built him a cabin of sods;
The gable is visible yet beside the bridge of Gleann na hUaighe.
Cattle were put on his farm, their leg-tendons were slit in the
night. . .
After seven years his case came on at the Assizes in Tralee
And he walked the whole twenty-six miles in there in his nailed
boots;
He couldn't pay a lawyer, he pleaded his own case in English
And won. His rent was slashed from six pounds a cow down
to two.

And his father before him again, that they called Seán of the
Women,
Who fell down dead as he worked out in his field.
The coroner came along driving his pony and trap
From Castlegregory, took the one look at him
And said, 'This is the body of a man seventy years old.'
'No,' said the neighbours, 'he was only fifty years of age.'
'No matter,' said the doctor, 'whatever age he was, this is an
old man's body' –
Worn out with perpetual labour, with the wet damp and the cold.

His son after him, Seán Caol the schoolmaster
Never soiled his hands with any kind of farming work.
He spent all his days in the struggle with heroic tasks of the
mind:
The teaching of grammar or solving enormous algebraic or
geometrical problems.
Learning and teaching were his eternal preoccupations,
And hammering mountains of English into the heads of his
pupils.
Well he knew that all their portion and capital for life
Would be sound learning, as they faced the emigrant ship to
America.

He warmed their hands, he made them dance without music,
He wielded his stick so memorably that at this day
in South Boston they say of anyone slow or ignorant,
'Easy to see he never spent any time with Seán Caol.'
He married a beautiful, gentle, pleasant woman,
Nano Rohan, but if so she had a hard time with him.
Six living words in English was all she'd get from him in
the morning:
'Water, Towel, Soap, Pinstuds, Breakfast at eight' and 'Polish
me boots.'

What wonder then that his own son couldn't stand him,
My Grandad, who joined the Irish Volunteers to get away
from him,
And from the Collège des Irlandais in Paris where he was
supposed to be studying for the priesthood.
It was thirty years before he could face going home to his father.
In the meantime he became an Inspector of Schools, much
against his nature,
A kind, gently spoken man (who had his dark side too,
A thirst for drink that could take him on the tear for weeks)
– A man who wrote dark poems full of gloom and self-loathing.

Eily, the one sister that he had in the world,
Was afraid neither of God nor man nor beast.
Her one terror on earth was the lightning would strike
The house, and she in it. She had a lead lightning-rod down
    through the chimney
As thick as a man's neck. I remember seeing it myself.
Any day that she would be raging round the house, whistling
With fury and bad temper, the boys needed only
To look up at the sky and suggest that there might be thunder

And she was down on her knees praying, beseeching the
    Blessèd Virgin,
Dousing the four corners of the house with holy water
And the rafters too.
                                What an inheritance for me,
What wonder then that when the fit strikes me
And I get out of bed as vicious as a bee
Fit to kick the cat and the dog if we had either,
That I feel my father's people are still with me
In the dark kitchen, waiting for the dawning day.

*Eiléan Ní Chuilleanáin*

## *The Hair Market*

Did you ever go to the Hair Market?
It's down on the right-hand side of the Bird Market.
You have to thread slowly through narrow streets
In a little medieval town in France.

It's there you'll hear the noise and fuss and uproar,
The auctioneers shouting over their megaphones,
Screaming the highest bid at the top of their voices,
Buying and selling, cutting deals at every turn.

And it's there you'll see plaits and chignons and ponytails
Flowing smooth or curling from ceiling to floor,
Heaps of tresses raked and teased out,
Servants combing them, armslength after armslength.

Were you ever in the Hair Market?
I went there once myself on a certain day.
They cut my long red locks close to my skull,
And sold them to a Sultan for the best price of all.

*Eiléan Ní Chuilleanáin*

## *Mermaid with Parish Priest*

Because she was so clever she wrote a brilliant essay
on 'Birds' for the Primary Cert Exam.
She had collected her knowledge from old copies of *National Geographic*
and other reference books she found at home.
She was crazy about birds, partly because they were so newfangled to her.
They were like fish, swimming in air like supernatural things.
It is small wonder that she lost the head over them.

The parish priest came into the school in the middle of the exam.
He picked up her essay and read it and was very taken with it.
A week later he asked the nun in charge of the class
to send the mermaid with a message of some kind to the Parochial House.

She would never forget the smell of his study.
The long lines of books and the musky smell in the air.
He spoke to her in Irish. He showed her Bedell's Bible.
Then he put her sitting on his lap
with her legs astride him on either side.

He pushed against her again and again
and he began to huff and puff and break out in a sweat.
His face went from dark to red to white
and then she felt something wet about his trousers.

She knew something was up but she couldn't make out what.
(She was only eleven and still totally ignorant of such things.)
But when the same thing began to happen again and again
on a weekly basis, she felt nausea and self-loathing.
In the end she refused point-blank to go over there again.
To her astonishment the nun made no comment whatsoever,
and another little victim was sent over in her stead.

There was only one other time he came on to her
when her application form
for the County Council Scholarship had gone missing
after her mother had warned her in no uncertain terms
not to forget to mail it. So she had to go
and pick up another one, which needed his signature
at the bottom of the form. She went up to the Parochial House
with her tiny little heart in her mouth, and her knees knocking
against each other.
She felt just like Isaac must have felt with the sacrificial wood
round his neck. And this time there was no convenient ram
with its horns caught in the bushes to let her off the hook.

He did his business, and she got the signature.
But she felt as if she had prostituted herself for it.
From that day on she lost complete faith in all adults
and six months later, when she took
first place in the county in the Scholarship exam,
it was a Pyrrhic victory. It was tainted with misery.
Especially when she could see that same man in the chapel
every Sunday where he thumped the pulpit
and fulminated against 'immodest dances'.
(He meant the Twist.) He was pawing and stamping like a bull.
She noticed something she remembered all too well,
how his face went from black to red to white.

That was the end of Mass for her.
Any time she went next nor near the church
she would fall down in a fainting fit.
Years later, after she'd lived abroad for a long time,
when she heard he'd died
at a County Hurling Championship, in Ennis, County Clare,
she didn't say a prayer for his soul but cursed him roundly.

But she wasn't free of him for a long time after
for he'd appear to her in dreams as a vampire
or bloodsucking fiend. He'd be standing on the balcony
outside the window of her bedroom
always asking leave
to come in. She used to wake up in a state of anxiety,
sweating profusely, her heart in her mouth,
terrified out of her wits, till she gradually realized
the bedroom she was in didn't have a balcony.

Little wonder that shortly afterwards she renounced the Irish language.
Never again did she set eyes on Bedell's Bible.
But the damage didn't just stop there. When she finally plucked up the courage,
years later, to tell her mother what had happened, the response
she got from her was 'Oh, the poor priest, isn't he a man
like any other?' 'Well,' said the mermaid inwardly,
'that's the last thing I'll ever tell you.'
And, as it happens, it was.

*Paul Muldoon*

## MAURICE SCULLY
## (*b.*1952)

### *from* Over & Through

#### *Sound*

I wish I had a house, wheedle and whine, I wish
I had a bit of money, closing the door,
opening the window. The soul's ability
to ripple through crisp watermarks – vertical
layers – mud and wattle cabins and a tidy
compound. Only a house. In. The.
Breathing. For instance. I wish I had a
roof, my two kids, my one wife. Less
nomadics, but then a whole haversack
of heartstopping examples: wash-basins,
wainscot, rain-pearls on a clothesline,
a clean spread of glasspane deep in its framebed,
whatever you've got, a folded view through
gold and developing veins underground,
small traditional poems – or even less
traditional poems even – or even less.

#### *Liking the Big Wheelbarrow*

We sat on the side of a mountain and muttered
something about the Basotho. We were dissatisfied.
We were given a part of something to understand,
our self-esteem under attack, daily nibblings
at the plinth. Fixing bridges, developing struts.
Wait. The instruction was to wait. Be still.

Dust particles collide and bounce away, collide
again elsewhere and stick until a thicker
filamentary delicate medium sinks to the central
plane of the disc which breaks into rings which
clump and accrete which orbit the core which spark
the beginning of the accretion of the solid cores
of the planets we know, from webs and threads
on magnetic bands. In theory. Only quietest
collisions. Clusters. Crystals and dust grains.
The four-year-old child who said to the pilot
on their way to the plane on the air ferry tarmac:
'I like your big wheelbarrow.'

## *from* D E F

### *Lullaby*

Yr father blank in a chair.
Bored tired deaf blind dirty.
Nurse calls in to the wrong ear.
Alert but not sure of the year.

Yr sister soaks a relative for money
yr brother terrified cuts & runs
yr wife yr children yr body ageing
bored tired deaf blind/damn it/all of these things –

sanity phones
listen this that
rubbish & bones
life is hate –

sit down then to concentrate this
hopelessness into an art that's
locked in to the point where the
key clicks yes but heart sinks –
bored tired deaf blind – down to all
these all of these all

of these things piled up to here do
you hear can you hear me me falling too
father yr head against the wall-wall
of yr room cracks with a bang & jammed
against the piano & the door I can't
get in

to you until we find the key to
life is easy isn't it piling up the past
in the mist deaf blind it ever occur
to you among world-things to look to
the place where the money screams then
blind deaf then
it's over
over?

Rubbish & bones
listen my love
listen to this
pass it on.

---

*I was a boy once, then a young man; now in middle age, both;*
*(the edge of the allegory twining the spine of the rentbook).*
*To fool a trout, Blue Lulu. To fool me, a peck of honesty.*

## MAURICE RIORDAN
## (*b.*1953)

### *The Sloe*

That he died alone in the gully
below the pass in a snowstorm, the first
of the year, in a lurch of the seasons
which became a change of climate;
that he died some three to five weeks
after an assault – from a wild beast
or fellow man – which shattered
his ribcage and sent him above
the tree-line, far from the settlements,
that he died really from
being alone, an injured man
relying on his few resources – which were,
however, both innate and military,
so that he carried about him
not only weapons and tools
but spares, medicine, and a sewing kit,
fire, and the means of fire,
and was observant and skilled
about stone, wood, grasses, skins,
about stag-horn and bone – knew for each
its properties and use, but he died
like Xenophon's comrades on the trek
home through Armenia, as soldiers
have died on all recorded
winter marches, not from lack of discipline
or the body's weakness, or not only,
but because of the slight
shortening of the odds which comes
with the unexpected comfort of snow;
so that prepared for the next day's climb,
his equipment in order,

the backpack, the axe, the two
birch-bark containers, one holding
tinder and flints, the other
insulated with damp sycamore leaves
(but no longer carrying live embers),
the quiver, and beside it the straight new bow
with its unused string, the bird net
spread, the pannier upright,
he ate the last of his food
– all except, oddly, a sloe –
then lay on his uninjured side
in the best available shelter
and pillowed his head, while the snow
(which would lull and warm him)
spiralled out of the night and marked,
as I've said, a change in the Tyrol,
a climatic glitch which lasted 5,000 years
until the thaw on the glacier two summers ago
brought him to our attention,
then here to the Institute;
so that, although I can tell you
nothing of his gods or language,
almost nothing of his way of life,
whether he was shepherd, headman,
or shaman, the last of his village
or employed on some delicate embassy;
whether he moved in the forest
among spirits and shades
or was himself almost a shadow
who with a visceral roar
fell on a victim and bludgeoned
his brains, whether on a raid
he would satisfy his need with a woman or child
or, contrariwise, was himself
husband and father,
a tender of flocks in the epoch
of transhumance: gregarious, hierarchical,
a transmitter of geographical lore,
of trails, cloud changes, windbreaks,

who sang at the camp fire –
though I can tell you nothing of this
I can tell exactly
how he died, how in his plight
he couldn't string the green yew stave,
he couldn't ignite the tinder
to roast the songbirds
and, from the decalcified traces
on the humerus, I can tell
he kept, those last weeks, one arm
crooked, in a virtual sling,
thus giving the broken ribs time
to knit (as indeed they were doing)
and can guess, in the interim, he hoped
for an Indian summer of nuts, mushrooms, fruit,
a fire not quite dead,
even a maggot-ridden carcass;
and for a hand with the bow stave
he would have given in exchange his knife
or his coloured tassel with its marble bead,
that one inutile item polished
so spherical and white
it seems, like the sloe,
extraneous . . . but everything
comes down to the sloe, the uneaten sloe:
herders from Anatolia to the Ötzal,
even to the present day, pick
these sour, purplish almost pith-less fruits
and, like my Grandfather Bögelmann
when he dropped one in his fob,
they say 'A frost will sweeten it'
– so it is grave goods, viaticum,
food for the soul on its journey,
in its flight from the tip
of the punctured heel or the slit
tattooed into the lumbar,
and when the temperature drops
and the body's anaesthetized,
as the brain sinks into its reverie

of log fires and song,
of dripping fat and tree sap,
even as the skin adheres to the earth,
the tannins and acids disintegrate
so that now, as I put the sloe back in the ice,
I tell you it is edible,
that, by morning, it was sweet.

## from *The Idylls*

### 2

Another day when they were sitting on the headland in the Small Fields, the men discussed the changes they had seen and a debate arose about what was the greatest change had happened in their lifetime.

'What do you think?' my father asked Dan-Jo.

'The steam tractor was a great change,' the trucker answered. 'And then the motor car. But the greatest of all to my mind was the cutter-and-binder.'

'That was a great change,' my father said. 'And you, Alf, what would you say?'

'When the dam was built at Ardnacrusha it flooded farmland in seven parishes,' said the Gully.

'Yes, that was a great and a terrible change,' my father agreed. 'Moss, you've seen more than any of us. What's your opinion?'

'Women's fashion,' the forester replied. 'Girls these days in next to nothing at Mass.'

My father nodded, 'That too is a great change.' And the rest chipped in and everyone had a different opinion about what was the greatest change in their lifetime: television, the creamery, penicillin, Shannon airport, the price of stout, false teeth, tourists, the electric fence, plastic bags, weedkiller.

'There are a lot of changes,' my father said.

Moss turned to him, 'Tell us, Martin, what you think.'

My father fished in his inside pocket and took out a small framed photo of a woman in a wide hat and veil, smiling happily.

'That,' he said, 'is my mother on her honeymoon.'

## DENNIS O'DRISCOLL
## (*b*.1954)

### from *Churchyard View: The New Estate*

Taking it all with us,
we move in.

*

On their side, inviolable silence.
On ours, hammering, pounding,
sawing, clawing out foundations
with the frenzy of someone buried alive.

*

We like our dead well-seasoned.
Newly-ground soil disturbs.

*

She could wind him round her little finger
that is now solid bone.

*

My halogen light with sensor
alert for resurrections.

*

Our houses, giant mausoleums,
dwarf their tombs to kennels.

*

Crab-apple windfalls
at the cemetery wall
no one collects for jelly.

*

The churchyard in shadow
like a north-facing garden.

*

A lip-puffed, ear-blocked, glow-nosed
head cold is what they feel nostalgia for.

*

How much it took to sustain their lives:
heaps of gravel, travel coupons, steel pads,
roll-on deodorants, bran flakes, tampons.

*

The dead seem more at ease in autumn
as the time to hibernate comes near.

*

In our pine bed, we hear them stirring
when floorboards creak, pipes cheep.

*

The prehensile clasp of the dead
grasping at prayer books
with straw-yellow claws.

*

Not a footprint dipped in churchyard snow.

*

The child's coffin
like a violin case.
A pitch which parents' ears
can hear through clay.

*

Scan the obit columns, uniform as war graves.
Check the maiden names, the regretting children.
Whole cities and towns wiped out.
A plague on all your houses.

*

Above prison-high walls,
the trees – up to their knees
in slaughter – protest their innocence
to the outside world.

*

Add the total suffering of these bodies.
Deduct their combined pleasure.
What doth it profit a man?

*

I stare at the graves
like a sailor gazing out to sea.

## THOMAS MCCARTHY

(*b.*1954)

### *Ellen Tobin McCarthy*

You were as psychic as my father
was confused. Nowadays I am haunted
by you and the menagerie of ghosts –
they are wings of loneliness.

*

Life was a mystery to you –
domestic life was a form of magic:
you always watched the ring of a cooker
as if it was the aurora borealis.

*

A gun behind the picture of The Sacred Heart;
the fear of uniforms. Your half-brother
lost a foot in some Monaghan skirmish –
our poor Republic! The poor always cop it.

*

Why should I love this dead town?
You were humiliated unto death.
The Rich wouldn't touch us with a ten-foot
pole, or even a number nine iron.

*

In moments of weakness when I believe in God
instead of the anarchist ideologue, Christ,

I recall the frightening of women by priests,
their Maria Corelli faces, their pitiful beads.

*

You are sitting in my father's lap;
it is a cold day in late October –
you rediscovered each other near the end,
but not before you broke our hearts.

*

I watch the minutes passing away:
the minutes are like bark of *olearia*
blowing along the grass after a storm:
each bark a negative of your dead face.

*

There is a fire burning in the bedroom
the night before my First Communion.
You re-enter, again and again,
to absorb the anointed firelight.

*

To be lucky in love is the best thing,
you insisted. Better than all the wealth
in Dungarvan. Which is why
you switched fiancés at seventeen.

*

I must have seen you crying often
after a Friday morning deluge of bills;
but it is your girl's infectious laugh
that reaches here through the years.

*

Leaves blown against the gutter,
bloodied leaves of Virginia creeper;
an untrained growth is void of conversation,
sterile as an unexamined life.

*

The Dáil assembles for a new session;
there's a Deputy still in prison.
How quickly you would have lit candles
for Gregory, as you did for Noel Browne.

*

Suffering anointed you for death.
You were adored at seventeen;
at thirty-seven you had the weight of love –
you were Mary without Elizabeth.

*

I visit your grave for the first time,
*Nel*, mother. The hardened earth
brings countless humiliations to mind –
no mystical blackbirds, no sparrows.

## *The Standing Trains*

*. . . and I thought how wonderful to miss one's connections;*
*soon I shall miss them all the time.*
Louis MacNeice, *The Strings Are False*

From the windows of a standing train
you can judge the artwork of our poor Republic.
The prominent ruins that make Limerick Junction
seem like Dresden in 1945

and the beaten-up coaches at Mallow Station,
the rusted side-tracks at Charleville,
have taken years of independent thought.
It takes decades to destroy a system
of stations. On the other hand, a few
well-placed hand-signals can destroy a whole
mode of life, a network of happiness.
This is our own Republic! O Memory,
O Patria, the shame of silenced junctions.
Time knew we'd rip the rails apart, we'd sell
emigrant tickets even while stripping
the ticket-office bare. The standing trains
of the future were backed against a wall.

Two hens peck seed from the bright platform,
hens roost in the signal-box.
Bilingual signs that caused a debate in the Senate
have been unbolted and used as gates:
it's late summer now in this dead station.
When I was twelve they unbolted the rails.
Now there's only the ghost of my father,
standing by the parcel-shed with his ghostly
suitcase. When he sees me walking towards him
he becomes upset. *Don't stop here!* he cries.
*Keep going, keep going! This place is dead.*

## RITA ANN HIGGINS

(*b.*1955)

### *Black Dog in My Docs Day*

Your mother rings from your grave.
I say where are you?

She says, I'm at Michael's grave
and it looks lovely today.

Duffy misses you,
Jennifer Lydon misses you.
You were grand until depression
slipped into your shoes –
after that you dragged your feet
big long giraffe strides. Slim-2 Speed.

When depression slept
you were up for anything,
go for it and you went for it –
times you got it, other times you lost it,
you didn't play the lyre,
you played the horses,
lady luck was often with you
you never looked back
William and Lara miss you.

When you were a few months old
I went to see you in hospital,
you had meningitis.
The nurse told me that I had to leave,
I told her you were my nephew,
she said you still had meningitis.
You had days months and years to go,
the crowd in Maxwell's miss you.

When your mother said,
Michael started school today
I thought you were too young,
you grew up without telling us,
you went to sleep small,
when you got up
you were kitchen-table tall,
you had fourteen years to go.

A messer in your Communion photos,
leaning against the wall in hidden valley
arms akimbo, one foot behind the other,
you were ready to trip the light fantastic
the body of Christ.

Odd times in Castle Park
when you were passing the house,
I'd said, Michael wait up
you'd say, no way José!
I've got the black dog in my shoes
I have to drag him half way across Ireland,
I have to do it today and it must be raining.

Our Jennifer misses you
Christy misses the long chats with you,
he wished you didn't talk so much in the bookies,
Heather misses you,
Larry didn't know you
but Larry misses you because Heather misses you.

Eleven years to go you dyed your hair,
your uncles didn't know you,
they didn't know what they were missing.
No school wanted you.
You wanted Nirvana, you wanted The Doors,
you wanted shoes you didn't have to drag
you wanted hush puppies or Gandhi's flip-flops
instead you got Docs with a difference
the joy-roy gang miss you.

For your Confirmation
you took Hercules as your middle name,
you wanted a sweatshirt and baggy pants,
you left your mother and George at the church,
kiss me there you said to your mother
pointing to your cheek
and you were off with your friends,

soldier of Christ.
Auntie Mary and Aidan miss you,
Johnny misses you,
Caroline Keady misses you.

Móinín na gCiseach Tech said you failed maths,
you went in yourself to set the record straight.
Your mother has the letter of apology the school sent.
No school wanted the boy with blue hair
Dana C. and Caroline L. miss you.

You did the junior cert
with 'Dóchas an Óige',
we went down on open day,
you made us cranky buns,
real conversation stoppers.
Bobby and Shane miss you.

The day you and I filled in
your passport application
your shoes were empty
except for your long dreamy feet,
they matched your fanciful answers.
Name: Michael drop-dead-gorgeous Mullins.
Who do you want to be when you grow up?
A rolling fucking stone baby
Keith The Buckfast Kid misses you,
Margaret and John miss you.

The black dog came and went,
he didn't answer to Lassie
but when you said, hey Cerberus!
an idiotic grin came over his dogface.
The tea-leaf who just got out misses you.

When I visited you in the Psych first
you were outside sitting next to
a bucketful of cigarette ends.
I said you'd need to cut down

on the fags or you'd end up killing yourself.
We laughed till we nearly cried.
Granny Bernie misses you
Alice and Brendan miss you
you had a year left give or take.

You talked a lot about your daughter Erin,
she was eighteen months you were eighteen years.
You were here she was over there.
You called to Father Frankie
and asked if one day you could have Erin baptized,
you were soaking to the skin that day,
you were always walking in the rain,
docs filled with despair day,
black dog in my Docs day.
Jackie from the Psych misses you.

The day you got out for the last time
you and I walked from our house to Carnmore.
We had a drink at the crossroads
You weren't supposed to with the medication.
Fuck it you said if all those smarties I took
didn't kill me a pint of pissie beer hardly will.

You showed me round the house,
you said it was spooky
and if you were going to top yourself
it would be here you'd do it, and you did.
Auntie Carmel in Florida misses you,
Jennifer said you had a girlfriend,
Linda misses you,
Claire from Waterside House misses you.

You wanted to fathom the world
but your legs were tired,
you had two months left.
Cookie and Jillian miss you.
You talked about the dark hole
you often found yourself in,

you were happy when you got out
but when you were in it,
there was no talking to you,
you had weeks to go.
The Rinnmore gang miss you.

You got a bad 'flu
and the 'flu got you
the Millennium Bug,
your days were numbered.

Depression and the 'flu didn't travel
but you did and you never came back.
On December the 9th 1999
you hanged yourself.
Paddy L. and Michael Flaherty miss you.

Your mother rings from your grave
I say where are you?
She says, I'm at Michael's grave
and it looks lovely today.

## CATHAL Ó SEARCAIGH

(*b.*1956)

### *A Runaway Cow*

*for Liam Ó Muirthile*

I'd say he'd had too much
of the desolation that trickles down
through the glens and the hillocks
steadily as a hearse;
of the lifeless villages in the foothills

as bare of young folk as of soil;
of the old codgers, the hummock-blasters
who turned the peat into good red earth
and who deafened him pink year after year
with their talk of the grand sods of the old days;

of the little white bungalows, attractive
as dandruff in the hairy armpit of the Glen;
of the young people trapped in their destinies
like caged animals out of touch with their instinct;
of the Three Sorrows of Storytelling
in the pity of unemployment, of low morale,
and of the remoteness and narrow-mindedness
of both sides of the Glen;
of the fine young things down in Rory's
who woke the man in him
but wouldn't give a curse for his attentions;

of clan boundaries, of old tribal ditches,
of pissing his frustration against the solid walls
race and religion built round him.
He'd had too much of being stuck in the Glen
and with a leap like a runaway cow's one spring
    morning
he *cleared* the walls and *hightailed* away.

*PC*

## *Lament*

*in memory of my mother*

I cried on my mother's breast, cried sore
The day Mollie died, our old pet ewe
Trapped on a rockface up at Beithí.
It was sultry heat, we'd been looking for her,
Sweating and panting, driving sheep back
From the cliff-edge when we saw her attacked

On a ledge far down. Crows and more crows
Were eating at her. We heard the cries
But couldn't get near. She was ripped to death
As we suffered her terrible, wild, last breath
And my child's heart broke. I couldn't be calmed
No matter how much she'd tighten her arms
And gather me close. I just cried on
Till she hushed me at last with a piggyback
And the promise of treats of potato-cake.

Today it's my language that's in its throes,
The poets' passion, my mothers' fathers'
Mothers' language, abandoned and trapped
On a fatal ledge that we won't attempt.
She's in agony, I can hear her heave
And gasp and struggle as they arrive,
The beaked and ravenous scavengers
Who are never far. Oh if only anger
Came howling wild out of her grief,
If only she'd bare the teeth of her love
And rout the pack. But she's giving in,
She's quivering badly, my mother's gone
And promises now won't ease the pain.

*Seamus Heaney*

## GREG DELANTY

(*b*.1958)

### *The Cure*

*to my father*

I drop into the printers and graft
to you with my hangover on hearing
the tall drinking tales of your craft
from an apprentice of yours, latching

on to the old typesetter days like myself.
He swore he could write a book.
I thought of how you were partial yourself
to a jorum or two, but you would look

down on my pint-swaggering and remind me
you kept your drinking to Saturday night,
barring births, weddings, deaths and maybe
the odd quick one if the company was right.

And for the most part I keep to that too,
but last night was a night I broke
and went on the rantan from bar to
bar, jawing with whichever bloke,

solving the world's problems drink by drink
and cigarette by cigarette, swigging
and puffing away the whole lousy stink.
You nagged away in my head about smoking

and how the butts did away with you.
But I swear the way I stood there
and yaketty-yakked, slagged and blew
smoke in the smoke-shrouded air,

coughing your smoker's cough,
I thought that you had turned into me
or I into you. I laughed your laugh
and then, knowing how you loved company,

I refused to quit the bar and leave you alone
or leave myself alone or whoever we were.
I raised my glass to your surprise return.
And now I hear you guffaw once more

as your apprentice continues to recount
printers' drink lore and asks if I know
comps at Signature O got a complimentary pint.
I joust our way out the door repeating O O O.

## *To My Mother, Eileen*

I'm threading the eye
        of the needle for you again. That is
my specially appointed task, my
                gift that you gave me. Ma, watch me slip this
                    camel of words through. Yes,
rich we are still even if your needlework
        has long since gone with the rag-and-bone man
                and Da never came home one day, our Dan.
    Work Work Work. Lose yourself in work.
            That's what he'd say.
                            Okay okay.
Ma, listen, I can hear the sticks of our fire spit
        like corn turning into popcorn
                with the brown insides of rotten teeth. We sit
in our old Slieve Mish house. Norman is just born.
        He's in the pen.
I raise the needle to the light and lick the thread
                to stiffen the limp words. I
peer through the eye, focus, put everything out of my head.
                I shut my right eye and thread.

I'm important now, a likely lad, instead
of the amadán at Dread School. I have the eye
haven't I, the knack?
I'm Prince Threader. I missed it that try.
Concentrate. Concentrate. Enough yaketty yak.
There, there, Ma, look, here's the threaded needle back.

## PETER MCDONALD
(*b.*1962)

### *The Hand*

1

A flat right hand: four fingers and a thumb,
and poised, as though to strike an instrument,
fend off a blow, or maybe stop the waves.

Each evening, it would blatter on the glass
of our front window like a thunderclap,
not breaking it, stretching our nerves past breaking.

2

Thirty years on, and I can't not drive
in this direction, just to see the place.
There's nothing much here, nobody about:

Stormont up in the hills, unearthly white
as ever, new houses eating up the fields;
but I forget more now than I remember.

Leaving, I see the parti-coloured kerbstones
with paint from last year or the year before
that fades into this almost-constant rain,

then, on one gable-wall, a raised right hand.

3

It took a full two minutes to run down
from the bus terminus to our front door:
in the last year, I skipped and swerved and darted

all the way back, with tiny ricochets
of stones at my legs and heels. All spring
I ran, and ran so fast I couldn't stop.

4

We lived in 44A Woodview Drive,
across the road, and just a few doors down
from an apprentice murderer, who learned

his trade in town, and then came home for tea.
The hard skin in my palm is like soft stone:
as I look at it now under the desk-light,

calloused and scuffed and bitten and worn-in,
this part of me is guiltless flesh and bone,
whatever it has done or might yet do.

5

Leaving means going away for the last time,
unnoticed now, hardly worth noticing:
up in the distance, Stormont, unearthly white.

I forget more than I remember – how
this road connects to that, the way to town,
the names of people who lived there, or there.

As I move faster, everything speeds up:
I make the rain stop by raising my hand,
and sunlight loses itself on the Castlereagh hills.

## COLETTE BRYCE

### (*b.*1970)

### *Self-Portrait in the Dark (with Cigarette)*

To sleep, perchance
to dream? No chance:
it's 4 a.m. and I'm wakeful
as an animal,
caught between your presence and the lack.
This is the realm insomniac.
On the window seat, I light a cigarette
from a slim flame and monitor the street –
a stilled film, bathed in amber,
softened now in the wake of a downpour.

Beyond the daffodils
on Magdalen Green, there's one slow vehicle
pushing its beam along Riverside Drive,
a sign of life;
and two months on
from 'moving on'
your car, that you haven't yet picked up,
waits, spattered in raindrops like bubble wrap.
Here, I could easily go off
on a riff

on how cars, like pets, look a little like their owners
but I won't 'go there',
as they say in America,
given it's a clapped-out Nissan Micra . . .
And you don't need to know that
I've been driving it illegally at night
in the lamp-lit silence of this city
– you'd only worry –
or, worse, that Morrissey
is jammed in the tape deck now and for eternity;

no. It's fine, all gleaming hubcaps,
seats like an upright, silhouetted couple;
from the dashboard, the wink
of that small red light I think
is a built-in security system.
In a poem
it could represent a heartbeat or a pulse.
Or loneliness: its vigilance.
Or simply the lighthouse-regular spark
of someone, somewhere, smoking in the dark.

## *The Poetry Bug*

is a moon-pale, lumpish creature
parcelled in translucent skin
papery as filo pastry
patterned faint as a fingerprint
is quite without face or feature
ear or eye or snout
has eight root-like
tentacles or feelers, rough
like knuckly tusks of ginger
clustered at the front.

Invisible to the naked eye
monstrous in microscopy
it loves the lovers' bed or couch
pillow, quilt or duvet
and feeds, *thrives* I should say
on human scurf and dander
indeed, is never happier
than feasting on the dust
of love's shucked husk
the micro-detritus of us.

## DAVID WHEATLEY
## (*b.*1970)

### *Sonnet*

stretch pants cashback pound shop store card

hubcaps tailfin souped-up Escort

breakbeat ringtone dole day cheques cashed

loan shark small change rat boys bag snatched

tin can tomcat backstreet dosshouse

TV late lunch warmed-up Chinese

black dog tongue stud real nails fake tan

red light road rage brain-dead Leeds fan

handbrake wheelspin pub crawl big screen

spiked drink lift home knocked up sixteen

knocked up knocked out well gone all gone

all day all week stay home what's on

chat shows pig out hard stuff hard case

hard luck fuck life fuck off now please

## *Drift*

In Whitby, through its gaping jaw,
I entered the whale, was swept from shore,

began to drift and smuggled my way
in a used coffin to Robin Hood's Bay,

my one endeavour to route my calls
through a satellite phone at Fylingdales

to where you stood on Whitby sands,
an ice cream cone in both your hands.

*

From Scarborough prom where donkeys roamed
I fled in a dodgem and made for home

until sparks flew and I came to grief
bumped up against Anne Brontë's grave,

and went to ground in a B&B,
where I watched the tide and bade goodbye

with a postcard and an unpaid bill
and jumped on a trawler, drifting still.

*

In Bempton of the guanoed cliffs
I lived on gulls' eggs and dry leaves,

the puffins made me a laughing stock
and heckled and pecked me off their rock

to Brid where I won you a teddy bear.
You get my drift. I was drifting far

but only in search of a tidal spate
to wash me up, washed up, at your feet.

*

In Withernsea, taking care to shun
a nightclub called *Oblivion*

I shaved on a wind farm's turbine blade
and watched the last of the coastline slide

to where land gave itself up for lost,
threw itself off itself in disgust,

on Spurn, long dreamt-of vanishing point,
end of the line, of the world: the end

*

of nothing, as it turned out. I went down
once, twice, thrice, and woke up thrown

on a beach that could only be Skegness.
All that coastal drift and mess

had merely relocated south.
I jumped back into the whale's huge mouth

to drift back north and start again.
You'd left me my ice cream. But you were gone.

## SINÉAD MORRISSEY

(*b*.1972)

### *Pilots*

It was black as the slick-stunned coast of Kuwait
over Belfast Lough when the whales came up
(bar the eyelights of aeroplanes, angling in into the airport
out of the east, like Venus on a kitestring being reeled
to earth). All night they surfaced and swam
among the detritus of Sellafield and the panic
of godwits and redshanks.

By morning
we'd counted fifty (species *Globicephala melaena*)
and Radio Ulster was construing a history. They'd left a sister
rotting on a Cornish beach, and then come here, to this dim
smoke-throated cistern, where the emptying tide leaves a scum
of musselshell and the smell of landfill and drains.
To mourn? Or to warn? Day drummed its thumbs
on their globular foreheads.

Neither due,
nor quarry, nor necessary, nor asked for, nor understood
upon arrival – what did we reckon to dress them in?
Nothing would fit. Not the man in oilskin working in the
warehouse
of a whale, from the film of Sir Shackleton's blasted *Endeavour*,
as though a hill had opened onto fairytale measures
of blubber and baleen, and this was the money-
god's recompense;

not the huge Blue
seen from the sky, its own floating eco-system, furred
at the edges with surf; nor the unbridgeable flick
of its three-storey tail, bidding goodbye to this angular world
before barrelling under. We remembered a kind of singing,
or rather our take on it: some dismal chorus of want and wistfulness
resounding around the planet, alarmed and prophetic,
with all the foresight we lack –

though not one of us
heard it from where we stood on the beaches and car-parks
and cycle-tracks skirting the water. What had they come for?
From Carrickfergus to Helen's Bay, birdwatchers with binoculars
held sway while the city sat empty. The whales grew frenzied.
Children sighed when they dived, then clapped as they rose
again, Christ-like and shining, from the sea, though they could have been
dying out there,

smack bang
in the middle of the ferries' trajectory, for all we knew.
Or attempting to die. These were Newfoundland whales,
radically adrift from their feeding grounds, but we took them
as a gift: as if our own lost magnificent ship
had re-entered the Lough, transformed and triumphant,
to visit us. As if those runaway fires on the spines of the hills
had been somehow extinguished . . .

For now,
they were here. And there was nothing whatsoever to be said.
New islands in the water between Eden and Holywood.

## ALAN GILLIS
(*b.*1973)

### *12th October, 1994*

I enter the Twilight Zone,
        the one run
by Frankie 'Ten Pints' Fraser, and slide the heptagon
        of my twenty
pence piece into its slot. The lights come on.
        Sam the Sham
and the Pharaohs are playing *Wooly Bully*.

A virtual combat zone lights up the green
        of my eyes,
my hand clammy on the joystick, as Johnny 'Book
        Keeper' McFeeter
saunters in and Smokey sings *The Tracks of My Tears*.
        He gives the nod
to Betty behind the bulletproof screen.

Love of my life, he says, and she says,
        ach Johnny,
when who do you know but Terry 'The Blaster' McMaster
        levels in
and B Bumble and the Stingers start playing *Nut Rocker*.
        I shoot down
a sniper and enter a higher level.

Betty buzzes Frankie who has a shifty
        look around,
poking his nut around a big blue door, through which
        I spy
Billy 'Warts' McBreeze drinking tea and tapping his toes
        to Randy
and The Rainbows' version of *Denise*.

On the screen I mutilate a double-agent
Ninja and collect
a bonus drum of kerosene. *Game of Love* by Wayne
Fontana pumps
out of the machine, when I have to catch my breath,
realizing Ricky
'Rottweiler' Rice is on my left

saying watch for the nifty fucker
with the cross-
bow on the right. Sweat-purls tease my spine, tensed ever
more rigidly,
when Ricky's joined by Andy 'No Knees' Tweed,
both of them
whistling merrily to The Crystals' *Then He Kissed Me.*

What the fuck is going on
here, asks
Victor 'Steel Plate' Hogg, as he slides through the fire
door. The kid's
on level 3, says Andy. At which point Frankie does his nut,
especially since
The Cramps are playing *Can Your Pussy Do the Dog?*

Betty puts on Curtis and the Clichés'
*Brush Against Me*
*Barbarella* instead, when the first helicopter shreds the air
to the left
of the screen. Gathering my wits and artillery, I might eclipse
the high score
of Markie 'Life Sentence' Prentice, set on October 6th.

I hear Benny 'Vindaloo' McVeigh say,
right we're going
to do this fucking thing. By now the smoke is so thick
the screen is almost grey.
The Shangri-Las are playing *Remember (Walkin' in the Sand).*
Frankie says
no, Victor, nobody's going to fucking disband.

Bob B Soxx and the Blue Jeans are playing
*Zip-A-Dee-Doo-Dah.*
Through a napalm blur I set the interns free. They wear US
marine khaki.
Jimmy 'Twelve Inch' Lynch says, son, not bad for 20p.
I leave the Zone and go
back to the fierce grey day. It looks like snow.

### *Progress*

They say that for years Belfast was backwards
and it's great now to see some progress.
So I guess we can look forward to taking boxes
from the earth. I guess that ambulances
will leave the dying back amidst the rubble
to be explosively healed. Given time,
one hundred thousand particles of glass
will create impossible patterns in the air
before coalescing into the clarity
of a window. Through which, a reassembled head
will look out and admire the shy young man
taking his bomb from the building and driving home.

## CAITRÍONA O'REILLY
## (*b*.1973)

### *A Lecture Upon the Bat*

of the species *Pipistrellus pipistrellus.*
Matchstick-sized, from the stumps of their tails
to the tips of their noses. On reversible toes,
dangling from gables like folded umbrellas.

Some of them live for thirty years
and die dangling. They hang on
like the leaves they pretended to be,
then like dying leaves turn dry.

*Suspicions amongst thoughts are like bats*
*amongst birds*, Francis Bacon writes,
*they fly ever by twilight*. But commonsense,
not sixth sense, makes them forage at night.

For the art of bat-pressing is not dead.
Inside numberless books, like tiny black flowers,
lie flattened bats. Even Shakespeare
was a keen bat-fowler, or so it's said.

In medieval beast books
extract of bat was a much-prized
depilator. *Reremice be blind as moles,*
*and lick powder and suck*

*oil out of lamps, and be most cold*
*of kind, therefore the blood*
*of a reremouse, nointed upon the legs,*
*suffereth not the hair to grow again.*

And how toothsome is fruit-bat soup
when boiled in the pot for an hour!
Small wonder then that the Mandarin
for both 'happiness' and 'bat' is 'fu'.

Bats have had a bad press.
Yet they snaffle bugs by the thousand
and carefully clean their babies' faces.
Their lives are quieter than this

bat lore would have us believe.
Bats overhead on frangible wings,
piping ultrasonic vespers. Bats
utterly wrapped up in themselves.

## *Heliotrope*

Past beautiful,
stuck in the dust

of a road, her thin
branched head

with its baby hair
and dozen white eyes

so anthropomorphized
and mute – her lover

going down the sky
daily in his flaming steps

and she with her
padlocked gaze –

eternal follower!
Yet the circle's story

fixes her
at its centre –

her greenish rooted
limbs keep company

with all the buried
girls and boys

whose lost testes
and ovules stir to life

again this month –
under the soft rain

of a god's grief
the hyacinth and lotus

come, with narcissus
on his sex-struck stem.

## LEONTIA FLYNN

(*b*.1974)

### *By My Skin*

*for Terry McGaughey*

Mr Bennet in *Pride and Prejudice – The Musical!*,
my father communicates with his family almost entirely through
song.
From the orange linoleum and trumpet-sized wallpaper flowers
of the late 1970s, he steps with a roll of cotton,
a soft-shoe routine, and a pound of soft white paraffin.

He sings 'Oft in the Stilly Night' and 'Believe Me, If All Those
Endearing Young Charms'.
He sings 'Edelweiss' and 'Cheek to Cheek' from *Top Hat*.
Disney-animals are swaying along the formica sink-top
where he gets me into a lather. He greases behind my knees
and the folds of my elbows; he wraps me in swaddling clothes.

Then lifts me up with his famous high-shouldered shuffle
– 'Yes Sir, That's My Baby!' – to the candlewick bunk.
The air is bright with a billion exfoliate flitters
as he changes track – one for his changeling child:
'Hauld Up Your Head My Bonnie Wee Lass and Dinnae
Look So Shy'.

He sings 'Put Your Shoes On, Lucy (Don't You Know You're
    In The City)'.
He sings 'Boolavogue' and 'Can't Help Loving that Man of Mine'
and 'Lily the Pink' and 'The Woods of Gortnamona'.
He sings – the lights are fading – 'Slievenamon'
and about the 'Boy Blue' (who awakens 'to angel song').

My father is Captain Von Trapp, Jean Valjean, Professor
    Henry Higgins –
gathering his repertoire, with the wheatgerm and cortisone,
like he's gathering up a dozen tribute roses.
Then, taking a bow, he lays these – just so – by my skin
which gets better and worse, and worse and better again.

## *Drive*

My mother's car is parked in the gravel drive
outside the house. A breeze springs
from the shore, and blows against this traffic sign
standing between the by-road and the main road
where somewhere a cricket ticks like a furious clock.
My mother's car is an estimable motor,

a boxy thing – the car in which my mother,
during a morning's work, will sometimes drive
to Dundrum, Ballykinlar, Seaford, Clough,
'Newcastle', 'Castlewellan', 'Analong'.
They drive along the old road and the new road –
my father, in beside her, reads the signs

as they escape him – for now they are empty signs,
now one name means as little as another;
the roads they drive along are fading roads.
– 'Dromore', 'Banbridge' (my father's going to drive
my mother to distraction). 'In Banbridge town . . .', he sings.
She turns the car round, glancing at the clock

and thinks for a moment, turning back the clock,
of early marriage – love! – under the sign
of youth and youthful fortunes – back, in the spring,
the first *great mystery*, of life together:
my mother's indefatigable drive
keeping them both on the straight and narrow road,

and, as they pass 'Killough' or 'Drumaroad',
she thinks of children – broods a while (cluck cluck),
on their beginnings (this last leg of this drive
leads back to the empty house which she takes as a sign) . . .
how does it work, she thinks, this little motor?
Where are its cogs, and parts and curly oiled springs

that make her now, improbably, the wellspring
of five full persons – out upon life's highroads:
a grown-up son, a gang of grown-up daughters,
prodigal, profligate – with 30 years on their clocks?
She doesn't know, and isn't one to assign
meaning to their ways, their worlds' bewildering drives –

though she tells this offspring she's nearing the end of the road
a clock ticks softly . . . the low pulse of some *drive* . . . ?
My mother watches. She's waiting for a sign . . .

## NICK LAIRD
## (*b.*1975)

### *Pedigree*

There are many of us.

My aunt,
the youngest sister,
is a reformed shoplifter.

An uncle breeds champion bantams.

Another, a pig-farmer,
has a racket smuggling cattle
back and forth and back across
the imaginary border.

Me, I've forty-seven cousins.

A scuffle over rustling sheep
became a stabbing in a bar outside Armagh,
and a murderer swings
from a branch high up in our family tree.

Which isn't a willow.

Instead,
an enormous unruly blackthorn hedge,

inside of which a corpse is tangled,
and sags from branch to branch,
like a dewy web:

a farmer jumped on the road, and strangled,
his pockets emptied
of the stock proceeds from the county fair
by two local Roman Catholic farmhands.

Riots in Donegal town when they were cleared.
And riots again when they were convicted.

I may be out on a limb.

One grandfather, the short-horn cattle dealer,
went bankrupt, calmly smoked his pipe,
and died at forty of lung cancer.

Martha, my grandmother, remade Heathhill a dairy farm
and when the rent man came
my mother'd hide behind the sofa with her brothers.

My father spent his boyhood fishing with a hook and
    tinfoil chocolate wrapper.

He coveted a Davy Crockett hat
and shined the medals of his legendary uncles
who'd all died at the Somme,
the Dragoon Guards of Inniskilling.

He left school without sitting his papers
and my mother dropped out to marry him.

Each evening after work and dinner,
she'd do her OU course,
and heave the brown suitcase of books
from out beneath the rickety, mythical bunks
I shared for ten years with my sister.

There is such a shelter in each other.

And you, you pad from the bathroom to Gershwin,
gentled with freckles and moisturized curves,
still dripping, made new, singing your footprints
as they singe the wood floor,
perfect in grammar and posture.

But before you passed me the phone
you were talking, and I couldn't help but note your tone,
as if you couldn't hear them right,
as if they were maybe calling
not from just across the water
but Timbuktu, or from the moon . . .

At least you can hear me, my darling,
I'm speaking so softly and clearly,
and this is a charge not a pleading.

# IX

# SONGS AND BALLADS SINCE 1801

*Shall the Harp then be silent?*

Thomas Moore,
'Shall the Harp Then be Silent'

## THOMAS MOORE

### *from* Irish Melodies

### *War Song: Remember the Glories of Brien the Brave*

Remember the glories of Brien the brave,
  Tho' the days of the hero are o'er;
Tho' lost to Mononia and cold in the grave
  He returns to Kinkora no more!
That star of the field, which so often has pour'd
  Its beam on the battle is set;
But enough of its glory remains on each sword,
  To light us to victory yet!

Mononia! when Nature embellish'd the tint
  Of thy fields, and thy mountains so fair,
Did she ever intend that a tryant should print
  The footstep of slavery there?
No, Freedom! whose smile we shall never resign,
  Go, tell our invaders, the Danes,
That 'tis sweeter to bleed for an age at thy shrine,
  Than to sleep but a moment in chains!

Forget not our wounded companions, who stood
  In the day of distress by our side;
While the moss of the valley grew red with their blood,
  They stirr'd not, but conquer'd and died!
That sun which now blesses our arms with his light,
  Saw them fall upon Ossory's plain!
Oh, let him not blush, when he leaves us tonight,
  To find that they fell there in vain!

## *The Song of Fionnuala*

Silent, oh Moyle! be the roar of thy water,
 Break not, ye breezes, your chain of repose,
While, murmuring mournfully, Lir's lonely daughter
 Tells to the night-star her tale of woes.
When shall the swan, her death-note singing,
 Sleep, with wings in darkness furl'd?
When will heaven, its sweet bell ringing,
 Call my spirit from this stormy world?

Sadly, oh Moyle! to thy winter wave weeping,
 Fate bids me languish long ages away;
Yet still in her darkness doth Erin lie sleeping,
 Still doth the pure light its dawning delay!
When will that day-star, mildly springing,
 Warm our isle with peace and love?
When will heaven, its sweet bell ringing,
 Call my spirit to the fields above?

## *She is Far from the Land*

She is far from the land where her young hero sleeps,
 And lovers are round her, sighing;
But coldly she turns from their gaze, and weeps,
 For her heart in his grave is lying!

She sings the wild song of her dear native plains,
 Every note which he lov'd awaking –
Ah! little they think who delight in her strains,
 How the heart of the minstrel is breaking!

He had liv'd for his love, for his country he died,
 They were all that to life had entwin'd him, –
Nor soon shall the tears of his country be dried,
 Nor long will his love stay behind him.

Oh! make her a grave, where the sun-beams rest,
  When they promise a glorious morrow;
They'll shine o'er her sleep, like a smile from the west,
  From her own lov'd island of sorrow!

## *'Tis the Last Rose of Summer*

'Tis the last rose of summer,
  Left blooming alone;
All her lovely companions
  Are faded and gone;
No flower of her kindred,
  No rose-bud is nigh,
To reflect back her blushes,
  Or give sigh for sigh!

I'll not leave thee, thou lone one!
  To pine on the stem;
Since the lovely are sleeping,
  Go, sleep thou with them;
Thus kindly I scatter
  Thy leaves o'er the bed,
Where thy mates of the garden
  Lie scentless and dead.

So soon may *I* follow,
  When friendships decay,
And from love's shining circle
  The gems drop away!
When true hearts lie wither'd,
  And fond ones are flown,
Oh! who would inhabit
  This bleak world alone?

## *Dear Harp of My Country*

Dear Harp of my country! in darkness I found thee,
  The cold chain of silence had hung o'er thee long,
When proudly, my own Island Harp! I unbound thee,
  And gave all thy chords to light, freedom, and song!
The warm lay of love and the light note of gladness
  Have waken'd thy fondest, thy liveliest thrill;
But, so oft hast thou echoed the deep sigh of sadness,
  That ev'n in thy mirth it will steal from thee still.

Dear Harp of my country! farewell to thy numbers,
  This sweet wreath of song is the last we shall twine;
Go, sleep, with the sunshine of Fame on thy slumbers,
  Till touch'd by some hand less unworthy than mine.
If the pulse of the patriot, soldier, or lover,
  Have throbb'd at our lay, 'tis thy glory alone;
I was *but* as the wind, passing heedlessly over.
  And all the wild sweetness I wak'd was thy own.

## *Shall the Harp Then be Silent*

Shall the Harp then be silent, when he who first gave
  To our country a name, is withdrawn from all eyes?
Shall a Minstrel of Erin stand mute by the grave,
  Where the first – where the last of her Patriots lies?

No – faint though the death-song may fall from his lips,
  Though his Harp, like his soul, may with shadows be crossed,
Yet, yet shall it sound, 'mid a nation's eclipse,
  And proclaim to the world what a star hath been lost; –

What a union of all the affections and powers
  By which life is exalted, embellished, refined,
Was embraced in that spirit – whose centre was ours,
  While its mighty circumference circled mankind.

Oh, who that loves Erin, or who that can see,
  Through the waste of her annals, that epoch sublime –
Like a pyramid raised in the desert – where he
  And his glory stand out to the eyes of all time;

That *one* lucid interval, snatched from the gloom
  And the madness of ages, when filled with his soul,
A Nation o'erleap'd the dark bounds of her doom,
  And for *one* sacred instant, touched Liberty's goal?

Who, that ever hath heard him – hath drank at the source
  Of that wonderful eloquence, all Erin's own,
In whose high-thoughted daring, the fire, and the force,
  And the yet untamed spring of her spirit are shown?

An eloquence rich, wheresoever its wave
  Wandered free and triumphant, with thoughts
    that shone through,
As clear as the brook's 'stone of lustre', and gave,
  With the flash of the gem, its solidity too.

Who, that ever approached him, when free from the crowd,
  In a home full of love, he delighted to tread
'Mong the trees which a nation had giv'n, and which bowed,
  As if each brought a new civic crown for his head –

Is there one, who hath thus, through his orbit of life
  But at distance observed him – through glory, through blame,
In the calm of retreat, in the grandeur of strife,
  Whether shining or clouded, still high and the same?

Oh no, not a heart, that e'er knew him, but mourns
Deep, deep o'er the grave, where such glory is shrined –
O'er a monument Fame will preserve, 'mong the urns
Of the wisest, the bravest, the best of mankind!

## *from* National Melodies

### *Then, Fare Thee Well*

Then, fare thee well, my own dear love,
This world has now for us
No greater grief, no pain above
The pain of parting thus,
Dear love!
The pain of parting thus.

Had we but known, since first we met,
Some few short hours of bliss,
We might, in numbering them, forget
The deep, deep pain of this,
Dear love!
The deep, deep pain of this.

But no, alas, we've never seen
One glimpse of pleasure's ray,
But still there came some cloud between,
And chased it all away,
Dear love!
And chased it all away.

Yet, ev'n could those sad moments last,
  Far dearer to my heart
Were hours of grief, together passed,
  Than years of mirth apart,
    Dear love!
  Than years of mirth apart.

Farewell! our hope was born in fears,
  And nursed 'mid vain regrets;
Like winter suns, it rose in tears,
  Like them in tears it sets,
    Dear love!
  Like them in tears it sets.

# LOVE

## ANONYMOUS

### *I Know My Love*

I know my love by his way of walking,
And I know my love by his way of talking,
And I know my love by his coat of blue,
And if my love leaves me, what will I do?
  And still she cried, 'I love him the best,
  But a troubled mind, sure, can know no rest,'
  And still she cried, 'Bonny boys are few,
  And if my love leaves me, what will I do?'

There is a dance house in Mardyke,
And it's there that my love goes every night;
To take a strange one upon his knee,
And don't you think, now, that vexes me?
  And still she cried, 'I love him the best,
  But a troubled mind, sure, can know no rest,'
  And still she cried, 'Bonny boys are few,
  And if my love leaves me, what will I do?'

If my love knew I could wash and wring,
And if my love knew I could weave and spin,
I would make a dress of the finest kind,
But the want of money, sure, leaves me behind.
  And still she cried, 'I love him the best,

But a troubled mind, sure, can know no rest,'
And still she cried, 'Bonny boys are few,
And if my love leaves me, what will I do?'

I know my love is an arrant rover,
And I know he'll roam the wide world over,
In dear old Ireland he'll no longer tarry,
And an English one he is sure to marry.
And still she cried, 'I love him the best,
And a troubled mind, sure, can know no rest,'
And still she cried, 'Bonny boys are few,
And if my love leaves me, what will I do?

## *The Dawning of the Day*

One morning early I walked forth
By the margin of Lough Lene;
The sunshine dressed the trees in green,
And summer bloomed again;
I left the town and wandered on
Through fields all green and gay;
And whom should I meet but a Cooleen-dhas,
By the dawning of the day.

No cap or cloak this maiden wore,
Her neck and feet were bare;
Down to the grass in ringlets fell
Her glossy golden hair;
A milking pail was in her hand,
She was lovely young and gay;
She bore the palm from Venus bright,
By the dawning of the day.

On a mossy bank I sat me down,
With the maiden by my side;
With gentle words I courted her,
And asked her for my bride;

She said, 'Young man, don't bring me blame,
  But let me go away,
For morning's light is shining bright,
  By the dawning of the day.'

*Patrick Weston Joyce*

## *The Drinan Dhun*

(*The Sloe Tree*)

My love he is fairer than a soft summer's day,
His breath it is sweeter than the new-mown hay;
His hair shines like gold when revived by the sun,
The name that they call him is the Drinan Dhun.

My boy he is gone to cross over the main,
May God send him safe to his true love again,
For I wander all day till the night-time comes on,
And I sleep on the leaves of the Drinan Dhun.

If I had a small cot on the ocean to row,
I would follow my true love wherever he'd go;
I'd rather have my darling for to sport and to play
Than all the gold treasures on land and on sea.

My love he is handsome and fair to be seen,
With his red rosy cheeks he is fit for a queen,
His two sparkling eyes are as bright as the sun,
He is fair as the blossom of the Drinan Dhun.

Impatient I wait for my love to return,
And for his long absence I ne'er cease to mourn,
I will join with the small birds when the summer comes on,
For to welcome the blossom of the Drinan Dhun.

## *The Butcher Boy*

In Moore Street once where I did dwell,
A butcher boy I loved right well;
He courted me my life away,
But alas with me he would not stay.

I wish, I wish, I wish in vain,
I wish I was a maid again;
But a maid again I ne'er will be
Till apples grow on an ivy tree.

I wish my baby it was born,
And smiling on his daddy's knee;
And I myself were dead and gone,
And the long green grass growing over me.

She went upstairs to make her bed,
And calling to her mother said:
'Give me a chair while I sit down,
And a pen and ink to write it down.'

At every line she shed a tear,
At every line cried, 'Willy, dear,
Oh, what a foolish girl was I,
To fall in love with a butcher boy.'

He went upstairs and the door he broke,
And found her hanging from a rope;
He took his knife and he cut her down,
And in her pocket these words he found:

Oh, dig my grave large, wide and deep,
With a marble slab at my head and feet,
And in the middle a turtle dove,
So the world may know I died for love.

## ANTOINE Ó RAIFTEIRÍ

### *Mary Hynes*

Going to Mass by the heavenly mercy,
    The day was rainy, the wind was wild;
I met a lady beside Kiltartan
    And fell in love with the lovely child;
My conversation was smooth and easy,
    And graciously she answered me
'Raftery dear, 'tis yourself that's welcome,
    So step beside me to Ballylee.'

This invitation there was no denying,
    I laughed with joy and my poor heart beat;
We had but to walk across a meadow,
    And in her dwelling I took my seat.
There was laid a table with a jug and glasses,
    And that sweet maiden sat down by me –
'Raftery drink and don't spare the liquor;
    There's a lengthy cellar in Ballylee.'

If I should travel France and England,
    And Spain and Greece and return once more
To study Ireland to the northern ocean,
    I would find no morsel the like of her.
If I was married to that youthful beauty
    I'd follow her through the open sea,
And wander coasts and winding roads
    With the shining pearl of Ballylee.

'Tis fine and bright on the mountainside,
    Looking down on Ballylee,
You can walk the woods, picking nuts and berries,
    And hear the birds sing merrily;

But where's the good if you got no tidings
    Of the flowering branch that resides below –
O summer sky, there's no denying
    It is for you that I ramble so.

My star of beauty, my sun of autumn,
    My golden hair, O my share of life!
Will you come with me this coming Sunday
    And tell the priest you will be my wife?
I'd not grudge you music, nor a feast at evening,
    Nor punch nor wine, if you'd have it be,
And King of Glory, dry up the roadway
    Till I find my posy at Ballylee!

*Frank O'Connor*

## *Brídín Vesey*

I would marry Brídín Vesey
Without a shoe or petticoat,
A comb, a cloak or dowry
Or even one clean shift;
And I would make novena
Or imitate the hermits
Who spend their lives in fasting
All for a Christmas gift.
O cheek like dogwood fruiting.
O cuckoo of the mountain,
I would send darkness packing
If you would rise and go
Against the ban of clergy
And the sour lips of your parents
And take me at an altar-stone
In spite of all Mayo.

That was the sullen morning
They told the cruel story
How scorning word or token
You rose and went away.
'Twas then my hands remembered,
My ears still heard you calling,
I smelt the gorse and heather
Where you first learned to pray.
What could they know, who named you,
Of jug and bed and table,
Hours slipping through our fingers,
Time banished from the room?
Or what of all the secrets
We knew among the rushes
Under the Reek when cuckoos
Brightened against the moon?

You are my first and last song,
The harp that lilts my fingers
Your lips like frozen honey,
Eyes like the mountain pool,
Shaped like the Reek your breast is,
Whiter than milk from Nephin,
And he who never saw you
Has lived and died a fool.
Oh, gone across the mearing
Dividing hope from sadness
What happy townland holds you?
In what country do you reign?
In spite of all the grinning lads
At corner and in haybarn,
I'll search all Ireland over
And bring you home again.

*Donagh MacDonagh*

## GERALD GRIFFIN
## (1803–40)

### *Eileen Aroon*

When, like the early rose,
*Eileen aroon!*
Beauty in childhood blows,
*Eileen aroon!*
When, like a diadem,
Buds blush around the stem,
Which is the fairest gem?
*Eileen aroon!*

Is it the laughing eye?
*Eileen aroon!*
Is it the timid sigh?
*Eileen aroon!*
Is it the tender tone,
Soft as the stringed harp's moan?
Oh! it is Truth alone,
*Eileen aroon!*

When, like the rising day,
*Eileen aroon!*
Love sends his early ray,
*Eileen aroon!*
What makes his dawning glow
Changeless through joy or woe? –
Only the constant know,
*Eileen aroon!*

I know a valley fair,
*Eileen aroon!*
I knew a cottage there,
*Eileen aroon!*

Far in that valley's shade
I knew a gentle maid,
Flower of a hazel glade,
*Eileen aroon!*

Who in the song so sweet?
*Eileen aroon!*
Who in the dance so fleet?
*Eileen aroon!*
Dear were her charms to me,
Dearer her laughter free,
Dearest her constancy,
*Eileen aroon!*

Youth must with time decay,
*Eileen aroon!*
Beauty must fade away,
*Eileen aroon!*
Castles are sacked in war,
Chieftains are scattered far
Truth is a fixèd star,
*Eileen aroon!*

## WILLIAM ALLINGHAM

### *Lovely Mary Donnelly*

Oh, lovely Mary Donnelly, my joy, my only best!
If fifty girls were round you, I'd hardly see the rest;
Be what it may the time o' day, the place be where it will,
Sweet looks o' Mary Donnelly, they bloom before me still.

Her eyes like mountain water that's flowing on a rock,
How clear they are, how dark they are! they give me many a
shock.
Red rowans warm in sunshine and wetted with a shower,
Could ne'er express the charming lip that has me in its power.

Her nose is straight and handsome, her eyebrows lifted up,
Her chin is very neat and pert, and smooth like a china cup,
Her hair's the brag of Ireland, so weighty and so fine;
It's rolling down upon her neck, and gather'd in a twine.

The dance o' last Whit-Monday night exceeded all before,
No pretty girl for miles about was missing from the floor;
But Mary kept the belt of love, and O but she was gay!
She danced a jig, she sung a song, that took my heart away.

When she stood up for dancing, her steps were so complete,
The music nearly killed itself to listen to her feet;
The fiddler moan'd his blindness, he heard her so much
praised,
But bless'd his luck to not be deaf when once her voice she
raised.

And evermore I'm whistling or lilting what you sung,
Your smile is always in my heart, your name beside my
tongue;
But you've as many sweethearts as you'd count on both your
hands,
And for myself there's not a thumb or little finger stands.

Oh, you're the flower o' womankind in country or in town;
The higher I exalt you, the lower I'm cast down.
If some great lord should come this way, and see your beauty
bright,
And you to be his lady, I'd own it was but right.

O might we live together in a lofty palace hall,
Where joyful music rises, and where scarlet curtains fall!
O might we live together in a cottage mean and small,
With sods o' grass the only roof, and mud the only wall!

O lovely Mary Donnelly, your beauty's my distress,
It's far too beauteous to be mine, but I'll never wish it less.
The proudest place would fit your face, and I am poor and
low;
But blessings be about you, dear, wherever you may go!

## ALFRED PERCEVAL GRAVES

## (1846–1931)

### *My Love's an Arbutus*

My love's an arbutus
By the borders of Lene,
So slender and shapely
In her girdle of green;
And I measure the pleasure
Of her eye's sapphire sheen
By the blue skies that sparkle
Through that soft branching screen.

But though ruddy the berry
And snowy the flower
That brighten together
The arbutus bower,
Perfuming and blooming
Through sunshine and shower,
Give *me* her bright lips
And her laugh's pearly dower.

Alas! fruit and blossom
Shall scatter the lea,
And Time's jealous fingers
Dim your young charms, machree.
But unranging, unchanging,
You'll still cling to me,
Like the evergreen leaf
To the arbutus tree.

## PERCY FRENCH

## (1854–1920)

### *McBreen's Heifer*

McBreen had two daughters, and each one in turn
Was offered in marriage to Jamsey O'Burn.
Now Kitty was pretty but Jane she was plain,
So to make up the differ, McBreen would explain,
He'd give the best heifer he had on the land,
As a sort of a bonus with Jane, understand.
But then Kitty would charrum a bird off a bush,
And that left the lad in a horrid non-plush.

CHORUS

Now there's no denyin' Kitty was remarkably pretty,
Tho' I can't say the same for Jane,
But still there's not the differ of the price of a heifer,
Between the pretty and the plain.

Entirely bothered was Jamsey O'Burn,
He thought that he'd give the schoolmaster a turn.
Sez he to wed Kitty is very good fun,
Still a heifer's a heifer when all's said an' done.
A girl she might lose her good looks anyhow,
And a heifer might grow to an elegant cow.
But still there's no price for the stock, d'ye mind,
And Jane has a face that the Divil designed.

CHORUS

Now there's no denyin' Kitty was remarkably pretty,
Tho' I can't say the same for Jane,
But still there's not the differ of the price of a heifer,
Between the pretty and the plain.

The schoolmaster said, with a good deal of sinse,
We'll reduce the two girls to shillin's an' pence;
Add the price of the heifer, then Jane, I'll be bound,
Will come out the top by a couple o' pound.
But still I'm forgettin' that down in Glengall,
The stock is just goin' for nothin' at all.
So Jim thought he'd wait till the end of the year,
Till girls might be cheaper or stock might be dear.

CHORUS

But when he came for Kitty, she was married to McVittie,
And McBlane had appropriated Jane,
So whether there's the differ of the price of a heifer,
Is a thing that he never could explain.

## WILLIAM BUTLER YEATS

### *Down by the Salley Gardens*

Down by the salley gardens my love and I did meet;
She passed the salley gardens with little snow-white feet.
She bid me take love easy, as the leaves grow on the tree;
But I, being young and foolish, with her would not agree.

In a field by the river my love and I did stand,
And on my leaning shoulder she laid her snow-white hand.
She bid me take life easy, as the grass grows on the weirs;
But I was young and foolish, and now am full of tears.

## JOSEPH CAMPBELL

### *My Lagan Love*

Where Lagan stream sings lullaby,
There blows a lily fair;
The twilight gleam is in her eye,
The night is on her hair.
But like a love-sick leanannsidhe,
She has my heart in thrall.
No life I own nor liberty,
For love is lord of all.

And often when the beetle's horn
Has lulled the eve to sleep;
I steal up to her sheiling lorn
And through the dooring peep;

There by the cricket's singing-stone
She spares the bogwood fire,
And sings in sad sweet undertone,
The song of heart's desire.

## PADRAIC COLUM

### *She Moved through the Fair*

My young love said to me, 'My brothers won't mind,
And my parents won't slight you for your lack of kind.'
Then she stepped away from me, and this she did say
'It will not be long, love, till our wedding day.'

She stepped away from me and she moved through
  the fair,
And fondly I watched her go here and go there,
Then she went her way homeward with one star awake,
As the swan in the evening moves over the lake.

The people were saying no two were e'er wed
But one had a sorrow that never was said,
And I smiled as she passed with her goods and her gear,
And that was the last that I saw of my dear.

I dreamt it last night that my young love came in,
So softly she entered, her feet made no din;
She came close beside me, and this she did say
'It will not be long, love, till our wedding day.'

## PATRICK KAVANAGH

### *On Raglan Road*

On Raglan Road on an autumn day I met her first and knew
That her dark hair would weave a snare that I might one day rue;
I saw the danger, yet I walked along the enchanted way,
And I said, let grief be a fallen leaf at the dawning of the day.

On Grafton Street in November we tripped lightly along the ledge
Of the deep ravine where can be seen the worth of passion's pledge,
The Queen of Hearts still making tarts and I not making hay –
O I loved too much and by such, by such, is happiness thrown away.

I gave her gifts of the mind, I gave her the secret sign that's known
To the artists who have known the true gods of sound and stone
And word and tint. I did not stint for I gave her poems to say
With her own name there and her own dark hair like clouds over fields of May.

On a quiet street where old ghosts meet I see her walking now
Away from me so hurriedly my reason must allow
That I had wooed not as I should a creature made of clay –
When the angel woos the clay he'd lose his wings at the dawn of day.

## DOMINIC BEHAN

## (1928–90)

### *Liverpool Lou*

*Oh Liverpool Lou, lovely Liverpool Lou,*
*Why don't you behave, love, like other girls do?*
*Why must my poor heart keep following you?*
*Stay home and love me, my Liverpool Lou.*

When I go a-walking, I hear people talking,
Schoolchildren playing, I hear what they're saying:
They're saying you'll grieve me, that you will deceive me,
Some morning you'll leave me, all woke up and gone.

*Oh Liverpool Lou,* etc.

The sounds from the river keep telling me ever
That I should forget you, like I'd never met you;
Tell me their song, love, was never more wrong, love;
Say I belong, love, to my Liverpool Lou.

*Oh Liverpool Lou,* etc.

## MACDARA WOODS

## (*b.*1942)

### *The Dark Sobrietee*

In the confines of the public park
and the blooming of sandragon trees

I met a fair-haired woman
who said soldier follow me
Ah then no my love I answered
for I know love's company
they would fix me and fact-find me
in the dark sobriety

By the confines of the ocean
and the serpentining sea
I met a dark-haired woman
who said sailor sail for me
Ah then no my love I answered
there are seven riding seas
and the course is reckoned dead dear
by the dark sobriety

In the confines of the city
and the evening flying free
I met the rarest woman
who said poet follow me
Ah then no my love I answered
I have prayed and drunk the lees
and what's left me now is searching
for the dark sobriety

# WAR, POLITICS, PRISON

## ANONYMOUS

### *Blarney Castle*

*Tune: 'O, hold your tongue, dear Sally!'*

O! Blarney Castle, my darling, you're nothing at all but
cold stone!
With a small little taste of old ivy, that up your side has grown.
Och, it's you that was once strong and ancient, and you
kept all the Sassenachs down:
And you sheltered the Lord of Clancarty, who then lived in
Dublin town.

Bad cess to that robber, old Cromwell, and to all his long
battering train,
Who rolled over here like a porpoise, in two or three hookers,
from Spain!
And because that he was a Freemason, he mounted a battering-ram,
And he loaded it up of dumb-powder, which in at its mouth
he did cram.

It was now the poor boys of the Castle looked over the
battlement wall,
And they there saw that ruffian, old Cromwell, a-feeding on
powder and ball;
And the fellow that married his daughter, with a great big
grape-shot in his jaw,
'Twas bold I-ER-TON they called him, and he was his
brother-in-law.

So they fired the bullet like thunder, and it flew through the air
like a snake;
And they hit the high walls of the Castle, which, like a young
curlew, did shake;
While the Irish had nothing to fire, but their bows and their
arrows – 'the *sowls!*'
Poor tools for shooting the Sassenachs, though mighty good for
wild fowls.

Now one of the boys in the Castle, he took up a Sassenach's
shot,
And he covered it up in turf ashes, and he watched it till it was
red-hot.
Then he carried it up in his fingers, and he threw it right over
the wall;
He'd have burned their tents all to tinder, if on them it happened
to fall.

The old Castle, it trembled all over, as you'd see a horse do
in July,
When just near the tail in his crupper, he's teased by a
pestering fly.
Black Cromwell, he made a dark signal, for in the black arts he
was deep;
So, though the eyes in the people stood open, they found
themselves all fast asleep.

With his jack-boots he stepped on the water, and he marched
right over the lake;
And his soldiers they all followed after, as dry as a duck or a
drake;
And he gave Squire Jeffreys the Castle, and the loch and the
rock close, they say;
Who both died there, and lived there in quiet, as his ancestors
do to this day.

## *The Relief of Derry, 1 August (old style) 1689*

*Tune: 'My ain kind dearie, O'*

The gloomy hour of trial's o'er,
  No longer cannons rattle O;
The tyrant's flag is seen no more,
  And James has lost the battle, O.
And here we are, renowned and free,
  By maiden walls surrounded O;
While all the knaves who'd make us slaves,
  Are baffled and confounded, O.

The Dartmouth spreads her snow-white sail,
  Her purple pendant flying, O;
While we the gallant Browning hail,
  Who saved us all from dying, O.
Like Noah's dove, sent from above,
  While foes would starve and grieve us, O,
Through floods and flame, an angel came,
  To comfort and relieve us, O.

Oh! when the vessel struck the boom,
  And pitched, and reeled, and stranded, O,
With shouts the foe denounced our doom,
  And open gates demanded, O.
And shrill and high arose the cry,
  Of anguish, grief and pity, O;
While, black with care, and deep despair,
  We mourned our falling city, O.

But, Heaven, her guide, with one broadside,
  The laden bark rebounded, O;
A favouring gale soon filled the sail,
  While hills and vales resounded, O.

The joy-bells ring, 'Long-live the King,'
  Adieu to grief and sadness, O;
To Heaven we raise the voice of praise,
  In heartfelt joy and gladness, O.

## *The Cow Ate the Piper*

In the year '98, when our troubles were great,
  It was treason to be a Milesian.
I can never forget the big black-whiskered set,
  The history books tell us were Hessians.
In them heart breaking times we had all sorts of crimes,
  And murdering never was rifer.
On the hill of Glencree, not an acre from me,
  Lived bould Dinny Byrne, the piper.

Neither wedding nor wake was worth an old shake,
  If Dinny was not first invited,
For at emptying kegs or squeezing the bags,
  He astonished as well as delighted.
In such times poor Dinny could not earn a penny,
  Martial law had a sting like a viper –
It kept Dinny within till his bones and his skin
  Were a-grin through the rags of the piper.

'Twas one heavenly night, with the moon shining bright,
  Coming home from the fair of Rathangan.
He happened to see, from the branch of a tree,
  The corpse of a Hessian there hanging;
Says Dinny, 'These rogues have fine boots, I've no brogues,'
  He laid on the heels such a griper,
They were so gallus tight, and he pulled with such might,
  Legs and boots came away with the piper.

So he tucked up the legs and he took to his pegs,
  Till he came to Tim Kavanagh's cabin,
'By the powers,' says Tim, 'I can't let you in,
  You'll be shot if you stop out there rappin'.'

He went round to the shed, where the cow was in bed,
  With a wisp he began for to wipe her –
They lay down together on the seven foot feather,
  And the cow fell to hugging the piper.

The daylight soon dawned, Dinny got up and yawned,
  Then he pulled on the boots of the Hessian;
The legs, by the law! he threw on the straw,
  And he gave them leg-bail on his mission.
When Tim's breakfast was done he sent out his son
  To make Dinny lep like a lamp-lighter –
When the two legs he saw, he roared like a daw
  'Oh Daddy, the cow ate de piper!'

'Sweet bad luck to the baste, she'd a musical taste,'
  Says Tim, 'to go eat such a chanter,
Here Padraic, avic, take this lump of a stick,
  Drive her up to Glenealy, I'll cant her.'
Mrs Kavanagh bawled – the neighbours were called,
  They began for to humbug and jibe her,
To the churchyard she walks with the legs in a box,
  Crying out, 'We'll be hanged for the piper.'

The cow then was drove just a mile or two off,
  To a fair by the side of Glenealy,
And the crathur was sold for four guineas in gold
  To the clerk of the parish, Tim Daly.
They went into a tent, and the luck-penny spent,
  (For the clerk was a woeful old swiper),
Who the divil was there, playing the Rakes of Kildare,
  But their friend, Dinny Byrne, the piper.

Then Tim gave a bolt like a half-broken colt,
  At the piper he gazed like a gommach;
Says he, 'By the powers, I thought these eight hours,
  You were playing in Dhrimindhu's stomach.'

But Dinny observed how the Hessian was served,
  So they all wished Nick's cure to the viper,
And for grá that they met, their whistles they wet,
  And like devils they danced round the piper.

## *A Lament for Kilcash*

Oh, sorrow the saddest and sorest!
  Kilcash's attractions are fled –
Felled lie the high trees of its forest,
  And its bells hang silent and dead.
There dwelt the fair Lady, the Vaunted,
  Who spread through the island her fame,
There the Mass and the Vespers were chaunted,
  And thither proud Princes came!

I am worn by an anguish unspoken
  As I gaze on its glories defaced,
Its beautiful gates lying broken,
  Its gardens all desert and waste.
Its courts, that in lightning and thunder
  Stood firm, are, alas! all decayed;
And the Lady Iveagh sleepeth under
  The sod, in the greenwood shade.

No more on a Summer-day sunny
  Shall I hear the thrush sing from his lair,
No more see the bee bearing honey
  At noon through the odorous air.
Hushed now in the thicket so shady,
  The dove hath forgotten her call,
And mute in the grave lies the Lady
  Whose voice was the sweetest of all!

As the deer from the brow of the mountain,
  When chased by the hunter and hound,
Looks down upon forest and fountain,
  And all the green scenery round;

So I on thy drear desolation
  Gaze, O, my Kilcash, upon thee!
On thy ruin and black devastation,
  So doleful and woeful to see!

There is mist on thy woods and thy meadows;
  The sun appears shorn of his beams;
Thy gardens are shrouded in shadows,
  And the beauty is gone from thy streams.
The hare has forsaken his cover;
  The wild fowl is lost to the lake;
Desolation hath shadowed thee over,
  And left thee – all briar and brake!

And I weep while I pen the sad story –
  Our Prince has gone over the main,
With a damsel, the pride and the glory
  Not more of Green Eire than Spain.
The Poor and the Helpless bewail her;
  The Cripple, the Blind, and the Old;
She never stood forth as their jailer,
  But gave them her silver and gold.

O, God! I beseech thee to send her
  Home here to the land of her birth!
We shall then have rejoicing and splendour,
  And revel in plenty and mirth,
And our land shall be highly exalted,
  And till the dread dawn of that day
When the race of Old Time shall have halted,
  It shall flourish in glory alway!

*James Clarence Mangan*

## *Johnny, I Hardly Knew You*

While going the road to sweet Athy,
    Hurroo! hurroo!
While going the road to sweet Athy,
    Hurroo! hurroo!
While going the road to sweet Athy,
A stick in my hand and a drop in my eye,
A doleful damsel I heard cry:
'Och, Johnny, I hardly knew you!'

'With drums and guns, and guns and drums,
    Hurroo! hurroo!
With drums and guns, and guns and drums,
    Hurroo! hurroo!
With drums and guns, and guns and drums,
The enemy nearly slew you;
My darling dear, you look so queer,
Och, Johnny, I hardly knew you!'

'Where are your eyes that looked so mild?
    Hurroo! hurroo!
Where are your eyes that looked so mild?
    Hurroo! hurroo!
Where are your eyes that looked so mild,
When my poor heart you first beguiled?
Why did you run from me and the child?
Och, Johnny, I hardly knew you!'

'With drums, etc.'

'Where are the legs with which you run?
    Hurroo! hurroo!
Where are the legs with which you run?
    Hurroo! hurroo!

Where are the legs with which you run
When first you went to carry a gun?
Indeed, your dancing days are done!
Och, Johnny, I hardly knew you!'

'With drums, etc.'

'It grieved my heart to see you sail,
Hurroo! hurroo!
It grieved my heart to see you sail,
Hurroo! hurroo!
It grieved my heart to see you sail,
As from my heart you took leg-bail;
Like a cod you're doubled up head and tail,
Och, Johnny, I hardly knew you!'

'With drums, etc.'

'You haven't an arm and you haven't a leg,
Hurroo! hurroo!
You haven't an arm and you haven't a leg,
Hurroo! hurroo!
You haven't an arm and you haven't a leg,
You're an eyeless, noseless, chickenless egg;
You'll have to be put with a bowl to beg:
Och, Johnny, I hardly knew you!'

'With drums, etc.'

'I'm happy for to see you home,
Hurroo! hurroo!
I'm happy for to see you home,
Hurroo! hurroo!
I'm happy for to see you home,
All from the Island of Sulloon;
So low in flesh, so high in bone;
Och, Johnny, I hardly knew you!'

'With drums, etc.'

'But sad it is to see you so,
    Hurroo! hurroo!
But sad it is to see you so,
    Hurroo! hurroo!
But sad it is to see you so,
And to think of you now as an object of woe,
Your Peggy'll still keep you on as her beau;
Och, Johnny, I hardly knew you!'

'With drums and guns, and guns and drums,
The enemy nearly slew you;
My darling dear, you look so queer,
Och, Johnny, I hardly knew you!'

## *Arthur MacBride*

Now me and me cousin, one Arthur MacBride
One day went a-walking down by the seaside;
And mark you what followed and what did betide,
It being on a Christmas morning.
For recreation, we went on a tramp
And we met Sergeant Napper and Corporal Cramp
And a little wee drummer, intending to camp,
The day being pleasant and charming.

'Good morning, Good morning,' the sergeant did cry
'And the same to you gentlemen,' we did reply,
Intending no harm but just to pass by,
It being on a Christmas morning;
But says he, 'My fine fellows, if you will enlist,
Ten guineas of gold I will slip in your fist
And a crown in the bargain for to kick up the dust
And drink the King's health in the morning.

'For a soldier he leads a very fine life
And he always is blessed with a charming young wife,
And he pays all his debts without sorrow or strife
And always lives pleasant and charming;

And a soldier he always is decent and clean
In the finest of clothing he's constantly seen
While other poor fellows go dirty and mean
And sup on thin gruel in the morning.'

'But,' says Arthur, 'I wouldn't be proud of your clothes
For you've only the lend of them, I suppose,
And you dare not change them for one night, you know,
If you do you'll be flogged in the morning.
And although it is true we are single and free
We take great delight in our own company;
We have no desire strange faces to see,
Although that your offers are charming.

'And we have no desire to take your advance,
All hazards and dangers we barter on chance;
And you'd have no scruples for to send us to France
Where we would get shot without warning.'
'Oh now!' says the sergeant 'I'll have no such chat
And I'll take it neither from spalpeen or brat,
And if you insult me with one other word
I'll cut off your heads in the morning.'

And then Arthur and I we soon drew our hods
And we scarce gave them time for to draw their own blades
When a trusty shillelagh came over their heads
And bade them take that as fair warning.
And their old rusty rapiers that hung by their side
We flung them as far as we could in the tide;
'Now take them out, Divils!' cried Arthur MacBride
'And temper their edge in the morning.'

And the little wee drummer we flattened his pow
And we made a football of his rowdey-dow-dow,
Threw it in the tide for to rock and to row
And bade it a tedious returning.

And, having no money, we paid them in cracks
And we showed no respect to their two bloody backs
For we lathered them there like a pair of wet sacks
And left them for dead in the morning.

And so to conclude and to finish disputes
We obligingly asked if they wanted recruits
For we were the lads who would give them hard clouts
And bid them look sharp in the morning.
Oh me and my cousin, one Arthur MacBride
As we went a-walking down by the seaside,
Now mark what followed and what did betide,
It being on Christmas morning.

## *The Peeler and the Goat*

Oh, the Bansha peeler went one night
On duty and patrolling, O;
He met a goat upon the road
He took for being a-strolling, O.
With bayonet fixed, he sallied forth
And caught him by the wizzen, O;
And then he swore a mighty oath
He'd send him off to prison, O.

'Have mercy, sir!' the goat replied
'And let me tell my story, O:
I am no rogue, no Ribbonman
No Croppy, Whig, or Tory, O!
I'm innocent of any crime,
Of petty or high treason, O,
For my tribe is active at this time
It is the mating season, O!'

'Do not complain,' the peeler said
'But give your tongue a bridle, O,
You're absent from your dwelling place,
Disorderly and idle, O.

Your hoary locks will not prevail
Nor your sublime oration, O;
The Peeler's Act will you transport
On your own information, O.'

'No penal law did I transgress
By deed or combination, O;
It's true I have no place of rest,
No home or habitation, O;
But Bansha is my dwelling place
Where I was bred and born, O,
Descendant of an honest race
Whose trade is all I've learned, O.'

'I will chastise your insolence
And violent behaviour, O,
In chains to Cashel you'll be sent
Where you will get no favour, O;
The magistrates will all consent
To sign your condemnation, O;
From there to Cork you will be sent
For speedy transportation, O.'

'This parish and this neighbourhood
Are peaceable and tranquil, O;
There's no disturbance here, thank God,
And long may it continue so.
I don't regard your oath a pin,
Or sign for my committal, O!
My jury will be gentlemen
Who'll grant me an acquittal, O.'

'The consequence be what it will,
A peeler's power I'll let you know,
I'll hand-cuff you, at all events,
And march you to the Bridewell, O;

And sure, you rogue, you can't deny
Before a judge and jury, O,
Intimidation with your horns
And threatening me with fury, O!'

'I'll wager, sir, that you are drunk
On whiskey, rum, and brandy, O,
Or you wouldn't have such gallant spunk
To be so bold and manly, O;
You readily would let me pass
If I had money handy, O,
To treat you to a poitín glass –
'Tis then I'd be the dandy, O!'

## *The Recruiting Sergeant*

As I was walking down the road
All feeling fine and larky, O,
A recruiting sergeant came up to me,
Said, 'You would look fine in khaki, O,
For the King he is in need of men,
Just read this proclamation, O;
A life in Flanders for you then
Would be a fine vacation, O!'

'That may be so,' says I to him,
'But tell me, Sergeant dearie-O,
If I had a pack stuck up on my back
Would I still look fine and cheery, O?
For you'd have me train and drill until
I looked like one of the Frenchies, O:
It may be warm in Flanders but
It's draughty in the trenches, O.'

The sergeant smiled and winked his eye,
And his smile was most provoking, O;
He twiddled and twirled his little moustache,
Says he, 'You're only joking, O,

For the sandbags are so warm and high
The wind you won't feel it blowing, O.'
Well I winked at a cailín passing by
And says I, 'What if it's snowing, O?

'Come rain or hail, come wind or snow,
I'm not going out to Flanders, O;
There's fighting in Ireland to be done –
Let your sergeants and commanders go;
Let Englishmen fight English wars
It's nearly time they started, O!'
I saluted the Sergeant a very good night
And there and then we parted, O.

## *By Memory Inspired*

By memory inspired,
And love of country fired,
The deeds of men I love to dwell upon;
And the patriotic glow
Of my spirit must bestow
A tribute to O'Connell that is gone, boys – gone:
Here's a memory to the friends that are gone!

In October Ninety-Seven –
May his soul find rest in Heaven! –
William Orr to execution was led on:
The jury, drunk, agreed
That Irish was his creed;
For perjury and threats drove them on, boys – on:
Here's the memory of John Mitchell that is gone!

In Ninety-Eight – the month July –
The informer's pay was high;
When Reynolds gave the gallows brave MacCann;
But MacCann was Reynolds' first –
One could not allay his thirst;
So he brought up Bond and Byrne, that are gone,
boys – gone:
Here's the memory of the friends that are gone!

We saw a nation's tears
Shed for John and Henry Shears;
Betrayed by Judas, Captain Armstrong;
We may forgive, but yet
We never can forget
The poisoning of Maguire that is gone, boys – gone:
Our high Star and true Apostle that is gone!

How did Lord Edward die?
Like a man, without a sigh;
But he left his handiwork on Major Swan!
But Sirr, with steel-clad breast,
And coward heart at best,
Left us cause to mourn Lord Edward that is gone,
boys – gone:
Here's the memory of our friends that are gone!

September, Eighteen-Three,
Closed this cruel history,
When Emmett's blood the scaffold flowed upon:
Oh, had their spirits been wise,
They might then realize
Their freedom! but we drink to Mitchell that is gone,
boys – gone:
Here's the memory of the friends that are gone!

# JEREMIAH JOSEPH CALLANAN

## *Wellington's Name*

How blest were the moments when liberty found thee
  The first in her cause on the fields of the brave,
When the young lines of ocean were charging around thee
  With the strength of their hills and the roar of their wave!

Oh, chieftain, what then was the throb of thy pride,
  When loud through the war-cloud exultingly came,
O'er the battle's red tide, which they swelled as they died,
  The shout of green Erin for Wellington's name!

How sweet, when thy country thy garland was wreathing,
  And the fires of thy triumph blazed brightly along,
Came the voice of its harp all its witchery breathing,
  And hallowed thy name with the light of her song!

And oh, 'twas a strain in each patriot breast
  That waked all the transport, that lit all the flame,
And raptured and blest was the Isle of the West
  When her own sweetest bard sang her Wellington's name!

But 'tis past – thou art false, and thy country's sad story
  Shall tell how she bled and she pleaded in vain;
How the arm that should lead her to freedom and glory,
  The child of her bosom, did rivet her chain!

Yet think not for ever her vengeance shall sleep,
  Wild harp that once praised him, sing louder his shame,
And where'er o'er the deep thy free numbers may sweep,
  Bear the curse of a nation on Wellington's name!

## THOMAS DAVIS

### *Clare's Dragoons*

*Air: 'Viva la'*

When, on Ramillies' bloody field,
The baffled French were forced to yield,
The victor Saxon backward reeled
  Before the charge of Clare's Dragoons.
The Flags, we conquered in that fray,
Look lone in Ypres' choir, they say,
We'll win them company today,
  Or bravely die like Clare's Dragoons.

CHORUS

*Viva la*, for Ireland's wrong!
  *Viva la*, for Ireland's right!
*Viva la*, in battle throng,
  For a Spanish steed, and sabre bright!

The brave old lord died near the fight,
But, for each drop he lost that night,
A Saxon cavalier shall bite
  The dust before Lord Clare's Dragoons.
For, never, when our spurs were set,
And never, when our sabres met,
Could we the Saxon soldiers get
To stand the shock of Clare's Dragoons.

CHORUS

*Viva la*, the New Brigade!
  *Viva la*, the Old One, too!
*Viva la*, the rose shall fade,
  And the shamrock shine for ever new!

Another Clare is here to lead,
The worthy son of such a breed;
The French expect some famous deed,
  When Clare leads on his bold Dragoons.
Our colonel comes from Brian's race,
His wounds are in his breast and face,
The *bearna baoghail* is still his place,
  The foremost of his bold Dragoons.

CHORUS

*Viva la*, the New Brigade!
  *Viva la*, the Old One, too!
*Viva la*, the rose shall fade,
  And the Shamrock shine for ever new!

There's not a man in squadron here
Was ever known to flinch or fear;
Though first in charge and last in rere,
  Have ever been Lord Clare's Dragoons;
But, see! we'll soon have work to do,
To shame our boasts, or prove them true,
For hither comes the English crew,
  To sweep away Lord Clare's Dragoons.

CHORUS

*Viva la*, for Ireland's wrong!
  *Viva la*, for Ireland's right!
*Viva la*, in battle throng,
  For a Spanish steed and sabre bright!

Oh! comrades! think how Ireland pines,
Her exiled lords, her rifled shrines,
Her dearest hope, the ordered lines,
  And bursting charge of Clare's Dragoons.
Then fling your Green Flag to the sky,
Be Limerick your battle-cry,
And charge, till blood floats fetlock-high,
  Around the track of Clare's Dragoons!

CHORUS
*Viva la*, the New Brigade!
*Viva la*, the Old One, too!
*Viva la*, the rose shall fade,
And the Shamrock shine for ever new!

## DION BOUCICAULT

(1820–90)

### *The Wearing of the Green*

O Paddy dear, and did you hear the news that's going round?
The shamrock is forbid by law to grow on Irish ground;
St Patrick's Day no more we'll keep, his colours can't be seen,
For there's a bloody law again the wearing of the Green.
I met with Napper Tandy, and he took me by the hand,
And he said, 'How's poor old Ireland, and how does she stand?'
She's the most distressful country that ever yet was seen,
They are hanging men and women for the wearing of the Green.

Then since the colour we must wear is England's cruel Red,
Sure Ireland's sons will ne'er forget the blood that they have shed.
You may take the shamrock from your hat and cast it on the sod,
But 'twill take root and flourish there, though under foot 'tis trod.
When law can stop the blades of grass from growing as they grow,
And when the leaves in summer-time their verdure dare not show,
Then I will change the colour that I wear in my caubeen,
But till that day, please God, I'll stick to wearing of the Green.

But if at last our colour should be torn from Ireland's heart,
Her sons with shame and sorrow from the dear old isle will
part;
I've heard a whisper of a country that lies beyond the sea,
Where rich and poor stand equal in the light of freedom's day.
O Erin, must we leave you, driven by a tyrant's hand?
Must we ask a mother's blessing from a strange and distant
land?
Where the cruel cross of England shall nevermore be seen,
And where, please God, we'll live and die still wearing of the
Green.

## 'CARROLL MALONE'
## (William McBurney, 182?–92)

### *The Croppy Boy*

*A Ballad of '98*

'Good men and true! in this house who dwell,
To a stranger *bouchal*, I pray you tell
Is the Priest at home? or may he be seen?
I would speak a word with Father Green.'

'The Priest's at home, boy, and may be seen;
'Tis easy speaking with Father Green;
But you must wait, till I go and see
If the holy Father alone may be.'

The youth has entered an empty hall –
What a lonely sound has his light foot-fall!
And the gloomy chamber's chill and bare,
With a vested Priest in a lonely chair.

The youth has knelt to tell his sins.
'*Nomine Dei*,' the youth begins:
At '*mea culpa*' he beats his breast,
And in broken murmurs he speaks the rest.

'At the siege of Ross did my father fall,
And at Gorey my loving brothers all.
I alone am left of my name and race;
I will go to Wexford and take their place.

'I cursed three times since last Easter Day –
At Mass-time once I went to play;
I passed the churchyard one day in haste,
And forgot to pray for my mother's rest.

'I bear no hate against living thing;
But I love my country above my King.
Now, Father! bless me, and let me go
To die, if God has ordained it so.'

The Priest said nought, but a rustling noise
Made the youth look above in wild surprise;
The robes were off, and in scarlet there
Sat a yeoman captain with fiery glare.

With fiery glare and with fury hoarse,
Instead of blessing, he breathed a curse:
''Twas a good thought, boy, to come here and shrive;
For one short hour is your time to live.

'Upon yon river three tenders float;
The Priest's in one, if he isn't shot;
We hold his house for our Lord the King,
And – Amen, say I – may all traitors swing!'

At Geneva barrack that young man died,
And at Passage they have his body laid.
Good people who live in peace and joy,
Breathe a prayer and a tear for the Croppy boy.

## JOHN KELLS INGRAM

(1823–1907)

### *The Memory of the Dead*

Who fears to speak of Ninety-Eight?
  Who blushes at the name?
When cowards mock the patriot's fate,
  Who hangs his head for shame?
He's all a knave or half a slave
  Who slights his country thus:
But a true man, like you, man,
  Will fill your glass with us.

We drink the memory of the brave,
  The faithful and the few –
Some lie far off beyond the wave,
  Some sleep in Ireland, too;
All, all are gone – but still lives on
  The fame of those who died;
And true men, like you, men,
  Remember them with pride.

Some on the shores of distant lands
  Their weary hearts have laid,
And by the stranger's heedless hands
  Their lonely graves were made;
But though their clay be far away
  Beyond the Atlantic foam,
In true men, like you, men,
  Their spirit's still at home.

The dust of some is Irish earth;
  Among their own they rest;
And the same land that gave them birth
  Has caught them to her breast;

And we will pray that from their clay
  Full many a race may start
Of true men, like you, men,
  To act as brave a part.

They rose in dark and evil days
  To right their native land;
They kindled here a living blaze
  That nothing shall withstand.
Alas! that Might can vanquish Right –
  *They* fell, and passed away;
But true men, like you, men,
  Are plenty here today.

Then here's their memory – may it be
  For us a guiding light,
To cheer our strife for liberty,
  And teach us to unite!
Through good and ill, be Ireland's still,
  Though sad as theirs, your fate;
And true men, be you, men,
  Like those of Ninety-Eight.

## JOHN TODHUNTER

### *Aghadoe*

There's a glen in Aghadoe, Aghadoe, Aghadoe,
There's a green and silent glade in Aghadoe,
  Where we met, my Love and I, Love's fair planet in the sky,
O'er that sweet and silent glen in Aghadoe.

There's a glen in Aghadoe, Aghadoe, Aghadoe,
There's a deep and secret glen in Aghadoe,
  Where I hid him from the eyes of the redcoats and their spies
That year the trouble came to Aghadoe!

Oh! my curse on one black heart in Aghadoe, Aghadoe,
On Shaun Dhuv, my mother's son in Aghadoe,
  When your throat fries in hell's drouth, salt the flame be in
    your mouth,
For the treachery you did in Aghadoe!

For they tracked me to that glen in Aghadoe, Aghadoe,
When the price was on his head in Aghadoe;
  O'er the mountain through the wood, as I stole to him
    with food,
When in hiding low he lay in Aghadoe.

But they never took him living in Aghadoe, Aghadoe;
With the bullets in his heart in Aghadoe,
  There he lay, the head – my breast keeps the warmth where
    once 'twould rest –
Gone, to win the traitor's gold from Aghadoe!

## OSCAR WILDE

### from *The Ballad of Reading Gaol*

He did not wear his scarlet coat,
  For blood and wine are red,
And blood and wine were on his hands
  When they found him with the dead,
The poor dead woman whom he loved,
  And murdered in her bed.

He walked amongst the Trial Men
  In a suit of shabby grey;
A cricket cap was on his head,
  And his step seemed light and gay;
But I never saw a man who looked
  So wistfully at the day.

I never saw a man who looked
  With such a wistful eye
Upon that little tent of blue
  Which prisoners call the sky,
And at every drifting cloud that went
  With sails of silver by.

I walked, with other souls in pain,
  Within another ring,
And was wondering if the man had done
  A great or little thing,
When a voice behind me whispered low,
  'That fellow's got to swing.'

Dear Christ! the very prison walls
  Suddenly seemed to reel,
And the sky above my head became
  Like a casque of scorching steel;
And, though I was a soul in pain,
  My pain I could not feel.

I only knew what hunted thought
  Quickened his step, and why
He looked upon the garish day
  With such a wistful eye;
The man had killed the thing he loved
  And so he had to die.

Yet each man kills the thing he loves
  By each let this be heard,
Some do it with a bitter look,
  Some with a flattering word,
The coward does it with a kiss,
  The brave man with a sword!

Some kill their love when they are young,
  And some when they are old;
Some strangle with the hands of Lust,
  Some with the hands of Gold:
The kindest use a knife, because
  The dead so soon grow cold.

Some love too little, some too long,
  Some sell, and others buy;
Some do the deed with many tears,
  And some without a sigh:
For each man kills the thing he loves,
  Yet each man does not die.

He does not die a death of shame
  On a day of dark disgrace,
Nor have a noose about his neck,
  Nor a cloth upon his face,
Nor drop feet foremost through the floor
  Into an empty space.

He does not sit with silent men
  Who watch him night and day;
Who watch him when he tries to weep,
  And when he tries to pray;
Who watch him lest himself should rob
  The prison of its prey.

He does not wake at dawn to see
  Dread figures throng his room,
The shivering Chaplain robed in white,
  The Sheriff stern with gloom,
And the Governor all in shiny black,
  With the yellow face of Doom.

## CANON CHARLES O'NEILL

## (1887–1941)

### *The Foggy Dew*

As down the glen one Easter morn
  Through a city fair rode I,
There armed lines of marching men,
  In squadrons passed me by;
No pipe did hum, no battle drum
  Did sound out its loud tattoo,
But the angelus bell o'er the Liffey's swell
  Rang out through the foggy dew.

Right proudly high o'er Dublin town
  They flung out the flag of war.
'Twas better to die 'neath an Irish sky,
  Than at Suvla or Sud el Bar.
And from the plains of royal Meath
  Strong men came hurrying through
While Britannia's Huns, with their long-range guns,
  Sailed into the foggy dew.

As the night fell black the rifle's crack,
  Made perfidious Albion reel;
Through that leaden hail seven tongues of flame
  Flashed out o'er the lines of steel.
By each shining blade a prayer was said,
  That to Ireland her sons be true,
And when morning broke still the green flag shook
  Out its folds in the foggy dew.

It was England bade our Wild Geese go,
  That small nations might be free
But their lonely graves are by Suvla's waves
  On the fringe of the great North Sea.
Oh, had they died by Pearse's side
  Or fought beside Cathal Brugha
Their names we would keep where the Fenians sleep,
  'Neath the shroud of the foggy dew.

But the bravest fell and the requiem knell
  Rang mournfully and clear
For those who died that Eastertide
  In the springtime of the year,
While the world did gaze with deep amaze,
  At those fearless men and few
Who bore the fight that freedom's light
  Might shine through the foggy dew.

Back through the glen I rode again
  And my heart with grief was sore
For I parted then from those valiant men
  Who I never shall see more;
As to and fro in my dreams I go
  I'll kneel and pray for you,
For Slavery fled, you glorious dead,
  When you fell in the foggy dew.

# PATRICK MACGILL

(1890–1963)

## *La Bassée Road*

*(Cuinchy,* 1915*)*

You'll see from the La Bassée Road, on any summer's day,
The children herding nanny-goats, the women making hay.
You'll see the soldiers, khaki clad, in column and platoon,
Come swinging up La Bassée Road from billets in Bethune.
There's hay to save and corn to cut, but harder work by far
Awaits the soldier boys who reap the harvest fields of war.
You'll see them swinging up the road where women work
at hay,
The straight long road, – La Bassée Road – on any summer day.

The night-breeze sweeps La Bassée Road, the night-dews
wet the hay,
The boys are coming back again, a straggling crowd are they.
The column's lines are broken, there are gaps in the platoon,
They'll not need many billets, now, for soldiers in Bethune,
For many boys, good lusty boys, who marched away so fine,
Have now got little homes of clay beside the firing line.
Good luck to them, God speed to them, the boys who march
away,
A-singing up La Bassée road each sunny summer day.

## *The Guns*

*(Shivery-shake Dug-out, Maroc.)*

There's a battery snug in the spinney,
A French seventy-five in the mine,
A big nine-point-two in the village
Three miles to the rear of the line.

The gunners will clean them at dawning
  And slumber beside them all day,
But the guns chant a chorus at sunset,
  And then you should hear what they say.

CHORUS

Whizz bang! pip squeak! ss-ss-st!
Big guns, little guns waken up to it.
We're in for heaps of trouble, dug-outs at the
    double,
And stretcher-bearers ready to tend the boys
    who're hit.

And then there's the little machine-gun, –
  A beggar for blood going large.
Go, fill up his belly with iron,
  And he'll spit in the face of a charge.
The foe fixed his ladders at daybreak,
  He's over the top with the sun;
He's waiting; for ever he's waiting,
  The pert little vigilant gun.

CHORUS

Its tit-tit! tit-tit! tit! tit! tit!
Hark the little terror bristling up to it!
See his victims lying, wounded sore and dying –
Red the field and volume on which his name is
    writ.

The howitzer lurks in an alley,
  (The howitzer isn't a fool,)
With a bearing of snub-nosed detachment
  He squats like a toad on a stool.
He's a close-lipped and masterly beggar,
  A fellow with little to say,
But the little he says he can say in
  A most irrepressible way.

CHORUS

OO–plonk! OO–plonk! plonk! plonk! plonk!
The bomb that bears the message riots through
the air.
The dug-outs topple over on the foemen under cover,
They'll slumber through revelly who get the message
there!

The battery barks in the spinney,
The howitzer *plonks* like the deuce,
The big nine-point-two speaks like thunder
And shatters the houses in Loos,
Sharp chatters the little machine-gun,
Oh! when will its chattering stop? –
At dawn, when we swarm up the ladders;
At dawn we go over the top!

CHORUS

Whizz bang! pip squeak! OO–plonk! sst!
Up the ladders! Over! And carry on with it!
The guns all chant their chorus, the shells go
whizzing o'er us:–
Forward, hearties! Forward to do our little bit!

## BRENDAN BEHAN

(1923–64)

### *from* The Quare Fellow

### *The Ould Triangle*

A hungry feeling came o'er me stealing
And the mice were squealing in my prison cell,
And that old triangle

Went jingle jangle,
Along the banks of the Royal Canal.

To begin the morning
The warder bawling
Get out of bed and clean up your cell,
And that old triangle
Went jingle jangle,
Along the banks of the Royal Canal.

On a fine spring evening,
The lag lay dreaming
The seagulls wheeling high above the wall,
And the old triangle
Went jingle jangle
Along the banks of the Royal Canal.

The screw was peeping
The lag was sleeping,
While he lay weeping for the girl Sal,
And that old triangle
Went jingle jangle,
Along the banks of the Royal Canal.

The wind was rising,
And the day declining
As I lay pining in my prison cell
And that old triangle
Went jingle jangle
Along the banks of the Royal Canal.

The day was dying
And the wind was sighing,
As I lay crying in my prison cell,
And the old triangle
Went jingle jangle
Along the banks of the Royal Canal.

In the female prison
There are seventy women
I wish it was with them that I did dwell,
Then that old triangle
Could jingle jangle
Along the banks of the Royal Canal.

## *from* The Hostage

### *The Captains and the Kings*

I remember in September,
When the final stumps were drawn,
And the shouts of crowds now silent
And the boys to tea were gone.
Let us, oh Lord above us,
Still remember simple things,
When all are dead who love us,
Oh the Captains and the Kings,
When all are dead who love us,
Oh the Captains and the Kings.

We have many goods for export,
Christian ethics and old port,
But our greatest boast is that
The Anglo-Saxon is a sport.
On the playing-fields of Eton
We still do thrilling things,
Do not think we'll ever weaken
Up the Captains and the Kings!
Do not think we'll ever weaken
Up the Captains and the Kings!

Far away in dear old Cyprus,
Or in Kenya's dusty land,
Where all bear the white man's burden
In many a strange land.
As we look across our shoulder
In West Belfast the school bell rings,
And we sigh for dear old England,
And the Captains and the Kings.
And we sigh for dear old England,
And the Captains and the Kings.

In our dreams we see old Harrow,
And we hear the crow's loud caw,
At the flower show our big marrow
Takes the prize from Evelyn Waugh.
Cups of tea or some dry sherry,
Vintage cars, these simple things,
So let's drink up and be merry
Oh, the Captains and the Kings.
So let's drink up and be merry
Oh, the Captains and the Kings.

I wandered in a nightmare
All around Great Windsor Park,
And what do you think I found there
As I stumbled in the dark?
'Twas an apple half-bitten,
And sweetest of all things,
Five baby teeth had written
Of the Captain and the Kings.
Five baby teeth had written
Of the Captains and the Kings.

By the moon that shines above us
In the misty morn and night,
Let us cease to run ourselves down
But praise God that we are white.
And better still we're English –
Tea and toast and muffin rings,

Old ladies with stern faces,
And the Captains and the Kings.
Old ladies with stern faces,
And the Captains and the Kings.

## DOMINIC BEHAN

### *The Patriot Game*

Come all you young rebels, and list while I sing,
For the love of one's country is a terrible thing.
It banishes fear with the speed of a flame,
And it makes us all part of the patriot game.

My name is O'Hanlon, and I've just turned sixteen.
My home is in Monaghan, that's where I was weaned.
I learned all my life cruel England to blame,
So now I am part of the patriot game.

It's nearly two years since I wandered away
With the local battalion of the bold IRA,
For I read of our heroes, and wanted the same
To play out my part in the patriot game.

I joined a battalion from dear Ballybay
And gave up my boyhood so happy and gay.
For now as a soldier I'd drill and I'd train
To play my full part in the patriot game.

They told me how Connolly was shot in his chair,
His wounds from the fighting all bloody and bare,
His fine body twisted, all battered and lame:
They soon made me part of the patriot game.

This Ireland of ours has long been half free.
Six counties are under John Bull's tyranny.
But still De Valera is greatly to blame
For shirking his part in the patriot game.

I don't mind a bit if I shoot down police
They are lackeys for war, never guardians of peace;
And yet at deserters I'm never let aim,
The rebels who sold out the patriot game.

And now as I lie here, my body all holes,
I think of those traitors who bargained and sold
And I wish that my rifle had given the same
To those Quislings who sold out the patriot game.

## SEAMUS HEANEY

### *Craig's Dragoons*

*Air: 'Dolly's Brae'*

Come all ye Ulster loyalists and in full chorus join,
Think on the deeds of Craig's Dragoons who strike below
the groin,
And drink a toast to the truncheon and the armoured water-
hose
That mowed a swathe through civil rights and spat on
Papish clothes.

We've gerrymandered Derry but Croppy won't lie down,
He calls himself a citizen and wants votes in the town.
But that Saturday in Duke Street we slipped the velvet glove –
The iron hand of Craig's Dragoons soon crunched a croppy
dove.

Big McAteer and Currie, Gerry Fitt and others too,
Were fool enough to lead the van, expecting to get through.
But our hero commandos, let loose at last to play,
Did annihilate the rights of man in noontime of a day.

They downed women with children, for Teagues all over-breed,
They used the baton on men's heads, for Craig would pay no heed,
And then the boys placed in plain clothes, they lent a loyal hand
To massacre those Derry ligs behind a Crossley van.

O William Craig, you are our love, our lily and our sash,
You have the boys who fear no noise, who'll batter and who'll bash.
They'll cordon and they'll baton-charge, they'll silence protest tunes,
They are the hounds of Ulster, boys, sweet William Craig's Dragoons.

# SOCIETY

## ANONYMOUS

### *In Praise of the City of Mullingar*

Ye may strain your muscles
To brag of Brussels,
        Of London, Paris or Timbuktu,
Constantinople,
Or Sebastabopal,
        Vienna, Naples, or Tongataboo,
Of Copenhagen,
Madrid, Kilbeggan,
        Or the Capital of the Rooshian Czar;
But they're all inferior
To the superior
    And gorgeous city of Mullingar.

That fair metropolis,
So great and populous,
        Adorns the region of sweet Westmeath,
That fertile county
Which nature's bounty
        Has richly gifted with bog and heath.
Them scenes so charming,
Where snipes a-swarming

Attract the sportsman that comes from far;
And whoever wishes
May catch fine fishes
In deep Loch Owel near Mullingar.

I could stray for ever
By Brusna's river,
And watch its waters in their sparkling fall,
And the ganders swimmin'
And lightly skimmin'
O'er the crystal bosom of the Royal Canal;
Or on Thursdays wander,
'Mid pigs so tender,
And geese and turkeys on many a car,
Exchangin' pleasantry
With the fine bold peasantry
That throng the market at Mullingar.

Ye Nine, inspire me,
And with rapture fire me
To sing the buildings, both old and new,
The majestic courthouse,
And spacious workhouse,
And the church and steeple which adorn the view;
Then there's barracks airy
For the military,
Where the brave repose from the toils of war;
Five schools, a nunnery,
And a thrivin' tannery,
In the gorgeous city of Mullingar.

The railway station
With admiration
I next must mention in terms of praise,
Where trains a-rollin'
And engines howlin'
Strike each beholder with wild amaze;
And then there's Main Street

That broad and clean street,
With its rows of gas-lamps that shine afar;
I could speak a lecture
On the architecture
Of the gorgeous city of Mullingar.

The men of genius,
Contemporaneous
Approach spontaneous this favoured spot,
Where good society
And great variety
Of entertainment are still their lot.
The neighbouring quality
For hospitality
And conviviality unequalled are;
And from December
Until November
There's still diversion in Mullingar.

Now, in conclusion,
I make allusion
To the beauteous females that here abound;
Celestial creatures
With lovely features,
And taper ankles that skim the ground;
But this suspends me,
The theme transcends me,
My muse's powers are too weak by far;
It would take Catullus,
Likewise Tibullus,
To sing the beauties of Mullingar.

## *The Nightcap*

Jolly Phœbus his car to the coach-house had driven,
And unharnessed his high-mettled horses of light;
He gave them a feed from the manger of heaven,
And rubbed them and littered them up for the night.

Then down to the kitchen he leisurely strode,
  Where Thetis, the housemaid, was sipping her tea;
He swore he was tired with that damn'd up-hill road,
  He'd have none of her slops nor hot water, not he.

So she took from the corner a little cruiskeen
  Well filled with the nectar Apollo loves best;
(From the neat Bog of Allen, some pretty poteen),
  And he tippled his quantum and staggered to rest.

His many-caped box-coat around him he threw,
  For his bed, faith, 'twas dampish, and none of the best;
All above him the clouds their bright fringed curtains drew,
  And the tuft of his nightcap lay red in the west.

## *Nell Flaherty's Drake*

Oh, my name it is Nell, quite candid I tell,
And I live near Clonmel, I will never deny,
I had a large drake, the truth for to speak,
My grandmother left me, and she going to die;
He was wholesome and sound, and he weighed twenty pound,
And the universe round I would rove for his sake.
Bad luck to the robber, whether drunken or sober,
That murdered Nell Flaherty's beautiful drake.

His neck it was green, he was rare to be seen,
He was fit for a queen of the highest degree.
His body so white, it would give you delight,
He was fat, plump and heavy, and brisk as a bee.
My dear little fellow, his legs, they were yellow,
He would fly like a swallow, and swim like a hake.
But some wicked savage, to grease his white cabbage,
Has murdered Nell Flaherty's beautiful drake.

May his pig never grunt, may his cat never hunt,
May a ghost him still haunt in the dead of the night.
May his hen never lay, may his ass never bray,
May his coat fly away like an old paper kite;
May the lice and the fleas the wretch ever tease,
And a bitter north breeze make him tremble and shake,
May a four-year-old bug make a nest in the lug
Of the monster that murdered Nell Flaherty's Drake.

May his cock never crow, may his bellows not blow,
His potatoes never grow – no not even one;
May his cradle not rock, may his chest have no lock,
May his wife have no smock to shield her back bone.
May his duck never quack, may his goose be turned black
And pull down his stack with her long yellow beak.
May scurvy and itch not depart from the breech
Of the monster that murdered Nell Flaherty's Drake.

May his pipe never smoke, may his teapot be broke,
And to add to the joke may his kettle not boil,
May he lie in his bed till the moment he's dead,
May he always be fed on lob-scouse and oil,
May he swell with the gout, may his grinders fall out,
May he roar, bawl and shout, with the horrid toothache.
May his temples wear horns, and all his toes corns,
The monster that murdered Nell Flaherty's Drake.

May his spade never dig, may his sow never pig,
May each nit in his wig be as big as a snail,
May his house have no thatch and his door have no latch,
May his turkey not hatch, may the rats eat his meal;
May every old fairy from Cork to Dunleary,
Dip him in snug and airy in pond or in lake,
Where the eel and the trout may dine out on the snout
Of the monster that murdered Nell Flaherty's Drake.

May his dog yelp and growl with hunger and cold,
May his wife always scold till his brain goes astray,
May the curse of each hag that ever carried a bag
Light on the wag till his beard it turns grey,
May monkeys still bite him, and mad dogs affright him,
And everyone slight him asleep or awake.
May weasels still gnaw him, and jackdaws still claw him,
The monster that murdered Nell Flaherty's Drake.

The only good news that I have to diffuse,
Is that Peter Hughes, and blind piper McPeake,
And big nosed Bob Manson, and buck-tooth Bob Hanson,
Each one has a grandson of my beautiful drake.
My bird he had dozens of nephews and cousins,
And one I must have or my heart it will break,
To keep my mind easy, or else I'll turn crazy,
And this ends the song of Nell Flaherty's Drake.

## *The Galway Races*

As I roved out through Galway town to seek for recreation,
On the seventeenth of August, my mind was elevated.
There were multitudes assembled with their tickets at the station,
My eyes began to dazzle and they goin' to see the races.
*With me whack fol-de-doo fal-de-diddlee-i-do-day.*

There were passengers from Limerick and passengers from Nenagh,
Passengers from Dublin and sportsmen from Tipperary.
There were passengers from Kerry and all quarters of the nation
And our member Mr Hasset for to join the Galway Blazers.
*With me whack fol-de-doo fal-de-diddlee-i-do-day.*

There were multitudes from Aran and members up from New Quay,
The boys from Connamara and the Clare unmarried maidens;
There were people from Cork city who were loyal, true and faithful

That brought home Fenian prisoners from dying in foreign
nations.
*With me whack fol-de-doo fal-de-diddlee-i-do-day.*

It's there you'll see confectioners with sugarsticks and dainties
And lozenges and oranges and lemonade and raisins,
And gingerbread and spices to accommodate the ladies
And a big crubeen for threepence to be picking while you're able.
*With me whack fol-de-doo fal-de-diddlee-i-do-day.*

It's there you'll see the gamblers, the thimbles and the garters
And the sporting Wheel of Fortune with the four and twenty
quarters;
There was others without scruple pelting wattles at poor Maggie
And her father well contented and he looking at his daughter.
*With me whack fol-de-doo fal-de-diddlee-i-do-day.*

It's there you'll see the pipers and the fiddlers competing
And the nimble-footed dancers and they tripping on the daisies;
There was others crying cigars and lights, and bills of all the
races
With the colours of the jockeys and the prize and horses' ages.
*With me whack fol-de-doo fal-de-diddlee-i-do-day.*

It's there you'll see the jockeys and they mounted on most stately
The pink, the blue, the red and the green, the emblem of our
nation.
When the bell was rung for starting, all the horses seemed
impatient,
I thought they never stood on ground, their speed was so amazing.
*With me whack fol-de-doo fal-de-diddlee-i-do-day.*

There was half a million people there of all denominations
The Catholic, the Protestant, the Jew, the Presbyterian.
There was yet no animosity, no matter what persuasion
But fáilte and hospitality inducing fresh acquaintance.
*With me whack fol-de-doo fal-de-diddlee-i-do-day.*

*With me whack fol-de-doo fal-de-diddlee-i-do-day.*

## *Brian O'Linn*

Brian O'Linn was a gentleman born,
His hair it was long and his beard was unshorn;
His teeth they went out and his eyes they went in –
'I have beautiful features,' said Brian O'Linn.

Brian O'Linn had no breeches to wear
So he found an old sheepskin to make him a pair,
With the fleshy side out and the woolly side in –
'They'll be pleasant and cool,' said Brian O'Linn.

Brian O'Linn had no shirt for his back
So he went to a neighbour and borrowed a sack;
He tucked up the meal bag right under his chin –
'Sure they'll take them for ruffles,' said Brian O'Linn.

Brian O'Linn was hard up for a coat
So he borrowed the skin of a generous goat;
When the horns stuck out from his oxters, right then
'They will think they are pistols,' said Brian O'Linn.

Brian O'Linn had no hat to put on
So he used an old beaver to make him a one;
There was none of the crown left, and less of the brim –
'I have fine ventilation,' said Brian O'Linn.

Brian O'Linn, with no brogues for his toes,
Hopped into two crab shells to serve him as those;
He split up two oysters the crab shells to twin –
'They will shine out like buckles,' said Brian O'Linn.

Brian O'Linn had no watch for to wear
So he took a big turnip and scooped it out fair;
He placed a live cricket in under the skin –
'They will take it for ticking," said Brian O'Linn.

Brian O'Linn went a-courting one night
And he set both a mother and daughter to fight;
To settle the matter they stripped to the skin –
'Sure I'll marry you both,' said Brian O'Linn.

Brian O'Linn and his wife and wife's mother
All lay down in the one bed together;
The sheets they were worn and the blankets were thin –
'Lie close to the wall,' said Brian O'Linn.

Brian O'Linn and his wife and wife's mother
Were all crossing over an old bridge together;
The bridge it broke down and the trio fell in –
'There is land at the bottom,' said Brian O'Linn.

## *Molly Malone*

In Dublin's fair city,
Where the girls are so pretty,
I first set my eyes on sweet Molly Malone
As she wheeled her wheel barrow
Through streets broad and narrow
Crying, 'Cockles and mussels alive, alive O!'
*Alive, alive O! Alive, alive O!*
*Crying, 'Cockles and mussels alive, alive O!'*

She was a fishmonger
And sure 'twas no wonder
For so were her father and mother before;
And they both wheeled their barrow
Through streets broad and narrow
Crying, 'Cockles and mussels alive, alive O!'
*Alive, alive O! Alive, alive O!*
*Crying, 'Cockles and mussels alive, alive O!'*

She died of a fever
And no one could save her
And that was the end of sweet Molly Malone;

Now her ghost wheels her barrow
Through streets broad and narrow
Crying, 'Cockles and mussels alive, alive O!'
*Alive, alive O! Alive, alive O!*
*Crying, 'Cockles and mussels alive, alive O!'*

## *The Bag of Nails*

You very merry people all, please listen just a minute,
For though my song is not too long, there's something comic
in it.
To sing of nails, if you permit, my sportive muse intends, Sirs,
A subject that right now I've got just at my finger-ends, Sirs.

This world is a big bag of nails, and there are very queer ones,
Some are flats and some are sharps, and some are very dear ones;
We've sprigs and spikes and sparables, and all nails great and
small, Sirs,
Some love nails with monstrous heads, and some love none at all,
Sirs.

A bachelor's a hobnail, and he rusts for want of use, Sirs,
And misers are no nails at all, they're just a pack of screws, Sirs;
My enemies will get some clouts, wherever they may roam, Sirs,
For Irishmen, like hammers, will be sure to drive them home,
Sirs.

The doctor nails you with his bill, that often proves a sore nail,
The coffin maker wishes you as dead as any doornail.
You'll often find an agent who is nailing his employer;
The lawyer nails his client, but the Devil nails the lawyer.

Dame Fortune is a bradawl, and she often does contrive it,
To make the nail go easy just where she likes to drive it;
And if I gain your kind applause for what I've sung or said, Sirs,
You will admit that I have hit the nail right on the head, Sirs.

## *William Bloat*

In a mean abode on the Skankill Road
  Lived a man named William Bloat;
He had a wife, the curse of his life,
  Who continually got on his goat.
So one day at dawn, with her nightdress on,
  He cut her bloody throat.

With a razor gash he settled her hash
  – Oh never was crime so quick –
But the drip, drip, drip on the pillowslip
  Of her life blood made him sick,
And the pool of her gore on the bedroom floor
  Grew clotted and cold and thick.

And yet he was glad he had done what he had
  When he saw her stiff and still
But a sudden awe of the angry law
  Struck his heart with an icy chill,
So to finish the fun so well begun
  He resolved himself to kill.

He took the sheet from his wife's cold feet
  And twisted it into a rope
And he hanged himself from the pantry shelf
  – 'Twas an easy end, I hope.
And in the face of death with his last breath
  He solemnly cursed the Pope.

But the strangest turn to the whole concern
  Was only just beginning:
He went to Hell but his wife got well
  And she's still alive and sinning;
For the razor blade was Dublin made
  But the sheet was Belfast linen.

## *Paddy on the Railway*

In eighteen hundred and forty-one
My corduroy breeches I put on,
My corduroy breeches I put on
To work upon the railway, the railway.
I'm weary of the railway,
Poor Paddy works on the railway.

In eighteen hundred and forty-two
From Hartlepool I moved to Crewe
And found myself a job to do,
Working on the railway.
*I was wearing corduroy breeches*
*Digging ditches, pulling switches*
*Dodging hitches, I*
*Was working on the railway.*

In eighteen hundred and forty-three
I broke the shovel across me knee
And went to work for the company
On the Leeds to Selby railway.
*I was wearing corduroy breeches*, etc.

In eighteen hundred and forty-four
I landed on the Liverpool shore;
My belly was empty, my hands were raw
From working on the railway, the railway.
I'm weary of the railway,
Poor Paddy works on the railway.

In eighteen hundred and forty-five
When Daniel O'Connell he was alive,
When Daniel O'Connell he was alive
I was working on the railway.
*I was wearing corduroy breeches*, etc.

In eighteen hundred and forty-six
I tried my hand at carrying bricks
But I changed my trade from carrying bricks
To working on the railway.
*I was wearing corduroy breeches*, etc.

In eighteen hundred and forty-seven
Poor Paddy was thinking of going to Heaven,
Poor Paddy was thinking of going to Heaven
To work upon the railway, the railway.
I'm weary of the railway
Poor Paddy works on the railway.
*I was wearing corduroy breeches*, etc.

I'm weary of the railway
Poor Paddy works on the railway.

## *Finnegan's Wake*

Tim Finnegan lived in Walkin Street,
  A gentleman Irish mighty odd;
He had a tongue both rich and sweet
  And to rise in the world he carried a hod.
Now Tim had a sort of tippling way,
  With the love of the liquor he was born,
And to help him on to work each day
  He'd a drop of the craythur every morn.
*Whack fol de dah, dance with your partner,*
*Welt the floor, your trotters shake,*
*Isn't it the truth I tell you?*
*Lots of fun at Finnegan's Wake.*

One morning Tim was rather full,
  His head felt heavy, and made him shake;
He fell off the ladder and he broke his skull
  And they carried him home his corpse to wake.

Well they rolled him up in a nice clean sheet
  And laid him out upon the bed,
With a bottle of whiskey at his feet
  And a barrel of porter at his head.
*Whack fol de dah*, etc.

Well his friends assembled at the wake
  And Mrs Finnegan called for lunch,
First they brought in tea and cake,
  Then pipes, tobacco and brandy punch.
Then Widow Malone began to cry,
  'Such a lovely corpse, did you ever see?
Arrah, Tim, Mavourneen, why did you die?'
  'Will you hould your gob?' said Biddy McGee.
*Whack fol de dah*, etc.

Well Mary O'Connor took up the job,
  'Biddy,' says she, 'you're wrong, I'm sure!'
But Biddy gave her a belt in the gob
  That left her sprawling on the floor.
A civil war did then engage,
  'Twas woman to woman and man to man,
Shillelagh law was all the rage
  As a row and a ruction soon began.
*Whack fol de dah*, etc.

Poor Micky Maloney raised his head,
  As a noggin of whiskey flew at him,
It missed and, landing on the bed,
  The whiskey scattered over Tim.
Bedad he revives, see how he rises,
  Tim Finnegan rising in the bed,
Saying, 'Whirl your whiskey around like blazes,
Tare-and-ages, girls, do ye think I'm dead?'
*Whack fol de dah*, etc.

## CHARLES O'FLAHERTY
## (*c.*1794–*c.*1828)

### *The Humours of Donnybrook Fair*

To Donnybrook steer, all you sons of Parnassus –
Poor painters, poor poets, poor newsmen, and knaves,
To see what the fun is, that all fun surpasses –
The sorrow and sadness of green Erin's slaves.
Oh, Donnybrook, jewel! full of mirth is your quiver,
Where all flock from Dublin to gape and to stare
At two elegant bridges, without e'er a river:
So, success to the humours of Donnybrook Fair!

O you lads that are witty, from famed Dublin city,
And you that in pastime take any delight,
To Donnybrook fly, for the time's drawing nigh
When fat pigs are hunted, and lean cobblers fight;
When maidens, so swift, run for a new shift;
Men, muffled in sacks, for a shirt they race there;
There jockeys well booted, and horses sure-footed,
All keep up the humours of Donnybrook Fair.

The mason does come, with his line and his plumb;
The sawyer and carpenter, brothers in chips;
There are carvers and gilders, and all sort of builders,
With soldiers from barracks and sailors from ships.
There confectioners, cooks, and printers of books,
There stampers of linen, and weavers, repair;
There widows and maids, and all sort of trades,
Go join in the humours of Donnybrook Fair.

There tinkers and nailers, and beggars and tailors,
And singers of ballads, and girls of the sieve;
With Barrack Street rangers, the known ones and strangers,
And many that no one can tell how they live:

There horsemen and walkers, and likewise fruit-hawkers,
And swindlers, the devil himself that would dare;
With pipers and fiddlers, and dandies and diddlers, –
All meet in the humours of Donnybrook Fair.

'Tis there are dogs dancing, and wild beasts a-prancing,
With neat bits of painting in red, yellow, and gold;
Toss-players and scramblers, and showmen and gamblers,
Pickpockets in plenty, both of young and of old.
There are brewers, and bakers, and jolly shoemakers,
With butchers, and porters, and men that cut hair;
There are mountebanks grinning, while others are sinning,
To keep up the humours of Donnybrook Fair.

Brisk lads and young lasses can there fill their glasses
With whisky, and send a full bumper around;
Jig it off in a tent till their money's all spent,
And spin like a top till they rest on the ground.
Oh, Donnybrook capers, to sweet catgut-scrapers,
They bother the vapours, and drive away care;
And what is more glorious – there's naught more uproarious –
Huzza for the humours of Donnybrook Fair!

## 'FATHER PROUT'

(John Sylvester O'Mahony, 1804–66)

### *The Town of Passage*

The town of Passage
Is both large and spacious,
And situated
Upon the *say*;
'Tis *nate* and *dacent*,
And quite adjacent,

To come from Cork
        On a summer's day.
There you may slip in,
To take a dipping,
Forenent the shipping,
        That at anchor ride;
Or in a wherry,
Cross o'er the ferry,
To 'Carrigaloe,
        On the other side.'

Mud cabins swarm in
This place so charming,
With sailors' garments
        Hung out to dry;
And each abode is
Snug and commodious,
With pigs melodious,
        In their straw-built sty.
'Tis there the turf is,
And lots of Murphies,
Dead sprats and herrings,
        And oyster-shells;
Nor any lack, oh!
Of good tobacco,
Though what is smuggled
        By far excels.

There are ships from Cadiz,
And from Barbadoes,
But the leading trade is
        In whisky-punch;
And you may go in
Where one Molly Bowen
Keeps a nate hotel
        For a quiet lunch.
But land or deck on,

You may safely reckon,
Whatsoever country
You come hither from,
On an invitation
To a jollification
With a parish priest,
That's called 'Father Tom'.

Of ships there's one fixt
For lodging convicts,
A floating 'stone jug'
Of amazing bulk;
The hake and salmon,
Playing at bagammon,
Swim for divarsion
All round this hulk;
There 'Saxon' jailers
Keep brave repailers,
Who soon with sailors
Must anchor weigh;
From th' em'rald island,
Ne'er to see dry land,
Until they spy land
In sweet Bot'ny Bay.

## CECIL FRANCES ALEXANDER
(1818–95)

### *All Things Bright and Beautiful*

All things bright and beautiful,
All creatures great and small,
All things wise and wonderful,
The Lord God made them all.

Each little flower that opens,
  Each little bird that sings,
He made their glowing colours,
  He made their tiny wings.

The rich man in his castle,
  The poor man at his gate,
God made them, high or lowly,
  And ordered their estate.

The purple-headed mountain,
  The river running by,
The sunset and the morning,
  That brightens up the sky;

The cold wind in the winter,
  The pleasant summer sun,
The ripe fruits in the garden –
  He made them every one;

The tall trees in the greenwood,
  The meadows where we play,
The rushes by the water,
  We gather every day:

He gave us eyes to see them,
  And lips that we might tell,
How great is God Almighty,
  Who has made all things well.

## *Once in Royal David's City*

Once in royal David's city
  Stood a lowly cattle shed,
Where a Mother laid her Baby
  In a manger for His bed.
Mary was that Mother mild,
Jesus Christ her little Child.

He came down to earth from Heaven
  Who is God and Lord of all,
And His shelter was a stable,
  And His cradle was a stall.
With the poor, and mean, and lowly,
Lived on earth our Saviour Holy.

And, through all His wondrous Childhood,
  He would honour and obey,
Love, and watch the lowly Maiden,
  In whose gentle arms He lay.
Christian children all must be
Mild, obedient, good as He.

For He is our childhood's pattern,
  Day by day like us He grew,
He was little, weak and helpless,
  Tears and smiles like us He knew.
And He feeleth for our sadness,
And He shareth in our gladness.

And our eyes at last shall see Him,
  Through His own redeeming love,
For that Child so dear and gentle
  Is our Lord in Heaven above;
And He leads His children on
To the place where He is gone.

Not in that poor lowly stable,
  With the oxen standing by,
We shall see Him, but in Heaven,
  Set at God's right hand on high;
When like stars His children crowned
All in white shall wait around.

## ALFRED PERCEVAL GRAVES

### *Herring is King*

Let all the fish that swim the sea,
Salmon and turbot, cod and ling,
Bow down the head, and bend the knee
To herring, their king! to herring, their king!
*Sing, Hugamar féin an sowra lin',*
*'Tis we have brought the summer in.*

The sun sank down so round and red
Upon the bay, upon the bay;
The sails shook idle overhead,
Becalmed we lay, becalmed we lay;
*Sing, Hugamar féin an sowra lin',*
*'Tis we have brought the summer in.*

Till Shawn, The Eagle, dropped on deck –
The bright-eyed boy, the bright-eyed boy;
'Tis he has spied your silver track,
Herring, our joy – herring, our joy;
*Sing, Hugamar féin an sowra lin',*
*'Tis we have brought the summer in.*

It was in with the sails and away to shore,
With the rise and swing, the rise and swing
Of two stout lads at each smoking oar,
After herring, our king – herring, our king;
*Sing, Hugamar féin an sowra lin',*
*'Tis we have brought the summer in.*

The Manx and the Cornish raised the shout,
  And joined the chase, and joined the chase;
But their fleets they fouled as they went about,
  And we won the race, we won the race;
*Sing, Hugamar féin an sowra lin',*
*'Tis we have brought the summer in.*

For we turned and faced you full to land,
  Down the góleen long, the góleen long,
And, after you, slipped from strand to strand
  Our nets so strong, our nets so strong;
*Sing, Hugamar féin an sowra lin',*
*'Tis we have brought the summer in.*

Then we called to our sweethearts and our wives,
  'Come welcome us home, welcome us home!'
Till they ran to meet us for their lives
  Into the foam, into the foam;
*Sing, Hugamar féin an sowra lin',*
*'Tis we have brought the summer in.*

O the kissing of hands and waving of caps
  From girl and boy, from girl and boy,
While you leapt by scores in the lasses' laps,
  Herring, our pride and joy;
*Sing, Hugamar féin an sowra lin',*
*'Tis we have brought the summer in.*

## JOHNNY TOM GLEESON
## (1853–1924)

### *The Bould Thady Quill*

Ye maids of Duhallow who are anxious for courtin'
A word of advice I will give unto ye,
Go down to Banteer to the athletic sporting,
And hand in your names to the club committee.
But do not commence any stretch of your progress
Till a carriage you see coming over the hill
And down through the valleys and hills of Kilcorney,
With that Muskerry sportsman the bould Thady Quill.

For ramblin', for rovin', for football or courtin',
For drinkin' black porter as fast as you'd fill,
In all your days rovin', you'd find none so jovial,
As our Muskerry sportsman the Bould Thady Quill.

Thady was famous in all sorts of places;
At the athletic meeting held out in Cloghroe,
He won the long jump without throwing off his braces,
Going fifty-four feet from the heel to the toe.
At the put of the shot was a Dublin man foremost,
But Thady out-reached and exceeded him still,
Around the whole field rang the wild ringing chorus,
'Here's luck to our hero, the Bould Thady Quill.'

For ramblin', etc.

At the great hurling match between Cork and Tipperary,
'Twas played in the park by the banks of the Lee,
Our own darling boys were afraid of being beaten,
So they sent for bould Thady to Ballinagree.

He hurled up the ball left and right in their faces,
And showed those Tipperary boys learning and skill,
If they came in his way, sure he surely would brain them,
And the papers were full of the praise of Thady Quill.

For ramblin', etc.

At the Cork exhibition there was a fine lady,
Whose fortune exceeded a million or more,
But a bad constitution had ruined her completely,
And medical treatment had failed o'er and o'er,
'Oh Mamma,' said she, 'I know what'll aise me,
And all me diseases most certainly kill,
Give over your doctors, your potions and treatment,
I'd rather one squeeze out of Bould Thady Quill.'

For ramblin', etc.

## PERCY FRENCH

### *Shlathery's Mounted Fut*

You've heard o' Julius Cæsar, an' the great Napoleon, too,
An' how the Cork Militia beat the Turks at Waterloo;
But there's a page of glory that, as yet, remains uncut,
An' that's the Martial story o' the Shlathery's Mounted Fut.
This gallant corps was organized by Shlathery's eldest son,
A noble-minded poacher, wid a double-breasted gun;
An' many a head was broken, aye, an' many an eye was shut,
Whin practisin' manœuvres in the Shlathery's Mounted Fut.

CHORUS

An' down from the mountains came the squadrons an' platoons,
Four-an'-twinty fightin' min, an' a couple o' sthout gossoons,
An' whin we marched behind the dhrum to patriotic tunes,
We felt that fame would gild the name o' Shlathery's Light
Dhragoons.

Well, first we reconnoithered round O'Sullivan's Shebeen –
It used to be 'The Shop House' but we call it 'The Canteen':
But there we saw a notice which the bravest heart unnerved –
'All liquor must be settled for before the dhrink is served.'
So on we marched, but soon again each warrior's heart grew
pale,
For risin' high in front o' us we saw the County Jail;
An' whin the army faced about, 'twas just in time to find
A couple o' policemin had surrounded us behind.

CHORUS

Still, from the mountains came the squadrons and platoons,
Four-an'-twinty fightin' min, an' a couple o' sthout gossoons;
Says Shlathery, 'We must circumvent these bludgeonin'
bosthoons,
Or else it sames they'll take the names o' Shlathery's Light
Dhragoons.

'We'll cross the ditch,' our leader cried, 'an' take the foe in
flank,'
But yells of consthernation here arose from every rank,
For posted high upon a tree we very plainly saw,
'Threspassers prosecuted, in accordance wid' the law.'
'We're foiled!' exclaimed bowld Shlathery, 'here ends our grand
campaign,
'Tis merely throwin' life away to face that mearin' dhrain,
I'm not as bold as lions, but I'm braver nor a hin,
An' he that fights and runs away will live to fight agin.'

CHORUS

An' back to the mountains went the squadrons and platoons,
Four-an'-twinty fightin' min an' a couple o' sthout gossoons;
The band was playing cautiously their patriotic tunes;
To sing the fame, if rather lame o' Shlathery's Light Dhragoons.

## JAMES JOYCE

### *from* Finnegans Wake

### *The Ballad of Persse O'Reilly*

Have you heard of one Humpty Dumpty
How he fell with a roll and a rumble
And curled up like Lord Olofa Crumple
By the butt of the Magazine Wall,
    (Chorus) Of the Magazine Wall,
        Hump, helmet and all?

He was one time our King of the Castle
Now he's kicked about like a rotten old parsnip.
And from Green street he'll be sent by order of His Worship
To the penal jail of Mountjoy
    (Chorus) To the jail of Mountjoy!
        Jail him and joy.

He was fafafather of all schemes for to bother us
Slow coaches and immaculate contraceptives for the populace,
Mare's milk for the sick, seven dry Sundays a week,
Openair love and religion's reform,
    (Chorus) And religious reform,
        Hideous in form.

Arrah, why, says you, couldn't he manage it?
I'll go bail, my fine dairyman darling,
Like the bumping bull of the Cassidys
All your butter is in your horns.
    (Chorus) His butter is in his horns.
        Butter his horns!

(Repeat) Hurrah there, Hosty, frosty Hosty, change that shirt on ye,
Rhyme the rann, the king of all ranns!

*Balbaccio, balbuccio!*

We had chaw chaw chops, chairs, chewing gum, the chickenpox and china chambers
Universally provided by this soffsoaping salesman.
Small wonder He'll Cheat E'erawan our local lads nicknamed him
When Chimpden first took the floor
    (Chorus) With his bucketshop store
        Down Bargainweg, Lower.

So snug he was in his hotel premises sumptuous
But soon we'll bonfire all his trash, tricks and trumpery
And 'tis short till sheriff Clancy'll be winding up his unlimited company
With the bailiff's bom at the door,
    (Chorus) Bimbam at the door.
        Then he'll bum no more.

Sweet bad luck on the waves washed to our island
The hooker of that hammerfast viking
And Gall's curse on the day when Eblana bay
Saw his black and tan man-o'-war.
    (Chorus) Saw his man-o'-war.
        On the harbour bar.

Where from? roars Poolbeg. Cookingha'pence, he bawls
    Donnez-moi scampitle, wick an wipin'fampiny
Fingal Mac Oscar Onesine Bargearse Boniface
Thok's min gammelhole Norveegickers moniker
Og as ay are at gammelhore Norveegickers cod.
        (Chorus) A Norwegian camel old cod.
                He is, begod.

Lift it, Hosty, lift it, ye devil ye! up with the rann, the rhyming
    rann!

It was during some fresh water garden pumping
Or, according to the *Nursing Mirror*, while admiring the
    monkeys
That our heavyweight heathen Humpharey
Made bold a maid to woo
        (Chorus) Woohoo, what'll she doo!
                The general lost her maidenloo!

He ought to blush for himself, the old hayheaded philosopher,
For to go and shove himself that way on top of her.
Begob, he's the crux of the catalogue
Of our antediluvial zoo,
        (Chorus) Messrs. Billing and Coo.
                Noah's larks, good as noo.

He was joulting by Wellinton's monument
Our rotorious hippopopotamuns
When some bugger let down the backtrap of the omnibus
And he caught his death of fusiliers,
        (Chorus) With his rent in his rears.
                Give him six years.

'Tis sore pity for his innocent poor children
But look out for his missus legitimate!
When that frew gets a grip of old Earwicker
Won't there be earwigs on the green?
(Chorus) Big earwigs on the green,
The largest ever you seen.

Suffoclose! Shikespower! Seudodanto! Anonymoses!

Then we'll have a free trade Gaels' band and mass meeting
For to sod the brave son of Scandiknavery.
And we'll bury him down in Oxmanstown
Along with the devil and Danes,
(Chorus) With the deaf and dumb Danes,
And all their remains.

And not all the king's men nor his horses
Will resurrect his corpus
For there's no true spell in Connacht or hell
(bis) That's able to raise a Cain.

## LOUIS MACNEICE

### *The Streets of Laredo*

O early one morning I walked out like Agag,
Early one morning to walk through the fire
Dodging the pythons that leaked on the pavements
With tinkle of glasses and tangle of wire;

When grimed to the eyebrows I met an old fireman
Who looked at me wryly and thus did he say:
'The streets of Laredo are closed to all traffic,
We won't never master this joker today.

'O hold the branch tightly and wield the axe brightly,
The bank is in powder, the banker's in hell,
But loot is still free on the streets of Laredo
And when we drive home we drive home on the bell.'

Then out from a doorway there sidled a cockney,
A rocking-chair rocking on top of his head:
'O fifty-five years I been feathering my love-nest
And look at it now – why, you'd sooner be dead.'

At which there arose from a wound in the asphalt,
His big wig a-smoulder, Sir Christopher Wren
Saying: 'Let them make hay of the streets of Laredo;
When your ground-rents expire I will build them again.'

Then twangling their bibles with wrath in their nostrils
From Bonehill Fields came Bunyan and Blake:
'Laredo the golden is fallen, is fallen;
Your flame shall not quench nor your thirst shall not slake.'

'I come to Laredo to find me asylum,'
Says Tom Dick and Harry the Wandering Jew;
'They tell me report at the first police station
But the station is pancaked – so what can I do?'

Thus eavesdropping sadly I strolled through Laredo
Perplexed by the dicta misfortunes inspire
Till one low last whisper inveigled my earhole –
The voice of the Angel, the voice of the fire:

*O late, very late, have I come to Laredo*
*A whimsical bride in my new scarlet dress*
*But at last I took pity on those who were waiting*
*To see my regalia and feel my caress.*

*Now ring the bells gaily and play the hose daily,*
*Put splints on your legs, put a gag on your breath;*
*O you streets of Laredo, you streets of Laredo,*
*Lay down the red carpet – my dowry is death.*

# CHRISTY MOORE

(*b.*1945)

## *Lisdoonvarna*

How's it goin' there everybody,
From Cork, New York, Dundalk, Gortahork and Glenamaddy?
Here we are in the County Clare,
It's a long, long way from here to there.
There's the Burren and the Cliffs of Moher,
The Tulla and the Kilfenora,
Micho Russell, Doctor Bill,
Willy Clancy, Noel Hill.
Flutes and fiddles everywhere.
If it's music you want,
You should go to Clare.
(Up the Banner!)

*Chorus:*
Oh, Lisdoonvarna
Lisdoon, Lisdoon, Lisdoon, Lisdoonvarna!

Everybody needs a break,
Climb a mountain or jump in a lake.
Some head off to exotic places,
Others go to the Galway Races.
Mattie goes to the South of France,
Jim to the dogs, Peter to the dance.
A cousin of mine goes pot-holin',
A cousin of hers loves Joe Dolan.
The summer comes around each year,
We go there and they come here.
Some jet off to Frijiliana,
But I always head for Lisdoonvarna.

*Chorus*

Normally leave of a Thursday night,
With me tent and groundsheet rolled up tight.
I like to get into Lisdoon,
In or around Friday afternoon.
This gives me time to get my tent up, get my gear together,
Don't need to worry about the weather.
Ramble in for a pint of stout,
You'd never know who'd be hangin' about!
There's a Dutchman playing a mandolin,
And a German looking for Liam Óg O'Floinn.
Adam and Bono and Garret Fitzgerald,
Gettin' their photos taken for the *Sunday World*.
Finbarr, Charlie and Jim Hand,
And they drinkin' pints to bate the band.
(Why wouldn't they, aren't they gettin' it for nothin'?)

*Chorus*

The multitudes they flocked in throngs
To hear the music and the songs.
On motorbikes and Hi-ace vans,
Bottles, barrels, flagons, cans.
Mighty crack, loads of frolics,
Pioneers and alcoholics,
PLAC, SPUC 'n' the FCA,
Free Nicky Kelly and the IRA,
Hairy chests and milk-white thighs,
Mickey-dodgers in disguise.
McGraths, O'Briens, Pippins, Coxes,
Massage parlours in horseboxes.
RTE are makin' tapes, takin' breaks and throwin' shapes.
Amhráns, bodhráns, amadáns,
Hairy Geeks, Arab Sheikhs, Hindu Sikhs, Jesus Freaks,
This is heaven, this is hell.
Who cares? Who can tell?
(Anyone for the last few choc ices?)

*Chorus*

A 747 for Jackson Browne,
They built a special runway just to get him down.
Before the Chieftains could start to play,
Seven creamy pints came out on a tray.
Seán Cannon was doin' the backstage cookin',
Shergar was ridden by Lord Lucan,
Mary O'Hara and Brush Shields,
Together singin' 'The Four Green Fields'.
Clannad were playin' 'Harry's Game',
Chris de Burgh singin' 'Lady in Red' on a Spanish train,
Van the Man, Emmy Lou,
Moving Hearts and Planxty too!

*Chorus*

Everybody needs a break,
Climb a mountain, jump in a lake.
Sean Doherty's down the Rose of Tralee,
Oliver J. Flanagan swimming naked in the Holy Sea.
But I like my music in the open air,
Every Summer I go to Clare.
Because Woodstock, Knock or the Feast of Cana,
Can't hold a match to . . . Lisdoonvarna!

*Chorus*

# Acknowledgements

Thanks for the existence of the book are due to Simon Winder at Penguin, who commissioned it; to Paul Keegan who championed it and whose *Penguin Book of English Verse* (2000) remained one of its inspirations from inception to completion; and to Alexis Kirschbaum, Director of Penguin Classics, who chivvied the manuscript on its way and whose unwavering support was crucial to the realization of my desire to present an appropriately large-scale account of Irish poetry. Ian Pindar, learned and eagle-eyed, was an unfailingly generous and acute copy editor, and Rebecca Lee a model of patience and acumen in overseeing the proofreading. Kristina Blagojevitch, permissions-seeker *par excellence*, kept me on an even keel during the nerve-racking final stages of production. Laura Barber, Marcella Edwards and Mariateresa Boffo were successively stalwart in their encouragement during the earlier phases of what ultimately proved a nine-year task.

Any anthology of Irish poetry contributes to a tradition of display that stretches back at least as far as the Victorian age and the four-volume *Cabinet of Irish Literature* (1879–80), and includes such assiduously meditated compilations as Stopford Brooke and T. W. Rolleston's *A Treasury of Irish Poetry in the English Tongue*, which grew through successive editions from 1900 to 1932. Three more recent anthologies stand directly behind the present volume – Brendan Kennelly's *Penguin Book of Irish Verse* (1970), with its generous attention to the poetry of early Ireland and its democratic treatment of the contemporary scene; John Montague's lively and various *Faber Book of Irish Verse* (1974), compiled when that poet-editor was my inspirational tutor at University College Cork; and Thomas Kinsella's *New Oxford Book of Irish Verse* (1986), the first anthology seriously to attempt an estimate of the scale of the Gaelic achievement via English translation. The larger scope and greater cultural pluralism of the present volume are to be understood in terms of evolutionary conversation rather than dispute with these groundbreaking books. Andrew Carpenter's more specialized *Verse in English from Eighteenth-Century Ireland* (1998) and *Verse in English from Tudor and Stuart Ireland* (2003) drew attention to a great deal of hitherto obscure material and proved invaluable resources in themselves, while also providing starting points for many research trails. Anybody who works on poetry in Irish must owe a huge debt to the visionary scholarship of Máirín Ní Dhonnchadha's sections of *The Field Day Anthology of Irish Writing*, Vol. IV (2002); I was greatly aided throughout all stages of the preparation of *The Penguin Book of Irish Poetry* by that distinguished editor's readiness to inform, clarify and advise in relation to various aspects of Gaelic literature and cultural practice. I thank her also for co-writing two of the translations.

I was fortunate in having my interest in poetry awoken at home in Fermoy by my great-aunt and godmother Honora O'Donoghue, and stirred at primary school by Brother Dónal Blake and the late Brother T. A. Farrell, and at St Colman's College by Michael Cannon, Seamus Cashman, the late Monsignor Christopher Twohig and – decisively – by Dr (later Prof.) Patrick Hannon. John Montague and the late Seán Lucy did much at University College Cork to maintain the momentum set by Pat Hannon. At secondary school and university I was blessed by the company of Maurice Riordan, a significant contributor to this book, and of Dermot Coakley and John Coakley. My time as a student and then a teacher in Cork featured animated discourse about poetry with those friends and with Seán Clerkin, Theo Dorgan, the late Seán Dunne, Paul Durcan, Willy Kelly, Anne Kelly, Tom Leonard, Thomas MacCarthy, Frank Murphy, Mike O'Brien, the late Gregory O'Donoghue and the late Robert O'Donoghue. In my visits to Scotland as a graduate student in the mid- and later 1970s I repeatedly enjoyed the inestimable privilege of the company of one of the founts of European poetry, the late Hugh MacDiarmid, and learned much also from the late Hamish Henderson, the late Norman McCaig, the late Sorley MacLean, Edwin Morgan (whose magnificent translation of the abecedarian poem attributed to Colum Cille is one of the glories of section I of the present book) and the late Alexander Scott, and from the critics the late Kenneth Buthlay and Ruth McQuillan. In Wales in the following decade the late Tudor Bevan, Tony Bianchi, the late Wyn Binding, George Boyce, Gillian Clarke, Katie Gramich, the late Dafydd Arthur Jones, the late Glyn Jones, Harri Pritchard Jones, John Pikoulis, Glyn Pursglove and M. Wynn Thomas kept the cauldron stirred.

The book has benefited from conversations with and other kinds of assistance from many poets, songwriters, critics, scholars and friends including Michael Alexander, Jonathan Allison, Fran Brearton, Terence Brown, James Campbell, Ciaran Carson, Philip Coleman, Neil Corcoran, Damian Walford Davies, Greg Delanty, Douglas Dunn, Leontia Flynn, Patrick K. Ford, John Wilson Foster, Roy Foster, Alan Gillis, Nicholas Grene, Tom Halpin, Liam Harte, Joe Hassett, Hugh Haughton, Marie Heaney,

Seamus Heaney, John Herdman, the late Mick Imlah, the late A. N. Jeffares, Christine Kelly, James Kelly, John Kelly, Elmer Kennedy-Andrews, Brendan Kennelly, John Kerrigan, Nick Laird, Edna Longley, Michael Longley, Peter McDonald, Medbh McGuckian, Liam McIlvanney, Andrew McNeillie, Aodán Mac Póilín, Alasdair Macrae, Elise Macrae, Christy Moore, David Norbrook, Ailbhe Ó Corráin, Donnchadh Ó Corráin, Bernard O'Donoghue, Heather O'Donoghue, Gitti Paulin, Tom Paulin, Alan Riach, Sean Ryder, John Scattergood, Bruce Stewart, Mary Shine Thompson, Fintan Vallely, Helen Vendler, Celia Watson, Roderick Watson, Tim Webb, Robert Welch, David Wheatley and David Wilson.

In Aberdeen I am grateful to Prof. Chris Gane, Head of the College of Arts and Social Sciences, who supplied me with an able and greatly needed research assistant during the submission phase. To that research assistant, Dr Dan Wall, I am deeply thankful for his tireless work in helping put the manuscript together. Without a semester's research leave granted by the School of Language and Literature in early 2009 the translations could not have been written or the book completed. I wish to record my thanks to the then Head of School, Prof. Chris Fynsk, and to all my colleagues in the School. I am particularly grateful to Dr Shane Alcobia-Murphy and Dr Wayne Price for their unfailing readiness to discuss aspects of the book and offer shrewd counsel. I am thankful also to Prof. Cairns Craig, Dr Stephen Dornan, Dr David Duff, Dr Barbara Fennell, Dr Andrew Gordon, Prof. David Hewitt, Dr Adrienne Janus, Dr Catherine Jones, Prof. Jeannette King, Dr Alison Lumsden, Mr Derrick McClure, Dr Ainsley McIntosh, Dr Robert McColl Millar, Prof. Isobel Murray, Dr Paul Shanks, Prof. Michael Syrotinski, Mrs Pam Thomson, Mrs Maureen Wilkie and Dr Tarrin Wills for support of important kinds. Elsewhere in the University I am grateful to Prof. Peter Davidson, Prof. David Dumville, Dr Ralph O'Connor and Prof. Jane Stevenson for so generously sharing their immense scholarship, and to Dr Michael Brown for his thoughtful comments on the Introduction. I owe a personal debt of gratitude to Sir Duncan Rice, Joanna Watson and above all to the late Prof. George Watson.

I wish to thank the staff of the Queen Mother Library and the Special Collections Library at the University of Aberdeen; of the National Library of Wales, Aberystwyth; of the University of Ulster libraries at Coleraine and Magee; and of the Cregan Library at St Patrick's College, Drumcondra. I am indebted also to Dr John Brannigan of University College Dublin for his help in tracking down fugitive material. Additionally, I wish to bless the mighty Internet for transforming the character of poem-hunting, though not utterly.

I owe special thanks to Tiffany Atkinson, Peter Davidson, Kit Fryatt, Seamus Heaney, Kathleen Jamie, Michael Longley, Bernard O'Donoghue, Maurice Riordan and David Wheatley for their new translations, and to

Seamus Heaney for his Preface. To Kit Fryatt, who lives the poetry life, I owe an additional and inestimable debt for her loving support during the period when the selections were being finalized and the translations and introduction composed.

*The editor and publisher gratefully acknowledge the following for permission to reprint copyright material:*

ANONYMOUS: 'Suibne in the Trees' trans. Paul Batchelor from *The Sinking Road* (Bloodaxe Books, 2008), reprinted by permission of the publisher (© Paul Batchelor, 2008); 'Adze-head', 'Writing Out of Doors' trans. James Carney from *Medieval Irish Lyrics with The Irish Bardic Poet* (The Dolmen Press, 1985), reprinted by permission of Mr Justice Paul Carney; 'Cu Chulainn's Lament over Fer Diad' and 'The Morrigan's Chant' trans. Ciaran Carson from *The Tain: a New Translation of the Tain Bao Cauailnge* (Penguin Classics, 2007), reprinted by permission of the publisher (© Ciaran Carson, 2007); 'Elegy for Richard Lynch, *d.* Salamanca 1679' trans. Peter Davidson (© Peter Davidson, 2010); 'At Mass', 'The Curse', 'The Dispraise of Absalom', 'He Praises His Wife When She Had Gone from Him' and 'Sadly the ousel sings . . .' trans. Robin Flower from *Poems and Translations* (Lilliput Press, 1994), reprinted by permission of Lilliput Press; 'The Complaints of Gormlaith' trans. Kit Fryatt (© Kit Fryatt, 2010); 'He is my love' trans. Michael Hartnett from *Translations: A Selection* (Gallery Press, 2003), reprinted by permission of the publisher (© The Estate of Michael Hartnett, 2003); 'Lynchseachan, you are a bother . . .' trans. Seamus Heaney from *Sweeney Astray* (Faber & Faber, 1984), reprinted by permission of the publisher (© Seamus Heaney, 1984); 'The Blackbird of Belfast Lough' trans. Seamus Heaney (© Seamus Heaney, 2010); 'My Grief on the Sea' trans. Douglas Hyde, reprinted by permission of Douglas Sealy; 'Fedelm's Vision of Cúchulainn' trans. Thomas Kinsella from *The Tain* (Oxford University Press, 1969), reprinted by permission of the translator (© Thomas Kinsella, 1969); 'Gaze North-East' and 'The Wooing of Etain' trans. John Montague, reprinted by permission of the Gallery Press (© John Montague, 1974); 'Aoibhinn, a leabhráin, do thriall' ('Delightful, book, your trip . . .') and 'Scél Lem Dúib' ('Here's a song . . .') trans. Flann O'Brien from *The Pleasures of Gaelic Poetry* (Penguin, 1982), reprinted by permission of A. M. Heath & Co. Ltd.; 'First Year in the Wilderness' trans. Flann O'Brien from *At Swim-Two-Birds* (Penguin Modern Classics, 2000), reprinted by permission of A. M. Heath & Co. Ltd. (© Flann O'Brien, 1968); 'Death and the Maiden', 'The Downfall of Heathendom', 'The Hermit's Song', 'A Jealous Man', 'Jealousy', 'The King of Connacht', 'Liadan', 'Patrick Sarsfield,

Lord Lucan', 'The Praise of Fionn', 'The Priest Rediscovers his Psalm-Book', 'Slievenamon', 'Storm at Sea' and 'Winter' trans. Frank O'Connor from *Kings, Lords, & Commons: An Anthology from the Irish* (Macmillan, 1961); 'Advice to Lovers', 'A History of Love' and 'Women' trans. Frank O'Connor from *The Little Monasteries* (The Dolmen Press, 1963), reprinted by permission of PFD on behalf of the Estate of Frank O'Connor (© The Estate of Frank O'Connor, 1959, 1963); 'Gormlaith's Last Lament' and 'On the Death of a Poet' trans. David Wheatley (© David Wheatley, 2010); BECCÁN THE HERMIT: 'Last Verses in Praise of Colum Cille' trans. Thomas Owen Clancy from *The Triumph Tree: Scotland's Earliest Poetry AD 550–1350* (Canongate, 1998), reprinted by permission of the translator. SAMUEL BECKETT: 'my way is in the sand flowing . . .', 'what would I do without this world faceless incurious . . .' and 'I would like my love to die . . .' from *Selected Poems 1930–89* (Faber & Faber, 2009), reprinted by permission of the publisher. BRENDAN BEHAN: 'The Captains and the Kings' from *The Hostage* (Methuen, 1958) and 'The Ould Triangle' from *The Quare Fellow* (Methuen, 1960), reprinted by permission of the Estate of Brendan Behan and the Sayle Literary Agency. DOMINIC BEHAN: 'Liverpool Lou' and 'The Patriot Game', reprinted by permission of the Estate of Dominic Behan. BLATHMAC SON OF CÚ BRETTAN: 'May I have from you my three petitions' trans. James Carney from *Medieval Irish Lyrics with The Irish Bardic Poet* (The Dolmen Press, 1985), reprinted by permission of Mr Justice Paul Carney. EAVAN BOLAND: 'Mise Eire' and 'From the Painting *Back from Market* by Chardin' from *Collected Poems* (Carcanet Press, 1995), reprinted by permission of the publisher (© Eavan Boland, 1995). COLETTE BRYCE: 'The Poetry Bug' and 'Self-Portrait in the Dark' from *Self-Portrait in the Dark* (Picador, 2008), reprinted by permission of Macmillan (© Colette Bryce, 2008). CIARAN CARSON: 'A Date Called *Eat Me*', 'Dresden', 'Part One: The Fetch' and 'Part Two: The Fetch', 'The Rising Sun', 'Trap' and 'Wake' from *Collected Poems* (The Gallery Press, 2008), reprinted by permission of the publisher (© Ciaran Carson, 2008). SÉATHRÚN CÉITINN: 'Dear Woman, With Your Wiles' trans. Maurice Riordan (© Maurice Riordan, 2010); 'No Sleep is Mine' trans. David Wheatley (© David Wheatley, 2010). COLUM CILLE (*attrib.*): 'Colum Cille's Exile' trans. James Carney from *Medieval Irish Lyrics with The Irish Bardic Poet* (The Dolmen Press, 1985), reprinted by permission of Mr Justice Paul Carney; 'The Maker on High' trans. Edwin Morgan from *Edwin Morgan: Collected Poems* (Carcanet Press, 1990), reprinted by permission of the publisher (© Edwin Morgan, 1990). AUSTIN CLARKE: 'The Blackbird of Derrycairn', 'The Lost Heifer', 'Martha Blake at Fifty-one', 'New Liberty Hall', 'Penal Law', 'The Planter's Daughter', 'The Scholar', 'The Straying Student', 'A Strong Wind', *Tiresias* (extract) from *Austin Clarke: Collected*

*Poems* (Carcanet Press and The Bridge Press, 2008), reprinted by permission of R. Dardis Clarke, 17 Oscar Square, Dublin 8. PADRAIC COLUM: 'A Drover', 'O woman shapely as the swan', 'The Poet', 'The Poor Girl's Meditation' and 'She Moved Through the Fair' from *Collected Poems* (Devin Adair, 1953), reprinted by permission of the Estate of Padraic Colum. COLUMBANUS: 'Hymn to the Trinity' trans. Kit Fryatt (© Kit Fryatt, 2010); CÚ CHUIMNE OF IONA: 'Hymn to the Virgin Mary' trans. Kit Fryatt (© Kit Fryatt, 2010). JOHN F. DEANE: 'The Instruments of Art' from *The Instruments of Art* (Carcanet Press, 2005), reprinted by permission of the publisher (© John F. Deane, 2005). GREG DELANTY: 'The Cure' and 'To My Mother, Eileen' from *Collected Poems* (Carcanet Press, 2006), reprinted by permission of the publisher (© Greg Delanty, 2006). PAUL DURCAN: 'Ireland 2001' from *The Art of Life* (Harvill Press, 2004); 'Give Him Bondi', 'Ireland 1972', 'Ireland 1977' and 'Ireland 2002' from *Life is a Dream: 40 Years Reading Poems 1967–2007* (Harvill Secker, 2009), reprinted by permission of Rogers, Coleridge & White, 20 Powis Mews, London W11 1JN (© Paul Durcan, 2004, 2009). PADRAIC FALLON: 'A Flask of Brandy' and 'Raftery's Dialogue with the Whiskey' from *Collected Poems* (Carcanet Press, 1990), reprinted by permission of the publisher (© Padraic Fallon, 1990). PETER FALLON: 'The Company of Horses' from *The Company of Horses* (The Gallery Press, 2007), reprinted by permission of the publisher (© Peter Fallon, 2007). LEONTIA FLYNN: 'By My Skin' from *These Days* (Jonathan Cape, 2004); 'Drive' from *Drives* (Jonathan Cape, 2008), reprinted by permission of The Random House Group Ltd (© Leontia Flynn, 2004, 2008). DALLÁN FORGAILL: 'Amra Colm Cille' trans. Thomas Owen Clancy from *The Triumph Tree: Scotland's Earliest Poetry* AD *550–1350* (Canongate, 1998), reprinted by permission of the translator. ALAN GILLIS: 'Progress' and '12th October, 1994' from *Somebody, Somewhere* (The Gallery Press, 2004), reprinted by permission of the publisher (© Alan Gillis, 2004). EAMON GRENNAN: '*because the body stops here because you can only reach out so far . . .*', 'Casual, prodigal, these piss-poor opportunists, the weeds . . .', 'Even under the rain that casts a fine white blanket over mountain and lake . . .' and 'When I see the quick ripple of a groundhog's back above the grass . . .' from *The Quick of It* (The Gallery Press, 2004), reprinted by permission of the publisher (© Eamon Grennan, 2004). PÁDRAIGÍN HAICÉAD: 'Dirge on the death of Éamon Mac Piarais Buitléir, 1640' trans. Michael Hartnett from *Haicéad: Translations from the Irish* (The Gallery Press, 1993), reprinted by permission of the publisher (© The Estate of Michael Hartnett, 1993). KERRY HARDIE: 'Ship of Death' from *A Furious Place* (The Gallery Press, 1996); 'Seal Morning' from *Cry for the Hot Belly* (The Gallery Press, 2000), reprinted by permission of the publisher (© Kerry Hardie 1996, 2000). MICHAEL HARTNETT:

'Bread', 'For My Grandmother, Bridget Halpin', *Inchicore Haiku* (extract), and *Notes on my Contemporaries* (extract) from *Collected Poems*, (The Gallery Press, 2001); 'Lament for Tadhg Cronin's Children' from *Translations: A Selection* (The Gallery Press, 2003), reprinted by permission of the publisher (© The Estate of Michael Hartnett, 2001, 2003). SEAMUS HEANEY: 'Bogland', 'Broagh', 'Death of a Naturalist', 'Hailstones', 'The Harvest Bow', 'The Peninsula', 'Postscript', 'Requiem for the Croppies', 'Settings', 'A Sofa in the Forties', 'Song', 'The Strand at Lough Beg', 'Sweeney Redivivus' and 'The Tollund Man' from *Opened Ground* (Faber & Faber, 1998); 'Perch' from *Electric Light* (Faber & Faber, 2001); 'The Blackbird of Glanmore' from *District and Circle* (Faber & Faber, 2006), reprinted by permission of the publisher (© Seamus Heaney 1998, 2001, 2006); 'Craig's Dragoons' (© Seamus Heaney, 2010). JOHN HEWITT: 'The Colony' from *The Selected Poems of John Hewitt* (Blackstaff Press, 2007), reprinted by permission of the publisher and the estate of John Hewitt. RITA ANN HIGGINS: 'Black Dog in My Docs Day' from *An Awful Racket* (Bloodaxe Books, 2001), reprinted by permission of the publisher (© Rita Ann Higgins, 2001). PEARSE HUTCHINSON: 'Petition to Release' from *Collected Poems* (The Gallery Press, 2002), reprinted by permission of the publisher (© Pearse Hutchinson, 2002). JAMES JOYCE: 'The Ballad of Persse O'Reilly' and 'The Ondt and the Gracehoper' from *Finnegans Wake*; 'Buy a book in brown paper', 'I hear an army charging upon the land' and 'Watching the Needleboats at San Sabba' from *Poems and Shorter Writings*, reprinted by permission of the Estate of James Joyce. TREVOR JOYCE: 'I once thought that the quiet speech . . .' from *With the first dream of fire they hunt the cold: A Body of Work 1966/2000* (New Writers' Press and Shearsman Books, 2001); 'all that is the case' and 'now then' from *What's in Store* (The Gig, 2007), reprinted by permission of the author (© Trevor Joyce, 2001, 2007). PATRICK KAVANAGH: 'A Christmas Childhood', 'Come Dance with Kitty Stobling', 'The Great Hunger', 'The Hospital', 'Inniskeen Road: July Evening', 'Innocence', 'Kerr's Ass', 'The One', 'On Raglan Road' and 'Threshing Morning' from *Collected Poems of Patrick Kavanagh* (Allen Lane, 2004), reprinted by permission of the Trustees of the Estate of the late Katherine B. Kavanagh, through the Jonathan Williams Literary Agency. BRENDAN KENNELLY: *The Book of Judas* (extract) and *The Man Made of Rain* (extract) from *Familiar Strangers: New and Selected Poems 1960–2004* (Bloodaxe Books, 2004), reprinted by permission of the publisher (© Brendan Kennelly, 2004); THOMAS KINSELLA: 'At the Western Ocean's Edge','Chrysalides', 'The Design', 'First Light', 'His Father's Hands', parts 2 and 5 of 'Nightwalker' 'Tao and Unfitness at Inistiogue on the River Nore' and '38 Phoenix Street' from *Collected Poems* (Carcanet Press, 2001), reprinted by permission of the publisher

(© Thomas Kinsella, 2001). NICK LAIRD: 'Pedigree' from *To a Fault* (Faber & Faber, 2005), reprinted by permission of the publisher (© Nick Laird, 2005). WALTER LAWLESS: 'To the most noble Lord, James Marquis of Ormonde . . . his humble servant Walter Lawles wishes happiness and prosperity' trans. Peter Davidson (© Peter Davidson, 2010). MICHAEL LONGLEY: 'Above Dooaghtry', 'Between Hovers', 'The Butchers', 'The Campfires', 'Ceasefire', 'The Evening Star', 'Form', 'In Memoriam', 'The Linen Industry', 'Overhead', 'Sleep & Death' and 'Wounds' from *Collected Poems* (Jonathan Cape, 2006); 'Whalsay' from *A Hundred Doors* (Jonathan Cape, 2011), reprinted by permission of The Random House Group Ltd (© Michael Longley, 2006, 2010). FEARGHAL ÓG MAC AN BHAIRD: 'A Letter of Complaint' trans. Bernard O'Donoghue (© Bernard O'Donoghue, 2010). LAOISEACH MAC AN BHAIRD: 'Brothers' trans. Seamus Heaney (© Seamus Heaney, 2010); 'A Man of Experience' trans. Frank O'Connor from *Kings, Lords, & Commons: An Anthology from the Irish* (Macmillan, 1961), reprinted by permission of PFD on behalf of the Estate of Frank O'Connor (© The Estate of Frank O'Connor, 1959); 'The Felling of a Sacred Tree' trans. Bernard O'Donoghue (© Bernard O'Donoghue, 2010). MOTHER OF DIARMAID MAC CÁRTHAIGH: 'A Lament for Diarmaid MacCarthy of Ráth Dubháin, Who Was a Butter-Merchant in Cork' trans. Angela Bourke from *The Field Day Anthology of Irish Writing,* Vol. IV (Cork University Press, 2002), reprinted by permission of the Jonathan Williams Literary Agency. THOMAS MCCARTHY: 'Ellen Tobin McCarthy' and 'The Standing Trains' from *Mr Dineen's Careful Parade: New and Selected Poems* (Anvil Press, 1999), reprinted by permission of the publisher. DONNCHADH RUA MAC CON MARA: 'Epitaph for Tadhg Gaedhealach Ó Súilleabháin' trans. Peter Davidson (© Peter Davidson, 2010). GIOLLA BRIGHDE MAC CON MIDHE: 'A Response to a Threat against Poetry' trans. Patrick K. Ford from *The Celtic Poets* (Belmont, MA: Ford and Bailie, 1999), reprinted by permission of the translator; 'Childless' trans. Frank O'Connor from *Kings, Lords, & Commons: An Anthology from the Irish* (Macmillan, 1961), reprinted by permission of PFD on behalf of the Estate of Frank O'Connor (© The Estate of Frank O'Connor, 1959). SÉAMAS DALL MAC CUARTA: 'The Drowned Blackbird' trans. Seamus Heaney (© Seamus Heaney, 2010). ART MAC CUMHAIGH: 'The Churchyard of Creggan' trans. Kit Fryatt (© Kit Fryatt, 2010). PETER MCDONALD: 'The Hand' from *The House of Clay* (Carcanet Press, 2007), reprinted by permission of the publisher (© Peter McDonald, 2007). PATRICK MACDONOGH: 'No Mean City' and 'O, Come to the Land' from *Poems* (The Gallery Press, 2001), reprinted by permission of the publisher (© Patrick MacDonogh, 2001). GEARÓID IARLA MAC GEARAILT: 'Woe to him who slanders women' trans. Thomas F. O'Rahilly in *Dánta Grádha: Anthology of Irish Love Poetry, 1350–1750* (Cork University Press, 1925), reprinted by permission of the publisher (© 1925). PATRICK MCGILL: 'La Baseé Road' and 'The Guns' from *The Navvy Poet* (Caliban, 1984), reprinted by permission of Peter Knight Associates. CATHAL BUÍ MAC GIOLLA GHUNNA: 'The Yellow Bittern' trans. Seamus Heaney from *The School Bag* (Faber & Faber, 1997), reprinted by permission of the publisher (© Seamus Heaney, 1997). MEDBH MCGUCKIAN: 'The Seed-Picture' from *The Flower Master* (The Gallery Press, 1993); 'The Sitting' from *Venus and the Rain* (The Gallery Press, 1994); 'Monody for Aghas' from *Drawing Ballerinas* (The Gallery Press, 2001); 'She is in the Past, She has this Grace' from *The Face of the Earth* (The Gallery Press, 2002), reprinted by permission of the publisher (© Medbh McGuckian, 1993, 1994, 2001, 2002). LOUIS MACNEICE: 'A Cataract Conceived as the March of Corpses', 'Autobiography', *Autumn Journal* (IX), 'Charon', 'The Introduction', 'Neutrality', 'Soap Suds', 'The Streets of Laredo', 'The Taxis' and 'Valediction' from *Collected Poems* (Faber & Faber, 2007), reprinted by permission of David Higham Associates; DEREK MAHON: An Bonnán Buí', 'Courtyards in Delft', 'A Disused Shed in Co. Wexford', 'Ecclesiastes', 'Glengormley' and 'An Image from Beckett' from *Collected Poems* (The Gallery Press, 1999); 'Things' from *Harbour Lights* (The Gallery Press, 2005); 'Biographia Literaria' from *Life on Earth* (The Gallery Press, 2008), reprinted by permission of the publisher (© Derek Mahon, 1999, 2005, 2008). BRIAN MERRIMAN: *The Midnight Court*: ''Twas my custom to stroll by a clear winding stream . . .' and 'The girl having listened to this peroration . . .' trans. Ciaran Carson from *The Midnight Court* (The Gallery Press, 2005), reprinted by permission of the publisher (© Ciaran Carson, 2005); 'To add to which, the whole assembly . . .' and 'Bathed in an aura of morning light . . .' trans. Seamus Heaney from *The Midnight Verdict: Translations from the Irish of Brian Merriman* (The Gallery Press, 1993), reprinted by permission of the publisher (© Seamus Heaney, 2003); 'By the time it strikes them to take a partner . . .' trans. Thomas Kinsella from *An Duanaire: Poems of the Dispossessed* (The Dolmen Press, 1981), reprinted by permission of the translator (© Thomas Kinsella, 1981); 'Then up there jumps from a neighbouring chair . . .' trans. Frank O'Connor from *Kings, Lords, & Commons: An Anthology from the Irish* (Macmillan, 1961), reprinted by permission of PFD on behalf of the Estate of Frank O'Connor (© The Estate of Frank O'Connor, 1959). DOROTHY MOLLOY: 'Gethsemane Day' and 'Ghost Train' from *Gethsemane Day* (Faber & Faber, 2006), reprinted by permission of the publisher (© Dorothy Molloy, 2006). JOHN MONTAGUE: 'All Legendary Obstacles', 'Herbert Street Revisited', 'Mount Eagle', 'She Cries', 'Sunset' 'The Trout', 'What a View' and 'Windharp' from *Collected Poems* (The Gallery Press, 1995), reprinted by permission of the publisher (© John Montague, 1995). CHRISTY MOORE: 'Lisdoonvarna', reprinted by permission of Christy Moore (IMRO), www.christymoore.com. SINÉAD MORRISSEY: 'Pilots' from *The State of the Prisons* (Carcanet Press, 2005), reprinted by permission of the publisher (© Sinéad Morrissey, 2005). PAUL MULDOON: 'Aisling', 'Anseo', 'Cuba', 'The Electric Orchard', 'Immram', 'Myself and Pangur', 'They That Wash on Thursday' and 'Third Epistle to Timothy' from *Poems 1968–1998* (Faber & Faber, 2001); 'The Breather' from *Moy Sand and Gravel* (Faber & Faber, 2002); 'Turkey Buzzards' from *Horse Latitudes* (Faber & Faber, 2006), reprinted by permission of the publisher (© Paul Muldoon, 2001, 2002, 2006). RICHARD MURPHY: 'Girl at the Seaside', 'Morning Call', 'Sailing to an Island', 'Seals at High Island' and 'Stormpetrel' from *New Selected Poems* (Faber & Faber, 1989); and *Collected Poems* (Wake Forest University Press and The Gallery Press, 2000), reprinted by permission of Dennis O'Driscoll. EILÉAN NÍ CHUILLEANÁIN: 'Deaths and Engines' from *The Second Voyage* (The Gallery Press, 1977, 1986); 'MacMoransbridge' from *The Magdalene Sermon* (The Gallery Press, 1989); 'Fireman's Lift' and 'The Real Thing' from *The Brazen Serpent* (The Gallery Press, 1994); 'A Capitulary' and 'Gloss/Clós/Glas' from *The Girl Who Married the Reindeer* (The Gallery Press, 2001), all reprinted by permission of the publisher (© Eiléan Ní Chuilleanáin, 1977, 1986, 1989, 1994, 2001). NUALA NI DHOMHNAILL: 'The Language Issue' trans. Paul Muldoon in *Pharaoh's Daughter* (The Gallery Press, 1990), reprinted by permission of the publisher (© Nuala Ni Dhomhnaill 1990; trans. © Paul Muldoon); 'My Father's People' and 'The Hair Market' trans. Eiléan Ní Chuilleanáin from *The Water Horse* (The Gallery Press, 1999), reprinted by permission of the publisher (© Nuala Ní Dhomhnaill, 1999; trans. © Eiléan Ní Chuilleanáin); 'Mermaid with Parish Priest' trans. Paul Muldoon from *The Fifty Minute Mermaid* (The Gallery Press, 2007), reprinted by permission of the publisher (© Nuala Ní Dhomhnaill, 2007; trans. © Paul Muldoon). DIARMAID Ó BRIAIN: 'The Shannon' trans. Robin Flower from *The Irish Tradition* (Lilliput Press 1994), reprinted by permission of the publisher. DÁIBHÍ Ó BRUADAIR: '*Adoramus te, Christe*' trans. Tiffany Atkinson (© Tiffany Atkinson, 2010); 'Eire' trans. Austin Clarke from *Austin Clarke: Collected Poems* (Carcanet Press and The Bridge Press, 2008), reprinted by permission of R. Dardis Clarke, 17 Oscar Square, Dublin 8; 'To them the state . . .' and 'To see the art of poetry lost' trans. Michael Hartnett from *O Bruadair* (The Gallery Press, 1985), reprinted by permission of the publisher (© The Estate of Michael Hartnett, 1985); 'A Glass of Beer' trans. James Stephens from *Collected Poems* (Macmillan, 1954), reprinted by permission of The Society of Authors. TOIRDHEALBHACH Ó CEARBHALLÁIN: 'Mabel Kelly' and 'Peggy Brown' trans. Austin Clarke from *Austin Clarke: Collected Poems* (Carcanet Press and The Bridge Press, 2008), reprinted by permission of R. Dardis Clarke, 17 Oscar Square, Dublin 8. GOFRAIDH FIONN Ó DÁLAIGH: 'Under Sorrow's Sign' trans. John Montague reprinted by permission of The Gallery Press (© John Montague, 1974); 'Praise of Maurice Fitz Maurice, Earl of Desmond' trans. David Wheatley (© David Wheatley, 2010). LOCHLAINN ÓG Ó DÁLAIGH: 'Praise for the Young O'Briens' trans. Maurice Riordan (© Maurice Riordan, 2010). MUIREADHACH ALBANACH Ó DÁLAIGH: 'A Poem Addressed to the Blessed Virgin' trans. Kathleen Jamie (© Kathleen Jamie, 2010); 'On the Death of his Wife' trans. Frank O'Connor from *The Little Monasteries* (The Dolmen Press, 1963), reprinted by permission of PFD on behalf of the Estate of Frank O'Connor (© The Estate of Frank O'Connor, 1963); 'On Cutting his Hair Before Going on Crusade' trans. Thomas Owen Clancy from *The Triumph Tree: Scotland's Earliest Poetry* AD *550–1350* (Canongate, 1998), reprinted by permission of the translator. PEADAR Ó DOIRNÍN: 'The Mother's Lament for Her Child' trans. Michael Longley (© Michael Longley, 2010); 'The Green Hill of Cian son of Cáinte' trans. Pádraigín Ní Uallacháin from *A Hidden Ulster* (Four Courts Press, 2003), reprinted by permission of the publisher (© Pádraigín Ní Uallacháin, 2003). BERNARD O'DONOGHUE: 'Casement on Banna' from *The Weakness* (Chatto & Windus, 1991), reprinted by permission of the author (© Bernard O'Donoghue, 1991); 'Ter Conatus' from *Here Nor There* (Chatto & Windus, 1999), reprinted by permission of The Random House Group Ltd (© Bernard O'Donoghue, 1999). DENNIS O'DRISCOLL: 'Churchyard View: The New Estate' from *New and Selected Poems* (Anvil Press, 2004), reprinted by permission of the publisher. EOCHAIDH Ó HEODHASA: 'The New Poetry' trans. Maurice Riordan (© Maurice Riordan, 2010). GIOLLA BRIGHDE (BONAVENTURA) Ó HEODHASA: 'In Memoriam Richard Nugent' trans. Tiffany Atkinson (© Tiffany Atkinson, 2010). TADHG DALL Ó HUIGÍNN: 'Enniskillen' trans. Patrick K. Ford from *The Celtic Poets* (Belmont, MA: Ford and Bailie, 1999), reprinted by permission of the translator. TADHG ÓG Ó HUIGÍNN: 'A School of Poetry Closes' trans. Seamus Heaney (© Seamus Heaney, 2010). SEÁN Ó NEACHTAIN: 'Ó Neachtain's Proposal to Úna Ní Bhroin' trans. Kit Fryatt (© Kit Fryatt, 2010). AODHAGÁN Ó RATHAILLE: 'The Ruin that Befell the Great Families of Ireland' and 'On a Gift of Shoes' trans. Michael Hartnett from *O Rathaille* (The Gallery Press, 1998), reprinted by permission of the publisher (© The Estate of Michael Hartnett, 1998); 'The Glamoured' trans. Seamus Heaney, reprinted by permission of the translator (© Seamus Heaney, 1998); 'A Grey Eye Weeping' trans. Frank O'Connor from *Kings, Lords, & Commons: An Anthology from the Irish* (Macmillan, 1961), reprinted by permission of PFD on behalf of the Estate of Frank O'Connor (© The Estate of Frank

O'Connor, 1959). CAITRÍONA O'REILLY: 'A Lecture Upon the Bat' from *The Nowhere Birds* (Bloodaxe Books, 2001); 'Heliotrope' from *The Sea Cabinet* (Bloodaxe Books, 2006), reprinted by permission of the publisher (© Caitríona O'Reilly, 2001, 2006). SEÁN Ó RÍORDÁIN: 'Despair' trans. David Wheatley (© David Wheatley, 2010). TADHG Ó RUAIRC: 'A Game of Cards and Dice' trans. Derek Mahon (The Gallery Press, 2002), reprinted by permission of the publisher (© Derek Mahon, 2002). CATHAL Ó SEARCAIGH: 'Lament' trans. Seamus Heaney from *Homecoming/ An Bealach 'na Bhaile* (Indreabhán, Co Galway: Cló Iar-Chonnachta Teo, 1993), reprinted by permission of the publisher. EOGHAN RUA Ó SÚILLEABHÁIN: 'Poet to Blacksmith' trans. Seamus Heaney from *District and Circle* (Faber & Faber, 2006), reprinted by permission of the publisher (© Seamus Heaney, 2006); 'A Magic Mist' trans. Thomas Kinsella from *An Duanaire: Poems of the Dispossessed* (The Dolmen Press, 1981), reprinted by permission of the translator (© Thomas Kinsella, 1981); 'The Volatile Kerryman' trans. Seán Ó Riada, reprinted by permission of Peadar Ó Riada. FRANK ORMSBY: 'The Gate' and 'The Whooper Swan' from *Fireflies* (Carcanet Press, 2009), reprinted by permission of the publisher (© Frank Ormsby, 2009). TOM PAULIN: 'A Written Answer' from *The Liberty Tree* (Faber & Faber, 1993); 'The Road to Inver' from *The Road to Inver* (Faber & Faber, 2004), reprinted by permission of the publisher (© Tom Paulin, 1993, 2004). ANTOINE RAIFTEIRÍ: 'Mary Hynes' trans. Frank O'Connor from *Kings, Lords, & Commons: An Anthology from the Irish* (Macmillan, 1961), reprinted by permission of PFD on behalf of the Estate of Frank O'Connor (© The Estate of Frank O'Connor, 1959). MAURICE RIORDAN: 'The Sloe' from *Floods* (Faber & Faber, 2000); *The Idylls* (extract) from *The Holy Land* (Faber & Faber, 2007), reprinted by permission of the publisher (© Maurice Riordan, 2000, 2007). W. R. RODGERS: 'The Net' from *Poems* (The Gallery Press, 1993), reprinted by permission of the publisher (© The Estate of W. R. Rodgers, 1993). EARL ROGNVALD OF ORKNEY: 'Irish Monks on a Rocky Island' trans. Kit Fryatt (© Kit Fryatt, 2010). BLANAID SALKELD: 'Art' and 'Role' from *Experiment in Error* (Hand & Flower Press, 1955), reprinted by permission of the Estate of Blanaid Salkeld. SEDULIUS SCOTTUS: 'He Complains to Bishop Hartgar of Thirst' trans. Helen Waddell from *Medieval Latin Lyrics* (Four Courts Press, 2008), reprinted by permission of the publisher (© Four Courts Press, 2008). MAURICE SCULLY: 'Liking the Big Wheelbarrow', 'Lullaby' and 'Sound' from *livelihood* (Wild Honey Press, 2004), reprinted by permission of the author (© Maurice Scully, 2004). JAMES STEPHENS: 'The Red-haired Man's Wife', 'The Street Behind Yours' and 'O Bruadair' from *Collected Poems* (Macmillan, 1954), reprinted by permission of The Society of Authors. DAVID WHEATLEY: 'Drift' and 'Sonnet' from

*Mocker* (The Gallery Press, 2006), reprinted by permission of the publisher (© David Wheatley, 2006). MACDARA WOODS: 'The Dark Sobrietee' from *Knowledge in the Blood: New and Selected Poems* (Dedalus Press, 2000), reprinted by permission of Dedalus Press.

*Every effort has been made to trace and contact the copyright-holders prior to publication. If notified, the publisher undertakes to rectify any errors or omissions at the earliest opportunity.*

# Index of Poets

# Index of First Lines

# Index of Titles